PICASSO

and the Invention of Cubism

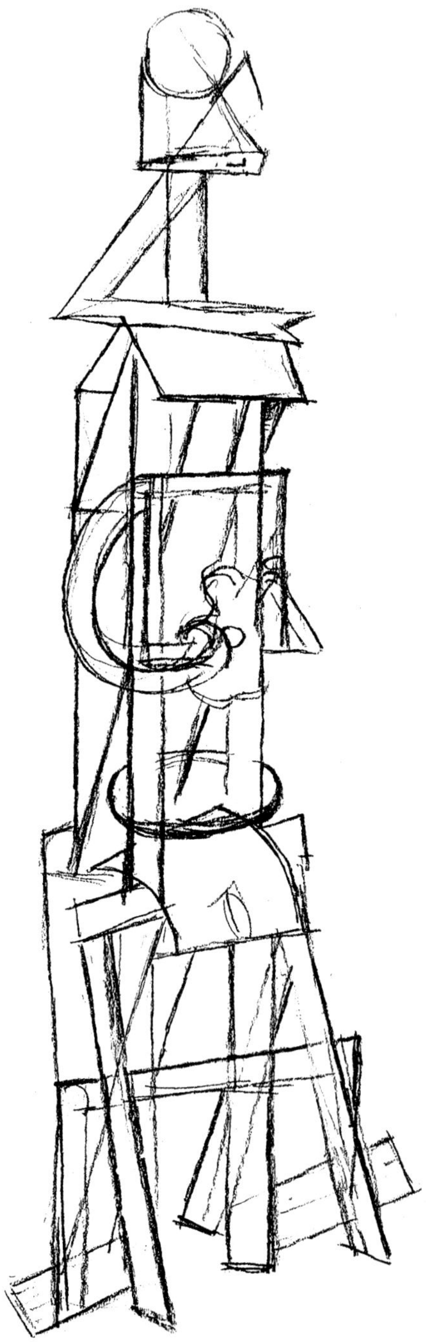

Pepe Karmel

PICASSO
and the Invention of Cubism

Yale University Press New Haven and London

For Carey

Designed by Gillian Malpass and Pepe Karmel

Printed in China

Library of Congress Cataloging-in-Publication Data

Karmel, Pepe.
Picasso and the invention of Cubism / Pepe Karmel.
p. cm.
Includes bibliographical references and index.
ISBN 0–300–09436–1 (cloth : alk. paper)
1. Picasso, Pablo, 1881–1973–Sources. 2. Cubism. I. Title.
ND553.P5 K265 2002
759.4–dc21 2002013603

A catalogue record for this book is available from
The British Library

Frontispiece
Picasso. *Seated Woman with Guitar (Study for a Construction).*
Sorgues, summer 1912.
Ink and lithographic crayon on paper, 31 × 19 cm.
Zervos XXVIII, 132; Richet 313. Musée Picasso, Paris

Contents

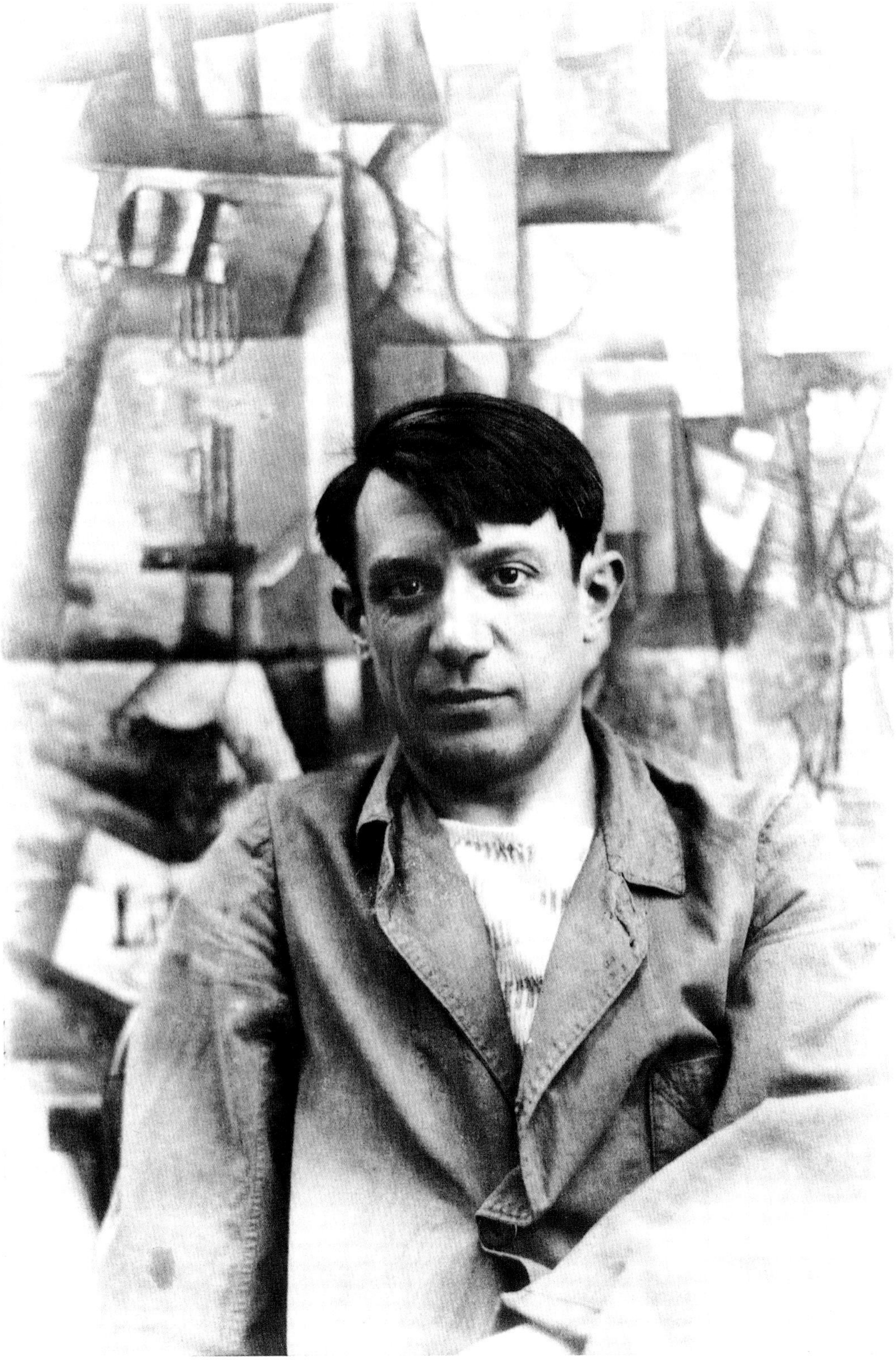

Picasso in front of *The Aficionado* (fig. 114). Sorgues, summer 1912

Preface

Form and Content in Cubism

In the last two decades there has been a virtual explosion in studies of Picasso and of Cubism. Social history has proven a particularly fruitful approach, yielding new insights into the links between Cubism and anarchism, the threat of war, the art market, entertainment, fashion, science, psychology, and philosophy.[1] The publication of the first two volumes of John Richardson and Marilyn McCully's magisterial *Life of Picasso* has tremendously enriched our understanding of the circumstances in which Cubism emerged, and of the private concerns hidden behind its façade of impersonal form.[2] Other scholars, drawing on the model of semiology, have argued that the key achievement of Cubism was Picasso's reinvention of painting as a system of arbitrary signs comparable to a written or spoken language.[3] What all of these approaches have in common is their opposition – or at least indifference – to the formalism that had previously dominated Cubist criticism.

This shift in the character of Cubist criticism corresponds to changes in the larger art world. Through much of the twentieth century, it seemed as if the story of modern art could be summed up as an evolution from representation to abstraction. Cubism's role in this story was to effect a formal revolution, replacing the natural shapes of figures and objects with a new language of abstract forms, and substituting a shallow space of overlapping planes for the deep space of Renaissance art. Picasso himself may have refused to abandon the goal of representation; later artists would be more radical, taking advantage of Cubism's discoveries to create a thoroughly abstract art.[4]

By 1980 this story was no longer credible. The human figure and the natural world had returned as important elements within "advanced" art. Pure abstraction no longer seemed revolutionary; on the contrary, it was widely perceived as the preferred style of the political establishment. What now seemed subversive in Cubism was precisely its impure combination of abstraction and representation.

The partisans of semiology and of social history have often attacked each other.[5] Nonetheless, for the last twenty years, their differing approaches to Cubism have functioned in a complementary fashion. Semiologists have argued that Cubism functions like a language, evoking the real world without having to represent it illusionistically, while social historians have explored the messages conveyed by this language. Today, it is Cubism's formal development that is unduly neglected. The social historians tend to regard this formal development as a "given" – something that needs to be interpreted but not to be explored in its own right. One might expect the semiologists to take a different view. However, their allegiance to the Saussurean doctrine of the arbitrariness of the sign has tended to close off this avenue of investigation: there is no reason to investigate the character or development of something that is deemed, *a priori*, to be arbitrary.[6] In practice, both social historians and semiologists have tended to regard the formal development of Cubism as a matter adequately described in earlier accounts.

There are two problems with this assumption. One is that it ignores the new visual evidence that has become available since the formulation of the "canonical" accounts of Cubism. Numerous drawings, paintings, and sculptures critical to the understanding of Picasso's development in the years 1906–13 were exhibited and published only after his death in 1973. Much of this material was simply unavailable to earlier authors, and requires significant revisions to their narratives. This process of revision was begun by Pierre Daix in his 1979 *catalogue raisonné* of Picasso's Cubist work but is far from complete, even today.[7]

The other problem is that the theoretical framework of the canonical accounts no longer seems adequate. Directly or indirectly, these accounts had been shaped by the writings of Clement Greenberg, which provided an almost inescapable point of reference for Anglo-American critics in the post-war era. As a practicing critic, discussing individual artists and movements, Greenberg was a subtle and varied writer. As a theoretician, however, he was highly reductive, defining modernism as an historically determined evolution toward a focus on the "medium" as the defining feature of art. In painting, this meant an insistence on the physical qualities of the medium, on the shape of the support, and – above all – on the flatness of the picture plane. Greenberg's theory imbued the innovations of Cubism with an air of historical necessity. The novel materials of collage and *papier collé*, the new formal language of geometric squared-off forms, the increasing shallowness of pictorial space – all these could be explained as a quasi-inevitable response to the historical situation of painting around 1910.[8]

This analysis no longer seems tenable. If Greenberg could convince himself that the evolution of modern art was a one-way street – a triumphal progress toward the promised land of abstraction – the passage of another fifty years has demonstrated that modern art does not so much evolve as revolve, adopting and discarding styles only to revive them in new combinations.[9] This process of ringing changes on the basic elements of modernism has only confirmed the importance of Cubism, which continues to provide the pictorial syntax for most contemporary art. But it has demolished the sense of historical determinism that made Greenbergian formalism so compelling. Cubism can no longer be seen as a step along a predetermined path toward abstraction, or as a necessary result of historical forces.

It is difficult to let go of this belief in historical necessity. Although art historians have rejected Greenbergian formalism, they have tended to substitute new kinds of determinism. For some, the fact that Cubism emerged in the same years that Ferdinand de Saussure outlined his theory of language suggests that both were the product of a new, semiological *zeitgeist*.[10] For others, the Cubist emphasis on formal elements at the expense of recognizable representation is a result of social and economic factors in French society.[11] But these determinist arguments are no more credible than Greenberg's.

Picasso invented Cubism with the assistance of Georges Braque. The detailed record of their work reveals a series of brilliant extrapolations and naïve misreadings, wrong turns and lucky breaks. It would be only a slight exaggeration to say that the invention of Cubism was a happy accident. There was nothing inevitable about it. It might very well not have happened. Furthermore, there is no evidence to suggest that anyone else would have invented Cubism if Picasso had not. Braque, Léger, and Gris – the other "essential" Cubists, as Douglas Cooper dubbed them[12] – all began their careers as Cubists by imitating Picasso. Without him, the course of modern art would have been completely different. The example of Cubism demonstrates the power of the human imagination to create something genuinely new.

This is not to say that Picasso invented Cubism out of whole cloth. He would never have been able to invent it if he had not had access to the rich formal and intellectual vocabulary of late nineteenth-century French art and culture. However, Cubism radically transformed its sources, to the extent that they are almost unrecognizable in Picasso's work of 1910–13. What emerged from this transformation was a new formal language that could serve equally well as a vehicle for pure estheticism or as an expression of social experience. A great variety of meanings – philosophical, political, or biographical – can be discovered in Cubist paintings and sculptures. But, for the most part, these meanings might equally well have been communicated in some other, more conventional way. The truly new and distinctive feature of Cubism is its formal language. The goal of this book is to show how Picasso invented that language in the years 1906 through 1913.

These dates perhaps require some explanation. Although Picasso's work of 1906 was in no sense Cubist, it was in the fall of this year that he began to explore the motifs that would lead to the development of Cubism. Conversely, all of the essential elements of Cubism had emerged by the end of 1913. Picasso continued to explore the potential of the Cubist style in the years that followed, but it might be argued that no fundamentally new element appeared in his Cubist work until the emergence of the curvilinear interlace in his work of 1923–26.

The first chapter of this book examines the ideas that seem actually to have played a role in the development of Cubism (as opposed to the ideas that became associated with it in later criticism). Three tendencies in nineteenth-century thought are important here. One is the "empiricist" theory of perception; the second is the idea of "decorative" design; the third, the Symbolist idea of the visual symbol as an "equivalent" for experience. These ideas were not taken over wholesale in Cubism, but were disassembled and recombined into a new synthesis; their influence remains visible in Picasso's and Braque's statements about Cubism, which are reviewed at the end of this chapter.

The second chapter traces the evolution of a distinctive Cubist space. This space is usually seen as a rejection of the perspectival space of the Renaissance tradition. In some ways, however, it is a return to the spatial organization typical of *trecento* and *quattrocento* painting. Cubist space thus seems at once revolutionary and archaic.

The third chapter follows Picasso's path toward the break-up of solid form into a series of independent lines and planes arranged in space. Although unprecedented in Western art, this break-up was rooted in Picasso's profound familiarity with academic representations of the human figure. It emerged, in a sense, from his investigation of different conventions for representing the body.

The final chapter attempts to clarify the "linguistic" character of the Cubist sign. Going back to the great philologists of the second half of the nineteenth century, it demonstrates how Saussure's ideas represent merely a selection from a larger body of linguistic thought. It is these broader analyses of the formation and development of language that provide the most useful models for understanding the Cubist sign.

* * *

This book has been taking shape since 1986. Its roots go back even further, to the extraordinary Picasso retrospective of 1980, organized by William Rubin for the Museum of Modern Art (MoMA), New York. A fledgling photography critic at the time, I would never have presumed to write about MoMA's exhibition. However, I did write an article for *Art in America* on a concurrent exhibition, "Looking for Picasso," at the International Center of Photography.[13] I am grateful to Elizabeth C. Baker, the editor of *Art in America*, for allowing a young, ignorant critic to educate himself in public. I am also grateful to Leo Rubinfien – photographer, critic, and friend – for encouraging me to write about art and photography in the first place.

In 1986, when the Pace Gallery held its revelatory exhibition of Picasso's sketchbooks, "Je Suis Le Cahier," I screwed up my courage to confront the artist directly, publishing a piece on "Picasso in Process," again in *Art in America*.[14] By this time I was in graduate school at the Institute of Fine Arts, New York University. Several friends – Molly Nesbit, Kenneth E. Silver, and Gertje Utley – had convinced me that I would enjoy studying the history of art in a more organized, scholarly fashion. My understanding of Picasso, and of modern art in general, has benefited tremendously from discussions with them over the years.

That fall, I had the extraordinary good fortune to take a seminar on Cubism with William Rubin, a magisterial scholar and an inspiring teacher. Since I had so recently written on Picasso's sketchbooks, Rubin insisted that I prepare a seminar report on Picasso's Cubist drawings. I trudged off toward the library with a heavy heart. The literature on Picasso and Cubism was so voluminous, and it seemed highly unlikely that a mere graduate student could make anything resembling an original discovery about the topic. Once I began to burrow through the stacks, however, I found that there was virtually no literature on Picasso's Cubist drawings, beyond a few entries in exhibition catalogues. Many (though far from all) of Picasso's Cubist drawings had been published in Christian Zervos's magnificent catalogue of Picasso's oeuvre, but they were often out of order, so that related works appeared on different pages or even in different volumes. With Rubin's encouragement, I quickly settled on Picasso's Cubist drawings as a dissertation topic.

That winter, I made the first of many visits to the Musée Picasso, which houses Picasso's archives as well as a unique collection of his work. Included in these archives is a complete photographic record of the drawings, paintings, and sculptures in Picasso's estate. This made it possible for me to study numerous unpublished works, and to reconstruct, bit by bit, the sequence of Picasso's drawings, and their relationship to works in other media. During this and many subsequent visits I received a warm greeting from the curators Michèle Richet, Brigitte Léal, Marie-Laure Bernadac, Hélène Klein, and Anne Baldassari. It is a tribute to Picasso's greatness that these exceptional scholars have devoted their efforts to researching, exhibiting, and publishing his work. I also benefited from the generous assistance of the Musée Picasso's librarians, especially Laurence Berthon, Jeanne-Yvette Sudour, Sylvie Fresuault, and Pierrot Eugène.

My initial research consisted largely of amassing and organizing reproductions of Picasso's drawings – a process that consumed uncountable hours of photocopying, scissoring, pasting and sorting, with enormous piles of paper arranged around the kitchen table, threatening frequently to topple to the floor. While this process was still underway, I was honored by William Rubin's request that I join the team working on the organization of MoMA's 1989 exhibition "Picasso and Braque: Pioneering Cubism." At the outset, I was principally responsible for suggesting the selection of Picasso's drawings. A few of the visual comparisons that I proposed in the catalogue of the same title are repeated here; others are cited in the notes.

Over time, my involvement broadened to include other aspects of the exhibition. This made it possible for me to study much of Picasso's and Braque's Cubist work at first hand, and not just from reproductions. I also benefited immeasurably from the opportunity to discuss this work with other scholars involved with the exhibition. Preeminent among these was of course William Rubin himself. It is one thing to read a book or a catalogue essay, another thing to hear a lecture, but there is nothing quite like working closely with a brilliant scholar on the subject closest to his heart. I also learned a tremendous amount from other members of the exhibition team, including the late Judith Cousins, curator of research; Lynn Zelevansky, curatorial assistant (now a distinguished curator at the Los Angeles County Museum of Art); and James Coddington, head of conservation. He and I made numerous after-hours visits to the exhibition in order to study at close hand the technique of Picasso's and Braque's paintings and *papiers collés*. Looking at pictures with a conservator teaches you things about art that you would never learn from books, and I have acquired from Jim a firm belief that you cannot really understand a work of art without understanding how it was made.

Two great scholars of Cubism – Pierre Daix and the late Edward Fry – served as advisors to the exhibition. Daix, needless to say, is the principal author of the *catalogue raisonné* of Picasso's Cubist paintings and of a library's worth of other books and essays about the artist.[15] His catalogue of the paintings provided the indispensable foundation for my own study of the drawings, his critical writings offer countless insights into Picasso's work, and I benefited greatly from our discussions. Edward Fry's *Cubism* combined a brilliant précis of the movement's evolution with a ground-breaking selection of contemporary criticism, while his later articles fundamentally transformed our understanding of Picasso's achievement.[16] Fry's good-humored and unconventional spirit made him a unique and delightful interlocutor.

As our work progressed, I acquired the additional responsibility of compiling information bearing on the dating of the works in the exhibition. This led me to the Galerie Louise Leiris, in Paris, the successor to the original Galerie Kahnweiler that represented Picasso and Braque during the Cubist years. Here I had the good fortune to meet Maurice Jardot and Quentin Laurens, past and present directors of the gallery, who permitted me to study Kahnweiler's stockbook, the photographic records of the works that passed through his hands, and some of the correspondence preserved in the gallery's archives.[17] Kahnweiler's records provide the foundation for all subsequent attempts to date the work of these years, and they have on occasion led me to revise the datings found in published catalogues. I also benefited, in Paris, from the advice of Claude Picasso, Brigitte Baer, and Etienne-Alain Hubert, and from the profound resources of the Bibliothèque Nationale and the Bibliothèque Jacques Doucet. Some of the information garnered during this time was included in an appendix to my dissertation; other elements of my research were summarized in the "Notes on the Dating of Works" that appeared as an appendix to the proceedings of a symposium organized by MoMA in conjunction with "Picasso and Braque: Pioneering Cubism."[18]

The papers presented at this symposium, and the lively discussion that followed them, made it clear that the semiological interpretation had become the new orthodoxy in Cubist studies. My ongoing research into Picasso's drawings and work in other media led me to feel that there were serious problems both with this interpretation and with the formalist interpretation it had supplanted.[19] These problems continued to preoccupy me as I worked on my dissertation, completed in 1993; this criticized the semiological approach to Cubism but did not propose an alternative. Benefiting from William Rubin's forceful criticisms, the final draft of the dissertation offered a narrative of the evolution of Cubism, as followed in Picasso's drawings.[20] Perhaps I should have published this text as it stood. However, I felt deeply dissatisfied with my own failure to forge a new positive reading of Cubism that would compensate for what I now saw as the serious flaws in existing interpretations.

As soon as I completed the dissertation, I therefore embarked upon a new phase of research, subsidized, in 1994–95, by a Jane and Morgan Whitney Fellowship from the Metropolitan Museum of Art. Searching for an intellectual framework corresponding to the innovations of

Cubism, I seized upon the Ariadne's thread offered by Kahnweiler's references, in *The Rise of Cubism*, to "tactile perceptions," the "stimulus" of "memory images," "associations," and "preperception."[21] These seemed to me to suggest a possible link between the ideas of the Cubists and nineteenth-century studies of perceptual psychology. Eventually, this investigation led me to explore nineteenth-century theories of language as well.

Pursuing these topics quickly took me beyond the borders of traditional Cubist scholarship. The writings of Richard Shiff and Jonathan Crary, tracing the links between perceptual psychology and nineteenth-century art, provided a valuable jumping-off point for this new research.[22] Molly Nesbit and Natasha Staller generously discussed with me their own research on language and avant-garde art.[23] I am particularly grateful to Molly Nesbit for directing me to the writings of Hans Aarsleff, who confirmed my intuition of a significant link between Hippolyte Taine and Saussure.[24]

Struggling to reformulate my thinking about the development of Cubism in general, I have benefited from the advice, assistance, and encouragement of numerous other colleagues, including Emily Braun, Michael Fitzgerald, Milly Glimcher, Lewis Kachur, Robert S. Lubar, Marilyn McCully, Linda Nochlin, John Richardson, Bernice Rose, Robert Rosenblum, Gertje Utley, and Jeffrey Weiss. I was also encouraged to refine my ideas by invitations to contribute to various catalogues. An essay written for "Picasso: Sculptor/Painter," the 1994 exhibition at the Tate Gallery, London, organized by John Golding and Elizabeth Cowling, allowed me to collect my thoughts on Cubist sculpture.[25] Cowling's probing questions and incisive editing forced me to clarify my ideas, contributing directly to the discussion of this topic in Chapter 4 here. Joséphine Matamoros, Chief Curator of the Musée d'Art Moderne de Ceret (the village where Picasso spent many productive months in 1911, 1912, and 1913), invited me to contribute an essay to the catalogue of her 1997 exhibition, "Picasso: Dessins et papiers collés."[26] I am also grateful for the warm hospitality extended by Matamoros and her staff during my visits to Céret in 1991 and 1997. More recently, I was given the opportunity to explore the American reception of Picasso's and Braque's 1912–13 work for the catalogue of Sarah Greenough's exhibition, "Modern Art and America: Alfred Stieglitz and His New York Galleries," seen at the National Gallery of Art, Washington, D.C., in 2001.[27]

I would also like to acknowledge the constant stimulus I have received from the writings of Daniel-Henry Kahnweiler, Alfred Barr, John Golding, Robert Rosenblum, Leo Steinberg, William Rubin, Pierre Daix, Rosalind Krauss, and Yve-Alain Bois. At one point or another, in the pages that follow, I have argued – sometimes explicitly, sometimes tacitly – with all of these writers. It is a mark of their brilliance that it has seemed worth arguing with them for so many years.

During my numerous research trips to Paris, my father and step-mother, Alex and Marianne Karmel, let me stay countless times in their apartment. The heavy hours in Parisian libraries were frequently lightened by the prospect of meeting them for dinner. I cannot forbear mentioning my father's delightful 1998 book, *A Corner in the Marais*, an historical memoir of their neighborhood, which he researched and wrote in considerably less time than it took me to complete this volume.[28]

Gillian Malpass, in the London office of Yale University Press, has displayed extraordinary patience in awaiting the arrival of a manuscript that took the better part of the decade to complete, has gently but firmly prodded me toward numerous necessary revisions, and, as designer, has coped brilliantly with the demands of an unreasonable author. It is only the ceaseless labors of Sarah Ganz Blythe that made it possible to obtain the numerous photographs reproduced here; I am not sure this book would ever have come into existence without her help. Jasmine Moorhead took on the tedious but essential task of compiling the index. In Paris, Anne Baldassari took time from her curatorial duties to help me obtain permission to reproduce many essential pictures, and arranged for a superb photographer, Jean Ravailler, to make the necessary copy prints.

Claude Picasso, together with Theodore H. Feder of the Arists Rights Society, helped me resolve difficult issues of artistic copyright. I am deeply grateful to both of them, and to the hard-working staff of ARS and Art Resource, especially Katie Stieglitz, Janet Hicks, and Ryan Jensen.

My fellow scholars Martha Carroll and Joan Pachner have demonstrated their extraordinary friendship and commitment to this project by reading and discussing draft after draft, year after year. Only those who have themselves provided such "hands-on" advice can appreciate the enormous time and effort it requires.

I cannot begin to express my gratitude to Kirk Varnedoe, who has played a critical role at every stage of this book's development. At the outset, when he first agreed to supervise my dissertation, he was still a professor at the Institute of Fine Arts. He continued to take an active interest in the project – criticizing each new draft of dissertation and book – even after assuming new and onerous responsibilities as Chief Curator in the Department of Painting and Sculpture at the Museum of Modern Art. His enthusiasm for the material has propelled me forward, while his probing skepticism has forced me constantly to refine my ideas and arguments. From 1996 through 1999, I enjoyed the privilege and pleasure of working with him on exhibitions of Picasso and of Jackson Pollock organized for MoMA.[29] Even when our extended discussions did not touch directly on the material of this book, they helped shape my understanding of Cubism and of modern art in general. As teacher, mentor, colleague, and friend, he has been a constant source of inspiration.

Above all, I am grateful to my wife, Carey Adina Karmel, and to our children, Remy and Caleb, who have tolerated far too many weeks and weekends when I abandoned them for the library or the computer. Their love has sustained me through the seemingly endless process of writing and rewriting, and their impatience has propelled me to complete it. I dedicate it to them.

Abbreviations

D.B.	Pierre Daix and Georges Boudaille, with Joan Rosselet. *Picasso, 1900–1906: catalogue raisonné de l'oeuvre peint.* Neuchâtel: Ides et Calendes, 1966. Rev. and trans. as *Picasso: The Blue and Rose Periods – A Catalogue Raisonné of the Paintings, 1900–1906.* Greenwich, Conn.: New York Graphic Society, 1967
D.R.	Pierre Daix and Joan Rosselet. *Le Cubisme de Picasso: catalogue raisonné de l'oeuvre peint, 1907–1916.* Neuchâtel: Ides et Calendes, 1979. Rev. and trans. as *Picasso: The Cubist Years, 1907–1916 – A Catalogue Raisonné of the Paintings and Related Works.* Boston: New York Graphic Society, 1979
Geiser/Baer	Bernhard Geiser and Brigitte Baer. *Picasso: peintre-graveur – catalogue raisonné de l'oeuvre gravé et lithographie et des monotypes, Vol. 1: 1899–1931.* Bern: Editions Kornfeld, 1990
Léal	Brigitte Léal. *Musée Picasso – Carnets: Catalogue des dessins.* Paris: Réunion des musées nationaux, 1996. 2 vols.
M.F./C.	Isabelle Monod-Fontaine and E. A. Carmean, Jr., eds. *Braque: The Papiers Collés.* Washington, D.C.: National Gallery of Art, 1982
Richet	Michèle Richet. *Musée Picasso – Catalogue sommaire des collections: Dessins, Aquarelles, Gouaches, Pastels.* Paris: Réunion des musées nationaux, 1987
Romilly	Nicole Worms de Romilly, with Jean Laude. *Braque: Cubism, 1907–1914.* Paris: Maeght, 1982
Seckel	Hélène Seckel, ed. *Les Demoiselles d'Avignon.* Paris: Musée Picasso, 1998. 2 vols.
Spies	Werner Spies. *Picasso: das plastische Werk.* Stuttgart: Gerd Hatje, 1983. Rev. and trans. as Werner Spies, with Christine Piot. *Picasso: sculpteur.* Paris: Editions du Centre Pompidou, 2000
Zervos	Christian Zervos. *Pablo Picasso.* Paris: Cahiers d'art, 1932–78. 33 vols.

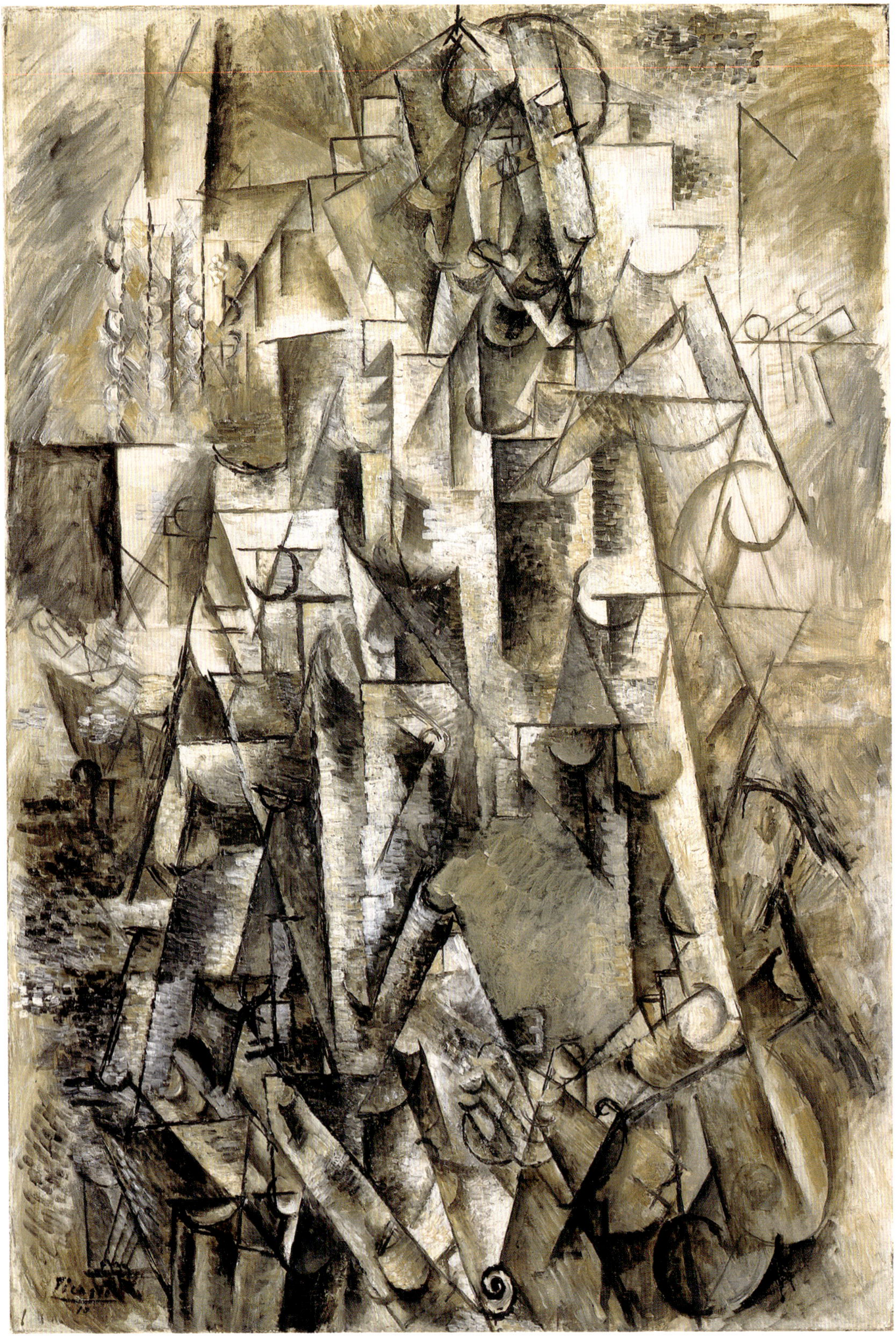

1 Picasso. *The Poet*. Céret, summer 1911. Oil on canvas, 131.2 × 89.5 cm. D.R. 423. The Solomon R. Guggenheim Foundation, New York. Peggy Guggenheim Collection, Venice, 1976

1

Ideas

In spring 1912 a journalist visited Picasso's dealer, Daniel-Henry Kahnweiler. Kahnweiler's first impulse was to send him away. He did not want his artists held up to mockery in the popular press. The journalist, Jacques de Gachons, persisted. He was writing an article about "The Art of the Future." It would begin with Cézanne, Gauguin, and Van Gogh and follow the development of the avant-garde up to the present. Gachons wanted to learn about Kahnweiler's artists because they were said to represent the "extreme" avant-garde. Kahnweiler relented, handing him albums of photographs of paintings by several artists he represented: Picasso, Braque, Vlaminck, and Derain.

Leafing through the album of Picasso's work, Gachons found the development of Cubism comprehensible up to the previous year:

> The earliest Picassos . . . look much like the work of Maurice Denis or Gauguin. Then the subjects become more individual, lines break up, angles are emphasized, bodies take on unexpected shapes. Finally, in 1911–12, the painter seems to have attained mastery of his approach. The well-intentioned layman is a bit like the turkey in the fable: he definitely sees something, but he's not sure what it is.
>
> The young and sympathetic dealer [Kahnweiler was then 27] comes to my aid: "Oh! I know that the reading of Picasso's and Braque's most recent works is quite difficult. Of course it's easier for me; I was there when the paintings were done. I know all about what the artist wanted to put in them. For instance, monsieur, this one represents *The Poet*. [fig. 1]
>
> "Ah!" (Good manners demand that I limit the expression of my total astonishment to this exclamation. I thought I was looking at a landscape, and it turned out to be a poet.)[1]

This sort of confusion was not uncommon among the early viewers of Cubism. The journalist André Salmon recounted a similar story in the *Paris-Journal* of July 14, 1911. Years later, the owner of the *Accordionist*, another 1911 Picasso, was said to have believed it was a landscape because it had the place name, "Céret," written on the back.[2]

Almost a century later, such anecdotes may seem quaint or amusing. But they remind us of something important: the sense of radical strangeness originally evoked by Cubism. In fact, a picture such as *The Poet*, with its welter of lines and curves, and its muted grays, browns, and whites seemingly placed at random, is not easy to decipher. Without the title for guidance, how many of us, today, would recognize it as a figure?

Picasso's motivation is no less mysterious than the finished canvas. Why did he choose to paint such a picture – one that was neither a comprehensible representation nor a decorative abstraction? The radical novelty of the composition presents us with an intellectual conundrum. Picasso cannot have taken any existing kind of picture as a model. Cubism is often said to derive from Cézanne, and there is much truth in this; but, by summer 1911, when Picasso painted *The Poet*, his work looked nothing like Cézanne's. Picasso must have had something in mind: a large, complex canvas such as this is not created simply as a joke or a random experiment. What was it? The challenge for the historian is to reconstruct the process by which the existing languages of Impressionism and Post-Impressionism were transformed into a fundamentally new and different visual language.

The evolution of this new formal language cannot be understood in purely formal terms. Cubism's transmutation of the formal elements of Impressionism and Post-Impressionism can be explained only by reference to the theories and ideas that had accompanied the development of these earlier movements. In effect, Picasso used the critical framework of existing avant-garde art to transform its visual elements into something virtually unrecognizable.

To understand Cubism, it is necessary to examine three key ideas associated with earlier avant-garde movements. One is the "empiricist" theory of perception, whose broad significance for Impressionism and other nineteenth-century art movements has been explored by Jonathan Crary in his book *Techniques of the Observer*.[3] Another is the Symbolist idea that the work of art should not imitate reality but should offer an "equivalent" for experience, expressed in a language of visual symbols; the linguistic aspect of Symbolism, in particular, has been the subject of important studies by Filiz Eda Burhan and Natasha Staller.[4] The third is the idea of "decorative" design, whose influence on modernism was traced in a ground-breaking 1976 article by Joseph Masheck.[5]

It cannot be said that any or all of these ideas "caused" the development of Cubism. They had already found adequate expression in the avant-garde art of preceding decades, and there was no trans-historical necessity for them to be expressed in a new formal language. On the other hand, Picasso and Braque would probably not have been able to invent Cubism without having these ideas available to provoke and justify what they were doing. As Pascal would have said, the ideas were necessary but not sufficient causes for the invention of Cubism.

Empiricism, Symbolism, and Decoration

Impressionism, as a movement, took as its point of departure the idea that painting should try to capture the artist's initial "impression" of his subject. But how was this naïve, uncensored impression to be distinguished from the artificial product of artistic training? Painters such as Monet and Pissarro turned to contemporary science to help them distinguish the signs of direct, unmediated sensation.[6] But the experiments of psychophysiologists like Helmholtz and Wundt were only the latest chapter in a long tradition of empiricist thought. And the conclusions that artists and critics drew from these experiments can only be understood in the light of this tradition.

It might be argued that the philosophy of empiricism derives from the scientific experiments of Johannes Kepler, who in 1604 published the first accurate description of the mechanism of vision. Kepler's analysis was a triumph for modern science – and a disaster for philosophy. The philosophical synthesis of the late Middle Ages and the Renaissance had regarded the projection of luminous images (and their reception by the eye) as an example of the more general process by which the Divine Will projected immaterial ideas or "species" into the material world. In the terminology of Neo-Platonism, the "multiplication of species" served equally well to describe the creation of objects and the propagation of images. The species emitted by objects were thought to travel to the eye along geometric guidelines known as visual rays. These were not rays of light, however. Light was thought to play only a marginal role in the process of vision. It made possible the perception of species but did not affect them. The species carried information that was independent of the process of transmission.[7]

The transmission of images, in the medieval world-view, was like the transmission of a digital file across the Internet today. The data remains the same whether it travels by copper wire, fiber-optic cable, radio wave, or infra-red beam. All that matters is that the receiving computer has the necessary software to decipher it. And God, in the medieval world-view, assured that all human beings were equipped with the same software.

What Kepler demonstrated was that vision depended on the transmission of light rays rather than species. He provided, for the first time, a mathematical explanation of how the lens of the eye focused incoming rays of light into an image projected onto the surface of the retina. Light now became the essential agent of vision, while the species, with all its Platonic implications, was banished. In effect, Kepler closed off the channel by which information flowed from the world to the brain. Since the eye was receptive only to light, it could absorb only as much information about objects as was provided by the light rays that bounced back and forth among them like balls on a billiard table.[8]

John Locke's *Essay Concerning Human Understanding*, published in 1690, confronts the philosophical challenge posed by Kepler's discovery: to explain how "bare naked perception" provides us with knowledge of an intelligible world.[9] He points out, for example, that, "When we set before our eyes a round globe of any uniform colour, e.g. gold, alabaster, or jet, it is certain that the idea thereby imprinted in our mind is of a flat circle, variously shadowed, with several degrees of light and brightness coming to our eyes." Although the actual object is spherical, the image imprinted on the retina by arriving light rays is effectively flat: "a plane variously coloured." It is, in effect, a "painting." What needs to be explained is how we come to interpret this flat image as a three-dimensional form, a globe.[10]

Locke's answer is that we have, by "habitual custom," formed an unconscious association between the three-dimensional form of a sphere, which we know from touch, and the two-dimensional shape it presents to the eye. We are so "accustomed to perceive what kind of appearance convex bodies are wont to make in us" that we no longer see the two-dimensional shapes that are actually imprinted on our eyes. Our mind "alters the appearances into their causes," so that we think we are seeing three-dimensional forms. Presented with "a flat circle, variously coloured," our judgment "frames to itself the perception of a convex figure and an uniform colour." The different colors of the optical image are seen as a single color modified by the effects of light and shade, and these in turn are translated into three-dimensional form.[11]

The analysis given by Locke privileges the sense of touch, which gives us real information about the form and position of objects. Vision is merely a substitute, a tool for inferring information about objects not accessible to touch. This analysis also leads him to divide the qualities of objects into two categories. Primary qualities discernible by touch, such as "solidity, extension, figure, motion or rest, and number," are inherent in objects themselves. In contrast, secondary qualities discernible by the other senses, such as "colours, sounds, tastes, etc.," are mere "sensations" existing in the mind of the observer, not in objects.[12]

Small wonder, then, that we constantly exchange the debased coinage of visual sensation for the solid currency of touch. Only under exceptional circumstances do we remain aware of the two-dimensional character of optical experience. Small children perceive light and dark as independent qualities, Locke suggests, because they have not yet formed the habit of instantly translating them into three-dimensional form.[13] Similarly, a blind man who suddenly regained his sight would perceive a flat field of color and light, because he would not have had the opportunity to build up mental associations between visual and tactile experience.[14] He might not recognize a shaded circle as a representation of a sphere because he would not know from experience, as we do, that a rounded, convex form often produces a gradated shadow.

These two counter-examples emphasize the unprecedented role of memory and association in Locke's theory of perception.[15] The theory implies that, even if two observers have identical retinal sensations, what they see will differ, because their retinal sensations will evoke different associations based on different past experiences. Without the intervention of memory and association, the process of perception will grind to a halt, for visual sensation alone is inadequate to produce a meaningful image. This reliance on previous experience rendered vision far more subjective than it had been in any previous account. The perception of the outside world had become entangled with the formation of the self.

The problem of vision became a central issue in eighteenth-century philosophy. It provided a perfect test case for empiricist philosophers such as Berkeley, Hume, and Condillac, who shared Locke's belief that our understanding of the world was shaped solely by experience, not by any innate ideas. If association could explain visual perception, it could probably explain most other forms of knowledge as well.

Berkeley, in particular, makes a significant addition to Locke's theory of vision. Like other empiricist writers, he insists that "what we properly and immediately see are only lights and colors." But he adds a novel linguistic dimension to the theory of vision. Lights and colors suggest the qualities of objects, he argues, "as words do things."[16] And just as the relation between letters and sounds is purely "arbitrary," so too is the relation between visual sensations and the actual objects they seem to represent. Indeed, "visible figures represent tangible figures much after the same manner that written words do sounds."[17] Although the signs of visual language are "constant and universal" (unlike the varying signs of spoken and written languages), the fact that a visual experience is often or invariably associated with a tactile experience does not mean that there is any "relation of similitude" between them.[18] A shaded circle is a common sign for a sphere because of the cause-and-effect relationship between convexity and gradated shading, not because there is any resemblance between one quality and the other.

The empiricist theory of vision began to play a role in French art only in the second half of the nineteenth century, after receiving what seemed to be objective verification from the experiments of Heinrich Helmholtz, the great psychophysiologist.[19] Avant-garde artists began to explore the idea that painting should recapitulate the process of perception. One by one, the elements of empiricist theory were examined for their esthetic potential.

Of these elements, the most influential was the idea that the visual field was, in itself, unintelligible – and hence non-representational. By the second half of the nineteenth century, this argument had become a cliché of contemporary philosophy. Hippolyte Taine, the most influential critic of the era (and the author of an immensely successful *Philosophy of Art*), noted in his 1870 treatise *On Intelligence* that, "Primitively, and in itself, the retina, when impressed, arouses sensations only of light, of obscurity, of successive and simultaneous colors."[20] Two hundred years earlier, John Locke had tried to define the purely visual by posing the imaginary case of a blind man who suddenly regained his sight. In the interim, several such cases had been recorded, and Taine reported that what the patients saw, upon recovering, was "variously colored patches more or less clear or obscure." Like Locke before him, Taine compared the experience of these formerly blind patients to that of "painters in color", whose art, he said, "consists in seeing their model as a *patch*, the only element of which is the more or less diversified, deadened, vivid, and mingled color."[21]

Indeed, avant-garde painters had already begun painting fields of color patches. In 1867, Emile Zola had defended Manet's "New Manner in Painting" by saying that the artist was trying to be faithful to his optical experience, and therefore represented his subject as an "ensemble of patches" or areas of color: "A head posed against a wall becomes nothing more than a more or less white patch on a more or less gray background; while the clothing juxtaposed to the head becomes, for example, a more or less blue patch side by side with the more or less white patch."[22]

From a philosophical point of view, the challenge posed by empiricist theory was to explain how we ever make the transition from seeing mere color patches to perceiving three-dimensional objects arranged in depth. As Taine wrote, the "sensations of the eye . . . taken alone, seem fit only to instruct us as to colors." How is it, then, that they "are capable of further instructing us . . . as to distance, extension and position"? His answer – a commonplace in nineteenth-century philosophy – was that these optical sensations become associated with "tactile and muscular sensations" that can and do provide knowledge about the three-dimensional world.[23] As another critic, Auguste Laugel, wrote in an 1869 treatise, *Optics and the Arts*, "The fingers undertake the slow and difficult education of sight."[24]

Once this education was completed, however, it seemed difficult to recover the "innocent eye" of childhood – that is, to experience visual sensations without immediately translating them into the language of three-dimensional form and space.[25] Lilla Cabot Perry, a wealthy American painter who befriended Monet in the 1890s, recalled his advice to "try to forget what objects you have before you, a tree, a house, a field or whatever. Merely think here is a little square of blue, here an oblong of pink, here a streak of yellow, and paint it just as it looks to you, the exact color and shape." Drawing on a philosophical example that had by then become a commonplace, Monet said that, "he wished he had been born blind and then had suddenly gained his sight [so] that he could have begun to paint in this way without knowing what the objects were that he saw before him." Paradoxically, painters could obtain a more faithful representation of visual experience by ignoring what it was they actually saw.[26]

The Impressionists had several techniques for postponing or suspending the viewer's recognition of the motif. One was to rely exclusively on color, suppressing contour and shading. The critic Jules Laforgue insisted that form, in Impressionist painting, should be "obtained not by line but solely by vibration and contrast of color." Line and shading were nothing but "illusions," their use sanctioned by academic "prejudice." Laforgue's rejection of line and shading is firmly rooted in empiricist theory. He recites the Lockean doctrine that the eye is inherently incapable of perceiving space or three-dimensional form, but has learned to interpret visual stimuli as signs for tactile sensations. Drawing is an artificial technique for giving visual expression to tactile experience, encouraging the illusion that we can see three-dimensional form. Since the eye "has lived, developed, and maintained itself in this state of illusion by centuries of line drawings," we tend to mistake it for the truth. But these drawn contours do not correspond to anything the eye ever actually perceives. All it perceives (according to empiricist theory) are patches of color. Line should therefore be banished from painting.[27] This opinion seems to have been shared by the painters themselves: Cézanne, for instance, told his son Paul that, "Line and modeling do not exist . . . Pure drawing is an abstraction."[28]

Another tactic, suggested by contemporary science, was to adopt an unfamiliar point of view. Helmholtz had noted that, "the instant we take an unusual position, and look at the landscape with the head under one arm, let us say, or between the legs, it all appears like a flat picture."[29] Similarly, the English researcher Ogden Rood observed that a landscape seen upside down "appears like a mass of beautiful patches of color heaped upon one another, and situated more or less in a vertical plane.[30]

Taine opened his 1870 volume *On Intelligence* with a description of the Champs Elysées seen from the top of the Arc de Triomphe. From this unfamiliar point of view, the people on the streets below appeared merely as "black or variously colored specks stirring about on the roadway or pavements."[31] Monet adopted the same tactic in 1873, showing the Boulevard des Capucines as seen from above. A contemporary critic described the figures in the eponymous painting as "innumerable black tongue-lickings . . . spots . . . obtained by the same method as that used to imitate marble: a bit here, a bit there, slapdash, any old way."[32] They had been reduced to mere specks, like Taine's pedestrians. Monet's shift to a distant and unfamiliar point of view interrupted the usually automatic process by which we recognize objects, and once this process had been interrupted, individual figures and objects reverted to mere patches of color.

How is the viewer to reconstruct an intelligible image from these patches? Evidently, by the same associative mechanism that makes it possible to interpret visual experience in the first place – by calling on the associations that will translate the purely optical sensations of color into the image of a three-dimensional world. As E. H. Gombrich put it in *Art and Illusion*, "the viewer must mobilize his memory of the visible world and project it into the mosaic of strokes and dabs on the canvas before him." This is the same act of projection that occurs (according to empiricist theory) every time we look at the world around us. The difference is that it now occurs consciously instead of unconsciously. The "beholder's share" in the image, as Gombrich called it, is greater, because the beholder has to do more work. The conventional signs of academic painting – the codified contours that evoke bodies and objects, the shading that describes three-dimensional form – have been omitted.[33]

The Impressionists called on empiricist theory to justify their suppression of line and shading. However, the same theory could also be invoked as a justification for a style that emphasized line and shading rather than color. The simplified drawing and shading of the Italian "Primitives" had heretofore been dismissed as a sign of their inability to capture optical experience. Art historians now began to reevaluate these early Renaissance painters as the authors of a style that deliberately concentrated on tactile form. Bernard Berenson, in 1894, invoked empiricist theory to praise Giotto for his "power to stimulate the tactile imagination." Rather than reproducing mere appearances, he said, Giotto's pictures "conveyed a *keener* sense of reality, of life-likeness than the objects themselves."[34]

This appreciation for a simplified, sculptural style also began to play a surreptitious role in the avant-garde painting of the 1880s and 1890s. Cézanne's work of these decades, for instance, functioned both as an extension of Impressionism and a reaction against it. On one hand, he strove incessantly to record his optical sensations. On the other, he departed from Impressionism by fitting his sensations of color into an ordered framework, and by supplementing them with lines and shading that provided a crude but powerful sense of three-dimensional form.[35] Depicting the human figure, Cézanne's drawing became aggressively sculptural. His cardplayers have the solidity of figures in a thirteenth-century fresco, their smocks falling in massive folds like the robes of Giotto's saints.

Cézanne's drawing led his admirers to praise his work for its "primitive" or "Gothic" qualities.[36] Berenson, who taught a new generation to appreciate the "primitive" painters of the early Renaissance, also played a key role in furthering Cézanne's reputation. What Berenson admired in Cézanne's landscapes was not their evanescent, optical brushwork but their "exquisite modelling" and "tactile values."[37] And it was Berenson who advised the Steins to buy Cézanne's work, starting them on the path that led to their patronage of Matisse and Picasso.[38]

For the most part, however, it was the optical style of Impressionism that continued to provide the point of departure for avant-garde painting around the turn of the twentieth century. The Impressionist belief that the purest form of artistic vision was to see without recognizing what was seen provided a powerful impetus toward abstraction. Kandinsky, in his *Reminiscences*, recalled seeing one of Monet's haystacks at an exhibition, and being particularly impressed by its brilliant color because he did not at first recognize its subject.[39] Another incident of defamiliarization occurred within his own studio. Returning at dusk, he was dumbstruck to discover a mysterious abstraction leaning against the wall: "Suddenly I saw an indescribably beautiful picture drenched with an inner glowing . . . I rushed toward this mysterious picture, of which I saw nothing but form and colors, and whose content was incomprehensible . . . It was a picture I had painted, leaning against the wall, standing on its side."[40] Here it was rotation that rendered the scene temporarily unrecognizable, and thereby made it possible to appreciate the composition purely in terms of form and colors. It becomes easier, in this context, to understand the reaction of Jacques de Gachons, who confronted Picasso's work at Kahnweiler's gallery in 1912. He was not unduly surprised to come upon an unintelligible canvas. He was merely surprised that it represented a human figure, rather than a landscape, as it would have in an Impressionist painting.

As noted earlier, the empiricist insistence on the primacy of the optical field implied that, even if we think we see three-dimensional figures and objects, these images are not the result of direct perception but are constructed from a combination of past and present sensations. Lucien Arréat, a conservative art critic, wrote in 1892 that: "All of our experience, insofar as it derives from visual sensation, represents a combination of new and old perceptions . . . what the artist sees at a given moment only provides him with a kind of skeleton; he has to flesh it out with old images."[41] For Taine, internal memory played such an important role in perception that so-called "external" perception might better be described as a "true hallucination . . . an internal dream which proves to be in harmony with external things."[42]

More soberly, Helmholtz argued that the perception of three-dimensional form depended on the synthesis of several different views: "The idea of a body in space, of a table, for instance, involves a quantity of separate observations. It comprises the whole series of images which this table would present to me in looking at it from different sides and at different distances."[43] The scientific study of vision demonstrated that only a small area of the visual field was in focus at any given moment so that it was only the synthesis of many successive acts of vision that produced the illusion that the visual field as a whole could be seen clearly.[44]

These ideas, too, could be applied by painters. Often, in late nineteenth-century painting, a face or a hand or patch of fabric is described with precise contours, while the rest of the composition is described by broad areas of diffuse color. This practice looks back to Rembrandt, but it also corresponds to "scientific" ideas about the eye's restricted field of sharp focus. Similarly, Helmholtz's description of how the image of a table is built up from successive observations corresponds to the multiple viewpoints of Cézanne's still lifes – and of early Cubism.

Behind these individual parallels between scientific theory and painterly practice lies the fundamental idea that we do not passively perceive the world but actively construct an image of it based on different sensations and associations, and that painting should recapitulate this process of active perception.[45] This shift toward an understanding of vision as a constructive process implied a corresponding change in the concept of the visual sign. For Locke and Berkeley the interpretation of visual sensations was an automatic process. The signs of visual language were "constant and universal," with no room for subjectivity or variation in their interpretation. Similarly, when a neo-empiricist like Taine wrote in 1870 that "our pure visual sensations are nothing more than signs," his goal was to stress the difference between these optical sensations and the tactile forms they represent.[46]

In the interim, however, the first stirrings of Symbolism had imbued the term "sign" with a new set of associations. Auguste Laugel in *Optics and the Arts* wrote that "visual images are the alphabet of the mystical language spoken by the world . . . the signs, the symbols by which our minds discover corporal entities." Although Laugel's basic point is the same as Taine's, it was rephrased in intentionally poetic terms.[47] Twenty years later, the Symbolist critic Georges Aurier, writing about Gauguin, declared that the true artist sees objects "only as *signs*. They are the letters of an enormous alphabet which only the man of genius knows how to spell."[48] Aurier echoes Laugel's description of visual images as the alphabet of a mystical language, but he now emphasizes the esoteric, mysterious quality of this alphabet.[49]

As Filiz Eda Burhan has stressed, Symbolism does not so much reject science as reinterpret it.[50] The Impressionists invoked the empiricist theory of perception to justify an art that would try to reproduce visual sensations as closely as possible. The following generation of avant-garde painters invoked the same theory to justify the making of deliberately unrealistic images. If visual sensations have only an indirect, symbolic relationship to reality, they reasoned, why should sensations be privileged over other kinds of visual signs? Any sign will do, so long as it functions as an equivalent for the original experience.

The shift from "sensation" to "equivalent" can be followed in the evolving rhetoric of avant-garde painting. In 1874, the critic Jules Castagnary justified the optical style of the Impressionists by saying that "They render not the landscape, but the sensation produced by the landscape."[51] (He was paraphrasing Mallarmé, who had proclaimed in 1864 that the goal of poetic language should be to evoke "not the thing itself but the effect it produces."[52]) Gauguin further generalized the idea of a visual "sensation," telling his followers that every work of art is "a transposition, a caricature, the passionate equivalent of a sensation received." He was quoted in a 1903 article by Maurice Denis, who returned to the topic in 1909, writing that:

> the emotions or spiritual states caused by any spectacle bring to the imagination of the artist symbols or plastic equivalents. These are capable of reproducing emotions or states of the spirit without it being necessary to provide the *copy* of the initial spectacle.[53]

Similarly, Matisse said in a 1913 interview that an artist "should not copy the walls, or objects on a table, but he should, above all, express a vision of color, the harmony of which corresponds to his feeling." Pressed for further explanation, he pointed to a jar of nasturtiums, sitting on a nearby table: "Take that table, for example . . . I do not literally paint that table, but the emotion it produces upon me."[54]

Instead of trying to capture "pure" visual sensation, the painters associated with Symbolism often turned to the decorative tradition, adopting a style of simplified outlines and unshaded colors. These anti-illusionist qualities signaled that the artist was searching for symbolic truth rather than literal reality. However, quite apart from its symbolic value, the decorative style exerted an important influence on the formal principles of modernist painting.[55] This influence can be divided into four main elements. One is flatness – the preservation of the integrity of the support against illusionism's tendency to "punch a hole" in the picture plane. The second is a deliberate simplification in the formal vocabulary of painting: the choice of shapes and colors is reduced to a handful, selected so that they contrast strongly with one another, or can be juxtaposed in simple but powerful harmonies. The third is the further pruning or modification of these shapes and colors so that they seem to derive from their material support rather than from artistic whim. The fourth is the stress on pattern rather than pictorial illusion as a compositional goal.

As Joseph Masheck demonstrates in "The Carpet Paradigm," the insistence on flatness became decorative dogma in the first half of the nineteenth century. It was already a subject for satire in Dickens's 1854 novel *Hard Times*, where a school inspector berates a little girl for saying that she would like a carpet with illusionistic flowers: the right-thinking inspector knows that only flat, non-pictorial designs are suitable for carpets.[56] Its crossover into figurative art is harder to trace. The seeming flatness of Manet's paintings of the 1860s reminded critics of *images d'Epinal*, cheap prints decorated with large areas of flat color. A few years later, the unbordered patches of color in Monet's Impressionist canvases provoked comparisons to wallpaper.[57]

The empiricist philosophy associated with Impressionism held that pure visual sensation consists of nothing more than color patches arrayed on the plane of the retina. However, this "retinal flatness" is something different from the absolute flatness of decorative design. Although Impressionist painting avoids the perspectival construction of the Renaissance tradition, the massing of the color patches, and the value contrasts between them, often create a strong sense of space.

It was Gauguin and his followers, in the 1880s, who first unequivocally established decorative flatness as a goal for figurative painting. The best-known statement of this goal appears in the "Definition of Neo-Traditionism" by Maurice Denis, who states that: "a painting – before it is a battle-horse, a nude woman, or some anecdote – is essentially a flat surface covered with colors assembled in a certain order."[58] As early as 1864, Taine had written:

> A picture is a colored surface in which the different tones and the different degrees of light are distributed with a certain selection . . . By themselves, and outside of their imitative purposes, colors, like lines, have a sense of their own. A gamut of colors which portray no real object may, like an arabesque of lines imitating no natural object, be either rich or meager, elegant or dull.

Conversely, even if colors and lines are "shaped into figures, draperies and architectural designs," this descriptive use does not cancel out their inherent expressive value.[59] As Masheck notes, Denis's more famous statement is essentially a paraphrase of Taine, but with a crucial shift of emphasis: instead of saying that an illusionistic image must also constitute a satisfying formal composition, he suggests that the flat, abstract composition is primary, the figurative value secondary.[60]

Since Gauguin, it has become almost axiomatic for modernist critics to identify "formal" analysis with the arrangment of lines and colors on a flat surface. However, formalism does not necessarily imply flatness. Before arriving at the topic of line and color, Taine discusses the expressive effect of changing the proportions of the human body. The artist may "select small heads and elongated bodies like Michael Angelo, simple and monumental lines like Fra Bartolomeo, undulating contours and varied inflexions like Correggio." Each of these will yield a different effect. Moving from the individual figure to the composition as a whole, Taine notes that the artist may choose among "balanced or disordered groups, upright or oblique attitudes, different planes and different compartments."[61] A more elaborate version of these categories provides the critical framework for Heinrich Wölfflin's *Principles of Art History*, published in 1915. In both cases, the arrangement of line and color upon a single plane appears as just one among a large repertory of possible formal structures. Similarly, Roger Fry, in his 1909 "Essay on Aesthetics," includes three-dimensional elements such as mass, space, and the inclination of individual planes in his list of art's purely formal characteristics, along with qualities such as order, variety, rhythm, light, shade, and color, which pertain more specifically to the arrangement of forms on a flat surface.[62] The exclusive identification between formalism and flatness is an assumption of the 1940s.

Decorative theory also seems to have been the source for the idea that artists should intentionally restrict and simplify their pictorial vocabulary, in order to make its formal character more evident. Maurice Denis criticized the mainstream Impressionists, such as Renoir, for their use of what he regarded as an excessive number of colors. "Impressionism," he wrote, "regarded color as nothing more than the result of an infinite number of contrasts; deconstructing with a prism, the Impressionists reconstructed reflections and nuances; for a given number of grays, they substituted an equal number of tints. This is Impressionism's fundamental vice." In contrast, Denis praised Manet's *Fife Player* for having been painted with only "four tones," and found in Cézanne "as much simplicity, austerity, and grandeur as in Manet," because Cézanne too deployed a severely reduced palette.[63] Emile Bernard, another of Gauguin's students, also praised Cézanne for working with a reduced palette, comparing him to a skilled weaver making a tapestry from colored threads.[64]

This idea of a simplified coloristic vocabulary touches on a terminological problem that is worth mentioning because it returned to haunt the criticism of Cubism. Denis described Renoir's use of color as "analytic," because Renoir analyzed his optical sensations into an "infinite" number of contrasting colors. Conversely, Denis described the simplified palette of Manet's *Fife Player* as "synthetic."[65] These terms "analytic" and "synthetic" were very much in vogue in the late nineteeth century. The problem is that their meanings are anything but consistent. Like Denis, Emile Zola had noted Manet's tendency to reduce complex colors and forms to a few "strong contrasts;" for Zola this made Manet into an "analytic" painter.[66] Evidently, the phenomenon of expressive simplification could be described as either "analytic" or "synthetic."

The idea of working with a limited, more harmonious palette played an important role in nineteenth-century decorative theory. In his influential opus, *Style in the Technical and Constructive Arts, or Practical Aesthetics*, published in 1860, Gottfried Semper argued that older tapestries were superior to modern ones precisely because earlier weavers worked with a small number of natural dyes, while modern weavers could choose from an unlimited number of colors, produced by modern chemistry. As if responding to Semper's argument, Aristide Maillol made his first reputation, in the 1890s, as a weaver working exclusively with natural dyes.[67]

By the end of the century, this idea of faithfulness to materials had been widely accepted. Masheck quotes the French theorist Bernard Bosanquet as writing that "Every form . . . has behind it a further form in the material itself; for this determines, as we say, 'what you can do with it.'"[68] Semper's earlier formulation had been more specific, however: he believed that each craft technique suggested its own characteristic formal vocabulary. For instance, he argued that the technique of weaving, with its repeated strands of warp and woof, arranged at right angles and overlapping in a regular pattern, lay at the origin of geometric pattern in general. When figurative imagery was overlaid on a woven support, as in embroidery, the geometric structure of the support tended to "constrain" the figuration to assume "geometric forms" that "could only arise from square elements."[69]

Within a few decades, Semper's descriptive analysis was taken by artists as a prescriptive manifesto. Around 1900, when the Norwegian artist Gerhard Munthe created a series of tapestries illustrating Norse legends, he adopted a style of quasi-abstract, rectilinear forms, with the result that his

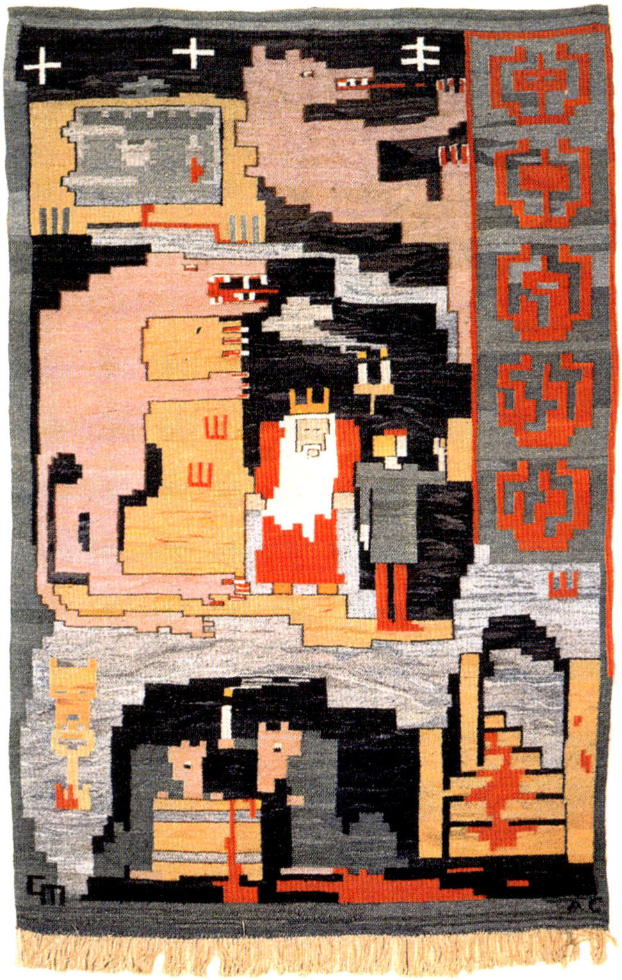

2 Gerhard Munthe. *The Tower of Blood.* 1902. Tapestry, 145 × 96 cm. Nordenfjeldske Kunstgewerbemuseum, Trondheim

kings and monsters look strangely like the pixilated characters from a primitive video game (fig. 2). A few years later, the Viennese designer Kolo Moser launched a new decorative style based on the grid; its Semperian origins are especially evident in Moser's furniture, which is often covered with a woven checkerboard of light and dark squares.[70]

It is difficult to determine the limits of Semper's influence. Mondrian adopted the short-title of Semper's treatise, *Der Stil*, as the label for his own school of geometric abstract painting.[71] The Greenbergian doctrine that the formal vocabulary of painting should reflect its basic features – that is, "the flat surface, the shape of the support, [and] the properties of the pigment" – also seems to derive from Semper, although probably at second- or thirdhand.[72] At a certain point, Semper's influence becomes indistinguishable from the influence of the decorative tradition as a whole.

The aspects of decorative style considered so far are mostly prohibitions: thou shalt not punch a hole in the plane, thou shalt not use too many colors. However, decoration also implies a number of positive commandments: guidelines for designing a decorative as opposed to an illusionistic composition. Semper refers to three basic elements of beauty – proportion, symmetry, and direction[73] – but the problem of defining the abstract principles of decoration is explored in greater depth by other critics. In the introduction to his *Grammar of the Decorative Arts*, originally published in 1882 and frequently reprinted thereafter, the influential critic Charles Blanc lists five "General Laws of Ornament," accompanied by another five corollary laws. The most basic principle is the repetition of a single motif; its corollary is consonance among the different motifs used in a design. The second principle is the regular alternation between two basic motifs; this can be intensified by creating a visible contrast between them. A symmetrical pattern can be enriched by being converted into one that spreads out in a generally symmetrical manner without forming a mirror image. A progression of similar elements growing larger or smaller by steps can be refined into a smooth gradation. And the decorative effects of casual confusion can be achieved deliberately by complication.[74] Although Blanc insists that designs for floors, carpets, tapestries, and wallpapers should avoid the illusion of depth, his "laws of ornament" are also applicable to designs for three-dimensional objects such as furniture. A regular alternation between spheres and cubes, for instance, provides a three-dimensional equivalent for the alternation of contrasting colors, such as orange and blue.[75]

Blanc's enumeration of the principles of decorative design makes it clear that there is something deeply problematic about the idea of applying decorative principles to figurative art. It is easy enough to obey the prohibitions – to avoid deep space, to use a restricted palette, for example. But the positive demands of decoration – for repetition, symmetry, complication, and others – pose a serious problem. While academic illusionism turns the space of painting into a kind of stage, with figures and props arranged asymmetrically for maximum dramatic impact, decorative art ignores the demands of narrative, sacrificing dramatic impact for the formal pleasures of color and pattern. Complication replaces clarity; symmetry replaces asymmetry; repetition and standardization replace individualization. Semper and his successors were able – just – to hold these qualities in balance. With the advent of Cubism, form definitively triumphed over narrative.

Theories of Cubism

It may seem a quixotic enterprise to ask how these nineteenth-century ideas influenced the development of Cubism, if only because Picasso is commonly believed to have invented Cubism in a quasi-unconscious fashion, without ever formulating a theory about what he was doing. Kahnweiler declared, "No one has ever really explained the theory for the simple reason that there was no theory." On another occasion, he recalled that, "In the years between 1908 and 1914, I saw Picasso almost every day, but I have to say that he never said much about his work or anything related to it."[76] Similarly, Fernande Olivier, Picasso's companion in the years 1904–12, wrote that he came to dislike visiting the Saturday salon of the collectors Gertrude and Leo Stein "because people were always trying to make him explain his position, which he found difficult to do, especially in French; and anyway he couldn't explain what he felt needed no explanation. He came away exasperated and furious."[77] In late 1911, Picasso told an interviewer from the *Paris-Journal*, "There is no such thing as Cubism."[78]

He had not always been so disdainful of theorizing, however. Leo Stein, one of his earliest patrons, later mocked the way that Picasso justified the geometrical constructions in his early Cubist paintings as a higher form of realism: "I would explain to him that what Plato and other philosophers meant by 'real thing' were not diagrams, that diagrams were abstract simplifications and not a whit more real than things with all their complexities, that Platonic ideas were worlds away from abstractions, and couldn't be pictured."[79] Another American, the journalist Gelett Burgess, interviewed Picasso in 1908 and described him as talking "of values and volumes, of the subjective and of the sentiment of emotion and instinct."[80] In early 1911, Picasso discussed his work at length with the Spanish-American critic, collector, and caricaturist Marius de Zayas, who summed up their conversations in a brochure published to accompany Picasso's first American exhibition, at Alfred Stieglitz's gallery *291*.[81]

Evidently, in these early years, Picasso felt that he needed to justify his practice in terms of a theory. Theoretical discussions also seem to have played an important role in Picasso's relationship with Georges Braque, the artist who was virtually his collaborator from 1907 to 1914. Picasso later told Françoise Gilot, "Almost every evening, either I went to Braque's studio or Braque came to mine. Each of us *had* to see what the other had done during the day." The poet Guillaume Apollinaire, who knew both men well, referred to Braque as the "verifier" who "corroborated" Picasso's discoveries. Their dialogue was carried on largely in their pictures, but it was also clearly theoretical. Picasso and Braque's correspondence of the Cubist years refers frequently to discussions of art, and when they were together in the south of France, Picasso apologized to another correspondent that he had little time to write because "Braque and I have had so many conversations about art."[82]

Years later, recalling these conversations, Braque told an interviewer that "Picasso and I said things to each other that will never be said again . . . that no one will ever be able to understand."[83] Indeed, it is impossible to reconstruct these conversations. But it seems likely that they involved the ideas that Picasso and Braque expressed in their public statements, some made during the early years of Cubism, others decades later. In many cases, they find close counterparts in remarks made by friends and associates during the Cubist epoch. By compiling and comparing these statements, it is possible to outline the ideas that Picasso and Braque seem to have developed in tandem with their work.

There was no one theory of Cubism. Rather, there were different theories, corresponding to the different kinds of work that the artists produced at different moments. In spring 1908, when there occurred the first interaction between Picasso's and Braque's works, the artists and their companions seem to have thought of the nascent style as essentially decorative. Discussing Picasso's work of winter 1907–08 Kahnweiler wrote that the artist was for several months "occupied only with the articulation of the color planes."[84] Kahnweiler here seems to be describing the style of the first studies (fig. 3) for the *Three Women*, executed during just these months.[85] By Charles Blanc's criteria, it is clearly a decorative style, based on the repetition of similar arcs throughout the composition. The use of the same curves to describe the figures, their garments, and their setting brings the different elements of the scene into formal consonance, but the monotony of the linear forms is offset

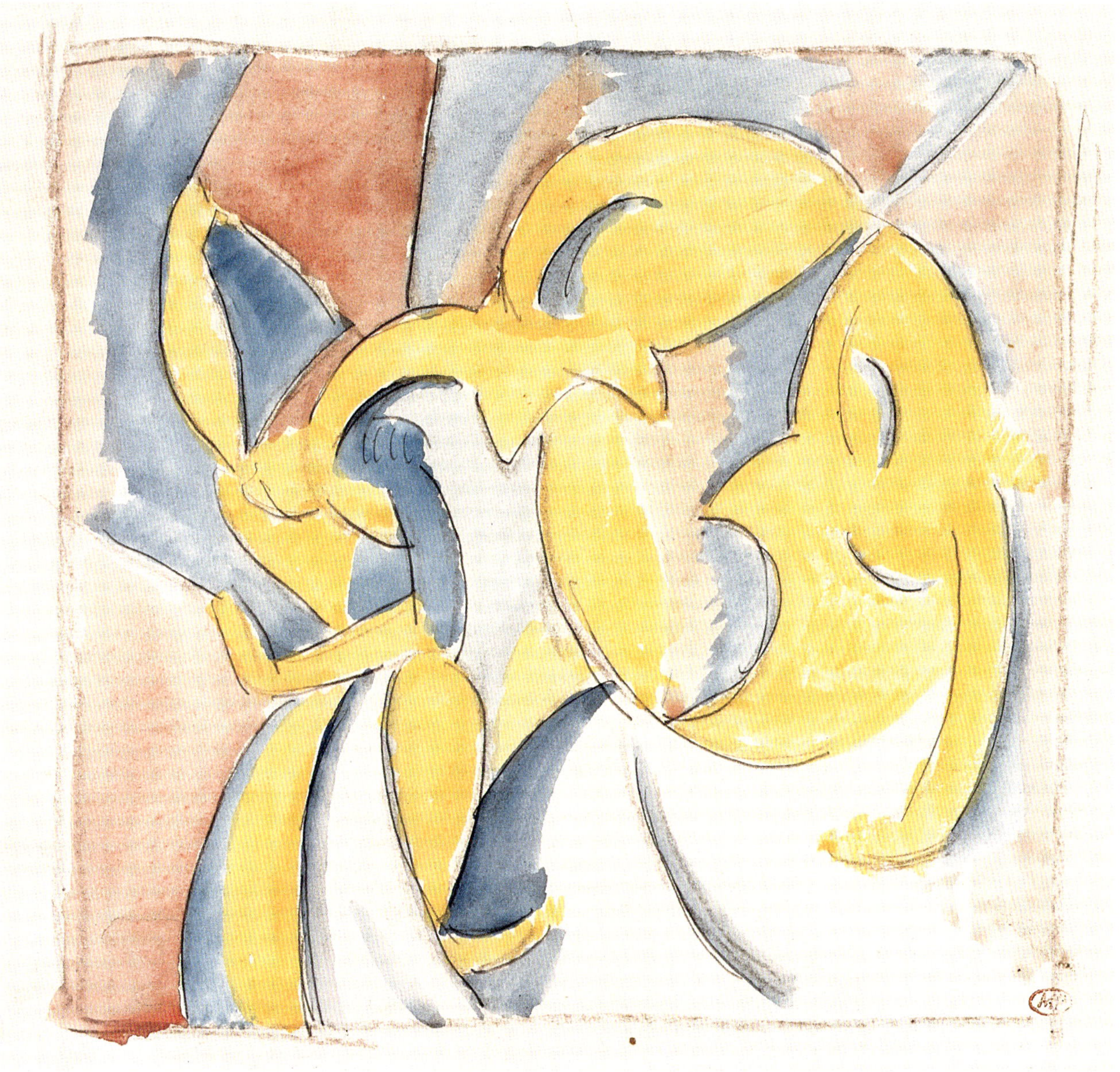

3 Picasso. *Three Women.* Paris, fall 1907. Watercolor, lead pencil, and charcoal on paper, sheet size 33 × 25 cm. Zervos XXVI, 337; Richet 188. Musée Picasso, Paris

by their alternating colors – blue and pink in the early drawings of this series, modulating into green and brick-red in the later drawings. The standing figure at center is flanked by two crouching figures at left and right, each with one raised arm, but strict symmetry is avoided in favor of complication. The composition as a whole (possibly inspired by Signac's portrait of Félix Fénéon) seems to be organized around pinwheeling curves emanating from the center, but the clockwise motion of the curves in the lower half of the composition is offset by a counter-clockwise motion of the curves in the upper half. The construction of the figures around interlacing lines recalls the pan-European style

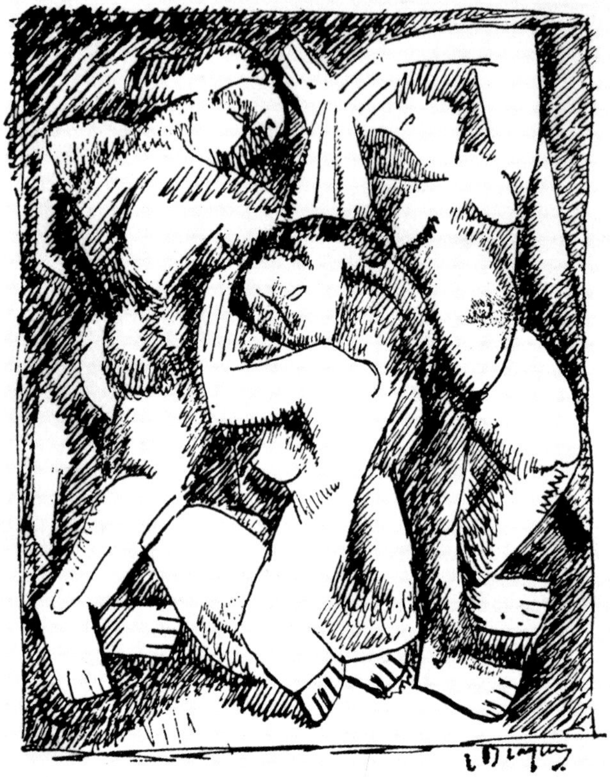

4 Braque. *Woman.* Paris, early 1908. Ink. Present whereabouts unknown. Formerly collection Gelett Burgess

known variously as Art Nouveau, Jugendstil, and "Modern-Style." Picasso himself later described Cubism as nothing more than a variant on the "Modern-Style." While this is clearly exaggeration, intended to provoke, the studies for the *Three Women* suggest a kernel of truth in his remark.[86]

Braque saw the unfinished canvas of the *Three Women* in Picasso's studio, and was so impressed that he painted his own version, a large canvas entitled *Woman,* exhibited at the spring 1908 Salon des Indépendants. The actual canvas is lost, but its composition has been preserved in the reproduction of a drawing (fig. 4) that Braque executed for Gelett Burgess. Burgess's account of his conversation with Braque offers the earliest instance of the Cubist idea of multiple perspectives. "To portray every physical aspect of such a figure, [Braque] said, required three figures, much as the representation of a house requires a plan, an elevation and a section." The distortion or abstraction of the figures was explained by Braque as the result of a quest for a new kind of decorative beauty. "Nature," he argued, "is a mere pretext for a decorative composition." However, Braque added, his goal was a "harmony of volume," not a "mere decorative effect."[87] This rejection of merely two-dimensional pattern is also apparent in Kahnweiler, who followed his remarks on Picasso's winter 1907–08 work by commenting that Picasso soon "perceived the danger of lowering his art to the level of ornament," and resumed his search for "the representation of the three-dimensional."[88]

The quest for a style that was both decorative and three-dimensional led Picasso to introduce the faceting visible in the finished version of the *Three Women* and in many of his summer 1909 paintings (fig. 5). This new style was justified, in turn, by reference to a Neo-Platonic theory that geometric forms could express the "real" forms of objects more clearly than did the naturalistic forms of conventional realism.[89] The human body, in these pictures, appears as a monolithic mass with crystalline contours. The shading is not meant to reproduce the appearance of the body under any actual lighting conditions, but to give an intensified sense of its three-dimensional form.[90]

When discussing Picasso's work of 1909–10, Kahnweiler cited John Locke, arguing that Picasso's goal was to represent what Locke had called the "primary" qualities of an object – "the object's form and its position in space" – without recourse to "secondary" qualities such as light and color.[91] At first glance, this seems paradoxical. A painting requires light to be seen; indeed, what distinguishes painting from sculpture is precisely its use of color and shade. What Kahnweiler was referring to, however, was Picasso's renunciation of traditional chiaroscuro – the technique of evoking three-dimensional form by reproducing the way that incident light plays across it, producing a sequence of highlights and shadows. Picasso apparently considered chiaroscuro a "dishonest" way of representing three-dimensional form.[92] He therefore turned to faceting as a means of describing three-dimensional form without using conventional shading. There is shading in the *Seated Woman* of summer 1909, but it does not correspond to the shadows cast by an imaginary light source within the space of the painting; it is, rather, an abstract alternation of light and dark facets, serving simply to set one plane off from the next.[93]

In the language of nineteenth-century empiricism, faceting is a device for communicating "tactile values" – for representing the actual three-dimensional forms of things

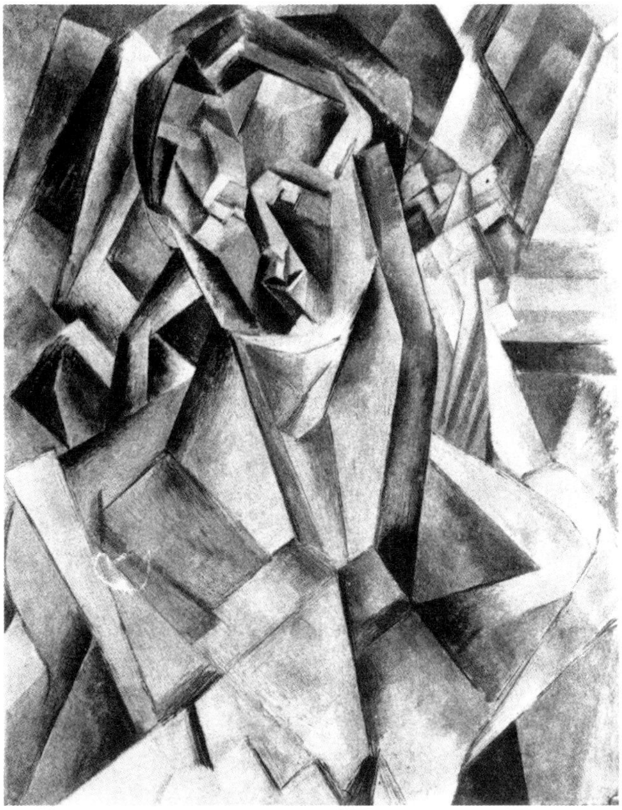

5 Picasso. *Seated Woman.* Horta de Ebro, summer 1909. Oil on canvas, 81 × 65 cm. D.R. 292. Private collection

rather than the optical sensations produced by them. For all their strangeness, Picasso's faceted figures of 1909 have a monumental quality that recalls Cézanne's card players or the figures of the Italian "Primitives." After the dematerialization of form in Impressionism, and the flattening of form in Post-Impressionism, this restoration of a sense of sculptural solidity (without a return to conventional realism) was a major achievement.

This sense of solidity soon began to dissolve, however. The continuous faceting of 1909 was replaced in 1910–12 by a new image of the body as an open scaffolding supporting a series of free-floating planes. For Kahnweiler, this breaking open of the "closed form" was the "decisive advance which set Cubism free from the language previously used by painting."[94]

It was in these years that the dialogue between Picasso and Braque seems to have been most intense, and that each artist's work most closely resembled the other's (figs. 6, 7). Although Picasso said little about his work of this period, Braque's more numerous statements may serve as a guide to the intentions of both artists. "In nature, there is a kind of tactile – I would almost say manual – space," Braque later said. The "materialization" of the new space satisfied his desire "to touch the object and not merely to see it . . . Fragmentation gave me a way to establish space, and movement in space, and I could only introduce the object after making the space for it." Fragmentation was a way for him "to get as close as possible to the object."[95] Read in isolation, Braque's remarks seem like the expression of a personal, idiosyncratic desire to make painting into an instrument of touch. Replaced in the context of nineteenth-century ideas about art and perception, they reveal themselves as a choice between two alternatives that were widely understood as polar opposites. Braque's earlier Fauve canvases had pursued the logic of optical sensation to one extreme; his new Cubist pictures explored the possibility of a pictorial syntax based instead on tactile sensation.[96]

Braque's goal in these years was the creation of a tactile space. Hence his dissatisfaction with "traditional perspective." "It's mechanical," Braque said, "it doesn't allow you to possess things fully."[97] What he seems to have meant by this was that traditional perspective, with its diagonals converging toward a vanishing point, made the things in the picture appear to recede from the viewer. It was therefore necessary to abandon perspective. "I said goodbye to the vanishing point . . . Instead of beginning with the foreground, I placed myself in the middle of the painting," Braque said. "Soon I even inverted perspective and its pyramid of forms, turning it around so that it came toward me – so that it came up to the viewer."[98]

Braque's new "interpretation . . . of surface and volume" was meant, he said, to re-establish "a tactile or palpable feeling. It's very nice to make people see something, but if you can make them touch it, that's better still!" This tactile sense had existed in painting before the high Renaissance: "You find it in Cimabue, in the Italian Primitives, in the early Flemish painters." Indeed, Cimabue seemed to Braque "almost of our own time . . . His concern with construction, his sense of monumental volume have always struck me. He used constructive elements whose qualities we would praise centuries later . . . His frontal vision, the models of his forms continue to provoke us moderns."[99]

What is surprising is that Braque should have invoked the ideas of tactile sensation and monumental volume to

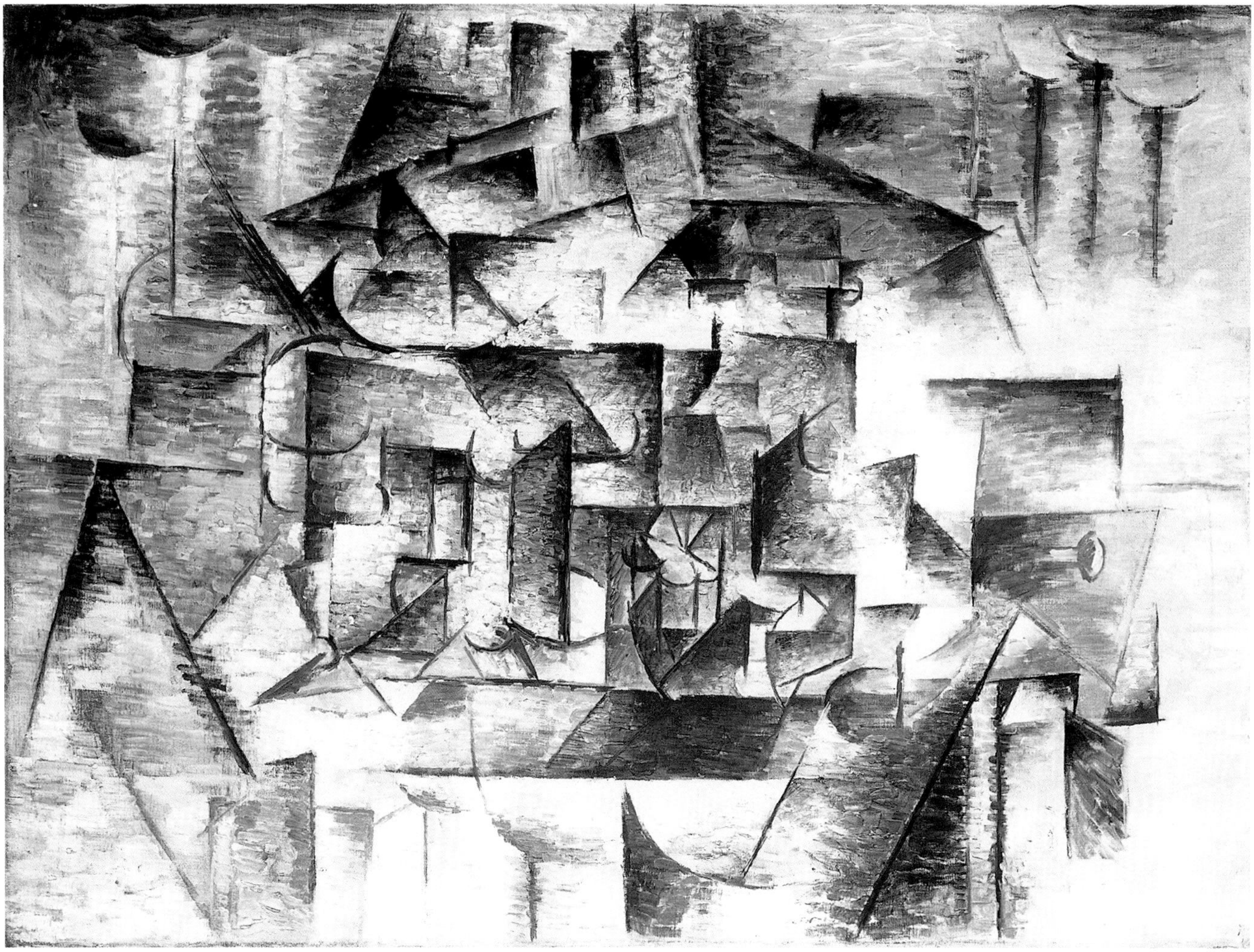

6 Picasso. *Still Life with Glass and Lemon.* Cadaqués, summer 1910. Oil on canvas, 73 × 100 cm. D.R. 357. Cincinnati Art Museum, Bequest of Mary E. Johnston

justify the new style of 1910–12 Cubism, which fragmented bodies and objects rather than reinforcing their sculptural solidity. It seemed to at least one contemporary observer that Picasso and Braque had merely substituted "an impressionism of form" for the original Impressionism of "color."[100] Other observers felt that Cubism added a new, "fourth dimension" to space – a "boundless sense of space or grandeur" that enlarged (rather than shrunk) the objects within it, enhancing their "plasticity."[101] Picasso and Braque themselves do not seem to have employed this language of the "fourth dimension," but Picasso alluded to it in a 1912 letter to Kahnweiler, recalling a moment in 1908 when he had tried to explain one of his faceted figures to Leo Stein, and Stein had reacted by saying, "But that's the fourth dimension!"[102]

It might be argued that the break-up of form in 1910–12 Cubism was an unavoidable by-product of the search for a new, projective space that would advance toward the viewer instead of receding. Braque's and Picasso's pictures of these years are organized around a rectilinear scaffolding, like a child's jungle-gym, with different elements of the image attached to different parts of the scaffolding, some nearer to the viewer, some farther away. In effect, Picasso and Braque replace the converging diagonals of traditional perspective

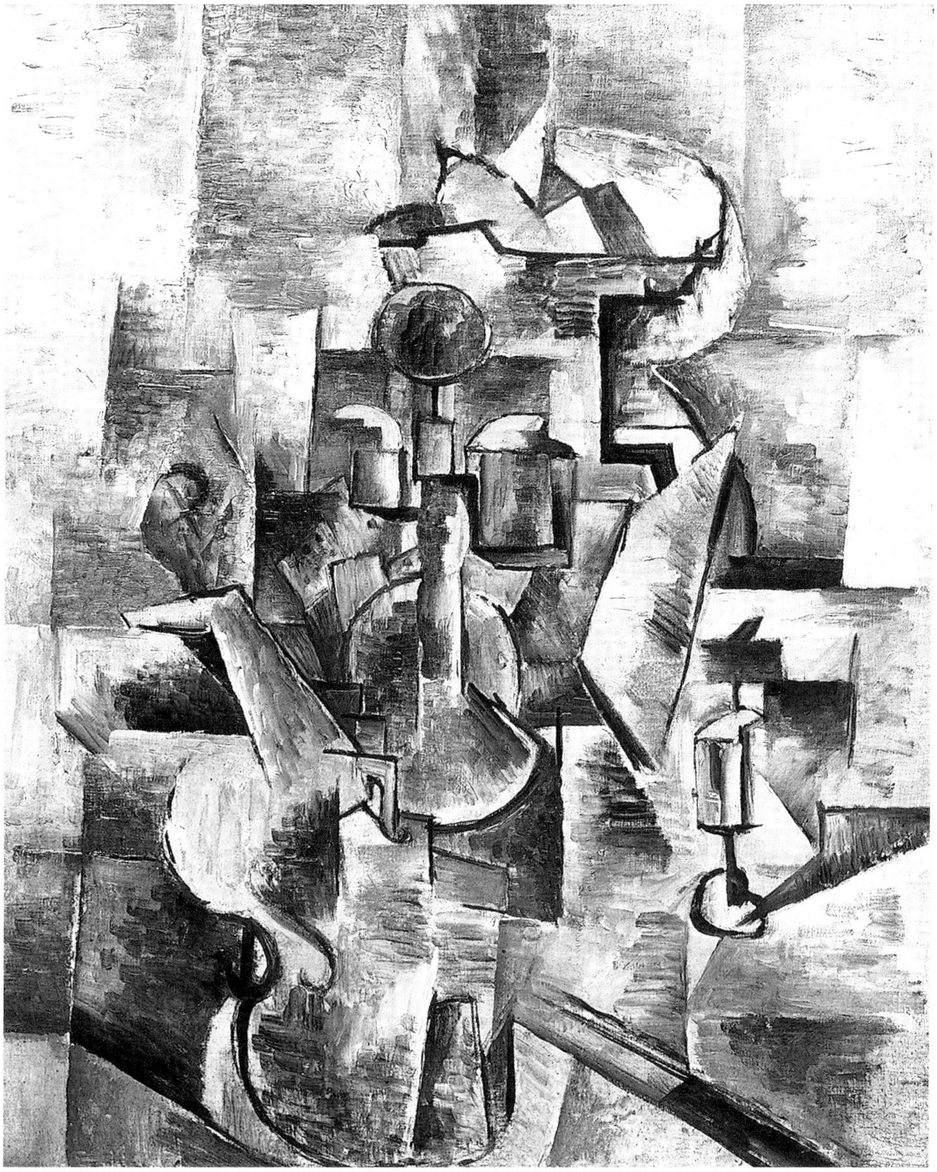

7 Braque. *Violin and Candlestick.* Paris, fall 1910. Oil on canvas, 61 × 50 cm. Romilly 63. San Francisco Museum of Modern Art. Gift of Rita B. Schreiber in loving memory of her husband, Taft Schreiber

with an arrangement of overlapping planes, supported by the scaffolding of the Cubist grid (figs. 6, 7). Braque described this development: "In order to avoid a recession toward infinity, I began superimposing planes one over the other, separated by slight distances. To make the viewer understand that things stand one in front of the other, rather than going back into space."[103] However, the price for this spatial reorganization was that everything in the picture had to be broken apart into individual planes that could be attached separately to the scaffolding of the grid.

A further result of this transformation was that the rectilinear scaffolding began to determine the placement and

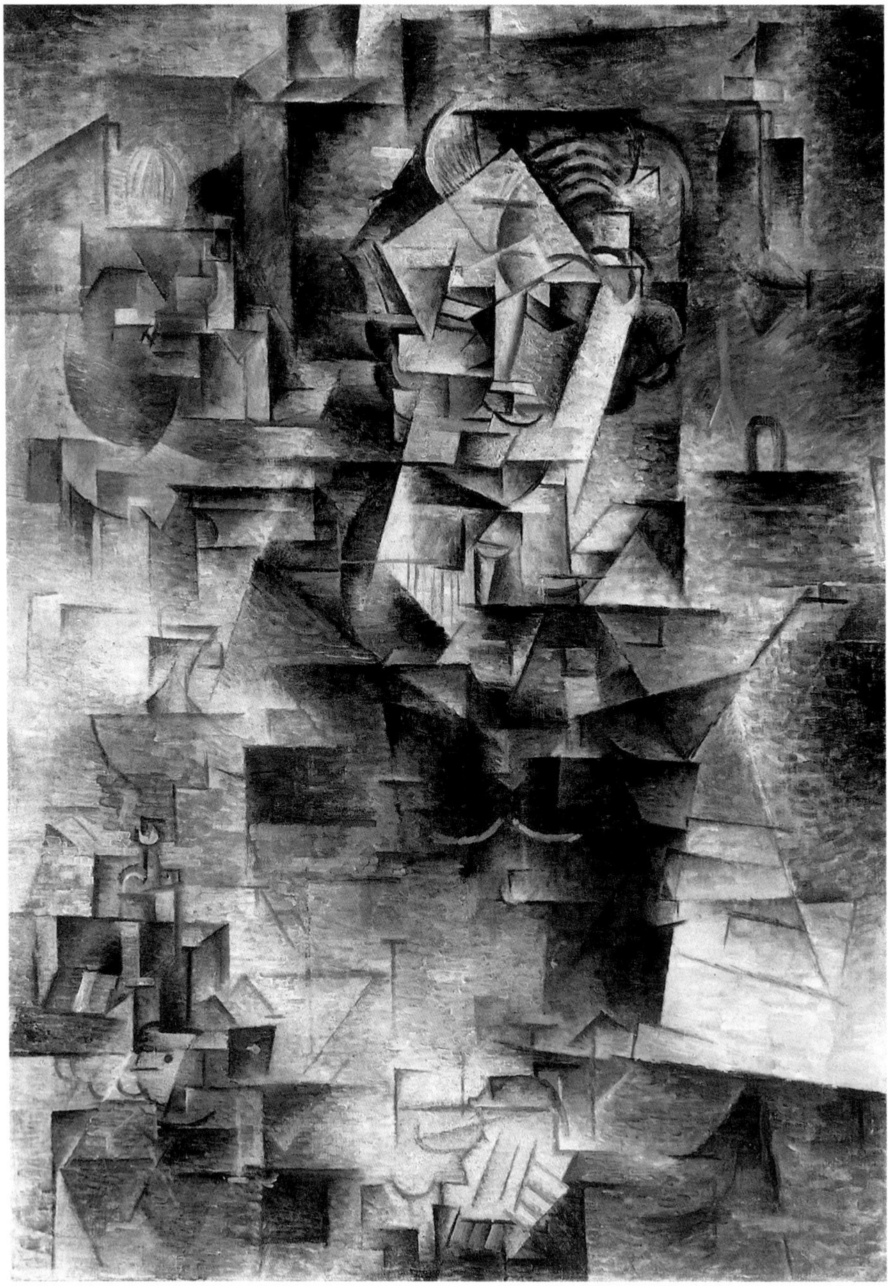

8 Picasso. *Daniel-Henry Kahnweiler.* Paris, fall–winter 1910. Oil on canvas, 100.6 × 72.8 cm. D.R. 368. The Art Institute of Chicago. Gift of Mrs. Gilbert W. Chapman in memory of Charles B. Goodspeed

structure of everything in the composition. As Kahnweiler wrote, "the Cubists sided resolutely with the canvas against the subject, and completely subordinated the part to the whole." The forms indicating particular objects "were bent to the strongly emphasized rhythm of the architecture."[104]

The idea of tactile space thus led step by step into the idea of an abstract structure that was determined even before the painter decided on his subject. "At that period," Picasso recalled, "I was doing painting for its own sake. It was really pure painting, and the composition was done as a composition." It was only in the later stages of work on a picture that he added "references to natural forms," intended "to bring one back to visual reality, recognizable to anyone." For instance, he said, his fall 1910 portrait of Kahnweiler (fig. 8) had originally seemed as indefinite as "smoke." So, Picasso said, "I added the attributes – a suggestion of eyes, the wave in the hair, an ear lobe, the clasped hands."[105]

Other avant-garde painters had approached abstraction by simplifying an originally realistic image. The Cubists began with an abstract image and modified it just enough to suggest reality. As one critic put it in a 1921 article: "Whereas Matisse reduces surrounding objects to patches of color, Braque transforms the patches of color into objects, which suggest themselves to his fancy. For example . . . he transforms a white patch into a sheet of music."[106] A staff and notes on a white patch could suggest sheet music; an *f*-shaped sound-hole, a violin; a moustache, a man's head.

If the representational component of the Cubist picture had been reduced to a few clues, scattered across the surface, how was the viewer supposed to recognize the subject? The answer, according to Kahnweiler, was that the clue would provide a "stimulus" evoking "memory images," and that the viewer would project these realistic images onto the abstract structure of the picture. The "desired physical representation" would thereby come into being not on canvas but "in the spectator's mind."[107]

Kahnweiler's explanation of Cubist representation, here, is essentially a restatement of the empiricist theory of guided projection that the Impressionists had invoked forty years earlier.[108] Then, it was optical sensations that provided the stimuli for tactile associations drawn from memory, making it possible for the viewer to reconstruct a three-dimensional image from two-dimensional clues. Now, it was samples of conventional drawing that allowed the viewer to reconstruct a recognizable image, projecting his "memory images" onto the field of geometric lines and planes.[109]

If the Cubists invoked the same perceptual theory as the Impressionists, they drew far more radical conclusions from it. Cézanne may have appealed to empiricism to justify his combination of multiple viewpoints within a single image. Picasso and Braque combined multiple kinds of information – contours, textures, written inscriptions – each one presented as an independent element within an image that now seemed to transcribe primarily the experience of memory rather than observation.

The poet Apollinaire – an intimate friend of the artists – reacted by describing Cubism as an "art of painting new configurations with elements borrowed, not from visual, but from conceptual reality."[110] The problem, as Apollinaire acknowledged, was that the resulting appearance of objects in Cubist paintings was "far different" from their normal appearance.[111] Indeed, Picasso and Braque could no longer count on viewers recognizing the subjects of their pictures. If the clues or stimuli did not evoke the appropriate memory images, viewers might not be able to make sense out of a picture, or might misconstrue it – mistaking a man for a landscape, for instance.[112] Acknowledging this possibility, Picasso claimed, in his 1911 interview with Marius de Zayas, that his goal was not, in fact, to represent an object or a scene but rather to present a "pictorial equivalent" corresponding to "the emotion or idea generated from the spectacle and not the spectacle itself."[113]

Picasso was falling back here on the Symbolistic esthetic of the previous generation, itself deeply rooted in empiricist philosophy. As noted above, Gauguin had introduced the idea that a painting was the "equivalent of a sensation received," and Maurice Denis had revived the idea in a 1909 article. For these Symbolists, the idea of the equivalent reflected their belief that the task of painting was not to reproduce appearances but to create expressive signs.[114] Although the precise term is absent, a similar idea appears in Burgess's 1908 interview with Braque, who says that he "looks at Nature in order to possess it emotionally." The "harmony" of his composition is meant to express a "spiritual sentiment."[115]

Neither Picasso nor Braque employed the term "sign" in the years 1910–13. Nonetheless, it seems clear that signs played an increasingly important role in their work of the time. In Picasso's spring 1912 *Head of Man with Pipe* (fig. 9), for instance, the individual features of the face are identified primarily by semi-abstract signs: the eyes are represented by circles or half-moons dangling from rods. It is these signs that carry the main burden of representation; the geometric planes of the composition have become mere supports onto which identifying signs or clues may be inscribed. The large geometrical elements thus play a less important – or at least a different – role than they played in Picasso's work of the preceding years. In his 1909 *Seated Woman* (see fig. 5), for instance, the crystalline facets had served to exaggerate and clarify the ridges and hollows of human anatomy. By 1912, it is much more difficult to define a one-to-one correspondence between the geometric forms

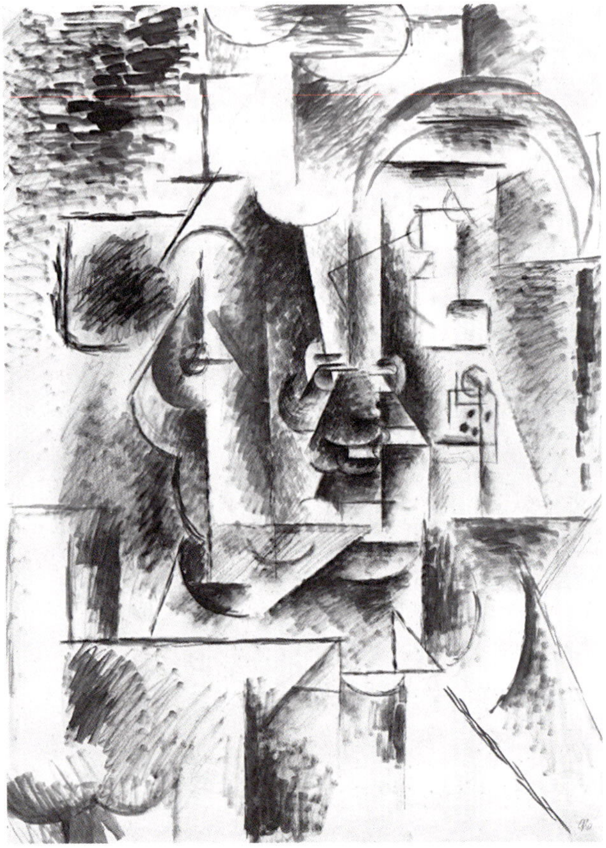

9 Picasso. *Head of Man with Pipe.* Paris, spring 1912. Chalk and oil wash, 64.2 × 46.7 cm. D.R. 420. Fogg Art Museum, Harvard University Art Museum, Annie S. Coburn Fund

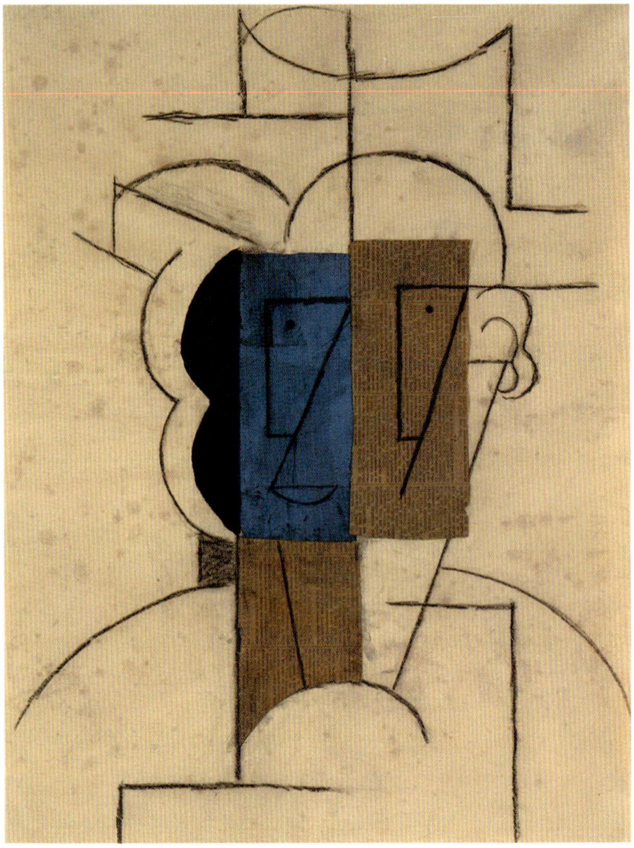

10 Picasso. *Man with a Hat.* Paris, after December 3, 1912. Posted paper, charcoal, and ink on paper, 62.2 × 47.3 cm. The Museum of Modern Art, New York. Purchase

of the composition and the real contours of the body they represent.

Picasso's *Man with a Hat* (fig. 10), executed in late 1912, displays a "semiological" character similar to that of his spring 1912 *Head of a Man.* In the intervening months, the shimmering chiaroscuro of 1910–11 Cubism has vanished, and the complex overlapping planes have been reduced to a few bare lines. The facial features are indicated by summary notations: a dot and an angle for eyes and nose, a small pair of loops for an ear at right, a more regular pair of semi-circles for the cheek and brow at left. The extreme simplicity of *Man with a Hat* seems calculated to provoke the ire of viewers accustomed to conventional realism. Years later, discussing another picture with simplified features, Picasso delighted in imagining the response of an angry viewer demanding: "How can that man put only two dots for the eyes, a button for the nose and a bit of line for the mouth?"[116]

Indeed, part of the pleasure of *Man with a Hat* lies in the way that it barely functions as a representation of a recognizable figure. The composition as a whole is virtually abstract: only the curves of the ear and mouth identify it unequivocally as a face. Deprived of these signs, and furnished instead with strings or a label, the same arrangement of planes might read as a guitar or a bottle – or both (fig. 11).

The "polysemy" of Picasso's forms (as Yve-Alain Bois has dubbed it) does not seem to have attracted critical attention at the time.[117] It was only a decade later, writing about Juan Gris rather than Picasso, that the critic Maurice Raynal took note of the role in Cubism of what he called "plastic metaphor" – that is, the use of the same form to represent

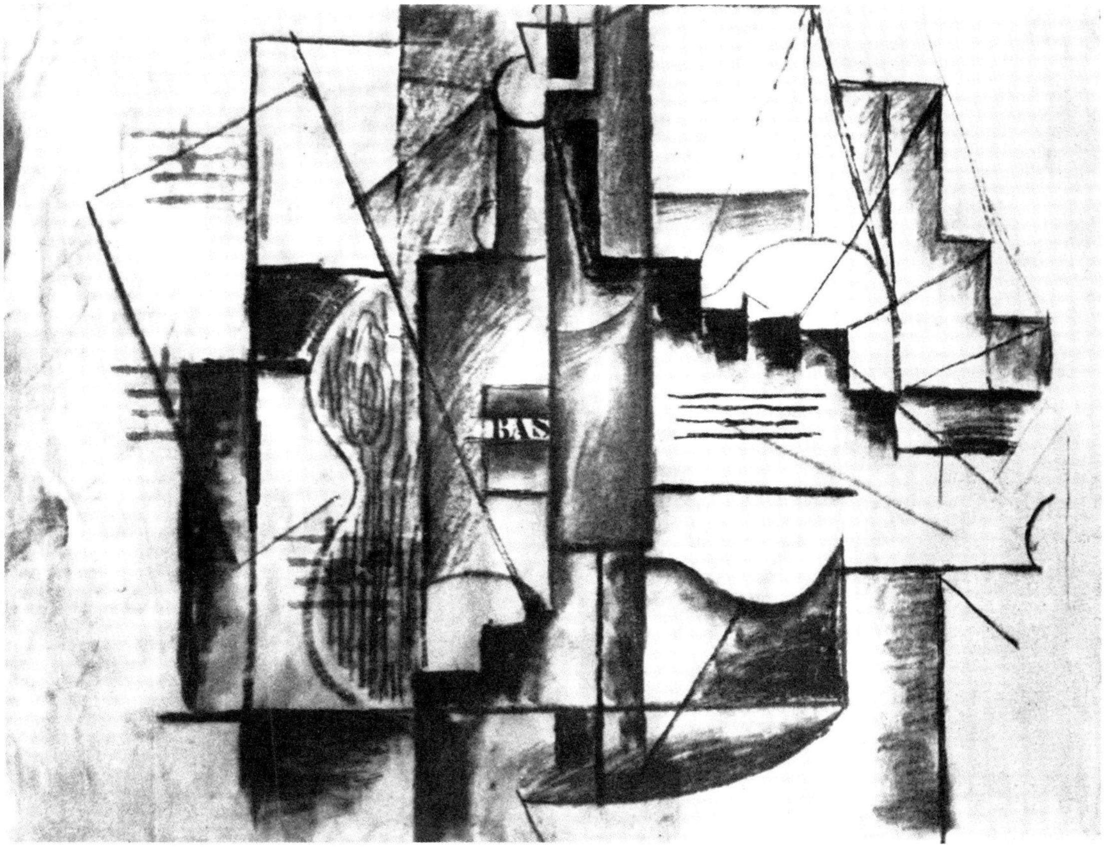

11 Picasso. *Bottle of Bass and Guitar.* Paris, fall 1912. Pastel, charcoal, and ink, 47.7 × 63.5 cm. D.R. 511. The Douglas Cooper Collection, Churchglade Ltd

two different motifs. The same back-and-forth curve may be used to represent both the side of a guitar and the contour of a range of hills; parallel lines may indicate both the strings of a guitar and the staff of a page of sheet music.[118] As Christopher Green has noted, this new, linguistic approach to the reading of Cubism derives, on one hand, from a renewed interest in the Symbolist poetry of Mallarmé and, on the other, from curiosity about the scientific discipline of linguistics.[119]

As Green demonstrates, Gris and Kahnweiler, in particular, seem to have shared a strong interest in linguistics, an interest that bore fruit in Kahnweiler's 1946 monograph, *Juan Gris,* which includes a long section devoted to a linguistic analysis of Cubism and art in general.[120] Evidently, Kahnweiler had discussed this topic with Picasso, who argued in a 1945 interview that nature "is only translatable into painting by signs" that offer an "equivalent" to it: "It has been agreed upon that a specific sign represents a tree, another a house, a man, a woman; exactly as in language, the word 'man' evokes the image of a man, the word 'house' a house and this in all languages although in every language the word varies."[121] The Symbolist idea of art as a system of signs was now revived in specifically linguistic terms.

Kahnweiler soon refined his linguistic analysis of art, arguing that the most important breakthrough in Cubism was Picasso's recognition that "Painting and sculpture are *forms of writing.* Their products are signs, emblems, and not a mirror, more or less distorted, of the external world. Once recognized, this evidence at one blow liberated the plastic arts from the slavery of illusionist style."[122]

Finally, it seems worth considering the terms "Analytic Cubism" and "Synthetic Cubism," which are used so routinely by art historians that it seems as if they must belong to the inner history of the movement, although in fact they were never employed by Picasso or Braque. Part of the confusion here stems from the adjectives "analytic" and "synthetic," which have been used in so many different ways that they have become virtually meaningless. In Kant's *Critique of Pure Reason*, they are associated with different kinds of logical judgments, but this usage has nothing to do with Cubism.[123] In empiricist discussions of perception, as we have seen, "analysis" was associated with the scientific quest to identify the most basic units of sensation, while "synthesis" served to describe the mind's activity in forging a single perception from the varied sensations triggered by a given object or experience. This scientific usage seems to have influenced Post-Impressionists such as Maurice Denis and Emile Bernard, who used "analysis" to describe the Impressionist quest to capture pure visual sensation and "synthesis" to describe their own simplified, decorative method of composition.

In his 1916 essay *The Rise of Cubism*, Kahnweiler contrasts the "analytical description of the object" in 1908–09 Cubism with the "synthesis" of 1910–11 Cubism. What is new here is the "analysis" of three-dimensional form rather than color – that is, the reference to tactile rather than optical sensation. As noted, this "analysis" takes place by the transformation of natural form into a series of geometric solids and planes (see fig. 5). According to Kahnweiler, Picasso and Braque "were disturbed by the unavoidable distortion of form" resulting from this process.[124]

The break-up of "closed form" in Picasso's work of summer 1910, and Braque's introduction of realistic "clues" around the same time provided a surprising answer to this problem. As long as there had been the "slightest verisimilitude" in the artists' pictures, the contrast between the represented form and the viewer's memory of natural form had produced the sensation of distortion. After summer 1910, however, the painting no longer had "the least resemblance to actuality." Instead, it offered a geometric "scheme of forms" and a series of "real details" that served as clues to the identity of the motif. These were to be be combined into a coherent image "in the mind of the spectator." Since there was no longer any coherent body or object in the picture, there was nothing to conflict with the viewer's memory of natural form, and therefore no sense of distortion. Kahnweiler summed up this process by saying that, "instead of an analytical description," this new approach allowed the artists to create a "synthesis of the object."[125] The idea of synthesis as non-illusionistic expression was still basically the same as in the decorative theory of Denis and Bernard, but the actual process was vastly more complex and elliptical.

The diffusion of the terms "analytic" and "synthetic" is usually attributed to Juan Gris, who responded to a 1924 questionnaire about Cubism by writing: "When it began Cubism was a sort of analysis which was no more painting than the description of physical phenomena was physics . . . but now . . . the analysis of yesterday has become a synthesis."[126] As Kenneth Silver has shown, Gris's use of these terms conformed to a broad trend, in post-war France, toward condemning what was seen as the Germanic tendency to excessive analysis, while praising the supposed Latin tendency to "synthesis."[127] At the same time, Gris's use of the terms "analysis" and "synthesis" corresponds to Kahnweiler's use of the same terms in his 1916 *Rise of Cubism*. There is no indication in Gris's comments that he intended to suggest a different chronological division of Picasso and Braque's development: "analytic" Cubism continued to refer to their work of 1908–09, while "synthetic" Cubism referred to their work of 1910 and after.

However, Gris, in conversation, also seems to have used the term "Analytical Cubism" to describe Picasso and Braque's practice of "analyzing" the form of an object by showing it from multiple perspectives.[128] In Kahnweiler's writing, this practice had previously been identified with the "synthetic" Cubism of 1910 and after. Gris's new usage therefore displaced the chronological meaning of "analytic" from the first period of Cubism to the second. By implication, "synthetic" would have to apply to a yet later phase.

In 1930, perhaps influenced by Gris (although he had died in 1927), the Surrealist journal *Documents* published a chronology of Picasso's career describing the years 1910–14 as the period of "Analytic Cubism" and the years 1914–18 as the period of "Synthetic Cubism."[129] It is only in Alfred Barr's catalogue to the 1939 Picasso retrospective at the Museum of Modern Art in New York that we find "analytic Cubism" used to describe the work of 1910–11, and "synthetic Cubism" to describe the work of 1912–14. Barr's new periodization corresponded to the perception that there was a distinct change in the appearance of Cubist pictures in mid-1912.[130] However, it is clear from Barr's text that the original meanings of the terms "analytic" and "synthetic" had been lost by 1939; indeed, he remarked that 1912–14

Cubism was called "synthetic" simply "for want of a better name."[131] The now canonical usage of "analytic Cubism" to refer to Picasso and Braque's work of 1910 through early 1912 and "synthetic Cubism" to refer to their work of later 1912 through 1914 cannot be reconciled with the original meanings of the terms. It seems more prudent simply to avoid them, relying instead on a chronological periodization: 1908–1909, 1910–1912, and later 1912 onwards.

* * *

In some ways, Cubism can be seen as a more radical expression of the same empiricist philosophy that served to justify the artistic innovations of Impressionism and Post-Impressionism. Empiricism held that "tactile" and "optical" sensation represented fundamentally different worlds of experience rather than two different ways of perceiving the same world. The Impressionists had used this idea to justify a purely "optical" style. Picasso, on the contrary, set out in 1908–09 to define a purely "tactile" style, one that would use the language of geometry to describe the "real" forms of bodies and objects without relying on the optical effects of incident light. Ironically, this quest proved self-defeating, as the geometric language of Cubism led within a few years to the dissolution of three-dimensional form.

This dissolution could, however, be rationalized in terms borrowed from Impressionism and Post-Impressionism. The seeming illegibility of Impressionist canvases, compared to academic paintings, could be seen as a precedent for the extreme "difficulty" of 1910–12 Cubism. Instead of using outline to describe three-dimensional forms, the Impressionists had reduced the visual field to an arrangement of color patches. Picasso and Braque reduced it, instead, to geometric shapes. Where the Impressionists were said to have "analyzed" optical experience, breaking it apart into countless individual sensations, the Post-Impressionists claimed to have arrived at a new "synthesis," making the image easier to seize by reducing it to a few basic shapes and colors. Cubism too could seen as a synthetic style, describing reality through a deliberately restricted vocabulary of forms organized into quasi-abstract patterns.

Impressionism and Post-Impressionism spelled an end to the transparency of the painted image. The canvas was no longer a window or a mirror that the viewer could look through, discovering an instantly recognizable image of the real world. Rather than a description, it offered an "equivalent" for experience. Cubism took this approach a step further, removing the last vestiges of resemblance and offering a composition that was explicitly a combination of abstract signs and isolated recognizable details. The painted image now needed to be read or decoded, and not merely seen. This new demand on the viewer could be justified by the argument that vision itself did not offer a direct experience of reality, but only a composite of memories and immediate sensations, so that the reading of a Cubist painting was merely a more self-conscious version of the normal process of visual perception.

Recognizing these roots in empiricism, Impressionism, and Post-Impressionism should not mean ignoring the profoundly new and radical elements of Cubism. If the projective space of 1908–09 Cubism looked back to the early Renaissance, there was no precedent for the reorganization of this space, in 1910, around the scaffolding of the "Cubist grid." Picasso's reinvention of the human body was equally revolutionary. Reduced to crystalline form in 1908–09, it shattered in 1910, breaking apart into geometric fragments. No longer linked by the conventions of classical anatomy, these fragments are anchored, instead, to the scaffolding of the grid. The Cubist geometricization of form exercised an overpowering influence on the art of the first half of the twentieth century. What has proven even more durable is the pictorial syntax of fragments arranged within a three-dimensional grid. The syntax of Cubism remains the syntax of art in the twenty-first century.

Finally, if Cubism inherited from Symbolism and Post-Impressionism the general idea of painting as a system of signs, it demonstrated a far more sophisticated analysis of the pictorial sign. The Symbolists stressed the importance of metaphor in expresssion, but remained content with a remarkably vague idea of how metaphor functioned. They simply ignored the extensive discussion of metaphor in contemporary linguistics. While it is unclear to what extent linguistics exerted a direct influence on Cubism, the Cubist analysis of the pictorial sign offers a series of striking parallels to the linguistic analyses of the 1890s. Between 1907 and 1913, Picasso explored how signs could evoke reality, how they could be created, and how they could be transformed.

The chapters that follow are devoted to these three topics: the reorganization of pictorial space, the fragmentation of the body, and the evolution of the Cubist sign.

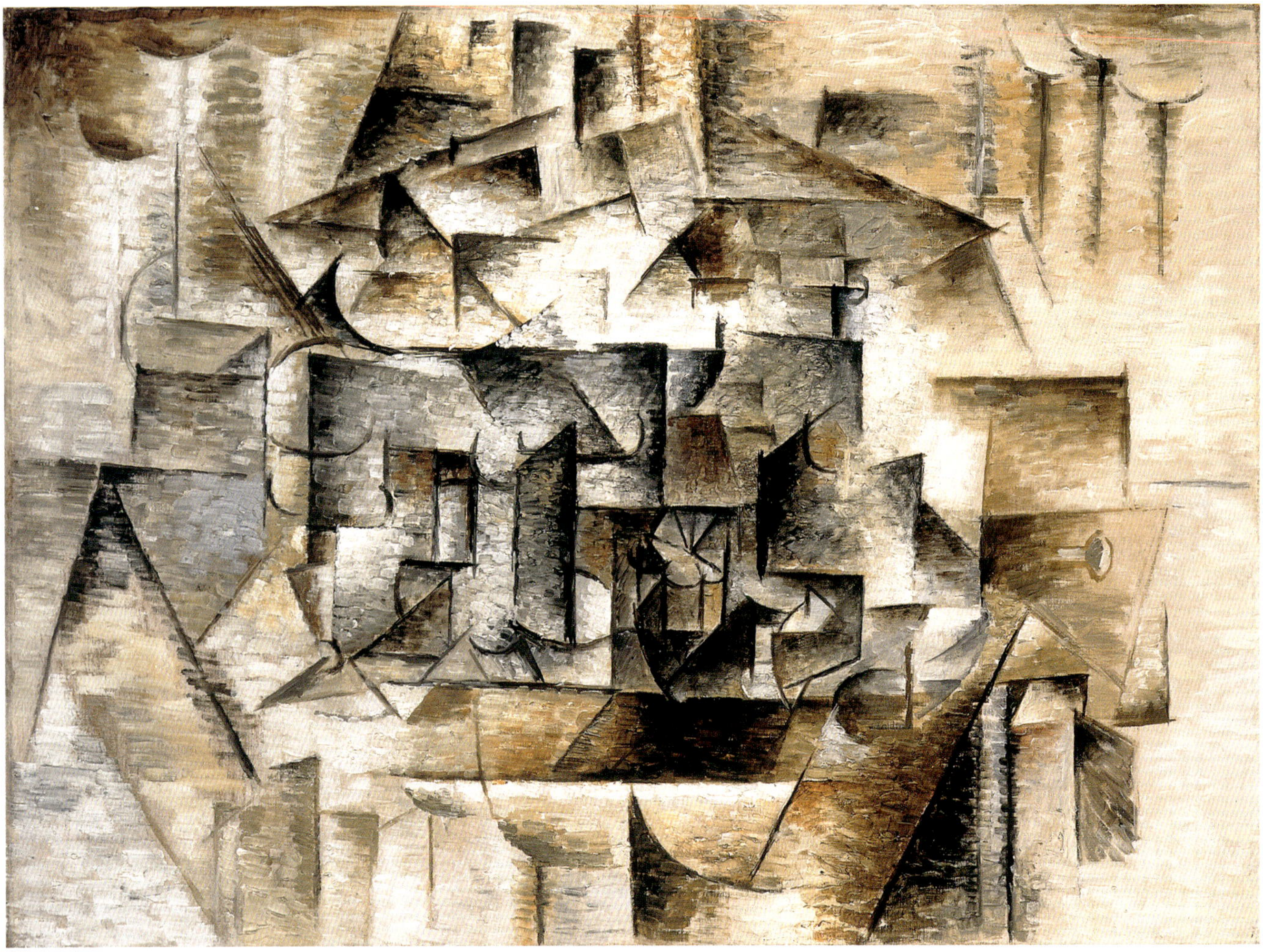

12 Picasso. *Still Life with Glass and Lemon.* Cadaqués, summer 1910. Oil on canvas, 73 × 100 cm. D.R. 357. Cincinnati Art Museum, Bequest of Mary E. Johnston

2

Spaces

Hidden among the geometric planes of Picasso's summer 1910 painting, *Still Life with Glass and Lemon* (fig. 12), the attentive viewer will discover a wineglass, a pedestal fruit bowl, and a lemon, resting on a table (fig. 13). The composition recalls numerous still lifes by Cézanne, with their characteristic peculiarities of arrangement and perspective. The rectangular table-top in Picasso's painting is indicated by a parallelogram whose sides seem to converge toward a point in front of the table, so that both its left and right sides are visible. This "reverse perspective" also suggests that the table is being seen from multiple viewpoints, like the wineglass at left, seen simultaneously from the side and from above. The drawer at right, with a protruding knob, is a particularly Cézannian touch. A cloth napkin drapes over the front edge of the table, its descending folds indicated by the reiterated motif of a curve atop a vertical rod. At the upper left and right corners, the same curve-plus-rod motif indicates curtains hanging in the background.

At first glance, little of this is visible in *Still Life with Glass and Lemon.* The painting seems to consist of an array of overlapping rectangular planes, floating in an indefinite space, and shaded randomly from light to dark. Several of Braque's paintings of 1910 (see fig. 7) display a similar spatial organization, and, as noted above, Braque later commented that he "began superimposing planes one over the other, separated by slight distances. To make the viewer understand that things stand one in front of the other, rather than going back into space . . . in order to avoid a recession toward infinity."[1]

Kahnweiler made the same point in his 1916 essay on Cubism, where he discussed how Picasso's "new method" of summer 1910 made it possible "to represent the dimension of depth without illusionistic methods." Describing this new method of spatial organization (in its perfected form of 1910–11), he wrote

> Instead of beginning from a defined foreground, and using perspective to create an illusion of apparent depth, the painter begins with a well defined background (a wall, for example), and then, in the clearest possible fashion, constructs an arrangement of forms (planes, etc.) in front of it. Thanks to their alignment and their positioning, one in front of another, these yield a strongly three-dimensional image.[2]

How did Picasso and Braque arrive at this new system of overlapping planes? And what, indeed, was the relationship between this new system and the space of traditional painting? Here, it is necessary to make a critical distinction. Picasso and Braque both spoke as if the spatial construction of traditional painting could be summed up in the word "perspective." This is a useful piece of shorthand, but it conceals the complexity and variety of the spatial models avail-

13 Picasso. *Still Life with Glass and Lemon.* Diagram highlighting "real" motifs

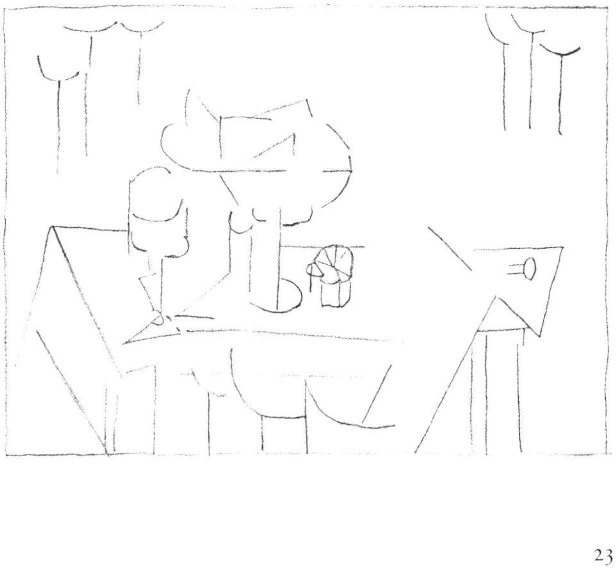

able in earlier art. In fact, Picasso took the first step toward the new space of Cubism by reviving the archaic space of fourteenth-century painting. Advancing simultaneously in the opposite direction, he transformed nineteenth-century Impressionism, with its mosaic of flat color patches evoking an indefinite space, into an arrangement of interlocking shapes bounded by lines. Finally, in 1910, Picasso and Braque together arrived at a revolutionary synthesis of depth and flatness, of tactility and opticality. But this synthesis can be understood only by examining each of its elements individually.

Stage Space

As Erwin Panofsky famously argued, perspective implies the conception of a homogeneous space – a space subject to uniform mathematical laws. It might seem reasonable to assume that painters must have arrived at the conception of such a uniform space before adopting the technique of perspective.[3] However, history demonstrates that this was not the case. The space of early Renaissance painting is visibly heterogeneous. Figures, buildings, and landscapes exist at radically different scales. Early Renaissance artists were obviously untroubled by spatial relationships that seem flagrantly inconsistent to modern eyes.

Perspective does not in fact follow from the prior emergence of a homogeneous space. Rather, the adoption of perspective creates the illusion of homogeneous space by imposing a new consistency on the various elements of the picture: figures and settings must conform to uniform laws of diminution and orientation. This formal consistency masks a persistent heterogeneity of space. If this heterogeneity has evaded discussion, it is in part because the triumph of perspective has tended to deprive critics of the language needed to discuss it. The conventional terms of spatial analysis – foreground, middle ground, and background – take it as a given that there is a single, uniform ground or space which is being divided artificially for the sake of discussion.[4] In fact, throughout the Renaissance and Baroque periods there is often a radical difference in character between one space and another – between the space of the foreground and the space of the background, for instance. But the conventional language for describing space offers no easy way to acknowledge this.

There are exceptions, of course. Writers often use the theatrical term "backdrop" to describe the background of a narrative painting, implicitly acknowledging that the space of this background is different from the space in which the narrative unfolds. Indeed, theater – with its vocabulary of stage, wings, backdrop, proscenium, scrim, curtain, and so on – offers a valuable resource for the analysis of pictorial space. This is not a coincidence. As the historians Pierre Francastel and George Kernodle observed, the interaction between theater and painting played a crucial role in defining the spatial structure of both Renaissance painting and the Renaissance stage. The history of theater, like the history

14 Duccio di Buoninsegna. *Entry into Jerusalem*, from the *Maestà* altarpiece. 1308–11. Museo dell'Opera Metropolitana, Siena

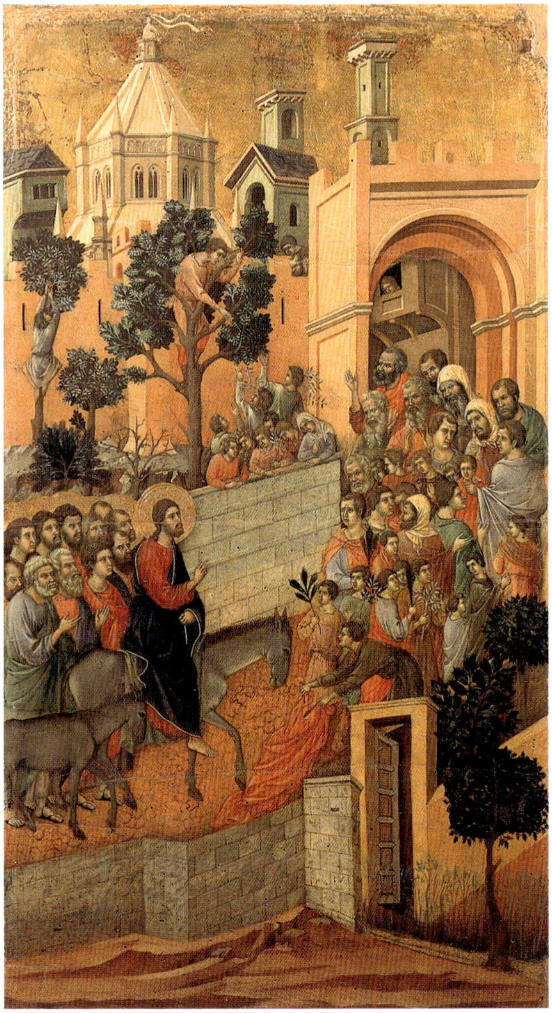

of art, usually emphasizes the transformations wrought by the invention of perspective. But earlier theatrical conventions continued to exercise an important influence on both stage and art.[5] It is worth pausing to examine these conventions, because the spatial structure of Picasso's and Braque's 1908–10 work was largely determined by them.

From the Middle Ages through the sixteenth century, religious festivals and processions constituted the most important kinds of theater. Religious dramas were enacted on fixed outdoor stages, which typically consisted of a wide, shallow platform extending in front of a more or less elaborate arcade. The bays of the arcade were usually closed off by a door or curtain to provide a backdrop for the actors, but these could be opened to reveal an inner stage with an interior scene or a painted vista.[6] These dramas were accompanied by *tableaux vivants* of biblical scenes, often presented on moving wagons – the ancestors of the floats in modern parades. The wagons could support a variety of symbolic props: an open-sided pavilion for a Nativity scene; a tree for the Garden of Eden; and so forth.[7] The same kind of symbolic props could be deployed on the fixed stage. As symbols, they might be larger or (more commonly) smaller than life; hence the seemingly inconsistent scale of figures and settings in paintings based on such dramatic representations.

This indebtedness to theatrical models is often frankly exposed in the settings of early Renaissance paintings, where the actors of the narrative are deployed on shallow stages, furnished with a symbolic architecture of open-sided "mansions," sometimes placed center stage and sometimes paired at either side of the stage. In early Renaissance paintings, these theatrical conventions alternate or co-exist with an archaic pictorial convention according to which depth is indicated by vertical displacement. The foreground occupies the lowest section of the picture and the background the highest, so that "up" equals "backwards" (fig. 14).

As the Renaissance progressed, painters found more subtle ways to define spatial relationships. Although the machinery of the medieval stage persisted at least until the end of the *quattrocento*, it was frequently disguised by a more "realistic" arrangement of props and mansions. Above all, the invention of linear perspective made it possible to deploy groups of figures in depth, from front to back, instead of spreading them out laterally across the width of the stage space. The new device of arranging figure groups into a "pyramid" combines the early Renaissance convention of "up equals backwards" with the perspectival convention of depth indicated by converging diagonals. Sophisticated painters such as Botticelli and Leonardo used perspective not to create dramatic architectural settings but to make some of their figures advance in front of others, so that their spatial relationship remains clear even when they overlap.

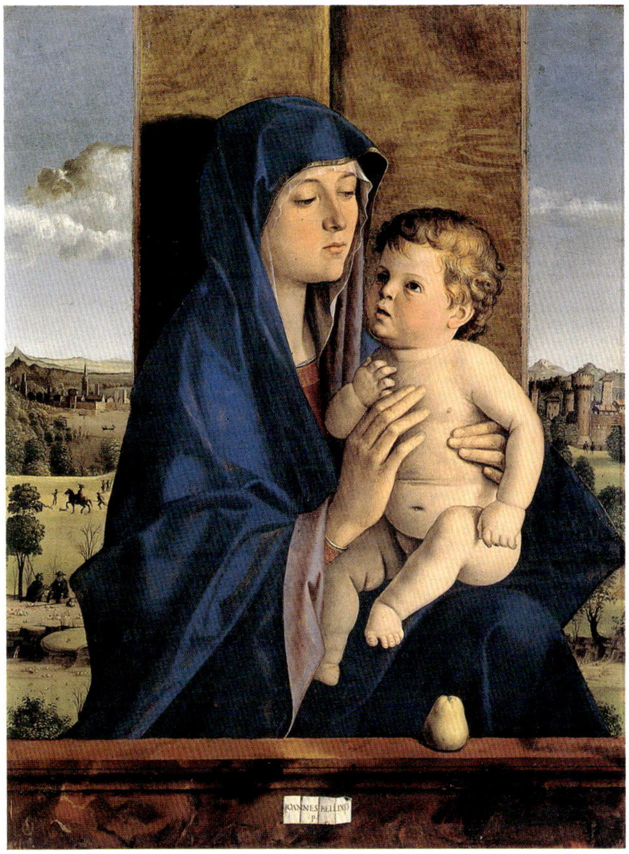

15 Giovanni Bellini. *Madonna and Child*. c. 1483. Distemper on wood, 47 × 34 cm. Accademia Carrara, Bergamo

The same effect of advancing forms could be achieved with even simpler means. In a *Madonna and Child* by Giovanni Bellini (fig. 15), the pavilion enclosing the figures has been reduced to a simple curtain hanging behind the Madonna, and the depth of the "stage" is indicated only by the ledge extending in front of her.[8] No converging diagonals or checkerboard pavements link the figure to its immediate setting or to the landscape background. And yet the composition gives a powerful sense of forms advancing in a perspectival space. The Virgin's head casts a strong shadow on the curtain behind her, while the middle-valued ledge strongly detaches itself from her dark blue robes. The Virgin's slightly enlarged hand and forearm move subtly but decisively in front of the oval of her face and neck.

The archaic convention of "up equals backwards" provided an important model for the spatial organization of 1908–09 Cubism. Bellini's more sophisticated arrangement of advancing and receding forms provided an equally important precedent for later Cubism. Indeed, Kahnweiler's description of Cubist painting from 1910 onward might serve equally well to describe this *Madonna and Child.* Bellini "begins with a well defined background . . . and then, in the clearest possible fashion, constructs an arrangement of forms . . . in front of it."

Landscape and Stage Space

If the conventions of perspectival stage space were first applied to religious scenes and narratives, they also proved adaptable to other genres. In the seventeenth century, Poussin and Claude Lorrain reconciled history painting and landscape by treating the foreground as a proscenium stage where actors could perform mythological or sacred dramas against a backdrop of idealized nature. However, it was within the genre of landscape painting that there arose the first serious challenge to the dominance of the conventions of stage space. Nineteenth-century landscape painters, beginning with the Barbizon school, displayed an increasing preference for pure landscape, stripped of narratives. The absence of "significant" figures meant that the proscenium of classical landscape could now be dispensed with. The remaining features of the landscape – trees, lakes, hills – no longer needed to be arranged around the sides and back of a stage-like space. But the rise of pure landscape presented a new problem: how to achieve the sense of formal closure previously produced by the conventions of stage space?

One answer was to reinstate at least some of these conventions – to use some element of the landscape to close off or limit the represented space. For Corot, this might be a scrim of trees at Ville d'Avray; for Courbet, a cliff face in the Auvergne; for Pissarro and Cézanne, a rising hillside at Pontoise or Montgeroult (fig. 16). On one hand, these rising landscapes look back to the elevated perspectives of early Renaissance painting (see fig. 14); on the other, they anticipate the spatial organization of Cubist pictures.

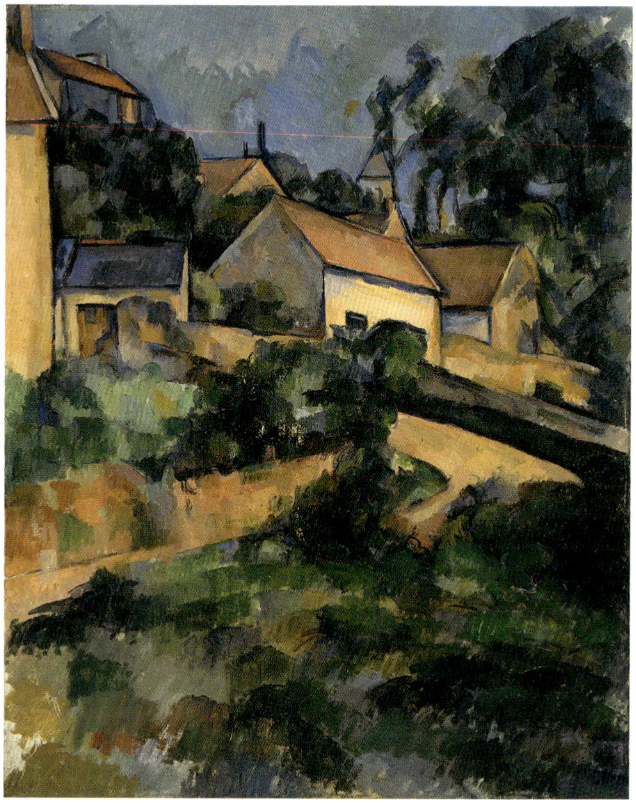

16 Paul Cézanne. *Bend in Road at Montgeroult.* 1898. Oil on canvas, 80 × 65 cm. The Museum of Modern Art, New York, Mrs. John Jay Whitney Bequest

The "bas-relief space" of Cézanne's rising landscapes (as William Rubin calls it[9]) was only one of the devices adopted by avant-garde artists as replacements for the spatial organization of "classical" landscape. Another device was to let the landscape extend into deep space, but to arrange its elements so that they formed a satisfying two-dimensional pattern on the surface of the canvas. This became the preferred solution of Impressionist landscape painters such as Monet, because it coincided perfectly with their goal of representing visual experience as a field of color patches.

The increasing disparity between the three-dimensional order of the represented scene and the two-dimensional order of the colors and brushwork in Impressionist painting yielded a variety of new pictorial effects. The alternation of light and dark tones could produce the illusion of a solid surface, unrelated to the space of the depicted scene, and located somewhere behind the actual surface of the

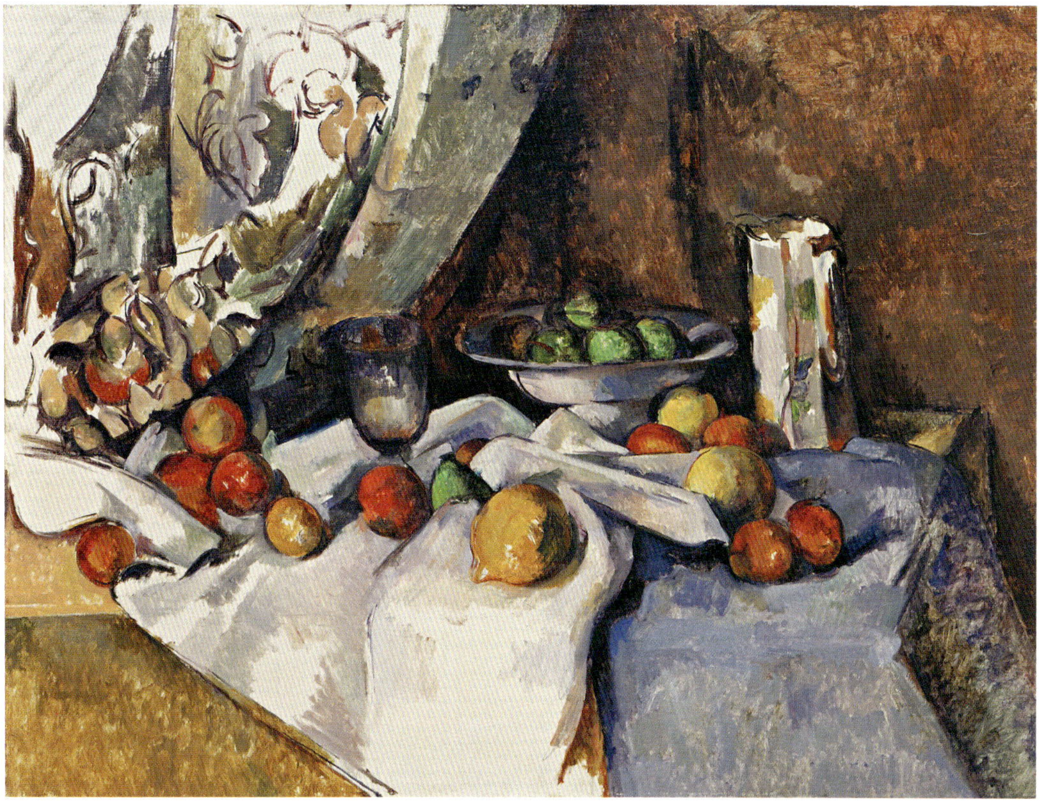

17 Paul Cézanne. *Still Life with Apples*. 1895–98. Oil on canvas, 68.6 × 92.7 cm. The Museum of Modern Art, New York. Lillie P. Bliss Bequest

canvas. In the work of Renoir, as Roger Fry noted, the alternation of light and dark hues created the impression that the colors were arranged in a series of rounded bumps or "bosses," each with a central highlight. "The picture," Fry wrote, "thus tends to take the form of a bas-relief in which the recessions are not into the profound distances of pictorial space, but only back, as it were, to the block out of which the bossed reliefs emerge."[10]

Similarly, Cézanne's constant modulation from light to dark hues often provides a suggestion of modeled forms in areas that would "realistically" be considered blank or formless, such as walls or skies.[11] (Hence Berenson's comment that he "gives the sky its tactile values as perfectly as Michelangelo has given them to the human figure."[12]) Verbally, at least, Cézanne adhered to Impressionist doctrine, insisting on the paramount importance of the optical sensation.[13] In practice, however, he almost always relied on drawing to describe three-dimensional form. Even in late paintings such as the *Bend in the Road at Montgeroult*, where the landscape seems to dissolve into a shimmer of colored brushstrokes, there are still a few crucial lines to anchor the work in what we traditionally understand as physical reality. Where an academic painter would have begun by drawing contours, then added shading, and finally introduced color as a supplementary, decorative element, Cézanne began by using color and then added line. As Maurice Denis wrote in 1907, "Contour comes only at the end, as a forceful accent, a liquid stroke underlining and isolating a form already made evident by the gradation of color."[14] Colored brushstrokes transcribe "optical" sensations while the dark lines transmit "tactile" information, so that the painting operates simultaneously in two different registers.[15]

Despite the revolutionary relationship between color and line in Cézanne's canvases, their spatial organization looks back to Renaissance models. In Cézanne's still lifes (fig. 17), as in Bellini's Madonnas, curtains serve to close off shallow spaces. Table-tops are tilted forward, like the landscapes in early Renaissance painting, the better to expose their contents. Cézanne's most ambitious painting, the *Large Bathers* now in Philadelphia (fig. 18), returns to the theatrical model of the high Renaissance: the figures are posed on a proscenium stage in front of a screen of trees, which parts to disclose a distant landscape.

Cézanne thus demonstrated that it was possible to be simultaneously modern and "classic." He is, in this sense, the progenitor both of Cubism and of its seeming antithesis, the return to classical forms evident around 1905. As Theodore Reff has noted, numerous avant-garde painters began to take an intense interest in Cézanne's work at this moment, because it provided a model of pictorial structure that could serve as a corrective to the formlessness of Impressionism and Fauvism.[16] The collector Leo Stein later recalled that "Hitherto Cézanne had been important only for the few; he was about to become important for everybody. At the Autumn Salon of 1905 people laughed themselves into hysterics before his pictures, in 1906 they were respectful, and in 1907 they were reverent. Cézanne had become the man of the moment."[17]

Projective Space, 1906–1909

It is a cliché that Cézanne's work was critical for the development of Cubism. But the cliché conceals a paradox. The aspect of his work that most obviously prefigures Cubism is his application of color in a series of rhythmic brushstrokes. At times, the pattern of Cézanne's brushwork seems to anticipate the structure of the Cubist grid. But Picasso, in 1905–10, only rarely imitated Cézanne's brushwork. What he imitated, rather, was the spatial construction of Cézanne's pictures: the proscenium space of his still lifes or the tilted up space of his landscapes. These are, in effect, the most traditional elements of Cézanne's work.

To make sense of this response, we need to rethink the conventional narrative of Picasso's development. Knowing in retrospect where Picasso was going, historians tend to focus their attention on the 1908–09 pictures that anticipate the fragmented forms and "allover" field of 1910–11 Cubism. However, as Leo Steinberg insists, Picasso's development cannot be reduced to a "linear stylistic progression."[18] The 1908 and 1909 works in which faceted objects seem to dissolve into an allover field are not his most characteristic works of these years. On the contrary, Picasso's main concern in 1908–09 was to intensify the presence of individual objects and figures. He experimented with the proscenium space of Cézanne's still lifes and the tilted up space of his landscapes because these are what might be called "projective" spaces, that is, spaces which seem to project the figures and objects within them toward the viewer. Picasso seems, in these years, to have had the same goal that Bernard Berenson attributed to Giotto: to evoke figures and objects with "a *keener* sense of reality, of life-likeness than the objects themselves."[19]

The discovery of Cézanne provoked a crisis in Picasso's work, but also demonstrated a way out of it. Up to the moment when Leo Stein began to acquire Picasso's paintings for the family collection on the Rue de Fleurus, Picasso had remained a fundamentally old-fashioned painter, engaged with literary themes rather than formal problems. Indeed, if Picasso had died in 1905, he would be known only as a minor exponent of 1890s-style Symbolism. Seeing his own work in the context of the Steins' collection of pictures by Cézanne and Matisse, and witnessing the *succès de scandale* achieved by Matisse and his Fauve followers at the 1905 Salon d'Automne, Picasso must have realized that his own work did not even begin to address the pictorial problems engaging the Parisian avant-garde.

Unwilling to imitate Matisse, he began to explore Cézanne's work as a guide to advanced art. "Around 1906," he later commented, "Cézanne's influence gradually flooded everything."[20] "Gradually" is a key word here. Picasso's confrontation with the pictorial problems posed by Cézanne and his followers extended over two years and two major canvases – *Les Demoiselles d'Avignon* of 1907 and the *Three Women* of 1908.

Vicissitudes of ownership and geography have tended to obscure the profound links between these two works. The *Demoiselles* was intended as a revolutionary manifesto – a demonstration that Picasso could, in a single bound, leap past his contemporaries and establish himself as the leader of the Parisian avant-garde. In the short run, the painting was an ignominious failure, rejected by precisely the audience Picasso had hoped to impress. Matisse denounced the picture as a hoax and an outrage, "an attempt to ridicule the modern movement." Derain remarked that it was a "desperate" enterprise and that "one fine morning we would find Picasso hanged behind his large canvas." Gertrude Stein described it as a "cataclysm." When she brought the Russian

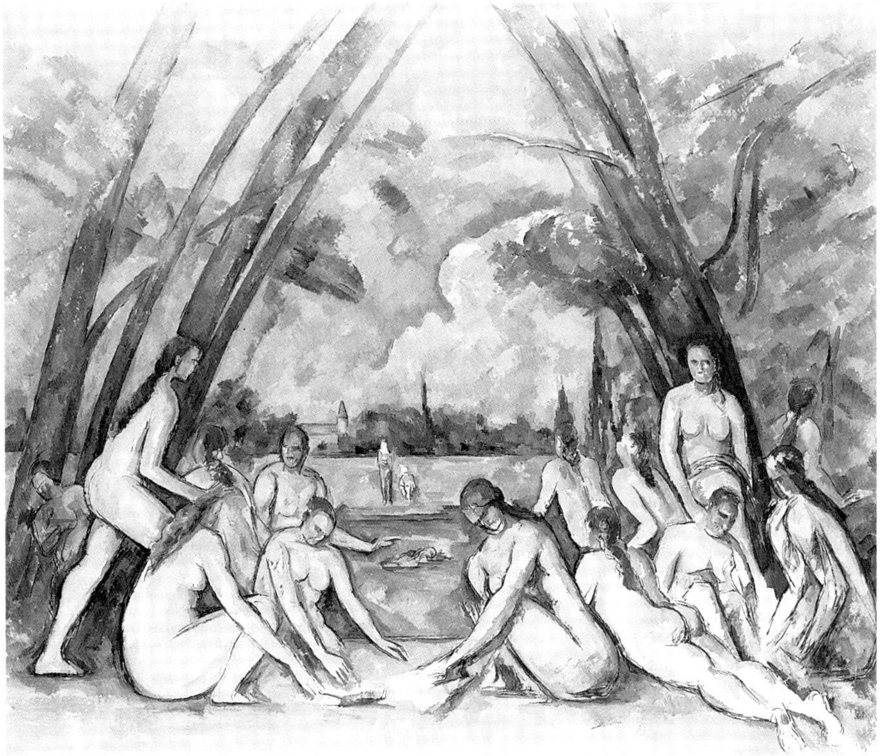

18 Paul Cézanne. *Large Bathers.* 1899–1906. Oil on canvas, 208 × 249 cm. Philadelphia Museum of Art: Purchase with the W. P. Wilstach Fund

19 Henri Matisse. *The Joy of Life.* Paris, autumn–winter 1905–06. Oil on canvas, 174 × 238.1 cm. The Barnes Foundation, Merion Station, Pennsylvania

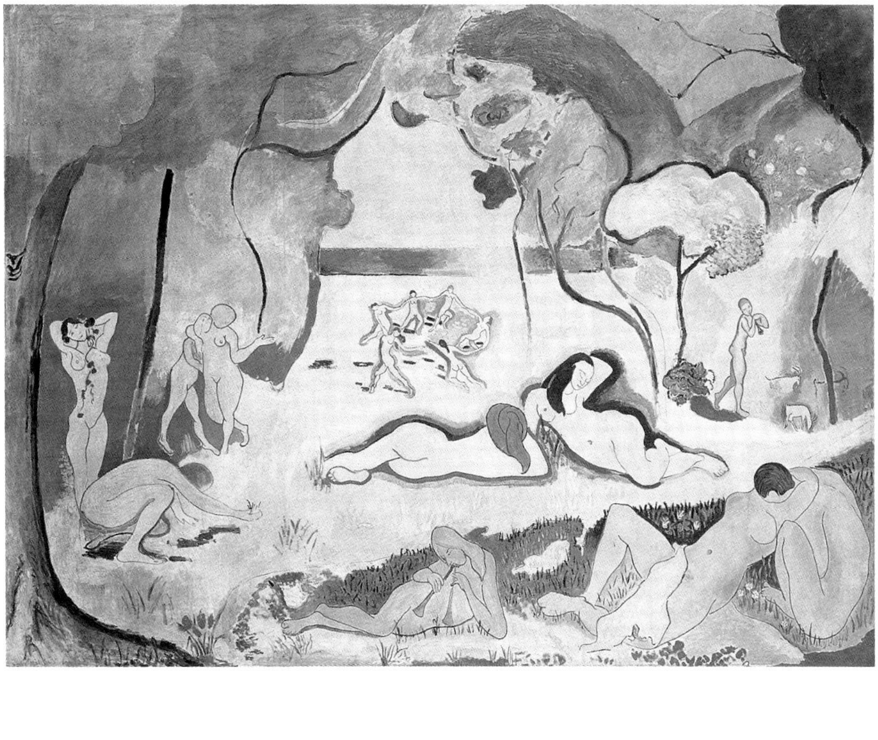

collector Sergei Shchukin to Picasso's studio, he remarked sadly, "what a loss for French art." Kahnweiler described the *Demoiselles* as a "failure," noting that everyone had disliked it at the time it was done. After languishing in Picasso's studio for almost a decade, the *Demoiselles* was finally exhibited publicly in 1916, and then sold to the couturier Jacques Doucet, who hung it in the back stairwell of his house because it was too indecent to put in his living room.[21]

The immediate reaction to the *Three Women* was almost exactly the contrary. Even before it was finished, it was recognized as a seminal masterpiece by contemporaries like Braque and Derain, who hastened to exploit Picasso's innovations in their own work. Visiting the Salon des Indépendants in the spring of 1908, Gertrude Stein took Alice B. Toklas to see the latest works by Braque and Derain, which showed that they "had become Picassoites and were definitely not Matisseites" any more.[22] Acquired by the Steins soon after its completion, the *Three Women* occupied pride of place in their influential salon, where it was seen (and imitated) by artists from literally all over the world. Within short order, Picasso had moved to the front ranks of the Parisian avant-garde.

Critical awareness of the two works changed radically in following decades, however. The *Three Women* vanished from the Parisian scene after 1913, when Kahnweiler arranged its sale to Sergei Shchukin in Moscow.[23] After the Russian Revolution, Shchukin's collection was seized by the state. The *Three Women* may have been displayed in Moscow during the liberal years of the 1920s, before Stalin's disapproval led to the suppression of modernist art. But it was no longer accessible to a Western audience and, until the 1970s, it was generally omitted from histories of Cubism.[24] In contrast, when the *Demoiselles* emerged from its seclusion in the Doucet collection, it was purchased by the Museum of Modern Art in New York. Virtually from the moment it went on display, in 1939, it was acclaimed as a defining masterpiece of modern art. But the *Demoiselles* and the *Three Women* have only rarely been seen together, so scholars have had little impetus to study their relationship.

As Leo Steinberg has famously argued, both pictures confront the viewer with archetypal figures embodying the primal power of sex.[25] The formal language of both pictures emerges from the same set of stylistic alternatives: possibilities explored in the studies for *Demoiselles*, but left unused, are taken up again in the studies for the *Three Women*, and

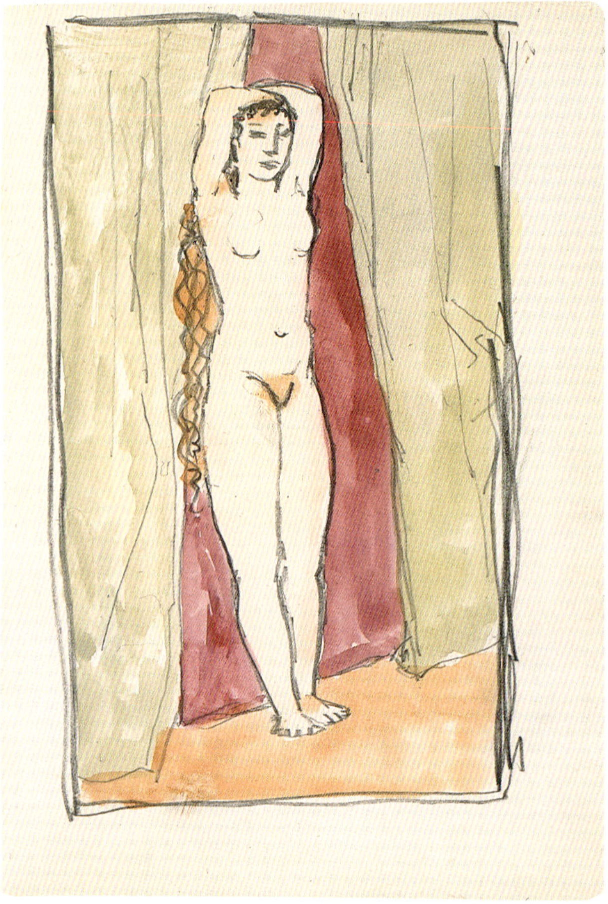

20 Picasso. *Nude with Raised Arms in Front of Parted Curtain.* Gosol, summer 1906. Graphite and gouache on sketchbook page, 17.5 × 12 cm. Seckel, carnet 6, p. 45r. Musée Picasso, Paris (M.P. 1857)

find their way into the finished canvas. And both pictures show Picasso wrestling with the dilemma of representing the human body effectively within an overall composition that seemed "modern" by the standards of Cézanne – specifically, by the standards of Cézanne's *Bathers*.

Matisse, who owned an earlier version of Cézanne's picture, had adopted a version of its proscenium-arch construction for *The Joy of Life*, his major canvas of 1905–06 (fig. 19). Here, a framework of trees divided the picture into three distinct spaces: proscenium, center stage, and background. The gamboling nude figures were distributed more or less evenly among the three spaces. Other ex-Fauves, such as Derain, Dufy, Braque, and Friesz, adapted the stage-like space of Cézanne's *Bathers* to the depiction of pure land-

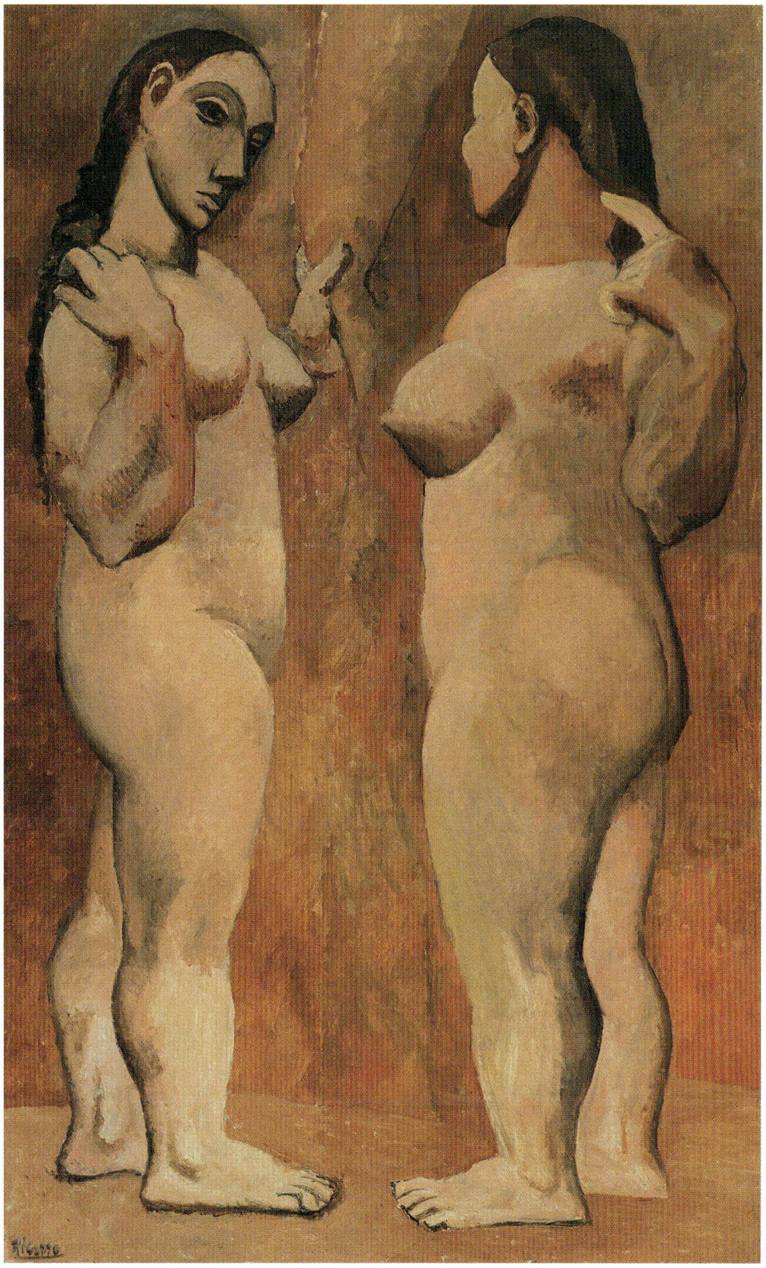

21 Picasso. *Two Nudes.* Paris, late 1906. Oil on canvas, 151.3 × 93 cm. Zervos I, 366. D.B. XVI, 15. Museum of Modern Art, New York. Gift of David Thompson in honor of Alfred H. Barr, Jr.

scape.[26] Rather than naturalizing Cézanne's composition, Picasso returned to its origins in theater. In one summer 1906 study (fig. 20), he posed a standing nude on a shallow stage, in front of a curtain parted to suggest a second, inner stage. His massive *Two Nudes* of late 1906 (fig. 21) were posed in a similar proscenium space, with one figure's hand extending to grasp the edge of a parted curtain.

In the winter of 1906–07, Picasso explored variations on this composition, replacing the standing figures with seated nudes, one modeled on the classical "Thorn-Puller" and seen from the front, the other seen from the rear.[27] A small notebook sketch (fig. 22) combining these figures on the shallow stage of the *Two Nudes* seems to have served as a starting point (if not *the* starting point) for the more

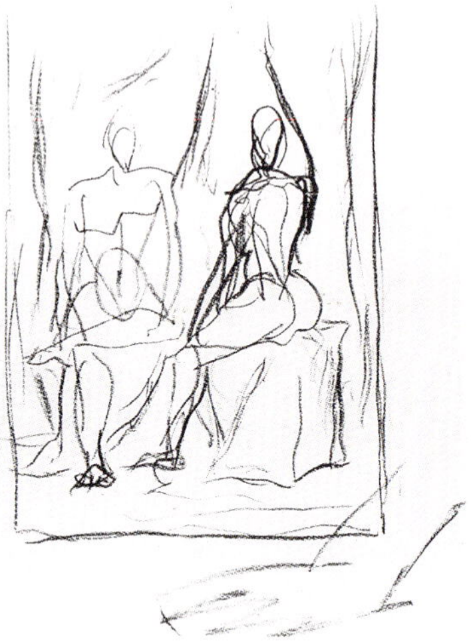

22 Picasso. *Two Seated Nudes, Face to Face in an Interior with Curtains, and Hand Study.* Paris, winter 1906–07. Pencil on sketchbook page, 14.7 × 10.6 cm. Seckel, carnet 2, p. 27v. Musée Picasso, Paris (M.P. 1859)

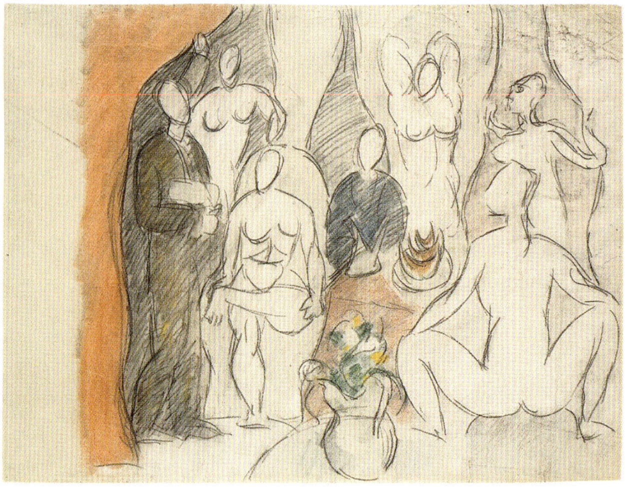

23 Picasso. Study for *Les Demoiselles d'Avignon.* Paris, March–April 1907 (?). Pencil and pastel on paper, 27.7 × 63.5 cm. Seckel, no. 22. Öffentliche Kunstsammlung Basel, Kupferstichkabinett. Bequest of the artist to the city of Basel, 1967

24 (*right*) Picasso. Ensemble study with one figure. Paris, March 1907. Pencil on sketchbook page, 19.3 × 24.2 cm. Seckel, carnet 3, p. 3r. Musée Picasso, Paris (M.P. 1861)

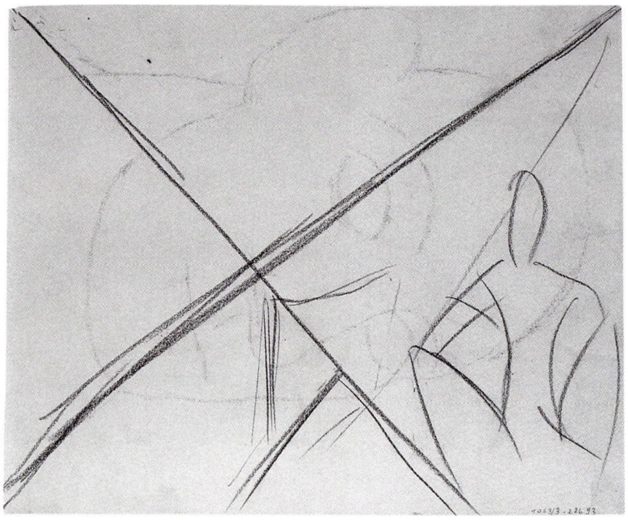

complex composition of the *Demoiselles d'Avignon.* In the early studies for this picture, the "Thorn-Puller" reappears on the left while the seated nude seen from the rear loses her cubic support and is forced instead to squat.[28] Accompanied by two men, and three additional women in the background, they occupy an enlarged version of the setting from the *Two Nudes.* Curtains like stage flats flank the left and right sides of the scene, while other curtains close off the back plane. The square table wedged between the figures is supplemented (and later supplanted) by another table at the near edge of the stage (fig. 23) – a repoussoir like the ledge in Bellini's Carrara *Madonna and Child* (see fig. 15).

If Picasso had executed the finished canvas at this moment in spring 1907 it would have looked much like his 1906 paintings, with graceful contours and sandy-rose coloring. Nothing here to shock or surprise his audience. That was a problem. To challenge his competitors in the Steins' circle, Picasso had to beat them at their own game – to be more extreme than they were. He therefore proceeded to radicalize the *Demoiselles* by geometricizing both the overall composition and the individual figures within it.

Picasso's first attempts at reworking the composition in a new "geometric" style appear in a May 1907 sketchbook, interspersed with drawings in the more naturalistic style of his earlier studies. He apparently wanted to fit the figures into the armature of a large *X* anchored to the corners of the composition (fig. 24). Ultimately, the *X* sank toward the

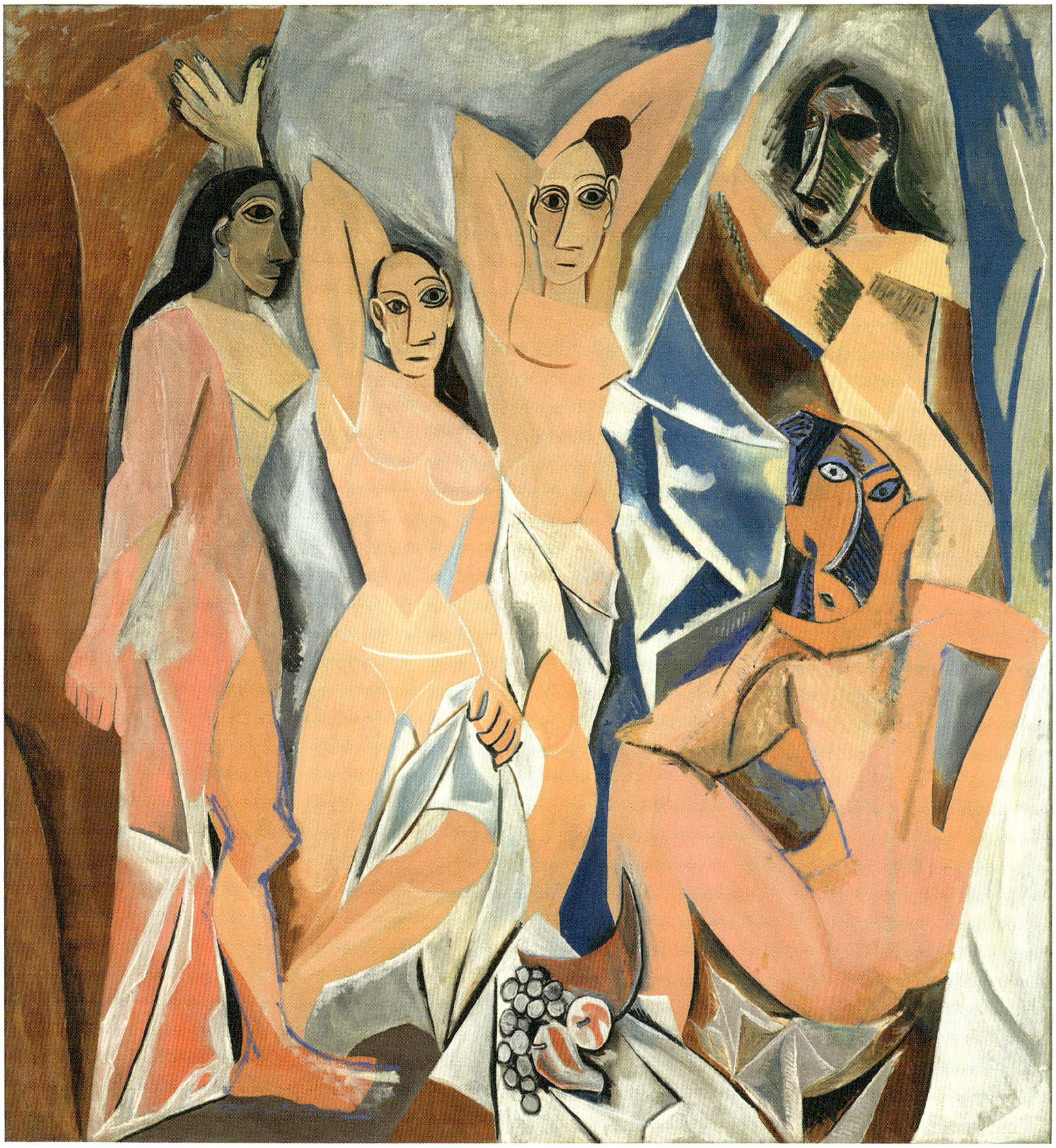

25 Picasso. *Les Demoiselles d'Avignon.* Paris, June–July 1907. Oil on canvas, 243.9 × 233.7 cm. Zervos II* 18. D.R. 47. The Museum of Modern Art, New York. Lillie P. Bliss Bequest

bottom, becoming something more like a *V.* The figures were now grouped within two rising triangles, to right and left, and a descending triangle at center.[29] The small table that had originally served as a repoussoir was absorbed into the vestigial base of the *X.* In the finished painting (fig. 25), this geometric framework is absorbed and hidden by the strong contrasts between the flesh tones of the figures and the blue-whites of the curtains in the background. The flattened, curvilinear forms of the two central figures seem to emerge violently from a multifold, three-dimensional space.

The stage setting of the earlier studies survives in the finished painting, but it has been fractured into a series of overlapping alcoves and niches.

Almost as soon as he completed the *Demoiselles*, Picasso began to plan its sequel, the *Three Women*.[30] More than any other single picture, this painting was responsible for Picasso's reputation as a leader of the avant-garde. Offering a unified, coherent solution to the pictorial problems first confronted in the *Demoiselles*, it instantly won over the critics of the earlier canvas. The evolution of the design can be followed in a series of sketches executed in the same medium-size format. In the early studies (see fig. 3), the pink figures occupy an enclosed space framed by bluish curtains, recalling the colors and composition of the *Demoiselles*.[31] Picasso sets himself a simpler problem here than he had in the *Demoiselles* by including only three figures instead of five or seven, and by eliminating even the vestigial narrative of the first canvas. There is no sense of action: none of the figures is turning or even seen in profile. Whether kneeling, standing, or crouching, they are all frontal, facing the viewer with a sense of hieratic solemnity.[32] Decorative harmony has replaced narrative: insofar as possible, Picasso tries to represent everything in the composition using the same graphic mark, a curve whose significance constantly changes, so that it represents an arm in one place, a thigh in a second, and a breast in a third.[33]

The figures are conceived from the outset as a single group, unified by long curves that pinwheel out toward the borders of the composition. These curves extend from limb to limb, and from figure to figure, so that the head of the kneeling woman at left runs into the shoulder of the standing woman at center, while the torso of the standing woman continues without interruption into the raised knee of the crouching woman at right. The details vary from one sketch to another, but the underlying idea remains constant. Signac's portrait of Félix Fénéon or the Art Nouveau posters of Alphonse Mucha may have inspired the interlacing lines of Picasso's composition. But there is no precedent for the extraordinarily close integration of the figures with one another and with the surrounding space. Indeed, the viewer seems first to perceive the unified pattern of lines, and only secondarily the individual figures.[34] Planes are set off from one another by their colors, but they are not modeled by shading. The spatial relationships of torsos and limbs are expressed instead by the juxtaposition or overlapping of flat shapes.

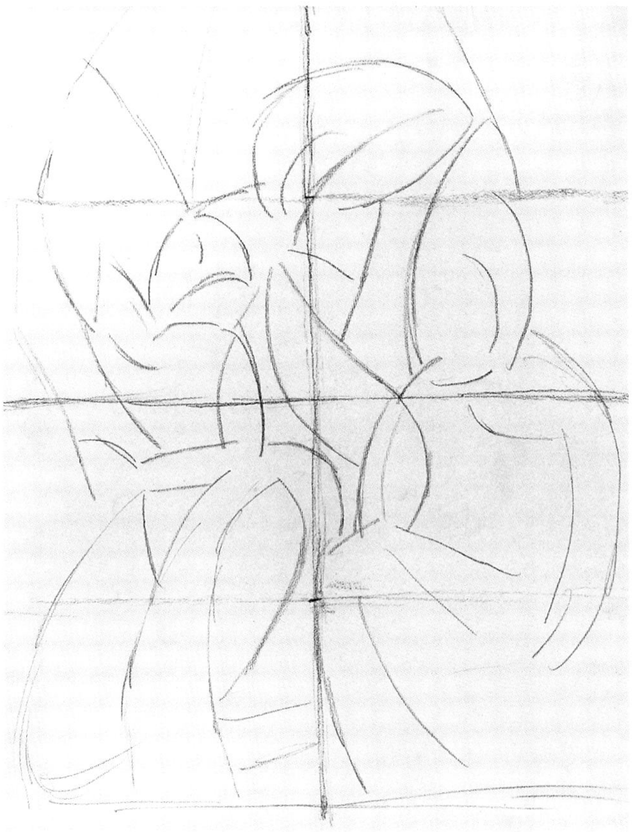

26 Picasso. *Three Women*. Paris, winter 1907–08. Charcoal on paper, 63 × 48.5 cm. Zervos XXVI, 319. Marina Picasso Collection. Courtesy Jan Krugier Gallery, Ditesheim & Cie, Geneva

There is no suggestion of geometric faceting in these studies, probably done in fall 1907. At this moment, Picasso was aiming for decorative unity, not for three-dimensional form. This still seems to have been the state of his thinking at the moment that he squared up the composition, in a large drawing (fig. 26) that anticipated its transfer to canvas (fig. 27).[35] Once the transfer had taken place, however, he became dissatisfied with the flat, decorative version of the *Three Women*. As noted above, Kahnweiler felt that Picasso, in the winter of 1907–08, had "been occupied only with the articulation of the color planes," but soon "perceived the danger of lowering his art to the level of ornament." In "the spring of 1908," Picasso "resumed his quest" for "the representation of the three-dimensional."[36]

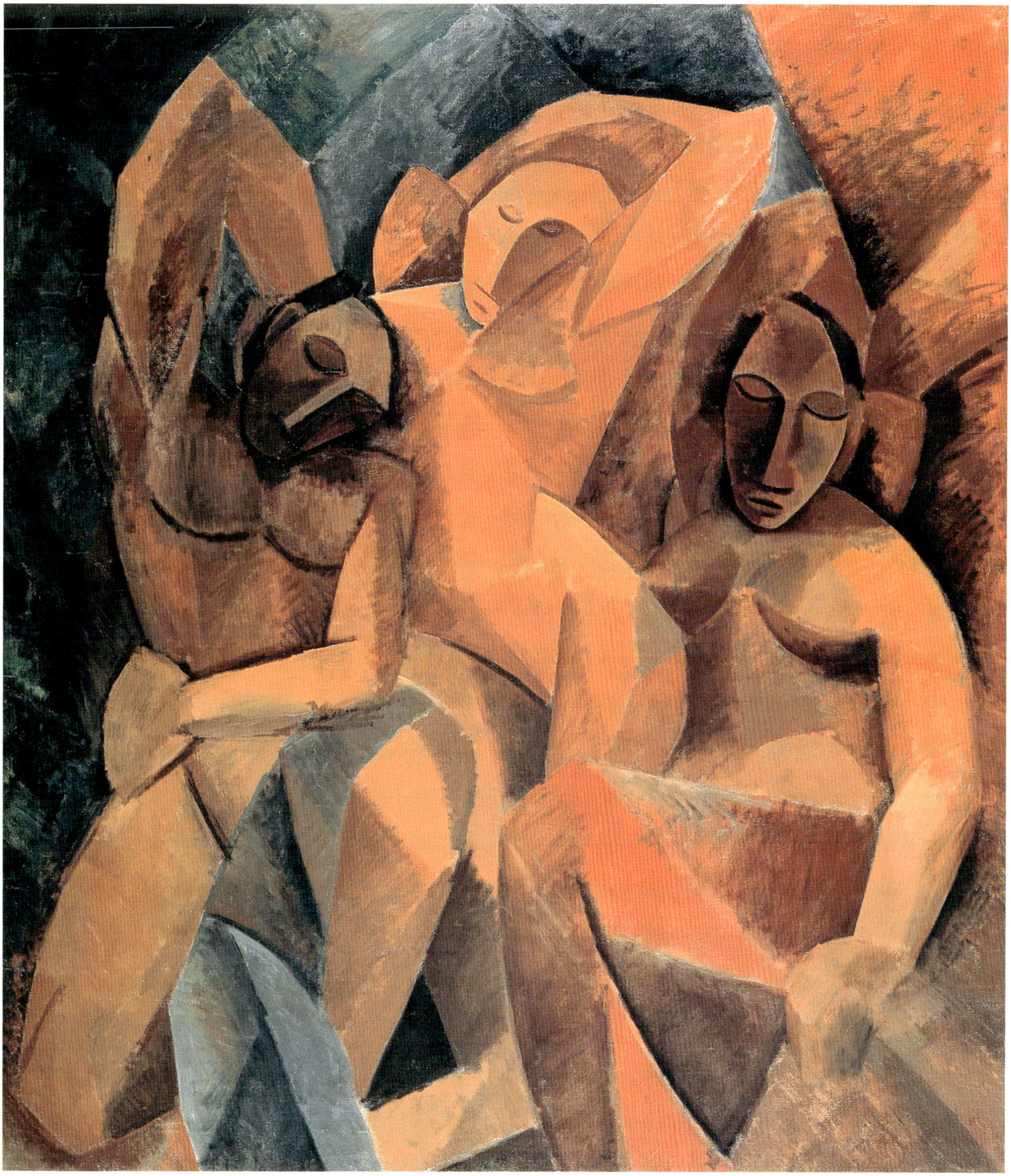

27 Picasso. *Three Women.* Paris, late 1907–spring 1908. Oil on canvas, 200 × 173 cm. D.R. 131. The State Hermitage Museum, St. Petersburg

The quest took the form of numerous studies and paintings exploring more sculptural versions of the figures in the painting. Picasso's solution, ultimately, was to preserve the outlines of the figures unchanged, but to divide them into a series of advancing and receding planes or facets, defined by linear edges and powerful shading. That there are no faceted studies for the composition of *Three Women* as a whole suggests that the revisions of this type were all undertaken after the composition had been transferred to canvas.

In carrying out these revisions, Picasso seems to have struggled to find the right balance between sculptural presence and decorative flatness. This aspect of the work is largely lost in reproduction, which greatly diminishes the picture's sculptural effect, in part because of the drastic reduction in size and in part because reproduction cannot convey the subtle interaction between shading and glazing. When the painting is seen firsthand (particularly under a strong light), it is clear that the facets of the figures were originally even more strongly modeled than they now appear, and that a series of glazes was subsequently added to reduce the three-dimensional effect of planes moving forward and back in space.

The *Three Women* clearly represents a turning point in Picasso's development, but it also presents a problem for the historiography of Cubism. Although the interlacing lines of the *Three Women* are curved rather than straight, they form a lattice defining the composition as a whole and breaking individual figures or objects into planar units. To this extent, they clearly anticipate the Cubist "grid" of 1910–12. The conventional history of Cubism tends, not unnaturally, to privilege this element of the picture. It then leaps from spring 1908 to summer 1909, when the lattice reappeared in Picasso's work. After that it makes another leap, to spring 1910, when the lattice made a third appearance, and was transformed into the rectilinear grid, which remained a constant feature of Picasso's work for the next five years.

This evolution from lattice to grid is a critical part of the history of Cubism, and will presently be examined in detail. However, focusing exclusively on the evolution of the lattice means neglecting a great deal of Picasso's work from the years 1908–10. It should be said that although Picasso's production in 1908–10 is extremely diverse and some of it is simply irrelevant to the development of Cubism, much of this work is critically important. It manifests Picasso's desire to describe the figure with the greatest possible sense of physical presence. The figures in the finished canvas of the *Three Women* are more powerfully three-dimensional than those in the *Demoiselles d'Avignon* – or, for that matter, any earlier painting by Picasso. Nevertheless, they still occupy a shallow stage space like that of the *Demoiselles.* Their setting pushes them forward toward the viewer. In the finished canvas, the background draperies are transformed into foliage by the simple expedient of painting them green, but the picture retains its claustrophobic sense of a box-like space contracting around the interlocking figures.

Evidently this was not what Picasso wanted, at this moment, to achieve. His subsequent work shows him abandoning the idea of total integration and searching, instead, for more dramatic ways to achieve a sense of spatial projection.[37] In a series of still lifes begun in summer 1908, such as *Carafe and Three Bowls* (fig. 28), bowls and pitcher are placed on a tilted table-top that serves as a kind of canted stage, and posed one in front of another so that they advance toward the viewer in a series of discrete steps. The humble motifs are monumentalized by their simplified forms and by the dramatic play of light and shade across their surfaces. The table-tops in these pictures are tilted more steeply than anything found in Cézanne's still lifes (see fig. 6); they are more like the hillside of his *Bend in the Road at Montgeroult* (see fig. 16). Indeed, Picasso's 1908 still lifes seem to look back to the elevated perspective of early Renaissance painting with its convention of indicating depth by vertical displacement, so that up stands for "backward" and down stands for "forward" (see fig. 14).

Picasso utilizes a similar projective space in fall 1909 pictures such as *Le Bock (Glass of Beer)*, with its vertiginous series of advancing forms (fig. 29). The table in the foreground is tilted steeply, and Picasso turns it so that a corner stabs outward at the viewer. The apples, carafe, and beer stein on the table are thrust forward; a surprisingly broad interval seems to separate the table from the fireplace mantel in the background. Despite the faceting of the apples and the crystal carafe, there is no place for this picture in the conventional history of Cubism. It strongly reinstates pictorial depth at a moment when the lattice or grid is supposed to be moving Picasso's pictures toward flatness.

* * *

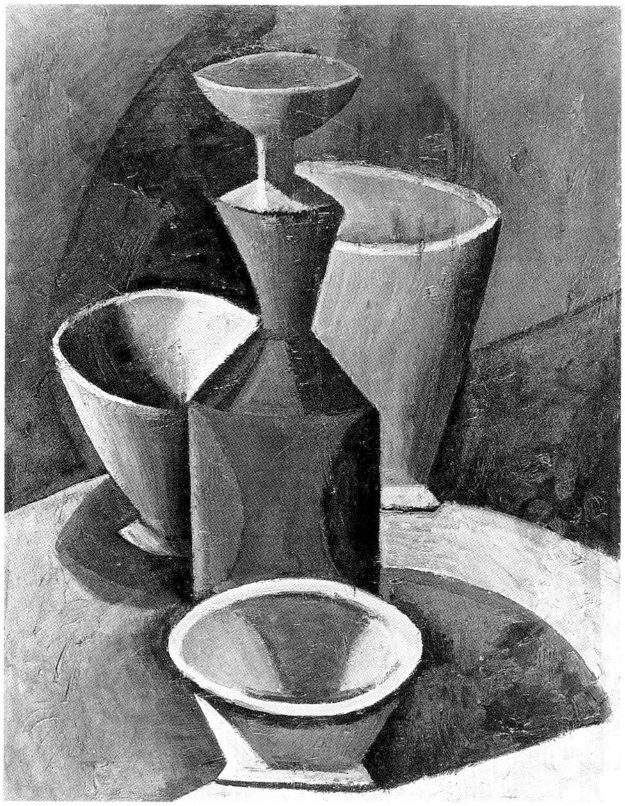

28 Picasso. *Carafe and Three Bowls*. Paris, summer 1908. Oil on cardboard, 66 × 50 cm. D.R. 176. The State Hermitage Museum, St. Petersburg

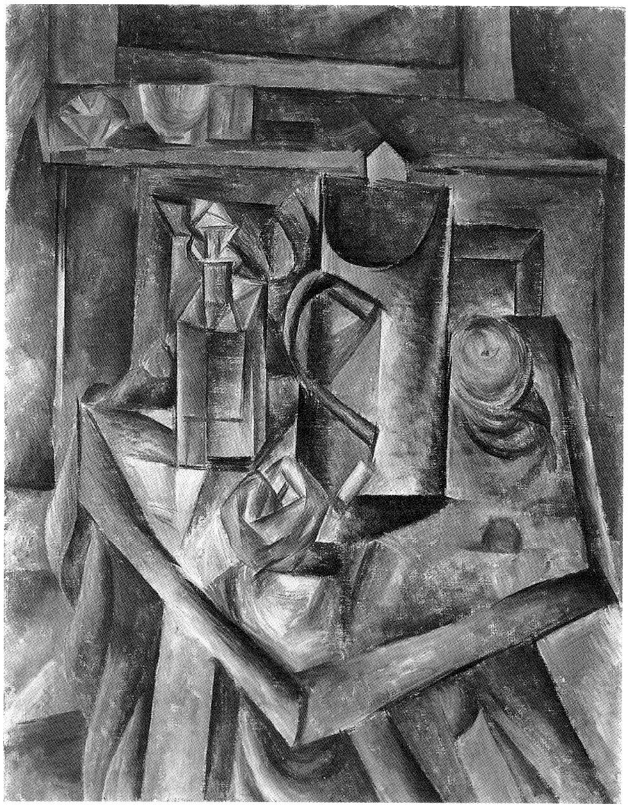

29 Picasso. *Le Bock (Glass of Beer)*. Paris, fall 1909. Oil on canvas, 81 × 65.6 cm. D.R. 312. Musée d'art moderne de Lille Métropole, Villeneuve-d'Ascq. Donation of Geneviève and Jean Masurel in 1979

The Two-Dimensional Lattice, 1908–1909

Indeed, the tension between the two dimensions of the lattice and the three dimensions of projective space dominates the development of Cubism from 1908 through 1910. It is in these years that Braque begins to play an important role as Picasso's interlocutor, adapting and reinterpreting his formal inventions and forcing him to reconsider their pictorial significance. It might almost be said that the revolutionary significance of Picasso's *Three Women* was only revealed by Braque's response to it. Picasso's idea of organizing a picture around a series of interlacing curves (see fig. 26) might well have ended where it started, as a clever variation on the flat, cloisonné designs of Art Nouveau. By superimposing facets on his original two-dimensional pattern (see fig. 27), Picasso made his figures pop out into bold relief, while the interlacing curves prevented them from separating into isolated forms. The combination of faceting with an interlocking design gave the impression that the picture as a whole formed a single continuous surface, modeled in three dimensions with tilting planes.

In effect, the *Three Women* demonstrated that it was possible to restore the sense of sculptural relief that had been sacrificed by Impressionism and Fauvism, without returning to the conventional language of academic painting. The lattice of interlocking curves satisfied the decorative demand that a painting should cohere as a two-dimensional design, while the alternation of light and dark facets simultaneously suggested the presence of three-dimensional forms. This innovative synthesis attracted the attention of Braque and Derain, inspiring the canvases that they showed at the Salon des Indépendants in March 1908. Braque's sketch of his now lost painting *Woman* (see fig. 4) shows that what he took from Picasso was not a system of hard-edged facets – most

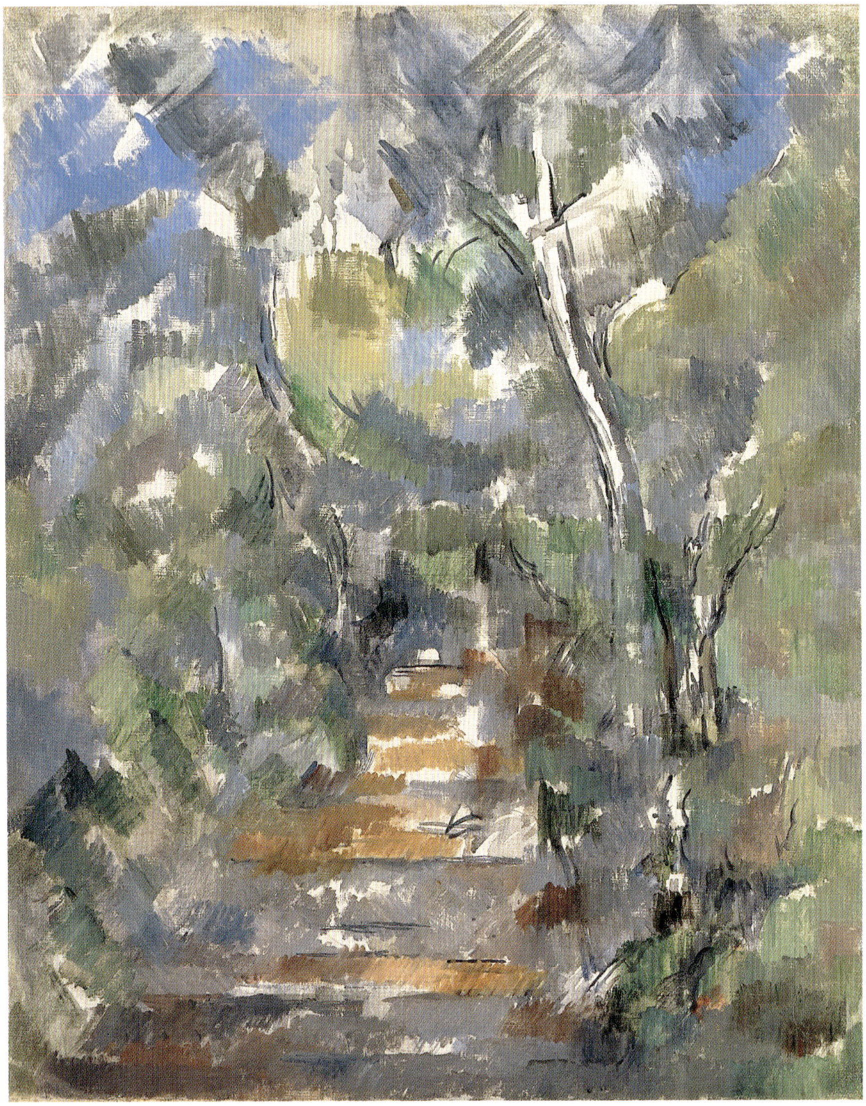

30 Paul Cézanne. *Forest Scene.* 1900–02. Oil on canvas, 79.5 × 64.5 cm. Rewald 884. Fondation Beyeler, Riehen/Basel

likely, these had not yet been imposed on the canvas of the *Three Women* – but the idea of a series of forms pushed up against one another within interlocking outlines, integrating figure and ground. Picasso reasserted three-dimensional form in the *Three Women* by vigorously shading the planes of the figures so that they tilted forward and backward in space. In contrast, Braque, in his paintings of the same months, adopted a "Cézannian" technique of laying in his colors with serried brushstrokes.[38]

The real link, however, between Cézanne and nascent Cubism was forged in Braque's landscapes of summer 1908, painted at L'Estaque. As Reff has suggested, Braque's accomplishment can be gauged by comparing one of his new landscapes with one of Cézanne's late forest scenes (figs. 30, 31).[39] In the Cézanne, dark lines describe tree-trunks, branches, and a few indentations in the forest path, but for the most part the forms of earth and foliage are indicated by the alternation of lighter and darker colors, applied in

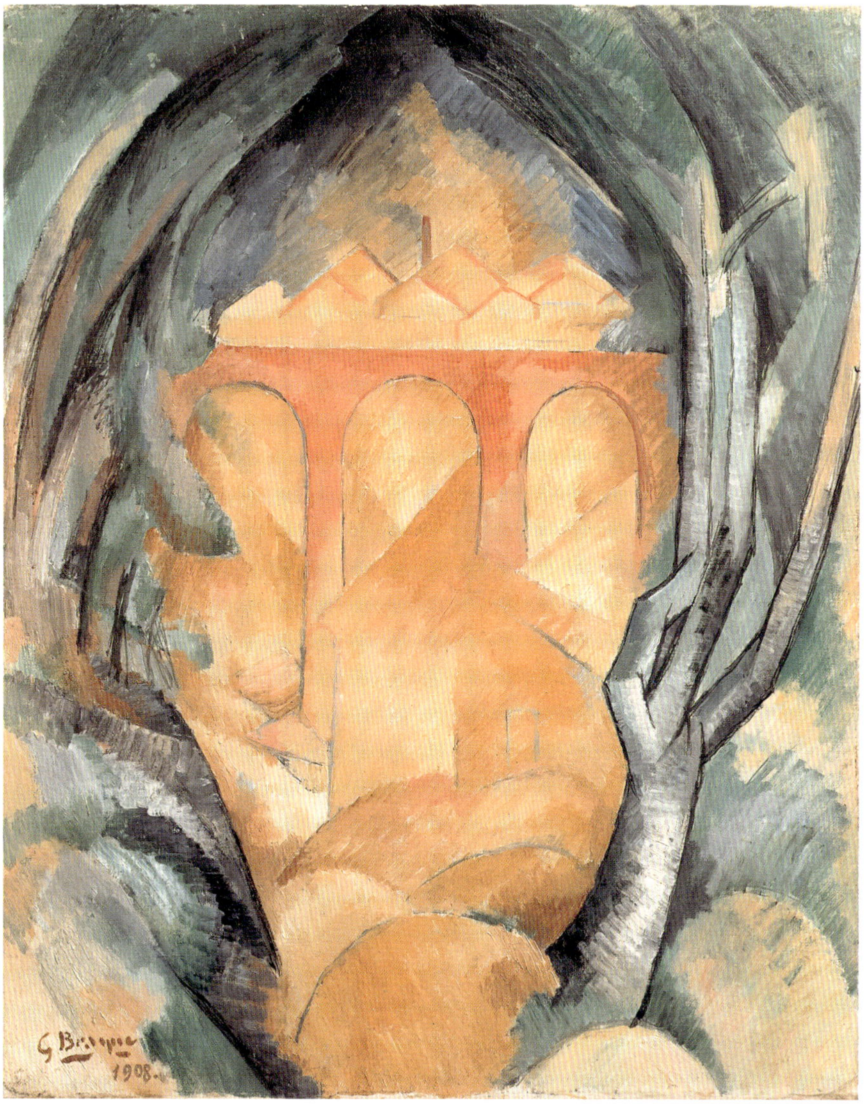

31 Braque. *Viaduct at L'Estaque.* L'Estaque, summer 1908. Oil on canvas, 73 × 60 cm. Romilly 21. Tel Aviv Museumof Art, Mizné Blumental Collection

irregular patches. What might otherwise seem an incoherent jumble of colors is given structure by the consistent rhythm of Cézanne's brushwork.

At first glance, Braque's composition seems strikingly similar. The trees framing the central aperture are bordered by dark contours, while the bulk of the picture is divided into alternating patches of light and dark greens and browns, laid down in regular diagonal strokes. However, Braque's color patches are no longer laid in on an ad hoc basis, in direct response to visual sensation. Close inspection of Braque's canvas (fig. 32) reveals that the borders of the patches were predetermined by an architectonic framework of lines, and that the colors were subsequently added within these outlines. This use of line is profoundly foreign to Cézanne, who expresses the undifferentiated experience of the optical field exclusively by color, reserving line for the description of particular forms. Braque, in contrast, expresses the unity of the optical field by means of an overall

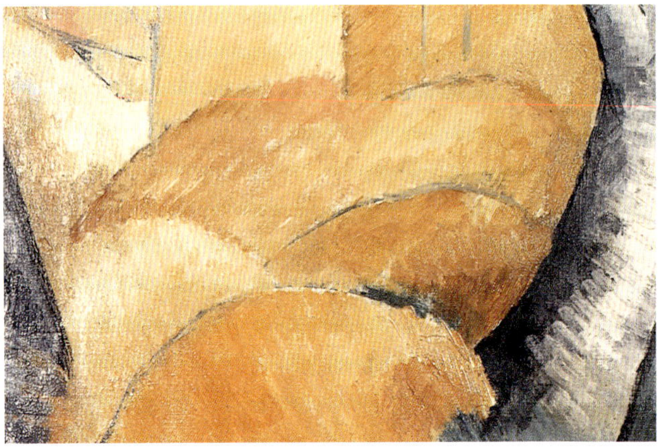

32 Braque. *Viaduct at L'Estaque.* Detail of fig. 31

lattice of lines. The Impressionist antithesis between optical color and tactile line breaks down here, and is replaced by a bizarre neologism: optical line.

The linear structure of Braque's *Viaduct at L'Estaque* clearly derives from the example of the *Three Women.* The picture plane is first divided by a lattice, and then colored and shaded to suggest three-dimensional forms. As in the *Three Women,* the color scheme has been reduced to a binary opposition of brown and green. In other respects, Braque's use of color remains close to Cézanne's practice, brilliantly analyzed by Lawrence Gowing, of modeling with color.[40] From one area to the next – and sometimes within a single area – the colors modulate from light to dark, giving the effect of three-dimensional form. But this modulation is repeated all across the surface of the picture, creating a flickering pattern of light and dark that the viewer perceives as a field, before perceiving any particular form within it.

The spatial organization of Braque's summer 1908 pictures looks back to Cézanne. *Viaduct at L'Estaque* borrows the framing arch of trees employed in Cézanne's *Forest Scene* and in his late *Large Bathers* (see fig. 18). The rising hillsides in *Viaduct at L'Estaque* and in *Houses at L'Estaque* (fig. 33) derive from pictures like *Bend in the Road at Montgeroult* (see fig. 16). They offer a landscape equivalent to the tilted space of contemporary still lifes by Picasso such as *Carafe and Three Bowls* (see fig. 28).

Braque's summer 1908 landscapes made a strong impression on contemporary observers such as the critic Louis Vauxcelles, who wrote that he "reduces everything, places and figures and houses, to geometrical schemes, to cubes" – hence the term "Cubism."[41] The only person who seems not to have been impressed by Braque's breakthrough was Picasso, whose work gives no hint of a response until May 1909. Only then, pausing in Barcelona on his way from Paris to Horta de Ebro, did he execute a series of drawings (fig. 34) whose cubic forms, arranged in a vertical frieze, clearly echo those of Braque's 1908 landscapes. Years later, discussing the development of Cubism, Picasso stressed the importance of these drawings, telling Pierre Daix: "That's where it all began. That's what I saw from my hotel window in Barcelona, and that's where I understood how far I could go . . ."[42] Picasso may have felt that he did not need to acknowledge Braque's precedent, since the Frenchman's landscapes were in turn indebted to his own earlier work. But the visual evidence seems clear enough. It was Braque who alerted Picasso to the fact that the pictorial construction of the *Three Women* could be applied not only to closely knit figure groups but also to landscape and other motifs.

Even so, Picasso's landscape paintings of summer 1909 (fig. 35) are consistently less "allover" than Braque's. The shading of his skies is relatively flat and even; only on the hillsides below does the repetition and alternation of light and dark planes create a fusion of optical and tactile signs equivalent to that of Braque's *Houses at L'Estaque.* Although the walls of the houses line up along common vertical axes, Picasso is not trying to knit the picture as a whole into a unified pattern like that of the *Three Women.* Rather, his goal here is to give a strong sense of forms projecting forward in space, as in his table-top still lifes (see figs. 28, 29).

Even in Braque's work of this period, the goal of creating a projective space tends to outweigh the quest for pictorial integration. In his *Violin and Pitcher* (fig. 36), painted early in 1910, the spatial relationships continue to be defined by the "primitive" convention of down = forward, while faceting is applied selectively to the foreground motifs rather than the setting. It is true, as critics have often remarked, that the clearly delineated shadow of the nail at the top makes it project strongly from the wall behind it. However, there is a sheet of music below and in front of the nail; there is a pitcher below and in front of the sheet music; and there is a violin below and in front of the pitcher. The still-life arrangement is anchored to the picture's lower edge, where it advances farthest forward, while the nail occupies the deepest space in the composition.

This is not to say that the faceting and fragmentation are unimportant. As shown earlier, Braque was attracted to

33 (*right*) Braque. *Houses at L'Estaque.* L'Estaque, summer 1908. Oil on canvas, 73 × 60 cm. Kunstmuseum Bern. Hermann and Margrit Rupf Foundation

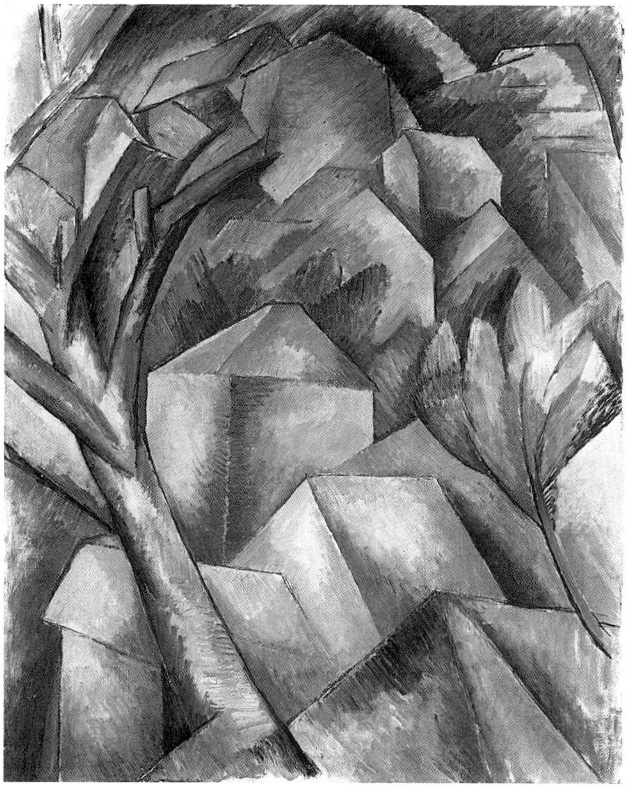

34 (*below left*) Picasso. *Houses and Palm Trees.* Barcelona, May 1909. Black ink on paper, 17 × 11 cm. Zervos VI, 1092. Richet 240. Musée Picasso, Paris

35 (*below right*) Picasso. *Reservoir at Horta.* Horta de Ebro, summer 1909. Oil on canvas, 60 × 50 cm. D.R. 280. The David and Peggy Rockefeller Collection

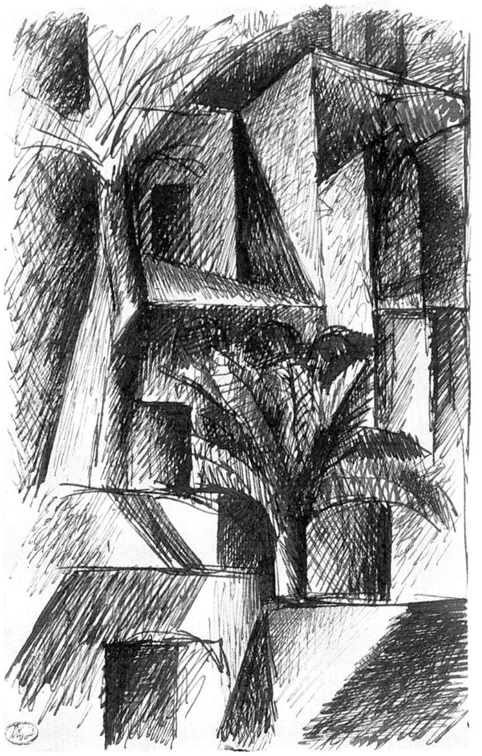

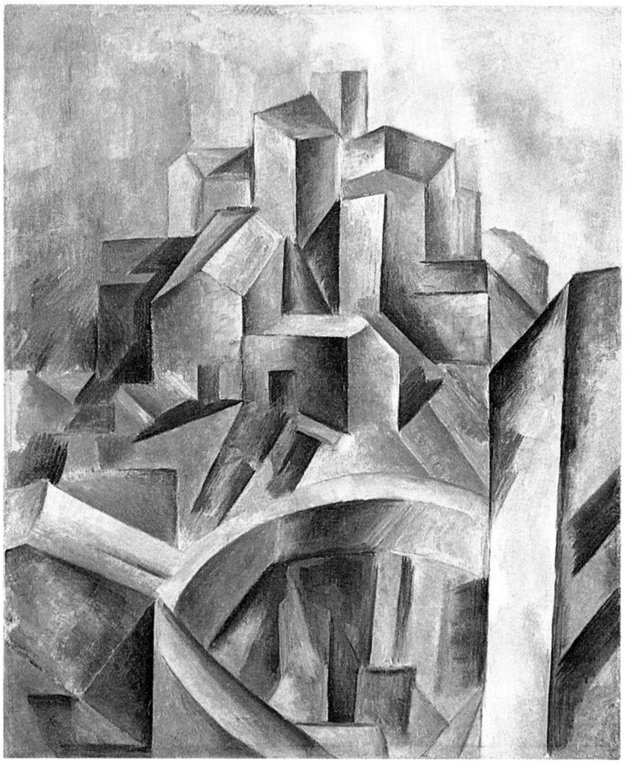

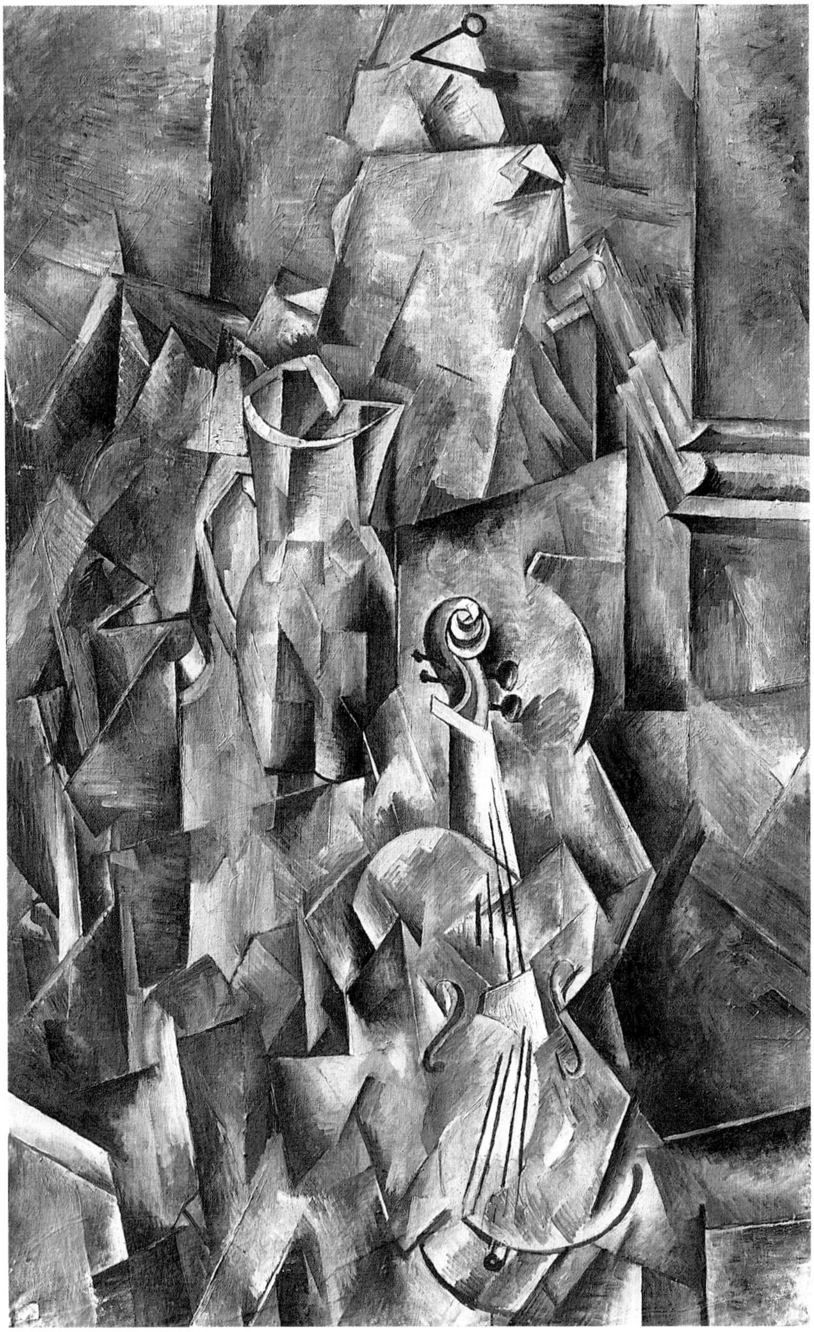

36 Braque. *Violin and Pitcher.* Paris, early 1910. Oil on canvas, 117 × 73 cm. Romilly 59. Oeffentliche Kunstsammlung, Basel, Kunstmuseum. Gift of Raoul La Roche, 1952

them because they made possible a new "materialization" of pictorial space.[43] In Braque's painting, the solid objects and the empty space around them are divided into the same hard-edged fragments, so that the violin and pitcher are nestled within an avalanche of crystalline boulders. By using geometry to describe both objects and the intervals between them in three-dimensional terms, Braque fused the two into a rugous, hard-edged surface of advancing and receding planes. This is the "tactile space" that answers his desire "to touch things, and not just to see them."[44]

The Three-Dimensional Grid, 1910–1912

Cubism, in winter 1909–10, still consisted of two contradictory elements. The sense of a projective space remained attached to the objects within the picture, whether houses and trees, carafes and bowls, or bodies and curtains. Conversely, the lattice remained a two-dimensional pattern, suspended like a scrim before the scene, and imposing its structure on the objects seen behind it. In Braque's *Mandola* (fig. 37) of this winter the musical instrument and jug are broken into shimmering, insubstantial shards, scattered across the picture plane. The imposition of geometric form can either reinforce the tactile presence of objects or reduce them to optical flickers. It may even, for a moment, do both. But the two goals remain fundamentally opposed.

37 Braque. *Mandola*. Paris, winter 1909–10. Oil on canvas, 71.1 × 55.9 cm. Romilly 55. Tate, London

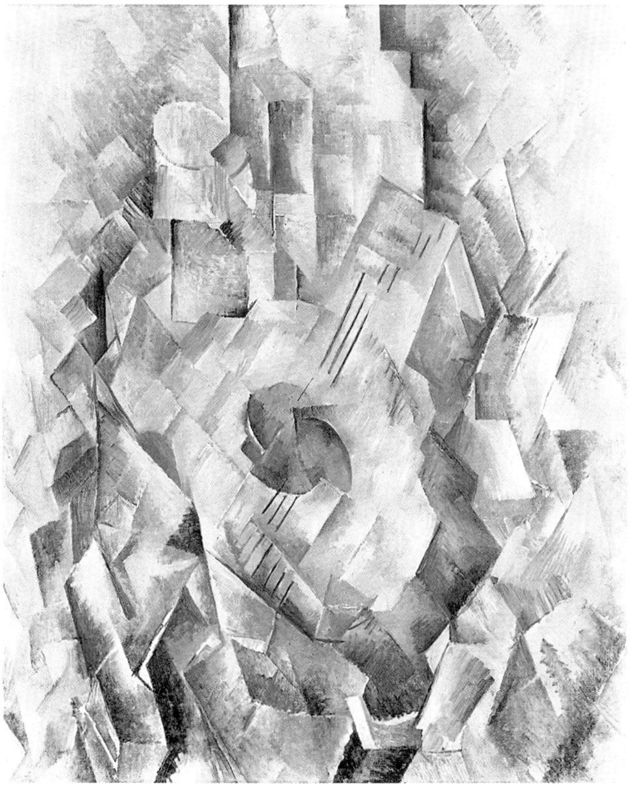

The solution to this dilemma is to make the lattice itself three-dimensional. But this expansion of the lattice into the third dimension is preceded by a different transformation – or, more precisely, a rotation. Sometime during the course of winter 1909–10 the diagonal lattice became a rectilinear grid. *Mandola* is organized around strong diagonal axes, breaking the forms within the lattice into diamonds and triangles. In contrast, Braque's cityscape *Le Sacré-Coeur* (fig. 38) is organized primarily around a series of verticals and horizontals, with diagonals and curves serving merely as accents.

38 Braque. *Le Sacré-Coeur*. Paris, winter 1909–10. Oil on canvas, 55 × 40.5 cm. Romilly 52. Musée d'art moderne de Lille Métropole, Villeneuve-d'Ascq. Donation of Geneviève and Jean Masurel in 1979

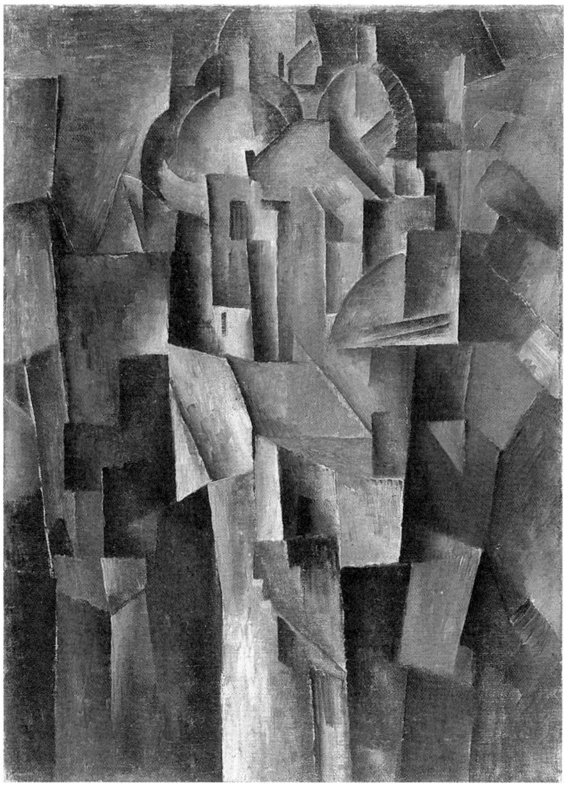

This transformation from lattice to grid remains one of the most mysterious episodes in the development of Cubism. Nothing anticipated it, and there is no obvious reason why it occurred. It is not even clear which artist, Braque or Picasso, first adopted the rectilinear grid. (On

balance, it seems likely that it was Braque, since a *Sacré-Coeur* painted by Picasso, apparently at the same time, is predominantly diagonal.[45])

Had the evolution of the lattice stopped there, however, Cubism would have remained within the formal universe of earlier art. Influenced by decorative theory, turn-of-the-century artists such as Gerhard Munthe and Kolo Moser often assigned the grid an important structural role, so much so that their work seems at moments to anticipate Cubism (see fig. 2). However, there is a fundamental difference between the grid employed by these artists and that utilized by Picasso and Braque: their grid is two-dimensional while the Cubist grid extends in three dimensions. In a picture like Picasso's summer 1910 *Still Life with Glass and Lemon* (see fig. 12), the irregular spacing of the horizontals and verticals breaks the composition into a series of independent planes, shaded to reinforce their separation in space. Indeed, the term "Cubist grid" is a misnomer, insofar as it suggests a regular, two-dimensional pattern of horizontals and verticals. Rather, what these lines form is a three-dimensional scaffolding like a child's jungle-gym. The planes and curves supported by this scaffolding do not advance and recede according to their place within the perspective of the underlying naturalistic composition (see fig. 13). Instead, the rectilinear scaffolding defines a series of overlapping planes, whose actual motion forward or backward in space is determined principally by their shading.

It should be said that this shading does not function according to conventional rules. Since the imaginary light source of a painting is usually somewhere in front of the picture, forms close to the viewer are usually more brightly illuminated than more distant forms. If two forms overlap, the nearer form blocks some of the light falling on the more distant one: it is thus bordered by its own cast shadow. This usual relation of light and dark is reversed in Picasso's *Still Life with Glass and Lemon*. Here, it is the shaded forms that seem to advance, and the light forms that seem to recede. The brownish planes of the table-top come forward, in front of the lighter spaces around them; and the cool gray-brown planes surrounding the fruit bowl seem to move in front of the warmer browns of the rest of the table.

The combination of overlapping forms and shading constitutes a new form of projective space, corresponding exactly to Braque's description of planes superimposed one over the other, or to Kahnweiler's analysis of forms arranged in front of a closed background.[46] However, this new pictorial structure co-existed, at first, with the older kinds of projective space explored in 1908–09 Cubism. The "reverse perspective" of the table-top in *Still Life with Glass and Lemon* recalls the projecting table-top of *Le Bock* (see fig. 29) and, even more closely, the roofs of the *Reservoir at Horta* (see fig. 35). Similarly, the steeply canted table in Braque's *Violin and Candlestick* (fig. 39), looks back to the tilted perspective of Picasso's *Carafe and Three Bowls* (see fig. 28). The new structure of overlapping planes supplemented, rather than replaced, the earlier form of projective space.

The organization of *Violin and Candlestick* offers a clue to the logic of Picasso's and Braque's development in spring–summer 1910. The objects here are arranged in accordance with the model of tilted up space, based on the convention that down equals forward. From this point of view, the base of the picture is the "leading edge" of the picture's fictional space. However, the shading of the picture creates a notably different impression. Unlike Picasso, Braque here did not reverse the conventional relationship between light and dark: when two planes overlap, the light seems to fall on the nearer one, which is silhouetted against a shaded area of the more distant one. The rear edge of the table, lower at left than at right, is marked by particularly prominent shadows. The strongly illuminated planes just below these shadows advance toward the viewer more forcefully than anything else in the picture – including the literal front edge of the table, indicated by a pair of diagonal edges near the bottom of the canvas.

The leading edge of the picture is thus relocated from its base to its mid-line, which comes to function as a kind of proxy for the base. This relocation is possible because of the rectilinear orientation of the pictorial lattice. If Braque had continued to employ the diagonal lattice of 1908–09, the edges of the planes formed by the lattice would not have echoed the lower edge of the picture, and would therefore not have been able to serve as proxies for it. To this extent, the invention of the rectilinear grid in spring 1910 was a prerequisite for the emergence of a new kind of projective space in summer 1910.

As Braque and Picasso gained confidence in this new pictorial architecture, they slowly abandoned their earlier models of projective space. By 1912, both artists began to arrange their motifs freely within the three-dimensional scaffolding of the Cubist grid. In Picasso's spring 1912 *Violin and Anchor* (fig. 40), for instance, it is impossible to define the "real" relationship among the objects represented.

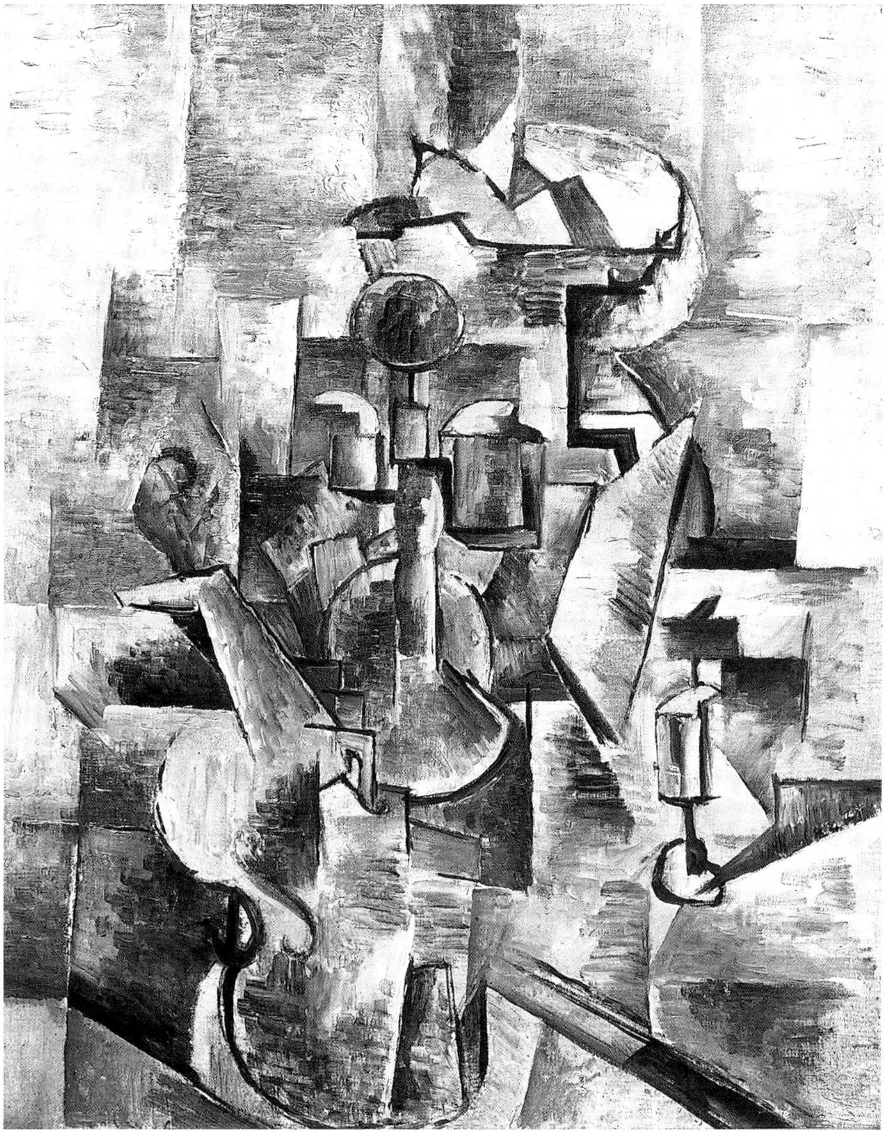

39 Braque. *Violin and Candlestick.* Paris, spring 1910. Oil on canvas, 61 × 50 cm. Romilly 63. San Francisco Museum of Modern Art. Gift of Rita Schreiber in loving memory of her husband, Taft Schreiber

Where is the violin in relation to the glasses? And what is the anchor doing here? Rather, the objects co-exist in a purely pictorial space.

This abandonment of earlier, more naturalistic forms of projective space also devalued the bottom edge, which was no longer the most forward element of the picture. Since the horizontal lines of the composition no longer needed to be emphasized as proxies for this bottom edge, the emphasis on the horizontal evident in 1910 pictures such as *Still Life with Glass and Lemon* and *Violin and Candlestick* (see figs. 12, 39) is replaced in *Violin and Anchor* by an emphasis on the vertical, evident in the long bands that traverse the picture from top to bottom. This reorientation of the grid into a series of vertical bands, first evident in fall 1911, led to Braque's *papiers collés* of summer–fall 1912, where the drawn vertical bands were supplemented by real strips

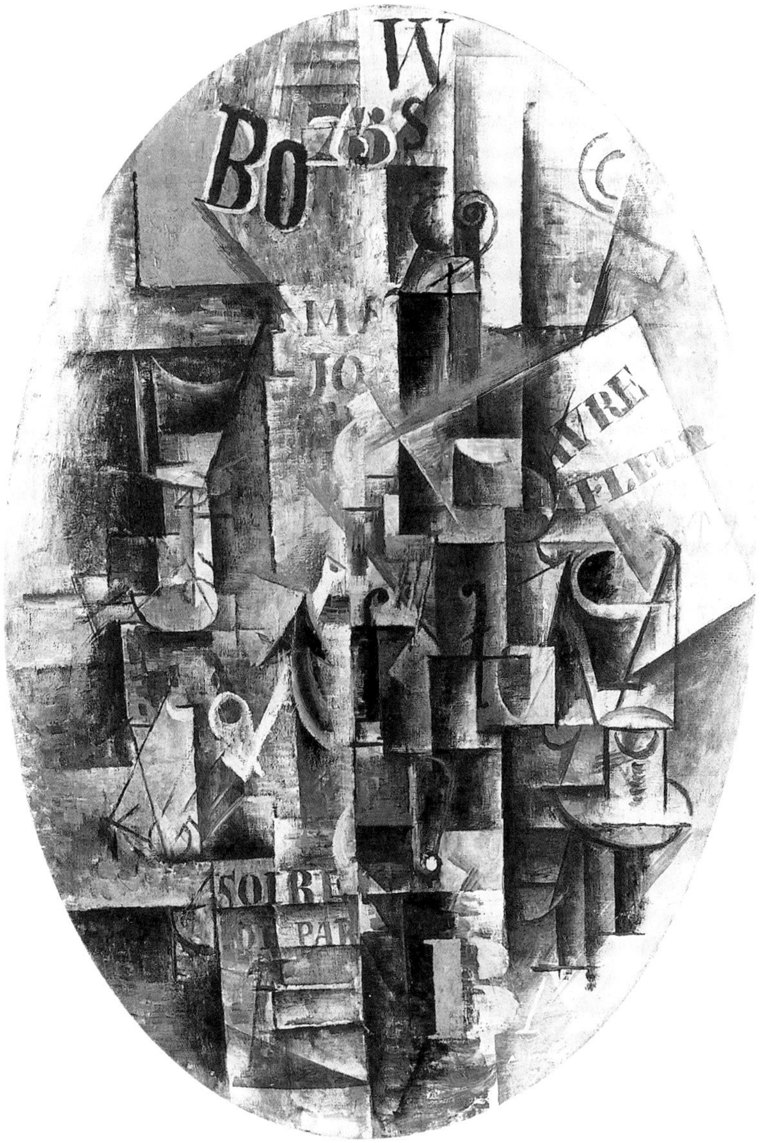

40 Picasso. *Violin and Anchor*. Paris, May 1912. Oil and enamel on canvas, 81 × 54 cm. D.R. 457. National Gallery in Prague

of wood-grained wallpaper (fig. 41). In effect, the new structure of vertical bands provided a template for the disposition of the pasted papers.

The restructuring of Cubist space, in 1910–12, had dramatic results for the bodies and objects in Picasso's and Braque's pictures. Fitting a solid object into the planes or bands of the grid meant breaking it into series of flat, rectilinear shapes. As Picasso told Kahnweiler, "Of course, when I want to make a cup, I'll show you that it is round, but the over-all rhythm of the picture, the structure, may force me to show this roundness as a square."[47] Already in 1908–09 the imposition of the diagonal lattice had encouraged Picasso and Braque to divide their motifs into triangular or diamond-shaped facets. But the rectilinear grid

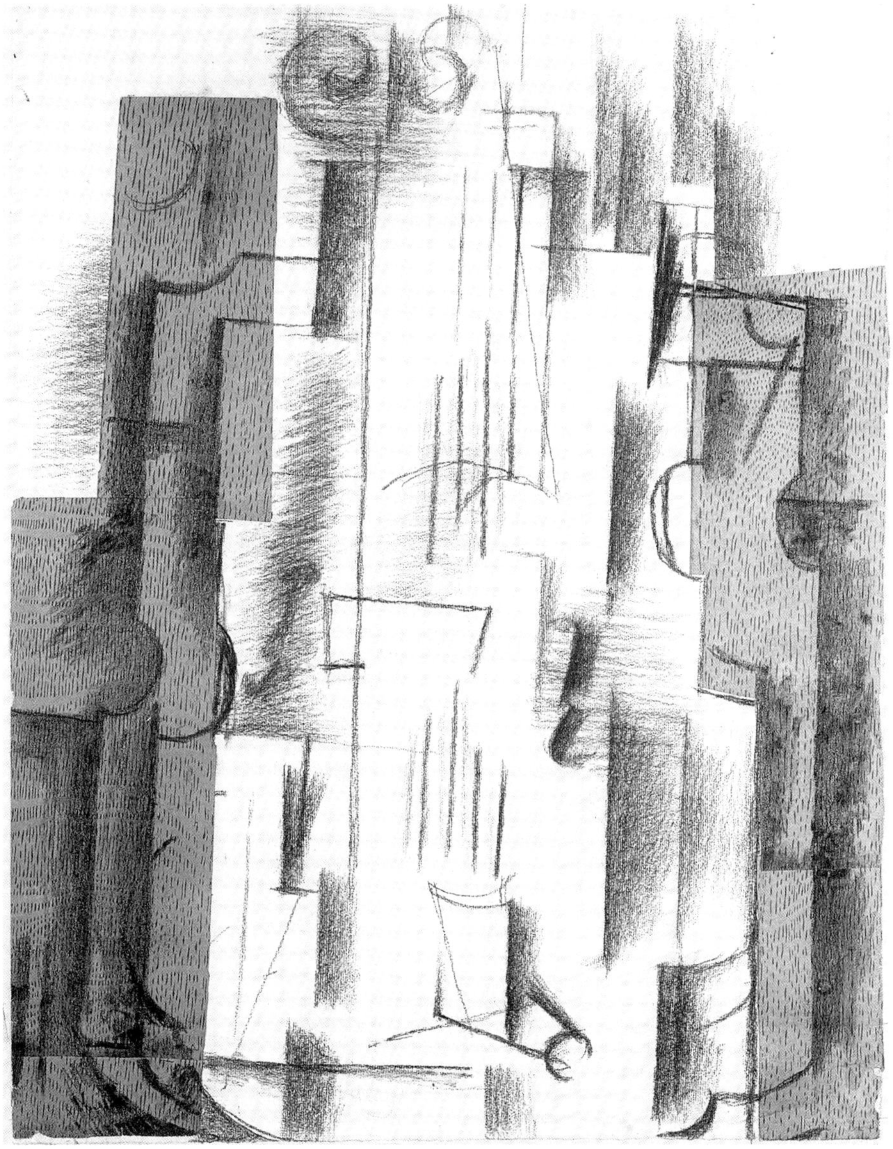

41 Braque. *Still Life with Violin.* Sorgues, fall 1912. Charcoal and pasted paper, 62.1 × 47.8 cm. M.-F./C. 9. Yale University Art Gallery, New Haven, Conn. The Leonard C. Hanna, Jr., B.A. 1913, Susan Vanderpoel Clark, and Edith M. K. Wetmore Funds

seemed to require a greater degree of distortion: the artists had literally to square the circle. The round lips of the wineglass and fruit bowl in *Still Life with Glass and Lemon* are evoked by curves, but their larger contours are indicated by overlapping, rectangular planes. The individual object had been reconfigured in terms of the open scaffolding of the picture as a whole. This development – the breaking open of the "closed form," as Kahnweiler called it – requires separate examination.

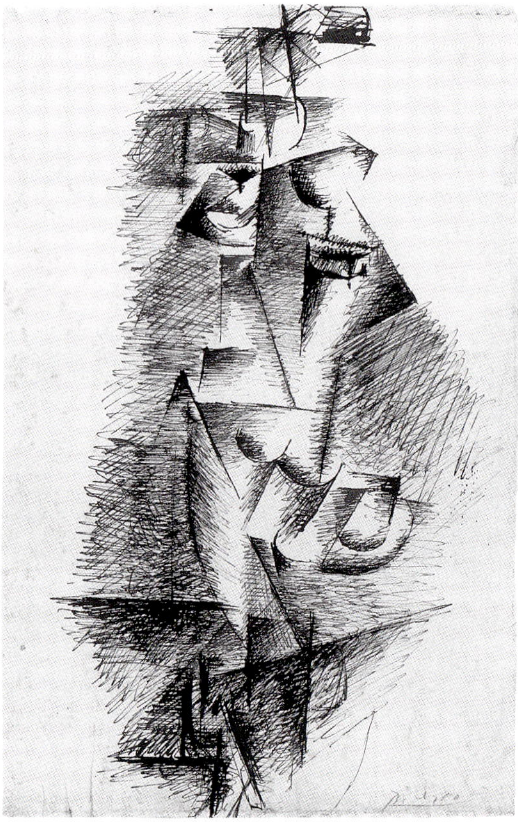

42 Picasso. *Standing Nude.* Cadaqués, summer 1910. Ink on paper, 32 × 23 cm. Zervos XXVIII, 20. Staatsgalerie, Stuttgart

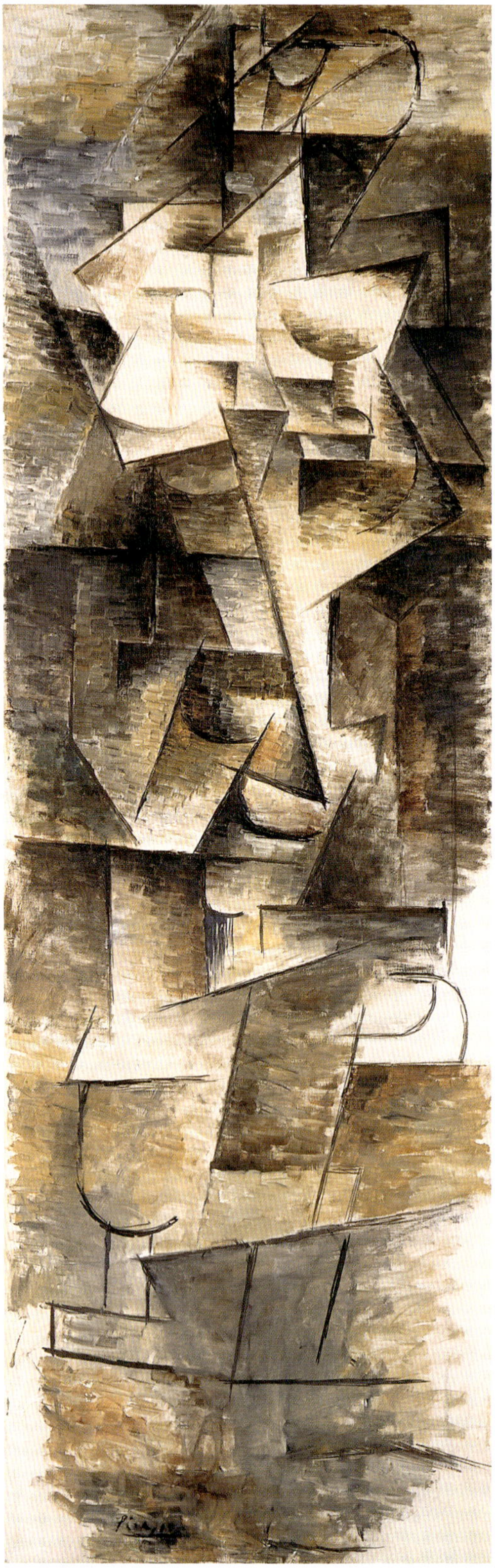

43 (*right*) Picasso. *Nude.* Cadaqués, summer 1910. Oil on canvas, 187.3 × 61 cm. D.R. 363. National Gallery of Art, Washington, D.C. Ailsa Mellon Bruce Fund

3

Bodies

In Picasso's paintings of summer 1910, the figure dissolves into an arrangement of free-floating lines and planes (figs. 42, 43). As Kahnweiler wrote, this was the "decisive advance which set Cubism free from the language previously used by painting." Traditional painting had represented bodies and objects "as contained by their own surfaces, viz., the skin." Picasso's revolutionary innovation was to pierce this "closed form," so that the body opened into the space around it, while space flowed into and through the body.[1] In hindsight, it is possible to identify important stages on the path to open form, but it is important to remember that Picasso had no way of knowing which ideas pointed "forward" and which did not.[2] Between 1900 and 1910, he experimented with a staggering variety of styles. To trace the path that led to Cubism therefore requires that the way be picked slowly and carefully through a complicated landscape. From 1901 through 1906, Picasso can be observed mostly trying to come to grips with Parisian modernism – trying, in other words, to overcome the limitations of his provincial education. From 1907 through 1909, he was focusing more clearly on the opposition between sculptural and decorative approaches to the human figure. But even in these years, when Picasso's work is conventionally described as "Cubist," there was no clear direction to his development. He devoted much time and energy to projects which seem in retrospect like splendid dead ends.

During this period, Picasso's experiments with different kinds of figuration ran parallel to his experiments with different kinds of projective space. Finally, in 1910, the two lines of investigation were brought together – and the result was open form. But there was nothing pre-ordained about it. There are no large general forces that can be invoked to explain it. This makes it all the harder to understand.

* * *

Against Impressionism

Three decades before Picasso arrived in Paris, the Impressionists had revolutionized painting by attempting to work in a manner corresponding to the latest scientific understanding of vision, which argued that "pure" optical sensation offered nothing more than a field of flat color patches. Trying to paint the optical field as a whole, an artist such as Monet was only secondarily concerned with the particular things found within it. Well past the turn of the century, this remained the defining idea of much avant-garde painting, especially that of Matisse and the Fauves.[3]

Picasso experimented with Impressionist color. But he seems to have been completely indifferent to the idea that the goal of painting was to transcribe the experience of the optical field as a whole. On the contrary, he remained deeply committed to representing particular things. Picasso's academic training oriented him toward an almost exclusive focus on the human. He then graduated to an "avant-garde" scene almost equally out of touch with the truly progressive art of the late 1890s. Instead, Barcelona *modernismo* was the local variant of the pan-European, decorative "Modern Style".

The studied poses, decorative colors, and literary subjects of Picasso's early paintings were compounded from Aubrey Beardsley and Maurice Denis. In his work of the Blue Period, Picasso defined a new, sculptural style that corresponded nonetheless to the empiricist theory dividing perception between optical and tactile sensations. Where the Impressionists had tried to achieve a purely "optical" style, Picasso opted instead for a purely "tactile" style of strong contours, massive three-dimensional forms, and monochrome coloring.

One of the attractions for Picasso of this new sculptural style was that it allowed him to continue to focus on the

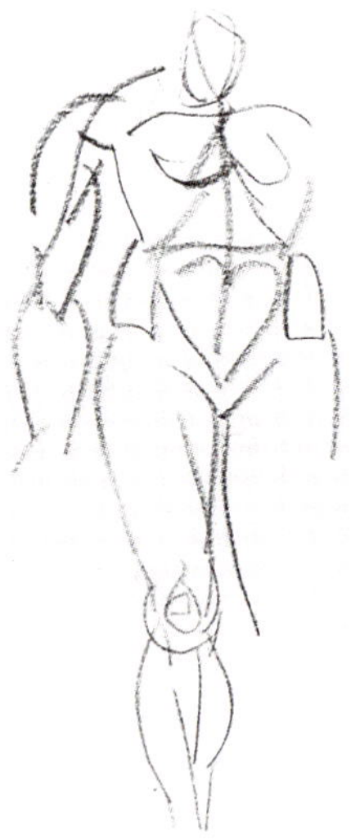

44 Picasso. Frontal view of a nude. Paris, early 1907. Pencil on sketchbook page, 14.7 × 10.6 cm. Seckel, carnet 2, p. 23v. Musée Picasso, Paris

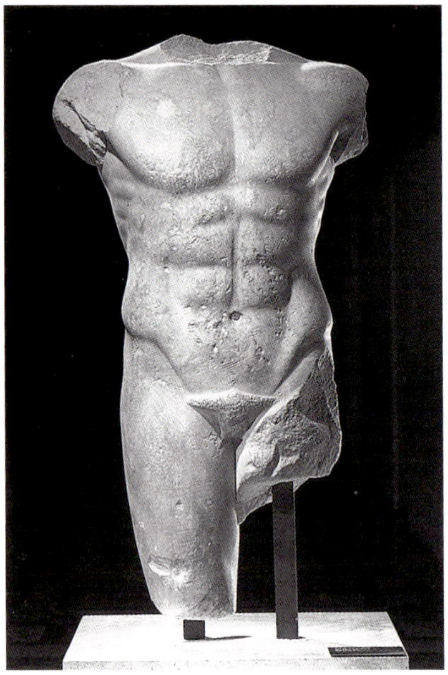

45 Male torso. Ionian style, after 479 B.C. Marble, h. 132 cm. Musée du Louvre, Paris

subject matter that interested him most, the human body. This preoccupation played a decisive role in Picasso's response to Cézanne. While Matisse studied Cézanne's paintings of female bathers, with multiple figures integrated into a complex composition (see figs. 18, 19), Picasso focused his attention on Cezanne's *Large Bather* of 1885, with its isolated, sculptural figure.[4] What Picasso gleaned from Cézanne was the idea of minimizing the internal contours of the body, and communicating its sculptural mass primarily by the inflection of its silhouette. This simplification of form was also encouraged by Picasso's study of several Hellenistic heads from Spain that had recently gone on display at the Louvre.[5] Their mask-like faces were often imitated in a series of 1906 paintings, culminating in the large canvas *Two Nudes* (see fig. 21). The bodies here were given a stronger sense of sculptural presence by the simple expedient of making them heftier.

Decorative vs. Sculptural Form, 1907

By the end of 1906, then, Picasso seemed firmly committed to a sculptural depiction of the human figure. The decorative elements of his earlier painting had been completely banished. Accordingly, in winter 1906–07, when he began planning the composition that became the *Demoiselles d'Avignon*, it was cast in the sculptural mode of the *Two Nudes*. The banished elements returned, however, in his studies of spring and summer 1907, setting off a long struggle between sculptural form and decorative design. This struggle continued, unabated, through the course of Picasso's work on the *Three Women* of spring 1908, and on into his varied experiments of later 1908 and 1909. It is worth examining Picasso's studies for the *Demoiselles d'Avignon* in painstaking detail, because some of the formal ideas explored in them provided the starting point for the treatment of the figure in the finished version of the *Three Women*. It is only a slight exaggeration to say that the faceted, "crystalline" Cubism of 1908–09 derived from ideas that Picasso considered – and rejected – in the course of his work on the *Demoiselles*.

As seen in the previous chapter, the overall composition of the *Demoiselles* seems to have evolved from a series of figure studies done as postscripts to the *Two Nudes* (see figs. 21–25). Although the face of the left-hand figure in the *Two Nudes* was drawn with razor-sharp clarity, the massive

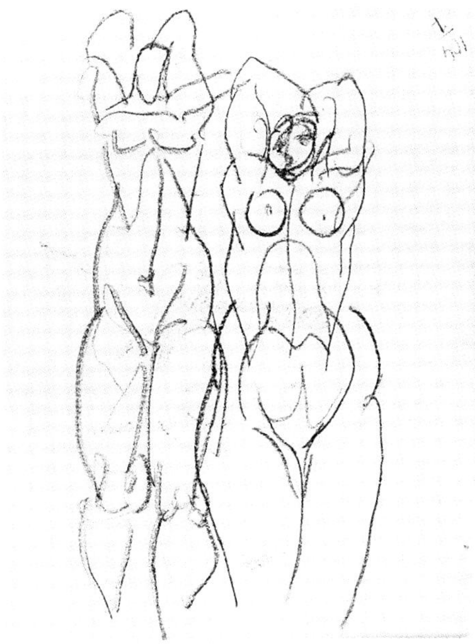

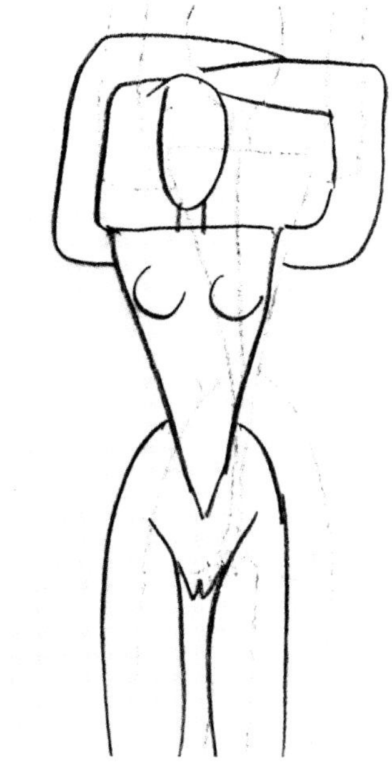

46 (*above left*) Picasso. Frontal view of nudes with raised arms (classical). Paris, winter 1906–07. Pencil on sketchbook page, 14.7 × 10.6 cm. Seckel, carnet 2, p. IV. Musée Picasso, Paris

47 (*above right*) Picasso. Frontal view of a nude with raised arms (geometric). Paris, March–April 1907. Pencil on sketchbook page, 16.5 × 11 cm. Seckel, carnet 4, p. 8v. Private collection

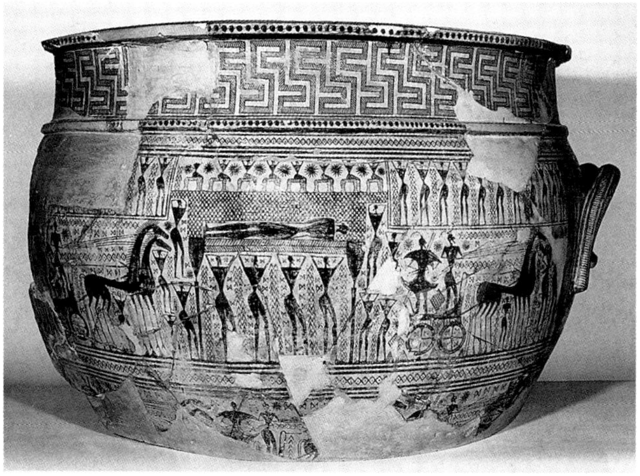

48 (*right*) Fragment of a krater. Funeral scene. Attic style, c. 750 B.C. Terracotta, h. c.58 cm. Musée du Louvre, Paris

bodies of the figures remained somewhat vague in structure. Picasso seems in his winter 1906–07 drawings (fig. 44) to be looking for a way to articulate the structure of the body as clearly as the face. Returning to the academic anatomy of his youth, he marks off the divisions of the pectorals and deltoids, the gluteus medius, the thigh, the kneecap, and the calf, as if his subject were a flayed figure. The abdomen is inscribed within a diamond, and divided by a cross.

The immediate impetus for this delineation of musculature may have been a visit to the Louvre, where Picasso could have studied the similar treatment of anatomy in a superb Ionian torso (fig. 45) or in classical vase paintings.[6] Applying this masculine anatomy to his female figures, he created a powerfully androgynous image of the human body, which served as the stock body type of the early sketches for the *Demoiselles*.[7]

At some point in early 1907, however, Picasso rejected this mode of figuration, probably because it seemed too naturalistic, compared with the bold distortions of his chief rival, Matisse. Under pressure to produce a more radical

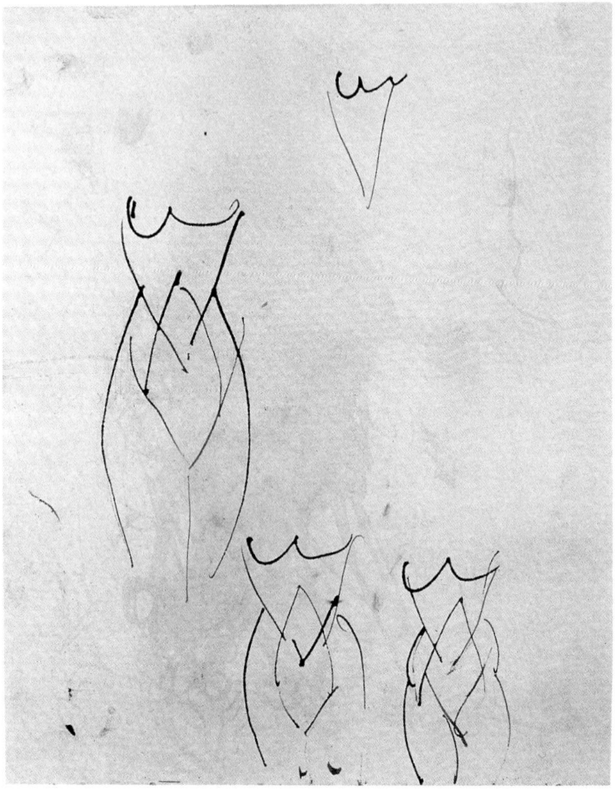

49 (*left*) Picasso. Studies of a nude, seen from the front. Paris, March 1907. Pencil on sketchbook page, 19.3 × 24.2 cm. Seckel, carnet 3, p. 23v. Musée Picasso, Paris

50 Picasso. Study for *Les Demoiselles d'Avignon*. Paris, March–May 1907. Ink on paper, 8.2 × 9 cm. Seckel, cat. 24. Musée Picasso, Paris

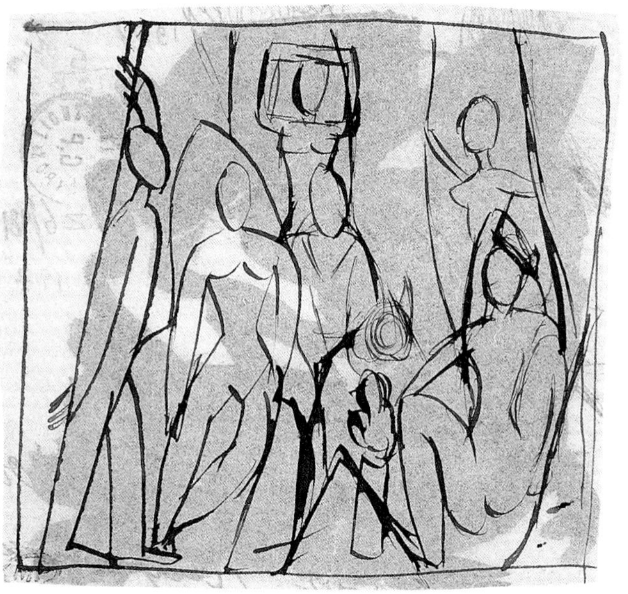

style, Picasso abandoned classical anatomy and redrew his figures in a new vocabulary of flat, geometric shapes (figs. 46, 47). The revised figures seem strikingly "modern." However, they may also derive from an antique source, specifically an eighth-century krater in the Greek galleries of the Louvre (fig. 48).[8] The silhouetted black figures on this krater, arranged in a frieze across the upper register, are drawn as flat silhouettes, with triangular torsos (seen frontally) perched atop curved hips (seen in profile). The figure in Picasso's notebook sketch is drawn with a similar combination of forms, although here both torso and hips are seen from the front. In another version (fig. 49), the triangle of the torso is combined with a diamond shape enclosing the muscles of the abdomen, as in his early "classical" sketches.

The contrasts between geometric shapes in these drawings recall one of Picasso's later comments about Cézanne: "Around 1906, Cézanne's influence gradually flooded everything, and the knowledge of composition, of the polarity of forms and of the rhythm of forms was open to all. I realized that painting had an intrinsic value, detached from any actual portrayal of objects . . ."[9] The idea of decoration was very much in the air at this time,[10] and the two qualities emphasized by Picasso – "polarity" and "rhythm" – would have been understood specifically as decorative qualities. In Blanc's *Grammar of the Decorative Arts*, rhythmic repetition is described as the fundamental principle of decoration. Repetition is then combined with its opposite, variety, to yield the secondary principle of alternation. "Two contrasting things, far from disrupting unity, will serve on the contrary to affirm it energetically," Blanc had written.[11]

From this point of view, the formal vocabulary of the revised studies for the *Demoiselles* can be understood as a decorative style based on oppositions among basic geometric shapes. Within a single figure (see fig. 47), Picasso contrasted the rectangle of the raised arms, the triangle of the torso, and the elliptical curve of the hips. A few years later, Fernand Léger adopted the "contrast of forms" as the key principle of his own version of Cubism.[12] In spring 1907, however, Picasso's new style of geometric shapes coexisted uneasily with the stage space of his original studies for the *Demoiselles*. As individual figures were transformed

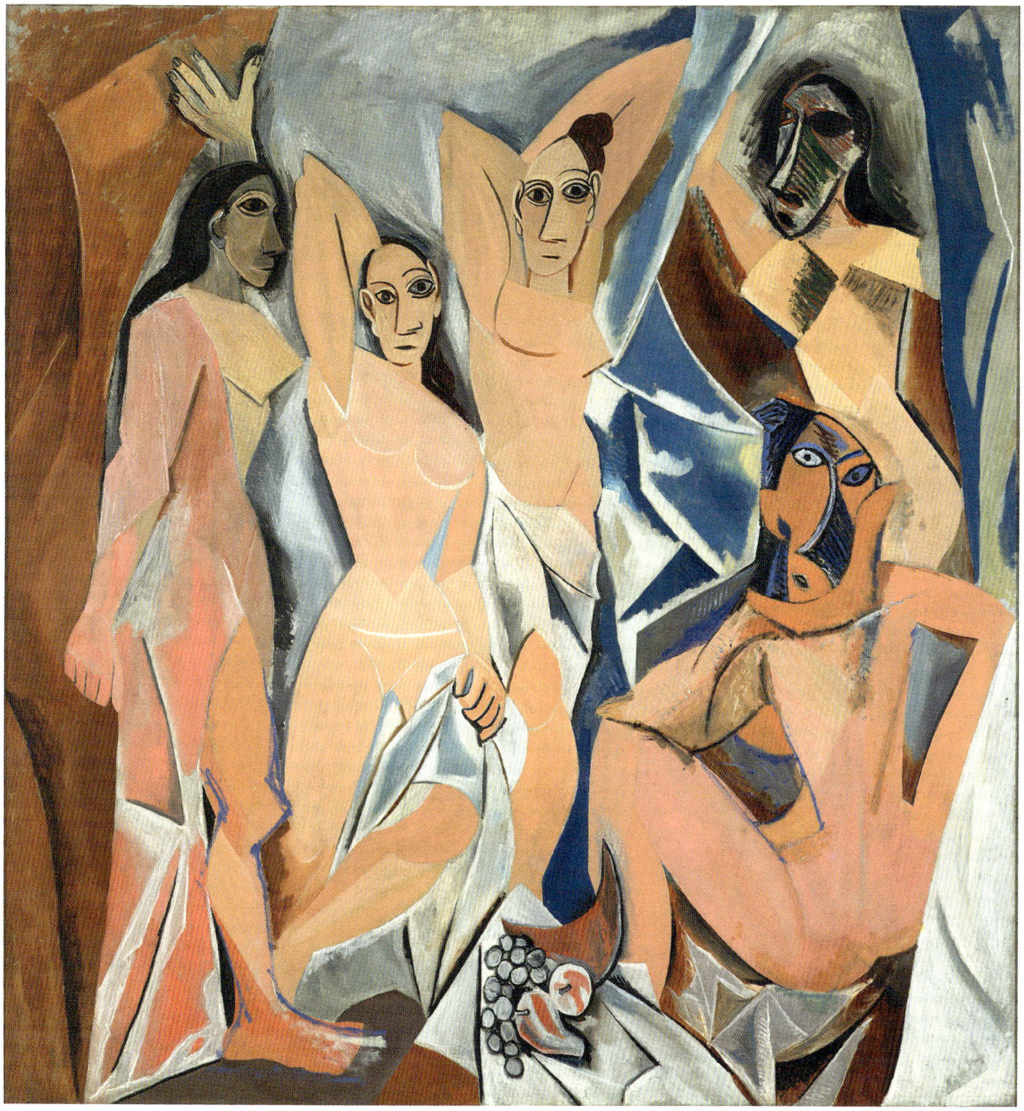

51 Picasso. *Les Demoiselles d'Avignon*. Paris, June–July 1907. Oil on canvas, 243.9 × 233.7 cm. The Museum of Modern Art, New York. Acquired through the Lillie P. Bliss Bequest

from three-dimensional bodies into flattened silhouettes, the composition as a whole had to be reorganized as a unified two-dimensional pattern. Picasso's first attempts at reworking the composition in his new "flattened" style appear in a May 1907 sketchbook. The poses of the figures had in turn to be adjusted to conform to the flatness of the revised composition. For instance, the crossed leg of the seated figure was redrawn so that it descended in the same plane as the other leg (fig. 50; see figs. 23, 25).

The contrast of rectangular, triangular, and curvilinear forms – which had worked successfully within a single figure – presented another problem. Once the composition as a whole had been aligned around the armature of an underlying *X* or *V* (as discussed in the previous chapter), the squared-off arms of the central figure stood out as a foreign element (see fig. 50). In the finished canvas, Picasso redrew the arms of this figure as curved lozenges that rhymed with the diagonals around them (fig. 51). Similarly, he raised one

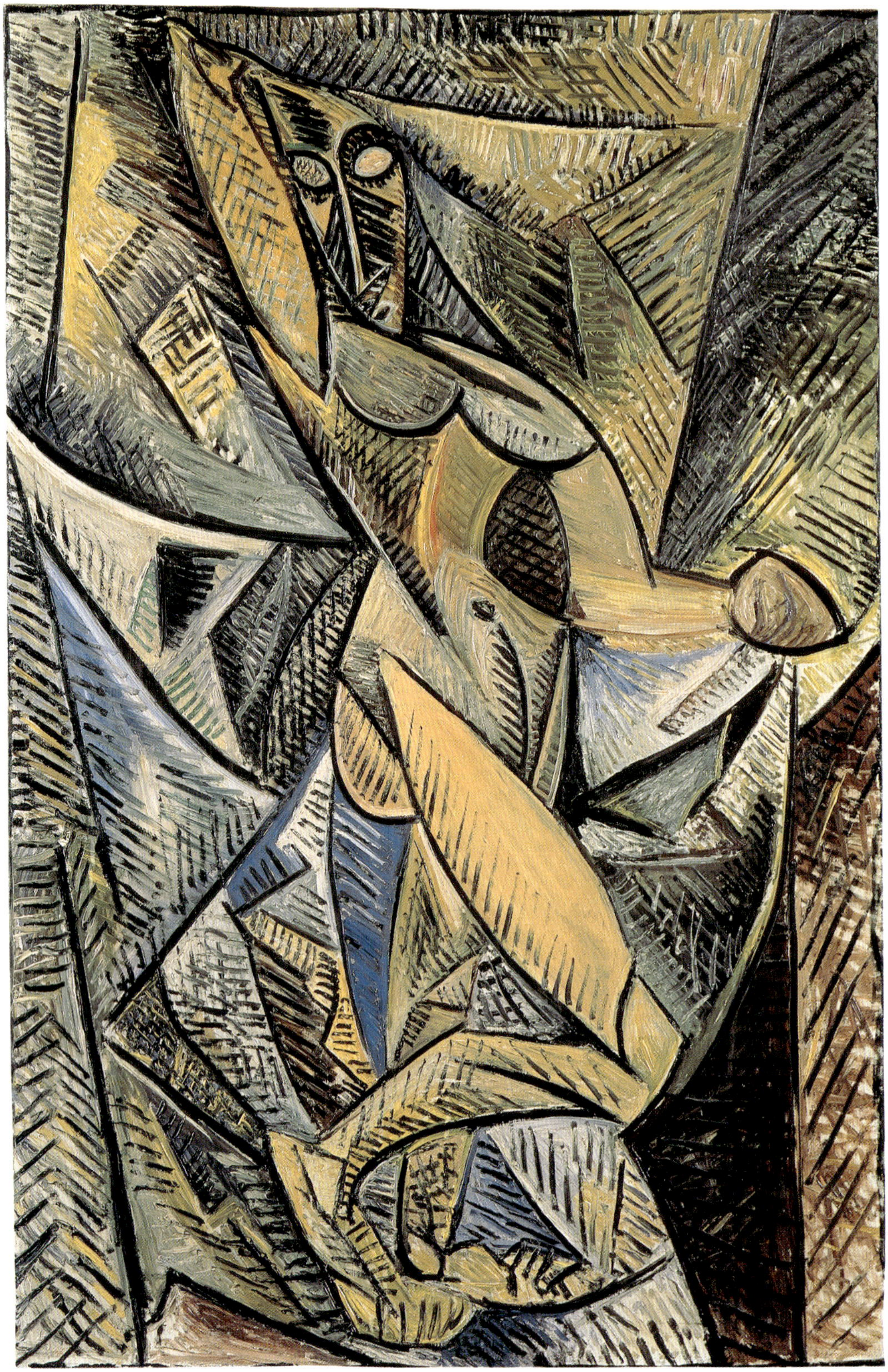

52 Picasso. *Nude with Drapery*. Paris, summer 1907. Oil on canvas, 152 × 101 cm. D.R. 95. The State Hermitage Museum, St. Petersburg

of the arms of the seated figure at left to align with the *V* of the picture's armature.

The "rhythm" of the forms thus triumphed over their "polarity." The drawing of the finished picture is dominated by a single unit: an almond-shaped lozenge with pointed ends, much like the traditional mandorla found on Gothic façades. Almost every form in the picture is a variant of the same shape. Large almonds indicate thighs, small ones arms. Even the curving curtain folds seem like sections of overlapping almonds. The triangular torsos, surviving from the earlier studies, and a few diamond-shaped breasts provide an understated contrast to the curved forms that surround them. Although the poses of the demoiselles are in fact quite varied, the concatenation of flat, curved shapes gives the impression that all five are seen frontally or in profile, reinforcing the archaic quality of their anatomy.[13]

If the *Demoiselles* had remained as it must have looked when first committed to canvas, with its clean outlines and its decorative color scheme of pink, brown, and blue, it would probably not have provoked the negative reactions that it did. Its flat colors and curved contours were no more outrageous than those of Matisse's *Young Sailor (II)*, painted in the second half of 1906; and Picasso's grouping of nudes had been anticipated in pictures like Derain's *The Dance* of 1906, with its arabesque of decorative figures. However, Picasso himself seems to have been dissatisfied with the picture, and continued to revise it through the spring and summer of 1907.

In abandoning the naturalistic style of his early studies for the picture, he had given up the descriptive power of classical anatomy, which had allowed him create an image of the body charged with physicality and sexuality. In contrast, the simplified, "archaic" forms of the revised composition tended to dematerialize and desexualize the image of the body. This palpable loss provoked Picasso to seek new ways of representing the body as a three-dimensional form. He wanted to reassert the power of sculptural form without giving up the pictorial coherence of his new decorative style.

In a series of spring–summer 1907 drawings, he developed a new, striated style, using hatch marks aligned in long rows to indicate surfaces turning in space. The culmination of these experiments was a major canvas, *Nude with Drapery* (fig. 52), in which the hatch marks functioned simultaneously as decorative and as sculptural elements. Picasso may have contemplated reworking the *Demoiselles* as a whole in the style of the *Nude with Drapery*. Indeed, Kahnweiler in 1916 described the *Demoiselles* as if this had happened, writing that Picasso "applied the colors in thread-like fashion to serve as lines of direction, and to build up, in conjunction with the drawing, the plastic effect."[14] In fact, more of the picture was at one moment covered with hatch marks, but some of these were overpainted with flat areas of color; in the end, striations appeared only on the faces of the two right-most figures.[15] If the entire canvas had been reworked in this fashion, it might have found a more appreciative audience. The *Nude with Drapery*, for instance, was quickly acquired by the Steins, and later by Sergei Shchukin. The partial revisions led many early viewers to dismiss the *Demoiselles* as an "unfinished" work.[16] In any case, Picasso himself soon abandoned the technique of rhythmic striations, instead pursuing other means to the same goal.

Faceting

Hatching transformed the appearance of the *Nude with Drapery* but the underlying composition was built up from the same "almond" module found in the *Demoiselles*. In his preparatory studies, however, Picasso had experimented with grouping muscles and bones into bulging, pod-like masses that proposed a new, three-dimensional module for the figure (fig. 53). Strikingly unattractive, these rubbery figures were fertile with implications for the future. As he reworked them, Picasso began, step by step, to evolve a new system of articulations, derived from classical anatomy but with its own structural logic. The gluteus maximus was set off from the gluteus medius, establishing two small forms that contrasted with the larger pods of the thigh and abdomen.[17] As the series progressed, the decorative principle of polarity reasserted itself: the smaller elements of breasts, buttocks, and knees became increasingly angular, so that they stood out from the curved forms that surrounded them (fig. 54).[18]

In retrospect, this introduction of angular geometric forms appears as a crucial step toward Cubism. It was not altogether without precedent in Picasso's work. He had used a kind of geometric shorthand to summarize the anatomical divisions of the body in his "classical" sketches of late 1906 (see fig. 44) and again in his first experiments with "archaic" imagery (see fig. 49). Here, the intersection between the "real" diamond of the abdomen and the "imaginary" triangle of the torso created a second, smaller

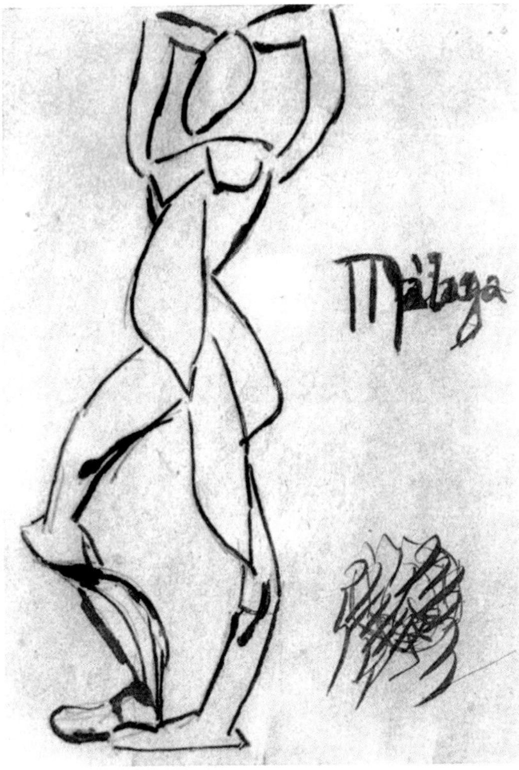

53 Picasso. *Standing Nude with Raised Arms.* Paris, May–early July 1907. Pencil and pink ink, reworked with purple ink, on sketchbook page, 22.4 × 17.5 cm. Seckel, carnet 9, inside back cover. Private collection

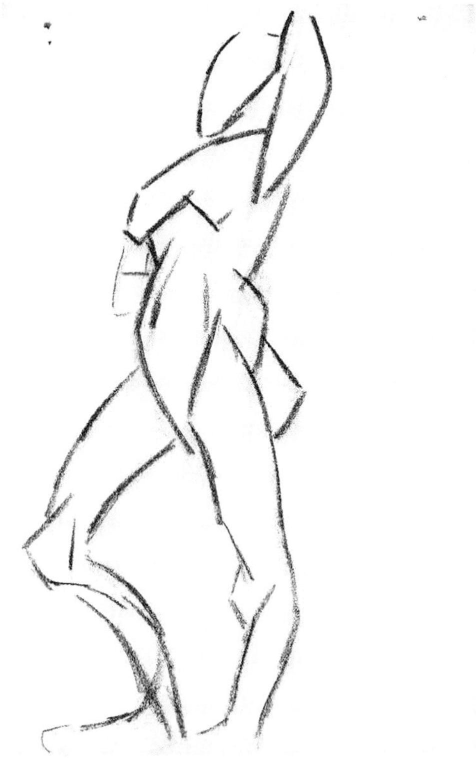

54 Picasso. *Nude with Raised Arm.* Paris, spring 1908? Pencil on sketchbook page, 13.3 × 21.3 cm. Seckel, carnet 16, p. 21r. Musée Picasso, Paris

55 (*facing page top left*) Picasso. *Standing Nude with Clasped Hands (Proportion Study).* Paris, April–May 1907. Pencil and black ink on page from Daumier exhibition catalogue, Seckel, carnet 5, p. IV. Private collection

56 (*facing page top right*) Diagram of the breast type found in the Venus de Milo. From Ernst Brücke, *The Human Figure: Its Beauties and Defects* (trans. London: H. Grevel, 1900), fig. 8

diamond that corresponded to no actual anatomical feature but was, rather, a by-product of the system of geometric representation. In spring 1907, Picasso returned to the idea of inscribing geometric forms on a naturalistic figure (fig. 55). The overlap of diamond-shaped abdomen and triangular torso was now repeated within a larger series of overlapping diamonds. One diamond extended from the top of the head to the navel; another from the neck to the groin; a third from the middle of the abdomen to the knees; and a fourth from the knees to the feet. This experiment, which has no immediate sequel in Picasso's work, seems to have been motivated by a kind of parodic logic.[19]

Geometric proportion was the ghost in the machine of classical anatomy. At bottom, the rules for the representation of the ideal body were arbitrary and contingent: a set of proportions derived from antiquity and modified by modern taste. But the attempt to define these rules geometrically gave them a semblance of objective justification. The sensual beauty of the visible body, it could be argued, corresponded to the ideal beauty of the Platonic forms hidden beneath the skin.

Picasso's diagram echoes and exaggerates academic procedures for using geometry to define body types. In a contemporary text on artistic anatomy, for instance, a discussion of different forms of breast found in ancient art begins with the type "set on the thorax like a cone, which, if cut through its axis, would exhibit an angle of 90° or

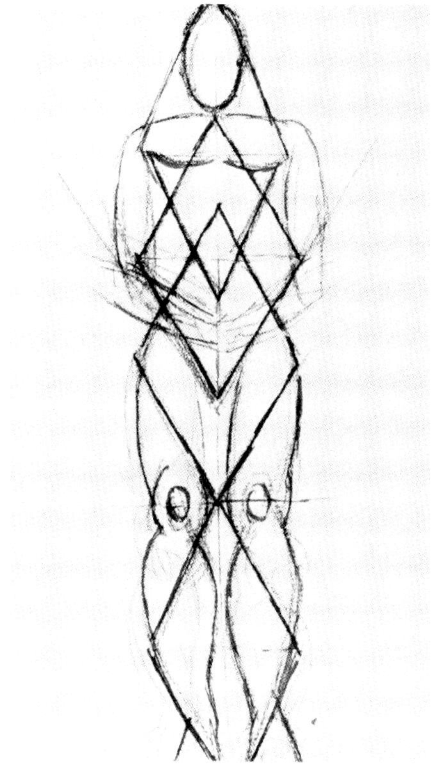

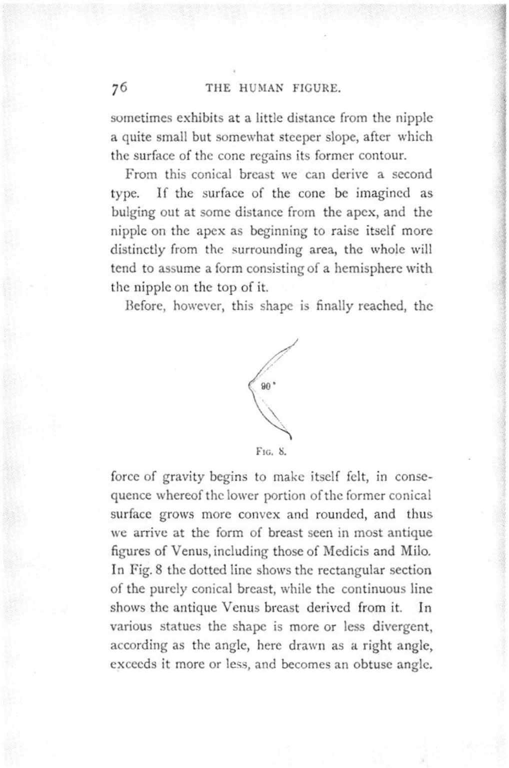

76 THE HUMAN FIGURE.

sometimes exhibits at a little distance from the nipple a quite small but somewhat steeper slope, after which the surface of the cone regains its former contour.

From this conical breast we can derive a second type. If the surface of the cone be imagined as bulging out at some distance from the apex, and the nipple on the apex as beginning to raise itself more distinctly from the surrounding area, the whole will tend to assume a form consisting of a hemisphere with the nipple on the top of it.

Before, however, this shape is finally reached, the

90°

FIG. 8.

force of gravity begins to make itself felt, in consequence whereof the lower portion of the former conical surface grows more convex and rounded, and thus we arrive at the form of breast seen in most antique figures of Venus, including those of Medicis and Milo. In Fig. 8 the dotted line shows the rectangular section of the purely conical breast, while the continuous line shows the antique Venus breast derived from it. In various statues the shape is more or less divergent, according as the angle, here drawn as a right angle, exceeds it more or less, and becomes an obtuse angle.

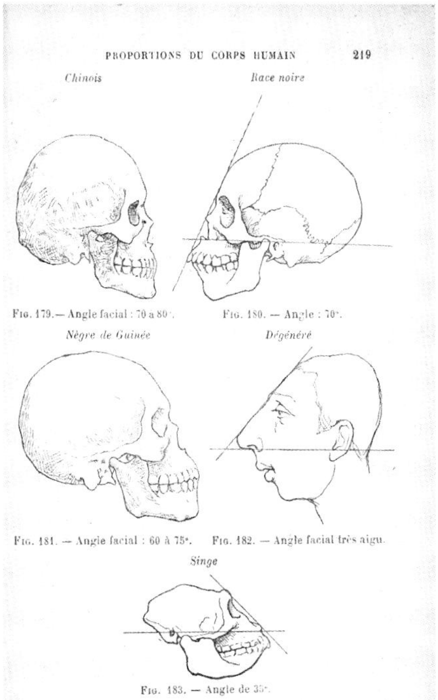

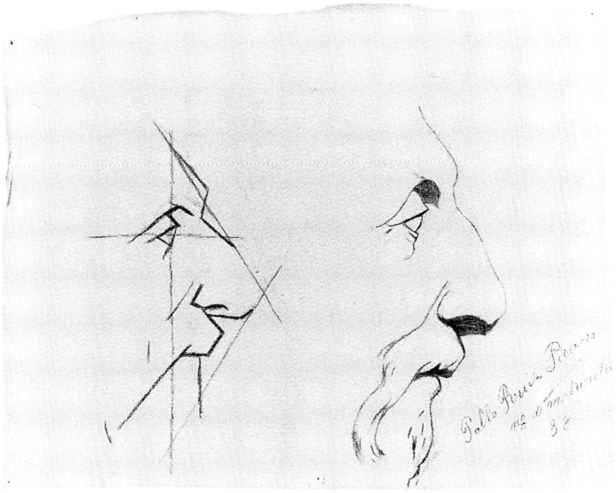

58 (*above*) Picasso. *Two Profile Studies of a Man.* 1892 (1888?). Charcoal on paper, 24 × 31 cm. Zervos VI, 10. Picasso estate (inv. 1)

57 (*left*) Angles of the facial plane. From Camille Bellanger, *L'Art du peintre: traité pratique du dessin et de la peinture* (Paris: Garnier Frères, 1909), p. 219

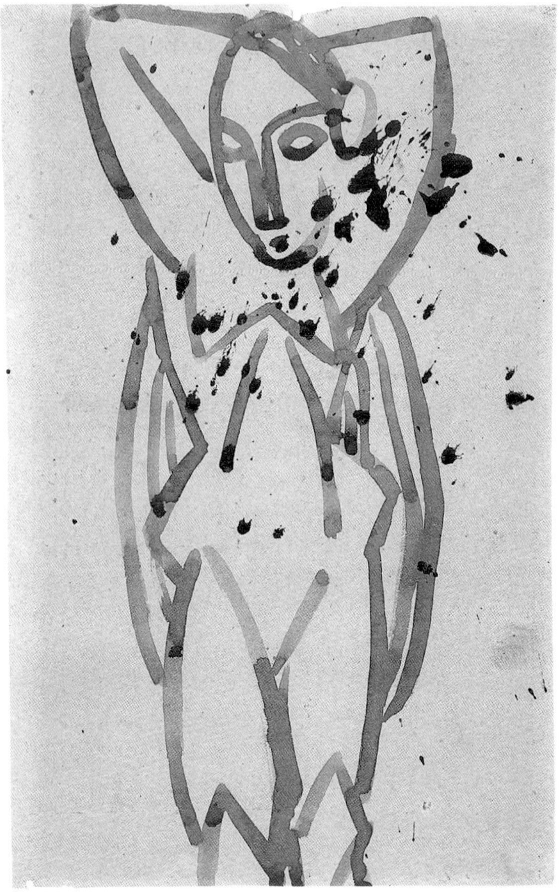

59 Picasso. *Standing Nude with Raised Arms.* Paris, spring 1907 (?). Brush and ink on paper, 30 × 19 cm. Zervos II*, 14. Chrysler Museum of Art, Norfolk, VA, Gift of Walter P. Chrysler, Jr.

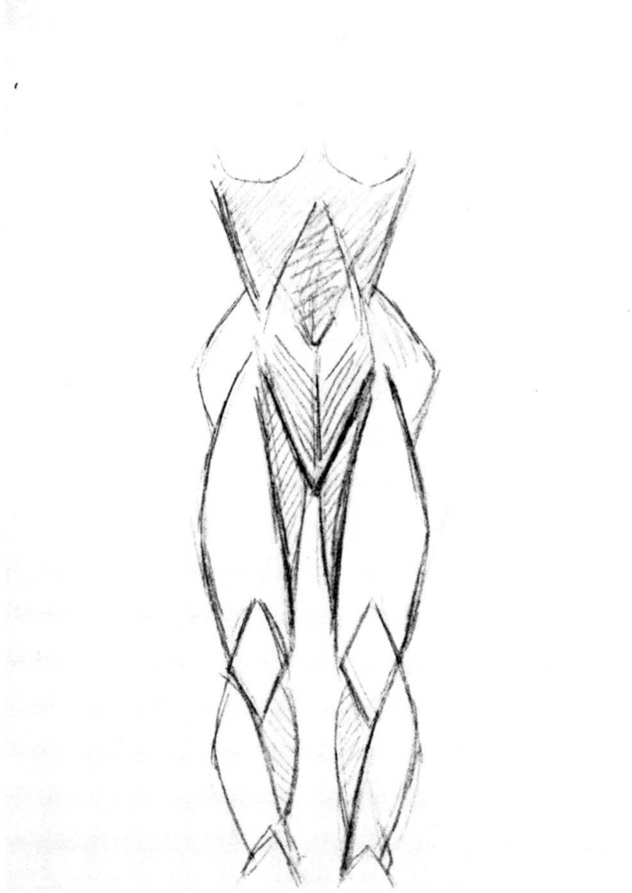

60 Picasso. *Standing Nude.* Paris, 1908 (?). 21 × 17 cm. Zervos XXVI, 346. Private collection

more." Such breasts are commonly found only in young girls, the author comments; as the force of gravity begins to make itself felt, "the lower portion of the former conical surface grows more convex and rounded," arriving finally at the form of breast found in the Venus de Milo.[20] The near-conical breast in the accompanying diagram (fig. 56) is precisely the kind of firm, high breast that appears in Picasso's *Two Nudes* and in Maillol's contemporary sculptures. The 90° angle inscribed within it justifies the choice of body type.

In another handbook of the period, the angle of the facial plane is calculated by measuring the intersection between a horizontal line and a diagonal line drawn from the nose to the brow (fig. 57). This type of measurement, invented by an eighteenth-century anthropologist to distinguish the facial types of different races, became a standard part of art education.[21] Picasso himself drew a similar diagram for one of his student examinations at the School of Fine Arts in Coruña (fig. 58).[22] Here too, geometry serves to justify the ideal forms of classical anatomy. The larger the angle, the "higher" the race. A "Greek" nose, descending in a straight line from brow to tip, and forming a 90° angle with the horizontal, would in theory represent the the highest point of racial evolution. Empirically, of course, it would look rather odd.

Picasso's "diamond" sketch of spring 1907 (see fig. 55) represents a kind of *reductio ad absurdum* of such academic devices, almost completely obscuring the natural figure

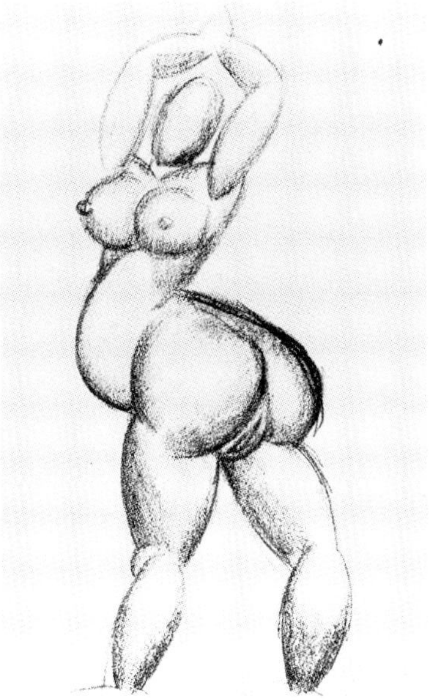

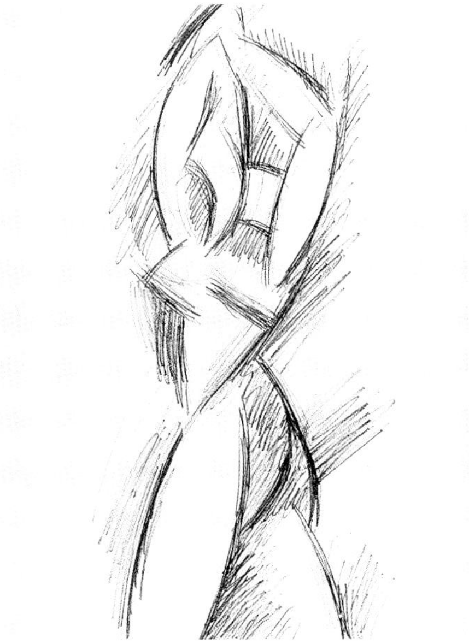

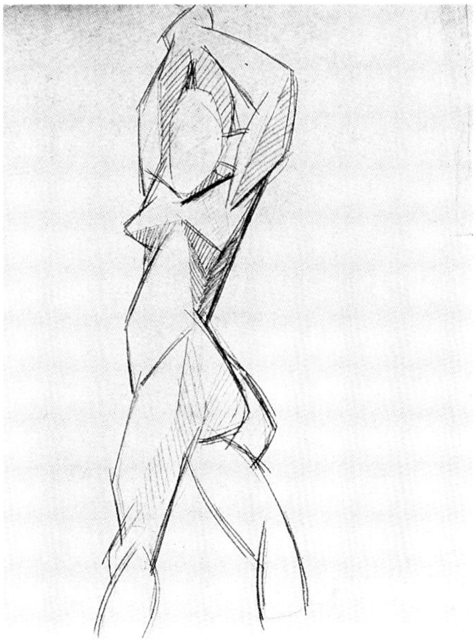

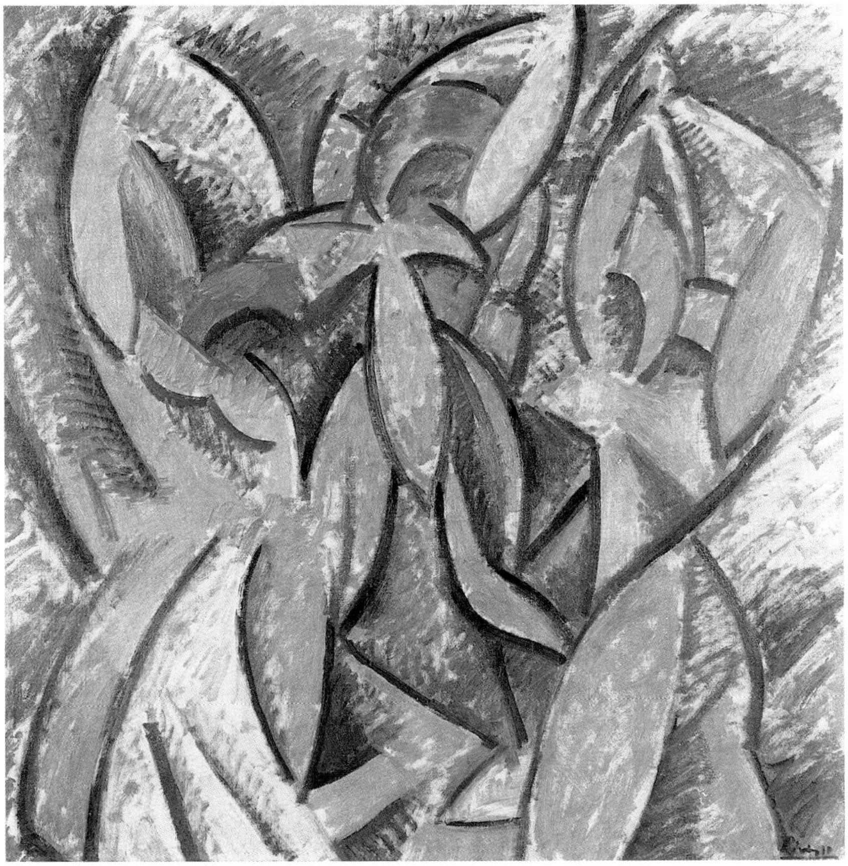

61 (*above left*) Picasso. *Turning Figure with Raised Arms.* Paris, early 1908. Charcoal on paper, 21 × 13.5 cm. Zervos XXVI, 379. Picasso estate (inv. 1090)

62 (*above centre*) Picasso. *Turning Figure with Raised Arms.* Paris, early 1908. Pencil on paper, 32.6 × 24.9 cm. Zervos XXVI, 312. Richet 170. Musée Picasso, Paris

63 (*above right*) Picasso. *Turning Figure with Raised Arms.* Paris, early 1908. Pencil on paper, 63 × 48 cm. Zervos XXVI, 297. Picasso estate (inv. 1022)

64 Picasso. *Three Women (Rhythmic Version).* Paris, early 1908. Oil on canvas, 91 × 91 cm. D.R. 123. Sprengel Museum, Hanover

behind an elaborate geometric scaffolding. More often, Picasso used geometric shapes sparingly, as a counterpoint to the relatively organic forms such as almond or pod. In a drawing of a nude with raised arms (fig. 59) – a variation on the central figure of the *Demoiselles* (see figs. 46, 51) – breasts, knees, and gluteus medius are depicted by sharp angles, in contrast to the gentler curves of the head, arms, abdomen, and thighs. In another version of this figure (fig. 60), the curvilinear forms of the abdomen, thighs, and calves are subdivided into sharp-edged planes, bringing them closer in character to the angular forms of the knees and gluteus.

It is this combination of hard-edged geometric shapes with an underlying anatomy of bulging, pod-like forms that produces the characteristic "faceting" of early Cubism. Picasso seems first to have experimented with this mixed angular and curvilinear style in late spring 1907, when he was thinking about revising the canvas of the *Demoiselles* to make it look more three-dimensional. He returned to it in early 1908, when he confronted the same tension between sculptural and decorative approaches in his work on the *Three Women.*

As seen earlier, the original studies for the *Three Women* were executed in a "decorative" style of color planes with interlacing contours (see figs. 3, 26). It was only after enlarging the composition onto canvas that Picasso became dissatisfied with the bland flatness of his original design, and began to look for ways to make the figures more energetic.

One solution was to add forceful hatching recalling the *Nude with Drapery* of summer 1907 (see fig. 52); another was to relax the interlacing of the composition so that the figures could move apart in space, becoming more three-dimensional. Picasso pursued both solutions simultaneously. In a hatched, "rhythmic" version of the composition (fig. 64), the central figure has been elevated and detached from her neighbors, while the squatting figure at right has been replaced by a standing nude with raised arms, turning vigorously in a kind of exaggerated contrapposto.

Picasso's sketches for this turning figure suggest that he was deliberating among several different styles in which he might have reworked the canvas of the *Three Women.* One sketch (fig. 61) is drawn with a kind of cartoon naturalism, exaggerating the curved bulges of breasts, belly, and buttocks. Offering the viewer simultaneous access to multiple areas of sexual interest, it exemplifies Picasso's penchant for "drawing as if to possess," as Leo Steinberg has dubbed it.[23] In another sketch (fig. 62), closer to the "rhythmic" version of the canvas, the model's contours are flattened into the familiar modules of the almond and the triangle. In a third (fig. 63), the curves are replaced by hard-edged forms. In effect, the curved bulges of the first sketch have been redrawn as faceted masses.

It was this muscular, geometric style of faceted planes that Picasso ultimately employed for the reworking of the large *Three Women.* It should be noted that there are no faceted studies for the composition as a whole. Picasso drew sketches of particularly complex details such as the arms and shoulders of the kneeling figure at left.[24] However, much of the faceting seems to have been worked out in an ad hoc fashion, on the canvas itself (see fig. 27).

In retrospect, the *Three Women* appears as a decisive turning point in the history of Cubism. It made a tremendous impression on the other members of Picasso's circle, achieving the success he had aimed for but failed to achieve with the *Demoiselles d'Avignon.* Specifically, what attracted the attention of Braque and other artists was the way that Picasso's combination of interlocking shapes and geometric faceting solved the problem of integrating figure and ground without sacrificing the sense of sculptural form. Surprisingly, this novel means of integrating figure and ground does not seem to have struck Picasso himself as an important discovery. For him, it was an expedient, a way of saving a large, ambitious canvas that had gone astray.

The Beginnings of Open Form, 1908–1909

During fall 1908, Picasso turned aside from the figure, concentrating instead on the problem of projective space, which he preferred at this moment to address in the genre of still life. When he did return to painting the human body, in early 1909, he addressed the isolated figure and not the interlocking group. And yet, it was his experiments with different ways of representing the isolated figure that led ultimately to the breakdown of the distinction between figure and ground – to the opening of the "closed form."

As John Richardson has pointed out, Picasso's *Bather* (fig. 65) of early 1909 seems to pose in front of – rather than within – the setting of empty beach, sea, and sky; indeed, the setting seems more like a painted backdrop than a real landscape.[25] With nothing else really to focus on, the viewer

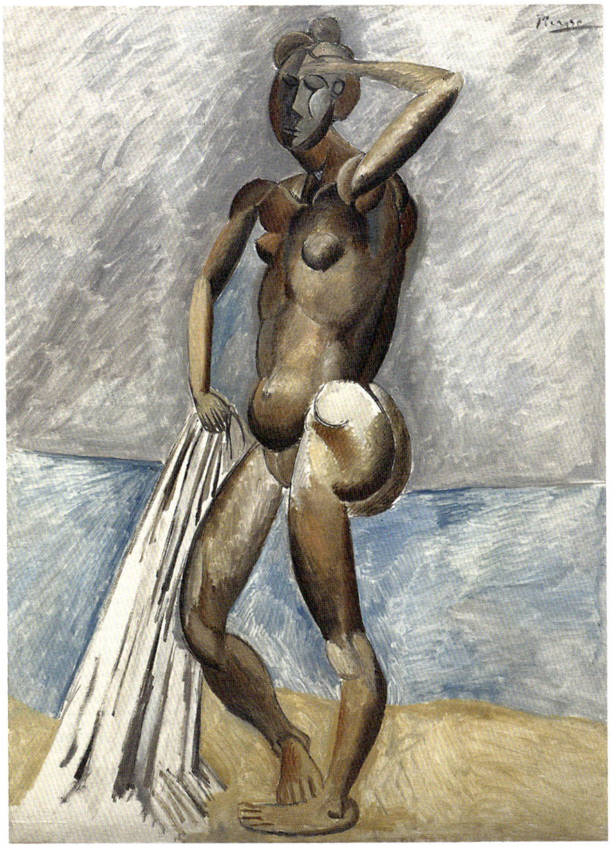

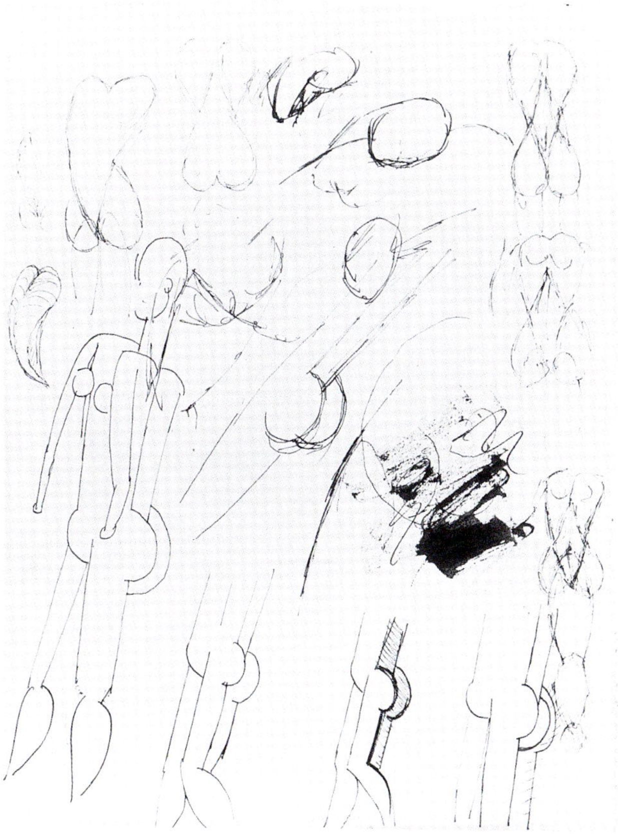

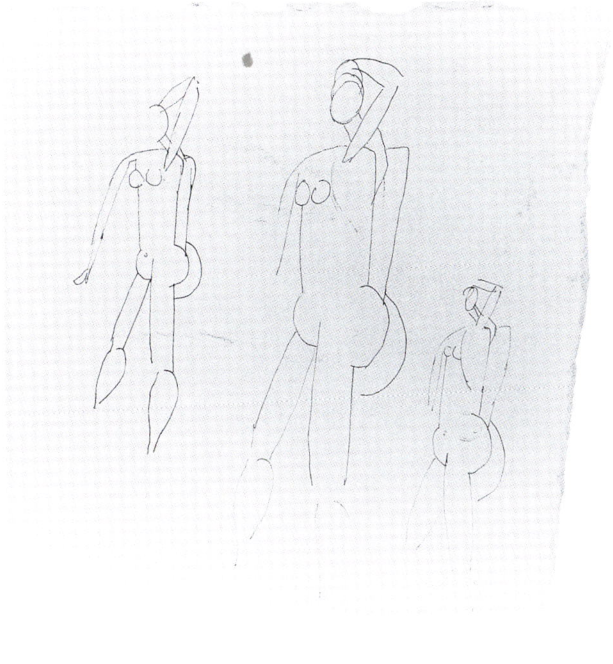

65 (*above left*) Picasso. *Bather*. Paris, early 1909. Oil on canvas, 130 × 97 cm. D.R. 239. The Museum of Modern Art, New York. Louis Reinhardt Smith Bequest

66 (*above right*) Picasso. Studies for *Bather*. Paris, early 1909. Drawing, dimensions unknown. Not in Zervos. Picasso estate (inv. 1092)

67 (*right*) Picasso. Figure studies. Paris, early 1909? Ink on paper, 32.2 × 24.7 cm. Zervos VI, 930.Picasso estate (inv. 1091)

is compelled to confront the extraordinary topography of the bather's body. Most of the contours of this fleshly landscape can be justified by reference to classical anatomy, but they have been resized and rearranged with disturbing freedom.

Once again, Picasso is "drawing as if to possess." The sexually charged areas of breasts, buttocks, and groin are simultaneously visible, as in the 1908 drawings of the *Turning Figure with Raised Arms.* But this obsessive visibility has been achieved by different means. Instead of having the model assume a pose that makes all these areas visible from a single point of view, Picasso seems to circle around the model, combining different viewpoints in order to depict her torso simultaneously from front, side, and back. The idea that our image of a given object is built up from a series of different perceptions was a commonplace of nineteenth-century philosophy, and Cézanne had already combined different viewpoints in his paintings of still lifes.[26] But nothing had quite anticipated the radical realization of this idea in Picasso's figure studies of spring 1909.

The anatomy of the figure, and even the pose, derives from Picasso's sketches of spring 1907 (see figs. 53, 54), where the muscles and bones of the body are divided into separate strands or merged into swelling pods. Indeed, the division of the buttock into gluteus maximus and gluteus medius in some of the 1907–08 drawings (fig. 54) may have provided the prototype for the double buttocks of the 1909 *Bather.* One kind of conceptual representation (academic anatomy) seems to have inspired another (multiple viewpoints).

With its combination of obsessive observation and disjunctive representation, the *Bather* stands at the head of a series of troubling and extraordinary figures that Picasso continued to create for another sixty years. It is also notable for the variety of the studies associated with it. In one unpublished drawing (fig. 67), the torso is reduced to a rectangular plane as flat as a playing card, attached to the circular disk of groin and hips. These planes overlap a second pair of identical planes, as if the body had been separated into front and back planes, like the placards of a sandwich-man wearing advertisements on a street-corner. In the painting, the doubled contours seem to indicate the far side of the back and buttocks, unveiled in accordance with the idea of multiple perspectives, but the figure retains its solidity and its closure. In the drawing, the body is no longer a closed mass, but an open volume defined by two parallel planes and the space between them. The doubled contour no longer seems to represent the two buttocks, seen one after the other, but rather the same buttock, seen twice. The overlapping silhouettes anticipate the principle of superimposed planes that became Cubism's replacement for the converging diagonals of traditional perspective. But Picasso was not yet ready to exploit this idea systematically.[27]

Instead, he moved on to invent yet another way of drawing the figure. On the same sheet as several of his "sandwich-man" figures, he used interlacing lines to draw symmetrical torsos built up from overlapping hearts (or repeated teardrops) representing both buttocks and shoulders (fig. 66). A related sheet (fig. 68) reveals how Picasso worked out the idea of having the contours of the back converge to a point and then curl back upon themselves, outlining the contours of the buttocks. Earlier, he had played with the idea of using a single interlacing line to draw animals; this idea was now applied to the human figure.[28]

It might have remained a kind of parlor game, except that Picasso had the further idea of visualizing his lines as if they were solid strands, twisting and turning in space. In a series of unpublished drawings, he visualized a figure constructed from curving strands. One sheet shows the figure's neck, shoulders, back, buttocks, and legs as if seen from the side (fig. 69). Another shows the same figure seen from the front (fig. 70). A third sheet moves in for a close-up of the head and neck (fig. 71), with strands outlining the chin, the tendons descending at either side of the neck, and the enclosing curve of the collarbone. In these studies, the figure ceases to be a solid mass and becomes instead a volume defined by the strands curving through and around it.

Picasso seemed to recoil from the revolutionary implications of this idea, however. He turned instead to its opposite: the reinforcement of monolithic mass by means of faceting (figs. 72, 73), as in the *Three Women* of 1908. However, there is a subtle difference between the faceting of 1908 and that of 1909. In the drawings associated with the *Three Women*, and in the finished canvas (see figs. 64, 27), the expressive elements were the facets themselves, corresponding to the advancing or receding planes of the body. As a rule, each plane was shaded with a single tone (light, medium, or dark), so that a shift in value coincided with the transition from one plane to another.

In the faceted pictures of 1909 (fig. 73), each individual plane tends to modulate from light to dark as if bending in space. Observing this distinctive shading, artists such as Léger and Kasimir Malevich went on to develop "Tubist" figures constructed from cones and cylinders. But Picasso's summer 1909 figures do not on the whole seem to be constructed from curved planes. Their shading is contradicted by the straight-edged borders of the planes, which insist on flatness. Picasso organizes the shading so that the light side of one plane abuts the dark side of another, emphasizing the border between them. The linear borders thus become the main expressive elements of the composition.[29] This new

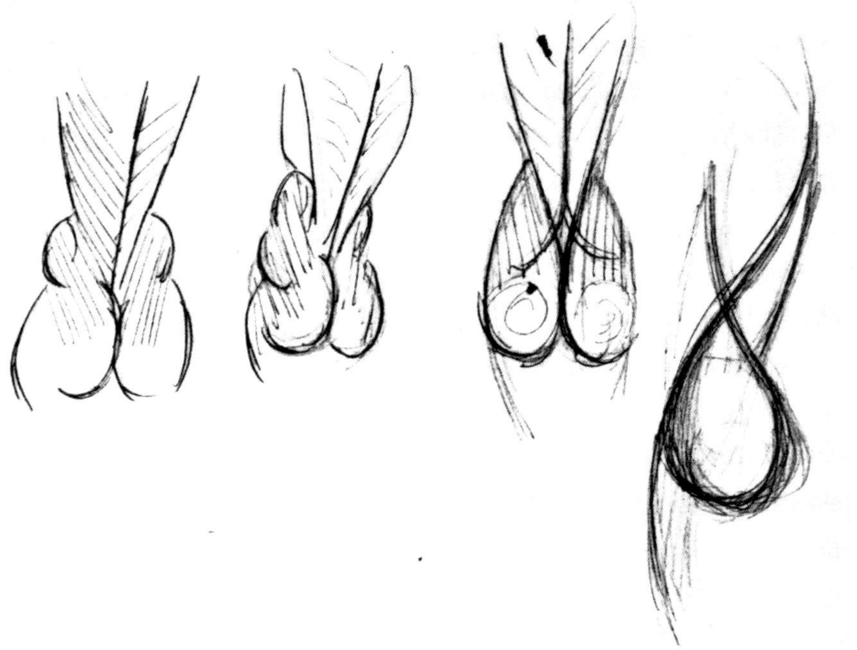

68 Picasso. Studies of torsos and buttocks. Paris, early 1909. India ink on paper, 32 × 49 cm. Zervos VI, 1116 (reproduced upside down). Picasso estate (inv. 1094)

69 (*below left*) Picasso. *Figure Constructed from Strands, Side View.* Paris, early 1909. Charcoal on paper, 32.5 × 22 cm. Not in Zervos. Picasso estate (inv. 1189)

70 (*below right*) Picasso. *Figure Constructed from Strands, Front View.* Paris, early 1909. Charcoal on paper, 32.5 × 22 cm. Not in Zervos. Picasso estate (inv. 1191)

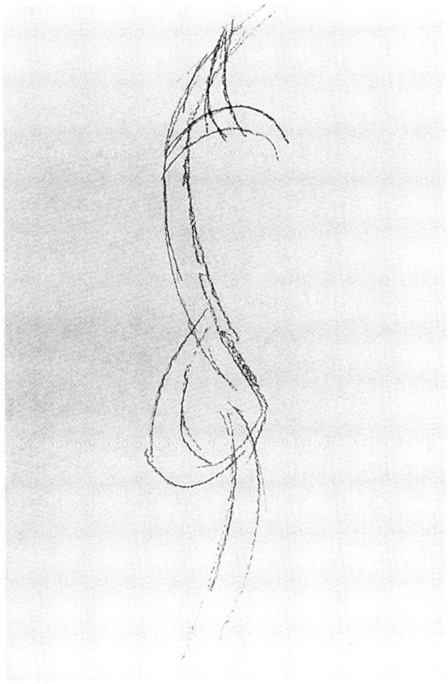

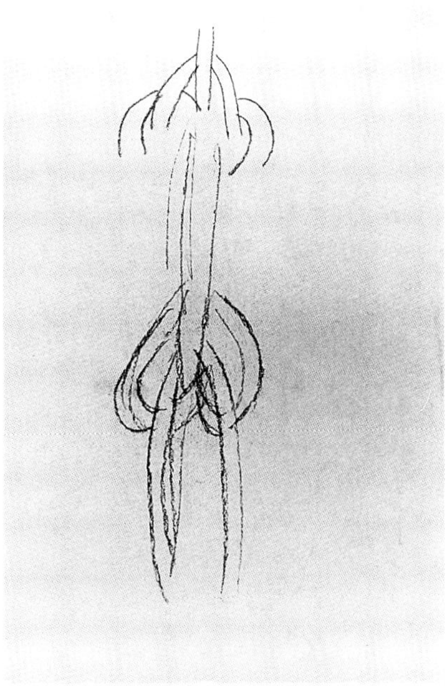

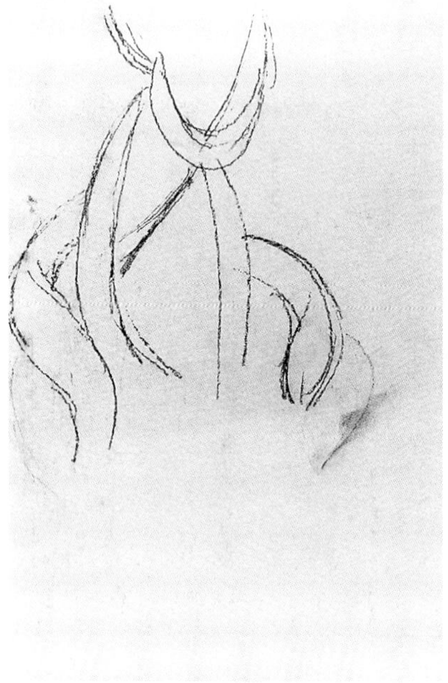

71 Picasso. *Bust Constructed from Strands.* Paris, early 1909. Charcoal on paper, 32.5 × 21.5 cm. Not in Zervos. Picasso estate (inv. 1190)

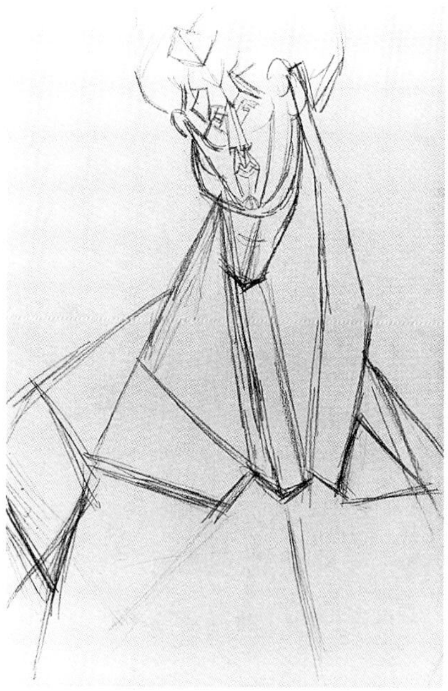

72 Picasso. *Head and Shoulders of a Woman.* Horta de Ebro, summer 1909. Charcoal on paper, 32.5 × 21.9 cm. Not in Zervos. Picasso estate (inv. 1180)

dominance of line is accompanied by a Michelangelesque exaggeration and distortion of form. The model's head is perched atop a hugely overdeveloped neck, with a strong emphasis on the tendons descending from the corners of the jaw to the center of the collarbone (figs. 72, 73). The neck is supported, in turn, by the even more massive promontory of the shoulders.

Other drawings work out the detailed faceting of mouth and nose (figs. 74, 75), reducing their anatomical complexity to a series of symmetrical, crystalline facets. Picasso himself seems to have justified the rigorously geometric language of these drawings as an expression of ideal, Platonic forms. As Leo Stein later recalled, "Picasso would stand before a Cézanne or a Renoir picture and say contemptuously, 'Is that a nose? No, this is a nose,' and then he would draw a pyramidal diagram."[30]

In other drawings, the crystalline facets of the face are softened into a series of intersecting curves. The head is divided into a series of curving ridges, coiled around one another like a symmetrical nest of snakes (fig. 76). Although some of the ridges have been shaded with brown and gray, they are defined primarily by the lines that run along their peaks. It was perhaps after his return to Paris, in September 1909, that Picasso began to consider making a sculpture based on these studies. His original intention may have been to create a sculpture that was a kind of cat's cradle of interlacing strands, with empty space between them. Many years later, he told Roland Penrose, "I thought that the curves you see on the surface should continue into the interior. I had the idea of doing them in wire."[31] The sculpture would thus have realized the idea suggested by his "strand" figures of early 1909 (see figs. 69–71).

Picasso's idea of using wire to draw in space was realized a few years later in Jean Crotti's caricatural *Portrait of Marcel Duchamp* (fig. 77). Picasso himself began making Cubist sculptures constructed from iron rods and wires in 1929, and the idea of "drawing in space" subsequently inspired sculptors such as Julio Gonzalez, Alexander Calder, Alberto Giacometti, and David Smith.[32] In 1909, however, Picasso did not pursue this idea, finding it "too intellectual, too much like painting."[33] For the moment, he was determined to preserve the sense of mass in his sculpture.

Ironically, his 1909 *Head* has often been seen as the opposite: a failed attempt to dissolve sculptural mass. This is

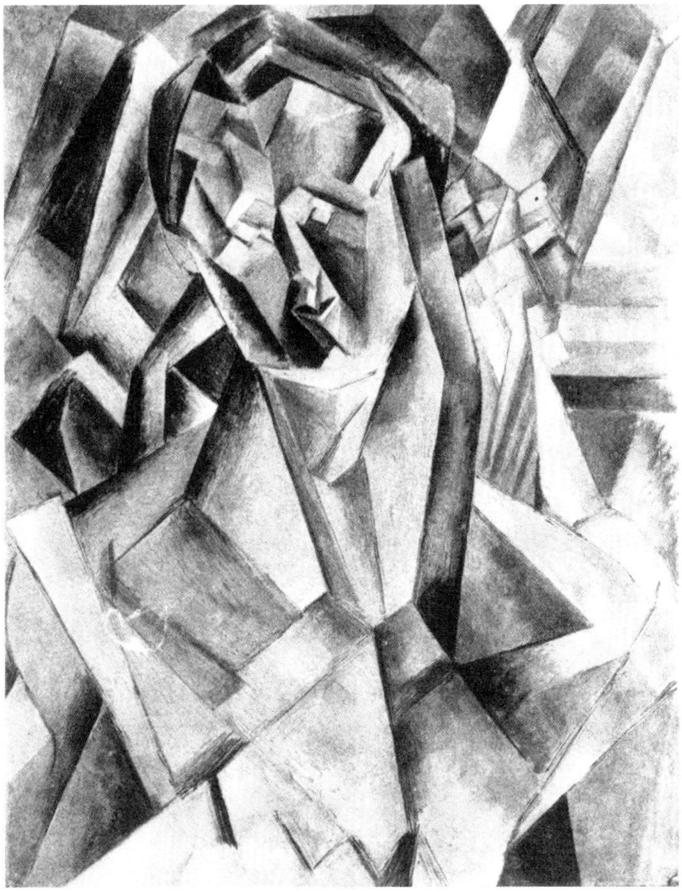

73 Picasso. *Seated Woman.* Horta de Ebro, summer 1909. Oil on canvas, 81 × 65 cm. D.R. 292. Private collection

74 (*below left*) Picasso. *Study of Nose, Mouth and Chin.* Horta de Ebro, summer 1909. Charcoal on paper, 32.5 × 22 cm. Picasso estate (inv. 1073)

75 (*below right*) Picasso *Study of Nose and Upper Lip.* Horta de Ebro, summer 1909. Charcoal on paper, 32.5 × 21.5 cm. Picasso estate (inv. 1072)

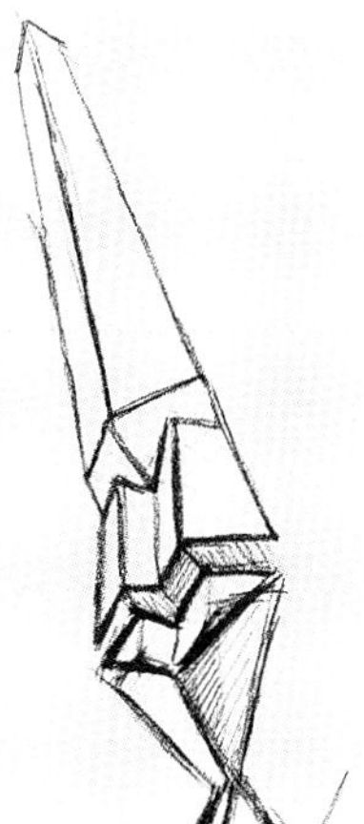

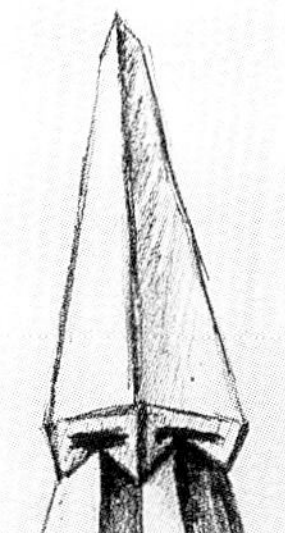

probably because it is known mostly from the bronze casts made by the dealers Ambroise Vollard and Heinz Berggruen (fig. 78).[34] As in the "Impressionist" sculptures of Auguste Rodin and Medardo Rosso, the play of light on the curving planes of the bronze diminishes its sense of solidity. However, the appearance of the bronze is seriously misleading. To evaluate Picasso's actual intentions, it is essential to remember that the appearance of the original plaster – specifically, the relationship between light and dark areas – was quite different. In the bronze, protruding areas are emphasized by glaring highlights, emphasizing the crest of the ridges atop the head. The incisions and indentations of the face below tend to merge indistinctly into the dark mass of the sculpture as a whole. In the plaster (fig. 79), on the contrary, the matte surface means that protruding areas display a relatively uniform degree of lightness, without pronounced highlights, while the shaded incisions and indentations of the face can be read more clearly against the lighter masses surrounding them. The plaster provides a much clearer idea of the actual three-dimensional form of the work. Since this was the object that Picasso actually worked on (he had no role in the creation of the bronzes), it should be taken as the guide to his artistic intentions.

It is evident from the plaster that Picasso worked the surface of the sculpture in two fundamentally different ways. For the most part, he shaped the plaster into geometric equivalents for the braids of the hair, the bulges of the brow, the beak of the nose, the tendons of the neck, and so on. In other areas, however, he treated the plaster as a surface to be incised with graphic signs that described three-dimensional features without actually reproducing their forms.

Both of these approaches find counterparts in the work of other contemporary sculptors. As early as 1905 or 1906, Elie Nadelman had arrived at a style which exaggerated every bulge into an independent form, demarcated by curving contours and ridges (fig. 80). Nadelman was another of the artists patronized by the Steins, and Picasso visited his studio with Leo Stein in late summer 1908. Picasso must have been struck by the similarity between Nadelman's curvilinear style and the more aggressive system of faceting that he himself had arrived at in the repainting of the *Three Women*. Nadelman subsequently became convinced that Picasso had "stolen" the idea of Cubism from him, and spent many years in a futile crusade to claim the credit he felt was rightfully his. The curvilinear faceting

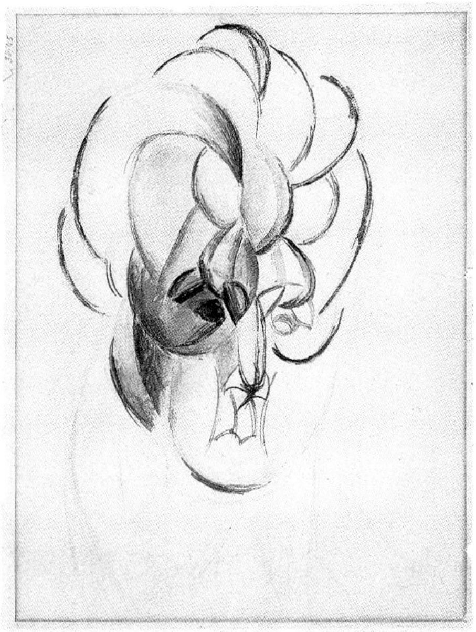

76 Picasso. *Woman's Head (Fernande)*. Horta de Ebro, summer 1909. Watercolor on tan wove paper, 33.2 × 25.6 cm. D.R. 289. The Art Institute of Chicago. Alfred Stieglitz Collection

77 Jean Crotti. *Portrait of Marcel Duchamp*. 1915. Lost work (photograph from the Philadelphia Museum of Art, gift of Ronny van de Velde)

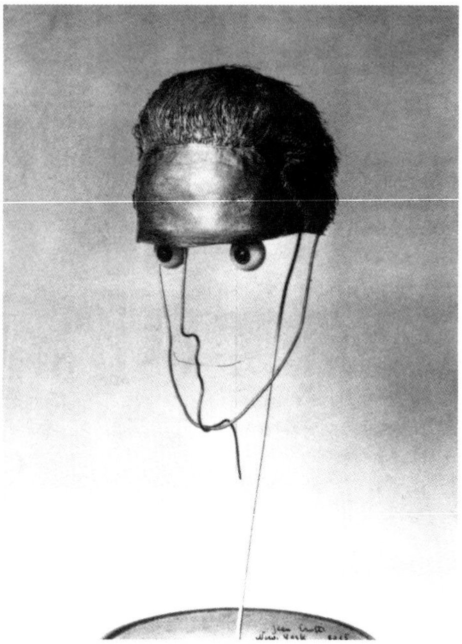

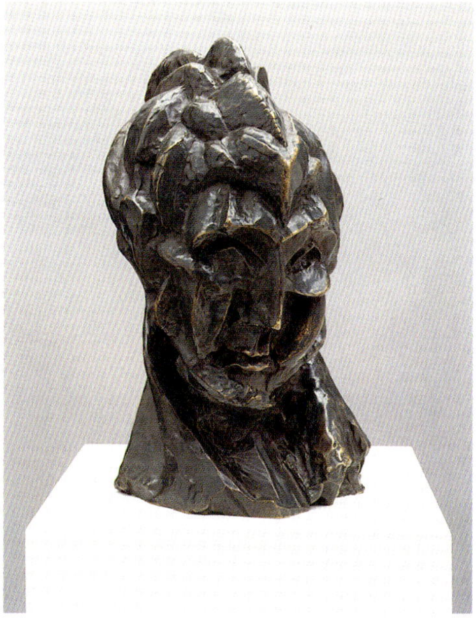

78 Picasso. *Woman's Head (Fernande).* Paris, fall 1909. Bronze, 41.3 × 24.7 × 26.6 cm. Spies 24. The Museum of Modern Art, New York. Purchase

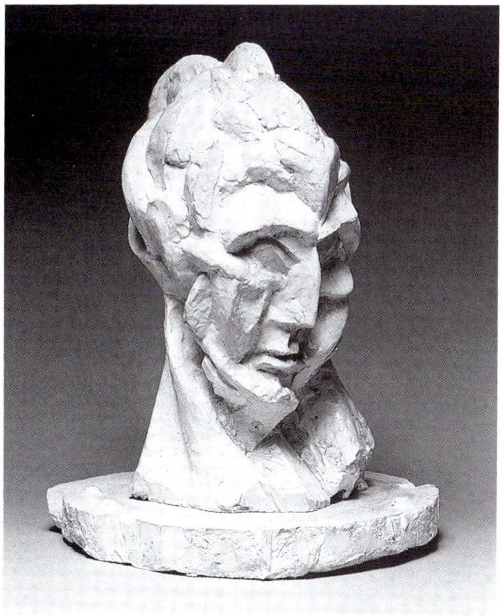

79 Picasso. *Woman's Head (Fernande).* Paris, fall 1909. Plaster, 47 × 35.9 × 34.9 cm. The Patsy R. and Raymond D. Nasher Collection, Dallas, Texas

80 Elie Nadelman. *Head.* c. 1906. Ink on paper, 18 × 12.7 cm. The Museum of Modern Art, New York

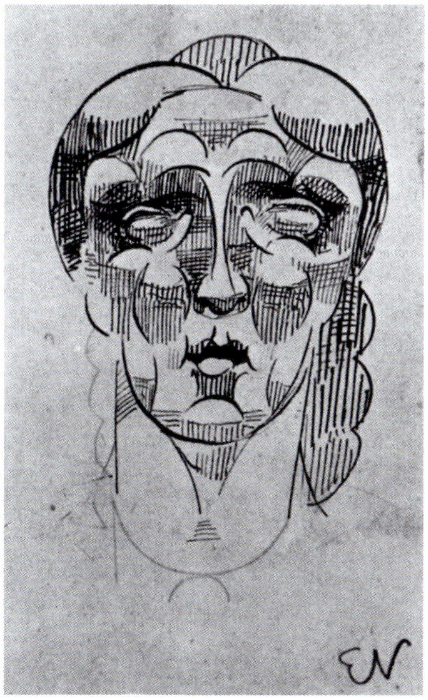

81 Grebo mask owned by Picasso. Wood, paint, vegetable fibers, h. 64 cm. Musée Picasso, Paris

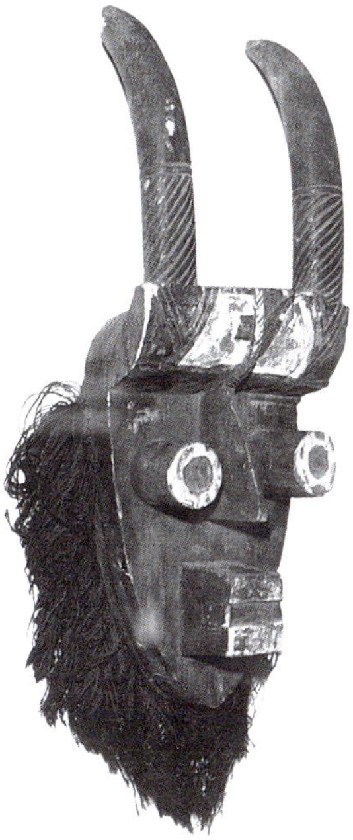

of Picasso's fall 1909 *Head* may well have profited from Nadelman's example. But the debt seems insignificant in retrospect because the meaning of faceting was transformed when it was translated back into painting.[35]

Sculptors who work by carving instead of modeling often incise a preliminary drawing onto the surface of the block. When Constantin Brancusi began to explore the esthetic of "direct carving" in 1907–08, he frequently represented facial features by incised lines while using carved masses to represent other anatomical features.[36] In the same years, Picasso executed several mask-like reliefs where the lines of the face were drawn with incised lines.[37] The contrast between these two methods is deliberately underscored in Picasso's 1909 *Head*, where one eyelid is defined as a projecting ridge above a hollowed-out eye, while the other eyelid is indicated by a deep-cut gouge above a solid mass where the eye should be. Many years later, Picasso told Françoise Gilot that:

> Everything is unique. Nature never produces the same thing twice. Hence my stress on seeking the *rapports de grand écart*: a small head on a large body; a large head on a small body. I want to draw the mind in a direction it's not used to and wake it up. I want to help the viewer discover something he wouldn't have discovered without me. That's why I stress the dissimilarity, for example, between the left eye and the right eye.[38]

The 1909 *Head* offers an early example of this principle, awakening the viewer's mind by using contrary forms to depict the exact same thing. The unrealism of one representation casts doubt on the realism of the other. If the gouge on one side of the face is an artificial "sign" for an eyelid, so too is the ridge on the other side.

It is thus at this moment, in 1909, that Picasso began to explore the idea that sculptural forms can be signs or emblems rather than more or less faithful reproductions of real forms. Critics usually date this discovery to several years later, linking it to the Grebo mask (fig. 81) that inspired Picasso's constructed *Guitar* of fall 1912. Kahnweiler described this mask as a sign system evoking the human face without resembling it. "The volume of the 'seen' face," he added, "is inscribed nowhere in the 'true' mask, which provides only the outline of this face. The volume is seen somewhere before the real mask. The epidermis of the seen face only exists in the consciousness of the viewer who 'imagines' or creates the volume of the face *in front* of the plane surface of the mask."[39]

This imagined, or "virtual," facial plane was already an important element in the 1909 *Head*, where the lower part of the face was deeply cut away on either side of the mouth and nose. The naturalistic contour of the face is indicated, in these areas, by the narrow ridges descending from eyes to jaw. The gouged out areas between ridges, mouth, and nose provide shaded areas from which the mouth and nose emerge more saliently. (They may also be meant to reveal the internal volume of the head, as in the later "Constructivist" heads of the Russian sculptor Naum Gabo.)

If the "sign" began to play an important role in the 1909 *Head*, it was not as a fixed or conventional unit of meaning. The gouge above the right eye may be a sign for "eyelid," but the gouged out areas of the lower face are not signs for anything in particular. They are blank spaces, equivalent to the blank areas in Picasso's preparatory drawing – places where the machinery of representation ceases to function. Together with the "positive" forms of the sculpture, these signs and spaces compel the viewer to take an active role in the process of perception. It is the viewer who constructs the image of a recognizable head from the fragmentary evidence available. According to nineteenth-century perceptual theory, every act of visual perception required a similar construction of the object from a series of visual signs. The difference here is that the process of construction ceases to be unconscious, and requires the viewer's active participation.

From Mass to Volume, Spring–Summer 1910

Kahnweiler dated the "decisive advance" of Cubism – the breaking open of the "closed form" – to the summer of 1910.[40] But this dating is misleading. Picasso had already considered opening up the figure, so that space would flow through as well as around it, in 1909. And he returned to the idea of the open figure not in summer but in spring 1910. It should be said that the course of Picasso's development in 1910 is extremely confusing. It is difficult to reconstruct the exact sequence of his work during these crucial months. It is even more difficult to reconstruct what he was thinking.

What seems to have happened, however, was that Picasso's two main lines of investigation now intersected. His search for sculptural mass had culminated in the

Woman's Head of fall 1909 (see fig. 79). His search for a new kind of projective space had culminated in the fall 1909 canvas *Le Bock* (see fig. 29). Now he wanted to know whether sculptural mass and projective space could be combined in a single picture.

He had, in fact, tried to combine these qualities in his paintings of summer 1909, integrating his massive, sculptural heads with their landscape or interior backgrounds by imposing a consistent system of faceting on both foreground and background (see fig. 73). But pictorial unity was achieved at the expense of pictorial space: the sensation of depth was squeezed out of the canvas as the interlinking facets merged into a two-dimensional lattice. At most, the figures occupied the limited, bas-relief space of the *Three Women*, not the deep projective space of *Le Bock*.

Picasso returned to this problem in early 1910, determined to integrate the figure and its surroundings without sacrificing the mass of one or the volume of the other. He seems, once more, to have turned to Cézanne as a guide – specifically to the portrait *Mme Cézanne in a Red Dress*, executed in 1890–94 (fig. 82). This had been one of the highlights of the Cézanne retrospective at the 1907 Salon d'Automne, and Picasso would subsequently have been able to study it in the stock of Vollard's gallery. It is an unusually complex picture. Mme Cézanne herself seems as flat as a Byzantine saint. Her red dress dissolves into a shimmerof brushstrokes, like the landscape in the foreground of the *Bend in Road at Montgeroult* (see fig. 16). However, this playing-card figure is framed by a kind of sculptural niche. The picture space is closed off at left by the fireplace mantel and mirror, and at right by large, swagged drapery. A chair-rail traverses the wall at an angle, so that the wall seems to swing backward, opening up an indefinite depth behind the armchair.

Picasso reprised Cézanne's composition in a spring 1910 *Woman Seated in an Armchair* (fig. 83). Here too the seated figure is evoked primarily by colored patches, while the setting is described in linear terms. Once again, the model is flanked on the right by a drapery swag festooned with flowers and baroque curlicues. Instead of a chair-rail, there is an oversized molding turning a corner above the model's head, while an opened door on the left stands in for the clock and mantel.

In effect, Picasso reinvented Cézanne's picture using props from his own studio. The floral drapery appears in the background of a 1911 photograph of Braque in military uniform, taken in Picasso's Boulevard Clichy studio (fig. 146).[41] In the painting, the floral pattern of the curtain is indicated by a series of curling strips that seem to strain forward into space. The molding, zigzagging across the wall and around a pillar in the corner, intensifies the sense of a deep space opening behind the figure. The door at left advances dramatically toward the viewer; the doorknob casts a sharp-edged shadow, while the door itself is drawn in reverse perspective.[42] The open door reveals the shadowy outline of another doorway in the distance – possibly the door of the apartment where Picasso then lived.[43] The anomalous element here is the figure, whose jagged, curving contours dissolve into hatched areas of gray and green. The room has far more tactile presence than the figure in it. The canvas thus poses the problem of combining sculptural mass and projective space, but it does not solve it.

Picasso's solution was to go back to the faceting of his summer 1909 canvases, but to change the nature of the faceting. The facets were now pried apart and rearranged into overlapping planes, instead of meeting edge to edge. The figure itself, as well as its setting, was now structured around a series of advancing planes. Sculptural mass was transformed into sculptural volume.

This solution was essayed in a second *Woman Seated in an Armchair* (fig. 84), now in the Centre Pompidou. The seated figure occupies the same studio setting, with an open door at left, a zigzagging molding in the background, and floral drapery at right. The physiognomy of the figure derives from Picasso's earlier faceted figures; the strongly marked tendons of the neck, for instance, can be traced back to spring and summer 1909 (see figs. 72, 73). The difference is that the facets no longer lock together to make a continuous skin. Individual planes and groups of planes indicate important anatomical features: a breast, an arm, an elbow. But they float independently in space, linked only intermittently with the planes around them. The figure is no longer a solid mass, with indentations gouged from it, as in the fall 1909 sculpture of a *Head* (see fig. 79). It is instead an open volume, divided and defined by a series of independent planes.

Picasso's attention in this canvas was clearly focused on the problem of representing the figure. However, the technique of discontinuous faceting was extended to the setting in a third version of the composition, now in the Tate Gallery (fig. 85). Here, the zigzagging molding has been reduced to a mere vestige, while the floral drapery and the

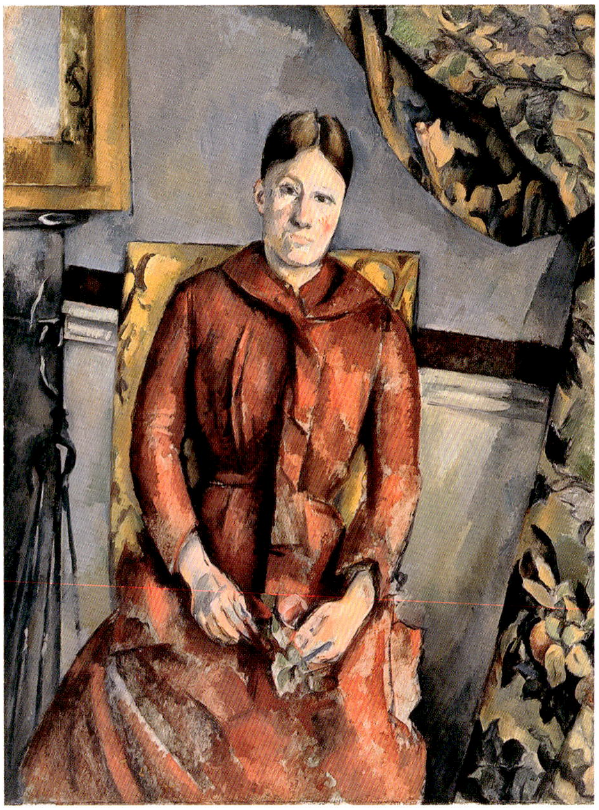

82 Paul Cézanne. *Mme Cézanne in a Red Dress.* 1888–90. Oil on canvas, 116.5 × 89.5 cm. Rewald 655. The Metropolitan Museum of Art, New York. The Mr. and Mrs. Henry Ittleson, Jr., Purchase Fund, 1962

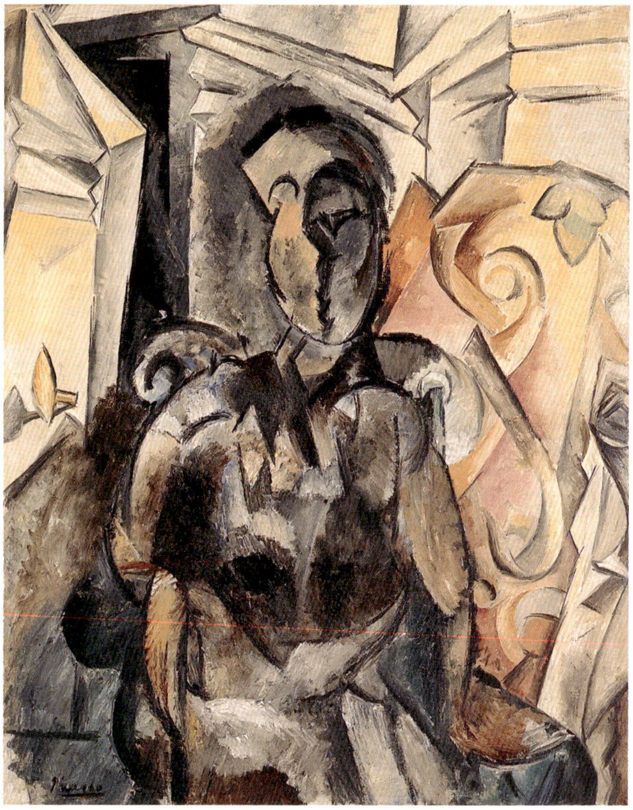

83 Picasso. *Woman Seated in an Armchair.* Paris, winter 1909–10. Oil on canvas, 81.3 × 63.5 cm. D.R. 333. The Metropolitan Museum of Art, New York. The Mr. and Mrs. Klaus G. Perls Collection, 1997

projecting door seem to have vanished (although the dark silhouette of the distant doorway remains visible at the top of the canvas). Figure and setting are described in a similar vocabulary of overlapping planes, but their integration no longer squeezes the depth out of the picture. The background appears as a series of open volumes, enclosing the volume of the figure. Picasso simplified the faceting of the figure to make it more self-contained and to keep it from dissolving into the setting. (It is also distinguished by a series of subtle highlights that play over the head, breast, and arms.) The sculptural presence of the figure and the projective space of the setting have both been preserved, although both have undergone a transformation.

The three versions of the *Woman Seated in an Armchair* provide the key models for Picasso's and Braque's production of the following year. The setting of Braque's *Violin and Pitcher* (see fig. 36), for instance, is clearly indebted to the first painting of this series (see fig. 83). Picasso's molding, turning around a pillar in the corner of a room, is quoted almost verbatim by Braque, while his projecting doorknob with its prominent shadow is transformed into a projecting nail with a prominent shadow. Braque also adopted the technique of discontinuous faceting invented in the later canvases of Picasso's series, breaking the violin in the foreground into a series of overlapping geometric volumes.

The invention of discontinuous faceting led Picasso to rethink the relationship between the figure and the space surrounding it. Traditionally, it was complementary; figures occupied the enclosed volume of a stage space, like objects in a container. But the rise of Impressionism had led to a fundamental change in this relationship. Manet relocated his figures in an amorphous space that provided a backdrop without containing them – a kind of "degree zero" of space.[44] Monet went even further. By reducing his subject

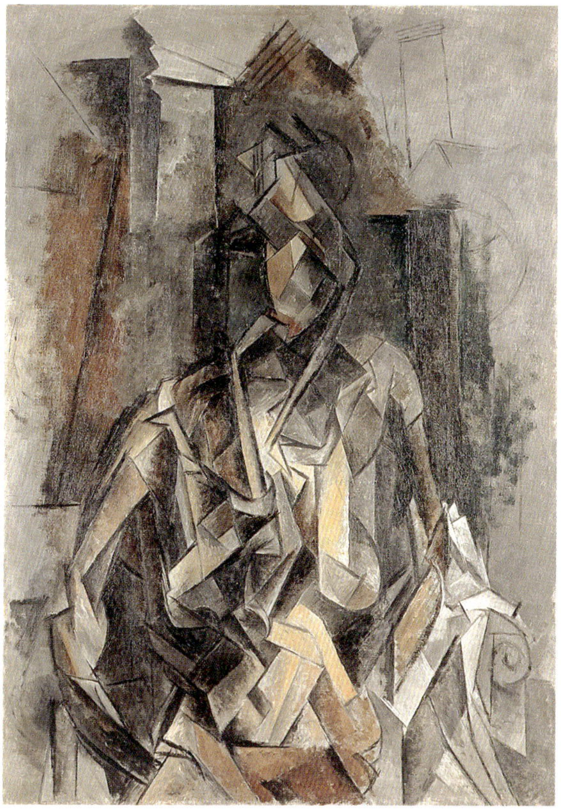

84 Picasso. *Woman Seated in an Armchair.* Paris, early 1910. Oil on canvas, 100 × 73 cm. D.R. 342. Centre Georges Pompidou, Musée National d'Art Moderne, Paris

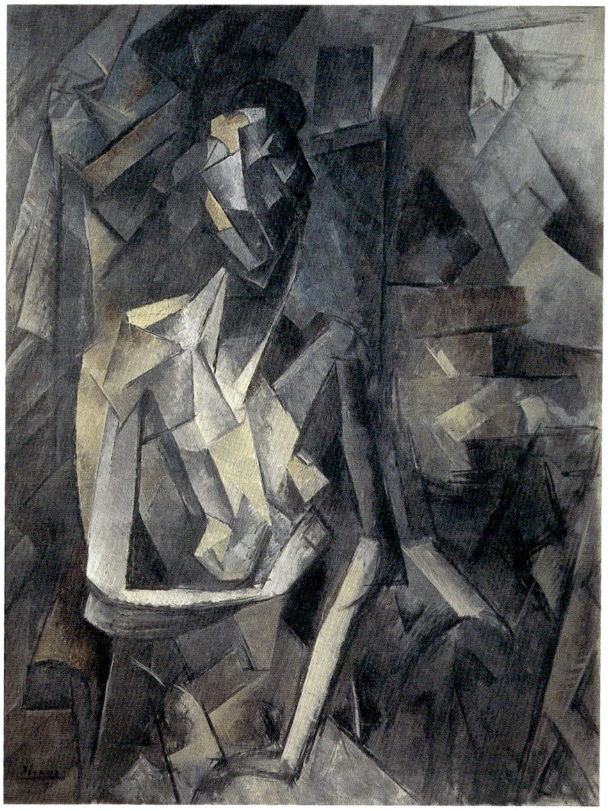

85 Picasso. *Seated Female Nude.* Paris, early 1910. Oil on canvas, 92 × 73 cm. D.R. 343. The Tate Gallery, London

matter to optical sensation, he minimized the distinction between figure and background. In theory, they were both reduced to color patches, replacing complementarity by homogeneity. In practice, there usually remained an obvious difference between the symmetrical shapes of figures or objects and the irregular shapes of the spaces surrounding them. The effect of Impressionism was to reformulate the problem of "negative space" in two dimensions rather than three. The intervals between solid forms were no longer treated as volumetric spaces, but as flat shapes to be integrated into the flat pattern of the composition.

Picasso's early work evinced little interest in the problem of negative space. He set his figures against amorphous backgrounds or within self-contained stage spaces. It was not until 1907 that he addressed the question of what to do with the empty spaces between figures. His first solution, in the *Demoiselles d'Avignon* (see fig. 51) was to fill them with zigzagging drapery, giving the intervening spaces an assertive shape and character. Beginning in 1909, the literal folds of drapery were replaced by the abstract rhythms of geometric faceting (see fig. 73). By extending the faceting more or less evenly across the surface of his compositions, Picasso created a lattice equivalent to the "optical field" of Impressionist painting.

Well into 1910, the relationship between figure and ground in Picasso's paintings remained ambiguous. If you focus on these pictures as representations, you perceive figures contained by a three-dimensional space. If you focus on the pictures as abstract compositions, you perceive homogeneous fields of geometric forms (see fig. 85). Braque's invention of the rectilinear grid, in spring 1910, seems to have tipped the balance in favor of the homogeneous field. But the grid played a surprisingly unimportant role in Picasso's work at this time. He continued to define

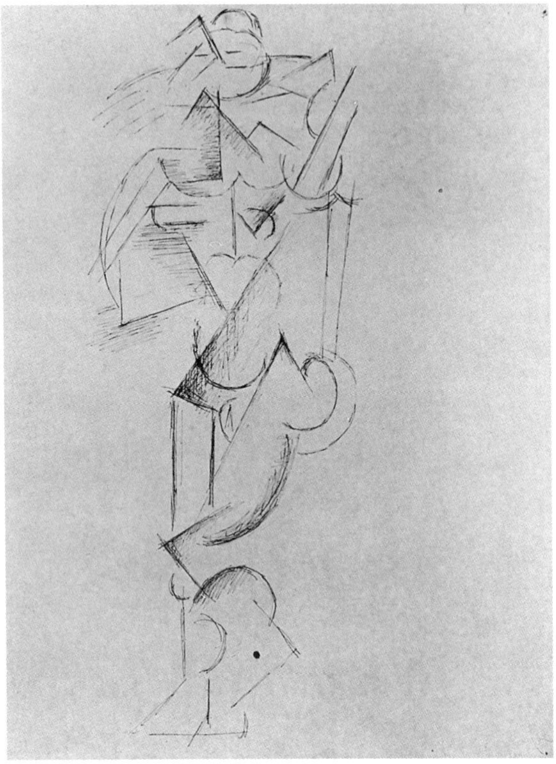

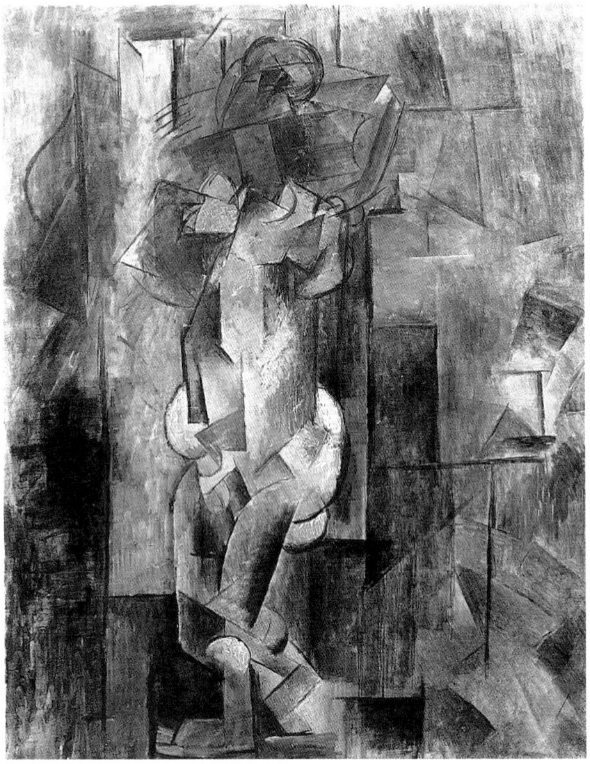

86 (*above left*) Picasso. *Standing Nude with Raised Arm.* Paris, spring 1910. India ink on paper, 63 × 48 cm. Zervos XXVIII, 16. Picasso estate (inv. 1266)

87 (*above right*) Picasso. *Nude.* Paris, late spring 1910. Oil on canvas, 99.1 × 78.1 cm. D.R. 349. Albright-Knox Art Gallery, Buffalo, New York. General Purchase Fund, 1954

the figure as an independent entity, adding a grid only when he transferred the figure to canvas (figs. 86, 87). Like the facets of 1909, the grid of 1910 offerred an expedient solution – a way to fill in the blank spaces of the composition and to create a superficial harmony between figure and ground. To this extent, Picasso's handling of negative space remained unchanged.

However, the shift from continuous to discontinuous faceting led Picasso to rethink the status of the space in the immediate vicinity of the figure. The opening of the closed form made the border between figure and space into a contested zone. On one hand, space began to circulate through the figure; on the other, the planes defining the figure began to incorporate the space around it. The "local" negative space began to take material form.

Picasso's spring 1910 drawing *Standing Nude with Raised Arm* (see fig. 86) offers an early example of this phenomenon. As Edward Fry noted, the figure's pose derives from an earlier *Bather* (see fig. 65).[45] In spring 1909, Picasso had used this bather to explore a variety of different figurations – for instance, depicting the body as a pair of overlapping planes, so that its mass became an open volume (see fig. 66). In retrospect, this 1909 drawing seems to prefigure the open volumes of spring 1910, and indeed the drawing of the back and buttocks in the 1910 study is almost identical to that of the early drawing.

The difference is that the rest of the body is no longer compressed into a single flat plane, but is represented by a series of discontinuous facets and independent planes. The breasts or pectoral muscles are represented by a pair of bowl-like curves stretching between the shoulders of the figure. (This was a convention that Picasso had already employed in the *Demoiselles d'Avignon*, *Three Women*, and related studies – see figs. 27, 51, 52, 60, 61.) However, the breasts are also represented a second time by a pair of forms just below these curves. One breast, on the left, is shown as a horizontal strip terminating in a curve. The other, on the

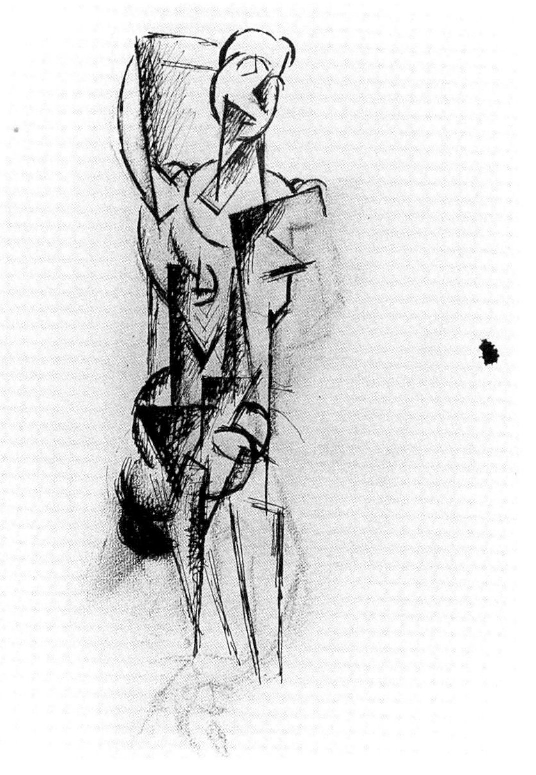

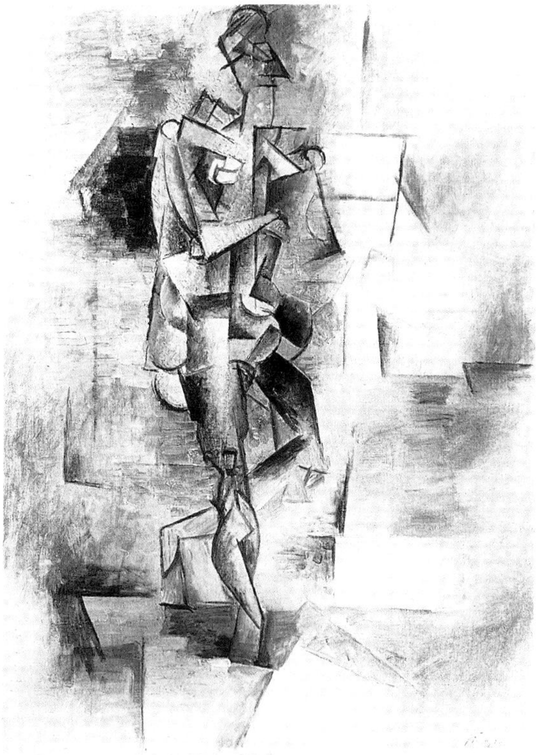

88 (*above left*) Picasso. *Standing Nude with Raised Arm.* Paris, spring 1910. Dimensions unknown. Picasso estate (inv. 1241)

89 (*above right*) Picasso. *Female Nude.* Paris, spring 1910. Oil on canvas, 73 × 53.9 cm. D.R. 348. The Menil Collection, Houston

90 (*right*) Picasso. *Nude.* Paris, spring 1910. Watercolor and ink on paper, 74 × 46.5 cm. D.R. 352. Private collection

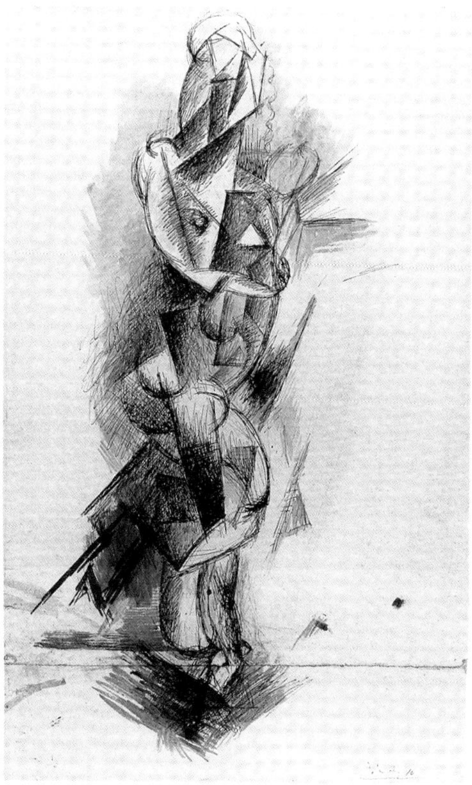

right, is shown as a descending triangle inscribed atop a curve. Similarly, one of the figure's knees is shown as a round knob, while the other is shown as a protruding angle.

Picasso's use of contrasting forms here echoes the differing treatment of the eyes in his 1909 sculpture *Woman's Head* (see fig. 79). As noted previously, Picasso told Françoise Gilot that he deliberately stressed the dissimilarity between the eyes in his figures. He also insisted that the other paired elements of the body should be handled differently:

> Every woman has two arms, two legs, two breasts, which may in real life be more or less symmetrical, but in painting they shouldn't be shown to have any similarity. In a

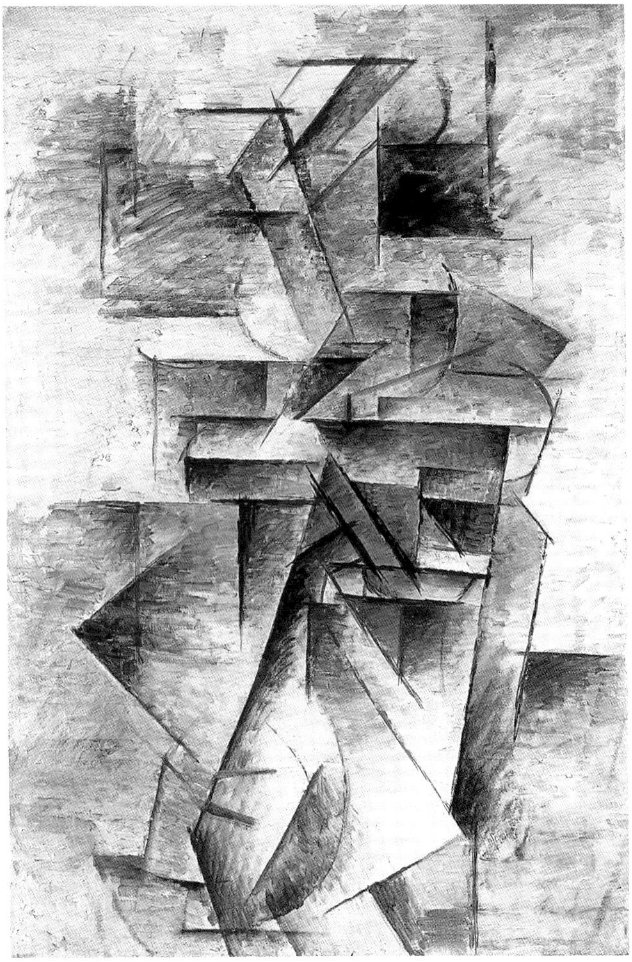

91 Picasso. *Woman with Mandolin.* Cadaqués, summer 1910. Oil on canvas, 91.5 × 59 cm. D.R. 361. Museum Ludwig, Cologne

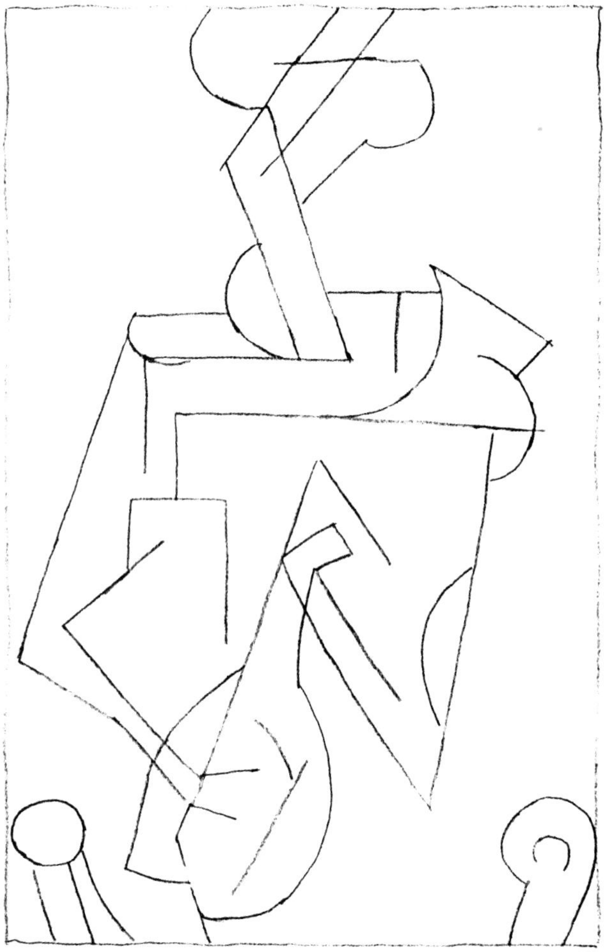

92 Picasso. *Woman with a Mandolin.* Diagram showing original composition before overpainting

naturalistic painting, it's the gesture that one arm or the other makes that differentiates them. They're drawn according to what they're doing. I individualize them by the different forms I give them, so that there often seems to be no relationship between them. From these differing forms one can infer that there is a gesture. But it isn't the gesture that determines the form. The form exists in its own right.[46]

This practice of deliberate asymmetry emerged in Picasso's work of 1909–10 and persisted to the end of his career.

The term "faceting" no longer seems adequate to describe Picasso's approach here. Rather than translating the naturalistic contours of the figure into a vocabulary of geometric facets, he completely re-imagined them as a series of free-floating lines and planes – a combination of curves, angles, and rectangular strips.

Some of these lines and planes, it should be noted, do not correspond to any particular element of the figure's anatomy. Beneath the figure's arm, on the left, for instance, there emerges a large angle, shaded to suggest an advancing plane. In effect, the negative space beneath the figure's arm has materialized into a plane, no less "real" than the planes that compose the body. Large shaded angles also appear at the figure's neck and abdomen. Rather than describing the body, they evoke the envelope of space surrounding it.

These tangential planes play an increasingly important role in subsequent drawings such as a *Standing Nude with*

Raised Arm (fig. 88) that faces right, reversing the pose of the *Bather*.[47] Here one tangential plane is inscribed over the raised arm, while another encloses the negative space between chin and collarbone. A third rises in front of the torso, on the right, with a triangular breast punching through it. A cluster of smaller vertical planes overlap the lower torso and hips.

The problem is that the profusion of unrelated tangential planes makes the figure awkward and incoherent. Picasso dealt with this problem in two different ways. First, he tried to bring some sense of order into the figure by setting it against a gridded backdrop (fig. 89). Some planes were brought into alignment with the surrounding grid; others were repositioned as diagonal accents, contrasting with their surroundings. Picasso dropped the figure's raised arm, and completed the figuration of the legs. But the result remains a somewhat awkward exercise.

Picasso also addressed the problem by creating internal rhymes and harmonies among the geometric elements composing the figure. In a third drawing (fig. 90), the lowered arm is adjusted so that it descends at the same angle as the weight-bearing leg below. The bent leg is redrawn so that it seems to circle in front of the straight, weight-bearing leg, imbuing the figure as a whole with a distinct sense of contrapposto. The cluster of tangential planes at the hip is reduced to a single plane leaning to the left at the same angle as the leg and arm. The tangential plane on the right of the torso, which had previously leaned slightly to the left, is now tilted to the right, so that it opposes and balances the other planes. The triangular breast no longer seems to emerge from this plane, but floats like a badge in front of it. Although the surrounding grid is more or less abandoned, the tangential planes overlapping the body are supplemented by additional planes extending into space at left and right, echoing the internal angles of the figure. This rhythmic integration yields a distinctly more graceful figure, which Picasso explored in a series of related sketches.[48]

Kahnweiler described the paintings done at Cadaqués in summer 1910 as a "decisive advance" over everything that Picasso had done before. But the large paintings from Cadaqués are actually a direct extension of the drawings and smaller canvases executed in Paris the previous spring. The difference is that the paintings of the summer are much harder to "read." This difficulty seems to be intentional.

When a canvas like *Woman with Mandolin* (fig. 91) is examined under a bright light, numerous pentimenti become visible, making it clear that the figure drawn on the canvas was originally more legible but was repainted to make it more abstract.

In the original lay-in (fig. 92), diagonal strips representing arms descended at either side of the rectangular torso. Trapezoidal hands grasped a schematic mandolin, with a rounded body and a crooked neck. As in several spring 1910 drawings (see figs. 86, 88), the shoulders were indicated by curves suggesting a cuff or socket. The neck ascended at an angle from the split curves of the collarbone. In the area of the head, three nearly parallel diagonals suggested the division of the face into two planes flanking the axis of the nose. The curves at either side of the face may indicate the woman's hair, or may be abstract signs for the rounded contours of the head as a whole.

In the *Woman with Mandolin*, as in other Cadaqués paintings, the lines of the initial design seem to have been laid in with black paint of a thin, wash-like consistency. These lines were then supplemented with horizontal strokes of thick white paint, covering the canvas like the tiles of a mosaic. This type of textured brushwork first appeared in Braque's paintings of spring 1910, and characterizes the canvases of both Braque and Picasso from summer 1910 through spring 1912. As William Rubin noted, the regular, rectangular brushstrokes, resembling a kind of brickwork, "echo the framing edge of the canvas."[49]

Braque and Picasso seem to have adapted this distinctive facture from the contemporary canvases of Paul Signac, who had evolved from the pointillist technique of his earlier Neo-Impressionist canvases to a style of widely separated horizontal strokes, laid in with thickly impastoed colors. Five years earlier, Matisse and Derain had utilized Signac's style as a model for the facture of their breakthrough Fauve canvases, copying his horizontal strokes of pure color while abandoning his impasto. Now, Picasso and Braque retained Signac's impasto but abandoned his bright colors.[50] The horizontal strokes of *Woman with Mandolin* seem to have been laid in with pure white paint. They were then tinted with brownish glazes, giving the picture a characteristically "blond" appearance. Although neither artist discussed this "brickwork" technique in detail, there is a 1911 letter from Picasso to Braque, in which he mentions a canvas he has just begun, commenting, "For the new painting, very liquid to start with and Signac-style methodical treatment only at the end."[51] "Signac-style" treatment, here, seems to mean filling in the composition with impastoed bricks.

The rows of bricks added to *Woman with Mandolin* were inserted, for the most part, between the lines of the original lay-in, converting a flat composition into a kind of bas-relief. The pronounced impasto of the bricks may have been intended to restore a sense of sculptural relief absent from the original linear design; in the daylight of Picasso's studio they may have been edged with shadows that disappear under the even illumination of museum lighting. (In 1909, Picasso had experimented with using bas-relief for this purpose.[52]) It seems likely, however, that even in the studio the white bricks of *Woman with Mandolin* did not cast shadows strong enough to impart a sense of modeling to the canvas as a whole. The brown glazes may have been added to compensate for this failure.

Even before this final revision Picasso had significantly modified his composition. In certain areas, he laid bricks over the lines of the original composition, deliberately rendering the existing form unintelligible. He overpainted the outer edges of the arm on the left of the canvas, letting it merge with the background. Within the angle formed by the remaining inner edges of this arm, he added dark shading, so that what had been a mere negative space became a positive shape – a tangential plane like those found in his spring 1909 drawings. A similar transformation occurred on the right side of the canvas. Here, Picasso added lines defining a triangle below the figure's raised forearm. Enclosing the round body of the mandolin and shaded so that it seems to protrude toward the viewer, this new triangle now appears as a kind of mirror-image of the triangle on the left of the canvas. Although it "represents" nothing but the negative space between the forearm and the mandolin, it effectively seizes the viewer's attention, rendering the bent arm above it virtually invisible. The bolstered cushions of the armchair, at lower left and right, were also overpainted, as was the curve on the left of the head.

The result, overall, is a composition that is abstract, not in the sense of being unrelated to natural forms, but in the sense of deriving from natural forms that have been reworked until they are unrecognizable. In Picasso's studies of spring 1910, the negative space around the figure solidified into tangential planes that accompanied other planes more directly derived from the naturalistic anatomy of the figure. In summer 1910 these tangential planes tended to replace anatomy. Paradoxically, they are more closely associated with the figure than with the surrounding space from which they seem to derive. Where the faceting of Picasso's 1908–09 canvases created a consistent pictorial texture, unifying figure and ground, the materialization of negative space in his 1910 pictures has no such unifying effect.

Reinventing Anatomy, Summer–Fall 1910

By summer 1910, Picasso's innovations had brought about a crisis in his work. The awkwardness of many figures of this period (see figs. 86, 88) seems to derive from the fact that Picasso was translating traditional anatomy into geometric terms on an ad hoc basis – using a rectangle or a curve here, a bare line or a shaded triangle there, without any compelling reason for choosing one form over another. As Kahnweiler put it, the presence of "even the slightest verisimilitude" in the work led the viewer to see the geometric figure as a distorted version of a more naturalistic one. As Kahnweiler wrote, "Picasso himself often repeated the ludicrous remark made by his friend, the sculptor Manolo, before one of his figure paintings: 'What would you say if your parents were to call for you at the Barcelona station with such faces?' "[53] Picasso's patrons seem to have shared his disquiet over the apparent distortions of his spring 1910 figures, as is evident in his sales for this period.

Between 1905 and 1909, Picasso had been supported principally by a small circle of collectors, above all the Steins, who had purchased thirty-five canvases ranging from the Blue Period to the faceted heads of summer 1909, and Kahnweiler, who had acquired approximately ninety paintings and drawings covering the same span of his career.[54] Picasso also sold to collectors and dealers such as Frank Haviland, Wilhelm Uhde, and Ambroise Vollard. By 1909, thanks to the patronage of this group, he had achieved a surprising degree of prosperity.[55]

However, Picasso's sales came virtually to a halt in spring 1910, at precisely the moment when he began seriously to explore the idea of open form.[56] Leo Stein later recalled that:

> In 1910 I bought my last picture from Picasso and that was one that I did not really want, but I had from time to time advanced him sums of money, and this cleared the account . . . Picasso was not pleased that I would have none of his cubism . . . Whenever we met he would recur to this and say, 'Why don't you like my painting?'[57]

It is difficult to identify the painting that "cleared the account," but it cannot have been one of Picasso's new pictures because the Stein collection never included any 1910 Picassos. Gertrude Stein's memoirs, written years later, give the impression that she continued to support Picasso's work even after Leo fell by the wayside. The reality, however, is that Gertrude did not buy another work from Picasso until 1912, when he waged a diplomatic campaign to win back her patronage.[58] Kahnweiler too responded negatively to Picasso's spring 1910 work, virtually suspending his purchases.[59] This meant a halt in sales to collectors who bought through Kahnweiler, such as Sergei Shchukin and Roger Dutilleul.[60]

Fortunately for Picasso, his new style proved less unpalatable to other patrons such as Frank Haviland and Wilhelm Uhde, who continued to buy new paintings.[61] Demonstrating his continued support for Picasso, Uhde in May 1910 mounted an exhibition of his 1908–10 work at a gallery on the Rue Notre-Dame des Champs, drawn primarily from his own and Haviland's collection.[62] Picasso's economic crisis was also mitigated in spring 1910 by the intervention of Vollard, who seized the occasion to buy most of the sculptures that Picasso had executed up to that date.[63]

Picasso's work of summer 1910 met an equally difficult reception. Despite his later description of the Cadaqués paintings as a "decisive advance," Kahnweiler regarded them as "unfinished," and declined to purchase any of them. Vollard, in contrast, bought three large figure paintings from Cadaqués, and a smaller still life. In December, these acquisitions were followed by a gallery show which seems to have combined this recent work with a number of earlier pictures.[64] Vollard was an exceptionally canny dealer, who had given Picasso his first exhibition in Paris in 1901, when he was a talented unknown just arrived from Spain. But, unlike Kahnweiler, Vollard had not consistently supported Picasso's work, and his fall 1910 purchases seem to have been made as speculative investments – just in case there turned out to be something to Cubism after all. Talking to the poet Max Jacob, one of Picasso's closest friends, Vollard gave voice to his real opinion: "He's gone mad, your friend."[65]

However "mad," the increasing abstraction of Picasso's new work at least provided an answer to the complaint that Cubism led to an intolerable distortion of the human figure. As Kahnweiler noted, Picasso seemed to have given up the idea that his Cubist figures needed to resemble the naturalistic image of the human body; and once "resemblance" had been abandoned, "the rhythmisation necessary for the coordination of the individual parts into the unity of the work of art [could] take place without producing disturbing distortions."[66]

Picasso did not, however, simply want to produce a pleasing abstract composition inspired by a human figure. The theory of the "equivalent" would certainly have justified his doing so, but Picasso's goal was to produce something recognizable as a figure. There were, he realized, two ways of doing this. One was to paint an essentially abstract composition and then to supplement it with a few recognizable details so that it could be identified as an image of something. Picasso took this route in pictures such as his fall 1910 *Daniel-Henry Kahnweiler* (see fig. 8), one of the "polyhedric Cubist portraits . . . in tones of white and gray and ocher" that he later discussed with Françoise Gilot. In the "early stages" of these pictures, he told her, there were practically no "references to natural forms . . . I painted them in afterwards."[67]

There was yet another way for Picasso to insure the legibility of the figure. This was to invent a new, geometric anatomy, with its own internal logic – something that could replace the traditional anatomical conventions that had dissolved in his recent work. A series of drawings and paintings done in summer and fall 1910 show precisely how Picasso went about inventing a new anatomical convention.

He began by looking back over his recent pictures, culling and combining their most important details. In one drawing, *Standing Nude* (fig. 93), the leaning planes of the head and the shaded angles of the arms are modeled closely on those of the summer 1910 *Woman with Mandolin* (see fig. 91). However, the treatment of the breasts – on the left, a short horizontal strip ending in a curve, and shaded; on the right, a downward-pointing triangle, again shaded – derives from the *Standing Nude with Raised Arm* of the spring (see fig. 86). The tangential plane that appeared in front of the torso in earlier drawings (see figs. 88, 90) now seems to rise through its center. Meanwhile, the curve that originally accompanied the triangular breast (see fig. 86) has been elongated into a tall, shaded cylinder, floating in front of the vertical plane of the torso. Below, on the left, a long descending curve, suggesting a woman's buttock seen in profile, encloses a horizontal line with two smaller curves depending from it, like a rear view of the same part of the body.

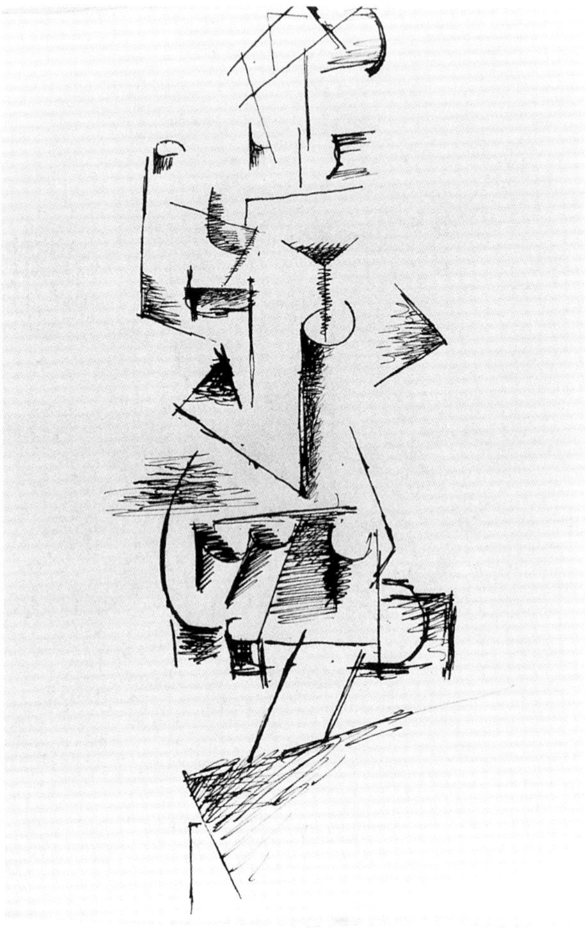

93 Picasso. *Standing Nude.* Cadaqués, summer 1910. Ink on paper, 31.8 × 21.8 cm. Not in Zervos. Private collection

Picasso drew eight different versions of this figure, reshuffling its elements and assigning them new meanings. In one drawing (fig. 94), the triangular planes suggesting arms sink down to the base of the torso, becoming signs for the figure's hips. The vertical cylinder now seems to rise through the center of the torso, dividing at the top where it emerges to become the base of the neck. The breasts are represented symmetrically, as bulges depending from "shelves" cantilevered at either side of the cylinder. At the top of the figure, an incomplete circle mounted on a stem – apparently representing the head – rhymes with the curves of the breasts, buttocks, and knees below. In a third drawing (fig. 95), the cantilevered breast on the left tilts downward, becoming a three-dimensional shape like a pendant slice of melon. This provided the point of departure for the large canvas of a *Nude* painted near the end of Picasso's stay at Cadaqués (see fig. 43).[68]

The problem of the figure was brought into even sharper focus by Kahnweiler's request for a suite of etchings to illustrate a fantastical novel, *Saint Matorel*, by Picasso's friend, the poet Max Jacob. Picasso accepted the commission and wrote Kahnweiler on July 28 that he was about to start work on the etchings.[69] Work seems to have begun at Cadaqués and continued after Picasso's return to Paris. Ultimately, he produced four etchings: a still life, a cityscape, and two versions of "Mademoiselle Léonie," a character from the novel, seen once standing and once seated.

The first etching, of a standing figure, seems to have required the most preparation. If this etching is reversed left to right to restore the orientation of the design that Picasso inscribed in the copper plate (figs. 96, 97), it reveals a number of affinities to the study (see fig. 95) for the large *Nude* (see fig. 43) painted at Cadaqués: the elongated strip of the neck; the curving "collar" enclosing the base of the neck; the sloping "melon slice" of the breast at left; the diagonal ascending gently to the other shoulder; the steeper diagonal enclosing the abdomen at right; and also at right the exaggerated silhouette of a buttock. The representation of one shoulder as a larger melon slice looks back even further, to the spring 1910 drawing *Standing Nude with Raised Arm* (see fig. 86) and beyond that to figures of 1907 (see fig. 52), where similar forms are used to represent breasts or pectoral muscles. The torso is divided by an elongated vertical, so that it advances on one side and recedes into shadows on the other, as in a *Standing Nude* from Cadaqués (see fig. 94). This sense of organization around a central axis is reiterated in the drawing of the face, divided by the bridge of the nose; in the printed version of the etching (fig. 97), this recalls the faces in the studies related to *Woman with Mandolin* (see figs. 91, 93).

The printed etching seems in turn to have served as the point of departure for other, independent studies of "Mademoiselle Léonie" (fig. 98). Here, Picasso repeats and codifies several distinctive features of the print: the long strip of the neck; the "melon slice" shoulder on the left; the protruding angle of the shoulder on the right; and the pendant breast on the left, its lower contour represented by a curve, its upper contour broken into a series of right-angled steps. However, the figuration of the lower part of the body is quite different from the print. On the left, Picasso returns

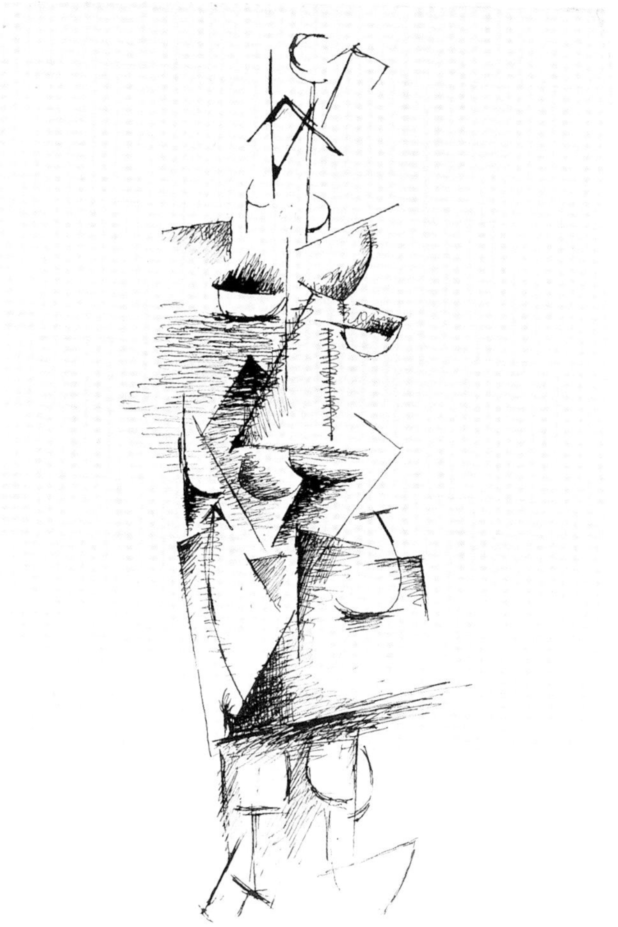

94 Picasso. *Standing Nude.* Cadaqués, summer 1910. Ink on paper, 31.5 × 21.5 cm. Not in Zervos. Richet 251. Musée Picasso, Paris (M.P. 645)

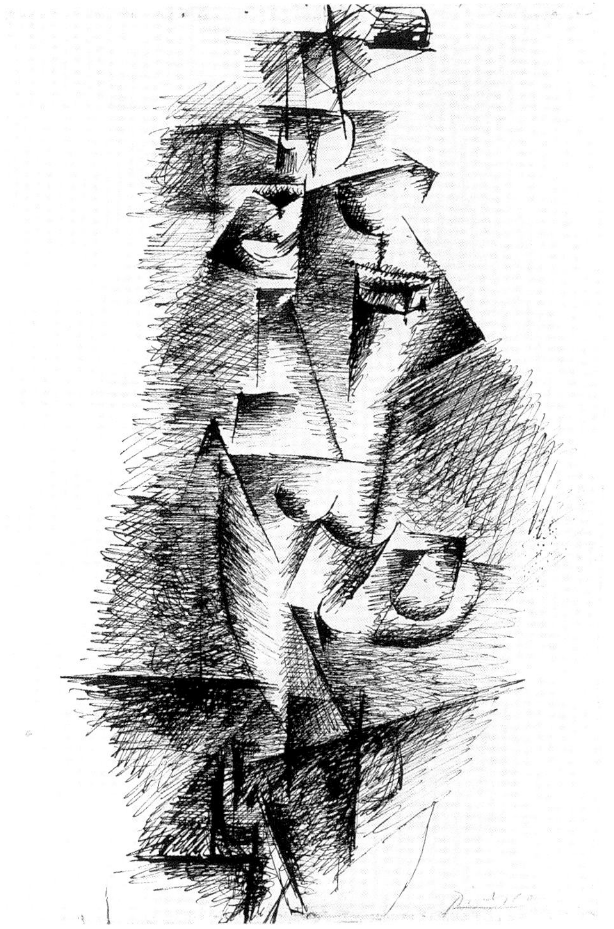

95 Picasso. *Standing Nude.* Cadaqués, summer 1910. Ink on paper, 32 × 23 cm. Zervos XXVIII, 20. Staatsgalerie Stuttgart

to the spring 1910 motif of a protruding black angle marking the hip (see fig. 88). On the right, he takes the vertical cylinder of one of the summer 1910 studies (see fig. 93) and turns it into a cone, pointing downward, which becomes the module defining the anatomy of the torso. The thigh, on the right, is indicated by one cone, cut in half; its curved upper edge suggests a hip. A second cone, rising from this aperture, indicates the abdomen. The chest is represented by a third curved plate, rising from the open mouth of the second cone, which also helps to form a socket where the arm is attached to the body. The arm on the left is omitted in this drawing, but in other versions it is represented by a pair of curving strips bent back at the elbow to form a right triangle.[70]

Many of the forms from the "Mademoiselle Léonie" series also appear in the celebrated canvas of a *Girl with Mandolin (Fanny Tellier)* (fig. 99). The place of this work in Picasso's oeuvre has long been confused. In the files of the Kahnweiler gallery, it was described as a "Woman with Mandolin" and dated to late 1910. Christian Zervos, in the 1942 volume of his Picasso catalogue, gave its title as "Young Girl with a Mandolin (Fanny Tellier)" and also dated it to late 1910.[71] Alfred Barr originally accepted this dating but then revised his opinion, arguing that the canvas "seems early 1910 in style."[72] The issue was further complicated by Roland Penrose, the longtime owner of the picture, who wrote in his 1958 biography of Picasso that *Girl with Mandolin* was painted "earlier" than the fall 1910 *Portrait*

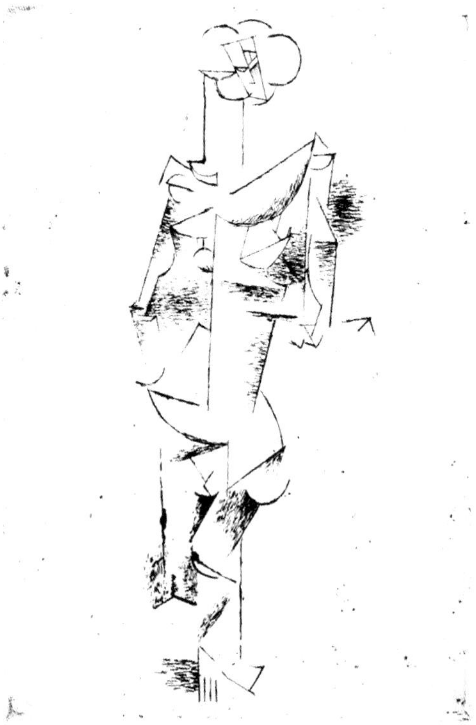

96 (*left*) Picasso. *Mademoiselle Léonie.* Plate 1 from *Saint Matorel.* Summer–fall 1910. Etching, 20 × 14.1 cm. Geiser/Baer 23. Reversed to show image as drawn on plate

99 (*facing page*) Picasso. *Girl with Mandolin (Fanny Tellier).* Paris, fall 1910. Oil on canvas, 100.3 × 73.6 cm. D.R. 346. The Museum of Modern Art, New York. Nelson A. Rockefeller Bequest

97 (*below left*) Picasso. *Mademoiselle Léonie.* Plate 1 from *Saint Matorel.* Summer–fall 1910. Etching, 20 × 14.1 cm. Geiser/Baer 23

98 (*below right*) Picasso. *Mademoiselle Léonie.* Paris, fall 1910. Ink on paper, 31.5 × 21.5 cm. Not in Zervos. Marina Picasso Collection (inv. 1236). Courtesy Jan Krugier Gallery, Geneva

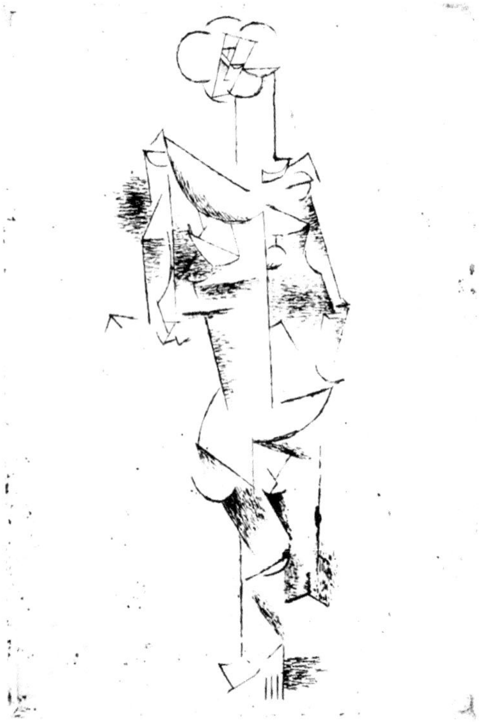

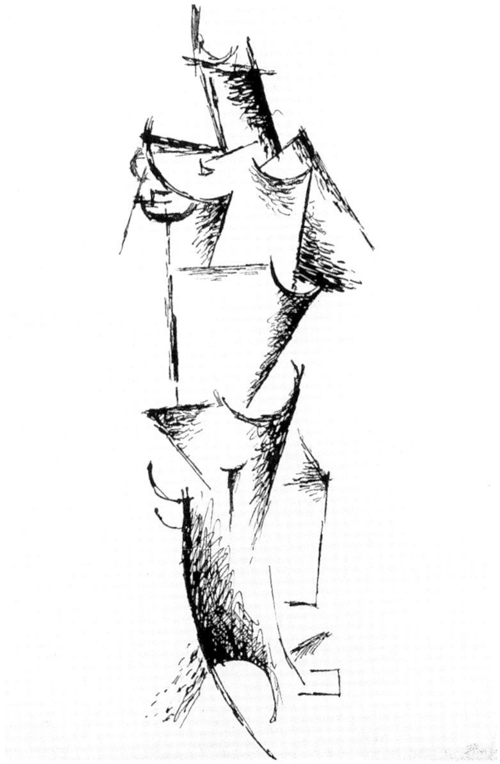

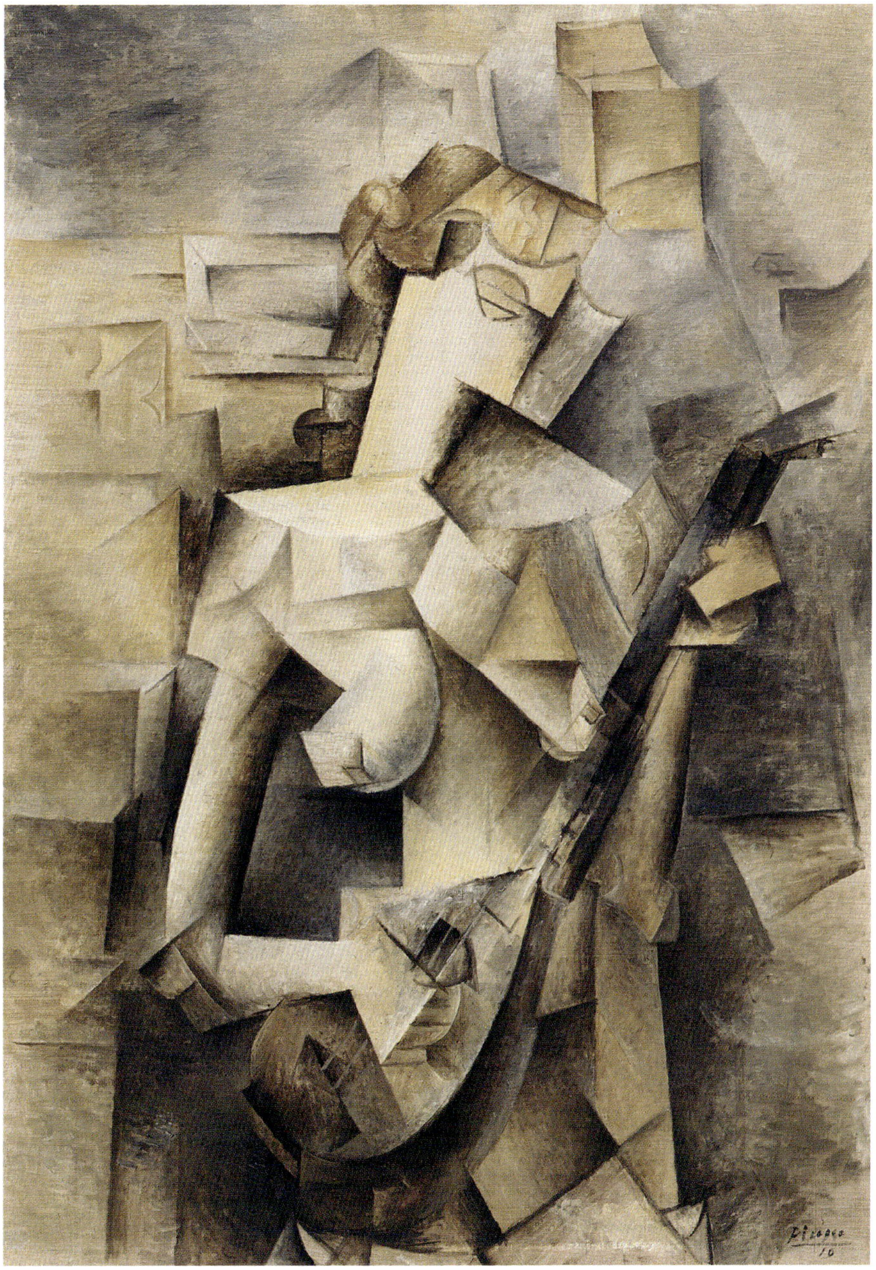

of Kahnweiler. Penrose also provided the details of the story behind the title given in Zervos:

> In this case, contrary to an increasing tendency to paint with the eye of his understanding rather than direct from nature, Picasso demanded many sittings from his model. A girl named Fanny Tellier, who had posed for many of his friends, offered her services to him and came persistently to pose. He found her presence, to which he was unaccustomed, somewhat embarassing, but did not let it interfere with prolonged concentration on his work, until finally it was the model who lost patience. After more sittings than she was in the habit of giving for a single painting she announced that she was indisposed

and could not come the following day. "I realised that she meant not to come back at all," Picasso told me, "and consequently I decided that I must leave the picture unfinished. But who knows," he added, "it may be just as well I left it as it is."[73]

For subsequent scholars, Penrose's tale has seemed to support Barr's view of *Girl with Mandolin* as a transitional work, painted just before Picasso stopped working from a live model. William Rubin, for instance, wrote that "Picasso's direct observation of the motif is still evident in *Girl with Mandolin*, which retains a semiorganic morphology in aspects of both the figure and the instrument." Pierre Daix described it as "the turning point from winter 1909–10 to the work of spring 1910," but also notes that the picture "foreshadows the abstract figuration of Cadaqués and of 1910–11."[74]

However, there is no reason not to accept Zervos and Kahnweiler's original dating of *Girl with Mandolin* to late 1910. Beyond the use of geometry, the formal vocabulary of the painting has almost nothing in common with the faceting of Picasso's early 1910 work. Rather, the treatment of the shoulders as a "melon slice" and an upward pointing angle, and the description of the arm on the left by two strips forming a right triangle, are virtually identical to the handling of the same anatomical elements in the "Mademoiselle Léonie" drawings of fall 1910 (see fig. 98). The pendant breast at left is a variant of the "stepped-down" breast in the same drawing.[75] The division of the face into a pair of overlapping planes looks back to the *Woman with Mandolin* painted at Cadaqués (see fig. 91).

Indeed, it seems that Picasso's goal in painting *Girl with Mandolin* was to create a more legible version of the earlier canvas. This is not surprising, considering the negative reaction which greeted *Woman with Mandolin* and the other highly "abstract" pictures painted at Cadaqués. Rather than being a transitional work between realism and abstraction, *Girl with Mandolin* represents a deliberate return toward realism: a demonstration that Picasso could still paint an appealing picture if he wanted to. The brushwork – a shimmering mosaic of transparent green, yellow, and gray, recalling Cézanne's late watercolors – is completely unlike anything else in Picasso's 1910 production, early or late. The picture was meant to be an exception, an obvious masterwork – and it is.

The role of the model, Fanny Tellier, remains mysterious. Penrose's account suggests that, by the time he began work on the canvas, Picasso was already "unaccustomed" to working with a live model, preferring instead to "paint with the eye of his understanding." The figure's anatomy, deriving from Picasso's studies of summer and fall 1910, clearly owes little or nothing to the model. (In any case, how would a live model suggest an abstract form like the "melon slice" shoulder?) It is possible that direct observation played some role in the coloring and shading of the picture – although this too could well have been arrived at abstractly. Or perhaps Picasso simply enjoyed having a naked model to look at while he worked. It is only the background, with its studio clutter of overlapping frames, that can be said with confidence to be based on observation.

Despite the success of *Girl with Mandolin*, purchased by Wilhelm Uhde soon after its completion, Picasso recognized that it represented a dead end.[76] The quest for a new anatomical convention led back toward an image of the body as self-sufficient and self-enclosed. The result was, inevitably, a geometric figure of the sort that other artists, inspired by Picasso's 1908–09 work, were already painting.[77] To go beyond this, Picasso realized, he would have to abandon the self-sufficient figure.

From Grid to Strip, 1911–1912

As seen in the previous chapter, the diagonal lattice of 1908–09 Cubism gave way in spring 1910 to a lattice of horizontal and vertical lines – the "Cubist grid." For some months, Picasso hesitated between two different uses of the grid. In some pictures, it is essentially a two-dimensional, decorative scrim, serving to unite the figure with its surroundings (see figs. 86, 87). In other pictures, it functions as a three-dimensional scaffolding, providing an armature for the figure.

The transition from one role to another can be seen in a large drawing of a *Standing Nude* (fig. 100) that was exhibited by Alfred Stieglitz at his New York gallery in the spring of 1911, and quickly became a touchstone of Cubist criticism, at least in the United States. The underlying figuration here is close to that of the "Madememoiselle Léonie" drawings (see fig. 88). The position of the body is indicated by a series of tangential planes evoking the torso, hips, thighs, and calves. Crucial junctures are indicated by "melon slices" at the shoulders, breast, hip, and knees. The arm at left is once again constructed from a pair of strips folded into a triangle, while the face is indicated by overlapping

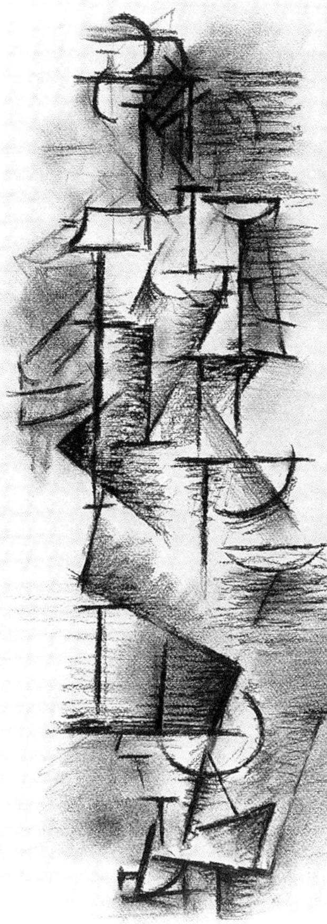

100 Picasso. *Standing Nude.* Paris, winter 1910–11. Charcoal on paper, 48.3 × 31.4 cm. Zervos II*, 208. The Metropolitan Museum of Art, New York. Alfred Stieglitz Collection, 1949

planes, as in *Fanny Tellier* and the earlier *Woman with Mandolin* (see figs. 99, 91). What is different in the *Standing Nude* is that this familiar figuration has now been supplemented by a loose grid of *T*-shaped marks, linking up with the "melon slices" and floating in front of the tangential planes.

Barr suggested that the grid of *T*s could be read either as a geometric "scaffolding" around a more naturalistic figure, or as a kind of X-ray view of the "skeleton" beneath the figure.[78] In the *Standing Nude*, as in the *Daniel-Henry Kahnweiler* (see fig. 8), the *T*s seem to function more as a scaffolding, but in the work of early 1911 the balance shifts rapidly toward the skeleton.[79] Several drawings of mandolin players show the *T*s merging into a continuous framework of vertical and horizontal lines (figs. 101, 102). The former are typically longer than the latter, so that the figure appears to be constructed primarily from vertical strips, overlapping or placed side by side. Individual parts of the body – shoulders, breasts, arms – are indicated by curves, "melon slices," and diagonals, cutting across and accenting the rectilinear structure.

Picasso's previous attempts to invent a new, geometric anatomy had foundered in part because he had not been able to invent a substitute for the actual structure – the internal skeleton – of the human body. The elements of the body might be translated into geometric forms, but the relationship among them was still basically naturalistic. In contrast, Picasso now seems to have realized, the grid was a radically inorganic structure. If it were used as an armature for the figure, perhaps it would provide a new, self-sufficient kind of "skeleton."

101 Picasso. *Woman with Mandolin.* Paris, early 1911. Ink and wash on paper, dimensions unknown. Not in Zervos. Picasso estate (inv. 1210)

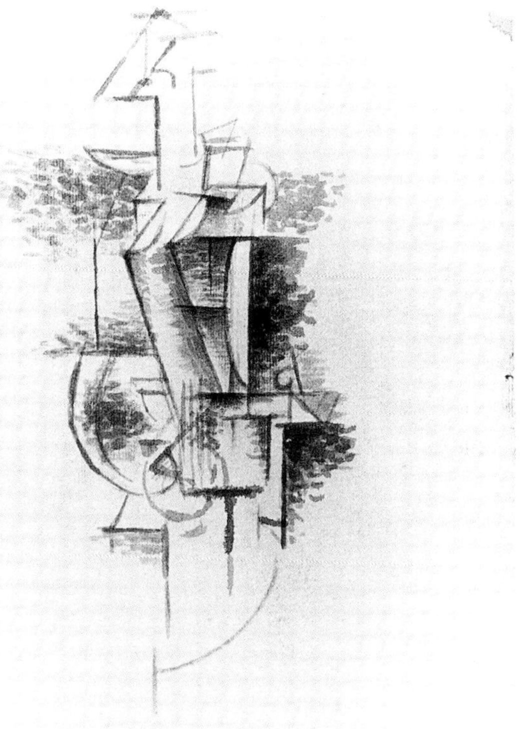

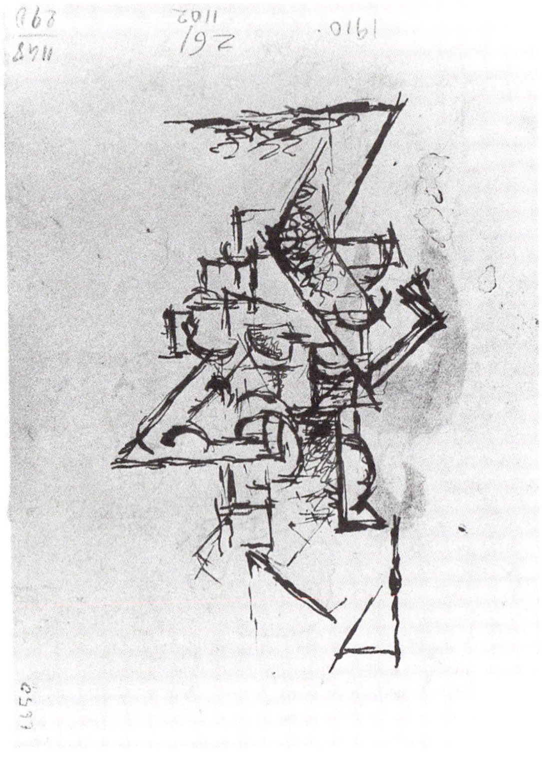

102 Picasso. *Woman with Mandolin.* Paris, early 1911. Ink on paper, 16.7 × 12.2 cm. Zervos VI, 1102. Picasso estate (inv. 1295 R)

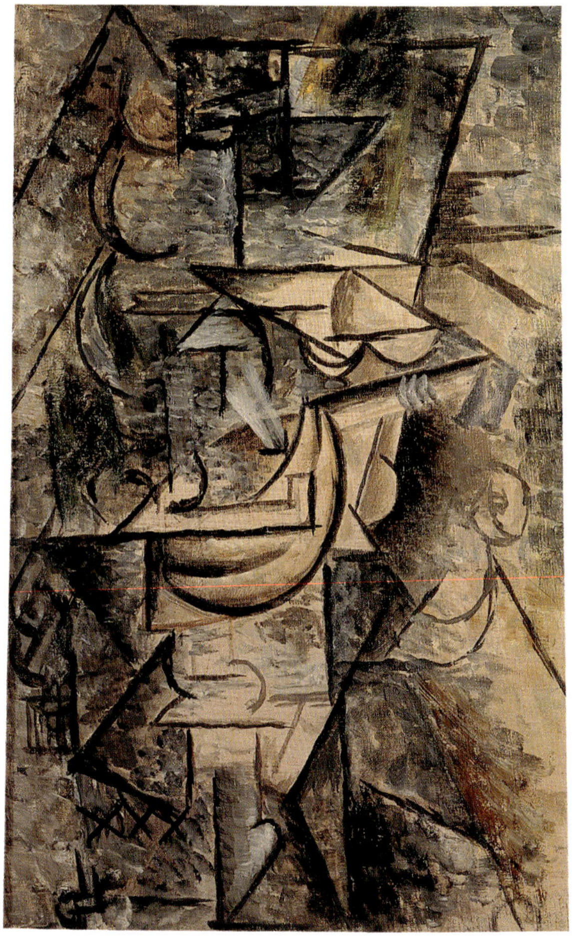

103 Picasso. *Seated Woman with a Mandolin.* Paris, early 1911. Oil on canvas, 38 × 24 cm. D.R. 397. Sidney Janis Gallery, New York

The grid also seemed to offer a ready-made solution to the problem of linking the figure with the space around it. Even if the grid was limited to the immediate vicinity of the figure, its vertical and horizontal axes echoed the edges of the surrounding sheet or canvas. Although the individual panels within the grid might move forward and backward in space, they remained parallel to the picture plane as a whole.

It was easier for Picasso to realize this gridded anatomy on paper than on canvas. Merely picking up a paintbrush was enough to revive the conventions of three-dimensional form. An early 1911 canvas, *Seated Woman with a Mandolin* (fig. 103), is clearly based on the gridded sketches, but Picasso was unable to resist the temptation to model the body and neck of the mandolin. The pose of the figure presents another problem. Two "melon slices" suggesting breasts appear just above the neck of the mandolin. The figure thus seems to be seen in three-quarter view, turning to the right, away from the viewer. This sense of rotation in depth is clearly at odds with the figure's gridded anatomy: since each plane within the figure is parallel to the picture plane, it seems logical that the figure as a whole should share the same orientation, facing forward toward the viewer.

Despite these tensions within the gridded figure, it serves effectively as an anchor for the composition as a whole. In his paintings of spring 1910, Picasso had felt compelled to compensate for the irregularity of his figures by surrounding them with a more or less regular grid (see figs. 87, 89). Here, with the gridded figure at center, he could arrange the borders of the composition more freely. Suddenly, there is a proliferation of semi-naturalistic details. Cascading curves and diagonals at left suggest a curtain hanging behind the mandolin player. Below this curtain hangs a small,

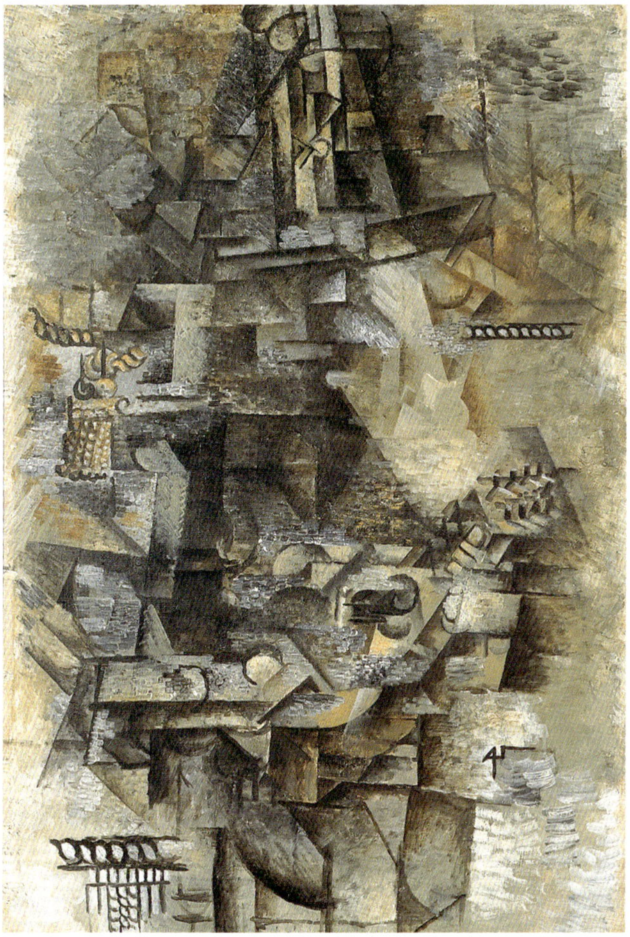

104 Picasso. *Mandolin Player.* Paris, early 1911. Oil on canvas, 100 × 65 cm. D.R. 425. Fondation Beyeler, Riehen/Basel

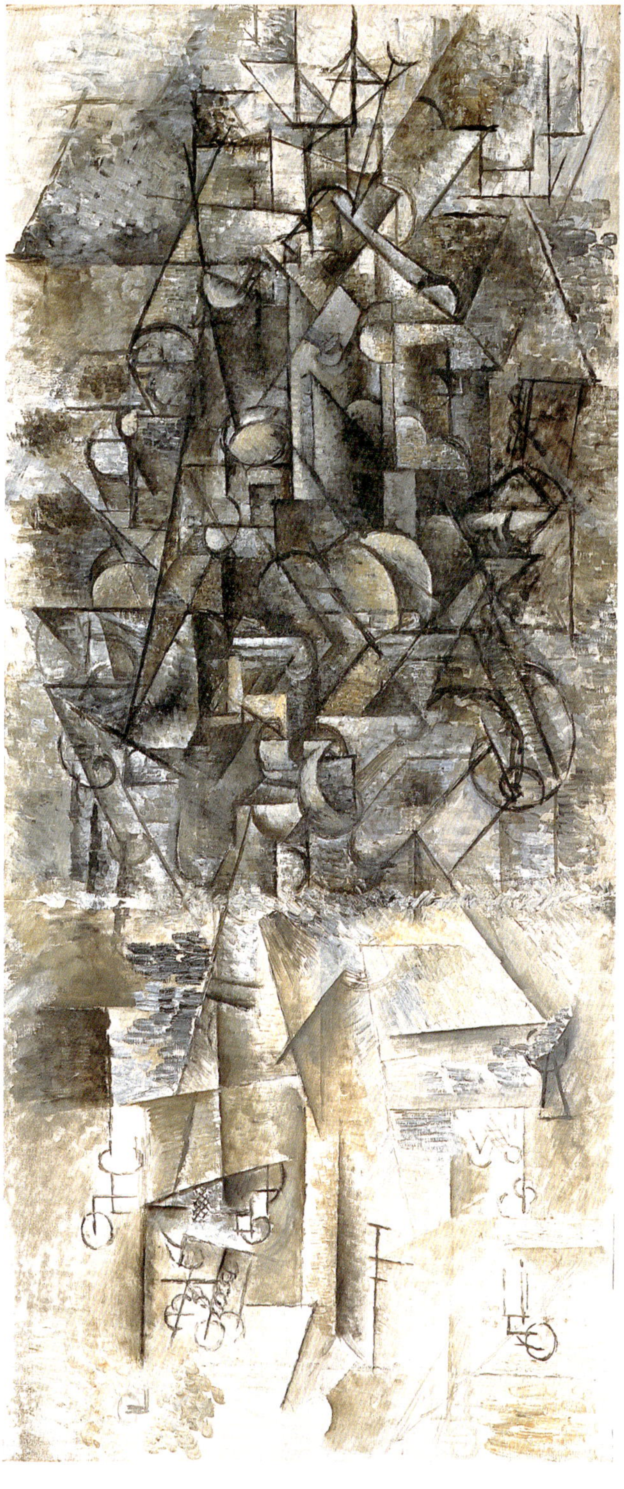

105 Picasso. *Man with Mandolin.* Paris, early 1911, reworked winter 1911–12. Oil on canvas, 99.5 × 71 cm. D.R. 428. Musée Picasso, Paris

schematic tassel – the first of countless tassels to appear in Picasso's 1911–12 work. The chair in which the mandolin player is seated corresponds to an actual armchair, visible in photographs of Picasso's studio (see, for example, fig. 160), with a scalloped back and a fringed seat. On the right, we see the chair's scrolled armrest; on the left, below the seat, three *X*s indicate a strip of fringe.

The tension between two- and three-dimensional form is brilliantly resolved in another, larger *Mandolin Player*, now in the Beyeler collection (fig. 104). The naturalistic details around the margins – tassel, fringe, rope – are drawn with cartoon-like exactness, as are the tuning pegs of the mandolin. Otherwise, the figure and the mandolin dissolve into a grid of rectangular planes, arranged in a series of predominantly vertical bands. The horizontal bar of the forearm, at lower left, makes a striking exception. The only other recognizable elements of the figure are the fingers of the other hand, grasping the neck of the mandolin, just below the tuning pegs. Devoid of mass, the figure occupies a shadowy volume, implied by the subtle fluctuation of light and dark between one plane and the next. As in the *Daniel-Henry Kahnweiler* (see fig. 8), the figure's contours are picked out by highlights; but these contours have been simplified into a vertical triangle, asserting the figure's presence without reproducing its naturalistic image. Picasso may also have intended this triangular outline as a geometric equivalent to the compositional "pyramid" of Renaissance painting.

The Beyeler painting is in fact just one from a large group of canvases, all devoted to the motif of mandolin players and mandolins, that Picasso began in early 1911.[80] Another member of this group, the *Man with Mandolin* now in the Musée Picasso, was subsequently enlarged by the addition of a panel of canvas along its bottom edge. However, the original, upper section (fig. 105) shows how the underlying schema of the mandolin player could be developed in a radically different fashion.[81]

Again, only the figure's hands and arms are recognizable. Fingers grasp the neck of the mandolin at right, atop a diagonal forearm repeated from the smaller study *Seated Woman with a Mandolin* (see fig. 103). On the left, the other forearm seems to appear twice, once as a light-colored horizontal bar and a second time as a pair of outlines tilting downward. Both versions of the forearm terminate in a prominent hand shaped like a lobster's claw, interpenetrating with the dark circle of the mandolin's sound-hole. At lower right, a spiraling curve indicates the armrest of the scallop-backed chair from Picasso's studio.

The man's body remains effectively indecipherable but every detail of its abstract anatomy is described with tremendous clarity. Where the corresponding area of the Beyeler *Mandolin Player* remains vague and mysterious, the torso of the *Man with Mandolin* is traversed by repeated lines, curves, and angles. Above and below the central area (presumably occupied by the curved body of the mandolin) the figure resolves into a series of vertical strips or bands with clear linear borders.

Recognizing that Picasso had achieved a breakthrough in the figurative use of the grid, Braque responded by painting a pair of musicians, *Le Portugais* and the so-called *Guitar Player*, echoing the stylistic polarity between Picasso's mandolin players.[82] Picasso himself returned to the motif of a seated musician in spring 1912, executing a series of drawings that borrowed freely from his and Braque's paintings of the previous year. By then, Picasso had decided definitively in favor of defining the body as a series of vertical strips (fig. 106). The horizontals in these 1912 compositions have clearly been subordinated to the verticals; like the curves, they serve as accents and termini, not as primary structural elements. This emphasis is even clearer in contemporary paintings such as the *Man with Violin* (fig. 107), where the vertical strips composing the figure are highlighted by their shading, alternately light and dark, gray and green. In effect, the vertical strip has taken over the role of the tangential plane as a substitute for conventional anatomy in Picasso's 1910

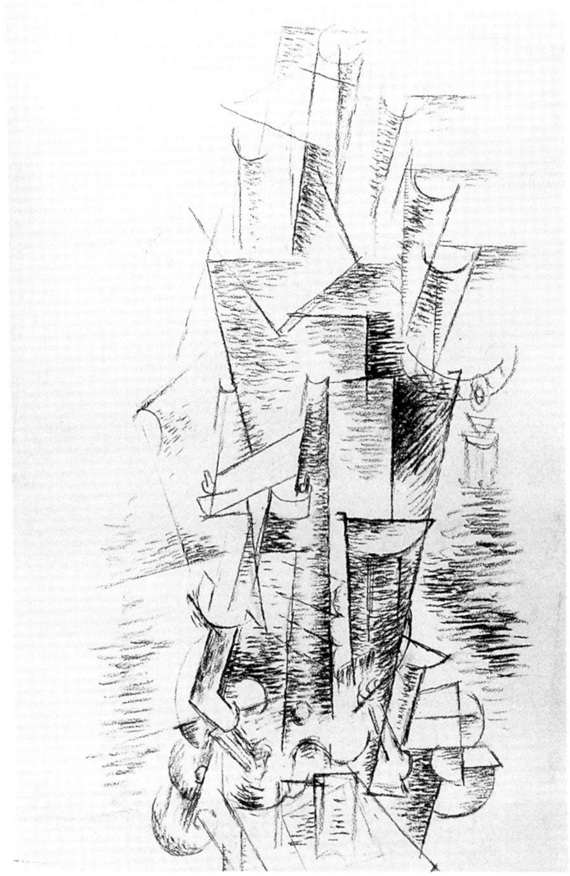

106 Picasso. *Seated Woman with Guitar*. Paris, spring 1912. Charcoal, 48.5 × 31.5 cm. Zervos XXVIII, 109. Richet 277. Musée Picasso, Paris

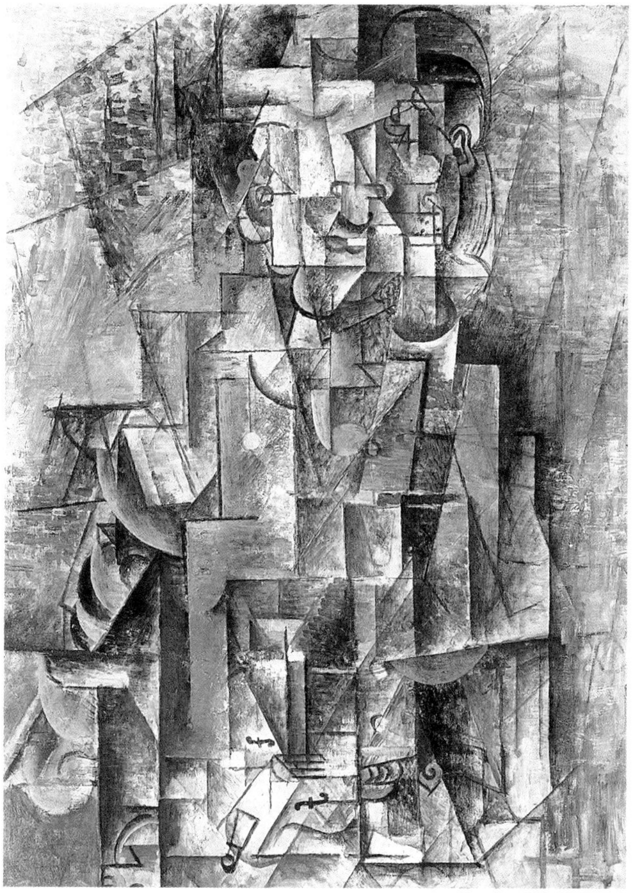

107 Picasso. *Man with Violin.* Paris, spring 1912. Oil on canvas, 100 × 73 cm. D.R. 470. Philadelphia Museum of Art. The Louise and Walter Arensberg Collection, 1950

figures (see figs. 88–90). Other features of these 1912 figures also seem to derive from 1910–11, especially the use of the "melon slice" as a sign for breasts and shoulders (see figs. 97–100, 106).

Superimposed Planes, 1911–1912

In itself, the figuration of the body as a series of vertical strips tended to flatten it into a single plane. But absolute flatness, eliminating volume as well as mass, was essentially antipathetic to Picasso. The evolution from grid to strip was therefore accompanied by the exploration of other formal devices reasserting the volume of both the figure and the space surrounding it.

One such device was the depiction of the figure in terms of diagonal planes tilted so that they angled forward and backward in space. A pair of summer 1911 drawings provides the clearest example (figs. 108, 109).[83] Here, the same arrangement of overlapping diagonal planes provides the armature both for a study of the overall figure and for a "close-up" of the figure's head. The diagonal planes have no descriptive value per se. It is the other elements of the composition – a few vertical strips, a pair of curves at left and right – that correspond to the recognizable features of the torso, forehead, and cranium. What the diagonal planes do provide is an indirect but powerful evocation of the volume of the body and head.

This armature of tilted planes rarely appears in isolation in Picasso's finished paintings, but is often combined with the more familiar structure of the grid. In the *Man with Mandolin* from the Musée Picasso, for instance (see fig. 105), the grid co-exists with several rows of angles pointing left and right, and linking into a large *S* that traverses the figure from head to hip. These correspond, in effect, to the projecting corners of the diagonal planes in the summer 1911 seated man (see fig. 108), except that the planes enclosed by the angles are no longer legible.

Picasso seems to have been troubled by the arbitrariness of the relation between armature and motif, and in a summer 1912 drawing he reworked the arrangement of tilted planes so that it had a more intelligible relationship to the real forms of the head (fig. 110). Two vertical lines, bordering the neck, serve as a back plane to the head. A long diagonal descends from ear to chin, and then turns a corner, so that it suggests a tilted plane, advancing in space, like those in the drawings of 1911. A third, shaded plane, slightly off-kilter, seems to represent the front of the face, with eyes, brows, nose, moustache, and mouth attached to its surface. A front plane, a back plane, and a diagonal plane linking them provide the armature of the head, embellished with more or less realistic details.

This tripartite schema also appears in a notebook sketch, drawn around the same time, of a man with a large round chin (fig. 111).[84] The facial features are now redistributed, so that one ear and one eye appear attached to the back plane while the other member of each pair appears on the advancing diagonal plane. Only the mouth seems firmly seated on the front plane of the chin.

When Picasso reworked this sketch as a full-scale presentation drawing (fig. 112), he eliminated the diagonal plane linking the front and back of the head. Diagonals rose from the body to the face, but they did not contribute to the spatial definition of the head. Instead, Picasso emphasized the front plane by consolidating its borders into a near-perfect square, and by regrouping the facial features in and around it. ("A head," he once said, "was a matter of eyes, nose, mouth, which could be distributed any way you like."[85]) Shading at left and right makes it clear that the square is floating in front of the back plane of the head.

In effect, this drawing represents the culmination of the evolution that began with the first gridded paintings of 1910. From the outset, Picasso had used shading to pry apart planes held together by the dense weave of the grid (see fig. 12). Over the course of 1911 and 1912, Picasso had loosened that weave, breaking the horizontal bands of the weft and freeing the vertical bands of the warp to move forward and backward in space (see fig. 107). Now the vertical bands too began to break into free-floating segments, overlapping within the advancing space of the composition as a whole. Braque adopted a similar structure in fall 1912 works such as *Still Life with Violin* (see fig. 41). Indeed, it was only at this moment that Cubism fully arrived at the spatial organization described in Braque's 1953 statement: "In order to avoid a recession toward infinity, I began superimposing planes one over the other, separated by slight distances. To make the viewer understand that things stand one in front of the other, rather than going back into space."[86]

This structure of superimposed planes virtually defined the pictorial syntax of twentieth-century painting. Its appearance in the work of Picasso and Braque led directly to the development of Constructivism, Suprematism, De Stijl, and related movements. Later in the century, it enjoyed a second life in the United States, thanks in large part to the teachings of Hans Hofmann, whose instructional diagrams provided a kind of primer showing how to create pictorial space and movement by arranging superimposed planes.[87] Nor is its influence limited to avant-garde or "high" art. The graphical interface of the modern computer, with its overlapping "windows" and "toolbars," almost exactly reproduces the structure of 1912 Cubism.

The technique of composing with superimposed planes was perfected in summer 1912, leading to a notable change in the appearance of Picasso's work. Through this summer, he typically began work on a composition by defining the mass or volume of a figure set against an empty stage. Then a kind of scrim was lowered in front of the figure, a lattice

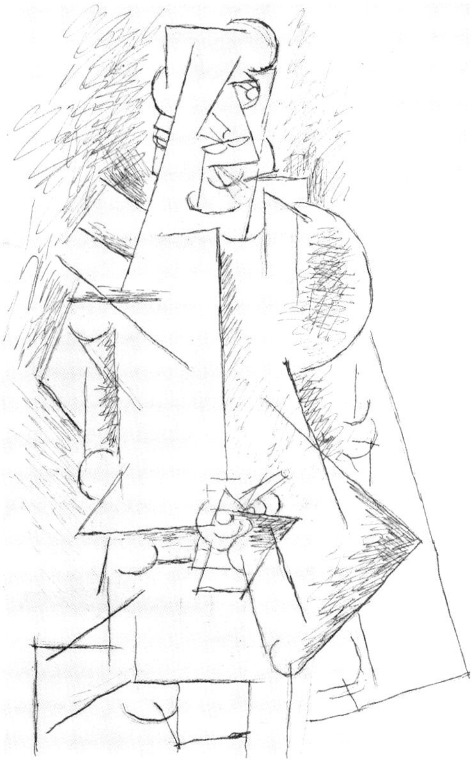

108 Picasso. *Man with Pipe*. Céret, summer 1911. Charcoal and India ink on paper, 31 × 19 cm. Zervos XXVIII, 99. Picasso estate (inv. 1374)

109 (*facing page top left*) Picasso. *Head of Man with Pipe*. Céret, summer 1911. Ink on paper, 21.3 × 13.3 cm. Zervos XXVIII, 68. Picasso estate (inv. 1561)

110 (*facing page top right*) Picasso. *Head of Man with Moustache*. Sorgues, summer 1912. Charcoal on paper, 60.5 × 46 cm. Zervos II*, 325. Formerly collection Mr. and Mrs. Richard C. Hedreen, Seattle

111 (*facing page bottom left*) Picasso. *Head of a Man*. Sorgues, summer 1912. Pencil on graph-paper page from notebook, 13 × 8.5 cm. Not in Zervos. Léal, carnet 16, p. 10v. Musée Picasso, Paris

112 (*facing page bottom right*) Picasso. *Head of a Man*. Sorgues, summer 1912. Charcoal and pastel on paper, 64 × 27 cm. Zervos II*, 327. Kunstmuseum Wintherthur. Bequest of C. and E. Friedrich-Jezler

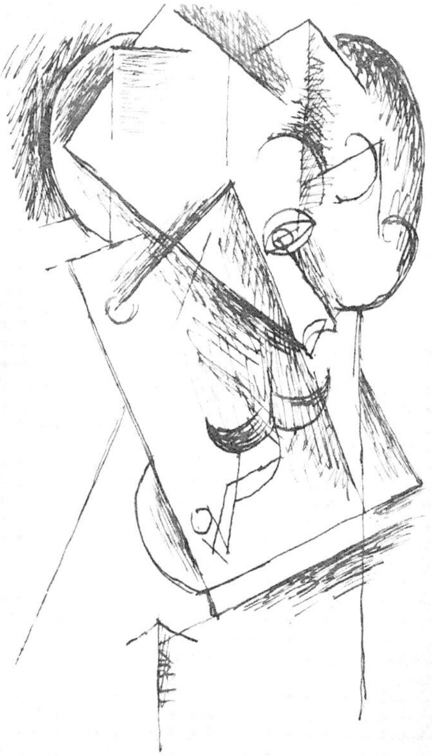

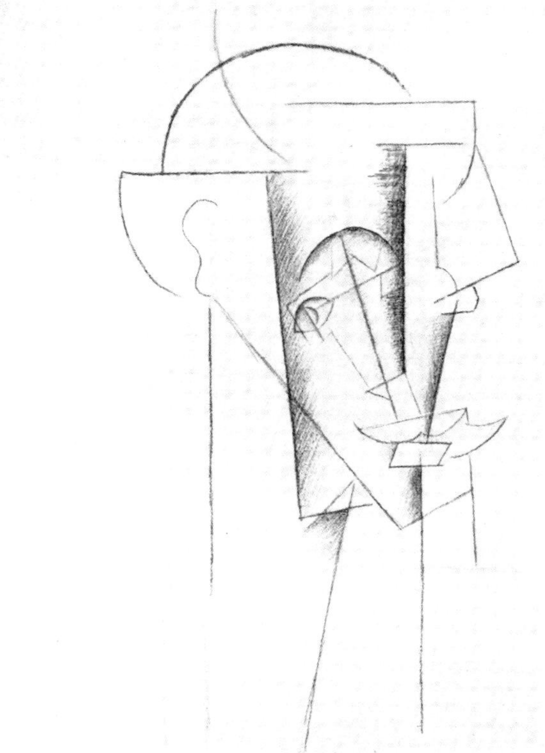

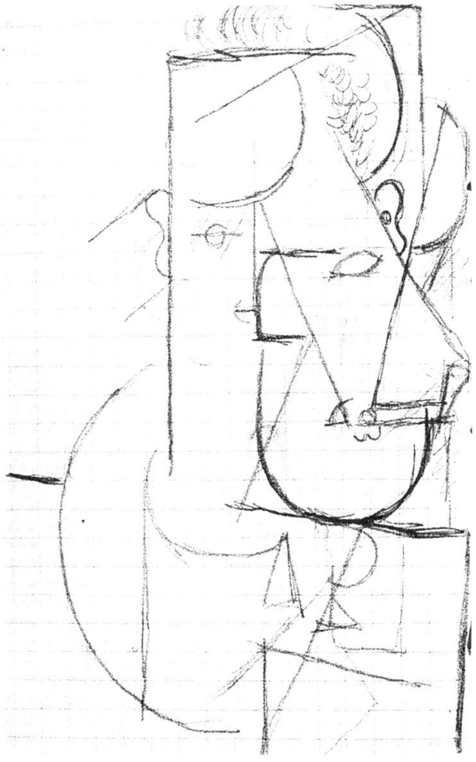

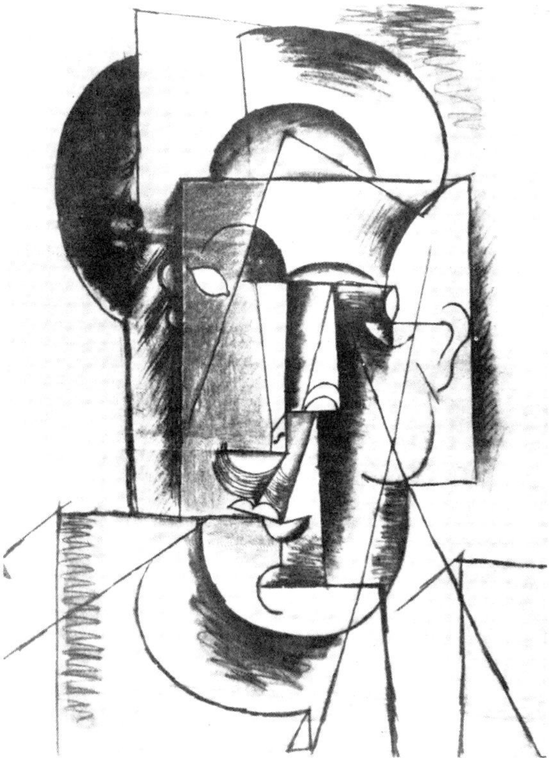

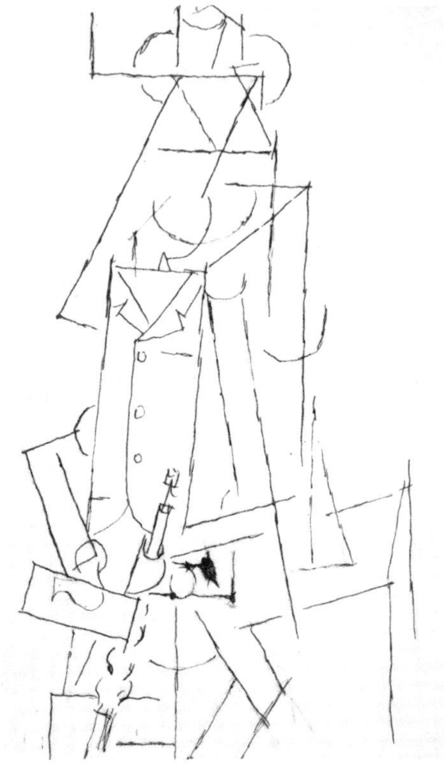

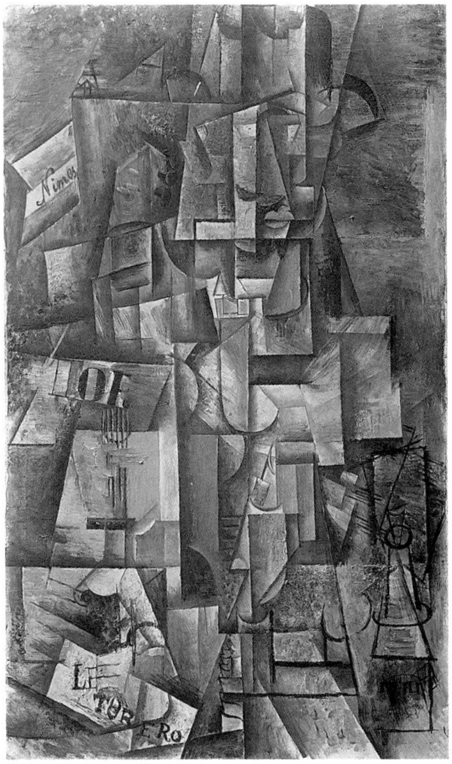
Nimes

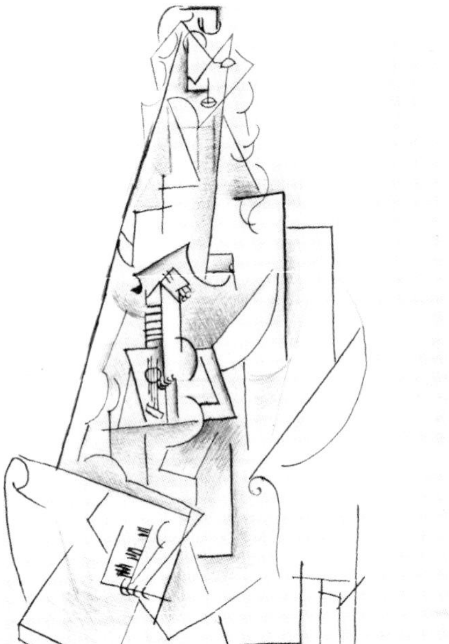

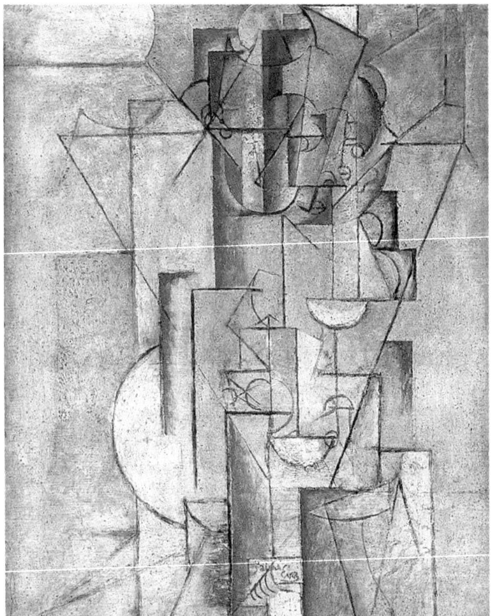

or grid uniting it with the space around it. I have already observed this process at work in his pictures of 1909 and 1910 (see figs. 72, 73, 86, 87), and it continued through the first half of 1912. That summer, Picasso drew a surprisingly legible figure of a seated man holding a banderilla and a newspaper (fig. 113). The man's jacket is drawn on the front of his box-like torso; his arms descend from the sides. In the finished painting called *The Aficionado* (fig. 114), the man's anatomy vanishes behind a scrim of shimmering planes and strips: it is no longer clear where he ends or where the surrounding space begins. In contrast, when another summer 1912 drawing (fig. 115) was translated to canvas after a delay of several months, the finished canvas (fig. 116) was little more than a painted version of the drawing – if anything, somewhat simplified by the omission of the lower part of the original composition. Although a few diagonal planes extend outward from the figure into the corners of the canvas, much of the background has simply been left blank. The monochrome surface is enlivened with a few patches of color, but there are no rapid alternations of light and dark to break up the figure and confuse it with its surroundings.

This change in Picasso's handling was noted, somewhat acerbically, by Leo Stein. Stein claimed that when he asked the reason for the "wavy shading all over the place" in a picture of 1911 or early 1912, Picasso responded that it "didn't mean anything except a sort of completion, since the lines which were the real picture were too bare." For Stein, this concession to "decorative exigencies" gave the lie to Cubism's philosophical pretensions. Nonetheless, he added with grudging admiration that Picasso "later . . . became more courageous and left the lines bare."[88] This was a step that Braque was never really willing to take. Even after 1912, he continued to use the grid to integrate his figures with their surroundings.[89]

The drawings of summer and fall 1912 mark the convergence of Picasso's two chief concerns of the preceding years: the definition of projective space and the reinvention of the body as a sculptural form. Construction with superimposed planes solved both of these problems. Picasso seems to have decided that since the structure of the Cubist figure was now identical with the structure of Cubist space, there was no longer any point in concealing it – or duplicating it. If the motif was constructed from planes attached to a three-dimensional armature, the viewer could be trusted to understand that the space around the motif was structured in the same fashion. The problem of pictorial space had been solved. It could therefore be ignored, freeing Picasso to focus his attention almost exclusively on his motifs.

Henceforth, Picasso advanced by inventing a series of new ways to represent the figure as a three-dimensional construction. Solutions worked out for the human figure were then applied to inanimate objects. Meanwhile, space could take care of itself. In effect, Picasso assumed that each new figuration he invented implied a new way of organizing the picture as a whole, as it had in the period 1908–12, and therefore constituted an artistic advance. Remarkably, this continued to be true for roughly three decades.

113 (*facing page top left*) Picasso. *Man with Banderilla.* Sorgues, summer 1912. Ink and pencil on paper, 30.5 × 19.5 cm. Zervos XXVIII, 110. Picasso estate (inv. 1371)

114 (*facing page top right*) Picasso. *The Aficionado.* Sorgues, summer 1912. Oil on canvas, 135 × 82 cm. D.R. 500. Oeffentliche Kunstsammlung, Basel, Kunstmuseum. Gift of Raoul La Roche, 1952

115 (*facing page bottom left*) Picasso. *Seated Woman with Guitar.* Sorgues, summer 1912. Ink and pencil on paper, 34 × 22 cm. Zervos XXVIII, 237. Picasso estate (inv. 1579)

116 (*facing page bottom right*) Picasso. *Female Nude: "J'Aime Eva".* Paris, winter 1912–13. Oil and sand on canvas, 75.6 × 66 cm. D.R. 541. Columbus Museum of Art, Ohio. Gift of Ferdinand Howald

New Anatomies, 1913–1914

The extraordinary breakthroughs of 1912 nonetheless left two questions unanswered. From 1910 through 1912, Picasso and Braque had worked with a deliberately limited vocabulary of forms and colors, so that they could focus on developing the syntax of Cubism. Once they had codified and perfected that syntax, could a wider range of forms and colors be added to Cubism's vocabulary? Similarly, the refinement of Cubism's form language had required that they virtually abandon the attempt to offer a recognizable representation of reality. Was there some way to bring back naturalistic imagery within the structure of Cubism, or at least to clarify the relation between natural form and its Cubist equivalent? These were the questions that henceforth impelled Picasso's work.

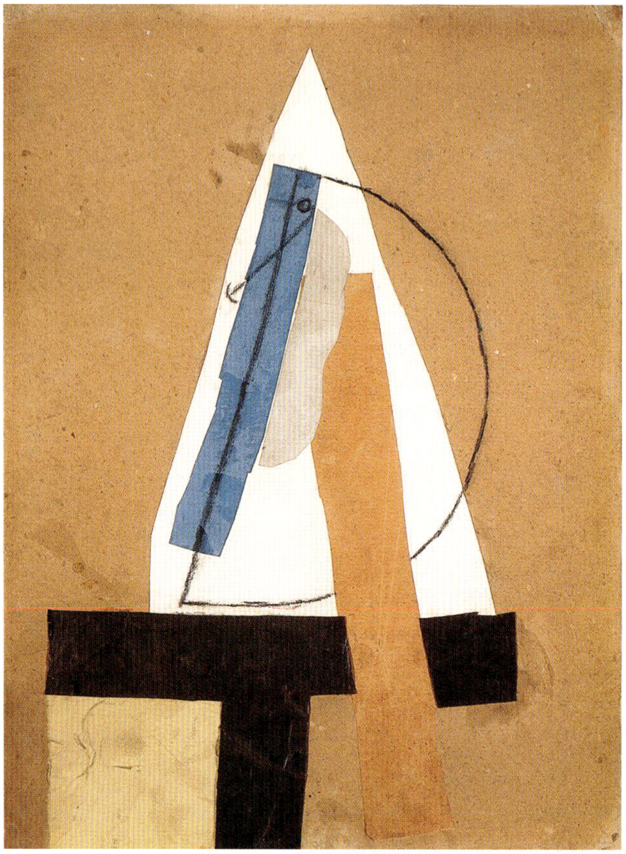

117 Picasso. *Head*. Céret, spring 1913. Pasted paper, charcoal, and pencil on cardboard, 43.5 × 33 cm. D.R. 595. Scottish National Gallery of Modern Art, Edinburgh

From 1910 through 1912, triangles and curves had served to accent the basic structure of the grid, indicating heads, shoulders, breasts, and other individual parts of the body. For a while, Picasso and Braque had used triangular outlines to indicate the figure as a whole (see fig. 104), but these outlines tended to disappear as the underlying structure of planes suspended from a rectilinear grid became more explicit. In spring 1913, Picasso began to explore the idea of using triangles and curves as the main elements of his figuration. In a typical work of this period (fig. 117), the overall shape of the head is a large white triangle, with a tilted rectangle of blue paper indicating the face.

However, the major drama of Picasso's 1913 work lies in his attempt to reinvent the Cubist figure as an assemblage of rounded rather than rectilinear planes. Bit by bit, the armature of vertical strips was enclosed by curves (figs. 118, 119). In spring 1913, he was not yet ready to return to a naturalistic depiction of the body. Nonetheless, the proliferation of rounded forms imbues the body with a sensual quality notably absent from his work of the previous three years.

This turn toward a more sensual form language clearly satisfied Picasso's long-suppressed desire for an eroticized image of the body. However, for the first time in several years, it may also have represented the influence on Picasso of a contemporary artist other than Georges Braque. Some of Picasso's 1913 drawings of female figures are strikingly similar to those drawn and painted by Fernand Léger in 1912 (fig. 120). Picasso would have been familiar with his work, since Léger too showed with Kahnweiler.

A prolonged illness in the summer of 1913 caused an unusual disruption in the continuity of Picasso's production. Nonetheless, his major enterprise of the fall, the *Woman with Chemise in an Armchair*, utilizes a formal vocabulary derived from his studies of the previous spring (figs. 121, 122). The head and neck are constructed around an acute triangle. A sideways-pointing angle traverses the body, extending upwards into a raised arm and downwards into the broad strip of a leg. The torso is a large, egg-shaped form. The breasts are represented twice, once as pointed ovoids – truncated "melon slices" – descending from the line of the angled shoulders, and a second time as semi-circles ascending from the same line.

The finished painting of *Woman with Chemise* (fig. 123) explicitly mobilizes the erotic potential of Picasso's new curvilinear vocabulary. The "realistic" details of the composition – the fringed armchair, the woman's undulating tresses, and the hair of her exposed armpit – lead the viewer to see the large curves of the woman's torso as suggesting shoulders, hips, buttocks, and belly, even if they do not correspond directly to these anatomical features. There is a kind of *fin-de-siècle* sensuality to the purple-ocher palette and the smoothly modulated shading. The pendulous breasts, with their brown-tipped nipples, and the exposed underarm demand that the viewer respond to the figure as a physical presence. According to Pierre Daix, when Picasso showed the painting to Braque, he asked him: "Is it a woman or a painting? Can you smell her armpits?" The crumpled chemise in the woman's lap only serves to emphasize her nakedness. Apollinaire told Picasso: "I always wanted to lift her chemise." He responded: "You can see it's a real woman. Even what's hidden is there."[90]

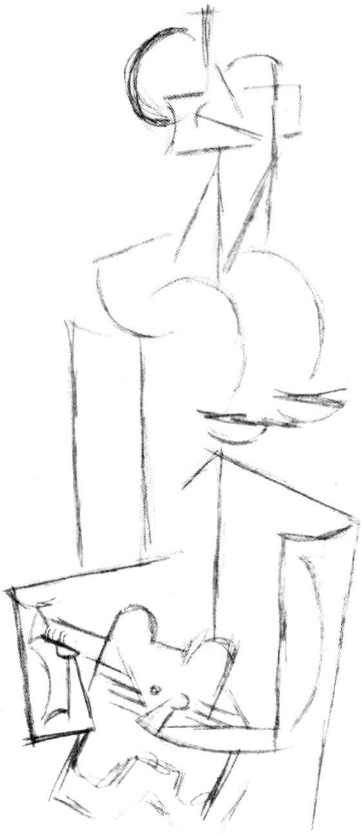

118 Picasso. *Woman with Guitar*. Céret, spring 1913. Lead pencil on paper, 27.5 × 21 cm. Zervos XXVIII, 172. Picasso estate (inv. 1564)

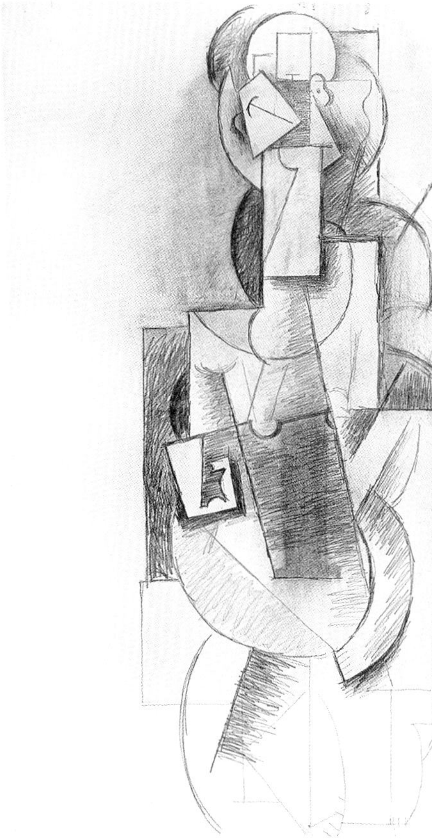

119 Picasso. *Woman with Guitar*. Céret, spring 1913. Lead pencil on paper, 63.5 × 47.6 cm. Zervos XXIX, 8. Solomon R. Guggenheim Museum, New York

Indeed, the shaded folds of the chemise crumpled in the woman's lap seem designed to remind the viewer of the anatomy they conceal. However, the hidden genitals may also be "there" in the sense of being represented elsewhere in the figure. At the top of the composition, the eyes, nose, and mouth are reduced to a narrow slit in the face. The symbolic meaning of this abstract form is underscored in a related study (fig. 124), where the "vaginal" features are flanked at either side by undulating hair.

Woman with Chemise in an Armchair was a favorite with the Surrealists. Writing in the 1940s, Paul Eluard praised "the enormous, sculptural mass of the woman, the head as large as that of the Sphinx, the breasts nailed to the chest."[91] The picture's agonized eroticism, which can find expression only by transgressing the limits of conventional representation, makes it, in effect, the first Surrealist painting. However, the aspect of the painting that Picasso continued to develop in 1914–15 was not its eroticism but its confrontation between naturalism and abstraction.

In 1910, Picasso had been propelled toward the use of an abstract armature by the disturbing effects of his geometric translations of traditional anatomy. The resulting figures seemed like distorted versions of more naturalistic figures. The solution had been to substitute the armature of the grid for the anatomy of the real body. From 1911 on, the Cubist figure no longer seemed strange because it suggested no naturalistic image for comparison.[92]

Beginning in fall 1913, Picasso reversed the evolution of 1910–11. By introducing curves and naturalistic details evoking the real body, he deliberately forced the viewer to confront the strangeness of his figures. In summer 1914, he took another deliberate step backward, returning to the pre-

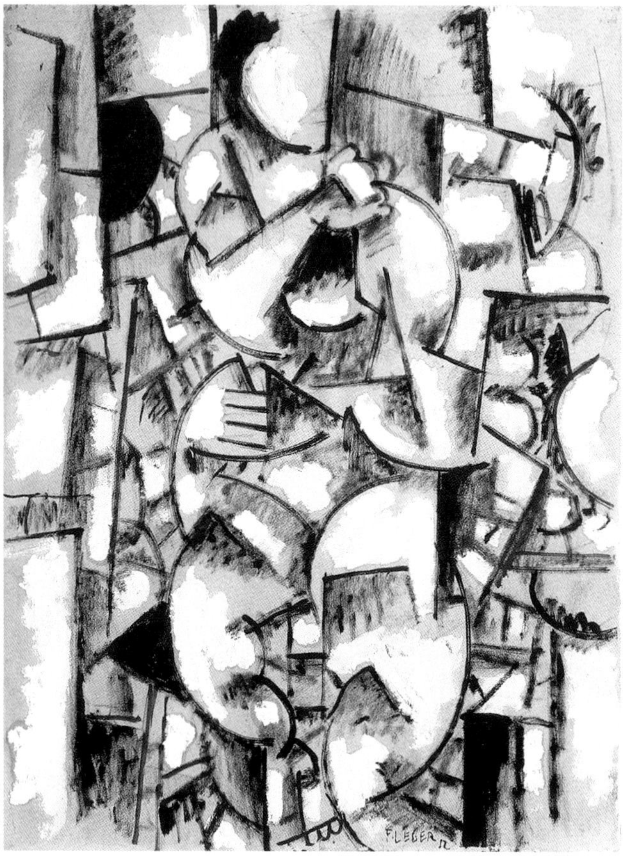

120 Fernand Léger. *Nude in the Studio.* 1912. Ink and gouache on paper, 61 × 50 cm. Centre Georges Pompidou, Musée National d'Art Moderne, Paris. Gift, Louise and Michel Leiris. 1984

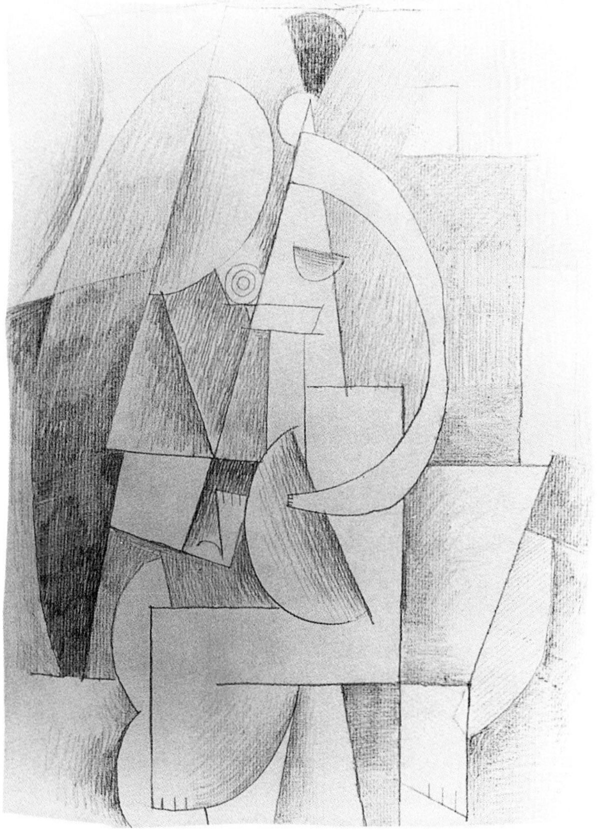

121 Picasso. *Woman with Guitar or Mandolin.* Céret, spring, or Paris, fall 1913. Pencil on paper, 30.5 × 22 cm. Zervos VI, 1250. Picasso estate (inv. 1766)

1911 system of translating the figure into geometric terms on a part-by-part basis, while allowing its overall configuration to be determined by its natural form. The difference is that Picasso's formal language of 1910 consisted mostly of straight lines, angles, triangles, and rectangles, with a few regular curves, while his formal language of summer 1914 consists largely of ovoids and free-form curves, with a few rectangular planes. The underlying structure of planes overlapping in space is the same as in 1911–12, but the appearance of the planes themselves is strikingly different.

For one of his test cases, Picasso chose the image of a moustachioed man leaning against a squared-off column (fig. 125). The contrapposto pose looks back to the figures of spring 1910 (see fig. 90). Rejecting the frontality that the grid had imposed on the Cubist figure of 1911–13, Picasso arranged the man's limbs to suggest rotating movement: one leg crosses leftward over the other, while an arm crosses the torso to the right. When the figure was translated into "abstract" terms (fig. 126), these limbs became curved or wavy strips, unfolding in opposite directions. The torso, expressed as a series of overlapping planes with (mostly) rounded corners looks back to Picasso's first, 1909 experiments with this mode of construction (see fig. 66).

This confrontation between realistic and abstract versions of the same figure casts important light on the "return to realism" in Picasso's work of the following decade, which has since become controversial. One writer has described the "new classicism" of Picasso's post-1913 pictures as a "transformation of art from the practice of the material and dialectical transgression of ideology to the static affirmation of the conditions of reification and their psychosexual origins in repression."[93] Another critic has denounced the "fraudu-

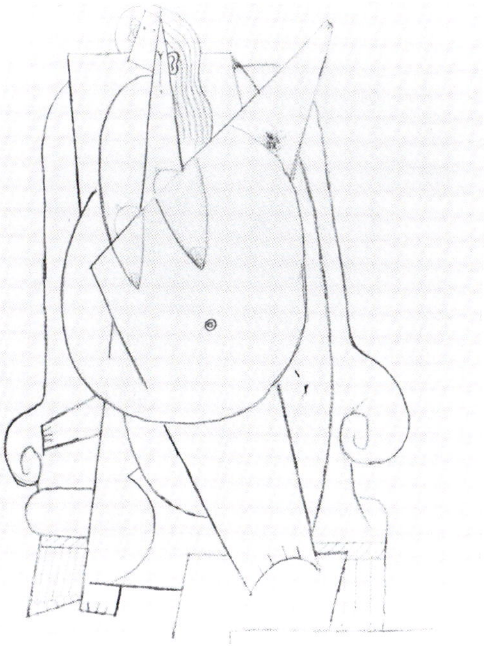

122 (*above*) Picasso. *Woman with Raised Arm.* Paris, fall 1913. Conté crayon on paper, 19 × 15 cm. Zervos VI, 1260. Picasso estate (inv. 1976)

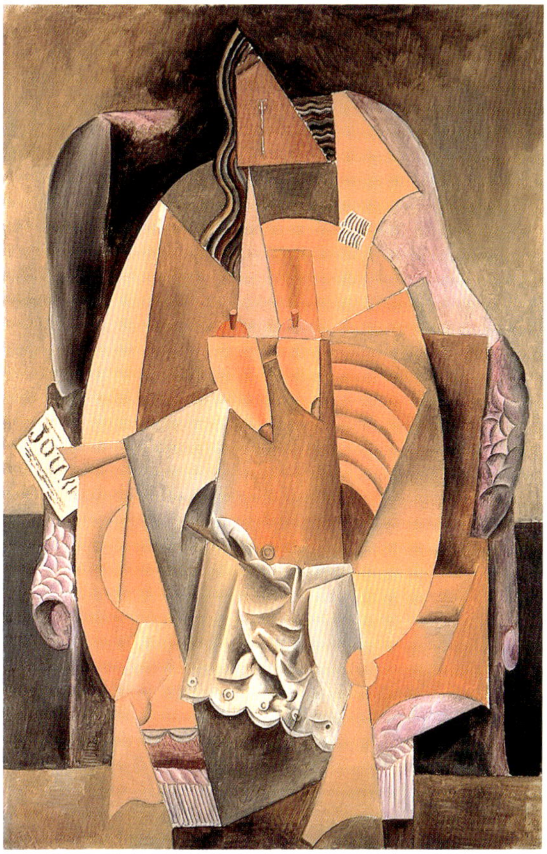

123 (*right*) Picasso. *Woman with Chemise in an Armchair.* Paris, fall 1913. Oil on canvas, 148 × 99 cm. D.R. 642. Private collection

lence" of Picasso's new naturalism as the sign of a kind of artistic bankruptcy. Exhausted by the quest for an original figuration, Picasso is said instead to have settled for the practice of pastiche, imitating the look of portraits by Ingres, nudes by Renoir, commercial photographs, and so on.[94]

There is no question that Picasso enjoyed rediscovering his own talent for realistic representation. Kahnweiler recalled that "In the spring of 1914 Picasso had shown me two drawings that were not Cubist, but classicist, two drawings of a seated man. He had said, 'Still, they're better than before, aren't they?'" What he meant, it seemed to Kahnweiler, was: "Better than the classicist, or, if you will, the naturalistic drawings that I did before."[95] Discussing Cubism with Leo Stein around this time, Picasso remarked: "Even if this new way is a mistake, it has prof-

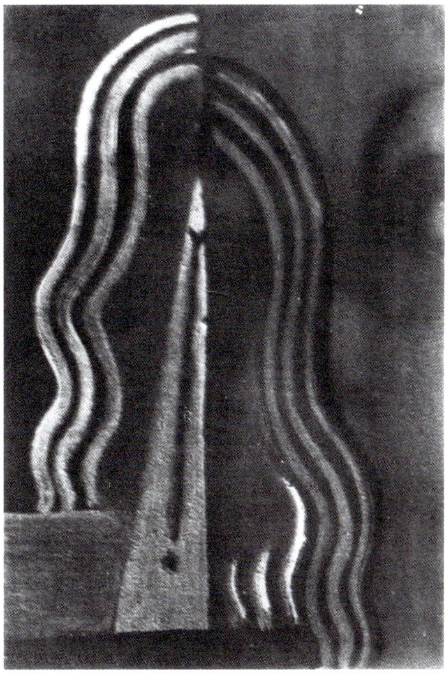

124 (*right*) Picasso. *Head of a Woman.* Paris, fall 1913. Oil on panel, 16 × 12 cm. D.R. 643. Private collection

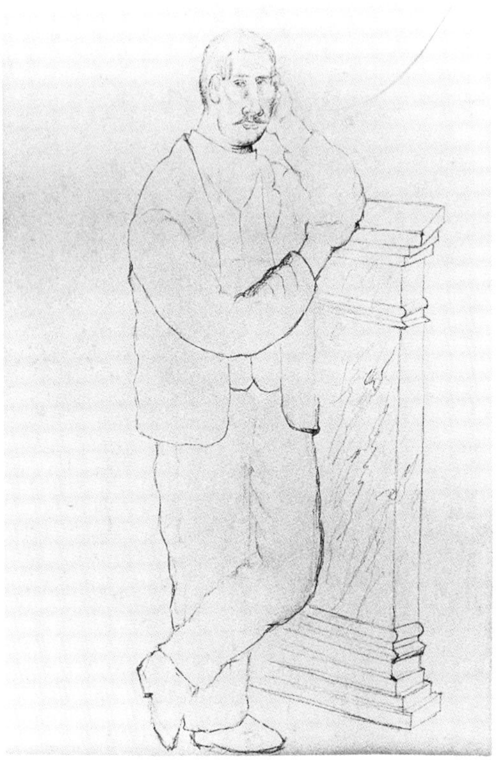

125 Picasso. *Man Leaning on a Column.* Avignon, summer 1914. Crayon on paper, 30 × 20 cm. Not in Zervos. Picasso estate (inv. 1678)

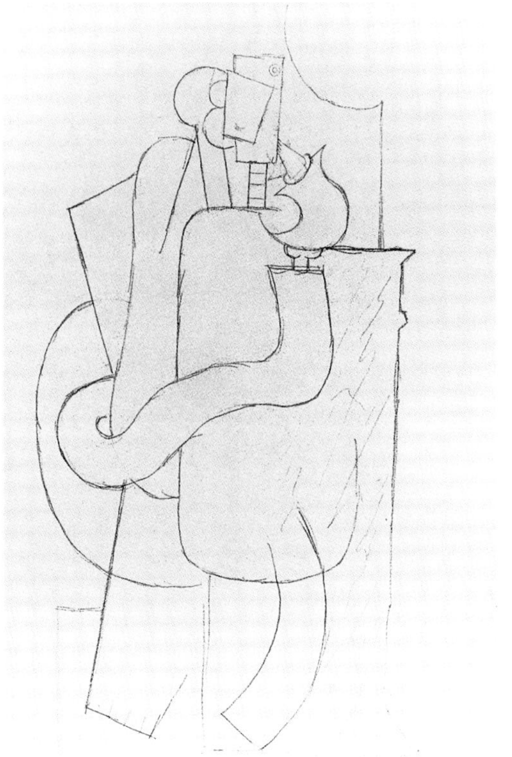

126 Picasso. *Man Leaning on a Column.* Avignon, summer 1914. Crayon on paper, 30 × 20 cm. Not in Zervos. Picasso estate (inv. 1700)

ited me, for I did a figure the other day and it was better than any I had done before."[96] This was quite true. Somehow, seven years of drawing and painting in a variety of geometric styles had greatly improved Picasso's talents as a realistic draftsman. The artificial elegance of the Blue and Rose periods had been succeeded by a more modest, descriptive style; the graceful awkwardness of Picasso's new line masked its extraordinary responsiveness to individual forms.

These new, naturalistic images do not emerge in isolation, however. They are part of an active dialogue between realism and Cubism.[97] Like the *Man Leaning on a Column*, the *Seated Man Leaning on a Table* appears as both a realist and an abstract figure. Indeed, Picasso seems to have drawn the realist versions (fig. 127) largely to set himself the challenge of translating them into geometric terms. On one sheet (fig. 128), we can see him searching for a new way to draw a bent arm. Geometric forms were superimposed on the naturalistic figure, and then repeated as an "abstract" configuration in the upper left corner of the sheet. Ultimately, each element of the man (and his setting) received its own distinctive figuration. The reinvented elements were then combined in a composition of summer 1914 as shadowy and complex as any picture of 1910–12, but with a vastly greater quantity of descriptive detail (fig. 129). The delineation of a realistic image posed a challenge, forcing Picasso to focus on numerous details that then had to be translated into the form language of Cubism. But each realist detail, in its ineluctable particularity, was also a potential source of abstract form.

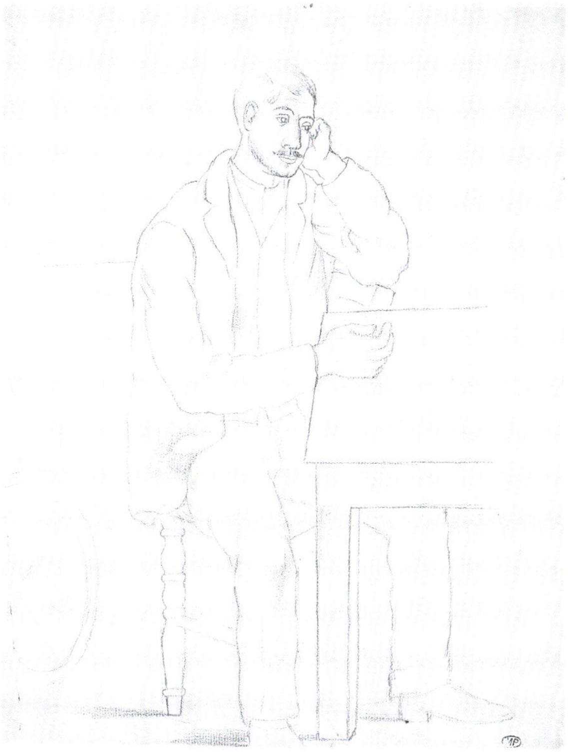

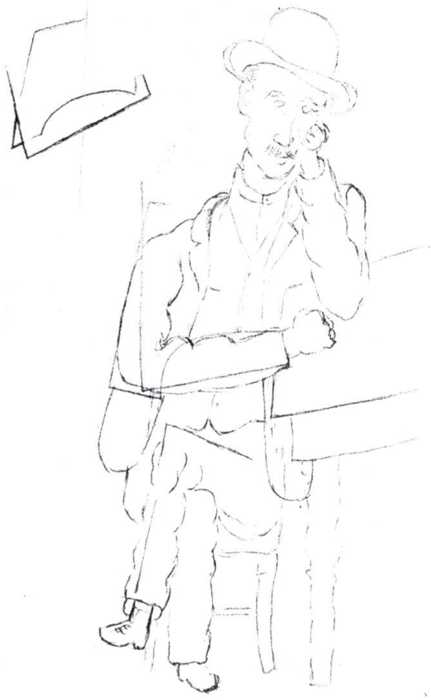

127 (*above left*) Picasso. *Seated Man Leaning on a Table.* Paris, spring, or Avignon, summer 1914. Lead pencil on paper, 31 × 24 cm. Zervos VI, 1198. Richet 359. Musée Picasso, Paris

128 (*above right*) Picasso. *Seated Man Leaning on a Table.* Paris, spring, or Avignon, summer 1914. Lead pencil on paper, 32 × 24.5 cm. Zervos VI, 1201. Picasso estate (inv. 17667)

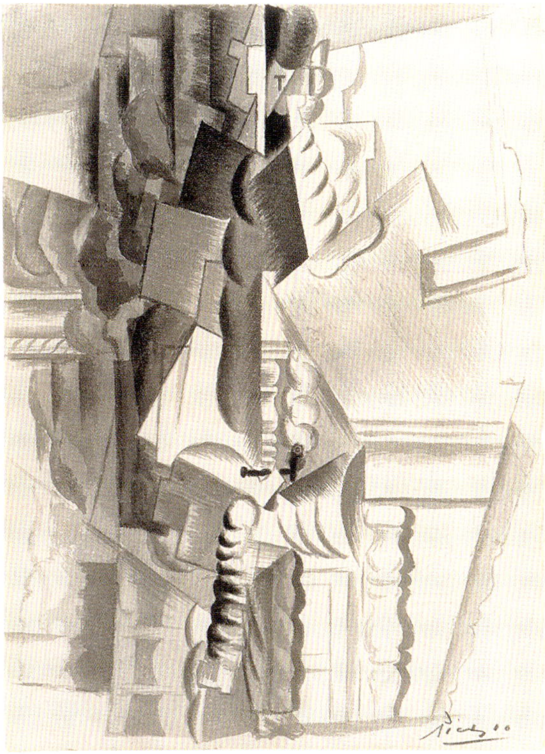

129 (*right*) Picasso. *Seated Man Leaning on a Table.* Avignon, summer 1914. Watercolor and ink on paper, 33 × 24 cm. D.R. 840. Collection Mr. and Mrs. Gustavo Cisneros

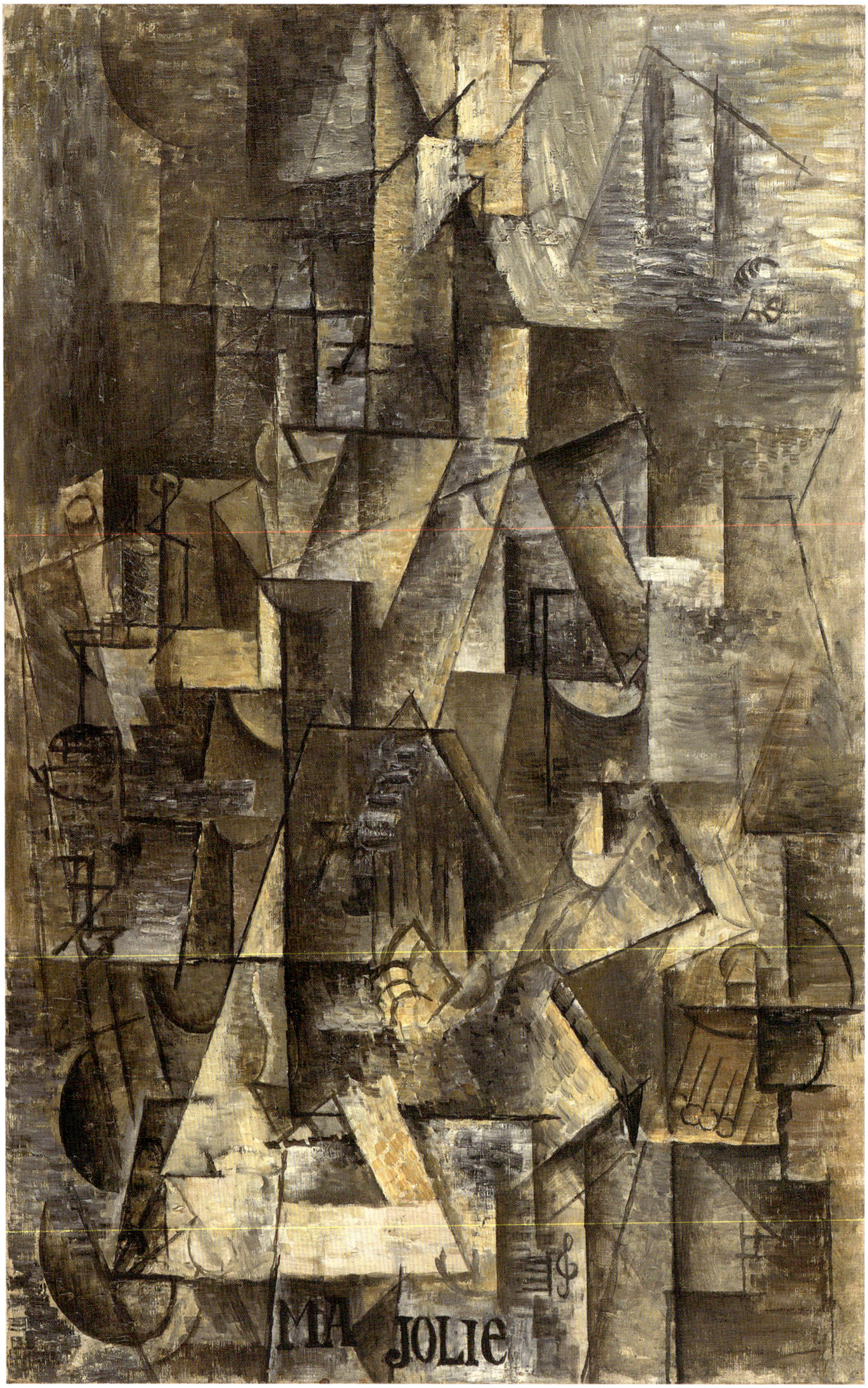

130 Picasso. *"Ma Jolie" (Woman with Zither)*. Paris, winter 1911–12. Oil on canvas, 100 × 65.4 cm. D.R. 430. The Museum of Modern Art, New York. Acquired through the Lillie P. Bliss Bequest

4
Signs

Picasso and the Sign

In June 1945, as the Paris art scene came back to life, a pair of exhibitions reasserted Picasso's position as leader of the avant-garde. An exhibition of 1911–18 Cubism, at the Galerie de France, reminded the public of the historic importance of his work of those years. A concurrent exhibition at the Galerie Louis Carré exposed his latest work. The journal *Arts* greeted the exhibitions with both a review and an interview. The reviewer, Raymond Cogniat, commented:

> Picasso! Braque! Nothing remains of the scandal of 1913: the provocation has evaporated, and one has the impression of standing in front of museum masterpieces . . . However, Picasso, more than any of the other former cubists, continues to arouse polemics. His past is accepted, but it doesn't make his present acceptable . . . The spirit which has driven Picasso through his successive metamorphoses remains as malevolent as ever.[1]

Responding to Cogniat's previous characterization of his work as "monstrous" and "inhuman," Picasso protested to his interviewer, André Warnod: "I'm astonished, because, on the contrary, I always try to observe nature . . . My goal is resemblance, but a resemblance more profound, more real than the real."[2] If this "super-realism" did not correspond to his viewers' expected image of realistic painting, that was not because of any willful distortion on his part, but because painting was inherently incapable of being realistic:

> Nature is one thing, painting another. Painting is an equivalent of nature. The image that we have of nature is something we owe to painters. We only perceive it through them. We usually accept the image of nature found in the classical painters, the painters of the seventeenth century, Poussin. The image they provide is accepted as being what nature really looks like, because their syntax is well established. But there's no proof that this image of nature is any more true than the images created at other epochs. Really, it is just a matter of signs. It has been agreed that this sign represents a tree, this other one a house, a man, a woman – just as, in language, the word 'man' evokes the image of a man in our minds; the word "house," a house; and so on in every language, although it's a different word in every language. It is a convention that's been agreed on; we communicate by using these customary signs.[3]

Leonardo da Vinci had insisted, famously, that painting was a *cosa mentale*, not just a mechanical skill. Likewise, Picasso told Warnod that "A painter's study should be a laboratory. He should invent, not just copy nature like an ape. Painting should be a *jeu d'esprit*."[4]

A similar analysis appears in the theoretical sections of Kahnweiler's 1946 monograph on Juan Gris. Echoing Picasso, Kahnweiler argues that "painters *create* the outer world in visible form, they make us *see* it in the likeness of their works." By inventing new signs or "graphic emblems," artists provide their contemporaries with the means to grasp the visual world around them. Like any other tool, these emblems wear out and need to be replaced. Indeed, "it is by inventing new graphic signs to replace those that are worn out that the painter proclaims his greatness and truly fulfills his role." This process of exhaustion and renewal of signs leads to a "perpetual evolution and alteration of style." No style is more "realistic" than another. Rather, each age finds its own style realistic: "the frescoes of Pompeii, Byzantine seventh-century mosaics, the works of Rembrandt and those of Courbet . . . have each in turn represented perfected 'likenesses' for contemporary spectators."[5] It is art that defines the "reality" of each epoch – except our own. "Why, from Impressionism to Cubism, has the art of our time only been comprehensible to certain people?" asks Kahnweiler. What has gone wrong, he argues, is that the establishment of an official Ecole des Beaux-Arts had frozen the normal evolution of graphic emblems: "the Ecole declared that only the emblems of the classical heritage of the Louis XVI period were valid and thereby established a perpetual convention . . . [It] artificially kept alive a vision that had been dead since the beginning of the nineteenth century and slowed up the reading of any new writing."[6]

Three years later, in his book on Picasso's sculpture, Kahnweiler returned to the argument: "Painting and sculpture are *forms of writing*. Their products are signs, emblems, and not a mirror, more or less distorted, of the external world." Kahnweiler now explicitly attributed this idea to Picasso, associating it with the artist's acquisition in 1912 of an African mask from the Ivory Coast (fig. 131). Studying this mask, Picasso realized that the "details of the sign" were unimportant: even though the face had been reduced to a flat plane adorned with a series of geometric shapes, the viewer could still "read" it as a face. The signs served as a stimulus to memory, so that the viewer constructed an imaginary image of a real face, floating "in front of the actual mask." Henceforth, Kahnweiler suggested, Picasso's work would function on the same principle.[7]

In this account, the relative illegibility of Cubist signs becomes a virtue rather than a defect. It means that viewers will see them first as signs, before seeing the things they signify. This implies, however, that it is not the fault of the Ecole des Beaux Arts that Cubism is hard to read. Cubist pictures and sculptures are hard to read because they are meant to be hard to read.

Here, as in Picasso's 1945 statement, the idea of the sign remains subordinated to the question of Cubism's "difficulty," and to the idea that "reading" a Cubist work depends on a process of mental association. Elsewhere, Picasso invoked the idea of the sign in order to stress the unimportance of the manual aspect of painting: "If I telephone one of my canvases to New York," he told Françoise Gilot, "any housepainter should be able to do it properly. A painting is a sign – just like the sign that indicates a one-way street."[8] The idea of the sign does not, in itself, seem to have carried much weight for Picasso or Kahnweiler; they merely invoked it to make a more important point about something else. Nor did it carry much weight for art historians of the 1950s. John Golding, for instance, in his 1959 history of Cubism, summarized Kahnweiler's account of the Grebo mask and its influence without ever mentioning the word "sign."[9]

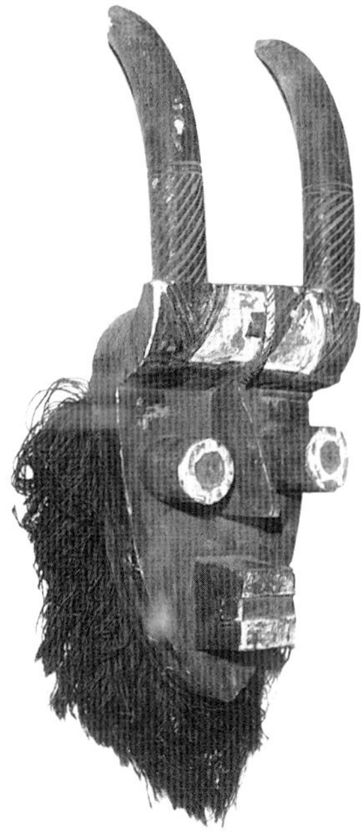

131 Grebo mask owned by Picasso. Wood, paint, vegetable fibers, h. 64 cm. Musée Picasso, Paris

When Robert Rosenblum revived the idea of the sign, in his *Cubism and Twentieth-Century Art* of 1960, he approached it from a completely different direction. Discussing the inscriptions in Cubist paintings such as "*Ma Jolie*" (*Woman with Zither*) (fig. 130), Rosenblum wrote:

> Confronted with these various alphabetical, numerical, and musical symbols, one realizes that the arcs and planes that surround them are also to be read as symbols, and that they are no more to be considered the visual counterpart of reality than a word is to be considered identical with the thing to which it refers . . . By this fusion of the traditional symbols for words, numbers, and music with the newly created geometric symbols of Cubism, Braque and Picasso offer a decisive rejection of one of the fundamentals of Western painting since the Renaissance, namely, that a picture presents an illusion of perceived reality. In its place, we have almost a reversion to a medieval viewpoint in which a pic-

torial image is a symbol and its relation to reality is conceptual.[10]

Where Picasso and Kahnweiler had argued that all art depended on signs to describe reality, Rosenblum proposed a fundamental opposition between conceptual and illusionistic styles. The Renaissance marked a swing of the pendulum from the first pole to the latter; the rise of Cubism revealed that the pendulum, five hundred years later, was swinging in the opposite direction.

The idea of the sign plays a similar role in William Rubin's 1972 discussion of Analytic and Synthetic Cubism. Rubin suggested that the pictorial elements of Analytic Cubism still derived from visual impressions of the object, while Synthetic Cubism utilized "an invented and semiautonomous – hence 'synthetic' – vocabulary of forms." Once he had invented this vocabulary, Picasso could then re-use it to construct new configurations of figures and objects "from preexisting signs and forms."[11] The importance of the sign, here, lay in the fact that it was a purely conceptual element, allowing Picasso to liberate himself from observed reality.

The Saussurean Sign

Meanwhile, philosophical and literary developments in France, seemingly unconnected to art history, were laying the groundwork for a dramatic re-evaluation of the importance of the sign in Cubism. The publication in 1958 of Claude Lévi-Strauss's *Structural Anthropology* sparked what seemed like a revolution in the "human sciences." Using a theoretical model derived from the ideas of the Swiss linguist Ferdinand de Saussure, Lévi-Strauss proposed revolutionary interpretations of traditional anthropological questions ranging from kinship structures and mythologies to tattoos. Beyond the inherent interest of Lévi-Strauss's interpretations, his approach seemed to offer a "structuralist" model that could be adapted to every area of the humanities.[12] The literary critic Roland Barthes, originally a champion of the "writing degree zero" of Alain Robbe-Grillet, then turned to the ideas of Saussure and his followers, summarizing them in a 1964 essay the "Elements of Semiology," followed by the ambitious "Introduction to the Structural Analysis of Narratives" (1966). In 1967, the philosopher Jacques Derrida, hitherto known as the author of a slim volume on Husserl, published a massive tome, *On Grammatology*, proposing a fundamental rethinking of Western metaphysics on the basis of Saussure's linguistics. The psychoanalyst Jacques Lacan, originally associated with the Surrealists, began in the 1950s to use Saussure to explicate Freud, but his approach became more widely influential after the publication of his selected essays in 1966 and his study, *The Four Fundamental Concepts of Psycho-Analysis*, in 1973. Of the founding fathers of structuralism, only Michel Foucault was not overwhelmingly indebted to Saussure.

Born in 1857, Saussure studied comparative philology at Leipzig. He spent the decade 1881–91 in Paris, and then assumed a professorship at the University of Geneva. His *Course in General Linguistics* was published posthumously in 1915. The opening lectures of the course are devoted to phonetics, and have provided the foundation for the modern study of this subject. However, it is the subsequent lectures on the sign and on "synchronic linguistics" that have exerted a broader influence on literary and artistic criticism, beginning with the Russian Formalists of the 1920s. Since Saussure's phonetics provided the model for his analysis of language and the sign, it is necessary to examine them together. Because the Saussurean model has exerted a strong influence on recent interpretations of Cubism, this examination will be especially detailed.

Beginning in the early nineteenth century, philologists realized that they could reconstruct the historical evolution of words and phonemes by comparing similar words from the languages and dialects of different epochs. Saussure felt that this "diachronic" approach, focusing on the evolution of individual words and sounds over a period of time, was inadequate. It neglected the way that a language, at any given moment in its development, functioned as a coherent system. The "diachronic" study of language therefore needed to be supplemented by a "synchronic" approach.

Saussure's synchronic approach to phonetics rests on a scientific taxonomy of the ways that vocal sounds may be produced and altered. All speech depends on the expiration of breath. However, there are seven different points, from the lips to the glottis, where the breath's pathway may be closed or narrowed, inflecting the sound. At any given point, the degree and sequence of aperture or closure will affect the sound produced. Furthermore, the basic act of expiration may be accompanied by vibration of the larynx or by nasal resonance. In principle, the total number of phonemes available for human communication might be calculated by multiplying all of these variables. In practice, any given language utilizes only a subset of these potential phonemes. Certain ways of generating and modifying sounds are emphasized while others are neglected. The phonemes of a given language form a system insofar as they are united by the distinctive features that define them. Conversely, the phonetic systems of different languages are distinguished by different sets of underlying features. A word or a sound cannot be imported from one language into another without being modified to fit into the phonetic system of the new language.[13]

This phonetics provides the model for Saussure's general theory of the sign. A language, he argues, is a system of signs, just as it is a phonetic system. Traditional philosophers focused on the relationship of signifier and signified within the individual sign. Saussure argues that this relationship can only be understood by examining the sign system as a whole. In any given language, the universe of possible phonemes is subdivided into a more limited set of actual phonemes. So, too, in any given language, the universe of possible meanings is subdivided into a more limited set of actual words. With words as with phonemes, this process of subdivision can proceed differently in different languages. Thus, French has one word, "*mouton*," where English has two, "sheep" and "mutton," one signifying the living animal, the other the meat derived from it.[14]

What are the semiological equivalents to the distinctive features of phonetics? The vocal apparatus structures the universe of possible phonemes; what comparable apparatus structures the universe of possible meanings? Saussure offers no answer to these fundamental questions. Instead, he offers a series of assertions based on the putative parallel between sign and phoneme. Earlier philosophers and philologists had argued that the relation between signifier and signified was purely arbitrary. However, as Saussure points out, the organization of language as a system sets a limit to this arbitrariness.[15] The arbitrariness of any given sign is limited, on one hand, by the fact that it belongs to a particular language, and, on the other, by the fact that it differs from all the other signs in that language. Saussure's logic thus demands that every sign within a given system be unique; otherwise, how could it be assigned a unique meaning?[16]

The idea that meaning is generated by difference is a fundamental feature of Saussure's system. In a famous passage, he writes: "In language, there are only differences. Even more important: a difference generally implies positive terms between which the difference is set up; but in language there are only differences *without positive terms*."[17] Saussure offers no evidence for this assertion that the meaning of words derives exclusively from the differences among them. Rather, the idea seems to be derived *a priori* from his phonetic model, summarized on the preceding page of the *Course* by the statement: "Phonemes are characterized not, as one might think, by their own positive quality but simply by the fact that they are distinct. Phonemes are above all else opposing, relative, and negative entities."[18]

Saussure's own analysis of the phoneme disproves this statement, since, as he demonstrates, any given phoneme can be defined positively as a combination of distinctive features. Insofar as a phoneme is defined by a unique combination of features, it may be said to be defined by its difference from all the other phonemes of the language, but this seems a rather tortured way of looking at the matter. Saussure's statement about "negative entities" may have been inspired by something more specific: the way that nasal resonance and vibration of the larynx function as distinctive features. As he points out on several occasions, these features may be either present or absent within a given phoneme, and their absence is generally as significant as their presence. In English, for instance, the phoneme "t" can be defined as a "d" minus the vibration of the larynx. The distinctive feature, in this case, has no material presence (that is, no sound) but exists as a pure difference, perceptible only because we are intuitively familiar with the larger system of English phonemes.[19] However, it is not the case that all phonemes include a purely negative element of this type, and even in the case of the "t" there are other defining features (alveolar point of occlusion, fricative expiration) that are unquestionably positive.

The idea that "phonemes are above all else opposing, relative, and negative entities" is thus a wildly inaccurate generalization; even more so, the idea that "in language there are only differences *without positive terms*." Saussure here seems to have been seduced by a glamorous philosophical idea that his own work does not really support. His use of other quasi-philosophical terms like "presence" and "absence" is also inconsistent. They are invoked, for instance, in his discussion of "Syntagmatic and Associative Relations." Syntagmatic relations are those governing the series of phonemes in a word or the series of words in a sentence. In contrast, associative relations link phonemes that might be substituted for one another within a word (forming a new but related word), or words that might be substituted for one another within a sentence (forming a new but related sentence). Saussure writes: "The syntagmatic relation is *in praesentia.* It is based on two or more terms that occur in effective series. Against this, the associative relation unites terms *in absentia* in a potential mnemonic series."[20] This seems clear enough.

In another passage of the *Course,* however, Saussure writes: "Language is a system of interdependent terms in which the value of each term results solely from the simultaneous presence of the others."[21] Evidently, he is discussing the importance of the associative relations among words – the way that the meaning of any given word depends on its similarity to and difference from other words associated with it. But Saussure seems to contradict himself by discussing these associations in terms of presence rather than absence.

Of course, the contradiction is superficial: what he means is that the related words are present in the memory of the listener, even if they are absent from the sentence in which the word is spoken. The contradiction is important only if you take "presence" and "absence" as metaphysical terms, and look for metaphysical significance in statements such as "language is a system of interdependent terms in which the value of each term results solely from the simultaneous presence of the others." Unfortunately, this is exactly the way in which Saussure has been read. The attractiveness of Saussurean linguistics as a model for criticism and philosophy rests precisely on the vast philosophical implications that seem to emerge from his analyses of language and the sign. The writings of Jacques Derrida, for instance, constitute a gigantic fugue expanding on Saussure's discussion of "difference," and the problems evident in Saussure's use of the term are multiplied many times over in the "deconstructionist" criticism deriving from Derrida.

Similarly, in his influential 1967 essay, "The Death of the Author," Roland Barthes used the idea of a self-contained system of language to argue that "it is language that speaks, not the author" – that there was no such thing as originality, because every text was merely "a tissue of quotations." The recombination of existing words and phrases, Barthes implied, could not possibly result in a new meaning.[22] In any case, the idea or feeling that the writer was trying to express could never be anything more than an entry from a "ready-formed" dictionary. "Life," Barthes declared, "never does more than imitate the book, and the book itself is only a tissue of signs, an imitation that is lost, infinitely deferred."[23] (Meanwhile, Barthes's American contemporary, Harold Bloom, argued in *The Anxiety of Influence* that great writers were precisely those who could rework the existing tradition in order to create something personal and new.[24])

For better or for worse, as the tidal wave of structuralism traveled outward in the 1960s and '70s, art critics and art historians began to re-examine the role of the sign in the visual arts. The structuralist interpretation of Cubism seems to have been launched by the critic Pierre Dufour in a 1969 article on "Cubism as Contemporary Art." Noting that 1907 was "the year both of the *Demoiselles d'Avignon* and of Saussure's first *Course,*" Dufour argued that Picasso's discovery of "the arbitrariness of forms" was the visual equivalent of Saussure's discovery of "the arbitrariness of the sign." Recalling Kahnweiler's analysis of Cubism as a form of "writing," Dufour described the Cubist revolution as a "liquidation" of the representational image "in favor of a construction assembled from relatively arbitrary elements." Traditional painting, an art of "nuance and resemblance" was exhausted; in its place, Picasso showed the way toward a "*painting of difference,* founded on the deliberate creation of a gap between the sign and the thing signified."[25]

However, Dufour argued, Picasso did not merely adopt a semiological model; he used Cubism to revise the nature of the sign. In an ordinary, utilitarian sign, Dufour noted, "the signifier serves merely to efficiently communicate the signified, but is in itself without interest or value." In the Cubist sign, however, "no sooner has the signified been communicated . . . than there is a turn back toward the signifier." Picasso and Braque chose banal subjects for their pictures, Dufour suggested, precisely so that the viewer could concentrate on "the originality of the sign."[26]

A 1973 colloquium at the Université de Saint-Etienne revealed the influence of Dufour's interpretation. Jean Laude opened the colloquium with a paper on "Picasso and Braque, 1910–1914: the Transformation of Signs." Following Dufour, Laude highlighted the importance of Kahnweiler's 1948 discussion of the Grebo mask, and argued that Picasso and Braque had adopted their simple, repetitious vocabulary of wineglasses, bottles, and musicians precisely in order to focus the viewer's interpretation on their sign language, and not on the things it represented. Laude's statement that a Cubist work "is a combination of signs whose meaning cannot be grasped outside of the work itself" echoed

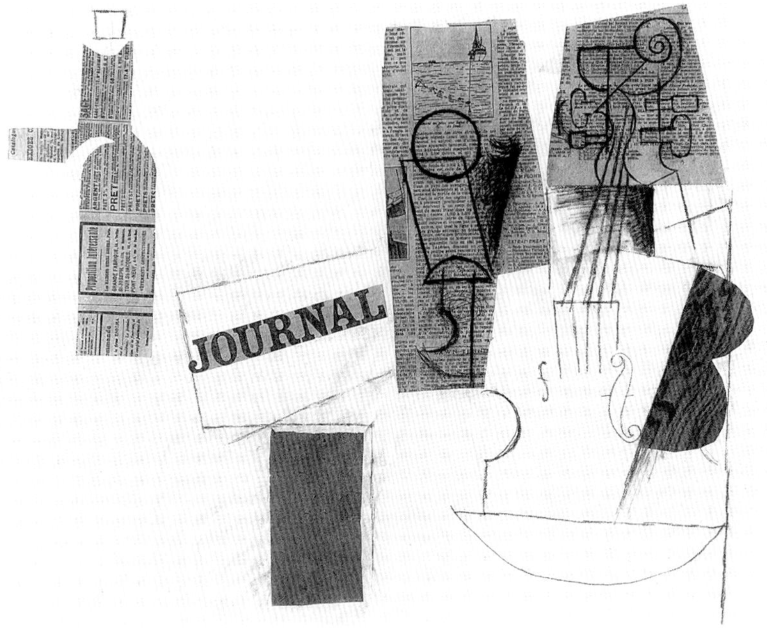

132 Picasso. *Siphon, Glass, Newspaper, and Violin.* Paris, after December 2, 1912. Charcoal and pasted papers on paper, 47 × 62.5 cm. Moderna Museet, Stockholm

Saussure's insistence that the meaning of an individual word can only be understood by analyzing its place within the language as a whole.[27] It was this "new conception of the sign," Laude argued, that led Picasso and Braque "to give up the practice of working from the motif" or even from a "mental image" of the motif. As Rubin had suggested, once they had arrived at a coherent visual language, they could create new images simply by re-arranging signs they had previously invented.[28]

Laude saw Cubism as an exemplar of the widespread tendency, after the turn of the century, to think "not about things but about the relationships among them," also evident in the pictures of Matisse and in the writings of Sigmund Freud, Marcel Mauss – and Ferdinand de Saussure.[29] Picasso and Braque had created their pioneering works before the publication of Saussure's lectures, so they could not possibly have been influenced by his ideas, even at secondhand. However, Laude pointed out, the parallels between Cubist practice and Saussurean theory were immediately perceived by the literary critics who became known as the Russian Formalists, and exerted an important influence on their thinking.[30]

Another paper at the Saint-Etienne symposium, delivered by Françoise Will-Levaillant, addressed "The Letter in Cubist Painting." For Will-Levaillant, too, the confrontation between "plastic" and "linguistic" signs in the Cubist paintings and *papiers collés* of 1911–13 manifested a fundamental shift from illusionism to a new mode of representation based on linguistic principles. Citing Rosenblum's argument that the "arcs and planes" of a painting like *Le Portugais* were "no more to be considered the visual counterpart of reality than a word is to be considered identical with the thing to which it refers," Will-Levaillant pointed out that the introduction of literal printed letters in the form of newspaper clippings was accompanied by an ironic subversion of their representational value. Although the headline "Journal" in *Siphon, Glass, Newspaper, and Violin* (fig. 132), indicates the presence of a newspaper, the surrounding fragments of newsprint serve to represent a siphon, a wineglass, and the head of a violin – anything but a newspaper. "The object," Will-Levaillant wrote, "thus contains an internal contradiction of a semantic nature. The object is simultaneously designated and negated. Present as material, it has lost its function."[31]

Unquestionably, Picasso's picture is intended as a *jeu d'esprit,* forcing the viewer to recognize the difference between the "presence" of the motif that is represented and the "presence" of the material used to represent it. But is there anything specifically linguistic or "semantic" about this *jeu d'esprit,* beyond the fact that Picasso has used a piece

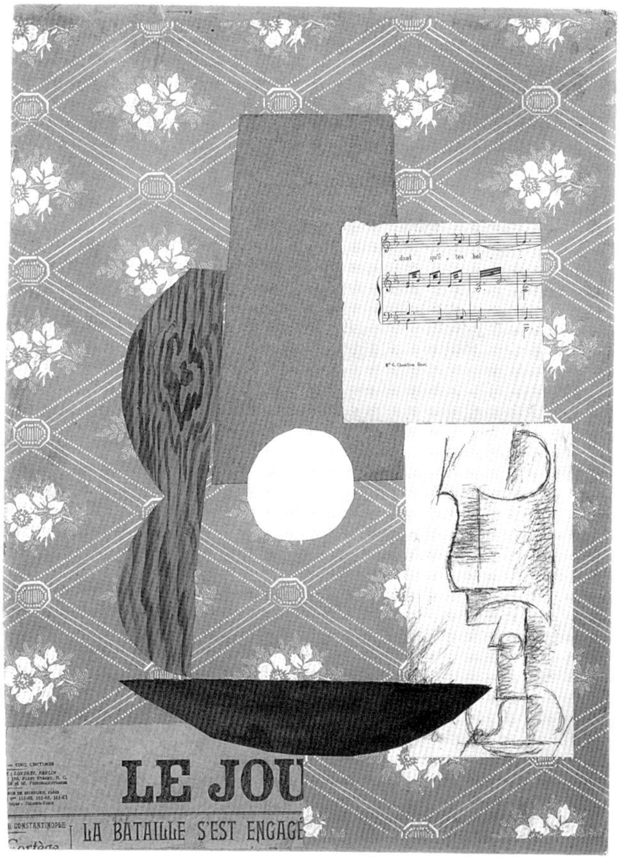

133 Picasso. *Guitar, Sheet Music, and Glass.* Paris, after November 18, 1912. Pasted paper, gouache, and charcoal on paper, 47.9 × 35.5 cm. D.R. 513. Collection of the McNay Art Museum, San Antonio, Bequest of Marion Koogler McNay

of newspaper? In another *papier collé* (fig. 133), the body of a guitar is represented, in part, by a piece of decorative wallpaper, while the adjacent newspaper simply represents itself. The visual joke is the same, but the materials of the *papier collé* can no longer be relied upon to argue that it is linguistic in character. Instead, you would have to make a broader argument. You might say, following Saussure, that it is in the nature of words to "represent" things quite different from themselves: the word "guitar," for instance, has nothing in common with the physical object it stands for. If you take this as a model of a linguistic relationship, then any sign that differs dramatically from its referent can be described as a linguistic sign. Furthermore, if you believe, following Saussure and Mallarmé, that the presence of the word "guitar" indicates the absence of the actual object, then you are entitled to say that the presence of the wallpaper in Picasso's *papier collé* indicates the absence of the guitar represented by it.[32] However, you might also say, with equal validity, that the presence of the wallpaper indicates the presence of the guitar in the picture.

Here, as in Saussure's text, the words "presence" and "absence" have effectively lost their meaning. What is actually happening, in the *papier collé* as in language, is that one thing is being associated with something else; the terms "presence" and "absence" do not add any actual information to the description of this relationship. Similarly, when Will-Levaillant writes that the newspaper in *Siphon, Glass, Newspaper, and Violin* "is simultaneously designated and negated. Present as material, it has lost its function," all she is really saying is that the newspaper no longer represents a newspaper, but stands for something else instead. There are no larger conclusions about "presence" and "absence" to be drawn from this fact.

The topic of signs and Cubism was reopened by Pierre Daix in the text accompanying the *catalogue raisonné* of Picasso's Cubist work that he and Joan Rosselet published in 1979. Like Will-Levaillant, Daix grafts a structuralist perspective onto Rosenblum's original perception that the "arcs and planes" in Picasso's pictures were just as much symbols as the inscriptions surrounding them.[33] To some extent, the language of structuralism here serves to recycle an earlier, formalist interpretation of modern art, as when Daix writes that

> Painting is reduced to the signifier, its material support. Neither the thing signified by perspective, nor the organizing anecdote, nor a resemblance to objects or persons intervenes in the way the spectator relates to the subject the artist submits to him. Here we have the final stage in the evolution initiated by Manet's pictorial silence.[34]

As the reference to Manet suggests, Daix is here reinscribing Cubism within the critical tradition that sees modern art as an evolution toward "pure" painting.

Elsewhere, however, the language of the sign facilitates observations that would be difficult to express in the older language of formalism. Daix writes, for instance, that "The remarkable thing about Braque's first *papier collé* (fig. 134) . . . is that the introduction of strips of frieze imitating wood is independent of the form . . . [The strips] convey the sign 'wood,' information about the presence of wood,

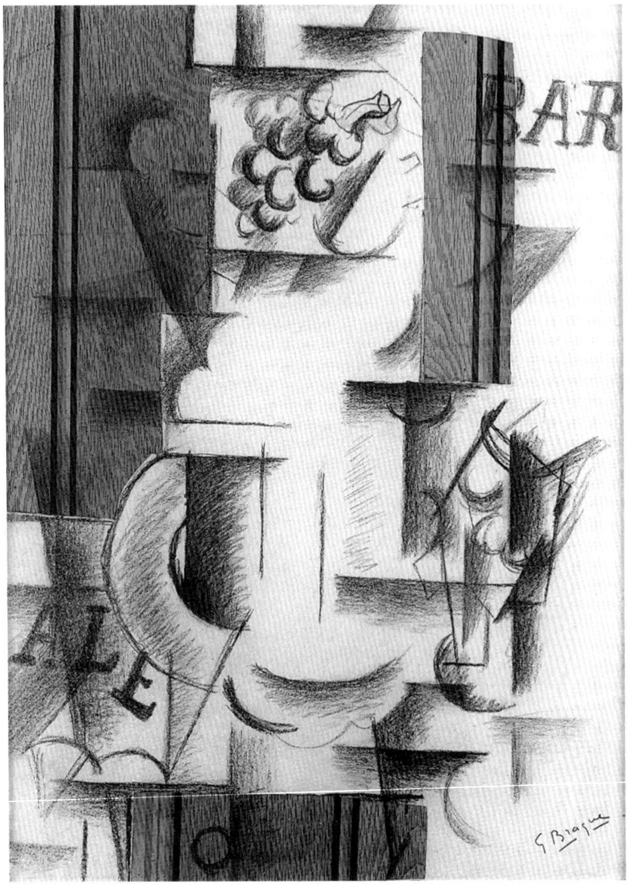

134 Braque. *Fruit Dish and Glass.* Sorgues, early September 1912. Charcoal and pasted paper on paper, 62 × 44.5 cm. M.-F./C. 1. Private collection

which we relate mentally to the table," even though they are not attached to the table.[35] There would be no simple way to express this idea in terms of the traditional opposition between representation and abstraction, since the strips are representational in one way (their texture) and abstract in another (their form). The term "sign" makes it possible to express their character and function clearly and concisely. It is not clear, however, that the wood-grained strips are Saussurean signs.

In contrast, Daix's analysis of Picasso's *Guitar, Sheet Music, and Glass* (see fig. 133) seems to draw directly on the Saussurean concept of the system. Picasso was learning, Daix writes, "that blanks can be expressed by filled-in areas, or vice-versa. It was not, then, the original nature of the elements that was decisive, but how they related to one another . . . The space of the guitar is indicated by a blank, a void; on the other hand, the round hole in the middle of the sound-box is painted in as a solid."[36] Daix echoes Laude's observation that Picasso, like Saussure, is thinking "not about things but about the relationships among them." His description of the disk representing the sound-hole also recalls Will-Levaillant's description of the newspaper in another *papier collé*: the disk is "present as material" but has "lost its function" in the sense that it now depicts an empty space instead of a solid object. Indeed, the only thing that keeps Daix's analysis from seeming thoroughly Saussurean is the absence of the word "sign."

The publication of the Daix-Rosselet catalogue in 1979, followed by the Museum of Modern Art's enormous Picasso retrospective of 1980, led American scholars to rethink many aspects of Picasso's career. It was at this moment that the structuralist interpretation of Cubism, inspired by Saussure, began to displace the formalist interpretation hitherto dominant in the United States and England.[37] Two articles by Rosalind Krauss, a formidable critic, and editor of the journal *October*, played a key role in this transition. Krauss credited Daix with advancing a Saussurean interpretation of Cubism, but criticized him for an insufficiently profound reading of Saussure.[38]

Krauss's reading focuses on four aspects of the Saussurean model. The first is simply the idea of language as a coherent system of signs, unified by an underlying set of distinctive features. Like Laude, Krauss sees this systemic approach as a feature linking Cubism with other intellectual phenomena of the turn of the century. To the examples given by Laude, she adds the system of art history itself, as formulated by Heinrich Wölfflin: "If we take Wölfflin as the father of art-historical structuralism, we realize that his 'principles of art history' amount to a code, a set of bipolar oppositions that constitute the formal language or system out of which art writes itself as history." The oppositions in question are those familiar to every graduate student: "line/color, closed/open, planarity/recession, unity/multiplicity, clear/indistinct." What is new is Krauss's assertion that the visual language of Cubism is generated by the same set of oppositions – a "differential system," as she calls it.[39]

Saussure began the *Course on General Linguistics* by listing the basic phonemes of the Indo-European languages.[40] If Cubism is a language, it presumably consists of corresponding units. Krauss does not attempt to enumerate these "graphemes," as one might call them. Nor does she explain exactly how they are derived from the Wölfflinian set of opposing qualities. Instead, she argues that Cubism is linguistic because it exemplifies Saussure's principle that "In language there are only differences . . . without positive terms." The sign is meaningful because it represents "a choice from a set of possibilities, with meaning determined by the very terms *not* chosen." To illustrate this play of pure difference, Krauss chooses the example of "the traffic-light system where red means 'stop' only in relation to an alternative of green as 'go.'"[41]

This is an unfortunate choice of example. The color language of traffic lights is quite clearly founded on the idea that red, the color of blood, indicates danger. In rural and suburban areas, a blinking red light often appears by itself as a "stop" sign. In cities, the same street-corner pole often supports both a traffic signal for cars, alternating between red, yellow, and green lights, and a "WALK/DON'T WALK" sign for pedestrians, where "DON'T WALK" is illuminated by a red light and "WALK" is illuminated by a white light. In both cases, red means "stop." The other colors are chosen to contrast with red; so "go" can be indicated by either white or green.

Next, Krauss sets out to illustrate "the systematic play of difference" in Cubism by discussing a *papier collé* of winter 1912–13, *Bowl with Fruit, Violin, and Wineglass* (fig. 135). As she notes, "the single patch of wood-grained paper ambiguously allocated to table and/or musical instrument composes the sign for open, as opposed to closed form. Yet the piece of wood graining terminates in a complex contour that produces the closed silhouette of a neighboring form." Here, as in other Cubist *papiers collés*, "each element is fully diacritical, instantiating both line and color, closure and openness, plane and recession. Each signifier thus yields a match pair of formal signifieds."[42] This may be true, but it does not prove what Krauss wants it to prove. If every element in a Cubist *papier collé* represents two contradictory qualities, then its real-world equivalent would be a traffic light in which "red" indicated both "stop" and "go." This "Cubist" traffic light would be an interesting object, but it would not demonstrate that "red" was defined by its opposition to "green."

To put it another way, if Krauss wants to prove that Cubism functions like a Saussurean system, she needs to demonstrate, not that "closed" is opposed to "open," but that "wood-graining" is opposed to some other signifier within the *papier collé* – say, to blank paper – and that this opposi-

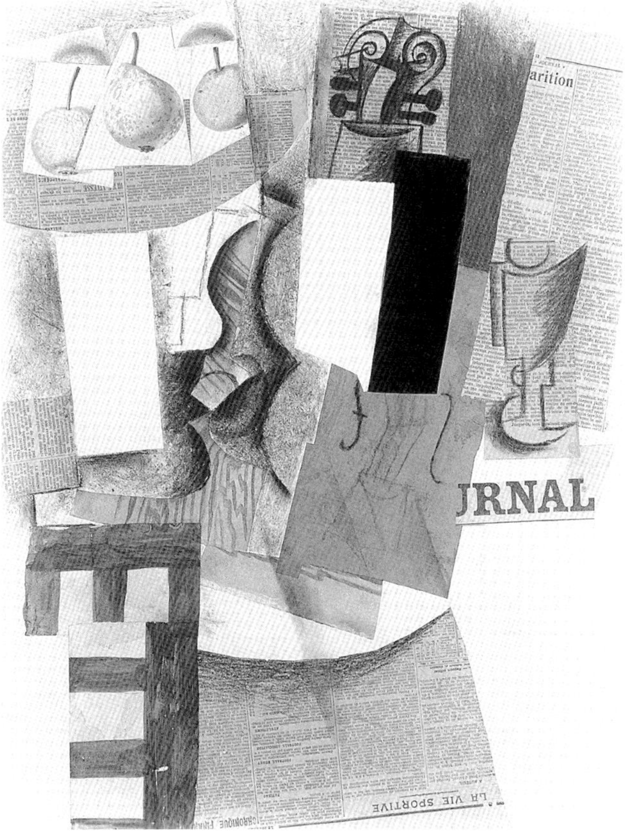

135 Picasso. *Bowl with Fruit, Violin, and Wineglass*. Paris, begun after December 2, 1912; completed after January 21, 1913. Pasted paper, watercolor, chalk, oil, and charcoal on cardboard, 65 × 50.5 cm. D.R. 530. Philadelphia Museum of Art. A. E. Gallatin Collection

tion between wood-graining and blankness serves consistently to signify something within the composition. It might be that wood-graining signified solid objects and blank paper signified empty space, or vice-versa. Consistency is all that matters: as Saussure said, everything relating to language comes down to "the limiting of arbitrariness."[43] What Krauss has demonstrated, on the contrary, is the efflorescence of arbitrariness within Cubism. The fact that wood-graining can mean one thing here and another thing there makes it precisely not like a Saussurean language.

The linguistic character of the Cubist sign is also manifest, for Krauss, in the opposition between the "material" nature of the signifier and the "immaterial" nature of the signified. For instance, an opaque piece of newsprint may be used "to construct space as penetrable or transparent."[44]

True – but it is not clear that this contrast between material sign and immaterial signified is limited to Cubism. In a painting by Rembrandt or Monet, a heavily impastoed brushstroke may represent an immaterial gleam of light. In support of her argument, Krauss also points out that Picasso often represents the sound-holes of his violins by two *f*-shaped marks of different sizes. The *f*s are flat, and they are often inscribed on a single, flat plane. However, she argues, their size difference functions as a sign for foreshortening, obliquely informing the viewer that the violin is turned in space, angling away from the picture plane. "'Depth' is thus written on the very place [the collaged plane] from which it is . . . most absent," she concludes.[45] (Perhaps, although since Picasso told Françoise Gilot that he always made a point of using different signs to represent the symmetrical features of the human body – eyes, breasts, and so on – it is also possible that he made the *f*s larger and smaller simply in order to vary them.[46]) But let us say that Krauss is correct, and the *f*s, drawn in different sizes, are material signs for the immaterial concept of depth. Then traditional perspective, which uses drawn or painted lines to evoke the transparent volume of space, must also qualify as a linguistic system.

Finally, Krauss argues that Cubist collage exemplifies "the *impersonal* operations of language." She supports her analysis by appealing to Daix's earlier structuralist analysis:

> In his discussion of classic collage, Daix repeatedly stresses the depersonalization of Picasso's drawings in these works, his use of preexistent, industrialized elements (which Daix goes so far as to call *readymade*), and his mechanization of the pictorial surfaces – in order to insist on the objective status of this art of language . . . language as a synchronic repertory of terms into which each individual must assimilate himself, so that from the point of view of structure, a speaker does not so much speak, as he is spoken by, language."[47]

Here, Krauss echoes the aphorism that Barthes had coined to sum up Saussure's ideas: "it is language that speaks, not the author." Poets writing in English or French do not invent new languages; they use the already existing vocabulary and syntax of English or French. So too, Krauss suggests, Picasso and Braque were utilizing a pre-existent visual language: their *papiers collés* of 1912–13 have a mechanical, impersonal look because they have given up trying to hide this fact.

It is true that Picasso and Braque cultivated a mechanical, impersonal look in some of their work of 1912–13.[48] However, Krauss seriously distorts the evidence in order to suggest that they were merely assimilating a ready-made language. When Daix says that Picasso and Braque used pre-existent signs, he is citing Rubin, who argued that 1912–13 Cubism utilized an "invented" vocabulary of forms, that these forms were "semiautonomous" from the real world, and that new compositions could therefore be constructed from these "preexisting signs" without the need for new observations of reality.[49] Indeed, signs and structures are repeated from one work to the next, in a way that compels the viewer to recognize Picasso's and Braque's use of a consistent visual language – but this language is one that the artists themselves have invented. The literary equivalent would be a poet who invented his own version of Esperanto, and then wrote a series of poems using it. This would demonstrate, not the "death of the author," but a tremendous expansion of authorial ambition. Indeed, Kahnweiler comments that, when Picasso employed the deliberately inartistic medium of *papier collé*,

> He was really concerned to be master of his means, to make his grip felt, to debunk the idea of "noble means," to prove that the painter can express his emotion just as well in terms of paper and cardboard . . . as in oil paint or gouache. It was one of those romantic, ironic gestures calculated to display the pre-eminence of the creator's personality over his creation.[50]

It is always Picasso who speaks, not tradition. (As for Daix's use of the term "ready-made," what he actually says is that Picasso's and Braque's collages sometimes include "ready-made fabric."[51])

After Krauss, the most important writer on Cubism and the sign has been Yve-Alain Bois, who addresses the subject in two major essays, "Kahnweiler's Lesson" and "The Semiology of Cubism," the first published in 1987 and the second in 1993.[52] Written with tremendous verve and erudition, these essays cover a broad range of topics from the influence of African sculpture on Cubism to the relation between Cubism and Russian Formalism. The heart of the first essay is an analysis of Kahnweiler's discussion of the Grebo mask, and its influence on Picasso. Bois argues that, when Kahnweiler said that the mask led Picasso to realize that "painting and sculpture are *forms of writing*," what he meant by "writing" was a system of signs akin to Saussure's linguistic model.[53]

In his second essay, Bois seems to turn from criticism to Cubism itself, focusing on a phenomenon that had received surprisingly little attention from earlier critics: the constant metamorphoses evident in Picasso's work of 1912–14. Bois points out that Picasso's development of a simplified sign language was accompanied by the discovery that "a bottle is like a guitar is like a face," or, more precisely, that the same forms used to describe a guitar could also be used to describe a face or a bottle.[54] This discovery of the possibility of visual metamorphosis was a key development, setting the stage both for Picasso's Cubist works of 1912–14 and for his Surrealist masterpieces of the 1920s and '30s. However, Bois seems to be less interested in tracing Picasso's visual exploration of metamorphosis than in arguing that it depends on a semiological model of representation.

There are two problems with this argument. One is that the tendency toward metamorphosis – which Bois refers to as "polysemy" or "metaphorical displacement"[55] – is evident in Picasso's work well before the moment in 1912 when the Grebo mask is said to have offered up its semiological revelation. As Bois himself notes, one of Picasso's studies for the *Demoiselles d'Avignon* seems to show a head becoming a torso, and another 1907 drawing shows an "African" head becoming both a leaf and a flowerpot.[56] And a certain lability of meaning seems inherent in the geometric language of 1908–11 Cubism. Bois's solution to this problem is to appeal to a different analysis of the sign – the analysis offered by the eccentric American philosopher Charles Sanders Peirce in his writings of the 1860s through '90s.

Peirce argued that a sign could be either an "icon," an "index," or a "symbol." An icon is a sign that resembles the thing it represents. An index is a sign that has a causal relationship with the object it represents; a bullet-hole, for instance, is an indexical "sign" of a shot. A symbol is a "conventional sign" such as a word, linked to its referent neither by resemblance nor by causality, but by the rules of a system or language.[57] What Peirce means by "symbol" is thus very close to what Saussure means by "sign." Beyond this, there is very little overlap in their ideas. Peirce is interested in signs insofar as they have a bearing on the empiricist theory of knowledge and perception, which he traces from William of Ockham, through Thomas Hobbes, down to Locke, Hume, and Berkeley.[58] Peirce is not interested in the conventions of language as such, and it does not occur to him to try to analyze them. In effect, Saussure's analysis begins where Peirce's leaves off.

Peirce is useful to Bois because the notion of the icon makes it possible to combine the old idea of resemblance with the new idea of signification. Even if the forms in early Cubism resemble their referents, they can nonetheless be called "signs." Bois thus explains the metamorphoses in Picasso's 1908–12 pictures as a result of "the elasticity of iconicity."[59] This allows Bois to distinguish between the metamorphoses of 1908–12 and those of 1912–13. The former can be explained by "the elasticity of iconicity," while the latter reflect "the transforming power of the semiological principle of the arbitrariness of the sign."[60]

This brings us to the second major problem with Bois's semiological reading of Cubism: the concept of the arbitrariness of the sign simply does not explain the phenomenon of metamorphosis that he wants it to explain. Trying to make it do so, Bois is forced to misrepresent the art in question. To prove that the Saussurean model is relevant, he argues that the Grebo mask (see fig. 131) demonstrates, not only that painting and sculpture are forms of writing, but that they are forms of writing capable of employing completely arbitrary signs. "There is no relationship of similarity," Bois writes, "between these protruding cylinders of the Grebo mask, and the eyes of any human being (in the generic sense), in the same way that there is no connection between the word 'tree,' and the mental image or concept we form of a tree when we hear or read that word."[61] Once Picasso has grasped this lesson, he begins making *papiers collés* like *Guitar, Sheet Music, and Glass* (see fig. 133) which exemplify a "new system" of figuration based on "the arbitrariness of the sign."[62]

However, the signs utilized in the works Bois cites are not completely arbitrary. He himself writes: "I have to admit that I have cheated. Speaking of the eyes of the Grebo mask, I have insisted on their nature as protruding cylinders to mark their arbitrary nature, and feigned to discard as irrelevant the fact their painted section, two concentric circles, bears a direct resemblance to the human eye."[63] Similarly, it is hard to locate any completely arbitrary signs in *Guitar, Sheet Music, and Glass.* The curved pieces of paper at left and bottom correspond to the curves of a guitar's body. The straight-edged trapezoid at top corresponds to its neck, straight-edged and gently narrowing. (The two rectangular sheets of paper at right are not curved, because they do not represent the guitar; one is a piece of sheet music, the other bears a drawing of a glass.) Like the eyes of the Grebo mask, each element of the *papier collé* has something in common with its real prototype, although its other qualities (color, texture, proportion) may differ. As Bois himself writes, Picasso is "interested in defining the minimum level of semantic articulation a shape is obliged to perform to be read as a sign."[64] In other words: what is the minimum of resemblance necessary for us to recognize a shape as a sign for something? We are still in the realm of the elastic icon, not the arbitrary sign.

The argument that 1912–13 Cubism employs arbitrary signs is in fact untenable. Instead of trying to defend it, Bois attempts to demonstrate that Picasso's pictorial language is semiological by dint of the "differential" nature of the signs composing it.[65] Bois explains the meaning of "differential" with the same unfortunate example as Krauss: "Signs are constituted by differences or oppositions, not by their substance . . . the red light means 'stop' only because it is opposed to the green light, meaning 'go.'"[66] Leaving aside the faulty example, Bois seems to mean that the units of a sign system, like the phonemes of a spoken language, are defined by a series of underlying oppositions,

Bois does not try to define these underlying oppositions, or to enumerate the units composing the language of Cubism. (Indeed, pressed on this question at the symposium where "The Semiology of Cubism" was first presented, Bois replied that, "Trying to find the phoneme in the Cubist painting would be atrociously stupid."[67]) Instead, he again follows Krauss in arguing that the linguistic character of a signifier may be demonstrated by the fact that it has multiple signifieds. "The differential nature of the sign," he writes, is demonstrated by its "exchangeability."[68] Pursuing this point, he discusses *Guitar, Sheet Music, and Glass* in a fashion that echoes both Daix and Krauss:

> The non-substantial character of the sign is emphasized via a general polysemy: the decorative pasted paper which constitutes the background is indeed materially present, but its trapezoid section sandwiched between the glass and the wood-grain paper becomes at once a sign of depth and, being utterly flat, its absolute negation. It becomes that paradox: an opaque yet transparent body.[69]

I have already noted the logical error here: proving that a red traffic light means both "stop" and "go" is not the same as proving that red is defined by its opposition to green.

However, Bois also offers two new arguments for the linguistic character of Cubism that deserve careful consideration. The first is that the meaning of the sign depends on its context. Kahnweiler and Laude had made the same observation about Cubism, but Bois was the first to link it to Saussure, who had suggested that the value of a given sign might depend not only on its place in the language as a whole but also on its position within a given sequence of signs – that is, its context.[70] Similarly, as Bois points out, the "section of a circle" near the bottom of *Guitar, Sheet Music, and Glass* appears with different meanings in different paintings. In Picasso's 1908–09 *Bread and Fruit Dish on a Table*, it stands for "the drop leaf of a table."[71] Through the "multiplicative" play of signs in *Guitar, Sheet Music, and Glass*, it comes instead to represent the bottom of a guitar.[72]

Bois also cites another passage from Saussure that seems uncannily appropriate to the Cubist sign. As noted earlier, Saussure thinks of meaning as something that arises from a process of division. New words are created as a language matures, drawing finer and finer distinctions. But this gain is also a loss. As Saussure says: "If you augment language by one sign, you diminish in the same proportion the [value] of the others. Reciprocally, if only two signs had been chosen . . . all the [concrete] significations would have had to be divided between these two signs. One would have designated one half of the objects, the other, the other half."[73]

This language with only two signs is obviously a fictional construct. But it corresponds in many ways to the visual language of Cubism, with its limited number of geometric forms, each possessing a broad range of potential meaning. As Bois writes:

> The more differentiated the value system is, the less ambiguous or rich will be the sign and the more rigid the rules governing the creation of new signs. The more open the system is, on the contrary, the greater the possibility of inventing new signs and, more important, of having the same sign performing entirely different functions and bearing entirely different significations.[74]

This seems to describe exactly how Cubism works: the deliberate abandonment of precise realistic description opens up an unprecedented potential for visual metaphor and metamorphosis.

These two ideas – the idea of a primitive language of ambiguous signs, and the dependence of meaning on context – are valuable contributions to the understanding of Cubism. However, it is not clear that they are valuable enough to make it worth adopting the complex theoretical apparatus of Saussurean linguistics, especially since so many elements of Saussure's system – the differential definition of the signs, its arbitrariness, the fixity of the code to which it belongs – do not correspond to anything in Cubism. There is also the chronological problem: even the proponents of a Saussurean interpretation of Cubism do not argue that Picasso could literally have been influenced by his ideas. Implicitly or explicitly, they fall back on Jean Laude's argument that both Cubism and Saussurean linguistics are examples of the tendency, after the turn of the twentieth century to think "not about things but about the relationships among them."

It is a mistake, however, to see this as an either/or situation, as if we had either to accept the Saussurean model or to reject the linguistic interpretation altogether. There are, after all, other ways of looking at language. More to the point, the late nineteenth century saw a rich and varied debate about the genesis and development of language. Saussure's system of structural linguistics, elaborated at the end of his career, was assembled from the ideas and observations of the earlier participants in this debate. If there are striking resonances between certain aspects of Cubism and certain elements of Saussure's doctrine, it may be because Picasso was influenced, at second or thirdhand, by some of the same ideas about language.

Language and the Sign

In the second half of the nineteenth century, two distinct groups of writers addressed the nature of the sign. For critics working in the tradition of associationist philosophy, the sign was the basic unit of human thought. Everything experienced via the senses was reduced, in the mind, to a sign; reactions between signs made up the process of thought, which could be expressed either as action or as speech. This associationist approach encouraged what might be called a psychological interpretation of language and the sign. In contrast, when linguists examined the relationship between sign and thought, their analyses reflected the principles of philology rather than psychology. The comparative study of modern and ancient languages had yielded astonishing insights into the evolution of phonetics, syntax, and etymology. Insofar as the process of thinking depended on words and signs, it seemed reasonable to believe that philology, rather than psychology, might prove itself the true "science of thought."[75]

The associationist approach to language is summed up in Hippolyte Taine's influential volume *On Intelligence*, published in 1870.[76] Taine here offers two different accounts of language, one describing its acquisition by the child, the other describing the birth and death of signs in the minds of adults.

According to Taine, the child's acquisition of language begins with a handful of words, each describing a broad category of things that seem similar to the child. For instance, adults may teach a child to use the word *papa* to refer to his own father, but: "When another person – that is, one similar in appearance, with a long coat, a beard, and loud voice – enters the room, he calls him also papa. The name was an individual one; he has made it general." In this case, the name's extension to a broader category is easy to understand; in other cases, the child creates categories using a logic markedly different from that of the adult world. Taine mentions a small boy he knew who used the term *fafer* (from *chemin-de-fer*, "railroad") to describe a steamboat and a coffeepot – "everything that hissed or smoked, or made a noise." Subjected to a liquid enema, the boy coined the word *zizi*, inspired by the noise of the syringe. Henceforth, "all long, hollow, slender objects – a scissors-sheath, a cigar-tube, a trumpet, were for him *zizi*, and he treated them all with distrust." For the little boy, Taine notes, "these two reigning ideas, the *zizi* and the *fafer*, were the two cardinal points of his intelligence, and from them he set out to comprehend and name other things."[77]

The logic of these fundamental categories is metaphorical: a coffeepot is a *fafer* because it is like a tiny locomotive. As the child masters adult language, Taine says, "the two or three dominant words lose their absolute preponderance, the general words limit their too extensive meaning, gain precision" and become arranged into "names of smaller classes." Taken to its logical extreme, this process would yield an adult language with a vocabulary large enough for every object to have its own unique name. But this linguistic precision would be purchased at the expense of metaphor.[78]

Where the categories of the child's thought derive from the perception of superficial similarities, the categories of adult thought are supposed to reflect the recognition of some essential quality linking all the members of a group. This is still a creative process. Indeed, Taine presents the artist's search for the essence of his motif as the prototype of linguistic creativity in general, stressing the extent to which it depends not merely on observation but on identification with the motif:

> The whole body speaks; often, if at a loss for a word, a gesture expresses the meaning; a grimace, a start, an imitative noise, becomes a sign in place of a name; to represent an avenue of old oaks, the stature becomes erect, the feet are planted firmly on the ground, the arms extend stiffly, or form sharp angles at the elbows.

"This mimicry," Taine comments, "is natural language."[79] But it is also the model for language in general: in "the imitative gesture of the artist, the metaphorical half-sight of the poet, the expressive pantomime of the savage, the animated tones of the impassioned man, the dry tone and abstract language of the calm reasoner . . . the mental operation is always the same." Even the cold, logical process of induction requires sentiment and metaphor. What exactly happens when we go through "a series of similar objects," seeking a "general idea" that unites them? Taine's answer is that, for each member of the series, we find "some principal and striking trait," which we note "by a familiar or exaggerated word." The result may be merely an "abstract name," but it will have been arrived at by "expressive comparisons and metaphors."[80]

At birth, therefore, the verbal sign is full of memories and sensations. As it is used and reused, however, these are emptied out, until the sign is reduced to a mere descriptive label. To illustrate this phenomenon, Taine tells a parable about hiring laborers to build a wall around his garden. At the outset, he sees them as living "workmen with their blouses and trowels." But when the job drags on, he decides he needs to hire more men, and sits down to calculate how many additional men it will take to finish the wall in a reasonable interval. Calculating the meters of wall constructed per man per day, he reduces the living, breathing human beings first to numbers and then to abstract signs in an algebraic equation. And the fate of the workmen is the fate of language in general: to be reduced from a living symbol to a mere formal notation.[81]

Elsewhere in his writings, Taine suggests that this is not the condition of language at all times and places. Rather, it is a result of the excessive civilization of modern European culture, which tends "to efface images more and more to the advantage of ideas." Analysis has replaced observation. To an artist of the Renaissance, the word *tree* conveyed "an instantaneous perception of the complete tree, the round and moving mass of bright foliage . . . its rugged trunk furrowed with big veins." In contrast, Taine says, "pronounce the same word *tree* to a modern . . . he lodges this sign in his brain . . . he knows that it does not signify a dog, a sheep, or a piece of furniture," but that is all it means to him. "Primitive observation" has faded away, giving way "to naked ideas, to terms well classified, to a sort of algebraic notation."[82]

Although the philologists were more interested in language than in psychology, they took note of many of the same phenomena. William Dwight Whitney, too, observed that "*papa* and *mamma* . . . are only signs for certain loving and caring individuals, distinguished most conspicuously by differences of dress; and the chance is . . . that [the child] will give the same names to other individuals showing like differences."[83] Similarly, the French lexicographer Arsène Darmesteter noted that "The simple mind of the child possesses only a few words; to these, he attaches ideas that grow broader and broader, covering a wider and wider range of newly perceived objects; then, inversely, as he learns more new words, he also learns to restrict the excessively broad generalizations which he had previously created."[84] And Michel Bréal, the inventor of the term "semantics," echoed Taine's comparison between verbal and numerical signs, noting that "The human intellect obtains from language, for its daily operations, the same services that it obtains from numbers for its calculations . . . It is easier for us to work upon the signs of ideas than upon the ideas themselves.[85]

The philologists themselves were divided into two camps. One camp, headed by the great Sanskrit scholar F. Max Müller, took historical evolution as the key to language. The study of Sanskrit and other ancient languages revealed the extent to which their vocabulary remained present in the "roots" of the modern European tongues. From this fact, Müller and his followers drew the conclusion that the world-view of Sanskrit still provided the intellectual framework of European thought:

> The eight hundred roots which supply our dictionary can be reduced to about one hundred and twenty concepts. These one hundred and twenty concepts are really the rivers that feed the whole ocean of thought and speech. There is no thought that passes through our mind, or that has passed through the mind of the greatest poets and prophets of old, that cannot directly or indirectly be derived from one of these fundamental concepts.[86]

For Müller, it was indisputable that the persistence of these roots proved the persistence of the concepts associated with them.[87] Furthermore, since language originated as a tool of social organization, it seemed valid to infer that the worldview of modern European thought reflected the social structure and activities of ancient Aryan society.[88]

This historical interpretation was firmly rejected by the members of what we might call the formalist camp, headed by William Dwight Whitney. Whitney, also a leading authority on Sanskrit, nonetheless attacked the assumption that the so-called "roots" of the Indo-European languages reflected the activities of a prehistoric era.[89] Bréal argued that the history of language was, in any case, irrelevant: "The actual and present value of a word exercises such a power over the mind that it deprives us of all feeling for the etymological signification."[90]

It was in this context that the "arbitrary sign," a shibboleth of Saussurean criticism, became a debated topic among philologists. The arbitrariness of the sign was not per se a new idea. On the contrary, it had been debated by Socrates and other antique philosophers, by the scholastics of the Middle Ages, and by seventeenth-century writers such as Thomas Hobbes and the followers of Descartes.[91] In the second half of the nineteenth century, writers interested in the social and historical origins of language tended to downplay the arbitrariness of the sign, by tracing the connections between words and the social activities from which they supposedly derived. Conversely, the formalists reasserted the arbitrariness of the sign in order to stress the independence of language from social reality.

The attention of the formalists was focused on the purely linguistic forces tending to modify the phonetic system, syntax, and vocabulary of languages. The evolution of phonemes seemed like a natural phenomenon, which could be described but not explained. Syntactic changes, on the other hand, could often be explained by "the force of analogy." Irregular verbs, for instance, tended over time to become regular, as they were modified to resemble other, more familiar patterns.[92] The creation and evolution of words also seemed to obey distinctive principles. Darmesteter argued that "every noun originally designates an object by a particular quality that it possesses." As a rule, he added, the name derives from some quality of an object, rather than the material of which it is composed. Since any given object tends to have several different aspects, it may receive radically different names in different languages. Thus the usual Latin and French words for river, *fluvius* and *fleuve*, express the fact that a river flows: "*quod fluit.*" In contrast, the English word "river" and the less common French *rivière* express the fact that it flows between banks – *ripa* in Latin, *rive* in French. In both cases, the actual substance that flows – water – goes unmentioned.[93]

The strange thing, Darmesteter remarked, was that there is no need for this descriptive term to correspond to anything "essential" about the object it qualified. A "soldier," for instance, is not described as a man who fights, but rather as a man who is paid (who receives a *solidus*). "The function of the name," he concluded, is "not to define the thing, but simply to awaken its image. The slightest, most imperfect, most incomplete sign will suffice to do this, as long as the speakers of the language agree that there is a relation between the sign and the thing it signifies."[94] Similarly, Bréal wrote that "It will be impossible for language to introduce into [a] word all the ideas which this entity or object awakens in the mind. Language is therefore compelled to choose. Out of all the ideas it can choose one only; it thus creates a name which is not long in becoming a mere sign."[95] This reduction makes possible a considerable economy of language, because, as Bréal wrote, "a sign can be cut, clipped, reduced by half; provided it is recognizable, it still fulfills its original function."[96]

Where Taine discusses the formation of new words in psychological terms, the formalists focus on their etymology. "Words are born in two ways," Darmesteter writes: by the creation of new words and by the creation of new meanings. "New words can be created by borrowing from foreign languages, or by adding prefixes or suffixes to an existing word, or by combining two or more words into one." The act of combining old words and fragments into a new whole produces a new meaning.[97] Conversely, words could remain unchanged and yet acquire new meanings by being applied in a figurative sense.

Darmesteter divides these figurative neologisms into three basic tropes, drawn from classical rhetoric: synecdoche, metonymy, and metaphor proper.[98] Of these, synecdoche, in which a part stands for a whole, or vice-versa, is closest to the basic mechanism of word formation, in which a qualifier takes the place of the thing it qualifies. For instance, *le papier journal* (the "daily paper"), which recounts the events of the day, becomes simply *le journal* (the "daily").[99] Similarly, metonymy seizes on a pair of closely associated terms, using one in place of the other. We say, "the house was in an uproar," when we mean that the people living in the house were upset.[100] Finally, metaphor, as Darmesteter writes, "transports a name from one object to another thanks to some quality common to both of them: the leaf [*feuille*] of a tree gives its name to a leaf of paper, because both of them are thin."[101]

Over time, these synecdochal, metonymic, and metaphoric transformations may be repeated, so that the word takes on a series of new meanings, forming a "chain" of related uses. As Darmesteter points out,

> In the formation of a chain, the original meaning of the word vanishes as the word is transferred to a new object. This new meaning then allows the word to move from the second object to a third; however, the new meaning vanishes in the transfer, and is replaced by yet another. And so on, indefinitely . . . [For instance,] *bureau*, a kind of sackcloth made from heavy green fabric, comes to designate a work table covered with the cloth, then any kind of furniture used for writing, then the room in which this furniture is found, then the people who occupy this room, etc.[102]

This concatenation of meanings, as Darmesteter notes, implies a cycle of invention and amnesia. At the moment that a new link is forged, speakers are aware that the word is being used metaphorically. After repeated use, however, the word is reduced to a mere label which seems to refer directly to its object. For instance, an English speaker will refer to a "sheet" of paper without thinking of the implied comparison between writing material and bed linen. Darmesteter's philological approach here intersects with Taine's psychological description of the transition from full to empty sign.[103]

Darmesteter goes beyond Taine in seeing this exhaustion of the sign as a motor of linguistic innovation. Once a word becomes "the exact sign for the thing it designates," it no longer seems adequate:

> Popular language cannot be satisfied by such precise, dry means of expression . . . Lively and picturesque, full of imagination, it demands metaphors and comparisons . . . When the word becomes a mere idea or simple image, popular language first neglects it, then rejects it, and finally replaces it with another term, which is diverted from its proper meaning and applied to the object in question.

Darmesteter gives an historical example – the replacement of the Latin *caput* (head) by *testa* (pottery shard), implicitly comparing the head to a pot – but, in stressing the imaginative quality of "popular language," he also seems to be thinking of modern slang (*argot*), which increasingly interested French linguists of his era.[104]

Where Müller and his followers emphasize the semantic continuity implied by the persistence of roots from antiquity to the present, the formalists stress the constant fluctuations in meaning produced by the metaphorical reuse of words and roots. Whitney notes the willingness of ordinary speakers "to forget the origin of a name when once it is won, to let drop the old associations and suggestions which belonged to it in virtue of its etymology, and invest it with a new set appertaining to its present use."[105] The formalist approach thus seems to anticipate Wittgenstein's argument that the true meaning of words lies in their use.

Furthermore, the successive transformations of a word often make it impossible to assign it a single, coherent meaning. As Whitney puts it, a word covers "not a point, but a territory that is irregular, heterogeneous and variable."[106] Whitney's attention here is still directed to the individual word. His followers begin to shift their attention to the interactions between related words. Thus Bréal, for instance, writes: "The signification of certain words becomes more and more restricted, because they have colleagues which are expanding their meaning."[107] This new emphasis on the relations among words seems to reflect Taine's influence. Bréal insists that "The history of Language is a series of differentiations. That, and that alone, takes place at the first lispings of a child; for it is by Differentiation that he applies little by little to distinct objects the syllables which he at first scatters impartially upon everything he meets."[108] Here, Taine's theory of the childhood acquisition of language becomes a model for the definition of language as a whole: instead of stressing the evolution of individual words, Bréal concentrates on the way that words divide up the domain of possible meanings, each one staking out a territory limited and defined by the territories of its neighbors.

It should by now be obvious how deeply Saussure was indebted to his German, American, and French colleagues. Indeed, it may be useful to re-examine his theories, not as a unified foundation for the edifice of structuralism, but as a composite construction, pieced together from the shared ideas of his era.

Saussure acknowledges the accomplishment of his German predecessors, and gives Whitney credit for insisting upon "the arbitrary nature of the sign," thereby placing linguistics "on its true axis."[109] His phonological analysis also seems to be modeled on Whitney's.[110] Otherwise, he is curiously silent about his contemporaries, and especially about the French linguists among whom he spent a decade of his career (Bréal, for instance, gave him his first teaching job in Paris[111]). This is especially curious because one of Saussure's main arguments – that words must be studied as a unified system of language, and not as a series of unrelated etymologies – is clearly anticipated in the writings of Whitney, Darmesteter, and Bréal.[112]

Yet, as Hans Aarsleff argued in a brilliant 1982 article, Saussure's chief impetus toward this systematic mode of thinking probably came from Taine, who had drawn the critical distinction between "the relationship among *simultaneous* events" and "the relationship among *successive* events."[113] Taine seems, too, to have been the source for Saussure's speculations about a primitive language in which "only two signs had been chosen," so that "all the [concrete] significations woud have had to be divided between these two signs. One would have designated half the objects, the other, the other half." This echoes, in more abstract terms, Taine's description of the boy for whom the "reigning ideas" of the "*zizi*" and the "*fafer*" were "the two cardinal points of his intelligence," from which "he set out to comprehend and name other things."

It might be said that Saussure's great achievement was to knit together these disparate observations into a coherent system. However, the creation of this system entailed significant sacrifices. Saussure saw the current state of language as something that could be studied apart from its history. He insisted on the "arbitrariness" of the sign in order to emphasize the degree to which the meaning of any given sign depended on the relationship among signifiers (that is, the relationship among words), rather than the relationship between individual signifier and individual signified.[114] But this desire for theoretical consistency forced Saussure to omit everything and anything that pointed to the non-arbitrary nature of the linguistic sign.

It is not by accident that the topic of "etymology" is given only a single page in the *Course*. For it is, after all, etymology that explains why we use this or that word to describe something, instead of using a random assortment of syllables. To this extent, etymology seems to disprove the doctrine of the arbitrariness of the sign. Saussure therefore chooses to ignore it. This is in striking contrast to his formalist precursors, such as Whitney, Darmesteter, and Bréal, who went to great lengths to tease apart the complicated strands of accident and necessity implicit in the history of words. As they demonstrated, etymology offers few if any cases of words that seemed to have been created by an arbitrary selection of sounds. Rather, most words are chosen from an already existing vocabulary to represent some aspect of the thing they represent. The signifier does not correspond to the "essence" of the signified, but neither is it completely arbitrary.

The subsequent evolution of a word is dependent on a series of metaphorical transformations. Again, these are both contingent and determined: there is no reason why a word should be adapted for this or that particular purpose, but there is always an historical link between the old and new meanings. Finally, the "fading" of the sign insures that its metaphorical origins will sooner or later be forgotten, so that it assumes the semblance of a purely arbitrary denomination. As Whitney writes, the "original value" of the word does not necessarily persist into its later uses. However, he adds, this fact "must not at all be understood as implying that there is no reason why anything is called as it is: there is in every case a reason; only the present use of the name is not dependent on it."[115] Saussure erases this complex understanding of linguistic value as doubly determined by history and by use, in order to assert the abstract principle that "Language is a system of interdependent terms in which the value of each term results *solely* from the simultaneous presence of the others" (emphasis added).[116]

Bréal observes that popular language rarely tolerates the persistence of exact synonyms, but tends to invent a difference between them.[117] Saussure generalizes this "Law of

Differentiation" into an exclusive mechanism for the generation of meaning.[118] In this case, the meaning of a given sign must be absolutely fixed by its difference from the other signs in the system. Otherwise, the system as a whole risks collapsing into semantic chaos. The differential definition of meaning thus implicitly excludes the possibility that a word will have multiple meanings. And, indeed, the term "polysemy" appears nowhere in Saussure's *Course.* Conversely, Bréal, who invented the term, explained it as the result of a series of metaphoric displacements that could transform a word into its opposite without suppressing its original meaning. Thus, *matura*, which originally signified "dawn" or "youth," came by a series of steps to signify "ripe," "wise," or simply "old."[119]

Indeed, the idea of metaphorical displacement, analyzed at length by Darmesteter, represents the most serious loss imposed by Saussure's exclusive insistence on difference as the source of meaning. Even his most devoted followers found this an unacceptable sacrifice. In fact, Roman Jakobson, the great Russian Formalist, devoted an influential essay to the argument that metaphor and metonymy (including synecdoche) represented the two fundamental mechanisms of language – indeed of thought.[120] This might be considered Darmesteter's revenge on Saussure.

Art and Language

What does it mean to say that Cubism is like a language, or is more like a language than the styles that preceded it? If one accepts Saussure's definition of language, then one should follow Krauss and Bois in examining Cubism for the use of arbitrary signs, or signs defined purely by differences. By these standards, Cubism does not qualify as a "linguistic" style. However, if the definition of language is broadened to include the phenomena analyzed by Saussure's precursors, one can identify other distinctively linguistic qualities of Cubism, specifically the representation of isolated aspects of the object rather than its overall appearance, visual ambiguity, and the invention of visual equivalents for rhetorical tropes such as synecdoche.

It is important to distinguish between language and the sign. The idea of the sign was already central to Impressionism. As discussed in Chapter I, the Impressionist quest for pure visual sensation reflected the empiricist belief that perception could be divided between tactile and visual sensations, and that the latter indicated the existence of solid objects only insofar as they could be associated with the former. Visual sensations, in other words, acted as signs for tactile sensations. By the middle of the nineteenth century, philosophers and critics such as Hippolyte Taine routinely referred to visual impressions as "signs."[121]

Taine's taste in art was conservative. His writings on art betray no awareness of – let alone sympathy for – Impressionism. Nonetheless, his analysis of perception provides a valuable key to the Impressionists' program. They wanted to reproduce solely the signs of visual sensation – and not to supplement those signs with additional information belonging to the realm of tactile sensation, as academic painters did. It seemed to them that the style of academic painting corresponded to the overly civilized condition of modern culture, in which every perception was reduced to a mere "algebraic notation." Instead, they wanted to recover the power of "primitive observation," with its capacity for detailed instantaneous perception. Hence, as quoted earlier, Monet's advice to Lilla Cabot Perry: "try to forget what objects you have before you, a tree, a house, a field or whatever. Merely think here is a little square of blue, here an oblong of pink, here a streak of yellow, and paint it just as it looks to you, the exact color and shape."[122] Monet's goal, in effect, was to replace the empty sign of the intellect with the full sign of naïve sensation.

From this perspective, the value of Impressionism lies in its role as a means of escaping from the realm of (mere) signs, and getting back to the world of actual sensations. It is in this sense phenomenological. But if it is true, as Taine argued, that visual sensations are themselves signs, then Impressionism is also semiological – and in a strictly Saussurean sense. The Impressionist brushstroke does not trace a contour but is applied in a consistent pattern or texture across the surface of the canvas. It is a perfectly arbitrary sign, unrelated to the character of the object it represents. In theory, drawing disappears from the painting. All that remains to distinguish one sign from another is color. This is a relational system, since each color assumes its specific value only in relation to its complementary color. The Impressionist sign is thus differential as well as arbitrary.

The idea of painting as a sign system was implicit in Impressionism; with Post-Impressionism, it became explicit. As noted above, the Symbolist critic Georges Aurier declared that the true artist sees objects "only as *signs.* They are the letters of an enormous alphabet which only the man of genius knows how to spell."[123] Aurier echoes Auguste Laugel's earlier statement that visible images are "the alphabet of the mystical language spoken by the world,"[124] as Laugel himself had echoed Baudelaire's poem "Correspondances":

> Nature is a temple where living pillars
> Sometimes let slip uncertain words
> Here, man passes through forests of symbols
> That study him with a familiar gaze.

However, the continuity of rhetoric here conceals the fact that the Post-Impressionists proposed a radically different relationship between sign and perception. For the Impressionists as for Taine, the goal of art had been to recover the perceptual richness of the full sign, undoing the process by which the sign was reduced to an algebraic or empty notation. In contrast, the Post-Impressionists took it as a given that the sign could never possess the richness of perception. For them, the sign was evocative precisely because it was an abstract notation. Mallarmé, for instance, said that the spoken word "flower" corresponds not to any seen contour but to the Platonic idea of a flower, something existing "in the absence of all bouquets." It is, for this reason, more powerfully evocative than any representation of an actual flower.[125]

Similarly, Maurice Denis pointed out in an 1890 essay that painting could never really reproduce "optical sensations." Mental habit made it impossible to see in the naïve fashion demanded by Impressionist doctrine, because "There is an inevitable tendency among painters to assimilate the appearance perceived in reality to the appearances in paintings already seen." Try as they might to regain the innocent eye of an infant or a blind person newly sighted, painters would inevitably see what they expected to see. No style of painting could claim a superior truth to nature or truth to sensation. Painting could not describe reality as it was; it could evoke it only by means of more or less artificial signs. It was thus more honest for painters to emphasize, rather than disguise, the conventional nature of their art.[126]

The challenge for Post-Impressionist painters was to create new signs that would seem at once personal and conventional. Aurier, in his essay on Gauguin, argued that the artist was entitled to "deform" or "exaggerate" shapes and colors in order to arrive at the necessary "simplification in the vocabulary of the sign."[127] Since it was hard to overcome the ingrained habit of representing things naturalistically, the Post-Impressionists therefore rejected the Impressionist doctrine of painting *en plein air*, directly confronting the motif. Instead, they created an art of recollection, hoping that their images would gain in expressiveness what they lost in precision. "It is better to paint from memory," Gauguin wrote, "for thus your work will be your own; your sensation, your intelligence, and your soul will triumph over the eye of the amateur."[128] Similarly, Emile Bernard stated, "One should not paint in front of things but by calling them back into the imagination that had acquired them, which preserved them in the idea."[129]

This emphasis on memory was not unique to the Symbolists but reflected a widely held belief, derived from empiricism, that memory played a central role in perception. Lucien Arréat – a conservative art critic – proclaimed in 1892 that "memory, as everyone knows, is the foundation of the whole psychic system," and that "all of our experience, insofar as it derives from the sense of vision, depends on a combination of new and old perceptions." An artist who wanted to do more than simply to reproduce the flux of visual sensation would have to draw on memory to produce a more meaningful and coherent picture: "Vision provides the artist with nothing more than a kind of skeleton, which he must clothe with old images."[130]

Like the Impressionists before them, the Post-Impressionists thus justified their practice by reference to the empiricist theory of perception. But they used it in an exactly contrary fashion. The Impressionists had rejected remembered experience in favor of immediate sensation; the Post-Impressionists (with the notable exception of Cézanne) rejected immediate sensation in favor of remembered experience. The Impressionists had employed pure colors and broken brushwork as signs for "purely optical" experience; the Post-Impressionists looked for new conventions that could serve as signs of remembrance. One answer was to suppress color while blurring forms into patches of light and dark, as in Seurat's drawings or the paintings of Eugène Carrière. Another answer was to reduce three-dimensional shapes to hard-edged silhouettes, seen either in profile or directly from in front. Like the pure colors of the Impressionists, this choice of silhouettes could be justified by reference to contemporary science, which taught that memory preserved only the most characteristic views of objects. The simplified quality of the memory image was invoked by scholars to explain the apparent distortions of Egyptian and early Greek art: their reliance on profiles, their tendency toward abstract geometric shapes. But it could also serve as a guide to the making of new art.[131]

The "infinite" color contrasts of Impressionism gave way in Post-Impressionism to a strictly limited palette organized around a few strong oppositions.[132] To this extent, it might be said that the Post-Impressionists underscored the differential nature of color as sign. However, their emphasis on contour reinstated the issue of resemblance that had been expelled from the Impressionism of Monet, Pissarro, and Renoir, and to this extent Post-Impressionism was clearly not an art of arbitrary signs. However stylized its deformations of form and color, they were still rooted in visual experience. It might be said that Post-Impressionism remained a "phenomenological" art, neither "semiological" in the Saussurean sense nor "linguistic" in the senses defined by Saussure's precursors. Indeed, it is only with Cubism that modern art began to find visual equivalents for the mechanisms of language isolated by the philologists and philosophers of the later nineteenth century.

Perhaps the most important of these is Darmesteter's analysis of the word, which suggests a profound rethinking of the nature of the sign. Historically, the sign had been thought to consist of two components: the signifier and the signified. Saussure retained this binary conception, although he privileged the signifier by discounting its link to the signified while emphasizing its links to other signifiers. Darmesteter, however, introduced a division into the signifier itself, distinguishing between the adjectival "qualifier" and the substantive "qualified" that together composed it. In Darmesteter's analysis, the sign thus has not two but three components, since neither the qualifier nor the qualified can by itself be identified with the signified. As Darmesteter pointed out, either the qualified or (more rarely) the qualifier often remains tacit, so that the word appears to take the form of a two-part sign. The "daily paper" becomes merely a "paper;" conversely, *le papier journal* becomes *le journal*. But the three-part construction – qualifier, qualified, and signified – remains latent even in the sign's reduced form. Neither the qualifier nor the qualified gives a comprehensive description of the signified. Even their combination remains incomplete (the phrase "daily paper," for instance, does not state that the publication in question reports on news of general interest). The individual components of the verbal sign might perfectly well describe something else; hence its potential for ambiguity or "polysemy."

The complexity and inherent ambiguity of the qualifier–qualified relationship provide a more powerful tool for understanding the nature of the Cubist sign than does the merely arbitrary relationship between Saussure's signifier and signified. However, a deeper analysis of the Cubist sign will need to call on other psychological and philological aspects of language.

For the psychological school deriving from Taine, the speech of children provided an example of a primitive language possessing only a few words but imbuing each one of them with a broad range of potential meaning. So too the geometric vocabulary of Cubism might be seen as a primitive visual language, in which each form can potentially represent many different objects. These primitive languages are not totally unstructured, however. According to Taine, the child's language is organized around a few basic oppositions, such as the contrast between *zizi* and *fafer*. This "law of differentiation" (to borrow Bréal's phrase) is also evident in the geometric language of Cubism, which quickly became structured around formal contrasts such as the opposition between curves and straight lines. It is in this sense that the Cubist sign may accurately be described as "differential."

The basic geometric forms of Cubism correspond to verbal metaphors based on resemblance. A rectangular plane looks like a guitar or a torso; a circle looks like a breast or a head. Of course, metaphor is just one of the rhetorical tropes that Darmesteter identified as crucial to the formation of new words. Cubism also employs a range of other signs that function like the tropes of synecdoche and metonymy. Of these, synecdoche seems to be the most fundamental in the formation of words. Insofar as the qualifier usually specifies a single aspect of the qualified, they stand in a synedochal relationship. Similarly, in the formation of a complex Cubist sign, a basic geometric form (the qualified) tends to be given a more precise meaning by a second sign (the qualifier) that suggests just one of its features: a facial plane, for instance, may be identified by the addition of an eye or a moustache. This, too, is a synecdochal relationship.

For the analysis of Cubism, what is valuable from the Saussurean model is not the concept of the arbitrary sign, but the idea of language as a system defined by innumerable repeated acts of speech.[133] Picasso had always tended to work out his pictorial ideas in long series of studies exploring endless variations on his figures and compositions. But these studies were subsumed in the final, definitive statement of a painting like the *Saltimbanques* of 1905. Beginning in 1910, the series itself became the statement. Almost every drawing and painting is intimately linked to the works that precede and follow it, and reveals its full meaning only when placed in that context.

Viewed as a whole, Picasso's work of the years 1910–14 is extraordinarily repetitive. But this repetitiveness is simultaneously the source of Picasso's seemingly boundless creativity. Each new work reiterates the logic of the system, as a spoken statement reveals the structure of the speaker's language. But, in reiterating the logic of the system, Picasso provides himself with something to react against. From one picture to another, he first transforms individual elements and then the system as a whole.

The "linguistic" character of 1910–13 Cubism was not enunciated by Picasso (or Braque) until the 1940s. It does, however, appear in Albert Gleizes and Jean Metzinger's 1912 text "On Cubism," where they discuss the need for the Cubist painter to balance personal (or "cabalistic") signs with conventional signs:

> If we condemn the exclusive use of common signs it is not at all because we think of replacing them with cabalistic ones. We will even willingly confess that it is impossible to write without using clichés, and to paint while disregarding familiar signs completely. It is up to each one to decide whether he should disseminate them throughout his work, mix them intimately with personal signs, or boldly plaster them, magical dissonances, tatters of the great collective lie, on a single point of the plane of higher reality which he sets aside for his art."[134]

Gleizes and Metzinger anticipated the later statements by Picasso and Kahnweiler both in their general description of painting as an arrangement of signs and in their more specific distinction between customary signs taken over from earlier art and personal signs invented by the artist. However, there is nothing specifically linguistic about Gleizes and Metzinger's idea of the sign; their text is, rather, a restatement of the Symbolist concept of the pictorial sign.[135]

The idea of Cubism as a language was taken up again by the critics of the post-war era. In 1921, for instance, Waldemar George described Juan Gris as "one of the most orthodox grammarians of the Cubist school."[136] To some extent, this is just a conventional phrase. Years earlier, Charles Blanc had titled his treatises "The Grammar of Design" and "The Grammar of the Decorative Arts," without therefore arguing that these arts were inherently linguistic in character. Similarly, Léon Werth, in his 1923 book, *Some Painters*, suggested that the essential distinction between sculpture and painting lay in the linguistic character of the latter. "A statue is an object," he wrote. "It weighs on the floor and occupies a real volume in space." In contrast, he argued, "a painting assembles a group of signs." This passage is introduced, however, by the statement that "A painting is a poem that we hang on our wall. The painter puts in it whatever he wishes of his thoughts, his feelings, his sensations." Evidently, Werth was continuing to use the term "sign" in a Symbolist rather than strictly linguistic sense.[137]

As Christopher Green has demonstrated, the post-war confluence between Cubism and linguistic theory seems to stem from the publication in 1921 of Joseph Vendryes's *Le Langage* and of Jacques de Morgan's *L'Humanité préhistorique*, which contained a chapter on the evolution of writing. These texts seem to have been read by Raynal and other members of the Cubist circle, and they are cited directly in Kahnweiler's 1946 monograph on Gris.[138] It is likely that in the interim Kahnweiler had verbally summarized their contents for Picasso. Through this channel, they may well have provided the basis for Picasso's 1945 statements on art and language.

Similar to Saussure's *Course in General Linguistics* but more comprehensive, Vendryes's book provides a concise overview of phonetics, philology, and the evolution of written language.[139] As a philologist, he adheres to Whitney's formalism rather than Müller's historicism. His discussion of words and their evolution is heavily indebted to Darmesteter and Bréal, but he criticizes Darmesteter for analyzing the life of individual words rather than the larger system of language. Although he does not use Saussure's terminology, his goal is a synchronic rather than a diachronic analysis.[140] His discussion of the transition from ideographic to phonetic writing stresses the use of objects as "emblems" rather than simple pictures: thus an oar may represent a sailor.[141] De Morgan also explored the ideographic char-acter of early writing in *L'Humanité préhistorique.*[142]

As Green notes, Raynal's review of a 1923 exhibition by Gris may represent the first deliberate application of linguistic theory to Cubism. Discussing the role of "plastic metaphor" in Gris's work, Raynal described this metaphor as a truth "derived from the confrontation of two elements of the same quality." The "orifice of a glass" and the "hole of a guitar," for instance, may both be represented by an abstract circle, which thus becomes a "metaphor" uniting them.[143] Raynal justified this practice of using one form to represent two different objects by comparing it to "the use of the same method in grammar" and specifically to the rhetorical trope of catachresis, which "enables the imagination to employ a known word in partial description of a new object," for instance in describing "a sheet of paper."[144]

Raynal's interest in linguistics may have been provoked by the publication of Vendryes's *Le Langage* in 1921. In this passage, however, he is citing Darmesteter, who used "catachresis" to describe the process by which frequent usage leads speakers to forget the metaphorical origins of their words, choosing the same example – a "sheet of paper" – found in Raynal.[145] Indeed, Darmesteter's slim volume *La Vie des mots* seems to have exerted a broad influence on French esthetics, providing the model for both the title and the argument of Henri Focillon's influential 1934 essay *La Vie des formes*.[146]

It is thus possible to reconstruct a chain of influence extending from Darmesteter and other nineteenth-century writers on language to the Cubist criticism of the 1920s, '30s, and '40s. What remains to be explored, however, is the way that these linguistic concepts found visual equivalents in Picasso's Cubist work of 1908–13.

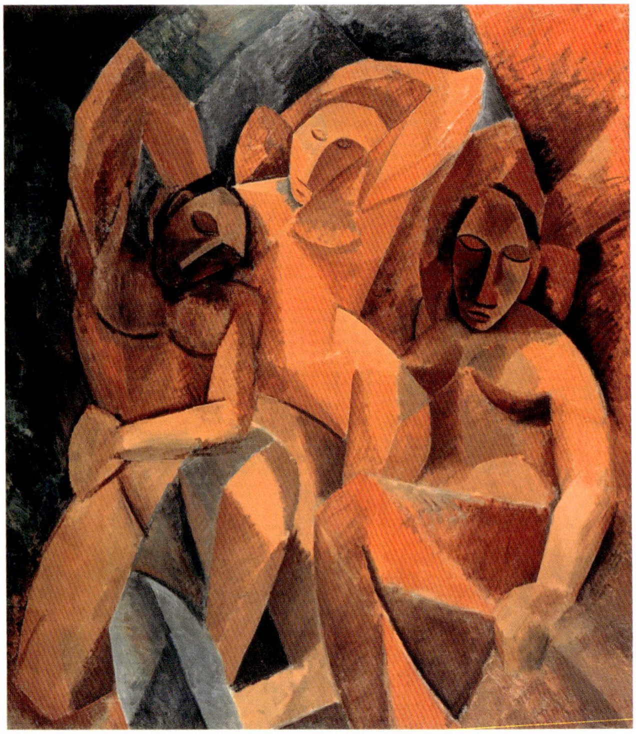

136 Picasso. *Three Women*. Paris, late 1907–spring 1908. Oil on canvas, 200 × 173 cm. D.R. 131. The State Hermitage Museum, St. Petersburg

Cubism as Language

The most obvious difference between the Cubism of 1908 and that of 1912 is the greater variety of geometric shapes employed in the latter. As Pierre Daix and Yve-Alain Bois have argued, Picasso in 1908 was pursuing "a unitary system of notation" – that is, a system that would allow him to use just one kind of mark (a more or less triangular facet) to describe all the different shapes in his pictures.[147] The unitary system of notation seems at first glance to constitute an even more primitive language than that envisioned by Taine – a language with only one word, repeated over and over. This is of course an inadequate description. The facets in a painting like *Three Women* (fig. 136) assume different meanings because their juxtapositions create a series of powerful contours, and because they are shaded differently; and these contours and shadings create additional categories of signs. Nonetheless, it seems clear that Picasso was trying to create the appearance of a visual language of utmost simplicity.

By summer–fall 1912, Picasso had arrived at a new kind of visual simplicity. He forsook the rich facture of his earlier work in favor of a spare, linear quality reflected in his preference for drawing and *papier collé* over painting. However, the simplicity of Picasso's execution belies the variety of his drawing, which carefully differentiates between straight lines and curves, orthogonal and diagonal axes, large and small marks, and so forth.

The individual facets of the *Three Women* are potentially interchangeable: the same facet that describes a breast at one location might equally describe a leg elsewhere. The meaning of the facet depends on its relationship to the larger contours of the composition. Similarly, the rectilinear strips and curved planes of the summer 1912 *Seated Woman with Guitar* (fig. 137) seem to take their representational value from their place in the figure as a whole. Viewed in

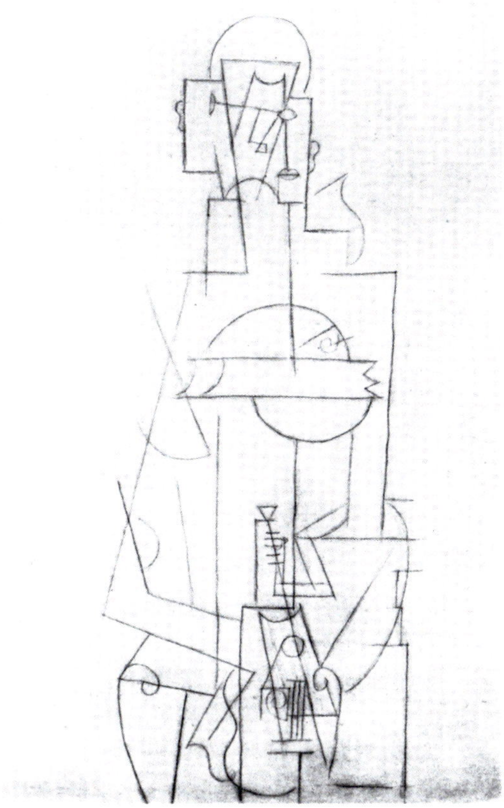

137 Picasso. *Seated Woman with Guitar.* Sorgues, summer 1912. Pencil and ink on paper, 61 × 47 cm. Zervos II*, 392. Yves Saint-Laurent and Pierre Bergé Collection

isolation, the local forms of the 1912 drawing are no more and no less ambiguous than the local forms of the 1908 painting. The difference lies in the ambiguity of the composition as a whole. Although the contours of the *Three Women* have been simplified and generalized, there is no mistaking them for the contours of anything except human figures. In contrast, the basic structure of *Seated Woman with Guitar* – two vertical strips, accompanied by a long diagonal, and topped by a shorter vertical strip – could represent any number of things. Later in 1912, Picasso used the

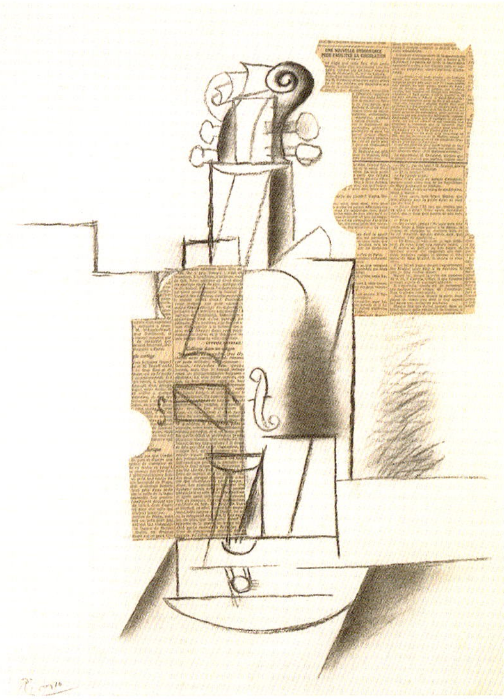

138 (*below left*) Picasso. *Violin.* Paris, after December 3, 1912. Pasted paper and charcoal on paper, 62 × 47 cm. D.R. 524. Centre Georges Pompidou, Musée National d'Art Moderne, Paris. Gift of Henri Laugier

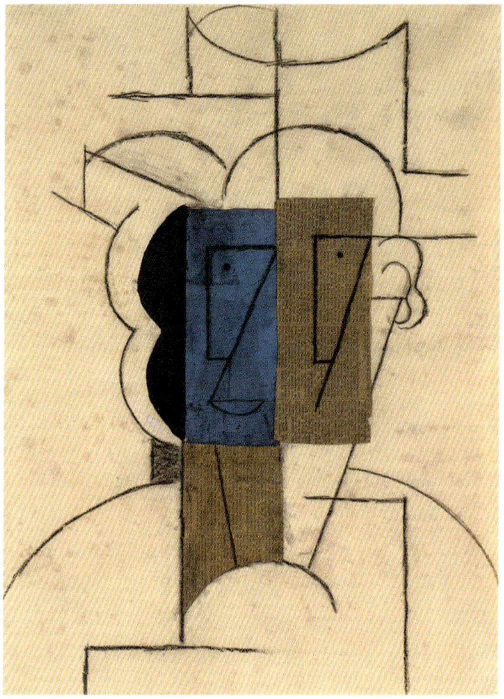

139 (*below right*) Picasso. *Man with a Hat.* Paris, after December 3, 1912. Pasted paper, charcoal, and ink on paper, 62.2 × 47.3 cm. D.R. 534. The Museum of Modern Art, New York. Purchase

same basic structure of lines and planes to represent both a violin and a head (figs. 138, 139). It is not just that the individual geometric forms are ambiguous. Their overall arrangement is ambiguous too.

What makes the woman, the violin, and the head distinguishable from one another is a series of smaller marks that accompany the larger geometric forms. In the drawing of the seated woman, the geometric forms of the head are ornamented with bee-stung lips and a pair of stylized ears; once this head has been recognized, the rest of the figure falls into place. The neck of the violin is topped by an exaggerated scroll, with tuning pegs at either side, while the instrument's body is incised with two *f*-shaped soundholes. An ear marks one side of the man's head, and his eyes are marked by dots – a simple but familiar convention.

Representation, in these pictures, results from the combination of two different kinds of marks. The larger geometric forms provide a kind of material substrate, indicating that there is something there, and giving a rough idea of its proportions. But they are too ambiguous – either individually or as an overall configuration – to complete the job of representation. As Kahnweiler wrote in 1916:

> If only this scheme of forms were to exist it would be impossible to see in the [picture] the "representation" of things from the outer world. One would only see an arrangement of planes, cylinders, quadrangles, etc. . . . [But] when : "real details" are thus introduced, the result is a stimulus which carries with it memory images. Combining the "real" stimulus and the scheme of forms, these images construct the finished object in the [viewer's] mind.[148]

The new structure of the Cubist "sign" corresponds to that of the verbal sign, with the larger geometric forms assuming the role of the substantive "qualified" in Darmesteter's analysis, and the smaller "realistic" marks assuming the role of the "qualifier." Together, they form a composite signifier, evoking the signified of a woman, a violin, or a head.

This composite signifier does not have an arbitrary relationship to its signified, nor do its constituent parts. The geometric forms that constitute the substrate of the image usually suggest the shape of the motif, albeit in a very general fashion. In the drawing of the seated woman, for instance, the vertical oblong of the torso is represented by vertical planes, while the ball of the head is suggested by a large section of a circle. Insofar as there is some resemblance between them, it might be said that the geometric forms act as metaphors for their referents. The smaller "qualifiers" sometimes have a kind of exaggerated, cartoon-like resemblance to the particular details they represent. However, they function primarily not as metaphors but as synecdoches, identifying the larger entities to which they belong. A more or less recognizable moustache evokes the face around it; *f*-shaped sound-holes evoke the larger configuration of a violin.

One troubling aspect of these composite signs is their incompleteness. Certain details of the motif are described with precision, while others must be guessed at. This kind of incomplete representation is acceptable in verbal language: it does not bother us that the word "river" refers to the river's banks without mentioning the water flowing between them. Visual language is different: it does bother us when an image of a face includes some details but omits others.

Another troubling feature is their inconsistency. A sophisticated viewer may shift without difficulty from the stylized "distortions" of Romanesque sculpture to the quasi-photographic "realism" of Neo-classical painting. Both styles offer a consistent set of "signs" for the human figure, although they vary greatly in their degree of stylization. If Picasso had established a fixed vocabulary of Cubist ideograms, the power of convention might have hidden their incompleteness. Viewers might absorb the meaning of the ideogram "woman" without thinking about its actual appearance, just as we read the word "river" without reflecting on its etymology. But this is not the case. The language of Cubism was always in flux. Picasso constantly changed the combination of metaphoric (geometric) and metonymic ("realistic") signs that he used, for instance, to indicate "woman." As a result, the viewer remains aware of the contingent, incomplete, and sometimes indecipherable character of the Cubist sign. In this respect, the "language" of Cubism is completely different from any spoken language.

Not all elements of the language of Cubism are equally unstable, however. From summer 1910 through early 1913, the geometric substrate of the Cubist sign remained strikingly consistent. Picasso reused the same limited vocabulary of rectangular strips, circles and arcs, angles and triangles. These forms proved to possess an almost inexhaustible metaphoric potential. But their stability also seems to reflect Picasso's success in forging them into a coherent system, organized around a simple but effective opposition between orthogonals, angles, and curves.

Differential Geometry

The "unitary system of notation" in the *Three Women* of 1908 (see fig. 136) was disrupted by fall 1909, when Picasso's sculpture of a woman's head (see fig. 79) represented the eyes in deliberately contrasting fashion, one indented while the other projects. Picasso sought such contrasts on principle.[149] His observation that "Every woman has two arms, two legs, two breasts, which may in real life be more or less symmetrical, but in painting they shouldn't be shown to have any similarity" is reflected in his spring 1910 drawing of a standing nude (see fig. 86), where the breast on the left is reduced to a horizontal strip, while the breast on the right is represented by a triangle inscribed over a curve.[150] However, this deliberate contrast is not repeated in the rest of the figure, which seems to have been constructed from lines, angles, and curves selected on a purely ad hoc basis. Picasso seems to react against this visual confusion by constructing subsequent figures from a more limited vocabulary of lines and angles, supplemented with occasional curves (see fig. 90).

As remarked earlier, the search for a coherent formal language culminated in the large drawing acquired by Alfred Stieglitz (fig. 140), where Picasso utilized just three basic

140 Picasso. *Standing Nude.* Paris, winter 1910–11. Charcoal on paper, 48.3 × 31.4 cm. Zervos II*, 208. The Metropolitan Museum of Art, New York. Alfred Stieglitz Collection, 1949

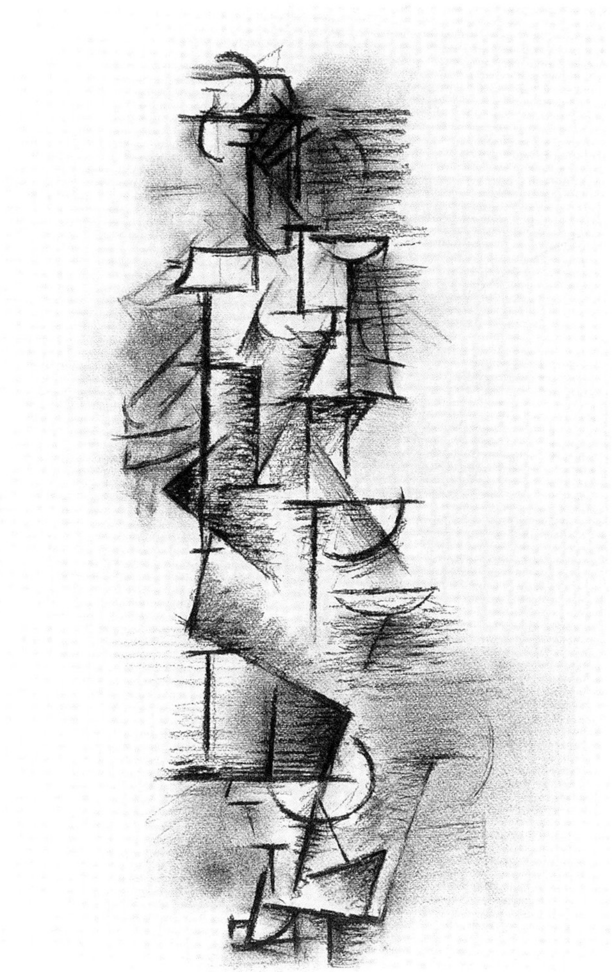

141 Piet Mondrian. *Composition.* 1913. Oil on canvas, 95.9 × 64.1 cm. Rijksmuseum Kröller-Müller, Otterlo

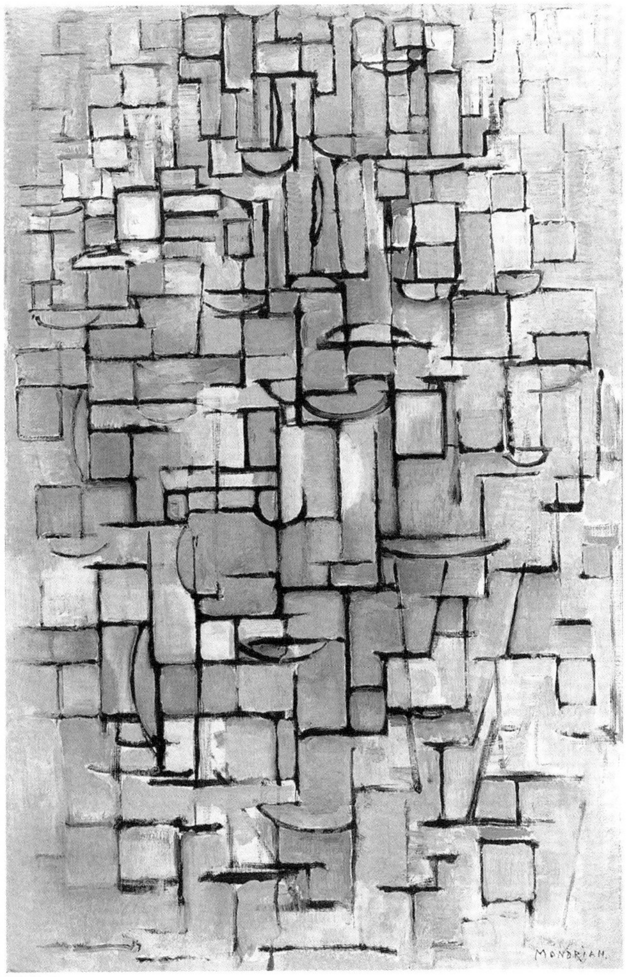

signs: overlapping diagonal planes, linear *T*s, and sections of curves. Each kind of sign seems to correspond to a different aspect of the figure. The diagonal planes mark the general disposition of the torso, hips, and legs. The curves indicate actual round forms (hair, breasts) but also points of articulation (shoulders, hips, knees). The *T*s imply the presence of a larger grid joining the figure to the space around it.

The clarity of the distinctions among different types of sign seems to have made a particularly strong impression on Picasso's contemporaries. In their 1912 book *On Cubism*, Gleizes and Metzinger wrote that "the art of drawing consists of creating relationships between curves and straight lines."[151] As if to illustrate this maxim, Piet Mondrian's early experiments with Cubism (fig. 141) utilized a rectilinear grid punctuated by shallow curves like those in the "Stieglitz" drawing.[152] Kasimir Malevich's equally acute study of Cubism is evident in many of the teaching diagrams he published in 1919.[153]

As these examples suggest, Bréal's "law of differentiation" is operative in Cubism not at the level of the qualifier, but at the level of the geometric substrate. It is clearly an oversimplification to say that the construction of 1910–11 Cubism can be reduced entirely to the contrast between straight line and curve, since diagonal lines and planes also play an important role. Still, a few basic elements, strongly contrasting with one another, seem sufficient to generate the system as a whole. However, this principle of systematic contrast does not serve to differentiate one complex sign from another in a Saussurean fashion. Picasso might have used the contrast between curves and straight lines, for instance, to distinguish between female and male figures, or between human beings and inanimate objects. But he did not in fact choose to do this. The signs that indicate the specific identity of his motifs (that is, the qualifiers, as opposed to the qualifieds) all seem to have been chosen on an ad hoc basis: the triangular breast of the spring 1910 *Standing Nude with Raised Arm* (see fig. 88); the bee-stung lips of the 1912 *Seated Woman* (see fig. 137); and the dotted eyes of the 1912 *Man with a Hat* (see fig. 139). These synecdochic signs were clearly chosen for their resemblance to particular anatomical features, rather than being determined by a larger system of contrasting forms.

* * *

The Synecdochical Setting

The "geometric forms" of Cubism, Kahnweiler argued, "are our categories of vision."[154] They correspond to the words of the primitive language described by Taine, dividing the world into a few large classes of things. From a philological point of view, they are metaphorical terms, insofar as they link things on the basis of a perceived resemblance. However, many of the signs in Cubist pictures correspond to other rhetorical tropes not based on resemblance. The most important of these is synecdoche, the evocation of an object by some part or aspect of it.

Most of the synecdochic signs in Cubist pictures are attached to specific geometric forms or configurations. Others seem to float, unrelated to any specific form in the composition. It is this second category that has received the most attention from critics. It was difficult to determine

142 Picasso. *Woman Seated in an Armchair*. Paris, winter 1909–10. Oil on canvas, 81.3 × 63.5 cm. D.R. 333. The Metropolitan Museum of Art, New York. The Mr. and Mrs. Klaus G. Perls Collection, 1997

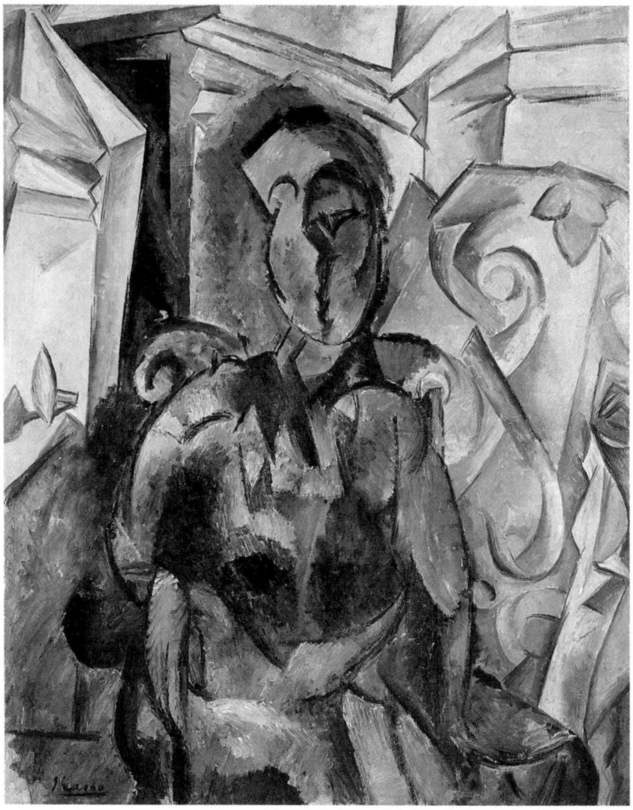

whether a given sign was or was not attached to a geometric form (in large part, because the forms themselves were hard to decipher). It therefore seemed simpler to assume *a priori* that most or all of the synecdochic signs were free-floating.

This assumption seemed justified, furthermore, by a delightful story in Fernande Olivier's memoirs. She and Picasso met a naval officer who told them how he had had his portrait drawn by an African artist, who represented him "in the traditional style of tribal figures." After the portrait was completed, however, the artist realized that he had omitted the shiny buttons of the officer's uniform. "The amusing part of the story," Olivier comments, was that "he saw no reason to put the buttons in their proper place. Instead, he surrounded the face with buttons! He did the same thing with the stripes, putting them at the side of the arms and over the head. It is scarcely necessary to go into the conclusions which were drawn from this story."[155] In fact, the buttons in Cubist pictures are generally right where they are supposed to be. In Picasso's summer 1912 drawing of a *Man with Banderilla*, for instance, the man's jacket is neatly fastened down the front (see fig. 113). The synecdochic signs that do appear in the margins of Cubist pictures are typically attached to the setting, not to the central figure. They are not really typical. But since they are the signs that viewers notice first, we may begin by examining them.

The placement of easily legible signs in the setting of Cubist pictures seems originally to have been motivated by an interest in projective space. The receding picture rail and protruding doorknob in Picasso's early 1910 *Woman Seated in an Armchair* (fig. 142), for instance, are signs indicating that, however amorphous the figure, its setting is fully three-dimensional. Braque uses a picture rail and a protruding

143 Braque. *Violin and Pitcher*. Paris, early 1910. Oil on canvas, 117 × 73 cm. Romilly 59. Oeffentliche Kunstsammlung Basel, Kunstmuseum. Gift of Raoul La Roche, 1952

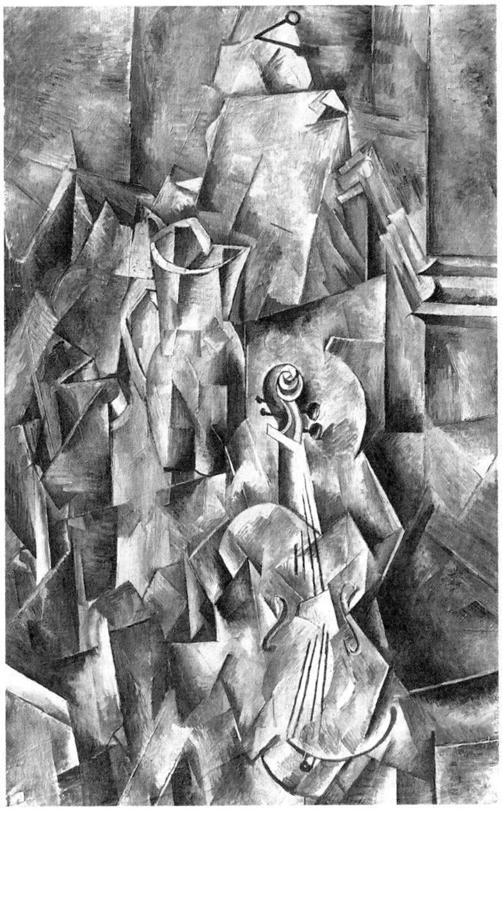

144 Picasso. *Guitar and Bottle of Bass*. Céret, spring 1913. Lead pencil and stumping on paper, 17.3 × 10.7 cm. Zervos XXVIII, 339. Richet 347. Musée Picasso, Paris

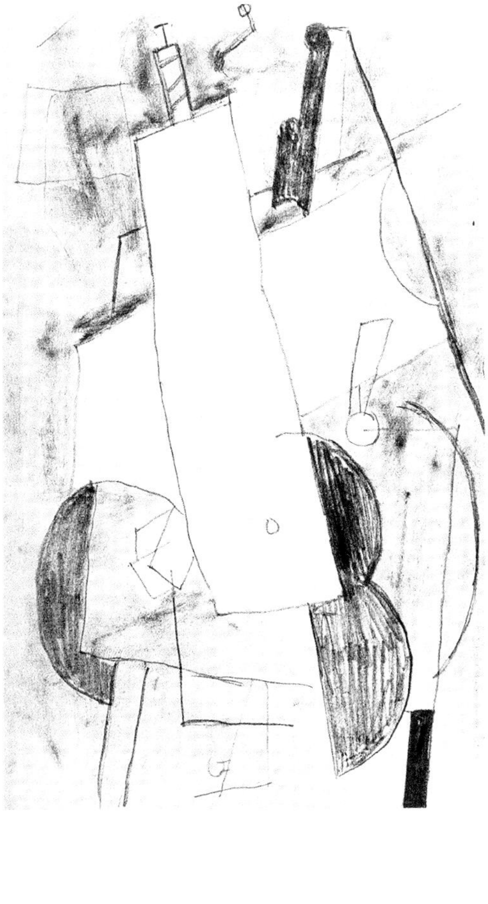

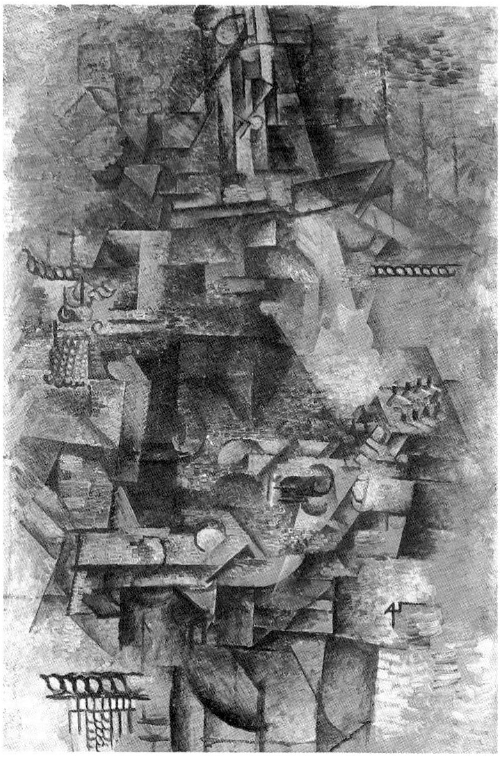

145 Picasso. *Mandolin Player.* Paris, spring 1911. Oil on canvas, 100 × 65 cm. D.R. 425. Fondation Beyeler, Riehen/Basel

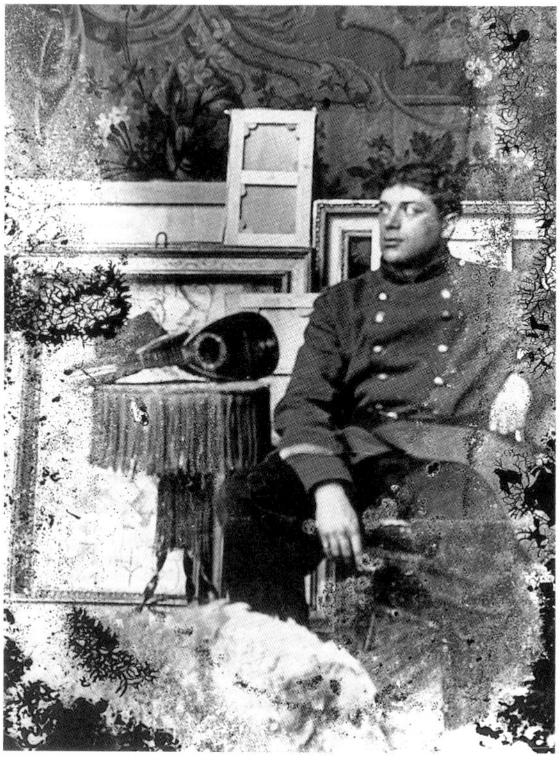

146 Photograph of Braque seated in Picasso's studio at 11, Boulevard Clichy. Paris, March–April 1911. Picasso Archives, Paris

nail for the same purpose in *Violin and Pitcher* (fig. 143), painted around the same time. In Braque's picture, the nail simultaneously asserts the depth of the pictorial space and suggests that the picture is merely a flat design, tacked to the wall.[156] Picasso seems to have been delighted with this paradox and frequently quoted Braque's nail in his own subsequent work. It appears, for instance, at the top of a spring 1913 sketch for a still life composition (fig. 144).

In the meantime, Picasso himself introduced new "environmental" motifs such as fringes, cords, and tassels. These often appear in 1911 pictures like the *Mandolin Player* (fig. 145). It should be noted that they do nothing at all to make the central figure more legible. They operate, instead, as synecdochic signs for the furnishings of Picasso's studio. Some of these can be identified. The cord with fringe at lower left belongs to the round pedestal table visible in a spring 1911 photograph of Braque (fig. 146). And the tassel and cord at upper left are presumably tying back a curtain. Their role in the picture is not to identify other forms, but simply to give a generalized sense of the concrete reality of the setting. The result is that the central figure seems relatively immaterial, much as in the spring 1910 *Woman Seated in an Armchair.*

Braque's response was to invent new kinds of signs that were similarly detached from the central motifs of his pictures. His spring 1911 canvas *Le Portugais* (fig. 147) reworks the compositional structure of Picasso's *Mandolin Player* and reproduces – twice – the motif of the curtain tieback. However, Braque also introduces an innovation – the large

149 (*facing page bottom left*) Ludwig Hohlwein. *Confection Kehl.* 1908. Lithograph, printed in color, 123.3 × 91.75 cm. The Museum of Modern Art, New York. Gift of Peter Müller-Munk

150 (*facing page bottom right*) Braque. *Man with Pipe.* Sorgues, early September 1912. Charcoal and pasted paper on paper, 61.9 × 49 cm. M.-F./C. 6. Oeffentliche Kunstsammlung Basel, Kupferstichkabinett. Gift of Raoul La Roche, 1952

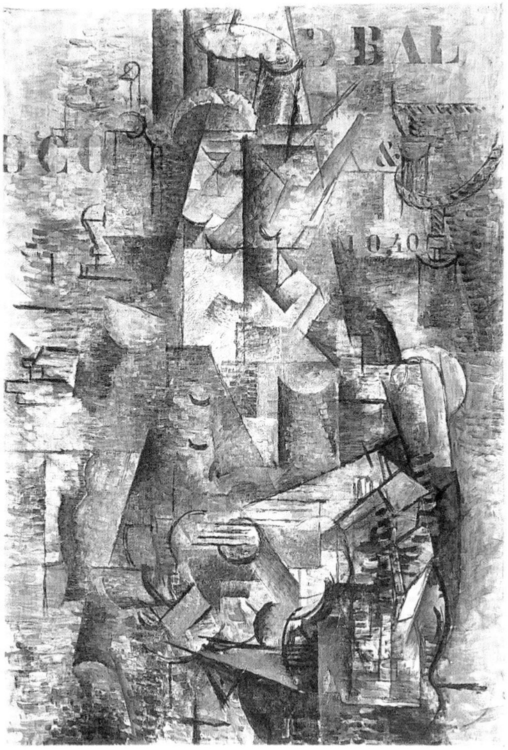

147 (*left*) Braque. *Le Portugais.* Paris, spring 1911. Oil on canvas, 117 × 81 cm. Romilly 80. Oeffentliche Kunstsammlung Basel, Kunstmuseum. Gift of Raoul La Roche, 1952

148 (*below*) Braque. *Homage to J. S. Bach.* Céret, winter 1911–12. Oil on canvas, 54 × 73 cm. Romilly 122. Collection of Carroll Janis, New York

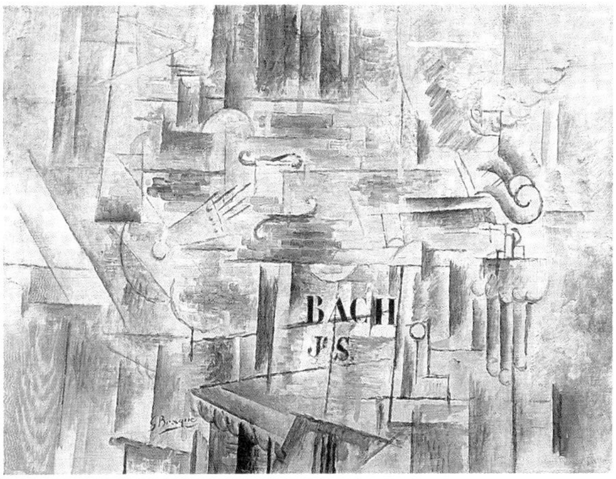

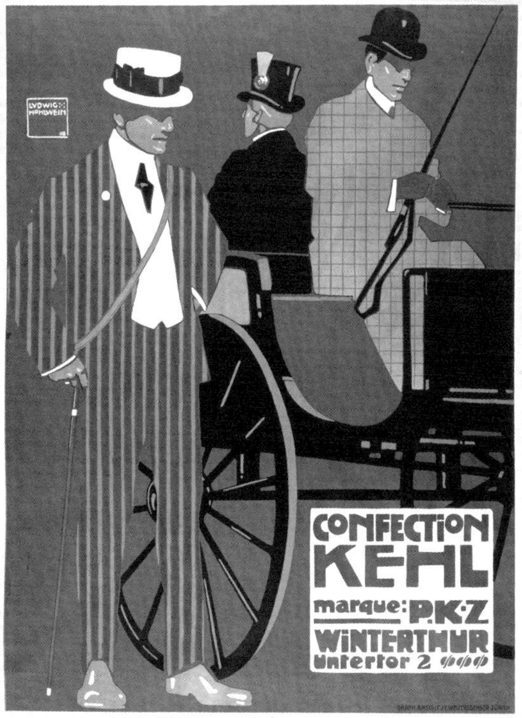

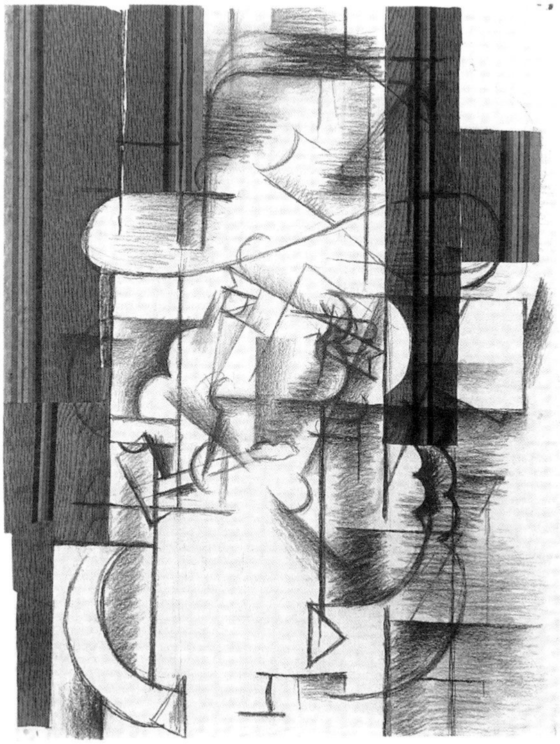

stenciled letters at upper left and right, reproducing portions of the phrases "GRAND CONCERT" and "GRAND BAL."[157] These are obviously not attached to the figure in the foreground. It is possible that they are meant to suggest glimpses of posters on a wall behind the figure. But the dark stenciled letters seem to float in space; it is not even clear whether they are behind or in front of the guitarist. Picasso responds, in turn, by inserting similar lettering in his canvas "*Ma Jolie*" *(Woman with Zither)* (see fig. 130). The phrase "ma jolie" comes from the chorus of "Dernière Chanson," a music-hall song popular at the time. Picasso makes it into the *leitmotif* of his feelings for his new inamorata, Eva Gouel. But the large letters of the inscription do not seem to be attached to the sheet music at the bottom of the composition. Like the letters in *Le Portugais*, they float in an indefinite space surrounding the dimly lit figure.

In the context of the painting's highly abstract, almost unreadable figuration (discussed in more detail below), the free-floating inscription gives the impression that "*Ma Jolie*" represents not a real figure located in a real space but a remembered figure located in a mental space. The flicker of light and dark planes, the occasional emergence of legible details (a hand, a breast), followed by a plunge back into obscurity, the allusive reference to "Ma Jolie" – these all seem to correspond to the movement of Picasso's thoughts, meditating simultaneously on the nature of passion and the nature of painting. As Rosenblum has noted, the canvas offers a visual equivalent to the sense of free association in contemporary novels by James Joyce and Virginia Woolf.[158]

Braque's still life *Homage to J. S. Bach* (fig. 148) of winter 1911–12 provides a comparable image of visual meditation. As in "*Ma Jolie*", the inscription ("BACH J. S.") presumably comes from a piece of sheet music, but this time the score is not visible anywhere in the painting. The major innovation of the canvas lies in the seemingly modest detail of the wood-graining that fills a vertical strip in the lower left corner of the composition. If there were more wood-graining, it might be interpreted as paneling in the background. But there is only an isolated strip. The most obvious explanation is that it "belongs" in some sense to the violin, even though it is not attached to it.

It is not clear why Braque chose to detach the wood-graining from the instrument. One explanation might be that if the wood-graining had been applied to the violin itself, it would then have been subjected to the usual distortions – shading and foreshortening – of three-dimensional representation. Transferred to a flat, rectangular strip in the corner of the painting, it could be presented as a pure, undistorted pattern. Of course, the same effect could in fact have been achieved without isolating the texture. In the 1890s, Bonnard and the Nabis had inserted expanses of flat pattern within three-dimensional contours, and by 1908 the same technique was being used in advertising posters (fig. 149). It seems, then, that Braque transferred the wood-graining from the violin to a separate area of the composition precisely in order to show that it could be separated, both visually and conceptually. That is, the different aspects of an object could be displayed as if they were literally separate objects – like the stripes and buttons separated from the naval officer's uniform in Fernande Olivier's story.

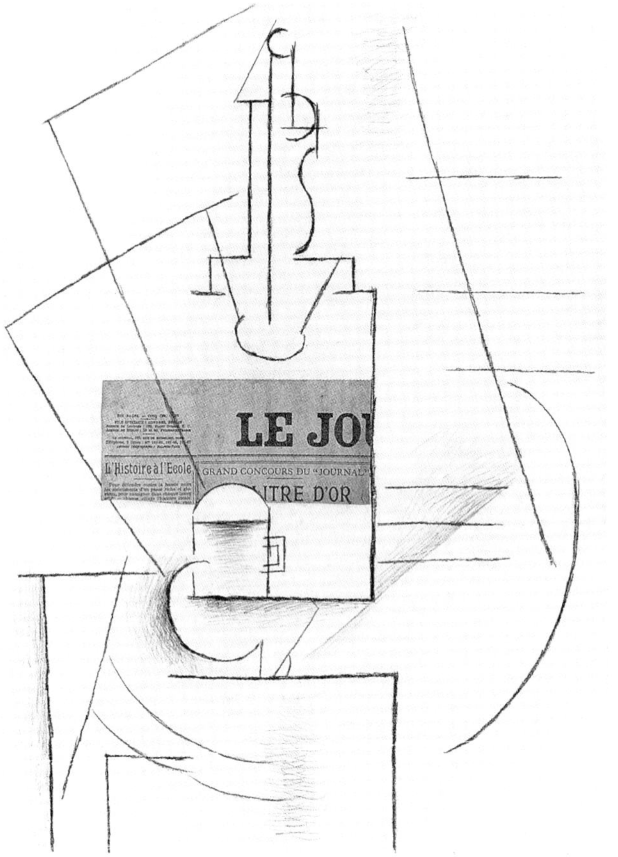

151 Picasso. *Bottle, Cup, and Newspaper*. Paris, after December 4, 1912. Pasted paper, charcoal and pencil on paper, 63 × 48 cm. D.R. 545. Museum Folkwang, Essen

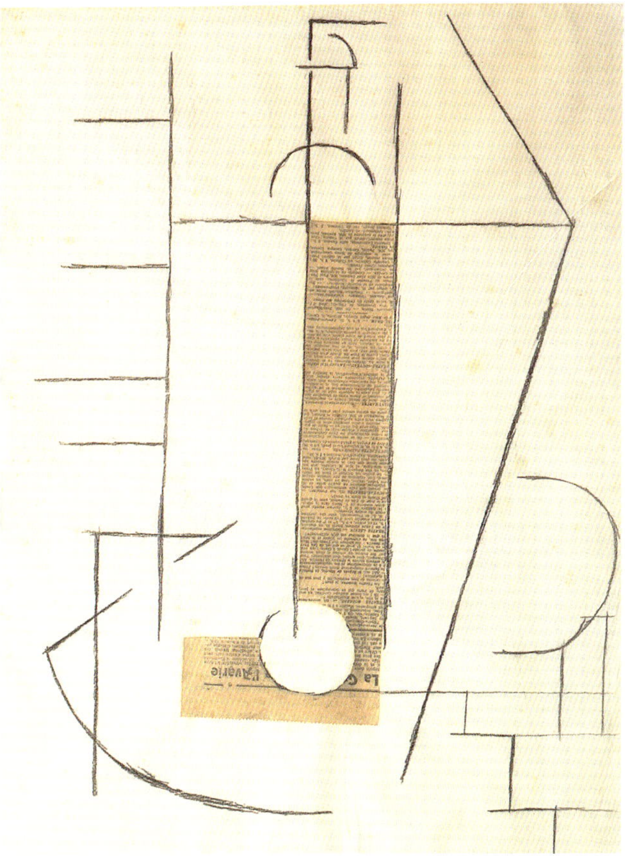

152 Picasso. *Bottle on Table.* Paris, after December 8, 1912. Pasted paper and charcoal on paper, 60 × 46 cm. D.R. 552. Fondation Beyeler, Riehen/Basel

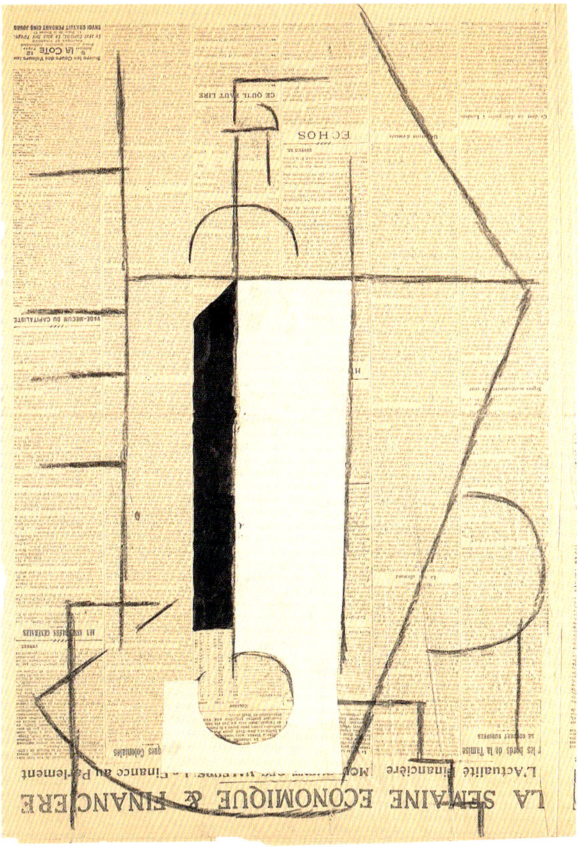

153 Picasso. *Bottle on Table.* Paris, after December 8, 1912. Pasted paper and charcoal on paper, 62 × 44 cm. D.R. 551. Musée Picasso, Paris

The displaced wood-graining of Braque's *Homage to J. S. Bach* clearly provides the antecedent for his first *papiers collés*, which are bordered by strips of wallpaper printed to resemble wood-paneling. The wood-graining in a work like *Man with Pipe* (fig. 150) does not seem to correspond to a displaced aspect of the central motif (presumably the man is made of flesh, not wood). Nor is the wallpaper meant to be read literally as wood-paneling in the background. Cut out to mold tightly to the heads and fruit dishes, it seems to represent simply a materialization of the space surrounding them.

In Picasso's *papiers collés* of December 1912, newsprint assumes the role of Braque's wood-grained wallpaper. Here, Picasso systematically explored the different kinds of relationship that might exist between a real material and a figurative composition. One work shows a circular café table supporting a coffee cup, a liqueur bottle, and a newspaper (fig. 151). The newspaper is drawn as a pair of overlapping planes, extending toward the upper left corner of the composition. But it is also represented by a literal piece of newsprint, cut out and pasted onto the middle of the composition. The newsprint acts as a synecdoche for the figured newspaper, although it has been displaced to occupy the position that belongs more properly to the bottle's label.

A few days later Picasso executed two additional *papiers collés* reworking this composition in more abstract form (figs. 152, 153). The café table and coffee cup survived only as fragmentary curves, while the drawn newspaper was reduced to a pair of long diagonals, enclosing the liqueur bottle on the right. In one version of this composition, the literal newsprint is again displaced from the figured newspaper to the bottle, whose volume it now almost fully occupies. The other version of *Bottle on Table* is almost a mirror-image of the first: the newsprint here serves as the support for the image, appearing through the outlines of everything except the bottle. It is now identified not only with the figured newspaper but also with all the space surrounding it. The series suggests, in effect, that there is no predestined limit to the displacement inherent in synecdoche. Once an aspect has been detached from the whole to which it originally belonged, it may shrink to occupy only part of that whole, it may emigrate to a neighboring object, or it may expand to occupy the entire environment. Picasso's newsprint, in the third member of this series, assumes the same spatial role as the wood-grained wall-paper in Braque's *Man with Pipe*.

The Synecdochic Figure

Cubist synecdoche does not usually take the inflationary form found in *Man with Pipe* or *Bottle on Table*. In most cases, the synecdochic sign lends representational value to a specific geometric form. They are paired as qualifier and qualified; if the first changes, so does the value of the second. This process has already been examined in Picasso's 1912 pictures of a woman with a guitar, a violin, and a head (see figs. 137–39). The same process can be found at work in a pair of drawings done in summer 1911 (figs. 154, 155). In one of these, an arrangement of overlapping planes and curves is supplemented with recognizable signs for an eye, nose, moustache, and pipe. The arrangement therefore comes to represent a head, even though the overlapping planes have little "natural" resemblance to an actual head. In the other drawing, the same arrangement of planes is supplemented with different forms suggesting trees and houses. It therefore becomes a landscape.

The synecdochic signs in the drawing of a man's head play the role ascribed by Kahnweiler to the "real details" of 1910–11 Cubism. Combining with the geometric "scheme of forms," they "construct" the head in the viewer's mind.[159] Yet it does not seem quite accurate to describe them as "real." Compared to the overlapping planes, the eye, nose, moustache, and pipe may seem real; compared to the real features they represent, they are quasi-abstract. More precisely, they are simplified, calligraphic, and caricatural.

As Adam Gopnik has observed, Picasso's penchant for caricature is already evident in his early drawings, many of which display "an allusive reduction of features to a telegraphic code of dots and dashes, suavely placed against blank white faces" (fig. 156).[160] Caricature began to play a role in his "serious" art only in 1906, when Picasso's discovery of "primitive" Iberian art allowed him to recognize how caricatural exaggeration might be used for artistic purposes. As Gopnik writes, "The move from low to high, the victory of the notebook over the easel, is accomplished through the Trojan horse of primitivism."[161] (Some critics, of course, recognized the Trojan horse for what it was: when the critic Félix Fénéon saw the *Demoiselles d'Avignon*, he advised Picasso to give up painting in favor of a career as a caricaturist.[162]) Obvious exaggeration seems to disappear from Picasso's work after 1909; but, Gopnik suggests, "the language of simplification in the great high Cubist portraits" involves "an adaptation of the elegant, dots-and-dashes style of the Parisian caricatures."[163]

How, exactly, Picasso adapted caricature to the purposes of Cubism becomes clearer if his 1905 sketch of Apollinaire is compared to a trio of drawings executed between summer 1912 and the beginning of 1913 (figs. 157–59). In the caricature, Apollinaire's head is reduced to a large pear, perched above a high, stiff collar. Its most distinctive features are the broad curve of the chin and jaw, and the flat bristle of hair atop the narrow brow. The facial features are crammed into the upper half of the pear, with anxiously descending brows echoing the elegant hook of the poet's nose.

The three drawings of 1912–13 seem in comparison like generic figures, constructed around an armature of vertical strips and slanted planes. In the first of them, a small sketchbook study (see fig. 157), the chin is indicated by a broad curve quite different from the squared-off chins of other summer 1912 figures (see fig. 172). The head is mounted above a tall wing collar, and terminates in a horizontal line topped by a series of curved strokes that seem to represent brushed-back hair. These three features – chin, collar, and hairline – distantly recall the 1905 caricature of Apollinaire, but since the overall effect of the drawing is completely different, it seems that these isolated points of resemblance might be accidental.

Certainly, the larger drawing (see fig. 158) based on this sketch looks nothing like the 1905 caricature. The broad

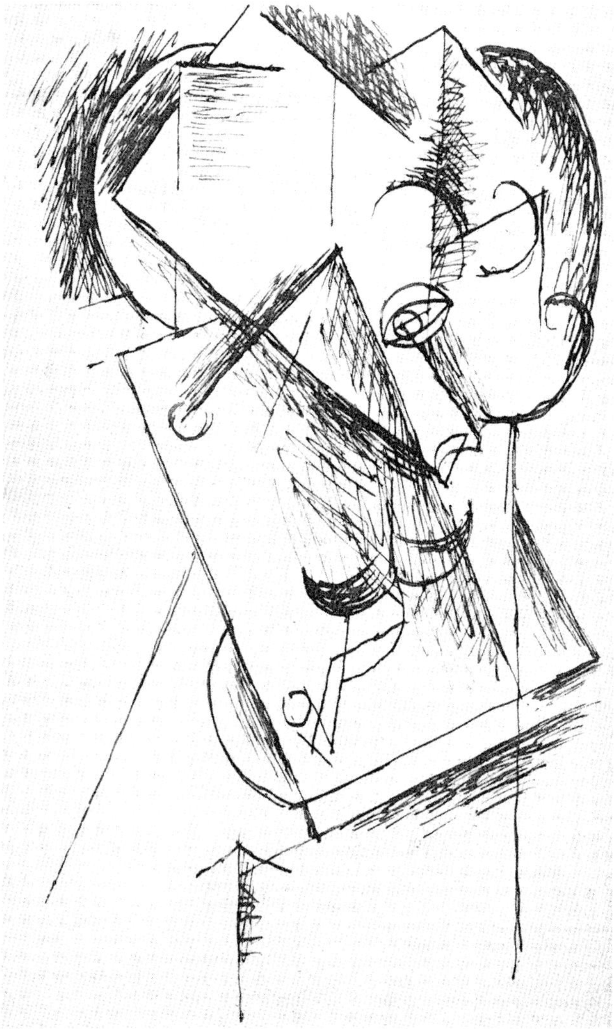

154 Picasso. *Head of Man with Pipe*. Céret, summer 1911. Ink on paper, 21.3 × 13.13 cm. Zervos XXVIII, 68. Picasso estate (inv. 1561)

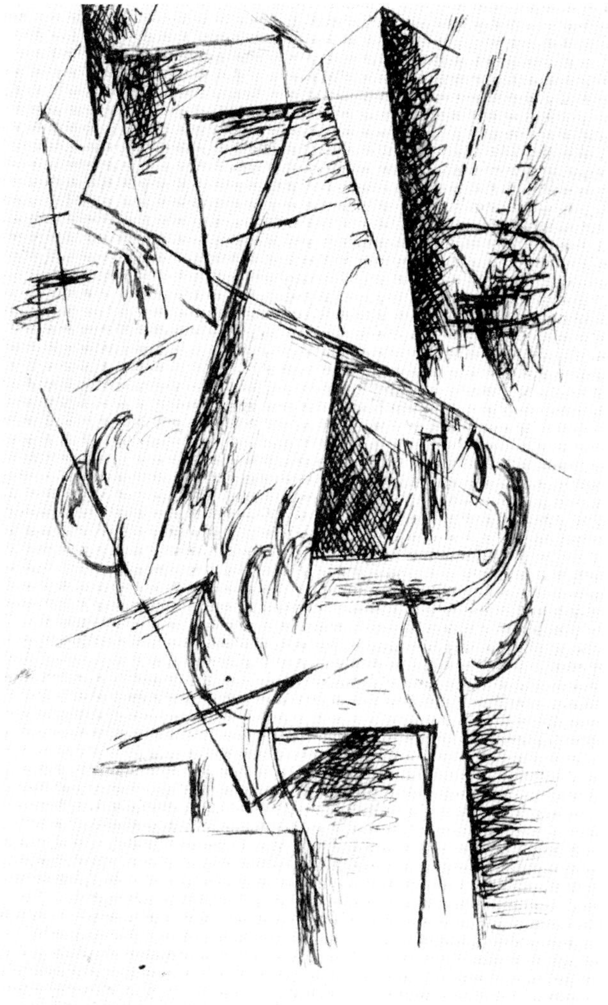

155 Picasso. *Landscape*. Céret, summer 1911. India ink on paper, 21 × 13.5 cm. Zervos XXVIII, 27. Picasso estate (inv. 1312)

curve of the chin is repeated, and even emphasized by shading; but the flat hairline vanishes and the tall wing collar is reduced to an unsupported curve. Furthermore, the figure is given an elegantly curled moustache, typical of the masculine heads in Picasso's 1911–13 work but unlike the small brush moustache in the 1905 sketch.

In the ink drawing done in early 1913 (see fig. 159), the curved chin remains prominent, the collar is once more attached to a strong vertical, and the curls of hair are again attached to a prominent horizontal line. In addition, the nose, indicated by a hooked curve, is more similar to the nose of the 1905 caricature than to the noses in either of the 1912 drawings. What is most telling about the 1913 drawing, however, is that it was executed in response to Apollinaire's request for a frontispiece to *Alcools*, his new collection of poems, and has traditionally been titled *Portrait of Guillaume Apollinaire*.

The small study from the summer 1912 sketchbook (see fig. 157) seems in retrospect to have been done with Apollinaire in mind, and this was why Picasso selected it as

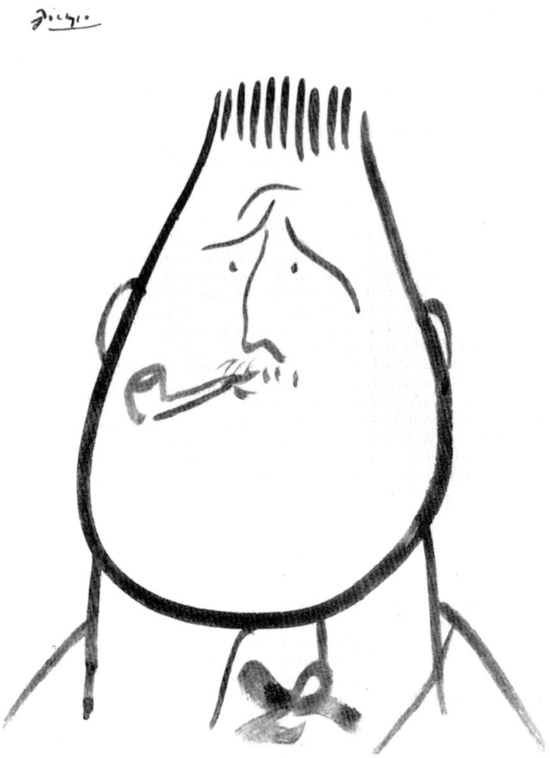
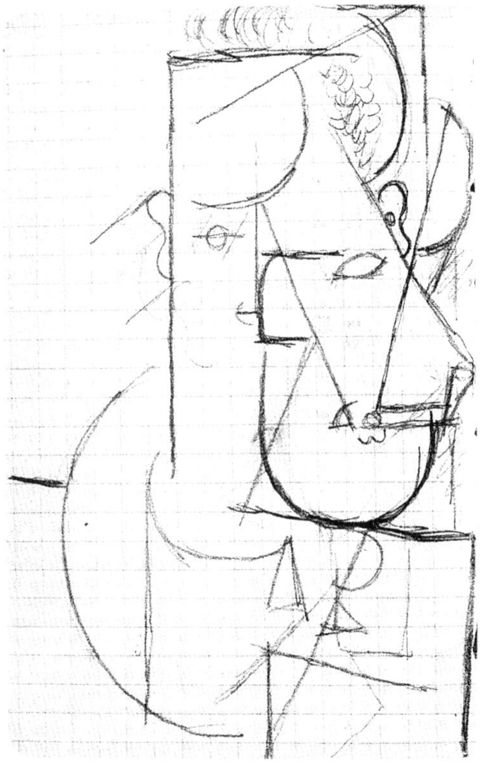
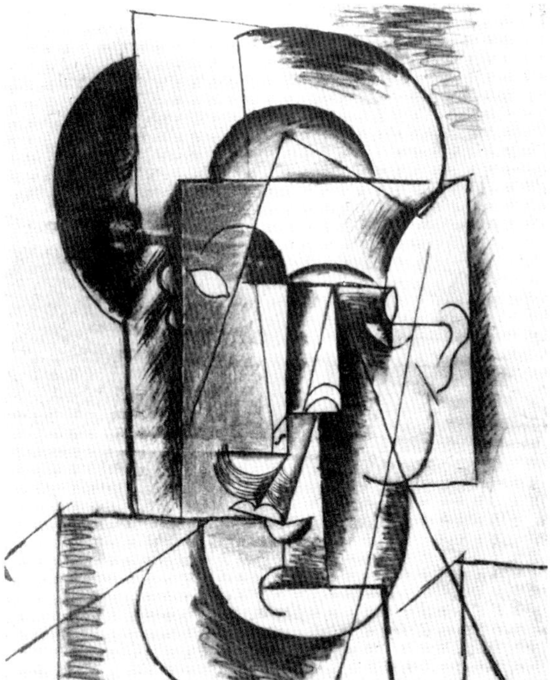
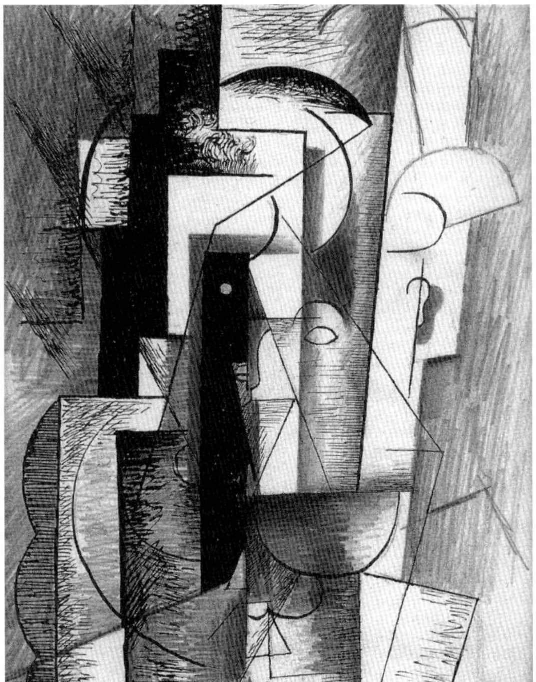

the model for his "official" portrait of 1913 (see fig. 159). dBesides the already noted descriptive features, the two drawings are linked by the identical relationship of the eyes (one a small circle, the other a large almond) and by the diagonal strip that emerges from the brow and descends to the right.

It would be inaccurate, nonetheless, to describe these two drawings as "caricatures" of Apollinaire. They are Cubist constructions that have assumed a particular representational value (in this case, as portraits) because of the insertion of caricatural details. The details act as a series of synecdoches for the integral image of Apollinaire, present in the 1905 caricature but absent in the 1912–13 drawings. As they demonstrate, the difference between a caricatural and a Cubist drawing is not merely one of degree; it is fundamental.

Even though the elements of the face are distorted in a caricature, the relationship among them remains basically naturalistic. The caricature is a transformed version of the naturalistic image as a whole. The Cubist face is not. In his 1912–13 drawings, Picasso discards most of the naturalistic elements of the face – and also the naturalistic relationship among them. He creates a geometric armature of vertical planes that have the potential to be read as equivalents for the planes of the human face. This geometric armature is then supplemented with synecdochic signs corresponding to fragments of a real face. These fragments often resemble the elements of a caricature – in this case, they actually derive from a caricature – but they are no longer linked together by the naturalistic relationship that makes a caricature seem "life-like" despite its distortions.

156 (*facing page top left*) Picasso. *Guillaume Apollinaire*. Paris, 1905. Pen and ink on paper, 31 × 23 cm. Zervos XXII, 294. Collection Family of Henry Brandon, Washington, D.C.

157 (*facing page top right*) Picasso. *Head of a Man*. Sorgues, summer 1912. Pencil on graph-paper page from notebook, 13 × 8.5 cm. Not in Zervos. Léal, carnet 16, p. 10v. Musée Picasso, Paris

158 (*facing page bottom left*) Picasso. *Head of a Man*. Sorgues, summer 1912. Charcoal and pastel on paper, 64 × 47 cm. Zervos II*, 327. Kunstmuseum Wintherthur. Bequest of C. and E. Friedrich-Jezler

159 (*facing page bottom right*) Picasso. *Portrait of Guillaume Apollinaire*. Paris, early 1913. Pencil and ink on paper, 21 × 15 cm. D.R. 579. Private collection

The large drawing of summer 1912 (see fig. 158) is instructive in this regard. Although it incorporates the broad, curving chin that serves elsewhere as a sign for "Apollinaire," it cannot really be seen as a portrait. Too many of the poet's distinctive features have vanished. Furthermore, the internal organization of the head is quite different from that of the sketchbook study: the diagonal strip has been replaced by a series of overlapping planes, both eyes are now represented by almonds, and so on. In terms of both structure and representational value, the large drawing is merely a variation on a theme suggested by Apollinaire.

The role of synecdoche in Cubist figuration is even more evident in a varied group of drawings deriving from an early 1912 photograph of the collector Frank Haviland seated in Picasso's Boulevard Clichy studio (fig. 160). Haviland had been an important patron for Picasso in 1908–10, and it was he who had first attracted the painter and his circle in 1911 to the summer retreat of Céret. He seems to have enjoyed sitting for his portrait: there is a pointillist canvas of him by Modigliani, a "classical" bust by Manolo Hugué, and a caricatural head by Jacques Lipchitz.[164] Picasso's carefully posed photograph may have been taken as the first step toward a portrait: Zervos's catalogue includes three studies labeled "Study for a Portrait of Frank Haviland," and there are five additional drawings clearly related to this project.[165]

Three different aspects of the photograph seem to have engaged Picasso's attention. One, not surprisingly, was Haviland's face, with its center-parted hair, high brow, ski-slope nose, and small, pointed chin. The second was his pose: seated in Picasso's familiar scallop-backed chair, with a cane projecting prominently from his lap. The third was the small oval canvas placed behind Haviland's right shoulder – the still life *Shells on a Piano*, seen here in an early, unfinished state.[166]

Picasso summarized the key details of Haviland's face in a caricature (fig. 161), its fundamental naturalism disguised by a series of heavily shaded diagonal planes. On a second sheet (fig. 162), the overall configuration of the face disintegrates and the stylized details are combined with a variety of non-naturalistic forms. Toward the top of the sheet, the curved "wings" of Haviland's center-parted hair are juxtaposed with a diagonal strip corresponding roughly to the facial plane of the caricature; lower down, these "wings" appear in tandem with the brows, nose, and chin, superimposed on a series of planes slanting to both right and left. The "wings" here seem to be mounted on a kind of stalk, rhyming with a series of plant-like forms that rise at left.

160 (*right*) Photograph of Frank Haviland in Picasso's studio at 11, Boulevard Clichy. Paris, early 1912, Picasso Archives, Paris

161 (*below left*) Picasso. *Head [Frank Haviland]*. Paris, early 1912. Lead pencil on paper, 29 × 23 cm. Zervos XXVIII, 168. Picasso estate (inv. 1113)

162 (*below right*) Picasso. *Study for a Portrait of Frank Haviland*. Paris, early 1912. India ink on paper, 24 × 16.5 cm. Zervos XXVIII, 28. Picasso estate (inv. 1303)

163 (*facing page top left*) Picasso. *Man in an Armchair [Frank Haviland]*. Paris, early 1912. Ink on paper, 31.5 × 20 cm. Zervos VI, 1161. Picasso estate (inv. 1335)

164 (*facing page top right*) Picasso. *Man in an Armchair by a Piano [Frank Haviland]*. Paris, early 1912. Ink on paper, 31.5 × 20 cm. Zervos XXVIII, 154. Picasso estate (inv. 1339)

165 (*facing page bottom left*) Picasso. *Woman at a Piano*. Sorgues, summer 1912. Ink and pencil on paper, 34 × 22 cm. Zervos XXVIII, 152. Musée Picasso, Paris

166 (*facing page bottom right*) Picasso. *Nude Leaning on a Sculpture Stand [Study for Artist's Model]*. Sorgues, summer 1912. India ink on paper, 34 × 22 km. Zervos XXVIII, 222. Picasso estate (inv. 1570)

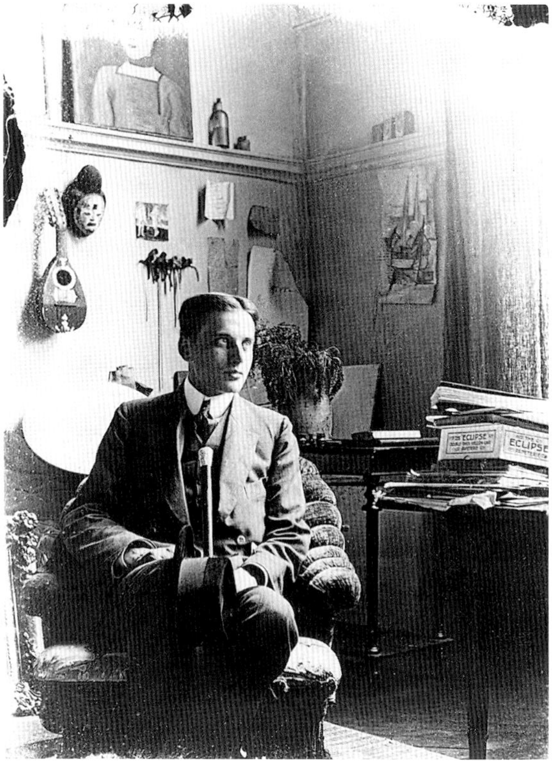

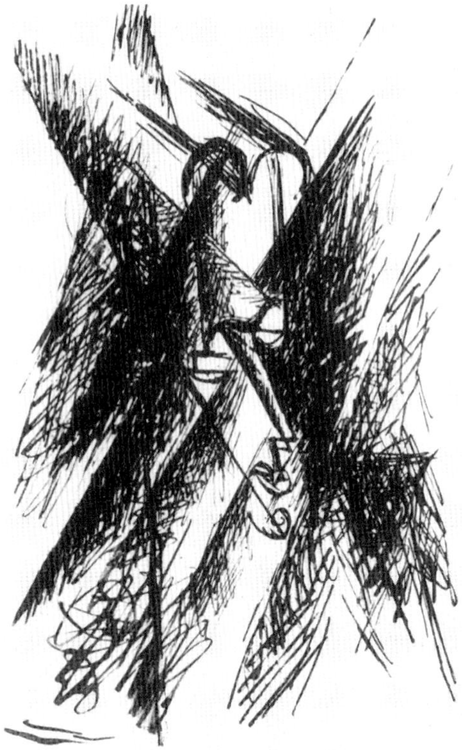

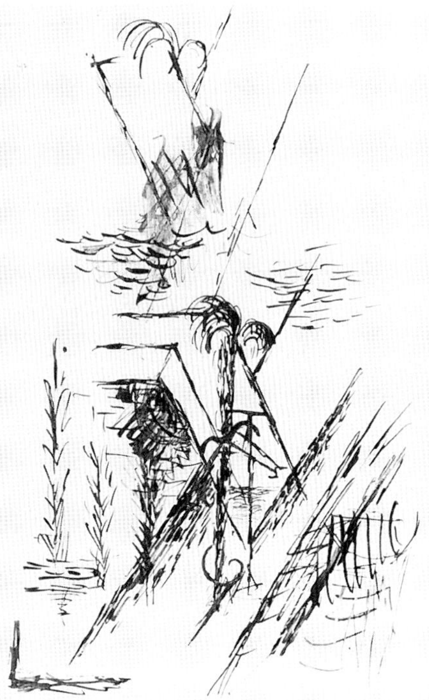

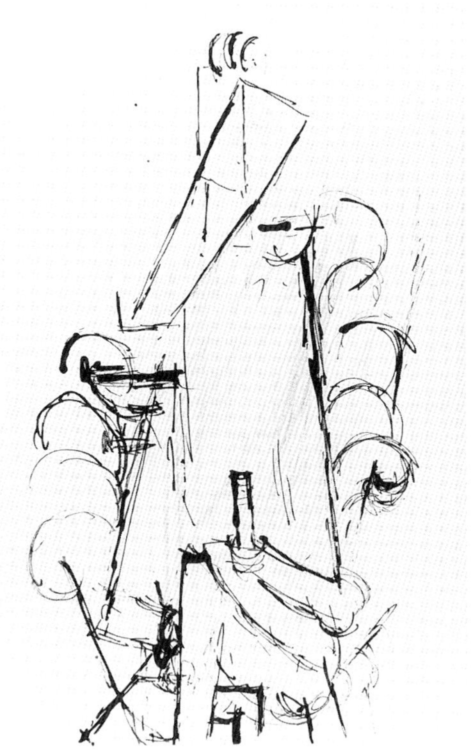

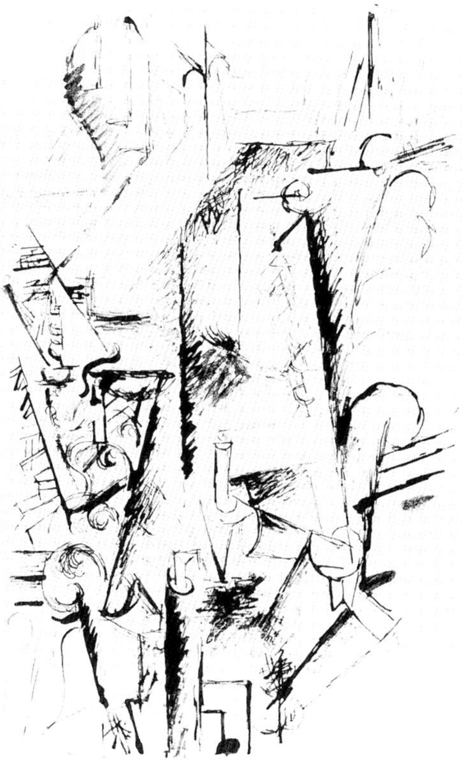

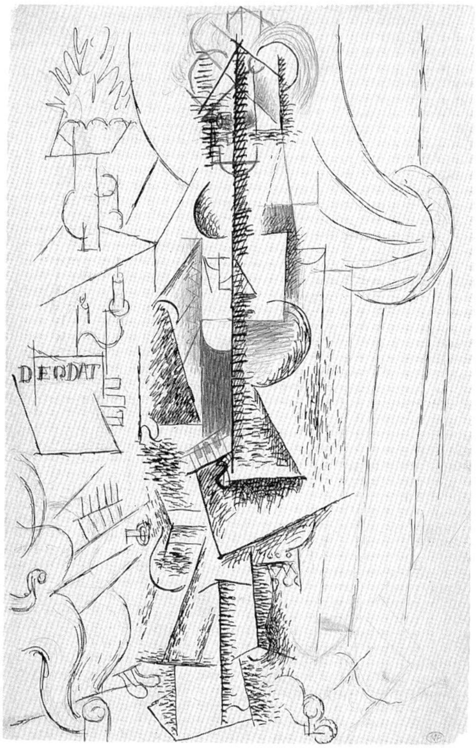

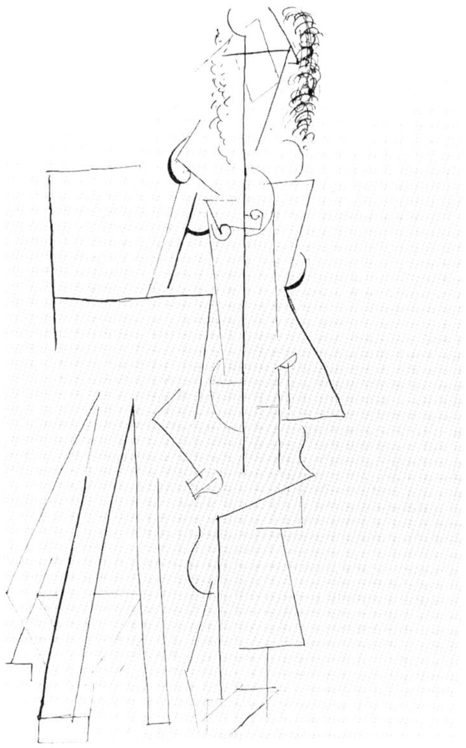

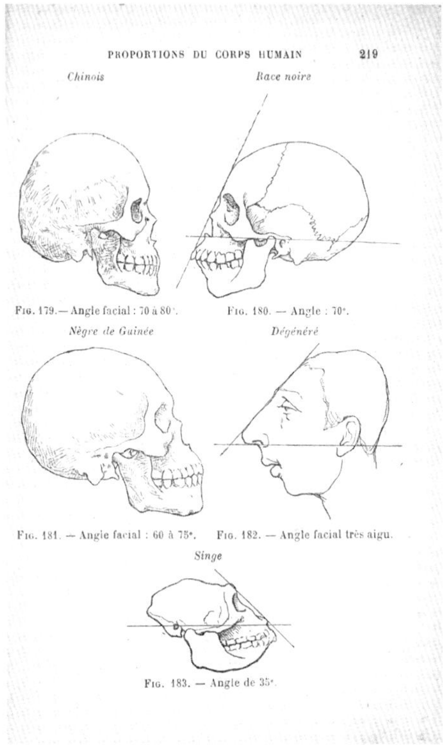

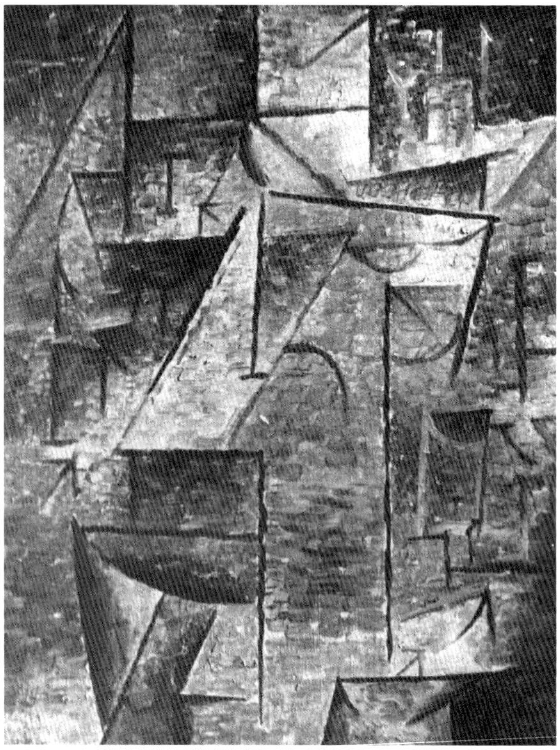

167 (*above left*) Angles of the facial plane. From Camille Bellanger, *L'Art du peintre: traité pratique du dessin et de la peinture* (Paris: Garnier Frères, 1909), p. 219

168 (*above right*) Picasso. *Head of Girl.* Paris, early 1911. Oil on canvas, 41 × 33 cm. D.R. 376. Collection Riccardo Jucker, Milan

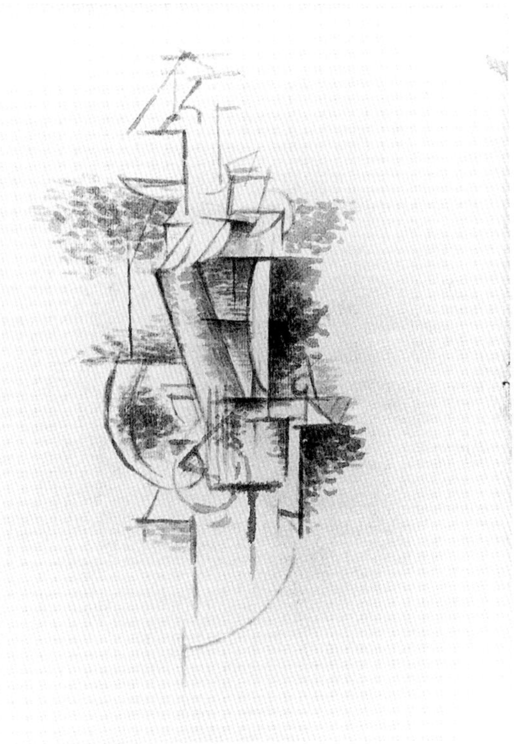

169 (*right*) Picasso. *Woman with Mandolin.* Paris, early 1911. Ink and wash on paper, dimensions unknown. Not in Zervos. Picasso estate (inv. 1210)

The overall image of Haviland seated in a chair provided the point of departure for a second series of drawings (fig. 163). Here, Picasso concentrated on the general outlines of Haviland's body, framed by the armchair's scalloped upholstery. He also emphasized the vertical stub of the cane, rising from between the knees. Conversely, Picasso ignored Haviland's facial features, treating the head as a blank trapezoid, topped by a few generic curves representing hair. On another sheet (fig. 164), Picasso elaborated this image in two distinct ways. The ideographic image of "wings on a stalk" was imported from the first series of drawings to serve as a synecdochic sign for Haviland's face and, more generally, identity. Appearing at the top of the composition, it is accompanied by a shaded, ghost-like curve suggesting the volume of the head. On the left, Picasso sketched in a disjointed image of an upright piano, with a curved leg to support the shelf-like keyboard, and an elaborate candelabra to illuminate the music stand.

The motif of the piano seems to have been suggested by the still life *Shells on a Piano* that appears in this location in the original photograph. This may be a deliberate piece of symbolism. Haviland was a talented pianist and had been introduced to Picasso's circle by the composer Déodat de Séverac.[167] It thus seems likely that the unfinished painting was placed prominently in the photograph specifically as a reference to Haviland's musical interests. It is, in effect, a conceptual synecdoche. In the drawing, the same point is made by including an actual piano, the Gaveau upright that stood in the drawing room of Picasso's apartment.[168]

The same kind of displacement of signs from one context to another is evident in a summer 1912 drawing, *Woman at a Piano* (fig. 165). The piano here is a more legible version of the piano in fig. 164, but the figure has nothing in common with the "portrait" of Haviland. Actually, the figuration of this drawing is even more complicated than it may at first appear. As he often did, Picasso first drew the composition in pencil, and then reinforced and elaborated it with pen and ink. The pencil underdrawing of the figure reveals a moustachioed figure resembling the composer Déodat de Séverac, whose name appears on the piano's music stand. The piano thus originally served as a symbol for the chain of friendships linking Picasso, Séverac, and Haviland. When Picasso redrew the standing figure in ink, however, he transformed it into a female nude similar to the figure in a composition he was then working on, showing a model standing next to a sculpture stand (fig. 166).

The signs linked to Apollinaire and Haviland in these drawings seem to have been created by a two-step process. First the subject's naturalistic image was reduced to a kind of caricature; then this caricature was broken up, and its fragments were exported to serve as signs of identity in new compositions that might or might not be linked to the original image. Caricature was just one device for generating signs, however. Equally often, Picasso proceeded by creating an abstract form corresponding to one or another aspect of the figure. Academic training relied on several geometric devices to define the naturalistic figure, and these provided Picasso with ready-made examples of abstraction.

As remarked earlier, Picasso borrowed the academic technique of measuring the angle formed by a line descending from brow to nose in early 1911, when he drew and painted several figures with their faces reduced to simple angles, defined by the intersection of diagonal and horizontal lines (figs. 167–69). Conceptually, this is a synecdochic sign more like the wood-graining of Braque's *Homage to J. S. Bach* (see fig. 148) than like the caricatural elements of the Apollinaire and Haviland pictures: the angle represents one aspect of the face, rather than one part of it. In effect, Picasso is selectively quoting an academic diagram of the human face, reproducing the geometric angle without reproducing the naturalistic profile it is supposed to describe. In other pictures, he parodies academic procedure by depicting the face as a plane traversed by a series of evenly spaced lines (fig. 170). This seems to allude to the academic belief that the human face can be divided into a series of even intervals between brow, eyes, nose, and chin (fig. 171). Here too Picasso reduces the face to a synecdochic sign derived from the conceptual analysis of form, not from visual experience.

These conceptual signs did not necessarily derive from academic theory: they could also emerge from the conventions of Cubism itself. This process can be followed in a series of drawings done between summer 1912 and spring 1913.

In summer 1912, as noted above, Picasso had evolved the convention of representing the face with a pair of planes, one descending diagonally from ear to chin, the other rising vertically from chin to forehead. The divergence between the two overlapping planes tended to create a sense of visual tension, which then affected the disposition of the other elements of the face. In a summer 1912 example of this type (fig. 172), the bridge of the nose inclines at an angle that seems to represent a compromise between the vertical of the face and the diagonal of the jaw. The eyes are attached to a crossbar at right angles to the line of the nose, while the eyebrows are indicated by an arc sitting atop this line. Together, eyebrows and nose form a shape like an upside-down anchor.

The summer 1912 head seems strongly three-dimensional, with the facial plane floating in front of the rest of the head, and the jaw receding behind it. By the beginning of 1913, however, Picasso had reworked this arrangement so that all of the planes lay parallel to the picture plane (fig. 173). The divergence between the facial plane and the plane of the jaw is now expressed in terms of a strictly two-dimen-

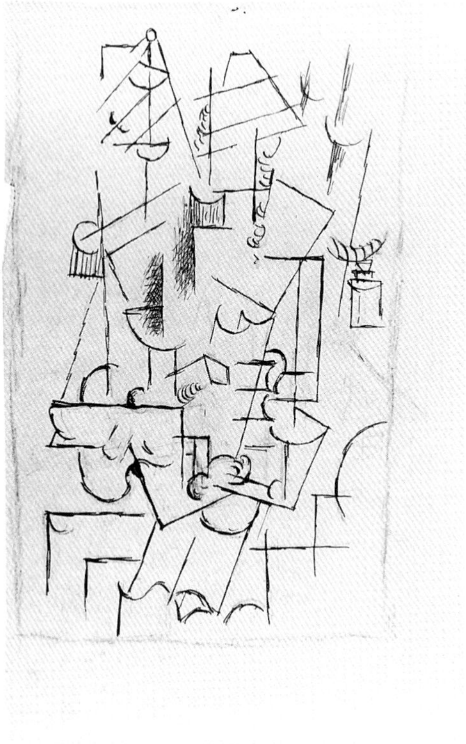

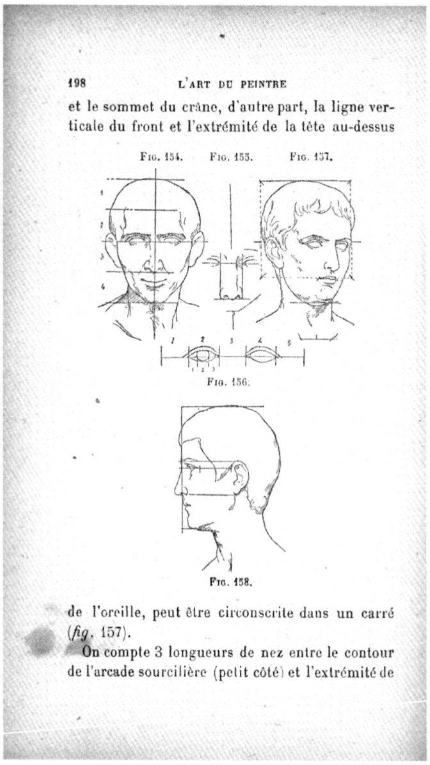

198 L'ART DU PEINTRE

et le sommet du crâne, d'autre part, la ligne verticale du front et l'extrémité de la tête au-dessus

Fig. 154. Fig. 155. Fig. 157.

Fig. 156.

Fig. 158.

de l'oreille, peut être circonscrite dans un carré (*fig.* 157).

On compte 3 longueurs de nez entre le contour de l'arcade sourcilière (petit côté) et l'extrémité de

sional pivoting movement. Otherwise, there is little to distinguish them. The "law of differentiation" has gone into reverse. Picasso acknowledges the new similarity between the facial plane and the plane of the jaw by allocating some of the facial features to each: the vertical plane gets the nose and eyes (represented by dots at either side of a vertical line), while the inclined plane gets the upside-down anchor representing nose and brows.

In a *papier collé* of around the same time (fig. 174), the dots-plus-line motif representing eyes and nose was again inscribed on the vertical plane of the face. But the plane of the jaw disappeared, surviving only in the inclination of the upside-down anchor. The original schema of overlapping planes was soon reduced to an ideographic arrangement of diverging axes (fig. 175), with only the dots of the eyes and the arc of the eyebrows to identify them as elements of a face. The diverging planes of the summer 1912 head, which had provided a geometric substrate supporting the linear signs for eyes and nose, now become linear signs: a pair of pivoting axes. This double-axis ideogram is a sign for the volume of the head and the larger body of which it is a part.

170 (*above left*) Picasso. Study for *Soldier and Girl.* Paris, spring 1912. Ink and charcoal on paper, 30.5 × 11.5 cm. Zervos XXVIII, 24. Picasso estate (inv. 1220)

171 (*above right*) Diagrams of facial proportions. From Camille Bellanger, *L'Art du peintre: traité pratique du dessin et de la peinture* (Paris: Garnier Frères, 1909), p. 198

172 (*facing page top left*) Picasso. *Head of Man with Moustache.* Sorgues, summer 1912. Charcoal, 60.5 × 46 cm. Zervos II*, 325. Formerly collection Mr. and Mrs. Richard C. Hedreen, Seattle

173 (*facing page top right*) Picasso. *Head of Man.* Paris, early 1913. Oil, charcoal, ink, and pencil on paper, 61.6 × 46.3 cm. D.R. 615. The Richard S. Zeisler Collection, New York

174 (*facing page bottom left*) Picasso. *Head of Harlequin.* Paris or Céret, winter–spring 1913. Charcoal and pasted paper on paper, 62.5 × 47 cm. D.R. 617. Musée Picasso, Paris

175 (*facing page bottom right*) Picasso. *Guitarist.* Céret, spring 1913. Pencil on graph-paper page from notebook, 13 × 8.5 cm. Not in Zervos. Léal, carnet 17, p. 7v. Musée Picasso, Paris

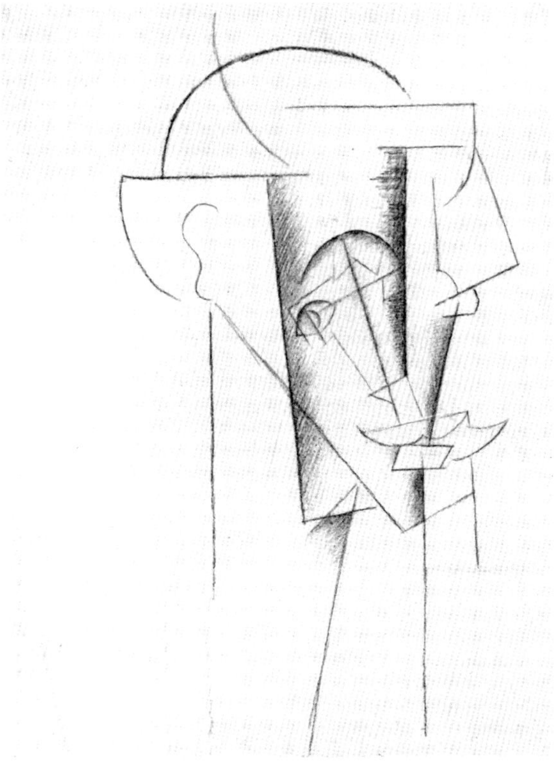

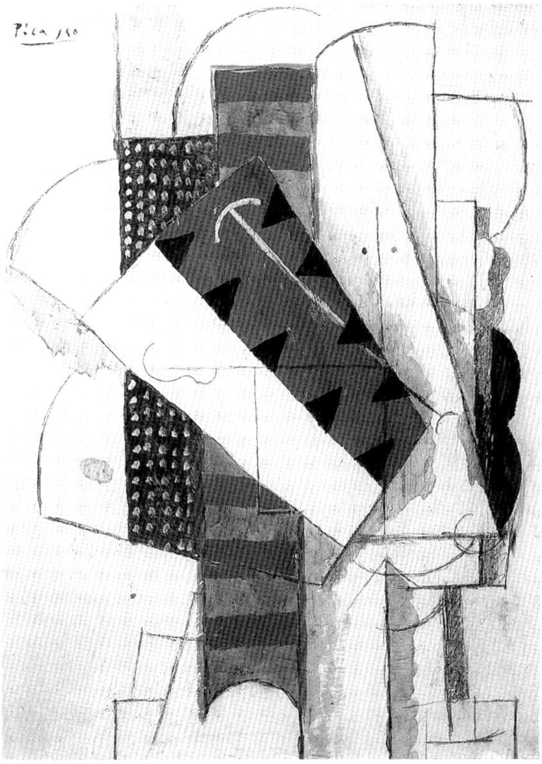

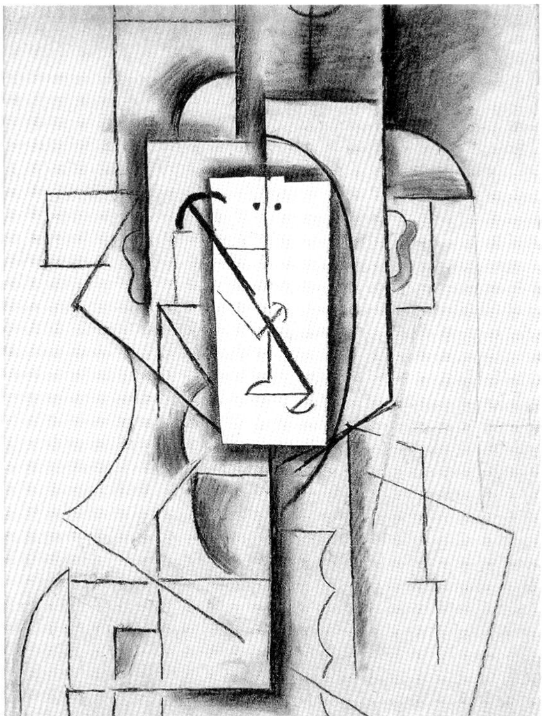

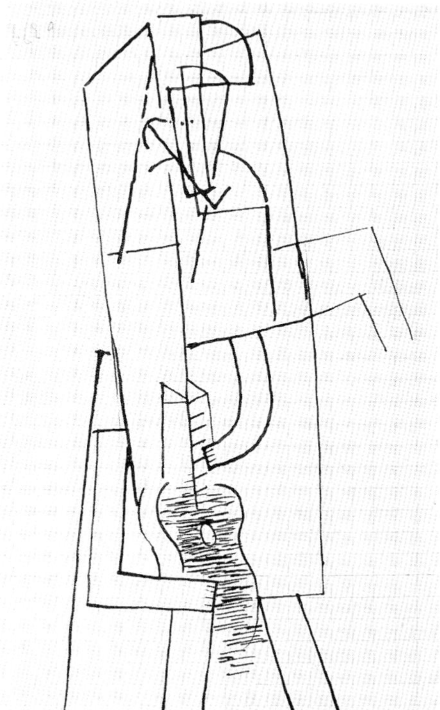

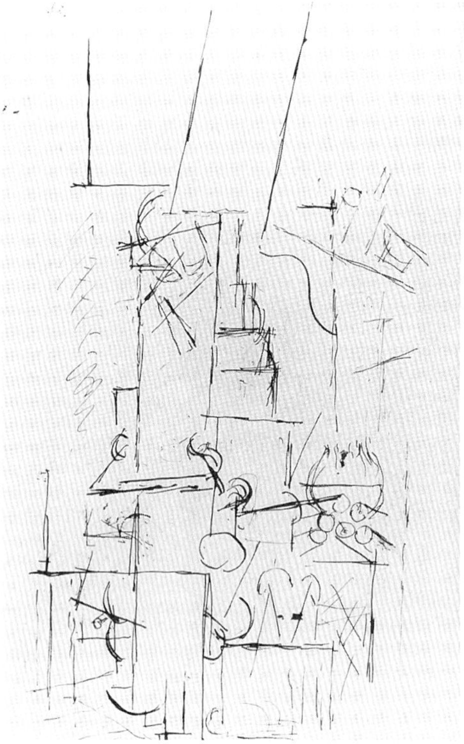

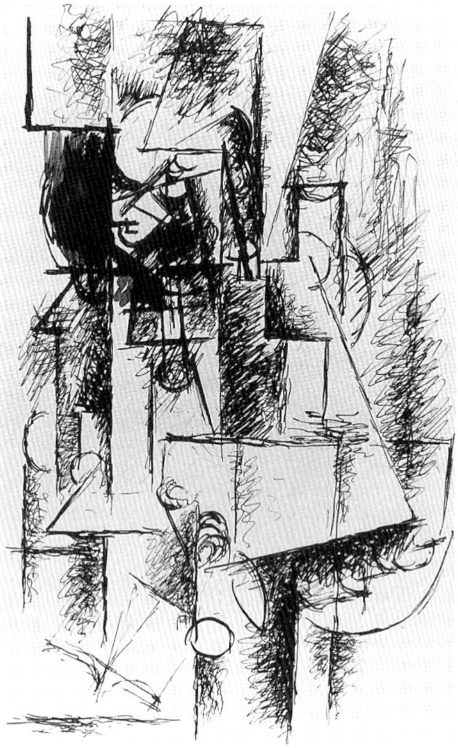

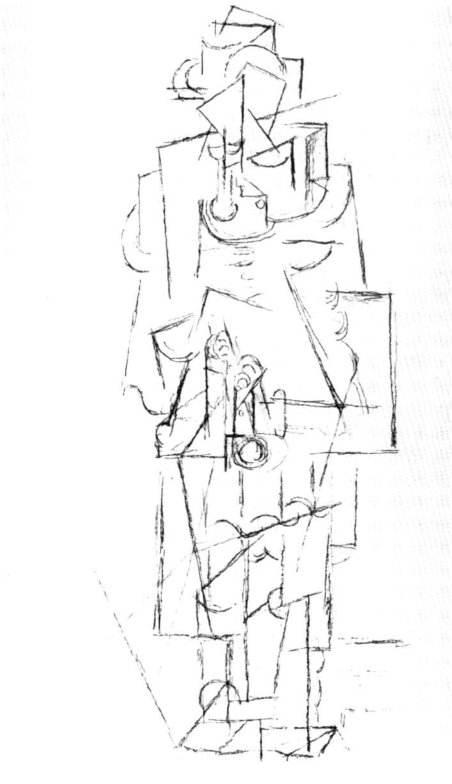

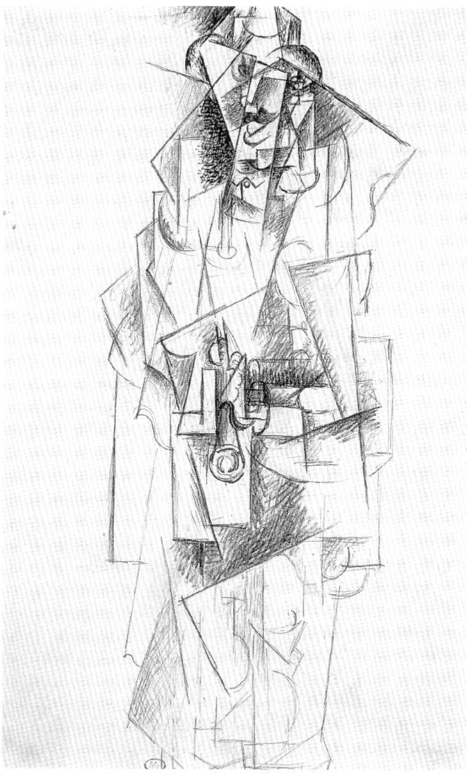

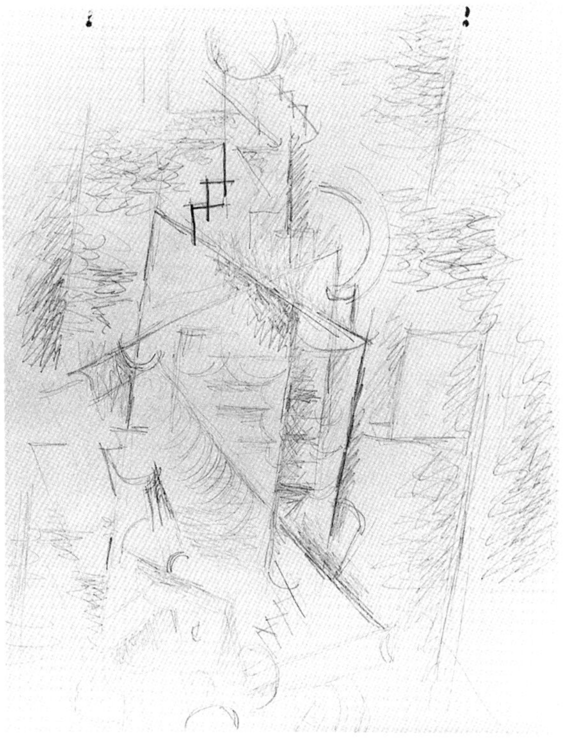

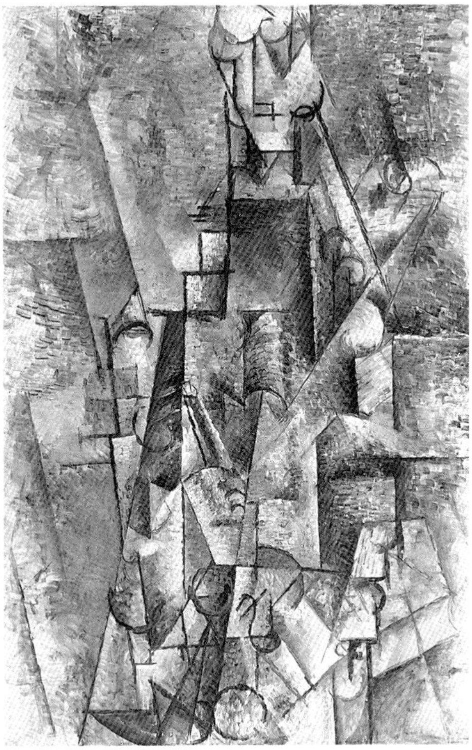

180 (*above left*) Picasso. *Woman with Tenora*. Paris, winter 1911–12. Lead pencil on paper, 29 × 23 cm. Zervos XXVIII, 45. Picasso estate (inv. 1284)

181 (*above right*) Picasso. *Man with Clarinet (Man with Tenora)*. Paris, winter 1911–spring 1912. Oil on canvas, 105 × 69 cm. D.R. 426. Museo Thyssen-Bornemisza, Madrid

176 (*facing page top left*) Picasso. *Figure with Tenora and Dog in Front of a Fire*. Paris, winter 1911–12. Ink on paper, 31 × 19 cm. Zervos XXIX, 74. Picasso estate (inv. 1563)

177 (*facing page top right*) Picasso. *Man with Tenora and Book*. Paris, winter 1911–12. Ink on paper, 30.5 × 19.5 cm. Zervos XXVIII, 47. Picasso estate (inv. 1312)

178 (*facing page bottom left*) Picasso. *Man with Tenora*. Paris, winter 1911–12. Lithographic crayon on paper, 30.5 × 19.5 cm. Zervos XXVIII, 43. Picasso estate (inv. 1563)

179 (*facing page bottom right*) Picasso. *Man with Tenora*. Paris, winter 1911–12. Lithographic crayon and India ink on paper, 30.5 × 19.5 cm. Zervos XXVIII, 48. Musée Picasso, Paris

Synecdoche and Superimposition

Artists have always created new pictures by repeating and varying earlier pictures. But the division of Cubist figuration into two different kinds of signs – synecdochic qualifiers and geometric qualifieds – added a new dimension to this process. Either element of the figuration might remain relatively stable while the other varied. The same geometric substrate could support different qualifiers. Or the same qualifiers could appear in tandem with a different set of geometric forms. The first of these possibilities finds many antecedents in earlier art, where compositional schemas invented for one purpose are often reused for another. The second yields something radically new, however – a series of pictures in which the subject and even its figuration remain the same, while the overall composition changes.

This process was at work in a series of drawings that seem to have been executed in winter 1911–12 (see figs. 176–79). Picasso's summer 1911 sojourn in the southwestern village of Céret had deeply impressed him, and his work of the following winter often drew on the Catalan culture that Céret shared with nearby Spain. Bullfighting and music provided two of the most picturesque elements of this culture, the first expressed primarily through images of local journals such as *Le Torero*, the second through images of the *tenora*, a distinctively raucous wind instrument. Picasso's friend Déodat de Séverac was a noted champion of the *tenora*; indeed, in spring 1911, he brought a group of *tenora* players from Céret to Paris to help perform his oratorio *Héliogabale*, presented to great acclaim in the Salle Gaveau. Although the wind instruments in Picasso's and Braque's 1911–12 pictures are usually identified as clarinets, they are in fact *tenoras*, as Patrick O'Brian and Lewis Kachur have noted.[169]

What seems to be the first of the drawings in this series (fig. 176) shows a standing figure playing a *tenora*. The dog at his side, the roaring fire behind him, and what appears to be a ceiling of low, broad beams all suggest a rustic setting. The *tenora* player himself is defined principally as a tall vertical strip. A sharply pointed elbow, at left, extends into a horizontal forearm, ending in a hand that curls back where it encounters the vertical cylinder of the *tenora*. The player's other hand grasps the outside edge of the instrument with scrawled, claw-like fingers. The bell of the instrument is represented by a flattened oval.

The player's elbow, forearm, and hands, and the bell of the *tenora* are recognizable on another sheet of identical dimensions (fig. 177), but everything else about the drawing is different. The vertical strip of the musician's body has been absorbed in a heavily shaded grid that expands to fill the entire sheet. The player seems to be wearing a hat with a high crown and a broad circular brim. A cylindrical form some distance below this hat seems to represent the mouthpiece of the *tenora*.

Both hat and mouthpiece reappear in a third drawing (fig. 178), along with the *tenora*'s bell and the musician's distinctive hands. But the overall grid disappears. More precisely, it contracts, so that it occupies only the area of the musician's body. In a fourth drawing (fig. 179), the shading is restored, and the musician is portrayed in greater detail. The moustache from the third drawing is colored in and a nose appears above it. A new figuration of arm and shoulder begins to take form in the third drawing and is clarified in the fourth drawing: the long horizontal forearm contracts to the base of a right triangle, while the shoulder above it is indicated by a "melon slice" deriving from the *Mademoiselle Léonie* figures of 1910 (see figs. 96–98).

The figuration of the *tenora* and of the player's hands and arms evolves only slightly from beginning to end of the

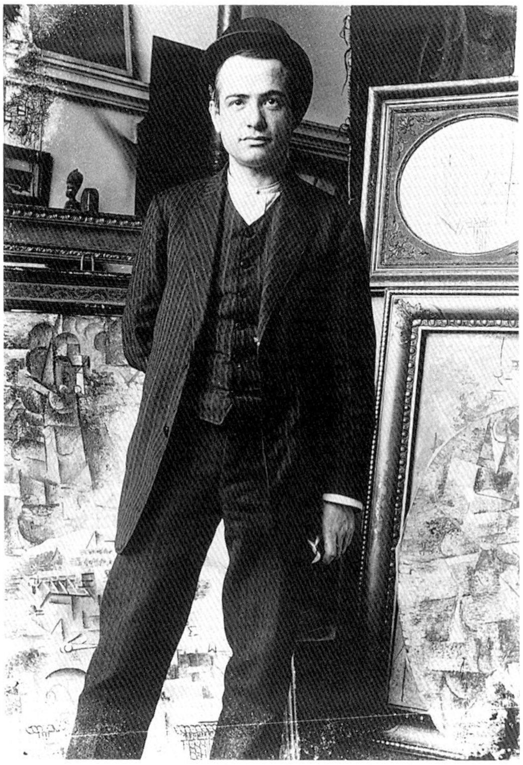

series. From one drawing to the next, however, they are attached to a very different substrate of geometrical forms. In effect, the qualifiers remain the same, while the qualifieds undergo radical change. As Picasso refined the composition, the original qualifiers were supplemented by new ones (the man's hat and moustache, the mouthpiece of the *tenora*), while some of the geometric forms (the arm on the left) began to crystallize into recognizable configurations, evolving from qualified into qualifier.

Meanwhile, in another series of drawings (on a different size of sheet), Picasso explored an alternative figuration of the *tenora* player (fig. 180). Here, the musician's head is indicated by a circle shaded to suggest an abstract ball, mounted atop a vertical strip flanked by rows of steps. A long straight line descends from left to right at the shoulders. Both arms are indicated by zigzagging diagonal strips, and the *tenora* between them is also placed on a diagonal. The finished painting known as *Man with Clarinet* (fig. 181) combines elements from both series of drawings. The arm on the left is a right triangle, as in the first series, while the arm on the right forms an angle like the arm in the second series. The lower section of the *tenora* is vertical, as in the

182 (*facing page*) Photograph of Auguste Herbin in Picasso's studio at 11, Boulevard Clichy. Paris, spring 1911. Picassso Archives, Paris

183 (*right*) Picasso. *Monk with Mandolin (Buffalo Bill)*. Paris, spring 1911. Oil on canvas, 98 × 77 cm. D.R. 389. Repainted as *Man with Guitar*, spring 1912, and 1913. Musée Picasso, Paris

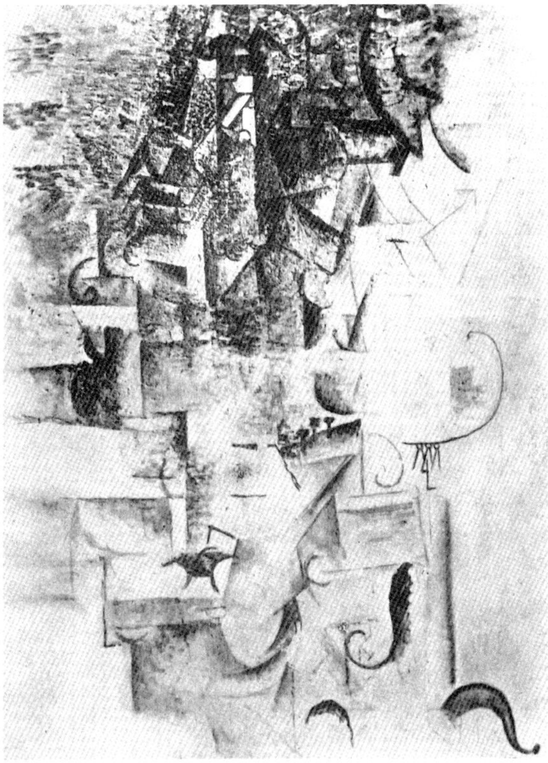

184 (*below left*) Diagram of the head in *Monk with Mandolin*, as seen in the photograph of Auguste Herbin

185 (*below right*) Diagram of the head in *Monk with Mandolin* as seen in the photograph from the Kahnweiler archives

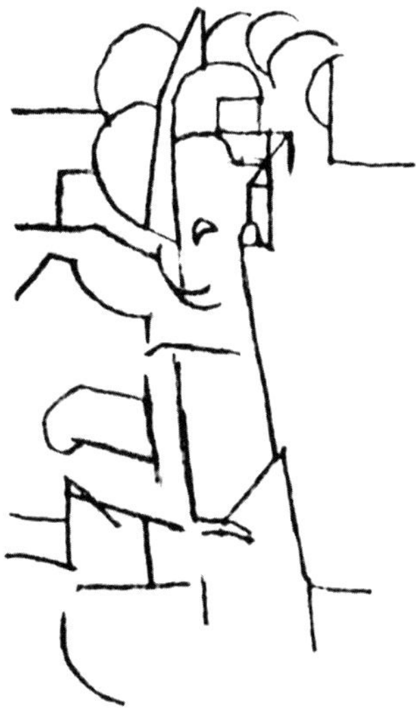

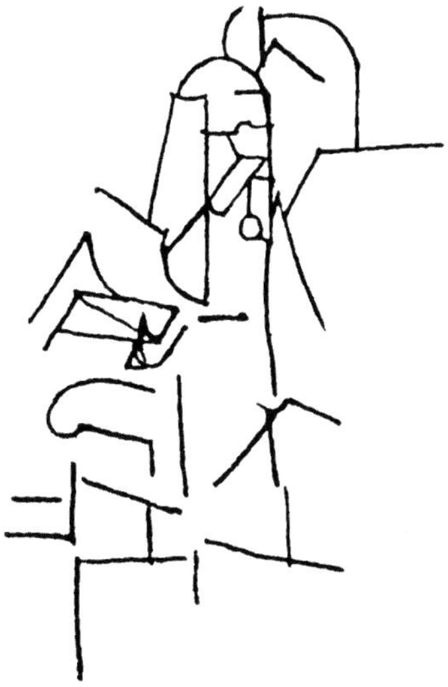

first series, but the upper section is tilted, as in the second series. The neck is flanked by little steps, as in the second series, but the figuration of the face differs from all of the preparatory drawings.

This independent evolution – and creative interaction – of sign and substrate was a permanent feature of Picasso's work from 1911 until virtually the end of his career.[170] Between spring 1911 and summer 1912, however, it resulted in pictures of a unique density, created by the layering of image upon image. The distinctive appearance of his work during these fifteen or so months was derived above all from the process of superimposition. It might be said that this process represents Picasso's appropriation, for the visual arts, of the endless combinatorial power of language. Once the distinction between signs and substrate had created visual equivalents for words and syntax, it became possible to repeat a syntactic construction with new words, or to reuse existing words in a new syntactic construction.

The series of mandolin players that Picasso painted in the course of 1911–12 offers the most complex example of this process of layering and reworking. As earlier seen, a small canvas of spring 1911 provided the template for a series of larger canvases painted and reworked over the following months (see figs. 103–05). The mandolin player motif was also explored in another canvas whose complex development can be traced through archival photographs. The earliest known state of this work is visible at left in a photograph of the painter Auguste Herbin, posing in Picasso's studio in spring 1911 (fig. 182).[171] The lower half of the canvas is concealed by an oval still life of a mandolin on a table, so that only the figure's head and shoulders are visible. Nonetheless, this is recognizably the same canvas that appears in the Kahnweiler gallery photograph of a spring 1911 painting known as *Monk with Mandolin* (fig. 183). (In Kahnweiler's stockbook, however, it is titled *Buffalo Bill*.[172]) Comparison between the two photographs suggests that Picasso reworked the canvas in the interval between the Herbin and Kahnweiler photographs. The differences in the figuration of the head are hard to summarize visually but can be indicated by drawings traced from the two photographs (figs. 184, 185).

Picasso sold *Monk with Mandolin* to Kahnweiler in spring 1911. During the time the canvas was visible at the gallery, it seems to have exercised a significant influence on other painters, providing the model, for instance, for Juan Gris's *Man in a Café*, which closely mimics Picasso's pedestal

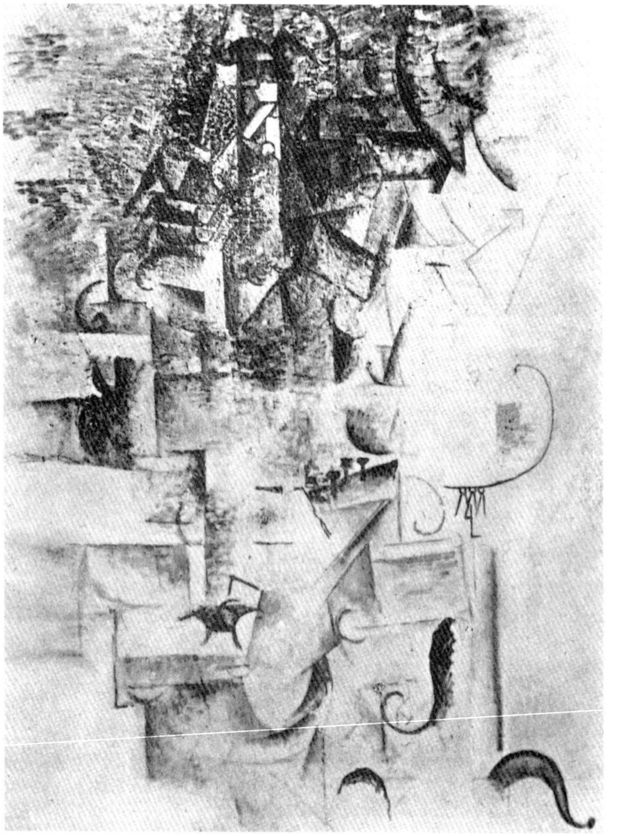

186 Picasso. *Monk with Mandolin (Buffalo Bill)*. Paris, spring 1911. Oil on canvas, 98 × 77 cm. D.R. 389. Repainted as *Man with Guitar*, spring 1912, and 1913. Musée Picasso, Paris

table with its distinctive arched foot.[173] Late in 1911 or early in 1912, however, Picasso reclaimed *Monk with Mandolin* and reworked it extensively, transforming it into a *Man with Guitar*. An inscription on the back of the reworked canvas reads, "K 11 & 12 / ET 13," indicating Kahnweiler's ownership and the three periods of work on the composition. Like the spring 1911 *Man with Mandolin*, the canvas was lengthened from 100 to just over 150 centimeters in height, but the added section was never finished, and the canvas remained in Picasso's studio at his death.[174] Comparison between the earlier and later states of the canvas (figs. 186–88) shows how the original composition, equally divided between vertical and horizontal bands, was revised so that it consisted almost exclusively of vertical strips. A wineglass appeared on the café table at right, but the table itself virtually disappeared, its tall pedestal base obscured by a broad plane descending

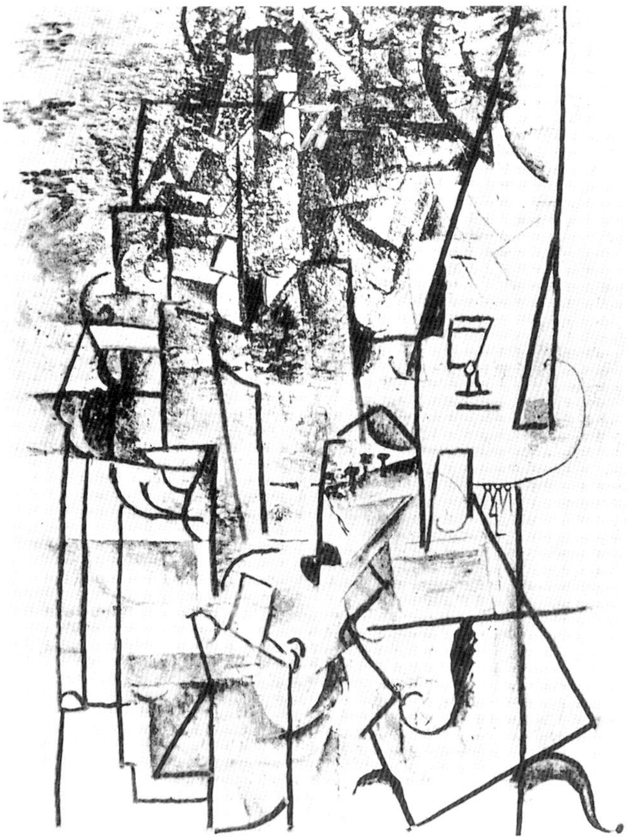

187 Diagram showing main lines added to *Monk with Mandolin* in the course of its transformation into *Man with Guitar*

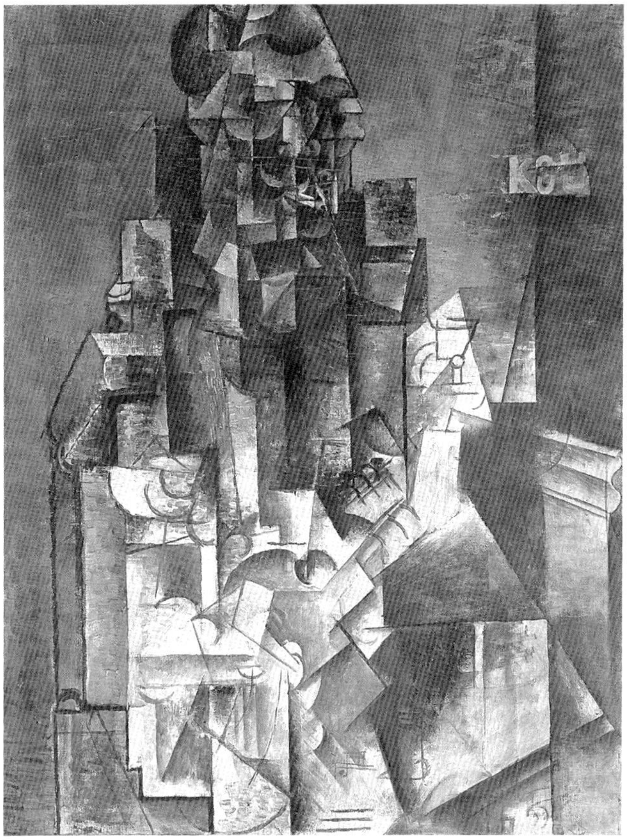

188 Picasso. *Man with Guitar.* Paris, spring 1911, spring 1912, and spring 1913. Oil on canvas, 154 × 77.5 cm. D.R. 427. Musée Picasso, Paris. Reproduction cropped to area of original canvas

at a diagonal toward the lower right corner. The tuning pegs remained unchanged, but the instrument they were attached to became nominally a guitar instead of a mandolin. A written inscription, "KOU," appeared in the upper right corner of the canvas, formerly occupied by drapery folds. In sum, the figure itself remained more or less the same, while its geometric substructure was revised and additional motifs were superimposed on the existing composition.

In the case of another painting, *"Ma Jolie" (Woman with Zither)* (see fig. 130), the finished canvas seems to combine figurations from two different sources. Once again, Picasso's starting point seems to have been the small mandolin player of spring 1911 (fig. 189). At some point – probably later that spring – Picasso drew a larger and more abstract version of this figure (fig. 190). The arm on the right, holding the neck of the mandolin, was modified only slightly; but Picasso reconfigured the arm on the left, chopping off the acute angle of the elbow and transferring it to the figure's hand. The naturalistic mandolin was replaced by an abstract collection of signs: a broken circle for the sound-hole, a diagonal rising from the circle for the tilt of the instrument's body, and a horizontal strip for the neck. In the drawing as in the painting, the breasts are depicted as semicircular arcs, cantilevered or suspended from the horizontal strip of the shoulders. A right triangle, accompanied by an incomplete circle, seems to indicate the presence of the head.

The distinctive figurations of arm and mandolin, and the breast suspended from the shoulder, all seem to recur in the canvas of *"Ma Jolie"* (fig. 191; see fig. 130), suggesting that, like *Monk with Mandolin*, it was begun in spring 1911 and then reworked in the winter of 1911–12. In this reworking,

Picasso seems to have drawn on the study of *Woman with Tenora* (see fig. 192) and the finished *Man with Clarinet* (see fig. 181), which provided the models for the stepped neck, the tilted shoulder terminating in a "melon slice," the right-angle arm at left, and the zigzag arm at right (fig. 193). The zither and the inscription "Ma Jolie" may have been added in a third campaign, influenced by the lyrics of Fragson's "Dernière Chanson," with its reference to (zither-playing) gypsy musicians, and its chorus, "Oh Manon ma jolie."[175] The finished canvas thus combines layer upon layer of forms and signs from different sources.

Simplification and Transformations

The superimposition of differing signs and structures is particularly characteristic of Picasso's work between early 1911 and summer 1912. Pictures from this period often include multiple versions of the same motif, and free-floating signs with no obvious connection to the forms surrounding them. The inexhaustible density and complexity of these pictures is achieved at the cost of their coherence and comprehensibility.

This seems to have troubled Picasso, and his work of summer–fall 1912 rejects density and complexity in favor of clarity and concision. What is most obvious about this new work is its relative simplicity. Picasso's paintings of late summer 1912 show that he was moving, gropingly, toward a new style of strong, unbroken lines and large, uninterrupted color planes. This development was confirmed by Braque's invention of the new medium of *papier collé* or "drawings with papers," as they were described in Braque's contract with Kahnweiler.[176]

It might be argued that this style was less new than it appeared to be – or, more precisely, that its novelty lay primarily in exposing the armature that had always been present in 1910–11 Cubism, although concealed by the superimposition of unrelated lines and forms. Evidently, summer–fall 1912 was the moment when this unveiling took place. As noted earlier, Leo Stein wrote that Picasso now "became more courageous and left the lines bare."[177]

The spare, linear drawing of his work from fall 1912 through early 1913 sometimes gives the impression that it might have been done by any reasonably skilled draftsman. Even before 1912, Picasso and Braque had stopped signing their pictures because, Picasso later said, "We felt the temptation, the hope of an anonymous art . . . We were trying to set up a new order and it had to express itself through different individuals. Nobody needed to know that it was so-and-so who had done this or that painting."[178] This impersonal quality made a particularly strong impression on

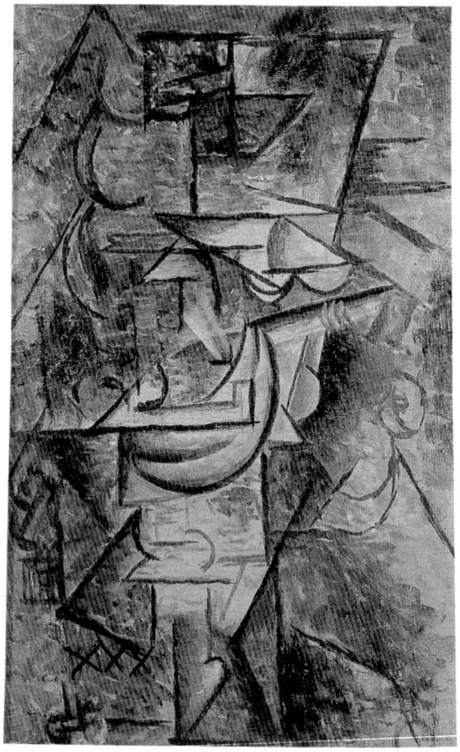

189 (*above*) Picasso. *Seated Woman with a Mandolin.* Paris, spring 1911. Oil on canvas, 38 × 24 cm. D.R. 397. Sidney Janis Gallery, New York

190 (*facing page top left*) Picasso. *Woman with Mandolin.* Paris, spring 1911. India ink on two sheets of paper, 80 × 48 cm. Zervos XXVII, 39. Picasso estate (inv. 1214)

191 (*facing page top right*) Diagram of *"Ma Jolie"* (*Woman with Zither*), with superimposed lines indicating "mandolin player"

192 (*facing page bottom left*) Picasso. *Woman with Tenora.* Paris, winter 1911–12. Lead pencil on paper, 29 × 23 cm. Zervos XXVIII, 45. Picasso estate (inv. 1284)

193 (*facing page bottom right*) Diagram of *"Ma Jolie"* (*Woman with Zither*), with superimposed lines indicating "tenora player" elements

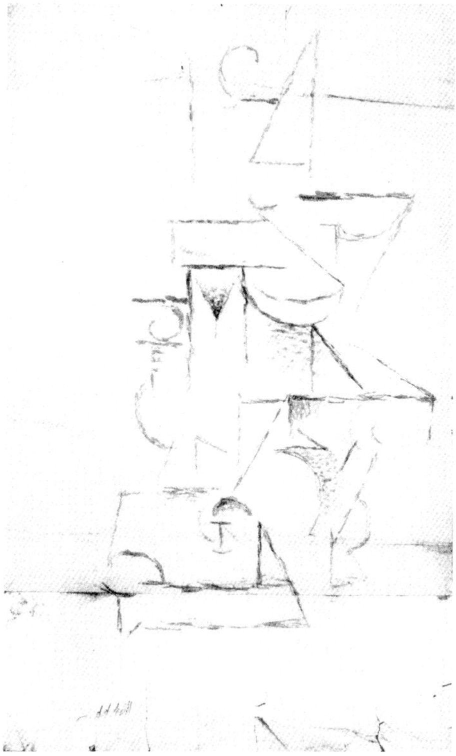

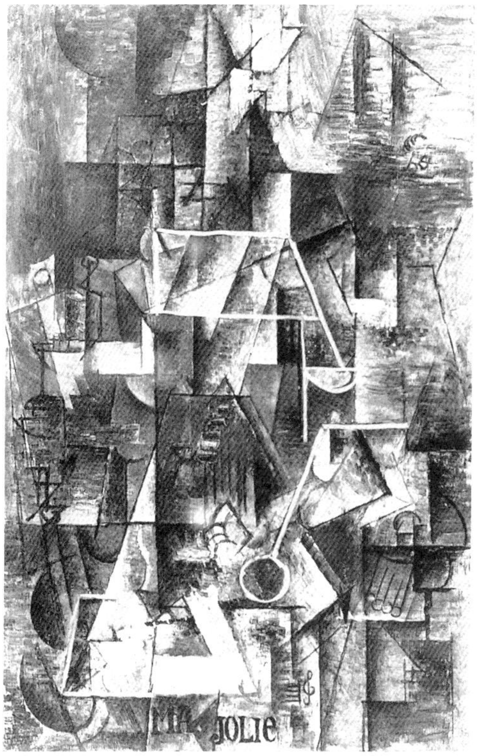
MA JOLIE

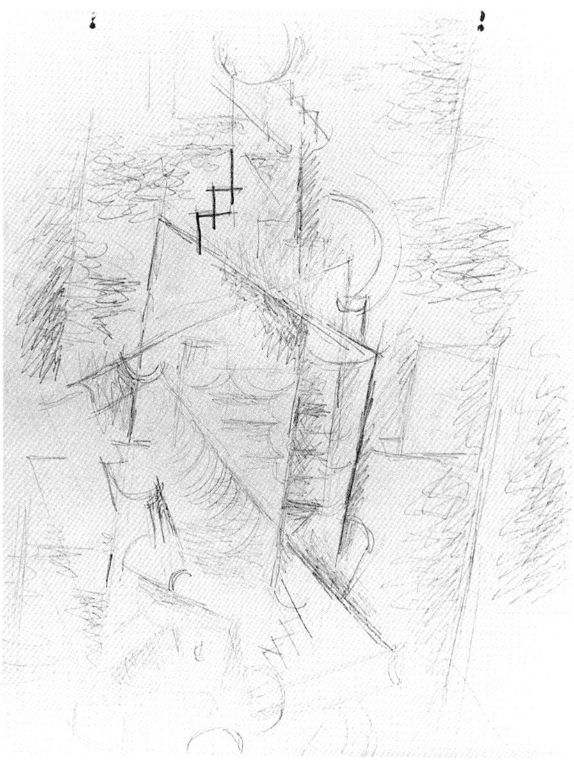

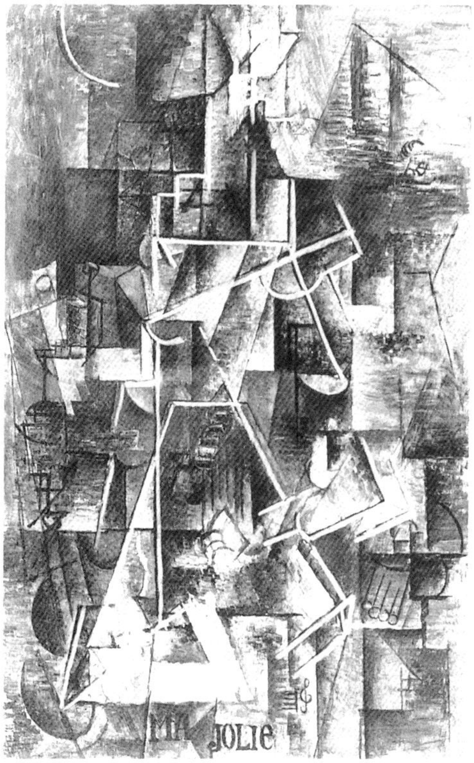
MA JOLIE

Marcel Duchamp and Francis Picabia, who saw in Picasso's and Braque's drawings a striking resemblance to the illustrations in technical manuals and the functional notations of scientific diagrams. Within a few years, this resemblance became the basis for the new "machine style" of Dada.[179]

It is probably a mistake to overestimate the social or political significance of the linear style in Picasso's and Braque's 1912–13 works. Their references to a quest for anonymity all date from the 1930s and '40s, when the polarization of French politics made the idea of anonymity into an expression of solidarity with the working class. As remarked before, Kahnweiler gave a more cynical, and probably more accurate, analysis of Picasso's motives when he wrote that Picasso's adoption of the medium of *papier collé* was "one of those romantic, ironic gestures calculated to display the pre-eminence of the creator's personality over his creation."[180]

In any case, it is not adequate to describe the new style of 1912–13 as merely a simplification or a laying bare of the elements of 1910–12 Cubism. The new style also involved a new relationship among signs. Instead of letting his synecdochic signs float freely on the surface of the image, Picasso began to tie them more directly to specific geometric forms – to create a more direct link between qualifier and qualified. Within the geometric substrate, Picasso began using similar arrangements of forms to represent both individual motifs and the larger complexes that they belonged to, so that the part would rhyme visually with the whole.

Ironically, the quest for greater coherence and specificity led to a new kind of mutability. The fact that the same forms could represent both part and whole suggested that they had no essential link to either. And the establishment of a closer link between sign and form ended by demonstrating how easily the value of a form could be modified, simply by changing the sign attached to it. At first, Picasso searched for ways to effect a rapid transformation of the motif from one picture to the next. Later, he experimented

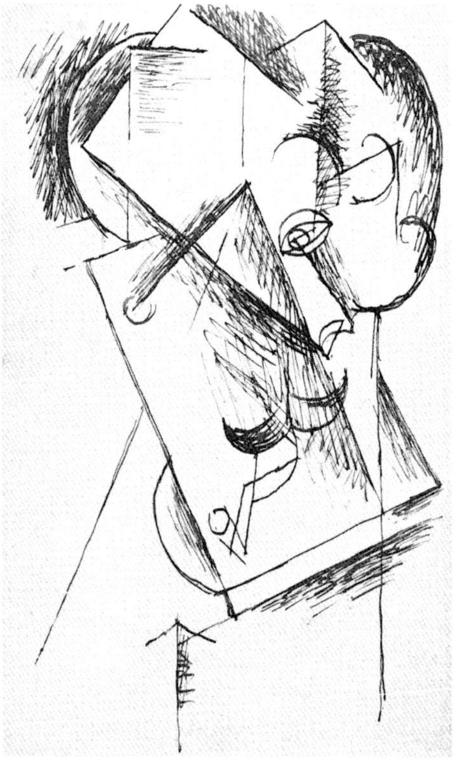

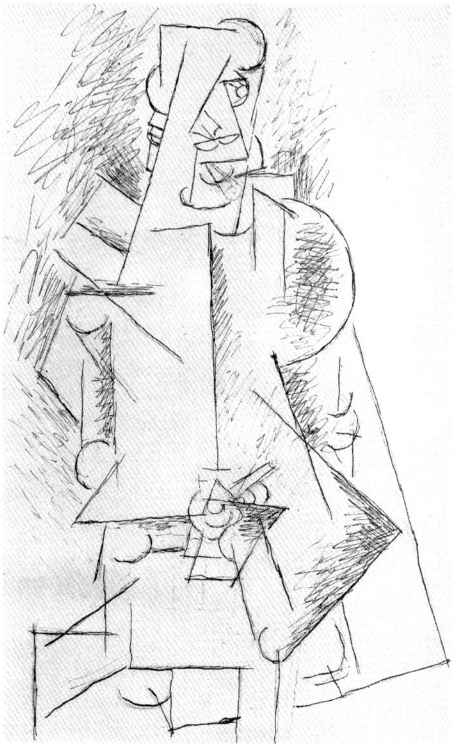

194 (*right top*) Picasso. *Head of Man with Pipe.* Céret, summer 1911. Ink on paper, 21.3 × 13.13 cm. Zervos XXVIII, 68. Picasso estate (inv. 1561)

195 (*right bottom*) Picasso. *Man with Pipe.* Céret, summer 1911. Charcoal and India ink on paper, 31 × 19 cm. Zervos XXVIII, 99. Formerly Marina Picasso Collection (inv. 1374)

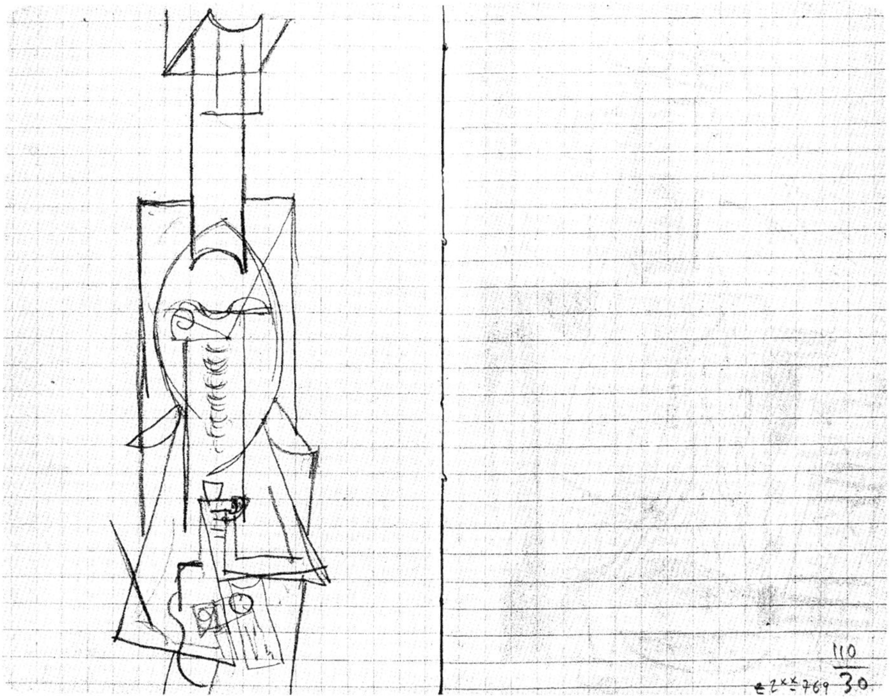

196 Picasso. *Seated Woman with Guitar.* Céret or Sorgues, summer 1912. Pencil on graph-paper page from notebook, 13 × 8.5 cm. Zervos II**, 760. Léal, carnet 16, pp. 18v and 19r. Musée Picasso, Paris

197 Picasso. *Violin.* Céret or Sorgues, summer 1912. Pencil on graph-paper page from notebook, 13 × 8.5 cm. Zervos II**, 769. Léal, carnet 16, pp. 19v and 20r. Musée Picasso, Paris

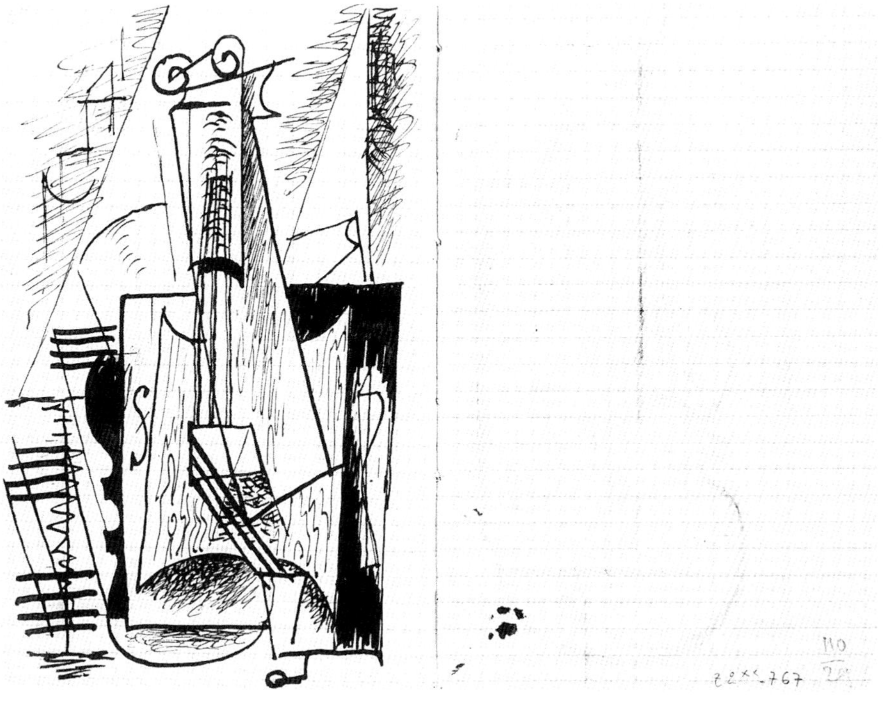

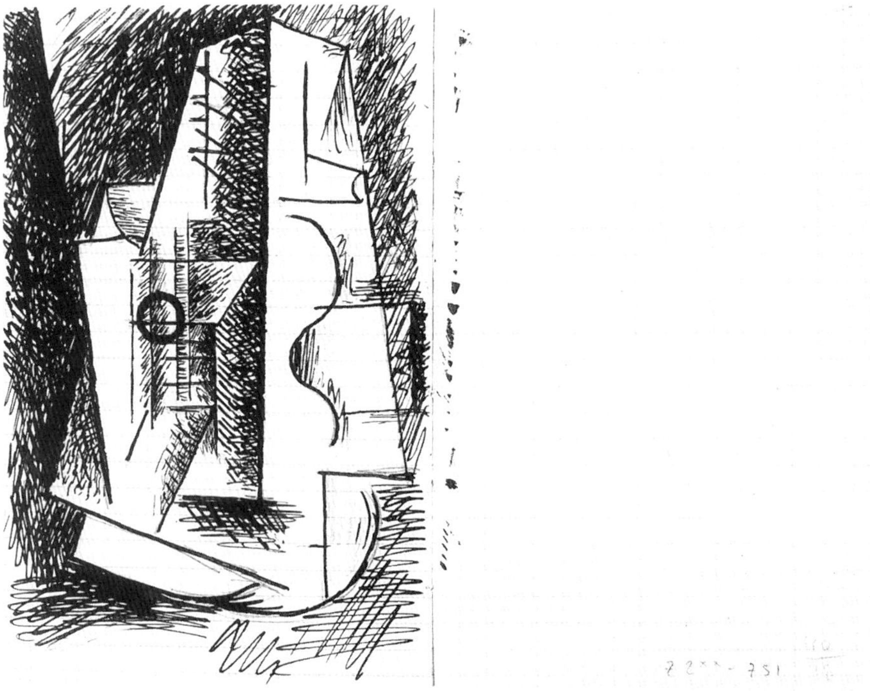

198 Picasso. *Guitar.* Sorgues, summer 1912. Pencil and black ink on graph-paper page from notebook, 13 × 8.5 cm. Zervos II**, 768. Léal, carnet 16, pp. 34v and 35r. Musée Picasso, Paris

199 Picasso. *Seated Woman with Violin.* Sorgues, summer 1912. Black ink and pencil on graph-paper page from notebook, 13 × 8.5 cm. Zervos II**, 751. Léal, carnet 16,pp. 35v and 36r. Musée Picasso, Paris

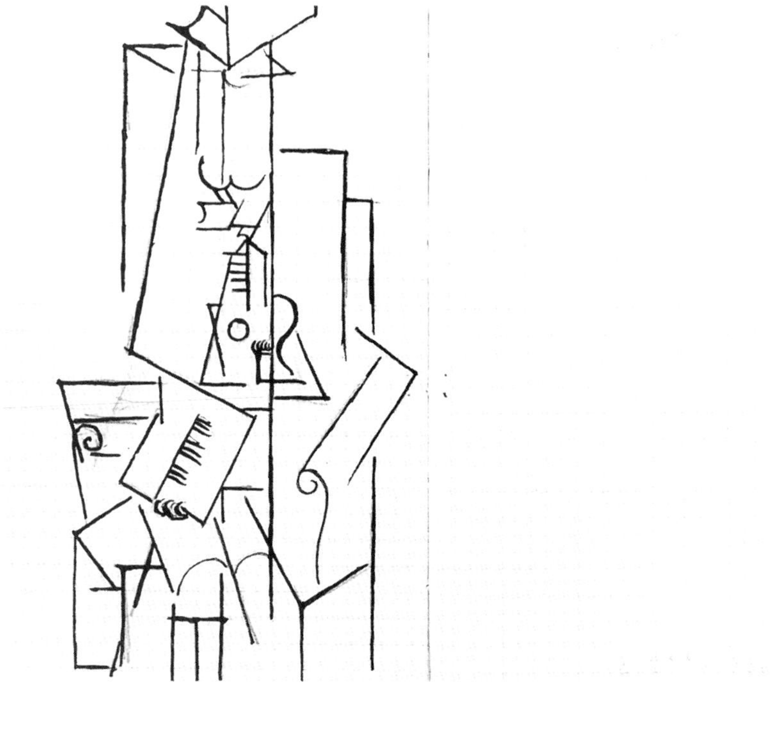

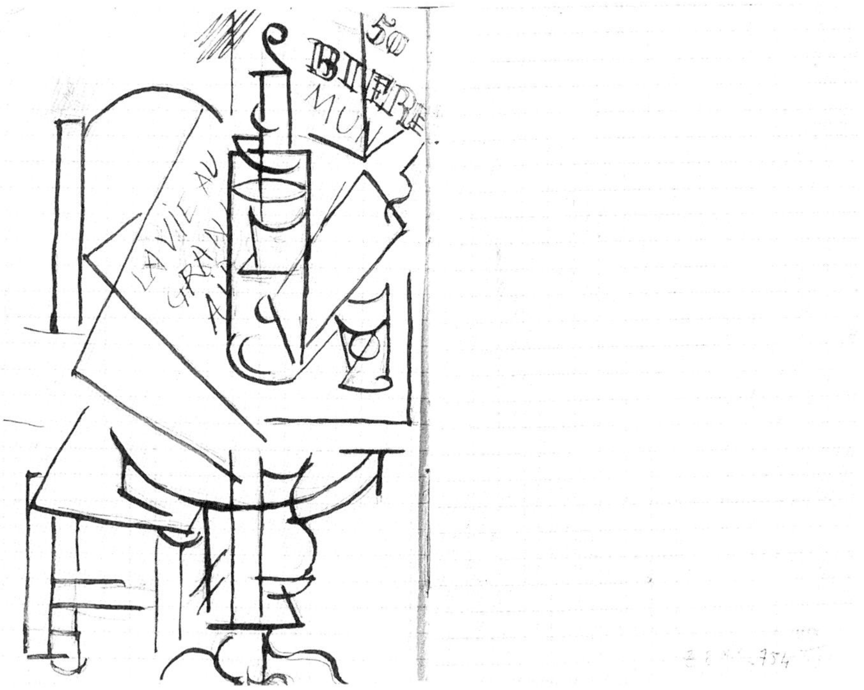

200 Picasso. *Bottle and Glass on Pedestal Table.* Sorgues, summer 1912. Black and brown ink and pencil on graph-paper page from notebook, 13 × 8.5 cm. Zervos II**, 753. Léal, carnet 16, pp. 41v and 42r. Musée Picasso, Paris

201 Picasso. *The Old Port of Marseille.* Sorgues, summer 1911. Black ink and pencil on graph-paper page from notebook, 13 × 8.5 cm. Zervos II**, 755. Léal, carnet 16, pp. 42v and 43r. Musée Picasso, Paris

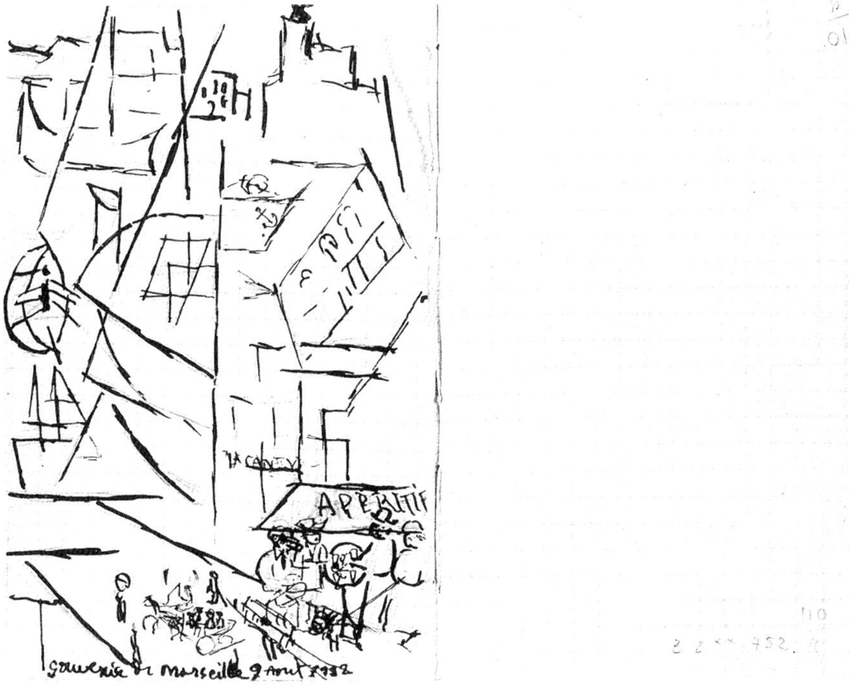

with gradual transformations, carried out over the course of a series of pictures.

Formal parallelism between part and whole seems to have emerged first in two drawings of summer 1911. It has already been seen how the summer 1911 *Head of Man with Pipe* shares its underlying structure with another drawing of a landscape (see figs. 154, 155). But Picasso also used this arrangement of planes and curves as the armature for a full-length drawing of the same *Man with Pipe* (figs. 194, 195). Here, the two inclined planes run through the torso, and the large curve at upper right stands for the shoulder rather than the ball of the head. The pipe occupies more or less the same place in the composition, but it has shifted from the man's mouth to his hand.

Picasso's summer 1912 sketchbook shows him pursuing this idea systematically. Contrary to his usual practice, Picasso drew primarily on the left-hand, verso pages of this sketchbook. The pages have now yellowed and become more opaque, but when they were new they seem to have been sufficiently translucent for Picasso to see whatever he had drawn on the previous page, as if he were working on a sheet of tracing paper. He seems repeatedly to have used elements from the drawing on one page as an armature for the drawing on the next. Sometimes, the two motifs are unrelated. More often, one is an element of the other. On the verso of page 18, for instance, Picasso drew a woman holding a vertical guitar in her lap (fig. 196); the woman's neck is represented as a long vertical strip with a concave base. On the verso of page 19, he drew a still-life version of the same guitar, halfway transformed into a violin (fig. 197); its neck coincides exactly with the neck of the woman on the previous page. On the verso of page 34, he drew a guitar with a strong vertical axis rising through its body and neck, culminating in an angle so that it looks like an upward-pointing arrow (fig. 198); long diagonals descend from either side of the arrow's head. On the verso of the following page he drew a seated woman holding the same guitar (fig. 199). Her body is traversed by the same vertical axis; and, on the left, a long diagonal descends from her head, retracing the diagonal that bordered the guitar on this side. The overall structure of the woman's body thus echoes the structure of the guitar that she holds in her lap.

On the verso of page 41, Picasso drew a still-life image of a bottle and newspaper (actually, a sporting magazine, *La Vie au grand air*) on a café table (fig. 200); the pages of the paper are spread out in a series of overlapping planes. On the verso of the next page, he drew a cityscape, labeled "Souvenir de Marseille" (fig. 201), with views of the café, boats in the harbor, buildings, and so on arranged around an armature consisting of the vertical axis and overlapping planes from the previous page. There is no sense of echoed forms within this second drawing, however, since the café table has diminished too much to "rhyme" with the structure surrounding it. The part-to-whole relationship exists only between the two drawings.

Picasso clearly showed these studies to Braque when the latter arrived in Sorgues in late July, for they had a decisive influence on the first *papiers collés*, which Braque created in early September. A brief detour is necessary to clarify the significance of this influence.

Braque and *Papier Collé*

In the course of the 1940s and '50s, Braque gave several interlocutors a similar account of his creation of the first *papier collé*. What is perhaps the earliest version appears in Jean Paulhan's short book, *Braque le patron*, first published in 1946:

> It was on the morning of September 13, 1912 that Braque, passing through Avignon, noticed in the window of a store some strips of wallpaper, which offered a superb imitation of the *faux-bois* done by house painters. He bought a roll, and, as soon as he returned to Sorgues, cut out three pieces which he glued onto a sheet of paper. Between them, he made a charcoal sketch of a pipe, a mandolin, and the surface of a table; then he added the letters ALE and BAR. It was the first *papier collé*.[181]

In a later version of this story, Braque explained that he did not in fact buy the wallpaper immediately upon seeing it in the shop window, but waited a few days until Picasso had left Sorgues for a brief visit to Paris. He then bought the wallpaper and went to work with it, so that the first *papier collé* was completed before Picasso's return.[182]

Three salient details emerge from these accounts. One is simply the identification of *Fruit Dish and Glass* as the first *papier collé*. The second is Braque's sense of rivalry with Picasso: he wanted to make the first *papier collé* in Picasso's absence, so that there would be absolutely no uncertainty about who invented the new medium.[183] The third is that the strips of wood-grained paper were laid down first, before the drawing. The importance of this third detail is underscored in a 1954 interview with Dora Vallier, where Braque says that his great achievement in the *papiers collés* was "to dissociate color from form." In these works, he said, "the color [that is, the wood-grained wallpaper] functions at the same time as the form, but has nothing to do with it."[184]

This dissociation between line and color became important to Miró's work in the early 1930s. It featured prominently in Léger's mural compositions of the 1940s and '50s. Indeed, by the 1950s, it was a standard element in "modern" decorative design. A historian might have traced its genesis back to Picasso's designs for the 1924 ballet *Mercure*.[185] By pointing to his *papiers collés* as the first example of dissociation between line and color, Braque was claiming priority over artists who by the 1950s loomed considerably larger than he did in the mind of the educated art audience.

Furthermore, the assertion that the strips of wood-grained paper were the first elements of the composition, glued into place before the addition of the drawn details and inscriptions, suggested that Braque had taken the first and most important step toward abstraction. Rather than deriving his geometric structures from the motif, he seemed to have started with a non-representational arrangement of colored forms, and only later added the details that transformed the composition into a representational image. This idea became part of the standard literature on Cubism.

John Golding, for instance, writes that the strips of wood-grained paper in *Fruit Dish and Glass* "boldly establish the basic composition of the picture to which the object is subsequently related by overdrawing."[186] Many of Braque's 1913–14 paintings, Golding suggests, were composed using this technique:

> Before he actually began to paint or draw on canvas, Braque experimented by laying strips of paper on it in various positions or combinations. Then, when he had decided upon the arrangement or composition that pleased him most, the pieces of paper were pinned to the canvas and lines were drawn around them, or their positions noted by pencil marks at the corner . . . The basic composition, worked out in terms of strips of paper, [existed] independently of the subject, which was superimposed or laid over it.[187]

Braque's insistence on the priority of the printed strips has tended to discourage scholars from looking carefully at the drawn elements of his *papiers collés*. Examination by naked eye and by transmitted light suggests that the printed strips were not the first elements of the composition. Rather, Braque drew his compositions in charcoal and then cut out pieces of paper corresponding to certain elements of the drawn composition.[188] If Braque's first *papiers collés* are examined as a group, it becomes apparent that his initial goal in these works was to explore the idea, suggested by Picasso, that the same geometrical forms could assume different representational values depending on the synecdochic signs associated with them. Examining these works as drawings – that is, without regard to their cut-paper elements – it is possible to place them in a sequence where the first drawing is the one that provides a representational rationale for the largest number of pictorial elements, the second repeats the same pictorial elements without assigning a representational meaning to all of them, and the third modifies these elements in order to provide new meanings for them.

Approached in this manner, the first drawing would be *Man with Pipe* (fig. 204). The human figure is an unusual motif for Braque, and his handling of it here seems to derive directly from the drawings that Picasso had done earlier in summer 1912. The eyes are indicated by a horizontal strip with indented ends, like the eyes of the figure in Picasso's study of a seated man holding a cane; and he wears a wing collar and a hat similar to the Kronstadt hat worn by the man in that study (see fig. 202). One of the studies associated with Apollinaire (see fig. 203) provides an even closer antecedent for Braque's drawing. Aside from the *papier collé* additions, the main innovation in Braque's picture is the pipe, with its smoke rising up in bubbles at either side of the man's neck and face.

Braque's figure in what seems to be the second drawing of this series (fig. 205) exchanges its wide-brimmed hat for the tricorne of a harlequin – a typical Picasso motif. The *Harlequin* is still wearing a wing collar with turned back, triangular tips. The bubbles of smoke remain at either side of his face, even though the pipe has disappeared.

In *Fruit Dish and Glass* (fig. 206), which seems to be the third member of this series, the human figure disappears but its geometric components remain. The man's wing collar becomes the circular base of the fruit dish, his neck becomes its pedestal, and the curving brim of his hat (on the left) becomes the open curve of its bowl. Although his pipe is absent, two smoke bubbles appear at left, between the pedestal and bowl of the dish. In brief, the eyes, pipe, and hat of the first drawing have been suppressed, replaced by a bunch of grapes. With this exchange of synedochic signs, what is essentially the same composition, formally, has assumed a new semantic value, so that it represents a fruit dish instead of a man's head.[189]

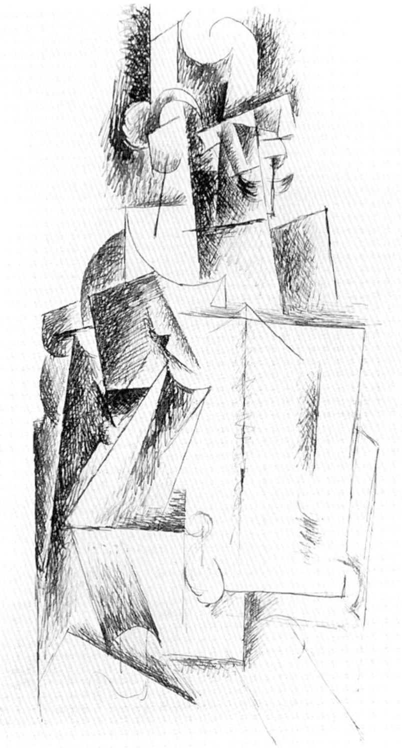
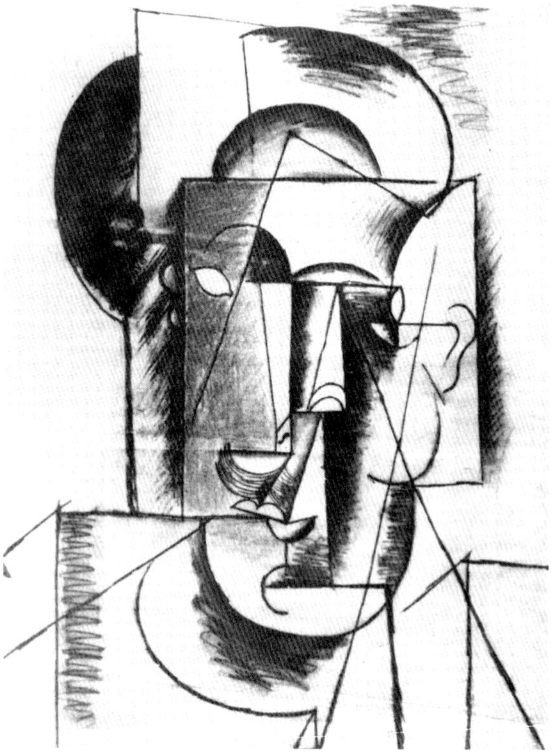
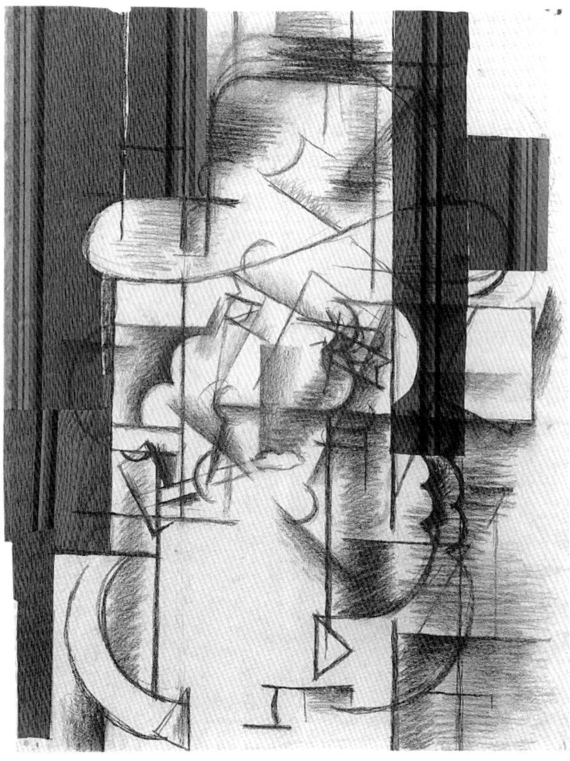
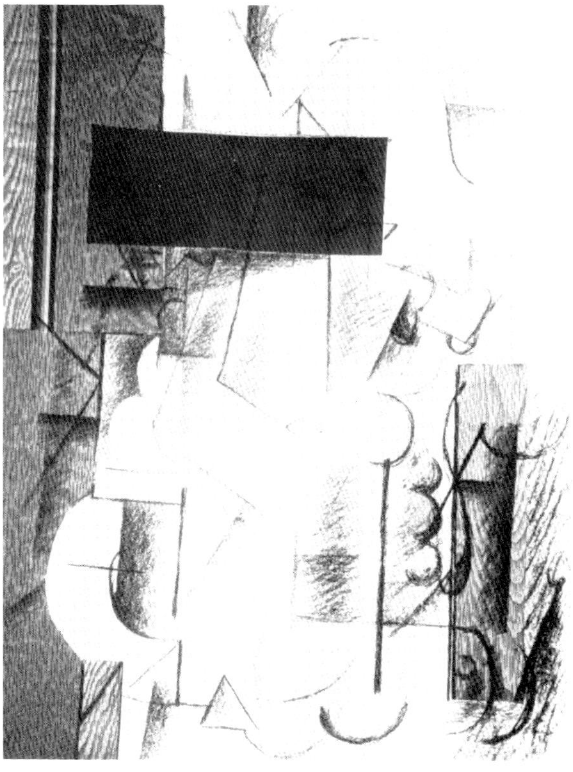

202 (*facing page top left*) Picasso. *Seated Man.* Sorgues, summer 1912. Ink on paper, 30.8 × 19.7 cm. The Metropolitan Museum of Art, New York. The Alfred Stieglitz Collection, 1949

203 (*facing page top right*) Picasso. *Head of Man.* Sorgues, summer 1912. Charcoal and pastel, 64 × 27 cm. Zervos II*, 327. Kunstmuseum Wintherthur. Bequest of C. and E. Friedrich-Jezler

204 (*facing page bottom left*) Braque. *Man with Pipe.* Sorgues, summer 1912. Charcoal and pasted paper on paper, 61.9 × 49 cm. M.-F./C. 6. Oeffentliche Kunstsammlung, Basel, Kupferstichkabinett. Gift of Raoul La Roche, 1963

205 (*facing page bottom right*) Braque. *Harlequin.* Sorgues, summer 1912. Charcoal and pasted paper on paper, 62 × 48 cm. M-F./C. 5. Collection unknown

206 (*below left*) Braque. *Fruit Dish and Glass.* Sorgues, early September 1912. Charcoal and pasted paper on paper, 62 × 44.5 cm. M.-F./C. 1. Private collection

207 (*below right*) Braque. *Fruit Dish: "Quotidien du Midi."* Sorgues, summer 1912. Oil and sand on canvas, 41 × 33 cm. Romilly 148. Private collection, courtesy Thomas Ammann Fine Art, Zurich

Evidently, the strips of wood-grained paper were not the first elements of the composition. Nor, in all likelihood, was *Fruit Dish and Glass* the first member of its group to be drawn, although it may have been the first of Braque's drawings to have wood-grained paper glued to it. What is more important is that there is nothing here to indicate that Braque's main goal, in *Fruit Dish and Glass* or any of his first *papiers collés*, was to establish the independence of color and form.

The meaning of the wood-grained strips is independent of the forms in the picture, in the sense that the strips do not necessarily represent objects made from wood (except for the horizontal strip at the bottom, which corresponds to the drawer of the table supporting the fruit dish). But wood-graining already functioned as an independent, "environmental" aspect of Braque's compositions, as in the fall 1911 *Homage to J. S. Bach* (see fig. 148) or in the 1912 canvas *Fruit Dish: "Quotidien du Midi"* (fig. 207), which very nearly duplicates the composition of the *papier collé*, except that it has been rationalized by the deletion of the details – the smoke bubbles and the angle of the wing collar – linking the composition to *Man with Pipe.*

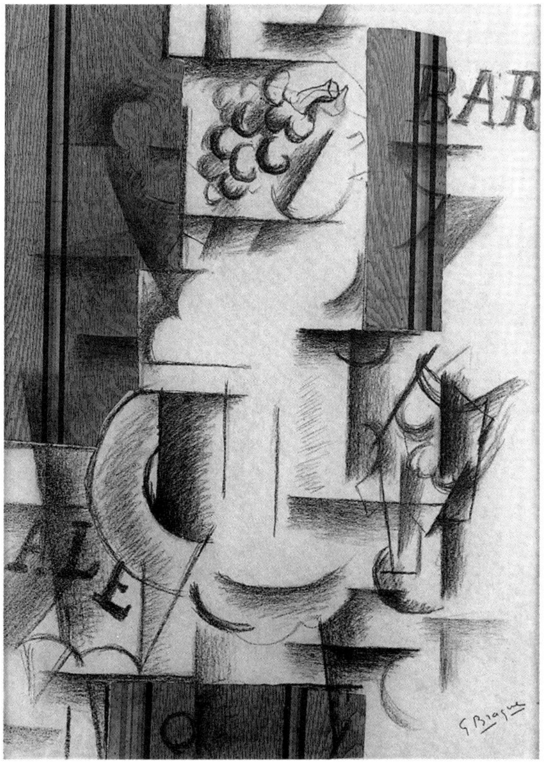

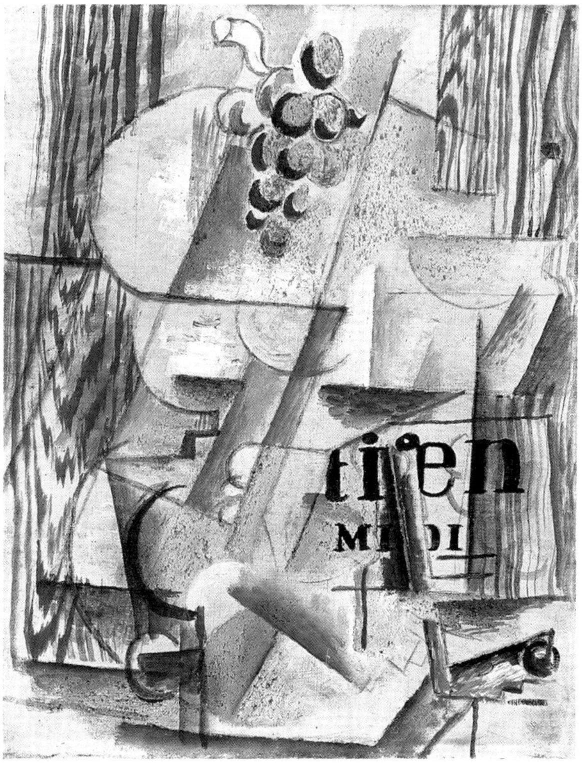

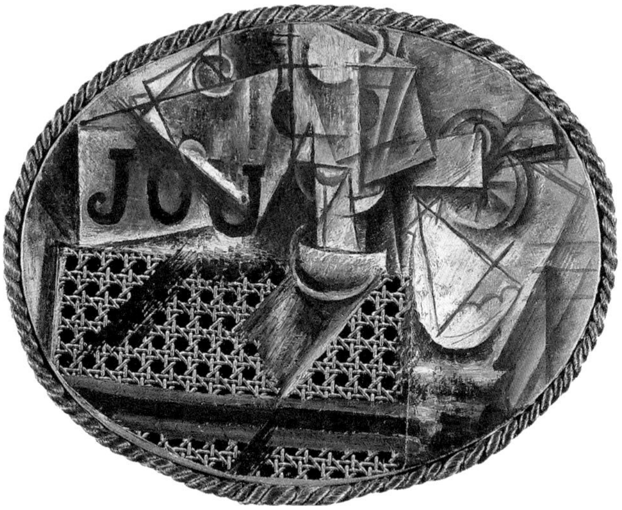

208 Picasso. *Still Life with Chair Caning.* Paris, spring 1912. Oil, oilcloth, and pasted paper on oval canvas, surrounded by rope, 27 × 35 cm. D.R. 466. Musée Picasso, Paris

Furthermore, the placement of the wood-grained strips is independent of the disposition of the synecdochic signs – grape cluster, bowl, inscriptions – in the picture. (Again, an exception must be made for the horizontal strip, which is clearly related to the table and which is absent in the first two works of this series, where there are no tables.) However, the independence of the strips, in this sense, is merely one more example of the independence of geometric forms and synecdochic signs which had characterized Cubism since 1910. The placement of the wood-grained strips is not independent of the disposition of the geometric forms in the picture. On the contrary, it was the organization of the Cubist picture into a series of vertical bands, in the course of 1911, that prepared the way for Braque's invention of *papier collé*.[190]

The wood-grained paper that Braque spotted in an Avignon shop window may have been displayed in a roll but, thanks to his early training as a house-painter, he would have been well aware that wallpaper is applied to walls in vertical strips. A comparison may have flashed through his mind, associating the large vertical strips of wallpaper with the smaller vertical strips of the compositions that he and Picasso had been designing during the previous year. Indeed, after buying the roll of wallpaper, he had to cut it into smaller strips that would fit into the bands in his drawings. But the association remained important. It seems relevant, in this regard, that Picasso's first *papiers collés* employ wallpaper (see fig. 209) and newsprint (see fig. 211), with its narrow columns of type. Such materials seemed to possess an inherent syntax similar to the geometric syntax of Cubism. This seems to be why both Picasso and Braque became so excited about the new technique, making dozens of *papiers collés* in the next few months. In contrast, Picasso's first collage, the *Still Life with Chair Caning* of spring 1912 (fig. 208), had remained a one-off, a singular experiment – probably because the uniform texture of the printed oilcloth did not possess an inherent structure related to the surrounding composition.

Series and Transformations

A *catalogue raisonné* is always valuable but the *catalogue raisonné* of Picasso's Cubist work, published by Pierre Daix and Joan Rosselet in 1979, is essential for understanding the evolution of Cubism in fall 1912. Before Daix and Rosselet corrected the mistaken datings in Zervos's earlier catalogue, and arranged Picasso's 1912–13 pictures into sequences of closely related works, it was virtually impossible to arrive at a full understanding of Picasso's goals and achievements during these months.

Picasso had always produced large numbers of closely related drawings, and his major paintings had often been accompanied by smaller canvases exploring variants or elements of the larger composition. However, this process of repetition and variation was justified by the goal of creating a "masterpiece" – a large, ambitious composition that would sum up and integrate the discoveries made in his studies. By 1912, Picasso had (temporarily) abandoned the idea of the masterpiece. The creation of a series of closely related works now became an end in itself.

Leo Stein took a characteristically dim view of the systematic character of Cubism. It seemed to him useful insofar as it stimulated inspiration – "just as rhymes may do when one is writing verse." But just as rhymes "carry on almost of themselves," so too with Picasso's inventions. "Often," Stein commented, "the end of one picture is the beginning of the next." This seemed to Stein to demonstrate that Picasso was "not essentially serious." On the other hand, the systematic approach had obvious benefits. It freed Picasso from the agony of "drifting and waiting for inspiration." He no longer needed "intervals of recharging." On the contrary, "his inventive genius was constantly productive," and his stream of formal inventions "served as a sufficient stimulus to his feelings."[191]

We may reject Stein's conclusion that the systematic and repetitive character of Picasso's Cubist work means that it is "not essentially serious." Still, Picasso's methodical approach and his production of numerous extremely similar pictures run counter to our usual assumptions about creativity and about the uniqueness of great art. This new working process implied that the individual picture was not a definitive statement but merely a provisional solution to a pictorial problem, and that the problem could be fully addressed only by exploring a series of solutions, each of them slightly different. Under these circumstances, the full value of any given work could be understood only in the context of the series as a whole. This aspect of Cubism seems to have been little understood at the time, perhaps because relatively few of Picasso's and Braque's pictures were sold or exhibited in the years before the outbreak of the First World War. The idea of the unified series remained latent within the various geometrical styles deriving from Cubism, but only began to play an important role in modern art fifty years later and a continent away.[192] Even its importance within Cubism was not really apparent until the publication of Daix and Rosselet's *catalogue raisonné*.

It is not practical here to illustrate more than a small fraction of the pictures that Picasso produced in fall and winter 1912–13. But some idea of their sequential character can be gained by looking at representative images from his series devoted to the motif of an upright guitar or violin (see figs. 209–12) and the motif of an isolated head (see figs. 214–16). The interest of these works does not lie simply in the individual pictures, but in the evolution of the composition from one picture to another. More precisely, the interest lies in seeing how the addition and subtraction of synecdochic signs gradually alters the value of the geometric forms they are attached to – or, in other cases, how the repetition of synecdochic signs permits the geometric forms to change and evolve. The result is a concatenated series of pictures, in which basically similar compositions assume a series of new meanings, much as the word "bureau" successively meant a fabric, a table, other kinds of furniture, a room, or a branch of government.

After returning to Paris in fall 1912, Picasso began to experiment with the new *papier collé* technique that Braque had invented. Curiously enough, *Guitar, Sheet Music, and Glass* (fig. 209), one of his first essays in the new medium, does not resemble Braque's efforts, which were essentially charcoal drawings enhanced by strips of patterned paper. Picasso, in contrast, "drew" his guitar by cutting out four pieces of paper: a trapezoidal piece of blue paper for its neck, a reversed "*B*" of wood-grained paper (handpainted) for its side, a white disk for its sound-hole, and a thin black section of a circle for its base. The diamond-patterned wallpaper of the background does double duty as the front of the guitar, below the sound-hole. There is an elegant drawing of a wineglass to the right of the guitar: the white sheet fits into the geometric configuration of the guitar, but the charcoal lines of the wineglass itself do not interact with it. Nor do the fragments of sheet music and newspaper at right and left enter into the figuration of the guitar, even though they are geometric forms similar to the blue trapezoid of the neck. They remain synecdochic signs, like the charcoal wineglass.

Picasso reproduced this composition almost exactly in a canvas known as *Small Violin* (fig. 210). The canvas repeats in painted form the central configuration of the guitar's trapezoidal blue neck, the reverse-*B* of its side, the white circle of the sound-hole, and the black section of its base. The front of the guitar once again seems to have been cut away, revealing a rectangle of brown paint mixed with sand. The sheet music and newspaper headline are faithfully reproduced as well. In terms of form, the only element that has really changed is the wineglass, which is now represented by a series of simple geometric forms, painted yellow and white. However, the representational value of the central configuration has now changed significantly, thanks to the addition of a series of synecdochic signs: the scrolled head and tuning pegs atop the neck, the black strings descending below them, and the *f*-shaped sound-hole superimposed on the reverse-*B* at left. The result is a kind of hybrid: half-violin (thanks to these new details) and half-guitar (thanks to the persistence of the reverse-B and the round sound-hole).

For another *Violin* (fig. 211), executed a few weeks later, Picasso adopted a technique closer to that of Braque's original *papiers collés*: the picture is essentially a charcoal drawing supplemented with strips of newsprint (rather than wallpaper).[193] The instrument's identity is now unequivocal. The scroll, tuning pegs, strings, and *f* sound-holes from the painting return, only slightly altered; but the circular sound-hole has vanished, and the reverse-*B* side has been

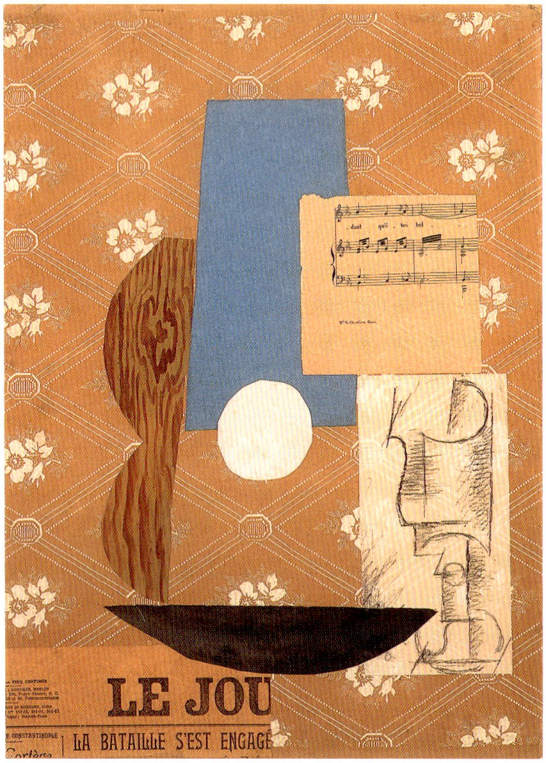

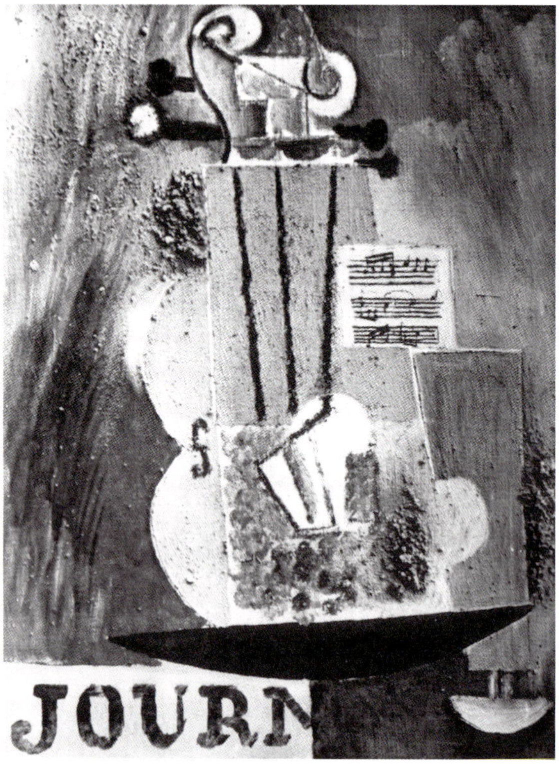

replaced by a roughly rectangular form with a semicircular indentation. Like the reverse-B of the guitar, this indented rectangle is not an arbitrary sign but a stylized version of the actual contour of a violin.

Up to this point, the geometric substrate of the instrument has remained relatively stable, while the synecdochic signs attached to it have changed. In 1913, however, more significant changes were made to the instrument's geometric structure. A sheet of studies from spring 1913 (fig. 212) shows Picasso experimenting with the form of an instrument described in Zervos as a guitar; but in the two largest studies on the sheet, the instrument's sound-holes seem equally to mark it as a violin. As in the *papier collé* of December 1912, the side of the violin is indicated by a rectangle with an indented side, but the indentation is now rectangular rather than semicircular. The sound-holes, too, are drawn with right angles rather than curves. (In one study they are supplemented by a central cube that is perhaps an heir to the circular sound-hole of the original guitar.) The neck has been reduced to a tall stick, culminating in a triangle topped by a dowel, like the handle of a shovel. It seems not impossible that Duchamp had this drawing in mind when he selected the snow shovel for his 1915 readymade, *In Advance of the Broken Arm* (fig. 213).

The radically new configuration of the violin in Picasso's 1913 drawings remains legible for two reasons. One is that at least one set of synecdochic markers survives, providing a guideline to the interpretation of the geometric signs. The other is that the geometric signs themselves are no longer located in an overall field of similar forms, but have contracted into a self-enclosed configuration, whose overall contour – a narrow neck atop a broader body – is similar to that of the real motif, even if its details are wildly distorted.

Over the same period of months, Picasso explored a parallel series of heads. Their configuration originates in the *Seated Woman with Guitar* (see fig. 137) that he drew repeatedly in summer 1912. However, Picasso soon began to explore the woman's head as an independent motif (fig. 214), constructed from a combination of overlapping shapes: square, ovoid, and conical. Returning to this configuration in December 1912, he extracted a simpler armature consisting of four or five basic shapes (fig. 215). Face and neck are merged into an upside-down cone, resting on the

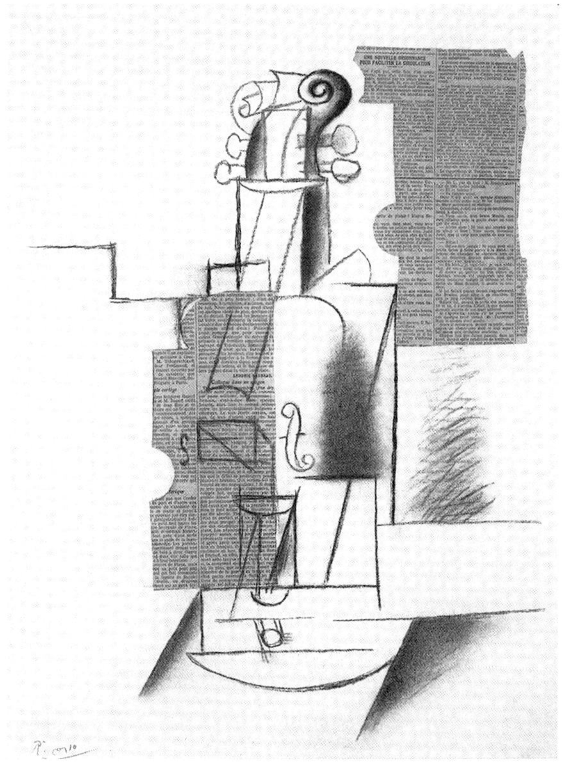

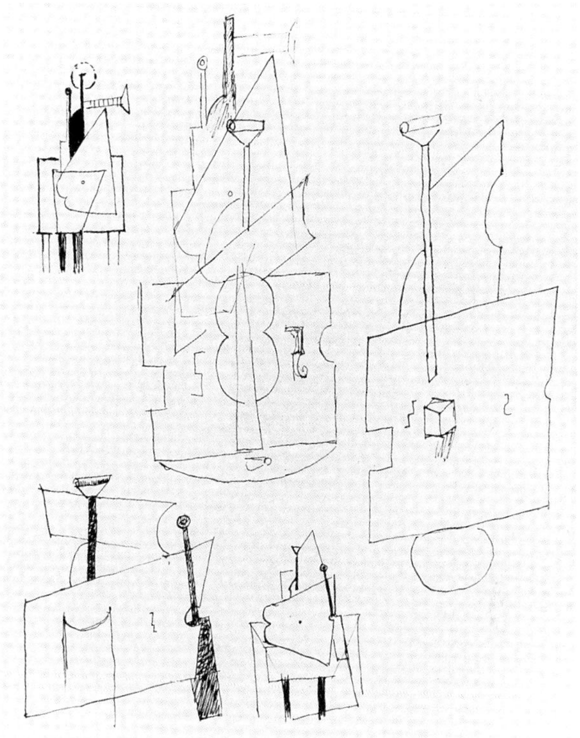

209 (*facing page left*) Picasso. *Guitar, Sheet Music, and Glass.* Paris, after November 18, 1912. Pasted paper, gouache, and charcoal on paper, 47.9 × 35.5 cm. D.R. 513. Collection of the McNay Art Museum, San Antonio, Bequest of Marion Koogler McNay

210 (*facing page right*) Picasso. *Small Violin.* Paris, fall 1912. Oil and sand on canvas, 35 × 27 cm. D.R. 514. Private collection

211 (*above left*) Picasso. *Violin.* Paris, after December 3, 1912. Pasted paper and charcoal on paper, 62 × 47 cm. D.R. 524. Centre Georges Pompidou, Musée National d'Art Moderne, Paris. Gift of Henri Laugier

212 (*above right*) Picasso. *Guitar and Bottle on Square Table (Studies for a Sculpture).* Céret, spring 1913. India ink on paper, 27.5 × 21 cm. Zervos XXVIII, 303. Picasso estate (inv. 1535)

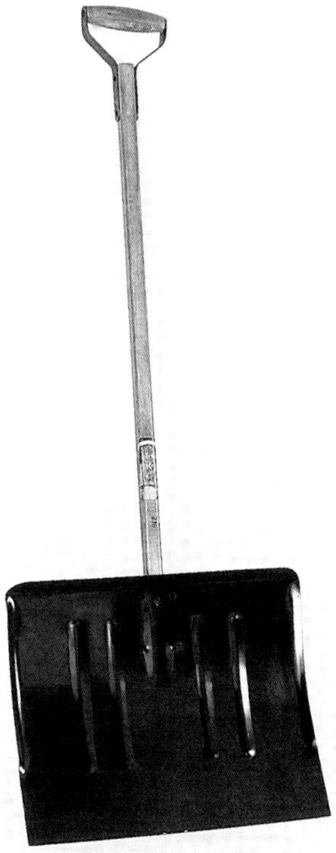

213 (*right*) Marcel Duchamp. *In Advance of the Broken Arm.* 1915 (remade 1945). H. 121.3 cm. Yale University Art Gallery. Gift of Katherine S. Dreier to the Collection Société Anonyme

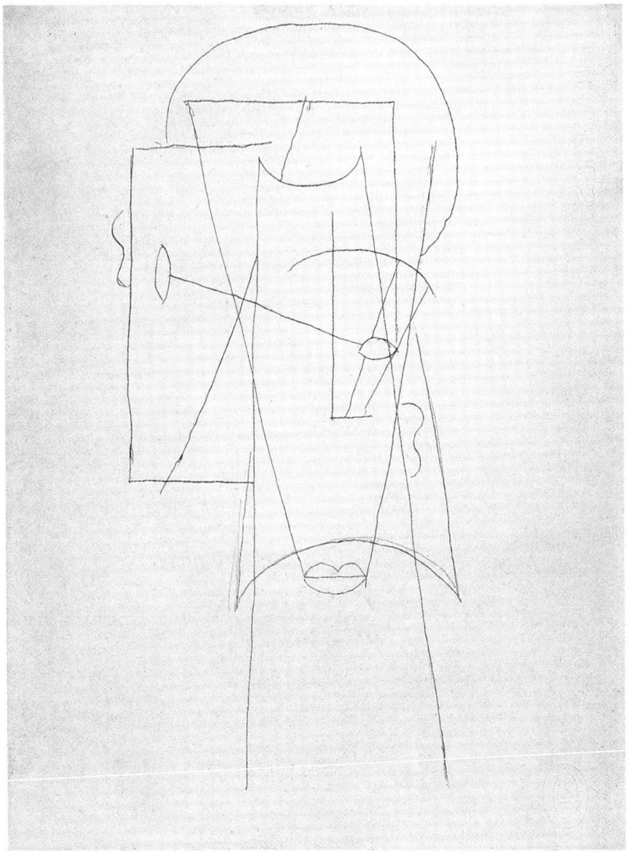

214 Picasso. *Head.* Sorgues, summer 1912. Ink on paper, 61 × 47 cm. Zervos II**, 387. Musée d'art moderne de Lille Métropole, Villeneuve d'Ascq. Donation of Geneviève and Jean Masurel in 1979

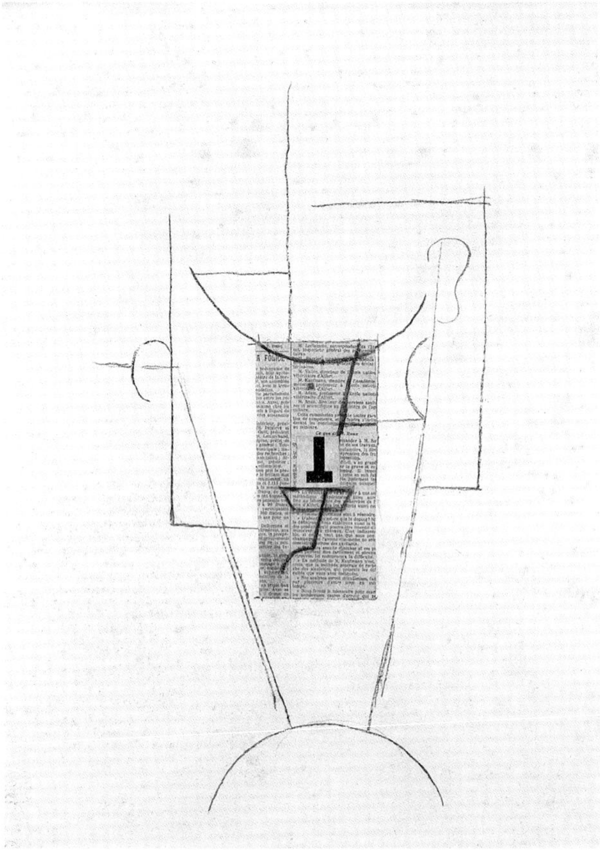

215 Picasso. *Head.* Paris, after December 9, 1912. Pasted papers and lead pencil on paper, 63 × 47 cm. D.R. 538. Musée d'art moderne de Lille Métropole, Villeneuve d'Ascq. Donation of Geneviève and Jean Masurel in 1979

arc of the shoulders. The back of the head is represented by two rectangles, offset on a vertical axis; curves at right and left suggest ears. A central rectangle of newsprint corresponds to the facial plane. This is decorated with a series of synecdochic signs: a dot for an eye, an upside-down *T* (presumably cut from an advertisement) for the nose, and an upside-down trapezoid for the mouth. A long diagonal suggests the incline of the nose, or of the face seen in profile.

In another *papier collé* done around the same time, Picasso constructed a more complex version of the head around the same basic armature (fig. 216). The head is topped by a hat and surrounded by a grid. Despite the increased complexity, the head is relatively poor in synecdochic signs, which are limited to the dot of the eye, at left, and the curve of the ear, at right. Otherwise, the figuration depends almost entirely on geometric, metaphoric signs. The vertical axis is extended and reinforced by shading to suggest the bilateral symmetry of the human face. On the left, an upside-down trapezoid seems to represent the nose. Further to the left, there appears the reverse-B shape from the earlier guitar pictures (see fig. 209): in this new context, however, it seems to become a sign for the man's brow and cheek seen in profile.

The still tentative elements of this figuration are simplified and resolved in a third *papier collé* (fig. 217). A conservator's report on this work reveals that, in its original version, it almost exactly repeated the figuration of the previous work, with a trapezoidal nose at left and a series of horizontal lines at right. The only major difference was

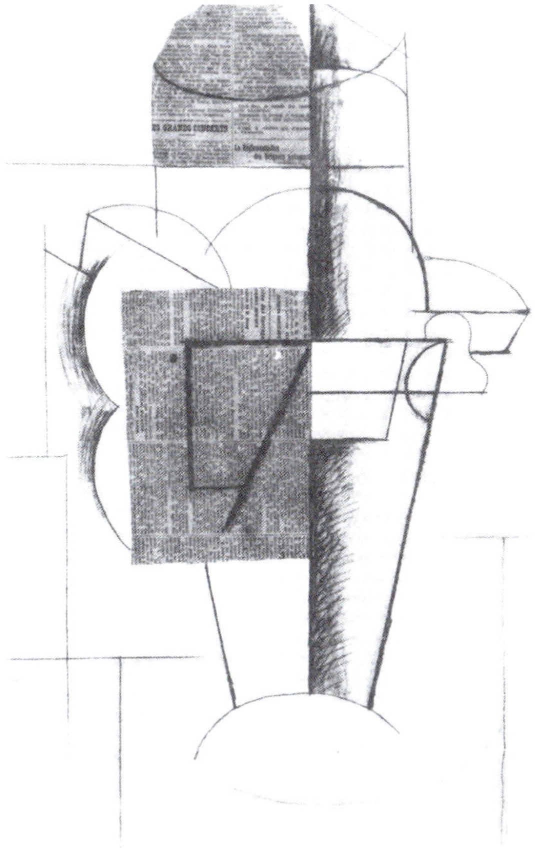

216 Picasso. *Head of Man in Bowler Hat.* Paris, after December 9, 1912. Pasted papers and charcoal on paper, 62.5 × 47 cm. D.R. 537. Private collection

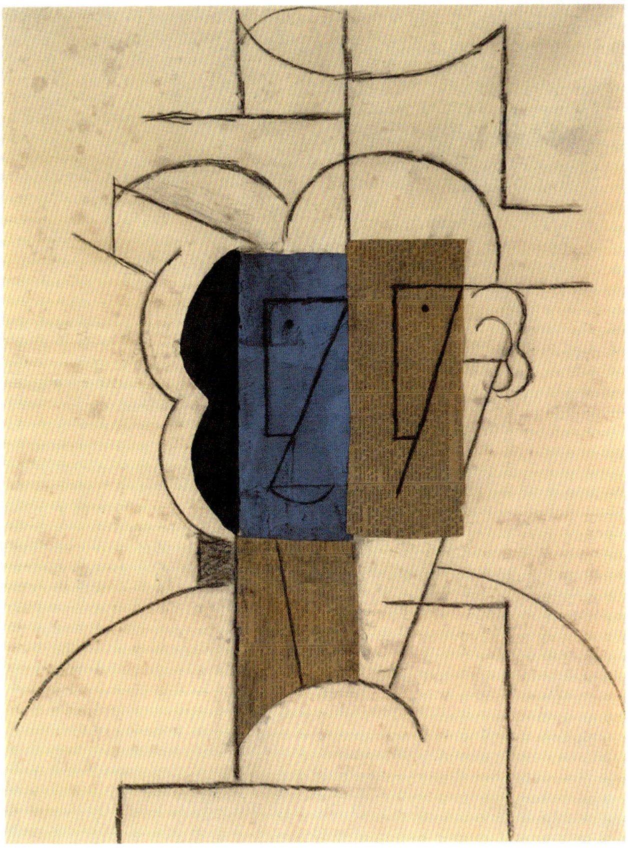

217 Picasso. *Man with a Hat.* Paris, after December 3, 1912. Pasted paper, charcoal, and ink on paper, 62.2 × 47.3 cm. D.R. 534. The Museum of Modern Art, New York. Purchase

that blue paper rather than newpaper was pasted onto the left side of the face. Picasso subsequently decided to cover over the right side of the face with a strip of newsprint, on which he drew another upside-down trapezoid almost exactly like the first. He also added dots for eyes within (rather than next to) each trapezoid.

The result is the visual equivalent of a play on words. The same geometric form is inscribed on both sides of the face, but its elements have a different representational value depending on whether they appear at left or at right. On the left, the vertical side of the trapezoid represents the outer edge of the eye socket, while the diagonal side represents the bridge of the nose. On the right, the vertical side of the trapezoid represents the juncture between nose and facial plane, while the diagonal represents the outer edge of the eye socket and the ridge of the cheekbone. The effect is rather like hearing someone say: "He knows a nose when he sees one." The sounds of the words "knows" and "nose" are identical, but they assume different meanings depending on their role within the sentence – one a verb, the other a noun.

This visual pun is complete within the work itself, although awareness of it is heightened by comparison to the earlier work where the two halves of the face are not identical. In contrast, recognition of the other visual pun here – the use of the reverse-B to represent the brow and cheek – depends on knowledge of the earlier works in which it represents the side of a guitar. To this extent, the image is no longer self-sufficient: to be fully understood, it needs to be seen as part of a series.

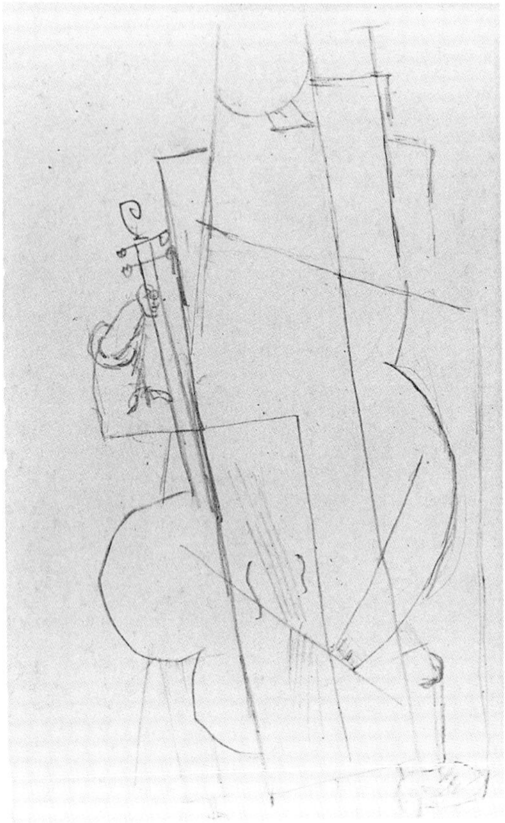

218 Picasso. *Figure with Double Bass.* Céret, spring 1913. Lead pencil on paper, 17 × 11 cm. Zervos XXVIII, 296. Picasso estate (inv. 1484)

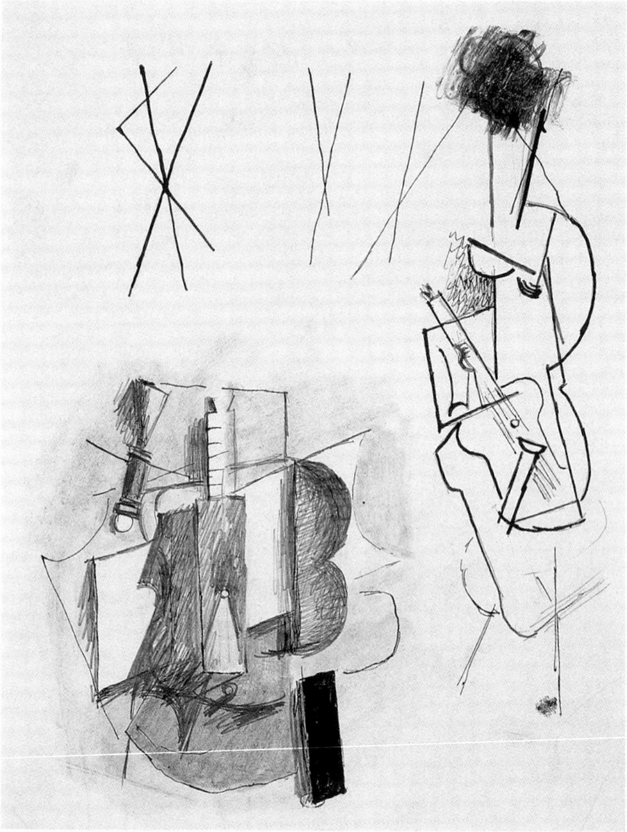

219 Picasso. *Guitar, Beer Glass, and Bottle of Bass, with Guitar Player.* Céret, spring 1913. India ink, lead pencil, and brown crayon on paper, 27.5 × 21 cm. Zervos XXVIII, 273. Richet 348. Musée Picasso, Paris

With these examples in mind, one can appreciate the significance of Leo Stein's observation that "the end of one picture is the beginning of the next." Repetition became a stimulus for creativity, because the existing composition provided Picasso with something to react against. He might introduce new signs, changing the meaning of the forms within the composition; or he might leave the signs unchanged while modifying the forms.

As seen above, repetition also made it possible to convert one kind of sign into another – typically, a geometric form into a synecdochic sign. Since their meaning depends on their place in the composition, geometric signs are relatively immobile. Through repeated use, however, they crystallize into synecdochic signs that can function in a variety of contexts. In Picasso's summer 1912 *Head of Man with Moustache* (see fig. 172), the two planes of the head are only legible as face and jaw because of the other signs around them. Once reduced to the ideographic sign of the "two-axis" face (see figs. 173–75), they become legible in almost any context.

With his usual perverse humor, Picasso no sooner established this principle than he proceeded to subvert it. The reverse-B crystallized in his summer 1912 work as a synecdochic sign for a guitar. By placing it in the new context of the head, he forced it to assume a new meaning, as if it were still an ambiguous geometric form. In his drawings of spring 1913 (figs. 218, 219), the B is seen in both normal and reversed orientations, indicating, on one side, the contour of a string instrument (a cello or bass) and, on the other, the contour of a body – one curve standing for the shoulder, the other for the arm below it. At this point the B has ceased to be a qualifying detail and has become instead a part of the

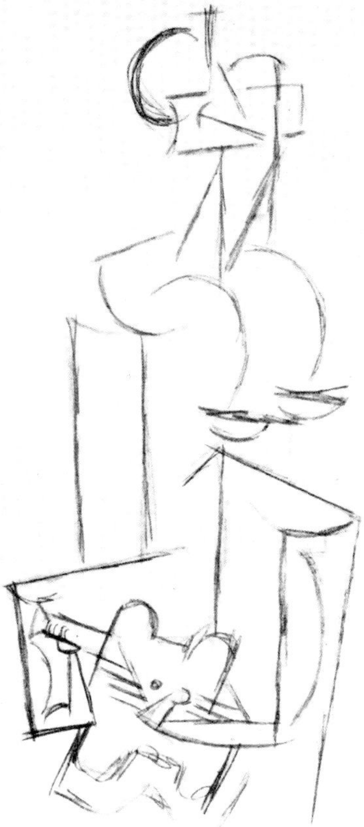

220 Picasso. *Woman with Guitar*. Céret, spring 1913. Lead pencil on paper, 27.5 × 21 cm. Zervos XXVIII, 172. Picasso estate (inv. 1564)

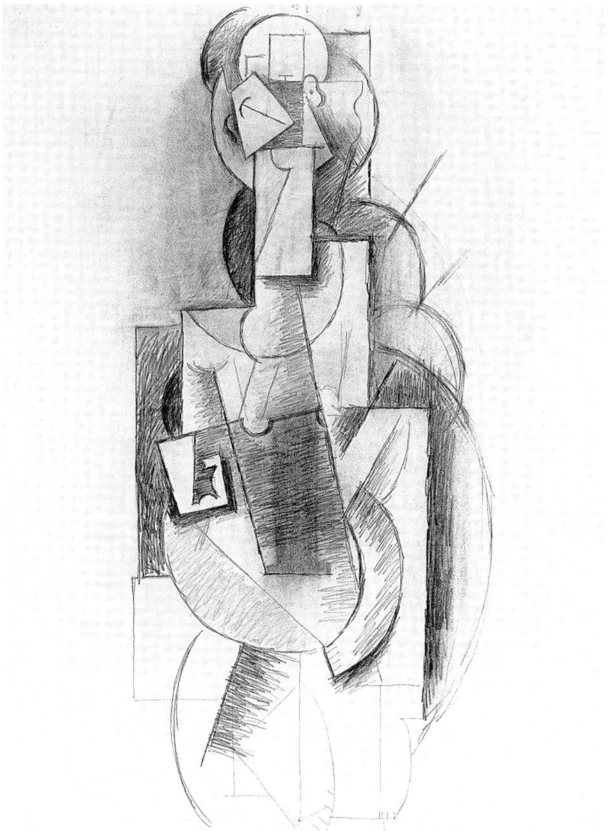

221 Picasso. *Woman with Guitar*. Céret, spring 1913. Lead pencil on paper, 63.5 × 47.6 cm. Zervos XXIX, 8. The Solomon R. Guggenheim Museum, New York

geometric substrate, experiencing a kind of reverse evolution from synecdochic to metaphorical sign. It is these experiments with the double curve of the B that led Picasso toward a new curvilinear vocabulary (figs. 220, 221) and the eroticized geometry of his fall 1913 *Woman with Chemise in an Armchair* (see fig. 123). Here the abstract curve does, in fact, become a symbol of femininity.

In spring 1913, however, Picasso remained chiefly preoccupied with the ideographic sign – that is, a configuration that derives from some real aspect of the motif but becomes abstract by dint of repetition. The operation of this process in the evolution of the "double-axis" face of early 1913 has been examined earlier. A few weeks later, in spring 1913, Picasso revised the "double-axis" face into a new ideogram – a long crossbar enclosed between narrow rectangular strips, accompanied by a version of the familiar B (fig. 222). He then tested its ability to function as a recognizable sign in a variety of different contexts, some highly abstract (fig. 223), others relatively realistic (fig. 224). The ideogram evolved as it was reused. Instead of representing the face as a whole, it came to represent just the eyes and nose. It forked at the bottom, suggesting nostrils, and was supplemented with a small square or cube representing the mouth. The pattern of its evolution then branched. In one series of drawings, Picasso kept some of its elements – the long rectangular strip with the forked base, accompanied by a B – but replaced others with new ones. The original crossbar gave way to an arrangement of strips representing the eyes and nose, while the small square of the mouth became a cylinder or cone suggesting a long, narrow chin. Picasso first explored this configuration in a series of studies for a constructed sculpture (fig. 225), and then turned it upside down

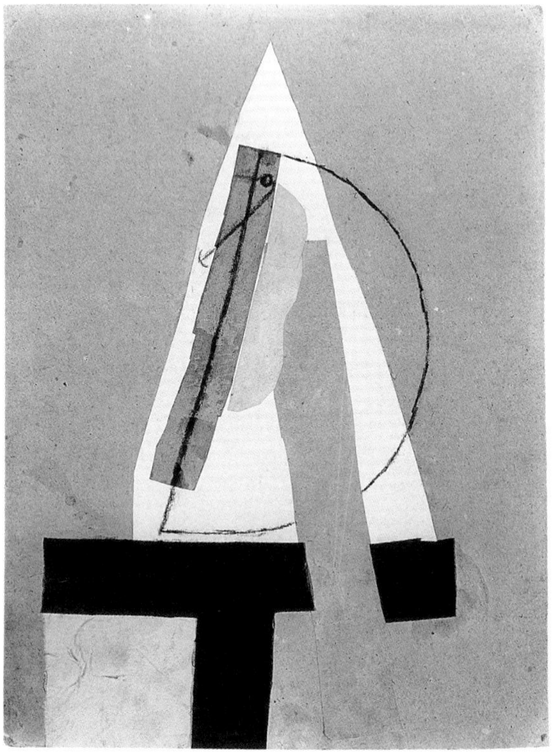

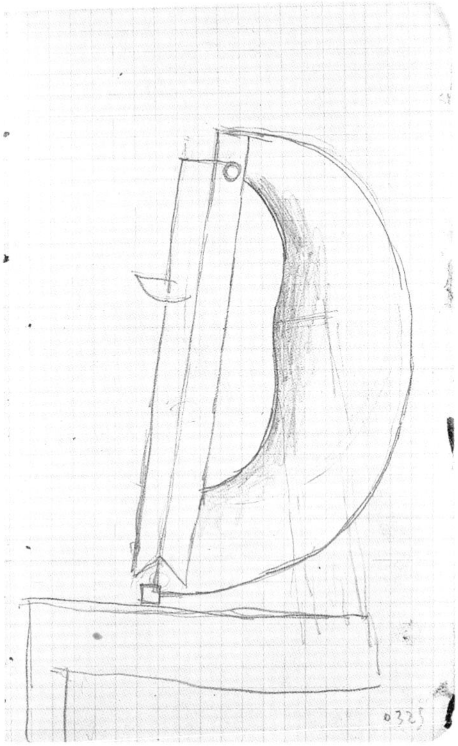

222 (*above left*) Picasso. *Head.* Céret, spring 1913. Pasted paper, charcoal, and pencil on cardboard, 43.5 × 33 cm. D.R. 595. Scottish National Gallery of Modern Art, Edinburgh

223 (*above right*) Picasso. *Head.* Céret, spring 1913. Lead pencil (?) on graph-paper page from notebook, 13 × 8.5 cm. Not in Zervos. Léal, carnet 17, p. 51r. Musée Picasso, Paris

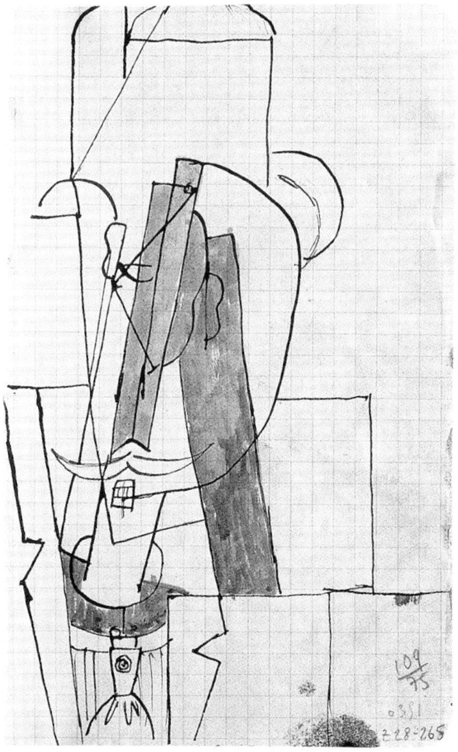

224 (*right*) Picasso. *Head.* Céret, spring 1913. Lead pencil (?) on graph-paper page from notebook, 13 × 8.5 cm. Zervos XXVIII, 265; Léal, carnet 17, p. 77r. Musée Picasso, Paris

225 (*facing page left*) Picasso. *Three Heads.* Céret, spring 1913. India ink on a sheet from an eighteenth-century tax register, 35.8 × 28.3 cm. Zervos XXVIII, 283. Formerly Maya Ruiz-Picasso Collection (inv. 1395)

226 (*facing page right*) Picasso. *Bottle on Table and Guitar on Table.* Céret, spring 1913. Ink on paper, 35 × 23 cm. Zervos XXVIII, 285. Picasso estate (inv. 1394)

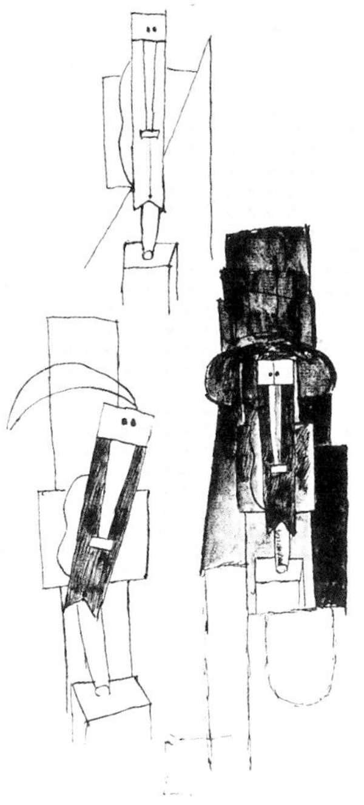

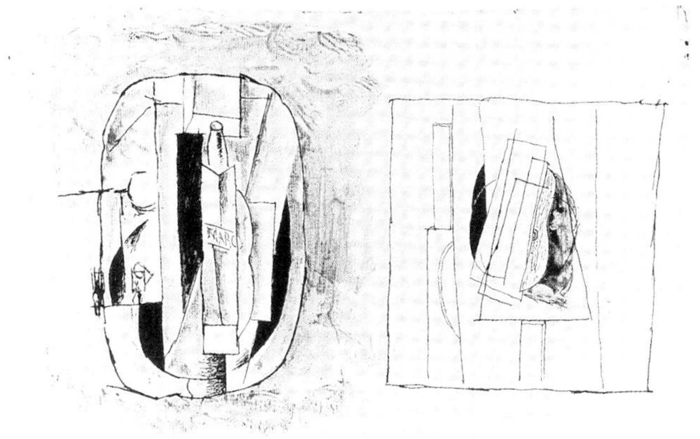

and used it to make a still-life arrangement of a bottle on a table (fig. 226, left side). The cylindrical chin became the neck of the bottle, while the horizontal strip of the nostrils became the label (inscribed "MARC"). In another study on the same sheet (fig. 226, right side), he went back to the earlier, "crossbar" version of the ideogram, which now became a guitar on a table rather than a head. Here, the B reverts to its original meaning as the side of a guitar, while the crossbar arrangement loses its function as a synecdoche for the face, becoming a mere geometrical arrangement.

Three different principles are at work in this sheet. One is the sequential and systematic character of Picasso's production. The bottle at left and the guitar at right both derive from the same ideogram, but their shared parentage is not obvious unless one is familiar with Picasso's other work of this period. Another is the devolution of the ideographic sign into an arrangement of geometric forms. This devolution has to take place before the ideogram can be transformed into a sign for something other than its original referent: a bottle or a guitar, instead of a face. The third is the convertibility of the ideogram between a graphic and a sculptural form. The "double-axis" and "crossbar" versions of the face were essentially graphic arrangements of lines and planes, but Picasso seems from the outset to have imagined the new "strip" face as a three-dimensional form. The squared-off bottle derived from this face is shaded to suggest volume, and even the ideographic guitar, in the drawing at right, is flanked by shading suggesting its spatial separation from the forms around it. Picasso's pursuit of the sign thus led him, not into the realm of graphic flatness, but back toward a sculptural view of form.

Signs and Constructions

The modest proportions and humble materials of Picasso's 1912–14 constructions belie their revolutionary importance. In them, Picasso broke with the formal assumptions that had dominated Western sculpture for millennia, assumptions to which sculptors had remained faithful even when they deviated from classical norms. Although the Romanesque artisans of the eleventh century had reduced their subjects to graphic outlines, although Bernini had unbalanced his figures and enfolded them in flickering

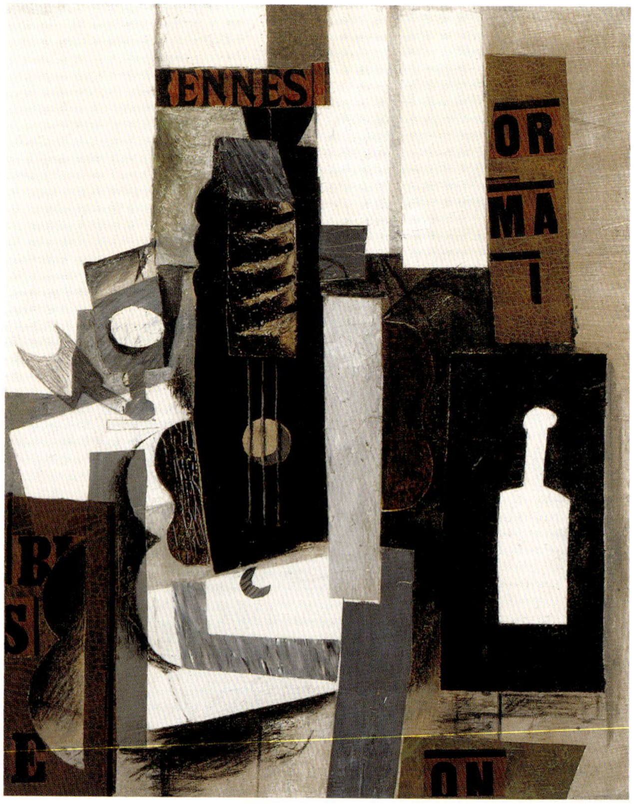

227 Picasso. *Glass, Guitar, and Bottle*. Paris, early 1913. Oil, pasted paper, gesso, and pencil on canvas, 65.4 × 53.6 cm. D.R. 570. The Museum of Modern Art, New York. The Sidney and Harriet Janis Collection

drapery, their sculptures had nonetheless continued to represent recognizable, solid figures. In discarding traditional techniques of modeling and carving, Picasso simultaneously discarded the underlying model of the body as a coherent mass with a continuous surface. His 1912–14 sculptures represent the beginning of a radically new approach to sculpture, subsequently explored by artists as diverse as Vladimir Tatlin and Henri Laurens, Julio Gonzalez and David Smith, Anthony Caro and Richard Serra.

The seminal role of Picasso's constructions is all the more surprising in that many of them were destroyed not long after their creation. Even those which survived were not exhibited publicly for decades. Their influence seems to have been diffused primarily through photographs such as those reproduced in the October 1913 issue of *Les Soirées de Paris*, and through their informal display in Picasso's studio. Unfortunately, it remains unclear to what extent Picasso opened his studio to artists outside his immediate circle. We do not know whether Tatlin's spring 1914 visit – which led directly to the inception of Russian Constructivism – was typical or exceptional.

As is often the case, the critical literature on Cubist construction derives from a few remarks by Kahnweiler, who focused on just two aspects of the subject. One was construction's relationship to *papier collé*, the other its relationship to the Grebo mask owned by Picasso. The first suggested a formalist reading of construction as an art of superimposed planes; the second a semiological reading as an anti-naturalistic art of arbitrary signs. Unfortunately, Kahnweiler's stress on these two issues has tended to narrow and even distort later critics' understanding of construction.

Kahnweiler on several occasions described the superimposed planes of Cubist painting as an 'imitation' of earlier relief sculptures made by Braque and Picasso, the former working with paper, the latter with cardboard, wood, and iron.[194] In these passages, Kahnweiler was rather vague about chronology, and it was not clear when exactly the sculptures in question had been made – especially since most of them were subsequently lost or destroyed. But, since several of Picasso's canvases from the winter of 1912–13 seem to be painted versions of wall reliefs visible in photographs of his studio (figs. 227, 228), it seems reasonable to assume that Kahnweiler was talking about this period.

In the general confusion over Cubist chronology that prevailed before the publication of Daix and Rosselet's *catalogue raisonné* in 1979, it also seemed reasonable to assume that the constructed *Guitar* (fig. 229) derived from these wall reliefs, extended somewhat further into the third dimension.[195] The problem with this interpretation was that the artists themselves said it was not true. Braque testified that sculpture preceded *papier collé* in his work: "I was making paper sculpture . . . Then I put the sculpture onto canvas. Those were my first *papiers collés*." Similarly, Picasso insisted that the constructed *Guitar* "had nothing to do with collage."[196] The publication of Daix and Rosselet's catalogue permitted Edward Fry to establish that the cardboard maquette for the "Guitar" was assembled in fall 1912, earlier than or at the same time as the reliefs cited by Kahnweiler.[197] Indeed, the photographs of Picasso's studio make it clear that the cardboard maquette was part of what seems to have been his first wall relief. Evidently, construct-

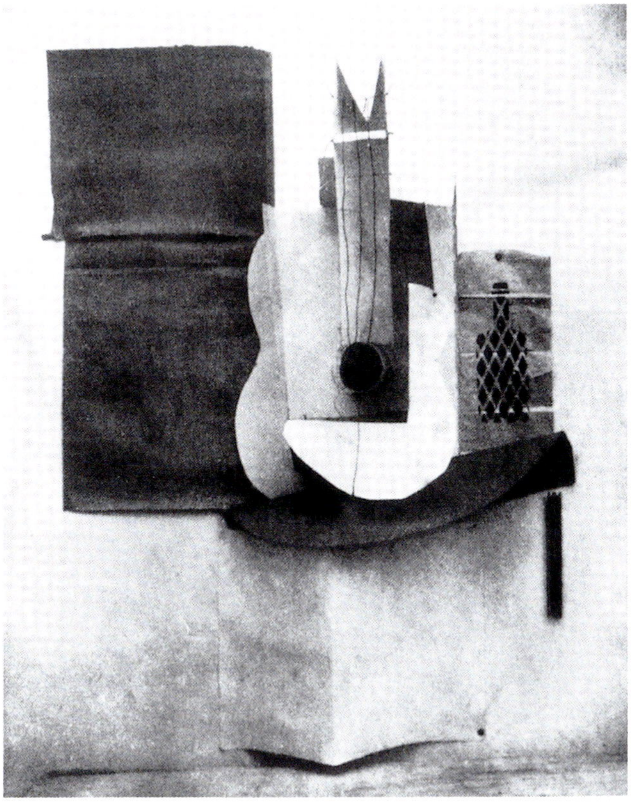

228 Photograph of relief construction mounted in Picasso's Boulevard Raspail studio, early 1913, including *Guitar.* Picasso Archives, Paris

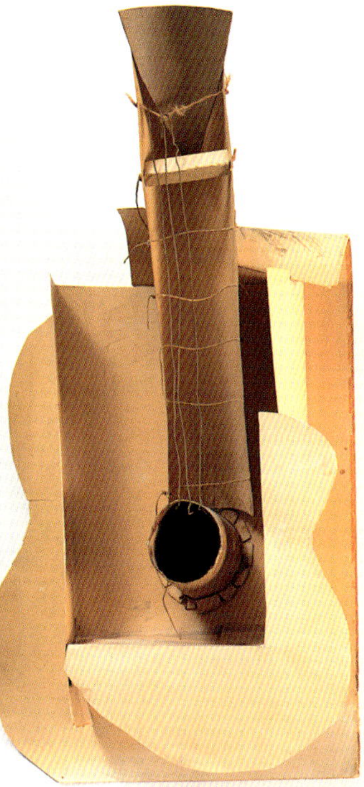

229 Picasso. *Guitar.* Paris, October 1912. Construction of cardboard, string, and wire (restored), 65.1 × 33 × 19 cm. Spies 27A. The Museum of Modern Art, New York. Gift of the artist

ed sculpture did not derive from *papier collé*; if anything, it was the other way round.

The whole discussion seems to have been befogged, in any case, by the tacit assumption that a material technique, such as pasting, could explain the formal vocabulary of the work created by that technique. In the short run, this idea was a legacy from Clement Greenberg's 1958 essay, "The Pasted Paper Revolution." Viewed in historical perspective, it reflected the persistent emphasis of the nineteenth-century scholar Gottfried Semper, who had argued in his influential treatise *Der Stil* that the formal vocabulary of the decorative arts derived from the technical processes of weaving, pottery, and other crafts.[198] In fact, as the subsequent history of Cubism showed, the techniques of *papier collé* and constructed sculpture could be adapted to a great variety of forms. This was a testament to their artistic fertility, but it demonstrated that technique per se had little explanatory value. In any case, this line of interpretation more or less vanished from Cubist criticism after 1980.

What replaced it was a semiological interpretation deriving from Kahnweiler's discussion of the Grebo mask (see fig. 233). It was the projecting eyes of this mask, Kahnweiler said, that provided the model for the projecting sound-hole of Picasso's *Guitar.* This element of Kahnweiler's interpretation was confirmed by Picasso in conversation with William Rubin in 1971. More fundamentally, Kahnweiler added, the mask demonstrated that "the true character of painting and sculpture is that of a script." Instead of imitating the "real" contours of the human face, it presented a series of signs – the cylindrical eyes, the box-like mouth, the narrow wedge of the nose – arrayed on the plane of the face. This too was confirmed by Picasso in 1971.[199] In his 1987 essay, "Kahnweiler's Lesson," Yve-Alain

Bois went a step further, arguing that it was the "non-substantial" character of the sign in the Grebo mask that provided the model for the description of a face or a guitar as an open volume rather than a closed mass.[200]

Bois's interpretation also seems to explain the timing of Picasso's invention of constructed sculpture. In an August 11, 1912 letter to Kahnweiler, Picasso mentions that he and Braque have visited Marseille, buying a number of "blacks" – that is, African sculptures. In particular, Picasso says, he purchased "a very good mask."[201] This trip is also documented in Picasso's sketchbook (see fig. 201), where the mask is visible under the café table. Picasso eventually came to own two Grebo masks, but it is not known where or when he bought the other.[202] It seems reasonable to conclude that the mask purchased in August 1912 was the first he acquired and that its acquisition led, a few weeks or months later, to the creation of the *Guitar* as described by Kahnweiler and Bois.

There are a few problems with this interpretation, however. For one thing, although "open" form may not appear in Picasso's sculpture until 1912, it is evident in his paintings and drawings of 1910 – as Kahnweiler noted in *The Rise of Cubism*.[203] Similarly, the idea of making an indentation stand for a projection appears in Picasso's work as early as 1909, in the sculpted *Woman's Head* (see fig. 79), where one eyebrow is represented by a curved ridge and the other by a curved trench. There is also a problem with Kahnweiler's argument that the viewer sees an imaginary facial plane at the height of the eye-cylinders in the Grebo mask: if this were true, most of the nose would be sunk within the face. Picasso's constructed *Guitar* may have a front plane, cut away to reveal the back plane, but the Grebo mask does not.

Furthermore, even if we imagine an invisible front plane to the mask, it cannot result from the "non-substantial" character of the signs, as Bois argues, because the signs in the mask are distinctly substantial. The eyes are two cylinders, the nose is a projecting fin, the mouth is a rectangular block inscribed with ridges indicating lips. Bois's description of them as "non-substantial" depends on the Saussurean reading according to which all signs are non-substantial, because they are defined purely by differences. Absent this verbal sleight of hand, and the signs in the Grebo mask revert to being what they actually are: chunks of wood, arranged on a plane.

To make sense of the development of Cubist construction, we need to look not only at Picasso's surviving constructions but also at the rich body of drawings related to them. These include numerous studies for now lost constructions, and even more numerous studies for constructions that Picasso never executed but that played an important role in his thinking about sculpture. From this perspective, Picasso's sculpture projects of 1912–13 fall into three major groups: studies for the figure of a never executed guitar player; studies linked to the constructed *Guitar*; and studies for constructed relief sculptures, most known only from photographs.

Picasso's first studies for constructions date from spring 1912. It is possible that they were prompted by some experiments with "paper sculpture" that Braque apparently made in fall 1911. We know about these exclusively from literary evidence. The only clue as to their actual appearance is that they seem to have reminded Picasso of the Wright Brothers' airplanes. (It was around this time that Picasso began jokingly to refer to Braque as "Wilbur.") Even if they did influence Picasso's first sculpture studies, there is no way of knowing how.[204]

Picasso was apparently thinking about making sculpture by the beginning of 1912. André Salmon's art column in the January 11, 1912 *Paris-Journal* contains the tantalizing comment: "Modern sculpture – the painter Picasso, without in any way throwing away his brushes, is undoubtedly going to execute some important sculptural works."[205] But none of Picasso's early 1912 studies seems to be related to sculpture projects. These first clearly identifiable sculpture studies emerge from a spring 1912 series of drawings depicting a female guitar player. Some of these show the guitarist in front of curtains or in a café setting (fig. 230); heavily shaded, they seem like studies for paintings. In others, the guitarist is presented against a blank backdrop (fig. 231); the near-absence of shading and the clarity of her anatomy make these look more like sculpture studies. The guitarist seems to be constructed around a kind of mast from which the other elements of the body are cantilevered or suspended.

Certain elements of this figuration can be traced back to Picasso's figures of 1910. For instance, in a sketch from the "Mademoiselle Léonie" series (see fig. 98), the shoulder on the left is depicted as a large circular segment, and the shoulder on the right as a sharp angle. Both of these forms return in a spring 1912 sculpture study (fig. 231), the angle as a pair of bent strips atop the shelf of the torso, the circular segment as curved "hinges" projecting at either side. But the most important feature of both figures is their broken, discontinuous contours. The "open" construction of the figure in Picasso's 1912 drawing derives directly from the open forms of his 1910 drawings and paintings.

The resemblance to Picasso's work of 1910 also points up the unusual sign language of the spring 1912 figure. In other figures of this period, such as the canvas "*Ma Jolie*" (see fig. 130), Picasso generally combines synecdochic signs based on caricature with a geometric armature that does not try to imitate the actual structure of the body. In contrast, the geometric structure of the figure in the sculpture study corresponds closely to the actual structure of the human body. The face is represented by a vertical plane, the mass of the head by a ball, and both of these are mounted on a horizontal plane serving as a jaw. A round collar encircles the neck. The upper edge of the torso is depicted as a kind of shelf, with semicircular flaps representing the figure's breasts rising from it. The volume of the torso is encircled by curving ribs and traversed by horizontal planes. The relatively naturalistic legs and feet are visible below the rectangular seat of a chair with four square legs. These are synecdochic signs, but most of them operate at an unusually high level of abstraction. There are no caricatural eyes, ears, nostrils, or moustaches to lend a more human quality to the geometric forms of the head, for instance. The absence of realistic or caricatural elements may reflect the continuing hold of the idea that sculpture should be made from a single material. In effect, Picasso limited himself to forms that could be constructed from bent or curved pieces of cardboard or sheet metal.

In another version of this figure (fig. 232), the torso is reduced to a large rectangle that rises from a horizontal plane supported by four legs. In effect, the guitarist has become identified with the chair in which she is seated. However, the flat plane of the body also recalls the flat facial plane of the Grebo mask, just as the two breasts, represented by dowels, recall the two cylindrical eyes of the mask (fig. 233). Another drawing from this series (fig. 234) shows a projecting brow, a wedge-shaped nose, and a rectangular mouth attached to a flat plane.[206] Both of these imaginary constructions seem to show the influence of a Grebo-type mask, suggesting that Picasso already owned such a mask by spring 1912 – several months before his visit to Marseille. They cast new light, furthermore, on what it was about the mask that interested him. Rubin recalled that Picasso "drew particular attention" to the "uninflected flat panel" of the face.[207] No doubt this struck him because it resembled his own practice of reducing the face or body to a series of vertical strips, which assumed a representational value thanks to the signs inscribed on them. As Picasso said on another occasion, the mask was a "witness" from a foreign culture, confirming an idea that he had already arrived at.[208] Where the Grebo mask differed from 1911–12 Cubism was in the nature of the signs mounted on its panel. Picasso had until then inscribed flat, graphic signs onto the vertical strips of his figures.[209] The mask suggested that these synecdochic signs might themselves take the form of solid, three-dimensional shapes. The dowel breasts of the spring 1912 drawing represent a first, tentative step in this direction, which did not come to fruition for another year.

This guitarist was clearly a transitional work but it already pointed to a new kind of metamorphosis, which became central to Picasso's later work, both Cubist and Surrealist. The metamorphoses in earlier "fantastic" pictures had usually followed what we might call the Arcimboldo model: what seemed at first glance to be a random assortment of fruits or farmyard implements would suddenly be revealed as an image of the human body. The "trick," so to speak, was that the outlines of the inanimate objects coincided with those of the face or limbs, naturalistically conceived.[210] Picasso's aim, in his spring 1912 sculpture study, is the exact opposite: not to arrange inanimate objects within the outlines of human anatomy, but to re-invent human anatomy on the model of inanimate objects. He does not make a chair look like a body. Rather, he asks: what would the human body look like if it were constructed like a chair? (He returned to this idea in 1933 in an etching, *Model and Surrealist Sculpture*, fig. 235.)

A similar idea is evident in some of Picasso's summer 1912 drawings, where a woman's body is compared, for instance, to a painter's easel (fig. 236). It was a different group of drawings and paintings, however, that led up to the constructed *Guitar*.[211] The curious thing about these pictures is that they anticipated the *Guitar*'s structure but do not look like studies for a sculpture. Apparently, it was only after they were completed that Picasso arrived at the decision to translate them into three dimensions.

The impetus for this decision seems to have come from Braque, who made several guitars and violins constructed

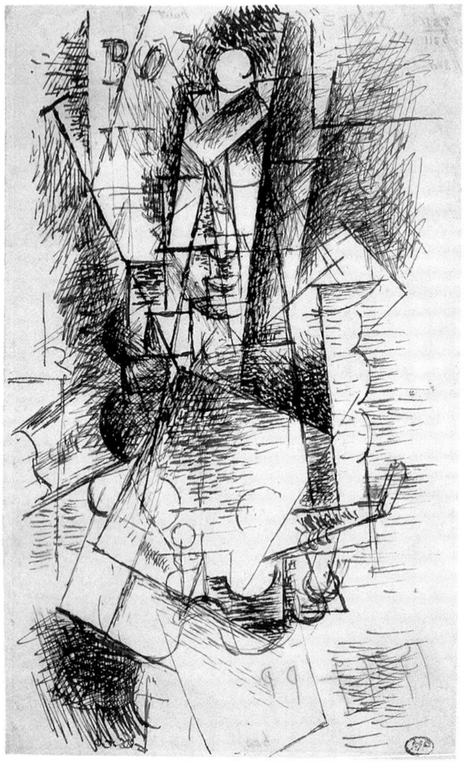

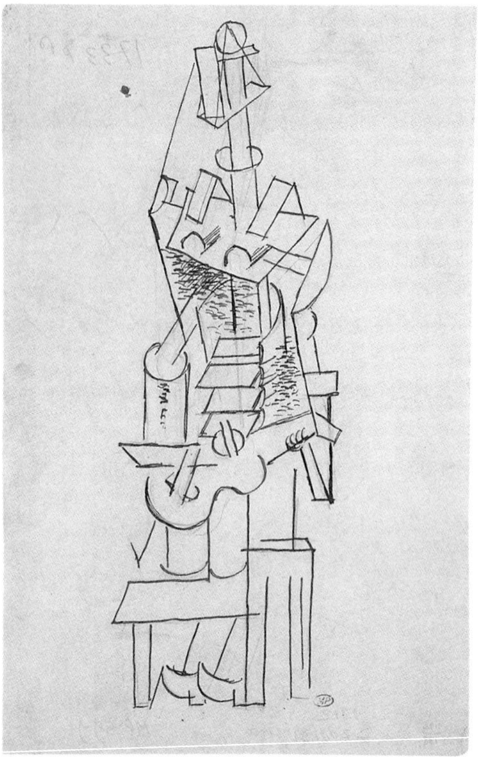

230 (*above left*) Picasso. *Seated Figure with Guitar.* Paris, spring 1912. Ink on paper, 21 × 13.5 cm. Zervos XXVIII, 65. Musée Picasso, Paris

231 (*above right*) Picasso. *Seated Woman with Guitar (Study for a Construction).* Paris, spring 1912. Brown ink over lead pencil on paper, 31 × 29 cm. Zervos XXVIII, 131; Richet 308. Musée Picasso, Paris

232 (*right*) Picasso. *Guitar and Seated Women with Guitars (Studies for Construction).* Paris, spring 1912. Brown ink on translucent paper, 21.2 × 13.2 cm. Zervos XXVIII, 129; Richet 311. Musée Picasso, Paris

233 (*facing page top left*) Grebo mask owned by Picasso. Wood, paint, vegetable fibers, h. 64 cm. Musée Picasso, Paris

234 (*facing page top right*) Picasso. *Head (Study for a Construction).* Paris, spring 1912. Lead pencil on paper, 29 × 23 cm. Zervos XXVIII, 137. Picasso estate (inv. 1403)

235 (*facing page bottom left*) Picasso. *Model and Surrealist Sculpture.* Paris, May 4, 1933. Etching, 26.7 × 19.4 cm. Geiser/Baer 346. The Museum of Modern Art, New York. Abby Aldrich Rockefeller Fund

236 (*facing page bottom right*) Picasso. *Seated Woman with Guitar (Study for a Construction).* Sorgues, summer 1912. Ink and lithographic crayon on paper, 31 × 19 cm. Zervos XXVIII, 132; Richet 313. Musée Picasso, Paris

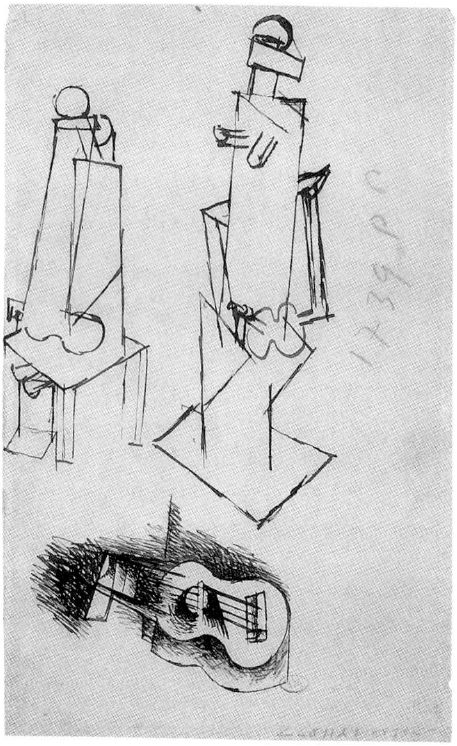

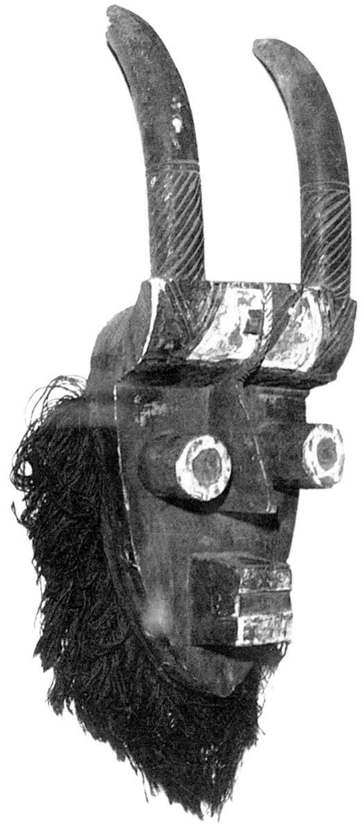

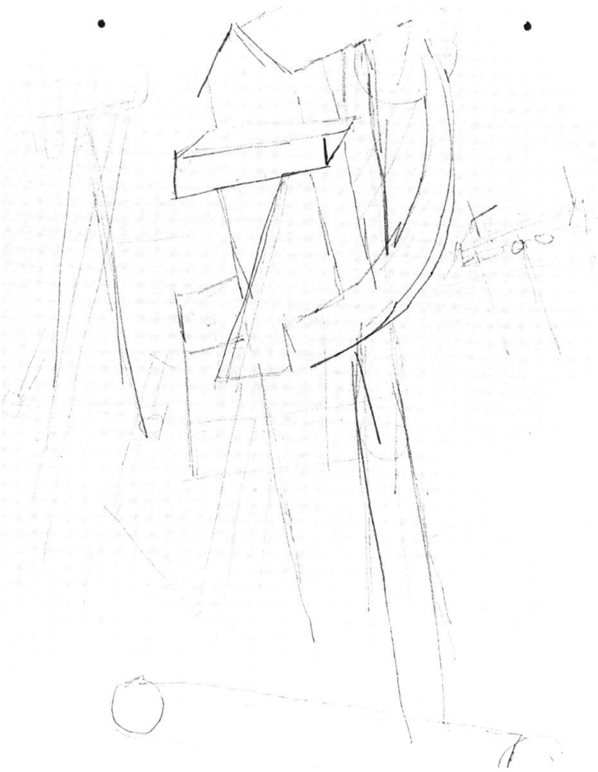

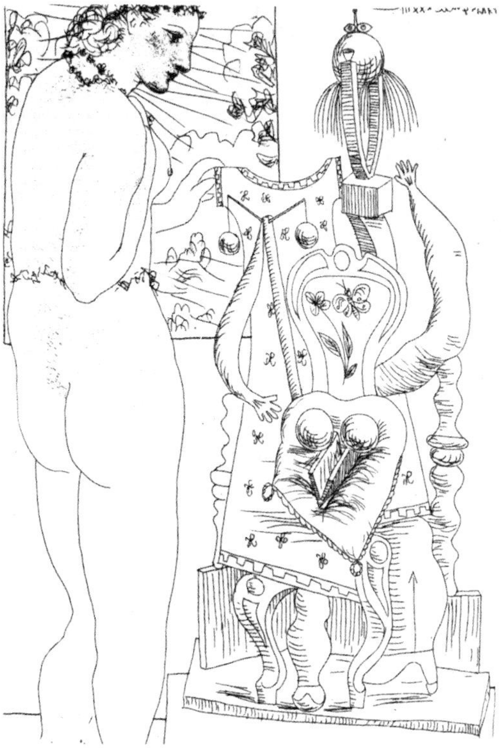

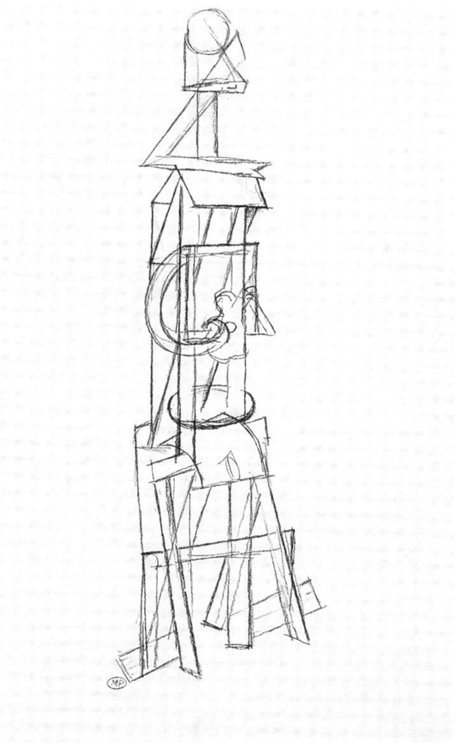

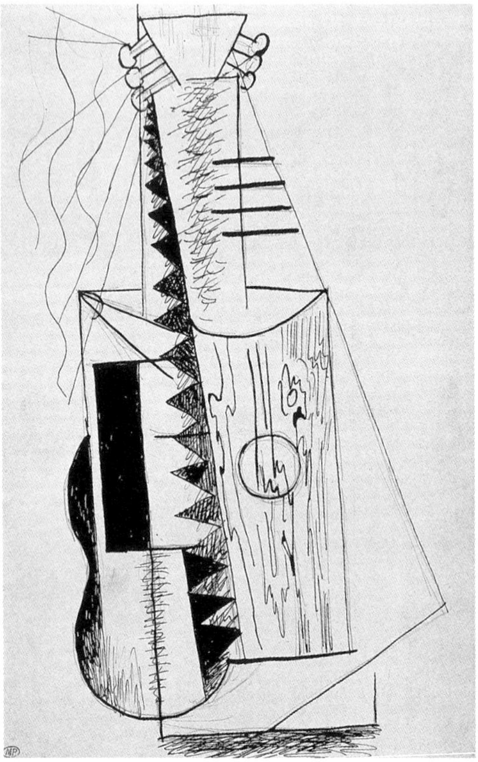

237 Picasso. *Guitar*. Sorgues, summer 1912. Ink and pencil on paper, 34.3 × 22.2 cm. Zervos XXVIII, 196; Richet 290. Musée Picasso, Paris

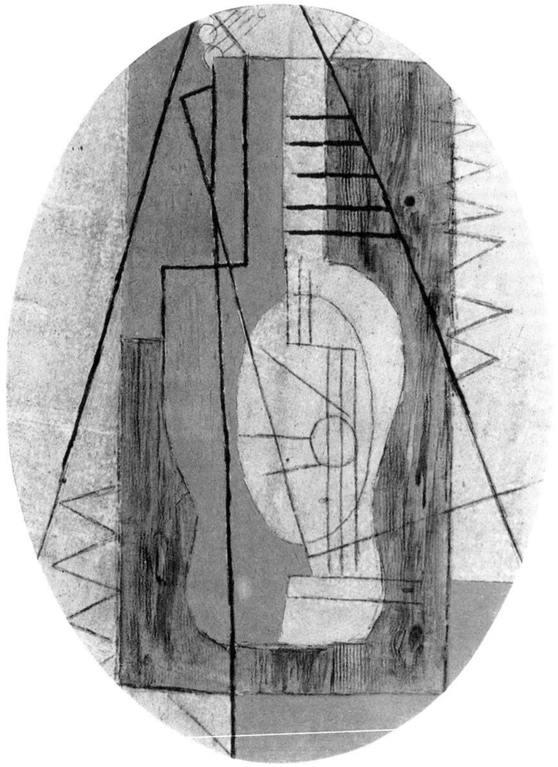

238 Picasso. *Guitar*. Sorgues, summer 1912. Oil on oval canvas, 64 × 50 cm. D.R. 488. Private collection

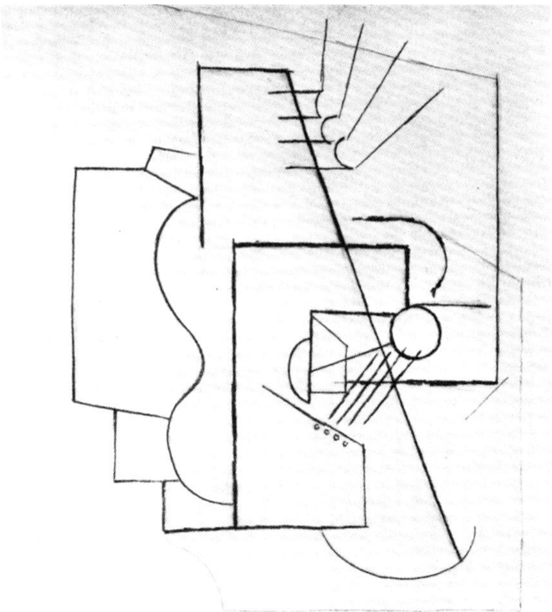

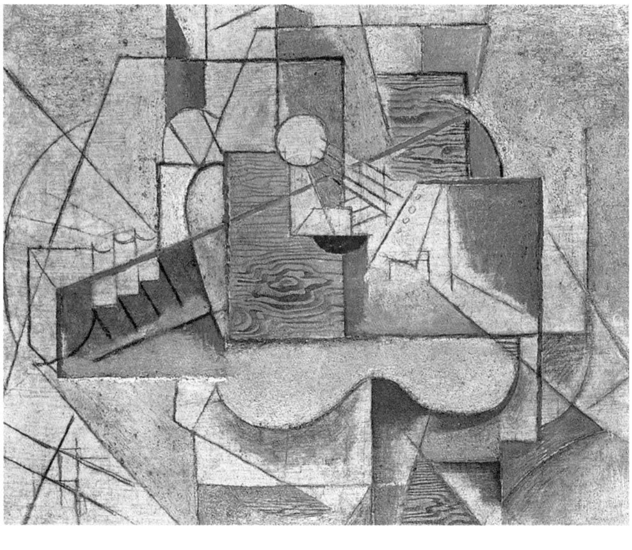

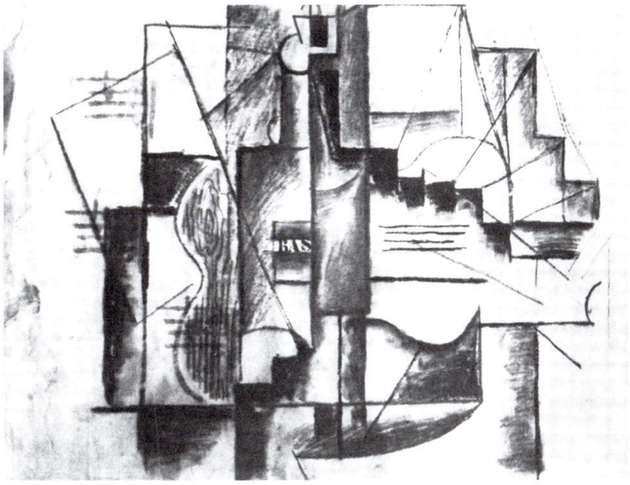

241 (*above*) Picasso. *Bottle of Bass and Guitar.* Paris, autumn 1912. Pastel, charcoal, and ink on paper, 47.7 × 63.5 cm. D.R. 511. The Douglas Cooper Collection, Churchglade Ltd

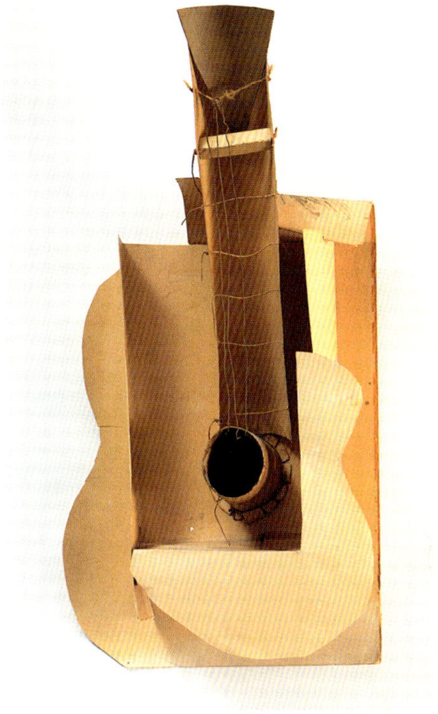

242 (*right*) Picasso. *Guitar.* Paris, October 1912. Construction of cardboard, string, and wire (restored), 65.1 × 33 × 19 cm. Spies 27A. The Museum of Modern Art, New York. Gift of the artist

from paper after his arrival at Sorgues in late July.[212] (Unfortunately, these are all lost.) Shortly after Picasso's return to Paris, he wrote to Braque: "I've been using your latest techniques for working with paper and dust. I'm thinking about imagining a guitar, and I'm using some dust on our horrible canvas."[213] The vehicle for these experiments was the guitar composition he had already begun to explore at Sorgues (figs. 237, 238). Picasso revised this in a large drawing sold to Gertrude Stein (fig. 239). He then transferred the composition to canvas, rotating it to a horizontal orientation (fig. 240) and adding sand ("dust") to his paint, as Braque had to several of his canvases from Sorgues. Playing with the metaphoric potential of his geometric armature, Picasso created another version that was simultaneously a vertical guitar, a horizontal guitar, and a bottle of Bass Ale (fig. 241). Finally, he explored Braque's sculptural procedures, translating the drawn and painted guitar into a construction of cardboard and string (fig. 242).

The tilted, overlapping planes of the drawn and painted studies seem to have been difficult to reproduce in this new medium. As a result, the main planes of the constructed *Guitar* are all either parallel or perpendicular to the wall on which it was mounted. The neck, however, is constructed from a curved strip, like a cylinder cut in half, and its head is indicated by a triangle that tilts downward at an angle. Picasso's contemporary paintings utilized a wide variety of colors and textures, but the *Guitar* construction was monochrome, with little variety of texture. Like his constructed guitarist, the *Guitar* employed a consistently abstract vocabulary, avoiding realistic or caricatural signs. Nonetheless, the shallow relief and closed backplane of the *Guitar* made it far more "pictorial" than the figures in Picasso's sculpture studies of the previous spring.

Picasso joked about selling the plan for the *Guitar,* so that other people could construct their own examples of the

239 (*facing page bottom left*) Picasso. Study for *Guitar on a Table.* Paris, October 1912. Crayon on paper, 63.5 × 48.6 cm. Previously collection Gertrude Stein

240 (*facing page bottom right*) Picasso. *Guitar on a Table.* Paris, October 1912. Oil, sand, and charcoal on canvas, 51.1 × 61.6 cm. D.R. 509. Hood Museum of Art, Hanover, New Hampshire. Gift of Nelson A. Rockefeller, Class of 1930

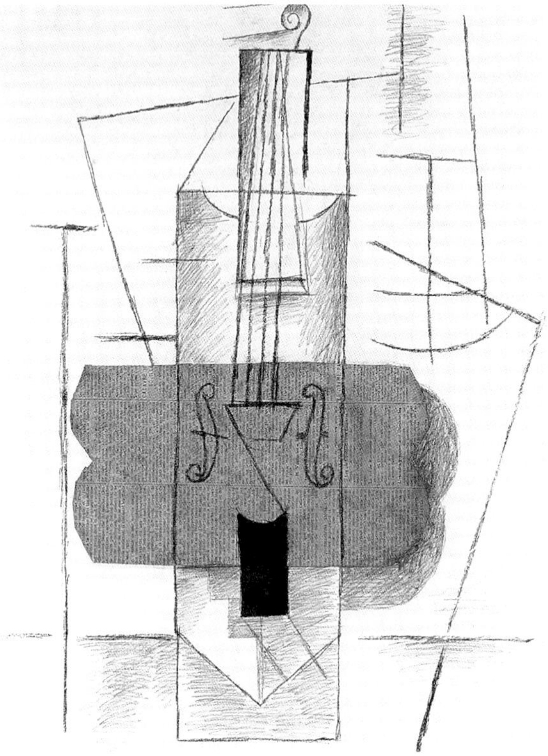

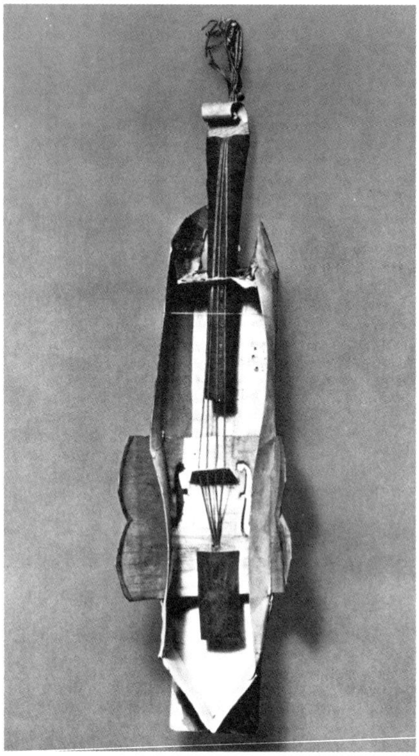

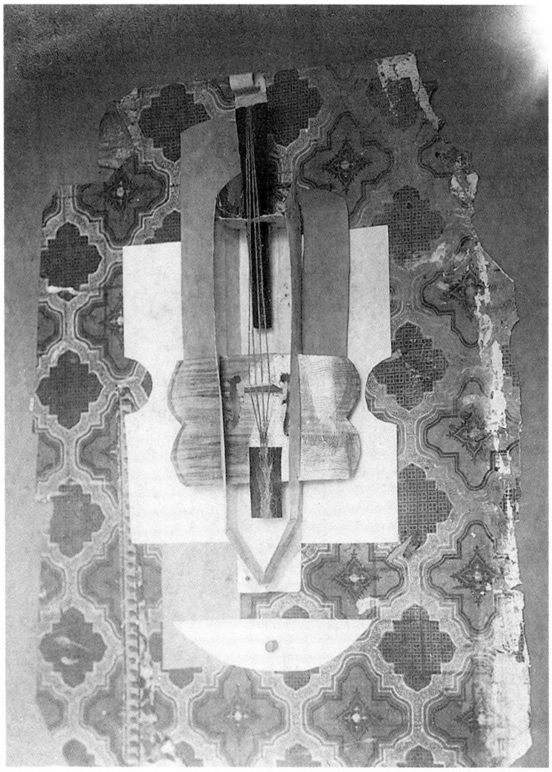

243 (*above left*) Picasso. *Violin.* Paris, after December 8, 1912. Pencil, charcoal, gouache, and pasted paper on paper, 61.1 × 46.5 cm. Not in Zervos. Private collection

244 (*above right*) Picasso. *Violin.* Paris, winter 1912–13. Cardboard and string, 58.5 × 21 × 7.5 cm. Spies 35. Staatsgalerie, Stuttgart

245 (*left*) Photograph of paper, cardboard, and string construction on the wall of Picasso's studio, Céret, spring 1913. Spies 34. No longer extant

sculpture.[214] He also at some point remade it in a more permanent, sheet-metal version. However, its primary role seems to have been to serve as a model for painting. As noted earlier, in the course of fall 1912 the *Guitar* was incorporated in a larger relief composition assembled in the Boulevard Raspail studio (see fig. 228). The ridged panel on the left of this relief appears to represent a wall with a chair-rail or molding, while the guitar and the cut-diamond bottle rest on a circular table with a single abstract tassel evoking its fringed tablecloth. This relief construction provided the model for at least five canvases, including *Glass, Guitar, and Bottle* (see fig. 227).[215]

It seems likely that Kahnweiler had this particular group of works in mind when he wrote that Picasso's 1912 (or rather 1912–13) paintings were "imitations" of his lost reliefs.[216] But insofar as the winter 1912–13 relief was based on paintings and drawings which Picasso had done the previous summer, its reinterpretation on canvas was, in effect, a return to the composition's original medium. Other works from this period seem to support the contention that constructed sculpture was derived from *papier collé*. A *papier collé* violin created on or after December 8, 1912 became the model for a three-dimensional construction, and was later incorporated in a more complex relief attached directly to the wall of Picasso's Céret studio (figs. 243–45). The only generalization that can safely be drawn from these examples is that the relationship between painting and sculpture was a two-way street. If Picasso wanted to use constructed sculpture as a source of pictorial ideas, he also wanted to translate the complex structures and sign language of his paintings into the medium of sculpture. This was the chief goal of his work of spring 1913.

Picasso spent spring 1913 back in Céret, where he elaborated a gigantic visual fugue composed on two familiar motifs – a man with a guitar, and a still-life arrangement of a guitar and a bottle on a table. New versions of these motifs had first been stated in a large construction (fig. 246) which Picasso assembled in his Boulevard Raspail studio early in the year, combining a drawn Cubist figure with newspaper limbs, a real guitar, and a table-top arrangement of real objects, including a bottle and newspaper. His subsequent variations on these themes extend through a 75-page notebook, over two hundred drawings on loose sheets, numerous *papiers collés*, and a comparatively small number of canvases. Many of the individual variations are unimpressive, but there is a hypnotic fascination in the constant metamorphoses leading from one work to the next. Figures are transformed into still lifes, still lifes into figures; sketches for paintings become sculpture studies, sculpture studies become sketches for paintings.[217]

The most important products of this labor were three large reliefs in which Picasso synthesized Cubist painting and constructed sculpture. Unfortunately, two of these reliefs were destroyed and the third survives only in altered form, so that this critical episode in Picasso's development must be understood primarily from studies and photographs, not from finished works.

In the early pages of Picasso's Céret sketchbook, the guitar player is depicted as a standing figure composed of vertical strips. After exploring several different versions of this figure, Picasso began to plan an elaborate construction based on this design, to be made from wood and other materials (figs. 247, 248). The torso in this design is reduced to a large vertical panel, with the back and arms of the chair attached to its reverse; the figure's arms attached to an independent framework in front of it. The spiky "beard" below the head was presumably inspired by the raffia fringes of the Grebo mask (see fig. 233). Above the head, an inverted L terminates in a large circle, corresponding to the top of the guitarist's stovepipe hat.

The basic structure of this figure derives from the spring 1912 sculpture study representing the body of the seated guitarist as a vertical plank rising from a horizontal plank (see fig. 232). But the three-dimensional signs for the other elements of the figure are more complicated than those in the earlier drawing. The head is itself a complex construction framed by cut-out Bs deriving from the *Guitar* drawings of summer 1912. The upper arm, at left, consists of a series of shaded, sculptural curves, while the forearm is a flat strip offering the mere silhouette of a sleeve. These sculptural signs have finally matched the complexity (and humor) of the synecdochic signs in Picasso's paintings.

Several of Picasso's sketches indicate the details of the joinery for this figure, and there is no way of knowing why he did not proceed to realize it. Either as a pendant to this construction or as a substitute for it, Picasso seems to have decided to convert the guitar player into a painting. A notebook sketch (fig. 249) shows how the wooden framework joining head and arms was transformed into a pattern of dark lines superimposed on a series of shaded strips. In other studies, Picasso's interest turned to problems of pattern and texture, and the large flat color areas of the finished painting (fig. 250) give no indication that the figure began as a sculptural composition.

Other notebook sketches show Picasso returning to this motif with the idea of realizing it as a wall relief rather than a free-standing construction.[218] Combining several early versions of the guitar player, Picasso created a large triangular figure, with target-like concentric circles indicating the face and the sound-hole of the guitar (fig. 251). The color of each element was carefully labeled, suggesting that this sketch was done specifically as a preparatory study for a

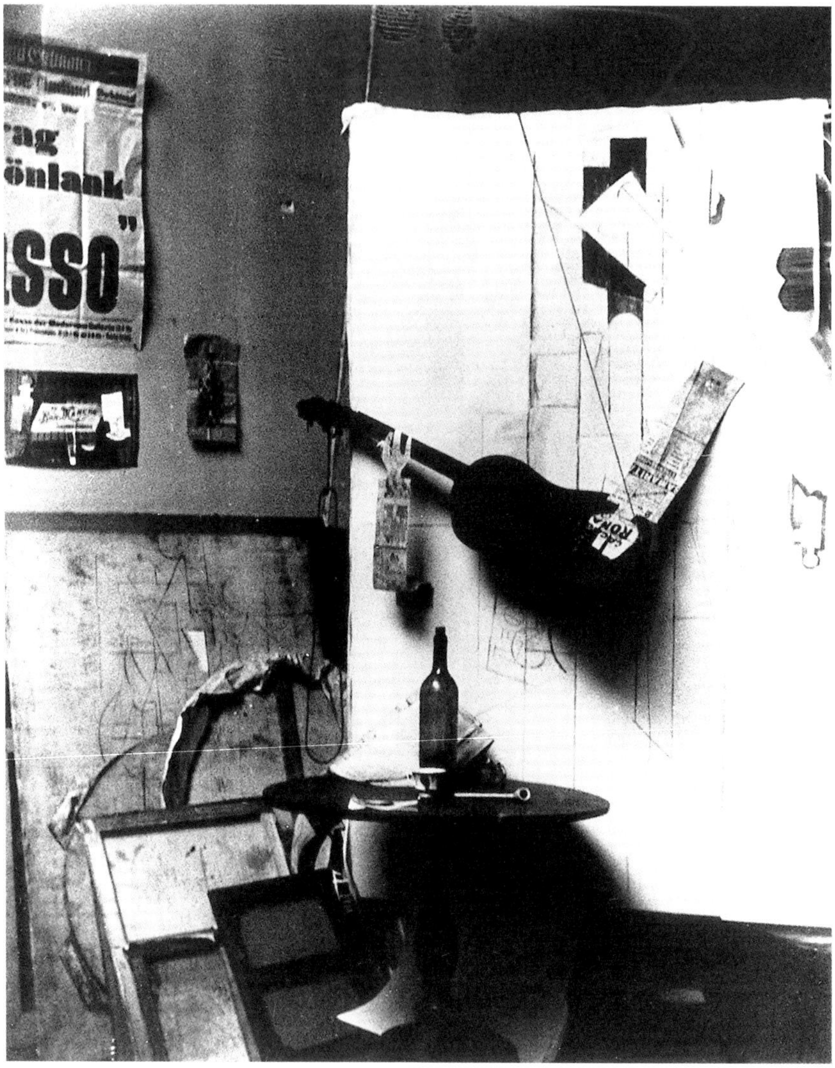

246 Photograph of construction in Picasso's studio, Boulevard Raspail, Paris, early 1913. Spies 28. No longer extant. Picasso Archives, Paris

larger work. A photograph in the Musée Picasso archives reveals that Picasso in fact assembled a wall relief (fig. 252) corresponding exactly to this drawing. If one gauges the size of this relief by the quarter-circle of newsprint at upper right, the relief as a whole seems to have been around 120 centimeters high and 80 wide – around the same size as the painted *Man with Guitar*.[219]

Picasso's sketches of spring 1913 also provided the models for two important panel reliefs. One derives from the draw-

247 (*facing page top left*) Picasso. *Head*. Céret, spring 1913. Lead pencil and India ink on graph-paper page from notebook, 13 × 8.5 cm. Zervos xxviii, 253. Léal, carnet 17, p. 43r. Musée Picasso, Paris

248 (*facing page top right*) Picasso. *Man with Guitar*. Céret, spring 1913. Lead pencil on paper, 42.5 × 28.5 cm. Zervos xxviii, 257. Private collection

249 (*facing page bottom left*) Picasso. *Man with Guitar*. Céret, spring 1913. Lead pencil on graph-paper page from notebook, 13 × 8.5 cm. Not in Zervos. Léal, carnet 17, p. 46r. Musée Picasso, Paris

250 (*facing page bottom right*) Picasso. *Man with Guitar*. Céret, spring 1913. Oil on canvas, 130.2 × 88.9 cm. D.R. 616. Private collection

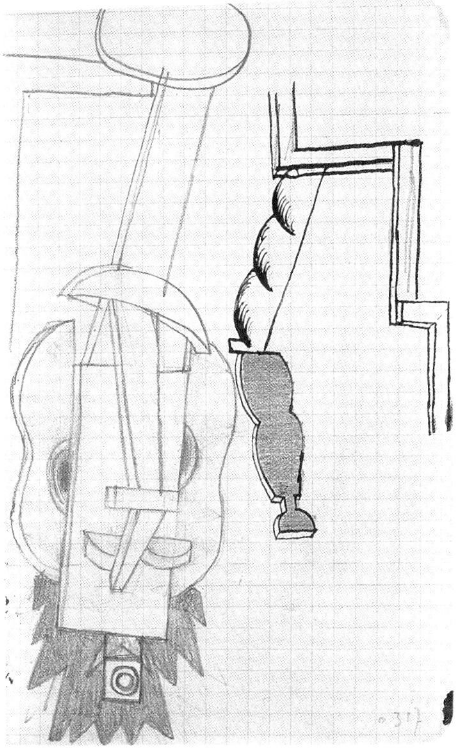

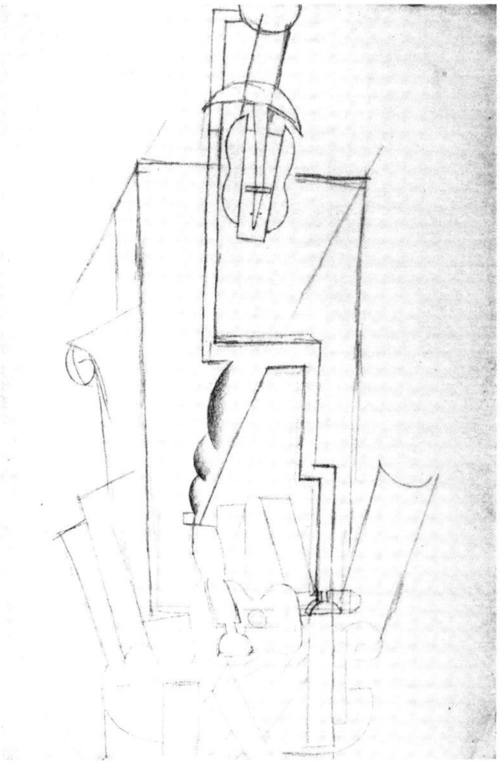

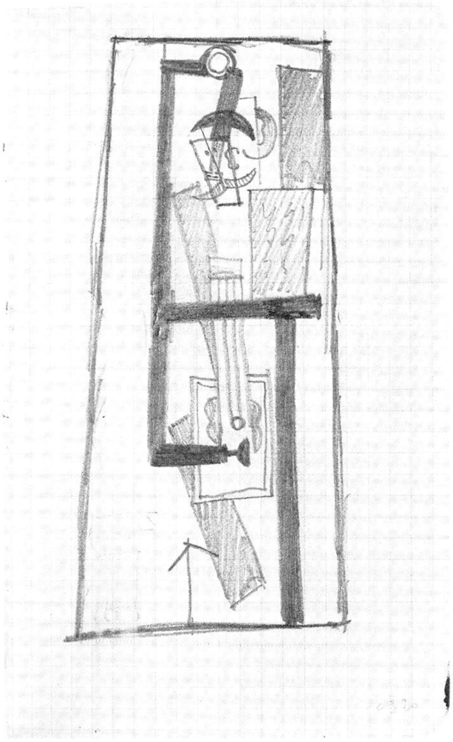

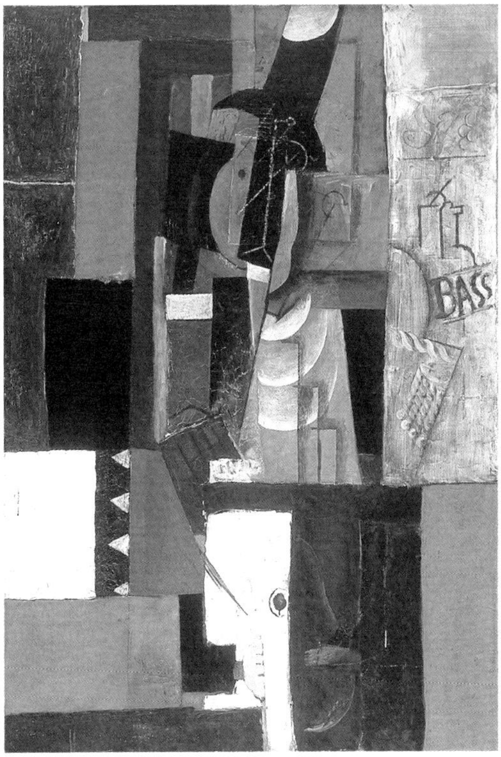
BASS

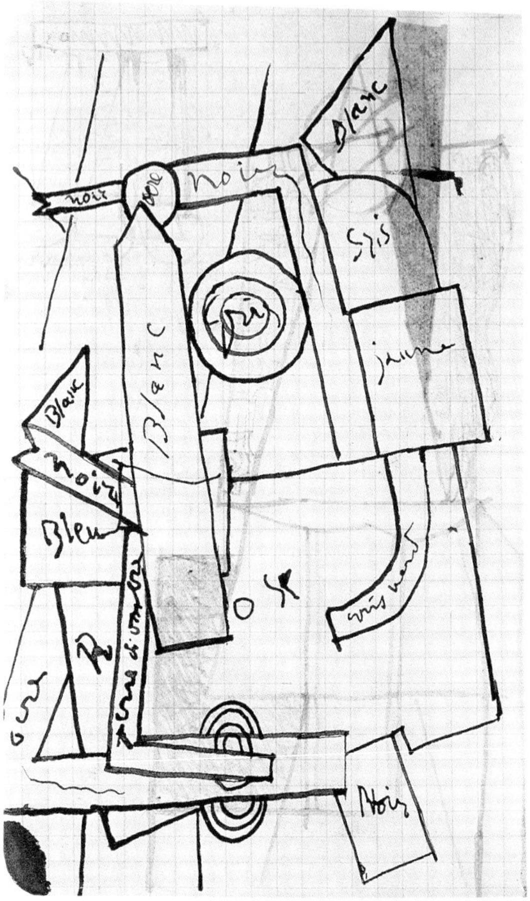

251 Picasso. *Guitar Player* (*Study for a* papier collé). Céret, spring 1913. Black ink on graph-paper page from notebook, 13 × 8.5 cm. Not in Zervos. Léal, carnet 17, p. 67v. Musée Picasso, Paris

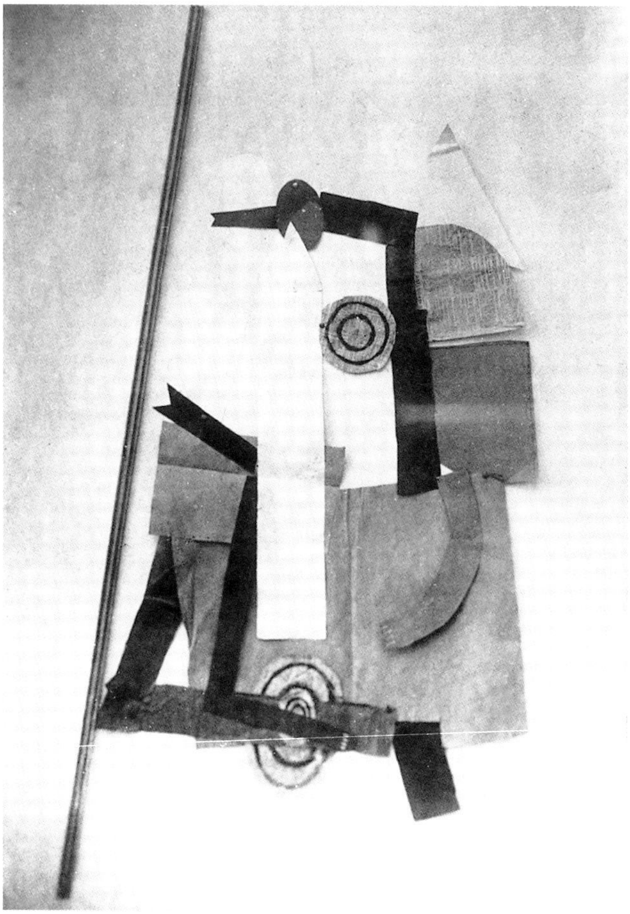

252 Photograph of lost *papier collé* mural in Picasso's studio, Ceret, spring 1913. Approx. 120 × 80 cm. Picasso Archives, Paris

ing already examined of a figure playing a double bass or cello (fig. 253), transformed in subsequent sketches into a table-top still life with a guitar and a bottle of Bass (figs. 254–58). Another evolves from a similar still life.[220] Mixing shaped and painted forms with found objects, these works look forward fifty years to the combines of Robert Rauschenberg. They might equally well be described as relief sculptures using the vocabulary of Cubist painting, or paintings made with three-dimensional elements.

This interchangeability of pictorial and sculptural ideas reflects the larger tendency toward metamorphosis in Picasso's work. As figures and objects are divided into a series of signs corresponding to different aspects of their form or appearance, their identity becomes increasingly unstable. Their isolated elements constantly assume new meanings as they shift from one context to another, from two dimensions to three, and back again. Recognizing the importance of Picasso's reliefs, Apollinaire published photographs of four of them in the November 1913 issue of *Les Soirées de Paris*, tracing their evolution from late 1912 through spring 1913.[221]

Picasso's work of fall 1913 includes an important coda to this evolution. Editing out most of the realist elements of his proto-Surrealist *Woman with Chemise in an Armchair* (see fig. 123), he rearranged the figure into an intricate composition of overlapping, curvilinear shapes, linked to its original configuration primarily by the trapezoid of the woman's arm, emerging at upper right (figs. 259–61). He then transformed the vertical strips of the woman's body into a clarinet, so that the composition became a still life (fig. 262). In another drawing (fig. 263), the clarinet (now horizontal) was accompanied by a large curve at center and a projecting trapezoid at upper right. These had previously corresponded to the woman's torso and extended arm, but now become the body and neck of a mandolin. Finally, Picasso transformed this drawing into a painted construction (fig. 264). Here, the use of paint allowed him to add specific, synecdochic signs to the geometric vocabulary of the wooden forms: a target marks the mouth of the clarinet, while the neck of the mandolin is given strings. Picasso positioned the boards of the construction at a variety of different angles, cutting out several large and small curves. In a particularly brilliant stroke, the negative space around the body of the mandolin is represented by a board, painted white, while the body itself is indicated by a curved cut-out. The technical restrictions evident in the constructed *Guitar* of 1912, with a limited repertory of parallel and perpendicular planes, have completely vanished.

Meanings and Pleasures

In February 1912, the satirical magazine *L'Assiette au beurre* greeted an exhibition of Picasso's and Braque's new works with the comment that "The Kahnweiler Gallery is offering its visitors a chance to solve a series of rebuses by Messrs. Pablo Picasso and Braque."[222] Despite its satirical tone, the anonymous comment contained a real insight into the nature of Cubist figuration. Just as the words in a rebus are broken into pieces, each represented by a separate image or symbol, so too the figures and objects in Cubist pictures were divided into independent aspects, represented by different signs. But, as the comparison suggested, the danger of creating an art of signs was that viewers would be unable – or unwilling – to read them.

Kahnweiler addressed this problem in his later writings on Cubism as a sign language. There, as discussed above, he argued that viewers had trouble reading the "graphic emblems" of Cubism only because they were unfamiliar with them. Viewers had been misled by the continued dominance of the Ecole des Beaux-Arts, which unnaturally perpetuated the sign language of seventeenth-century classicism. Writing at the end of World War II, Kahnweiler was convinced that this situation would change:

> The modern poster . . . the window displays and catalogues of the chain stores, are accustoming even the provincial spectator to the appearance of Cubist and later painting, thus slowly re-creating for him the world in the image of the new art. There is therefore reason to hope that we shall soon see the end of the isolation of the painters from their contemporaries.[223]

History has given a mixed verdict on this prediction. It is true, as Kahnweiler suggests, that Cubism has been absorbed into the vernacular language of design and decoration. However, it is not true that Cubism has become the dominant visual language of our time. If anything, the ubiquity of photographic reproduction has reinforced the dominance of naturalism: the photograph has become our yardstick of what things "really" look like. Nor has the diffusion of a simplified version of Cubism into popular design made it any easier for viewers to decipher real Cubism. For most viewers, Picasso's and Braque's paintings and sculptures seem as strange and hermetic today as they did in 1946 or 1912.

In a sense, Kahnweiler's earlier writings provided a more useful analysis of Cubist representation. Distinguishing between the different kinds of signs employed by Picasso and Braque, Kahnweiler acknowledged that geometric forms alone might not suffice to create a recognizable image. There was a risk that the viewer would see only "an arrangement of planes, cylinders, quadrangles, etc." However, the introduction of "real details" provided a "stimulus" evoking "memory images." Projecting these images onto the geometric forms, the viewer would "construct the finished object" in his or her mind.[224]

In describing the complex process of reading a Cubist painting, Kahnweiler seems at least implicitly to acknowledge its inherent difficulty and uncertainty. As a rule, the "real details" in Cubism are fragmentary and incomplete. How can the viewer be sure that the memory images they evoke in his or her mind are the images that the painter intended? And, even if they are the right images, will the viewer know how to project them correctly onto the geometric forms of the composition? In Picasso's paintings of 1911, individual features can be picked out – an elbow here, a shoulder there – but the figures remain mostly indecipherable. Which forms if any represent their faces or torsos?

Furthermore, where is the pleasure in looking at such difficult pictures? It is certainly not the pleasure of looking at

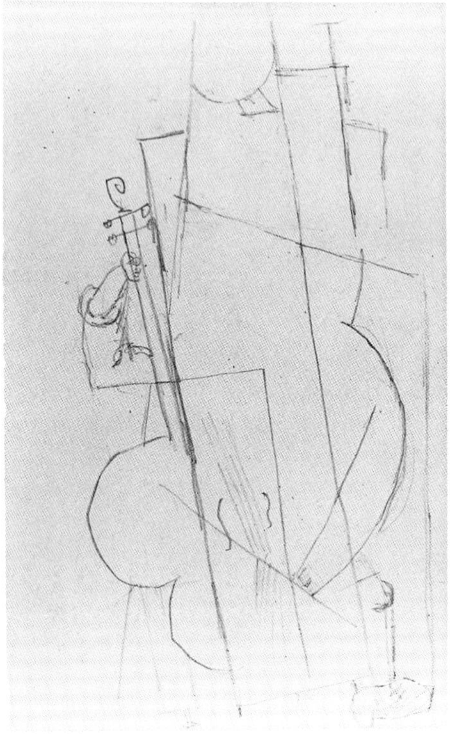

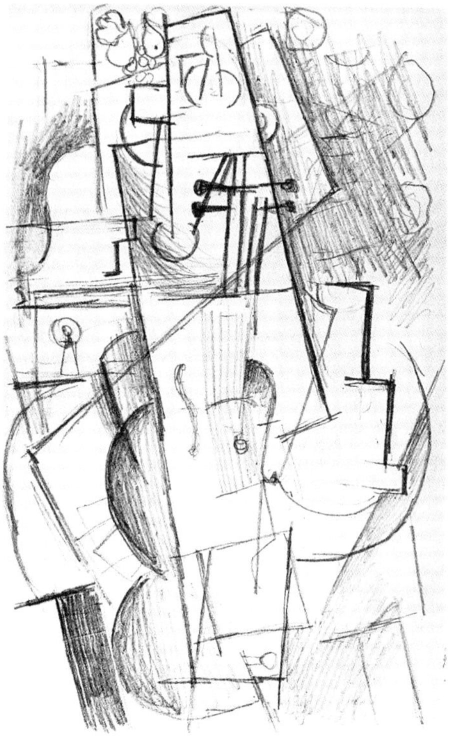

253 (*above left*) Picasso. *Figure with Double Bass.* Céret, spring 1913. Lead pencil on paper, 17 × 11 cm. Zervos XXVIII, 288. Picasso estate (inv. 1484)

254 (*above right*) Picasso. *Double Bass and Fruit Bowl.* Céret, spring 1913. Lead pencil on paper, 17 × 11 cm. Zervos XXVIII, 337; Richet 329. Musée Picasso, Paris

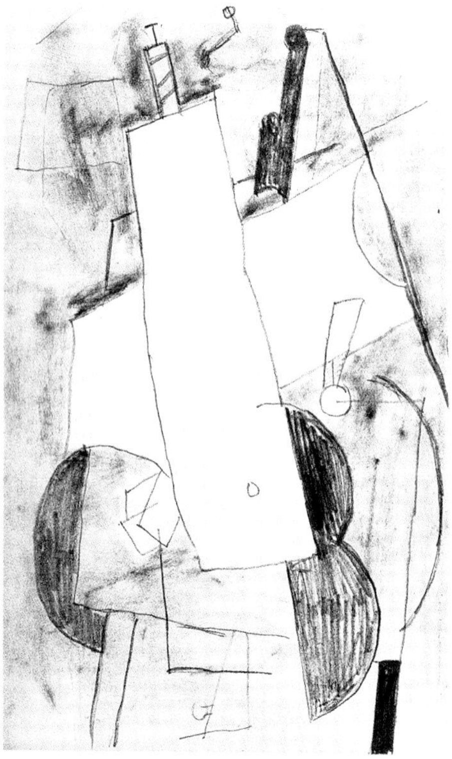

255 (*left*) Picasso. *Guitar and Bottle of Bass.* Céret, spring 1913. Lead pencil and stumping on paper, 17.3 × 10.7 cm. Zervos XXVIII, 339; Richet 347. Musée Picasso, Paris

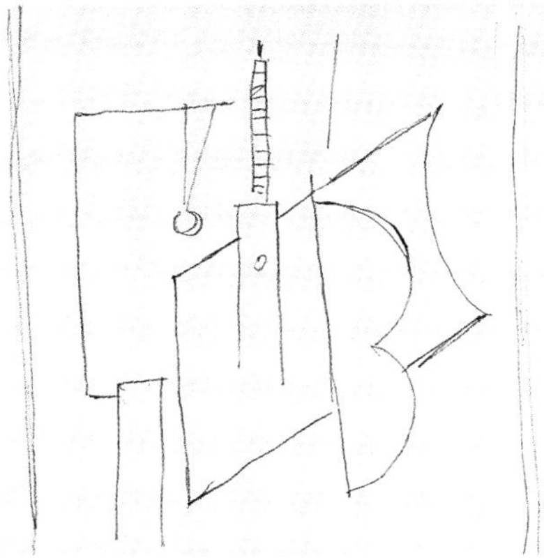

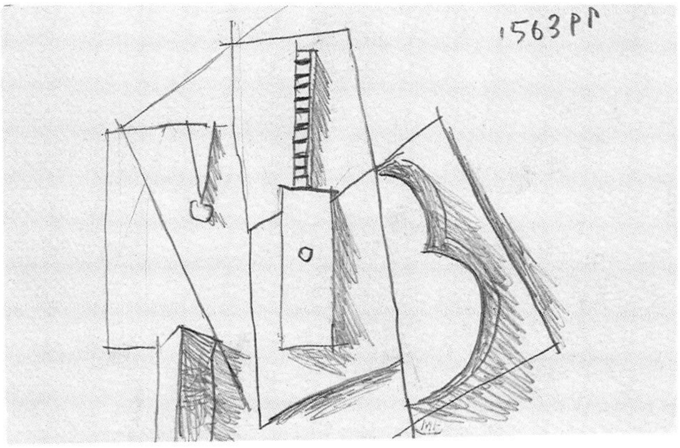

256 (*above left*) Picasso. *Guitar and Beer Glass.* Céret, spring 1913. Lead pencil on paper, 11 × 17.5 cm. Zervos XXVIII, 182; Richet 336. Musée Picasso, Paris

257 (*above right*) Picasso. *Guitar and Beer Glass.* Céret, spring 1913. Lead pencil on paper, 11 × 17.5 cm. Zervos XXVIII, 184; Richet 340. Musée Picasso, Paris

258 (*right*) Picasso. *Guitar, Beer Glass, and Bottle of Bass.* Céret, after April 23, 1913. Wood, newspaper, charcoal, and nails on wood panel, 89.5 × 80 × 14 cm. Spies 33A. Bernadac/Richet/Seckel 241. Musée Picasso, Paris. Object survives in modified condition

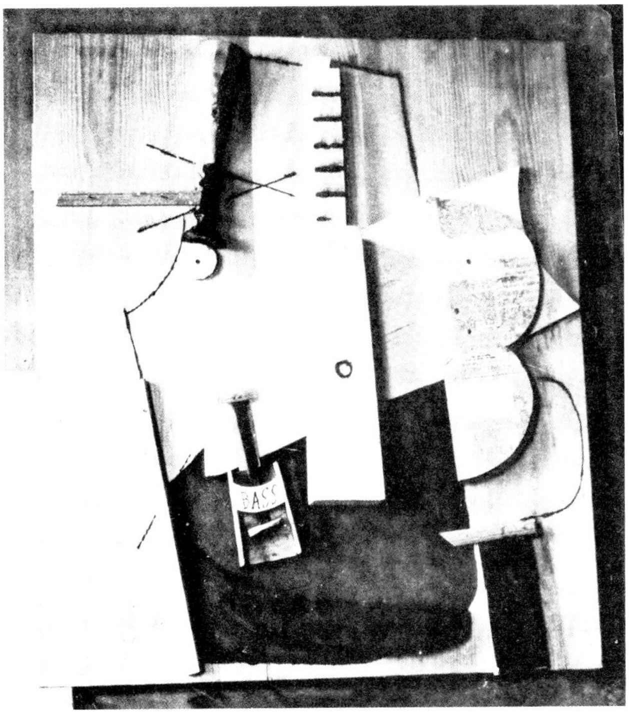

a beautiful figure or object, since the figures and objects are mostly indecipherable. It might be said that the viewer takes pleasure in the pictures as "abstract" compositions. This implies that the abstract composition is what is important in these pictures, and the figurative content is secondary. Mondrian and Malevich are often said to have drawn this conclusion from their study of Cubism, so that they abandoned figuration in favor of pure abstraction. (This story no longer seems quite credible.) In any case, Picasso and Braque always insisted that their goal was representation. To treat their pictures as abstractions is to say, in effect, that they did not know what they were doing. Conversely, if we take them at their word, we are forced to the conclusions that Picasso and Braque were making pictures that did not make sense unless they were read as figurative images, but were intentionally difficult to read. Why would they do this?

This question can be answered if Kahnweiler's analysis of Cubist representation is reconsidered in relation to Impressionism. It appears, in this light, as a kind of parody.

Impressionism, as noted earlier, took as its starting point the empiricist belief that we do not actually see figures or objects. As Berkeley, for instance, wrote, "what we properly and immediately see are only lights and colors."[225] These lights and colors function as signs, recalling the tactile sensations that inform us about the actual shapes of things. Because we do this so routinely – the theory holds – the process becomes automatic: we think we are seeing the shape of an object when we are really constructing its three-dimensional image in our mind. According to Taine and his

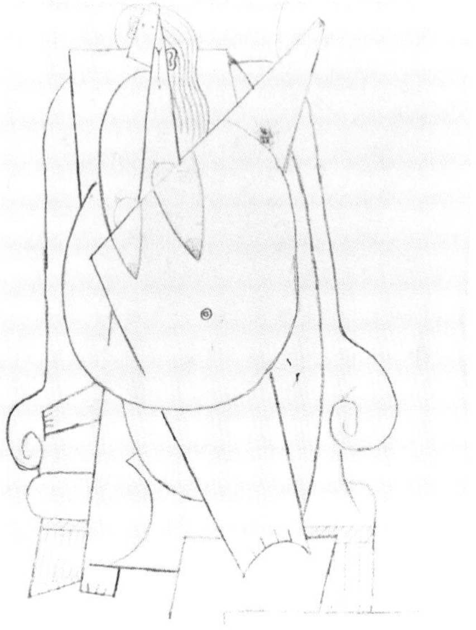

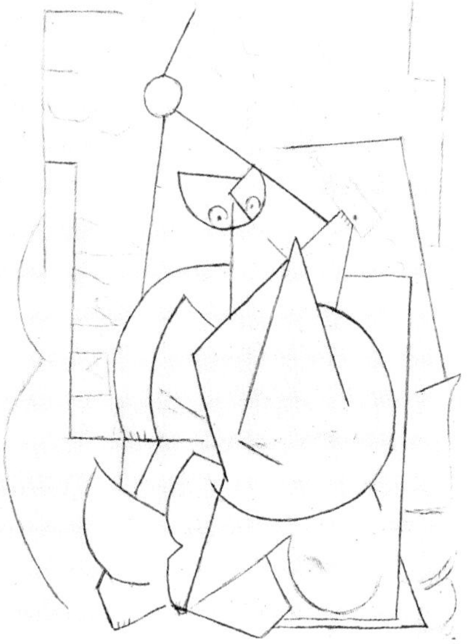

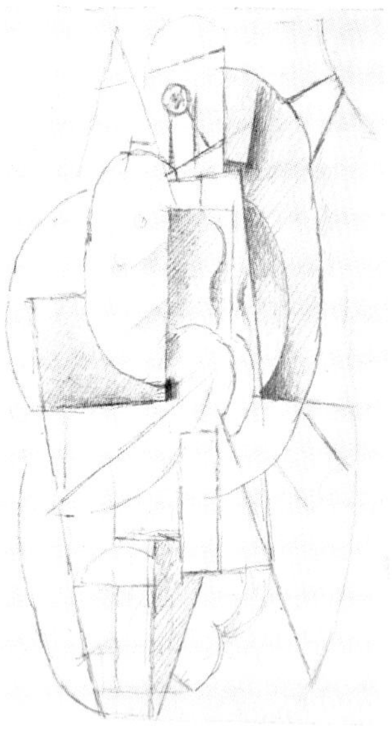

259 (*above left*) Picasso. *Woman with Raised Arm.* Paris, fall 1913. Conte crayon on paper, 19 × 15 cm. Zervos VI, 1260. Picasso estate (inv. 1976)

260 (*above centre*) Picasso. *Woman with Raised Arm.* Paris, fall 1913. Lead pencil on paper, 27.4 × 22 cm. Zervos VI, 1240. Picasso estate (inv. 1773)

261 (*above right*) Picasso. *Woman with Raised Arm (Still Life with Bottle).* Paris, fall 1913. Lead pencil on paper, 31.5 × 20 cm. Zervos VI, 1237. Picasso estate (inv. 1763)

followers, this process of automatic association proceeded even further in the mind of the modern European, and a verbal "label" came to replace both the visual and the tactile sensation.

The champions of Impressionism and Post-Impressionism made this point over and over again. Conrad Fiedler in 1876 argued that the demands of "conceptual thinking" lead people to ignore their actual "perceptual experience." For the true artist, Fiedler wrote, "the world is but a thing of appearances. He approaches it as a whole and tries to recreate it as a visual whole."[226] Discussing contemporary society, Henri Bergson wrote in 1900:

> The individuality of things or of beings escapes us . . . we do not see the actual things themselves; in most cases we confine ourselves to reading the labels affixed to them . . . We move amidst generalities and symbols . . . Art, whether it be painting or sculpture, poetry or music, has no other object than to brush aside the utilitarian symbols, the conventional and socially accepted generalities, in short, everything that veils reality from us, in order to bring us face to face with reality itself."[227]

The artist, Bergson said, is "wedded to art . . . through one of his senses." A painter is someone who "loves colour for colour and form for form," and can therefore represent the actual appearances of things instead of merely reproducing their labels.[228]

Roger Fry in 1909 followed Bergson in using the term "label" to describe the empty sign of everyday thought and perception:

> We learn to see only so much as is needful for our purposes; but this is in fact very little, just enough to recognise and identify each object or person; that done, they go into an entry in our mental catalogue and are no more really seen. In actual life the normal person really only reads the labels as it were on the objects around him and troubles no further . . . This specialisation of vision goes so far that ordinary people have almost no idea of what things really look like . . . The only things they have ever really *looked* at being other pictures; the moment an artist who has looked at nature brings to them a clear report of something definitely seen by him,

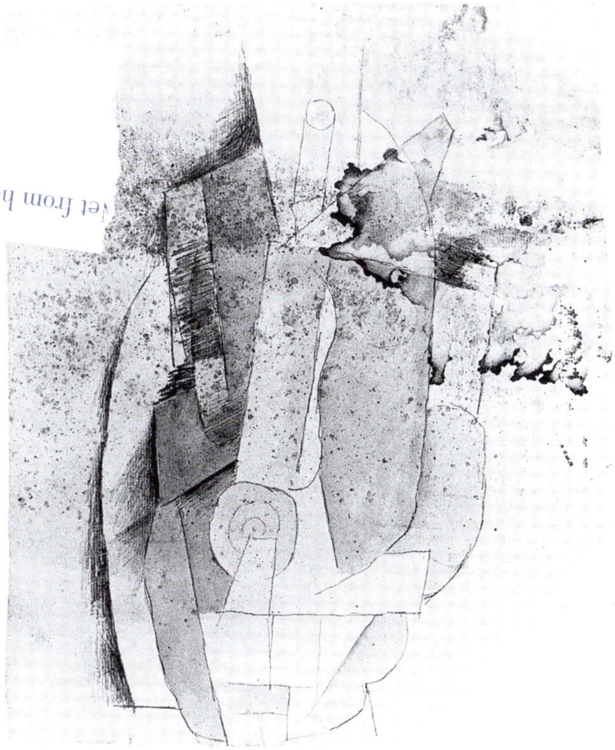

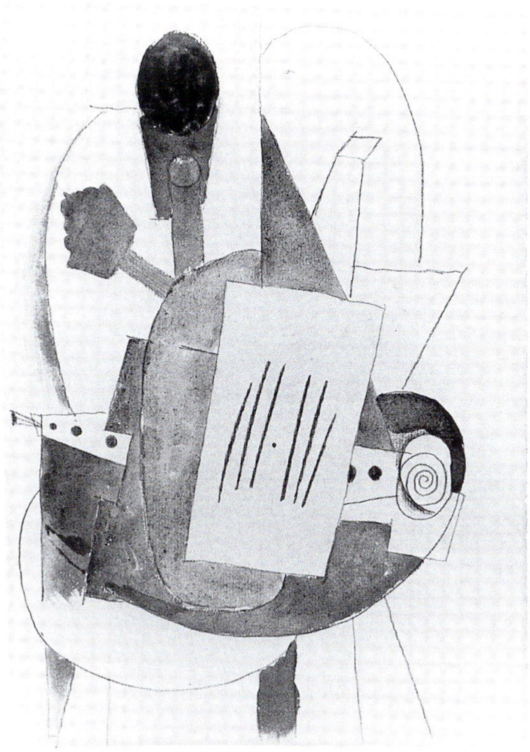

262 (*above left*) Picasso. *Still Life with Clarinet (Still Life with Bottle)*. Paris, fall 1913. Lead pencil and watercolor on paper, 31.5 × 26 cm. Zervos XXIX, 102. Picasso estate (inv. 1764)

263 (*above right*) Picasso. *Guitar and Clarinet on Table*. Paris, fall 1913. Lead pencil and watercolor on paper, 32 × 24.5 cm. D.R. 818. Picasso estate (inv. 1801)

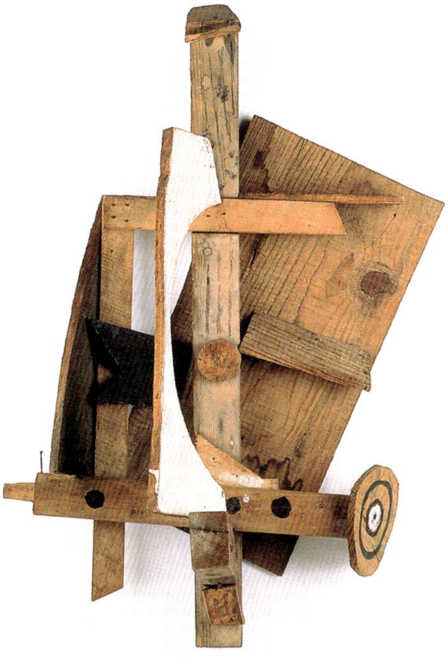

264 (*right*) Picasso. *Mandolin and Clarinet*. Paris, fall 1913. Wood and paint, 60 × 36 × 20 cm. Spies 54. Musée Picasso, Paris

> they are wildly indignant at its untruth to nature. . . . One instance will suffice. Monet is an artist whose chief claim to recognition lies in the fact of his astonishing power of faithfully reproducing certain aspects of nature, but his really naïve innocence and sincerity were taken by the public to be the most audacious humbug.[229]

Impressionism is thus "pure" painting, in the sense that it aims to reproduce purely optical sensations. The pleasure yielded by an Impressionist painting comes not merely from its decorative arrangement of colors but from its recovery of a primal sensation suppressed by thought.

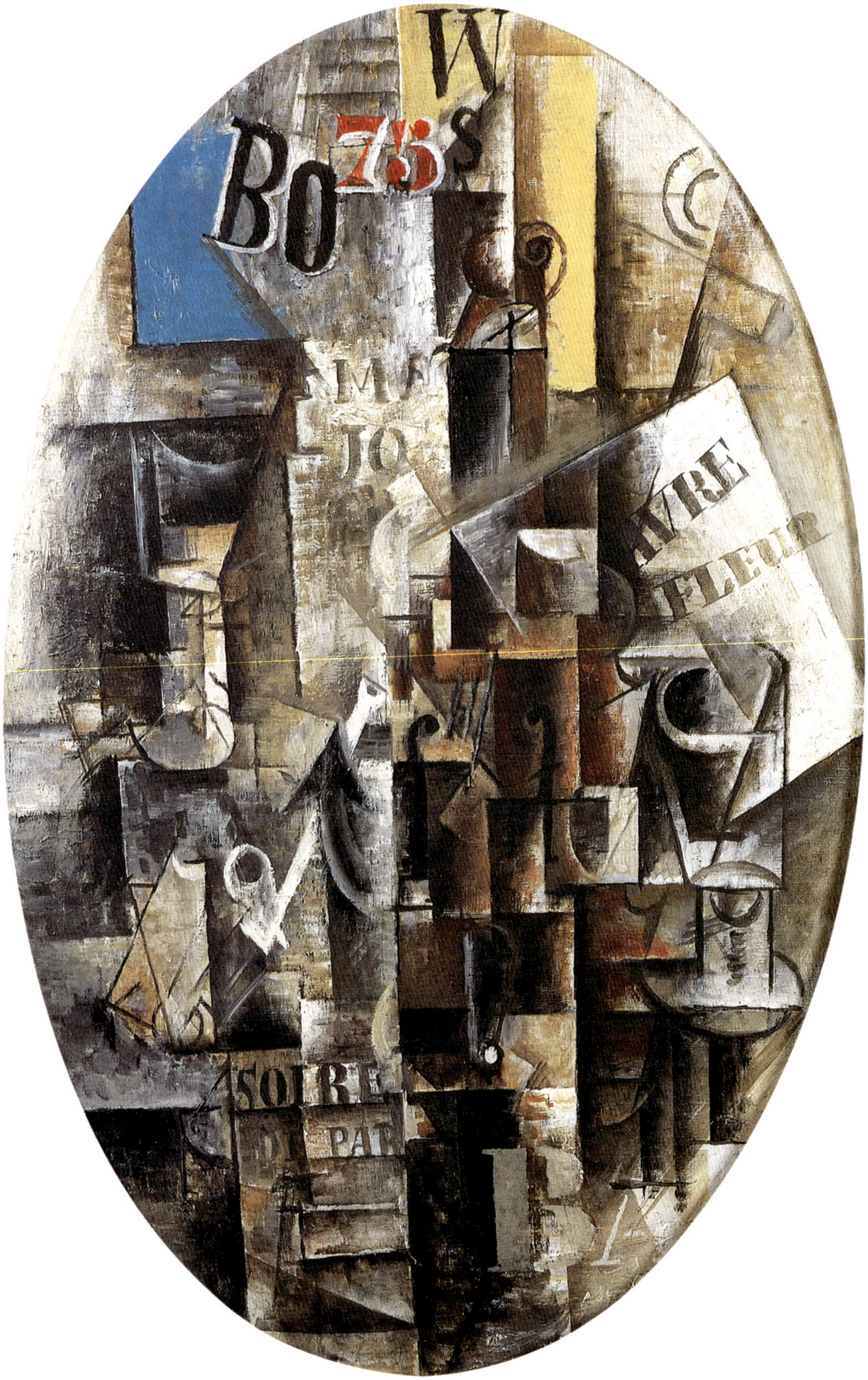

265 Picasso. *Violin and Anchor.* Paris, spring 1912. Oil on oval canvas, 81 × 54 cm. D.R. 457.
National Gallery in Prague

Impressionism might be said to anticipate Cubism insofar as the artist, in both cases, deliberately neglects the "natural" form of the object in order to represent some other aspect of its appearance. The object's presence in the picture is implied indirectly, by the signs on which the artists have focused their attention. But the signs that interest Picasso and Braque are very different from the signs that interest the Impressionists. Indeed, they are precisely the signs rejected by the Impressionists: tactile signs, verbal signs, and conceptual signs.

From 1910 onward, it is not clear how these signs relate to actual perceptual experience. They are the product of reflection, a composite compiled from different experiences and different analyses. Here, Kahnweiler's method for reconstructing the subject by projecting memory images onto geometric forms breaks down altogether. Since the painted image often includes different figurations superimposed one over the other, there may be no single original subject to reconstruct.

In addition to the difficulty or impossibility of deciphering a "natural" image behind the palimpsest of signs, there is also the problem of evaluating what a Cubist picture "means." Are the nudes and musicians, glasses and bottles, guitars and violins merely stock motifs, or are they imbued with personal meaning? From one picture to the next, the answer seems to change. And what of the inscriptions that became increasingly important after 1910? "JOURNAL" may just announce another article of daily life – the newspaper – but when whole phrases or advertisements or columns of newsprint appear, it is hard to avoid the conclusion that they meant something to the artist.[230]

If there is one picture that seems to sum up this problem of interpretation, it is Picasso's spring 1912 canvas, *Violin and Anchor* (fig. 265). It is replete with symbols and biographical allusions; whether these add up to a meaning, or any kind of paraphrasable content, is another question.

Most of the motifs in *Violin and Anchor* are not hard to recognize. There are a violin and an anchor, obviously. These are accompanied by a pair of wineglasses, a clay pipe, and a series of inscriptions, some easily decipherable ("[H]AVRE," "[HON]FLEUR"), some not ("BO"). However, the armature of vertical strips supporting the objects has the effect of breaking them into a series of interpenetrating fragments, and it is difficult or impossible to recontruct their "real-life" arrangement – if indeed there was one. The scroll of the violin is visible near the top of the canvas; its curved

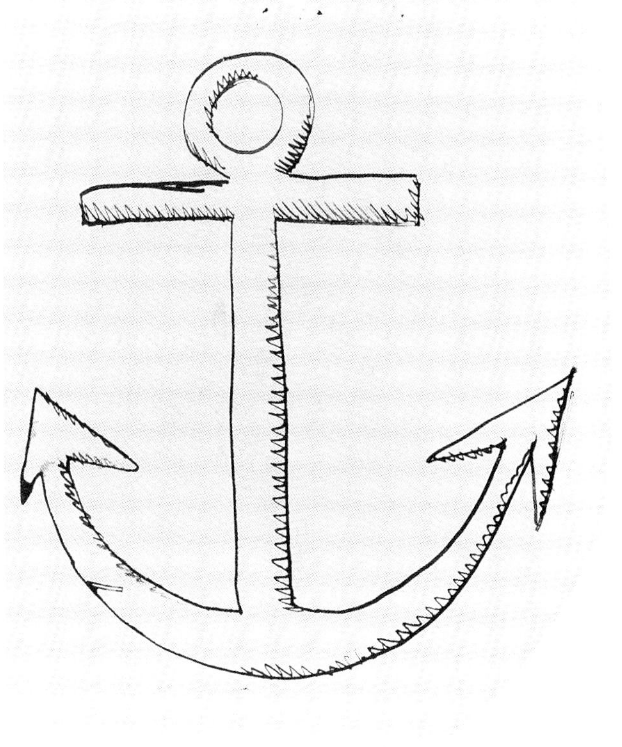

266 Picasso. *Anchor*. Paris, spring 1912. Ink on paper, dimensions unknown. Not in Zervos. Picasso estate (inv. 1242)

shoulder appears at right, obscuring the initial letters of "HAVRE" and "HONFLEUR;" and its *f*-shaped sound-holes float in space, near the center of the picture. An unbroken version of the anchor appears in an unpublished sketch (fig. 266), but in the canvas only its head and spiked arm are visible, the former at upper right, the latter just left of center, overlapping the pipe. The wineglasses – similar to those that Picasso had been drawing and painting since 1910 – frame the composition as a whole, one appearing at left, just above the picture's median; the other at right, just below it.

The significance of this grouping is not immediately obvious. What do a violin, an anchor, a pipe, and some wineglasses have in common? How are they related to the cryptic inscriptions around them? In fact, with a certain amount of detective work, the individual components of this rebus can be read, and some of the relationships among them clarified.

Prior to winter 1911–12, the motif of the violin had appeared only once in Picasso's Cubist work. At first glance, it seems an odd choice for Picasso, whose musical tastes can be gauged by Fernande Olivier's comments about the orchestra at the Brasserie de l'Ermitage, which they frequented in 1910–12. The Picasso circle, she says,

> sat in their corner on the right side of the café, not too near the orchestra, which they found tiresome; though its leader, who was a good violinist, played excellent music and was really playing for their benefit. If that poor bandleader still harbours any illusions about this, may he be instantly disabused: not one of them ever listened to him . . . Braque only liked the accordion and Picasso only liked the guitar . . . as for serious music, I think they were all pretty well unmoved by it.[231]

What then impelled Picasso and Braque to represent violins? One possible explanation is given by the title the painting has in Kahnweiler's stockbook, where it was originally listed as "Le Violon d'Ingres." This was subsequently modified to the descriptive title "Le Violon & ancre." However, in a June 5, 1912 letter to Kahnweiler, Picasso referred to what was presumably the same work as a "violon d'Ingres with ripolin" – that is, the red, yellow, and blue enamel paint that appears near the top of the canvas.[232]

The phrase "violon d'Ingres" conventionally refers to a hobby pursued with as much intensity as someone's main vocation. But "violon d'Ingres" was not, for Picasso and Braque, a purely conventional phrase. The previous April, during the great Ingres exhibition at the Galeries Georges Petit, the famed violinist Jean Kubelik had given a performance on Ingres's own instrument, which was then placed on display for the duration of the exhibition.[233] Although it is unlikely that Picasso and Braque were included in the aristocratic audience at this event, they would certainly have been aware of it, since the concert was announced by Picasso's friend André Salmon in the "Studio Newsletter" that he wrote for the *Paris-Journal*.[234] It is probably not a coincidence that Braque painted a large oval *Violin* around this time. A few months later, at Céret, Picasso responded with his own *Wineglass, Fan, and Violin.* Braque painted numerous violins in the following year, but the motif disappeared from Picasso's work until spring 1912. Something then happened to remind him and Braque of Kubelik's concert, for it was at this time that Braque painted a violin with the inscription "MOZART/KUBELICK" (sic), while Picasso painted his "Violon d'Ingres." Each artist also painted a large *Man with a Violin*; it is possible that these canvases, too, were intended as souvenirs of Kubelik's concert.[235]

The written inscriptions in *Violin and Anchor* introduce several new themes which seem, at first glance, unrelated to the central motif of the "violon d'Ingres." "MA . . . JO" clearly stands for "Ma Jolie," Picasso's habitual way of referring to his new companion, Eva Gouel. "SOIRE . . . DE PARIS," at lower left, alludes to *Les Soirées de Paris*, the new literary journal edited by Picasso's friends Apollinaire and Salmon. Although the inscription may simply have been meant to celebrate the appearance of their journal, which began publishing in February 1912, it could also be construed as a subtle rebuke to Apollinaire.[236]

Apollinaire's essay "On the Subject in Modern Painting," published in the first issue of *Les Soirées de Paris*, proclaimed that Cubism demonstrated the arrival of "pure painting," in which "verisimilitude" no longer had any importance and the "artistic sensations" produced by the painting were "due exclusively to the harmony of lights and shades."[237] A few days after the appearance of Apollinaire's essay, the Galeries Bernheim-Jeune opened a large exhibition of the Italian Futurists, who borrowed the formal language of Cubism but used it to paint what they called "states of mind." Apollinaire rushed to condemn them as "awkward pupils" of the Cubists, and declared that their allegiance to the "subject" marked their work as fundamentally reactionary.[238] This may have been a case of being holier than the Pope. Picasso, who struck up friendships with several of the Futurists, seems to have been attracted to the idea of painting states of mind, and it is probably not a coincidence that the two Cubist paintings richest in personal allusions – *Violin and Anchor* and its pendant, *Souvenir du Havre* [239] – were both painted in spring 1912, after the Futurist exhibition.[240]

The inscriptions "HAVRE" and "HONFLEUR," which appear in both of these canvases, seem to be related to a trip that Picasso took with Braque in April 1912.[241] Apollinaire alluded to "that famous return from Le Havre" in his 1913 volume on *The Cubist Painters*, and the trip is often mentioned in the literature on Cubism, but nothing certain is known about it beyond the fact that it occurred. We do know that Braque, who came from Le Havre, returned there frequently to see his family, and to visit the bars catering to sailors.[242] On balance, it seems likely that Picasso had begun work on *Violin and Anchor* well before his visit to Le Havre in late April; the anchor and the place names seem to have been added in the comparatively brief interval between his return from Le Havre and his departure for Céret in late May.[243] (The *Souvenir du Havre*, in contrast, seems to

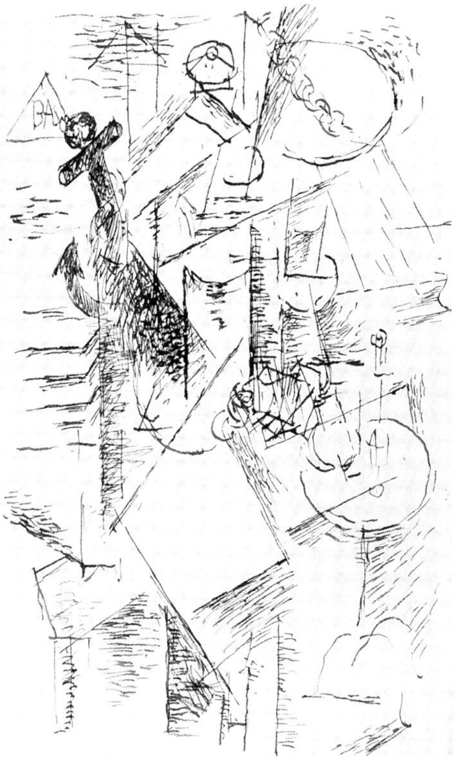

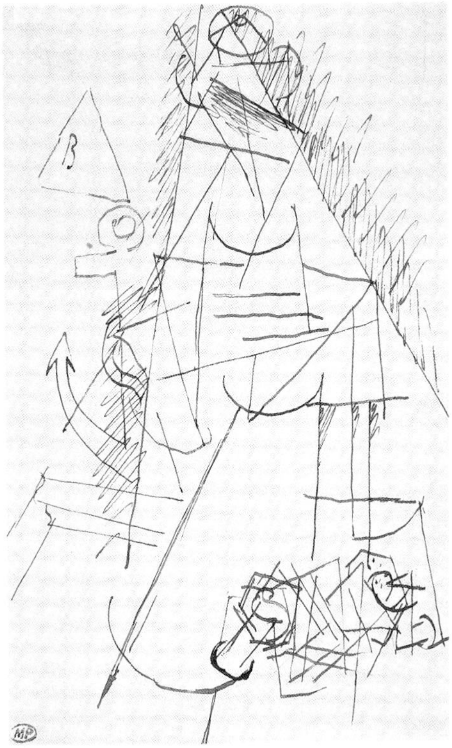

267 (*above left*) Picasso. *Souvenir du Havre (Accordionist).* Paris, spring 1912. Ink on paper, 21 × 13.5 cm. Zervos XXVIII, 205. Richet 276. Musée Picasso, Paris

268 (*above right*) Picasso. *Accordionist.* Paris, spring 1912. Ink on paper, 21 × 13.5 cm. Zervos XXVIII, 207. Richet 275. Musée Picasso, Paris

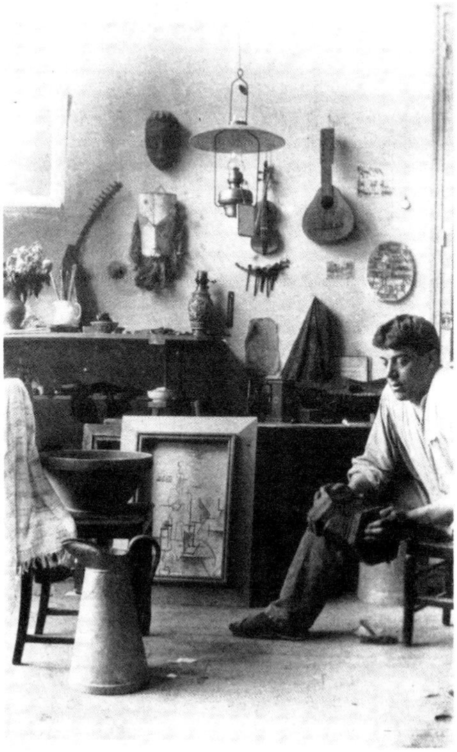

269 (*right*) Photograph of Braque in his studio. Paris, spring 1911

have been begun after Picasso's return from Le Havre and completed in fall 1912, after his return from the south of France.[244])

The cluster of associations here – between Braque, bars, sailors, and music – corresponds to the imagery associated with Le Havre in Picasso's drawings of spring 1912. A drawing entitled *Souvenir du Havre* in Zervos shows a figure playing a concertina, seated next to a pedestal table with a wineglass (fig. 267). In the background are an anchor, a chain, and a large triangle enclosing the letters "BAS," apparently from a poster for Bass Ale. (A similar triangle appears on Bass Ale labels even today.) The figure and the concertina are more legible in a second drawing that appears in Zervos under the title *Sailor Playing the Accordion* (fig. 268). The horizontal lines across the figure's torso recall the striped sweaters worn by French sailors. However, it seems likely that the musician is also meant to suggest Braque himself.

The instrument held by the "sailor" in Picasso's drawings is strikingly similar to the hexagonal concertina held by Braque in a 1911 studio photograph (fig. 269). As it happens, Braque's performances on the concertina were a regular entertainment in the Picasso circle. H. P. Roché said: "He often had with him a little hexagonal accordion of brown wood, on which he would play whenever the urge took him, no matter where he was; his repertory ranged from circus music to Sebastian Bach."[245] And Braque himself reacted to a brief profile by Salmon in the October 13, 1911 issue of *Paris-Journal* by saying that the only thing missing was his accordion.[246] The juxtaposition of Le Havre imagery with the violin in *Violin and Anchor* may thus be intended to make the point that the concertina was Braque's "violon d'Ingres."

In other drawings and in a related print the accordionist becomes a guitar player seated in a bar or café (figs. 270–73). These pictures also lead back to Braque by various routes. The wall in the background is inscribed with the same cryptic inscriptions – "BO" and "W" – found in *Violin and Anchor*.[247] In this context, they seem to belong to posters like those in the background of Braque's *Le Portugais* (see fig. 147). (This connection is reinforced by the stenciled letters "BA" at the lower right of *Violin and Anchor*, which are virtually a quotation from the stencilled "BAL" in Braque's canvas.)

Furthermore, if the letters in the print and drawing are combined, they form an extended inscription reading: "BOX . . . WI . . . S." This may refer to a match featuring the well-known American boxer Willie Lewis, who fought the French champion Georges Carpentier on December 13, 1911 at the Cirque de Paris (fig. 274).[248] It seems likely that Picasso would have been aware of this match as he was an avid boxing fan. Fernande Olivier wrote that "Picasso was attracted by boxing. He enjoyed going to fights and he used to follow them keenly . . . Physical strength staggered him and compelled his admiration. He was affected by the beauty of a fight as by a work of art."[249] Indeed, Picasso devoted several drawings to the sport in winter 1911–12 (figs. 275, 276), depicting a pair of boxers both close up and from a distance, in the ring. This reference, too, leads back to Braque, who was an avid amateur boxer (fig. 277). In the *Paris-Journal*, Salmon said that "each morning, before painting, he loosens up at the punching bag," and his friend H. P. Roché, another amateur boxer, recalled that he had "an impenetrable English defense."[250]

Many elements of *Violin and Anchor* thus seem to lead back to Braque – as a boxer, a musician, a native of Le Havre, an inventor of new Cubist devices, and a fellow admirer of Ingres. This proliferation of symbols recalls the Dutch tradition of allegorical still life. However, traditional still lifes relied on a public language of conventional symbols – candles for death, oysters for lust, and so on. In contrast, Picasso's painting utilizes an essentially private language. Even at the time it was done, it was probably comprehensible only to the members of his immediate circle. Even if we can crack the code and decipher Picasso's private language, there does not seem to be any specific message communicated by the painting. It is not a rebus whose elements correctly translated form a readable sen-

270 (*facing page top left*) Picasso. *Seated Woman with Guitar*, state I. Paris, spring 1912. Drypoint etching, 19.8 × 14.1 cm. Geiser/Baer 31.

271 (*facing page top right*) Picasso. *Seated Woman with Guitar*, state IV. Paris, spring 1912. Drypoint etching, 19.8 × 14.1 cm. Geiser/Baer 31

272 (*facing page bottom left*) Picasso. *Seated Woman with Guitar*. Paris, spring 1912. Charcoal on paper, 48.5 × 31.5 cm. Zervos XXVIII, 109; Richet 277. Musée Picasso, Paris

273 (*facing page bottom right*) Picasso. *Seated Figure with Guitar*. Paris, spring 1912. Ink on paper, 21 × 13.5 cm. Zervos XXVIII, 65. Musée Picasso, Paris

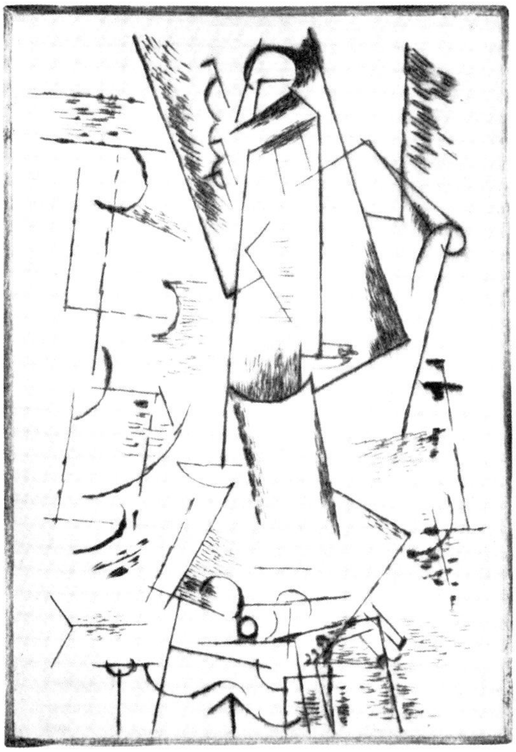

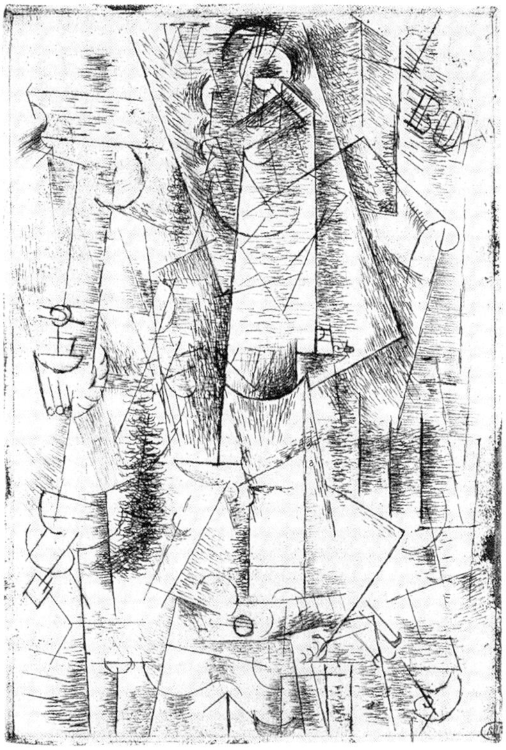
BO

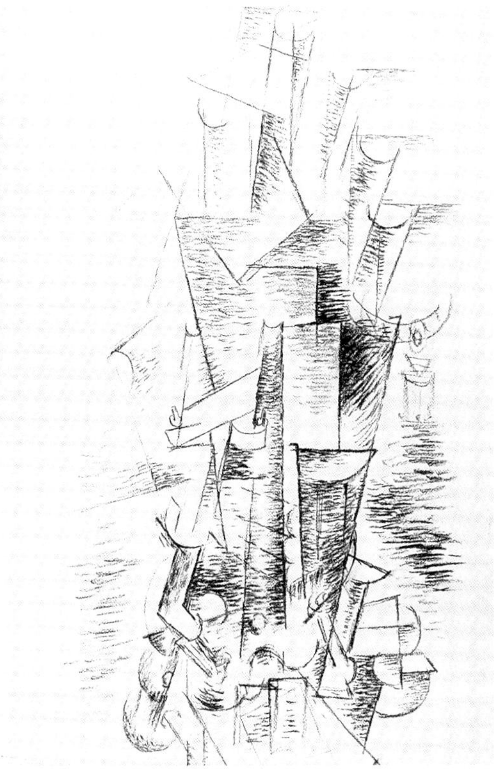

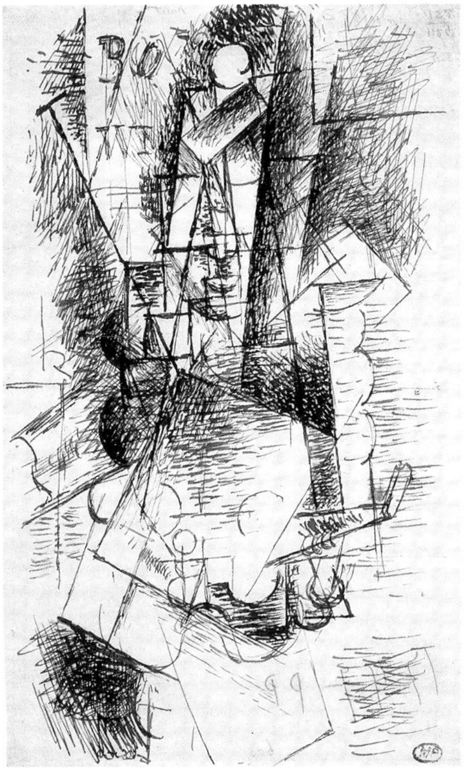
BO

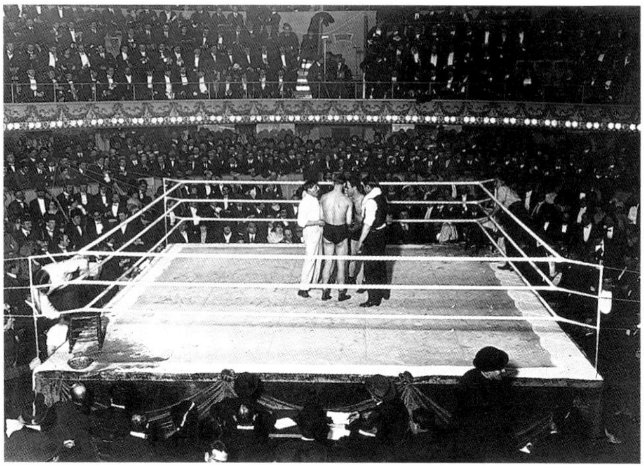

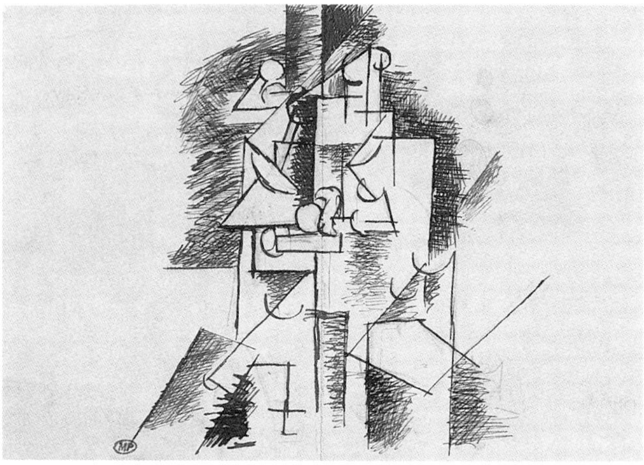

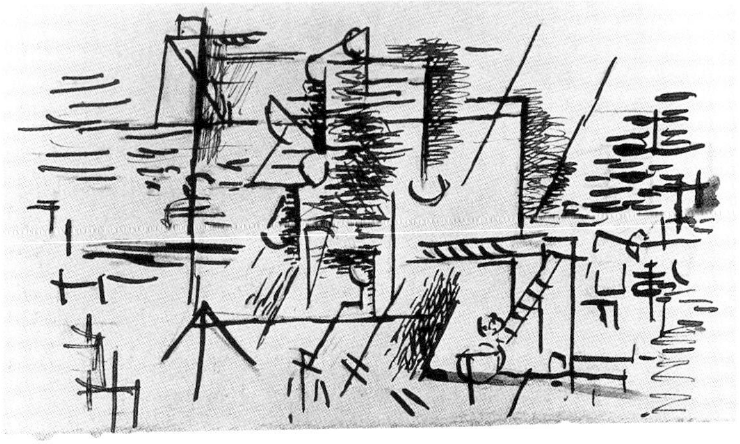

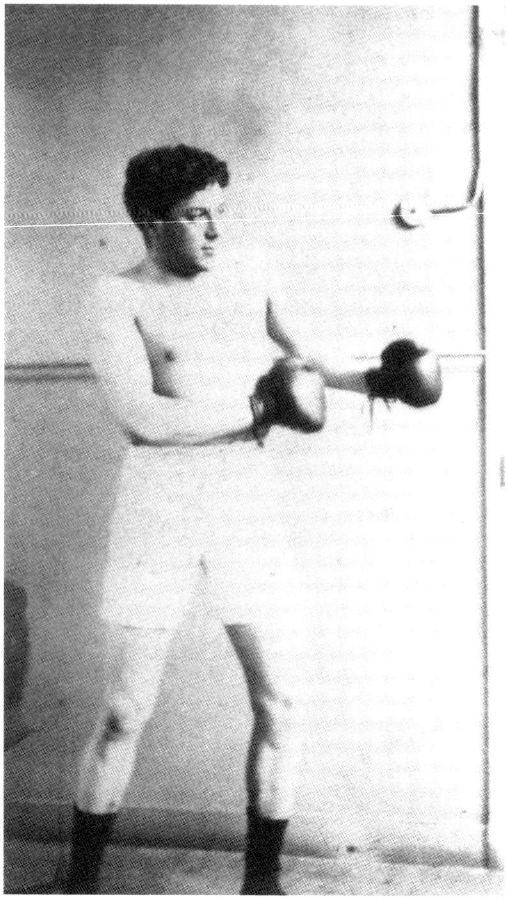

274 (*top left*) Photograph of boxing match between Willie Lewis and Georges Carpentier. Cirque de Paris, December 13, 1911.

275 (*top right*) Picasso. *Boxers.* Paris, winter 1911–12. Black ink over black crayon on paper, 16.9 × 24.3 cm. Zervos XXVIII, 18; Richet 263. Musée Picasso, Paris

276 (*above*) Picasso. *Boxing Ring.* Paris, winter 1911–12. Ink on paper, 9 × 15.5 cm. Zervos XXVIII, 32. Private collection. Formerly Marina Picasso Collection.

277 (*right*) Photograph of Georges Braque in boxing trunks and gloves, c. 1911.

tence. It is perhaps a kind of "Homage to Braque." Beyond this, it is impossible to extract any specific meaning from the composition. On the contrary, its Cubist syntax works to defeat the possibility of logical meaning. Narrative is suppressed. Motifs and fragments are superimposed so that the viewer cannot define the relationship among them. Inscriptions are removed from their original context, truncated and rearranged.

It seems that Picasso's goal here was not to communicate a message but to paint an image of consciousness. The picture's manifold spatial relationships provide a visual metaphor for memory's open-ended web of associations, while its stubborn unintelligibility recalls the essential incommunicability of subjective consciousness. Although this deliberate lack of resolution is frustrating, it is also a source of esthetic pleasure.

The Russian Formalists seem to have been the first critics to recognize this. They eagerly attended Cubist exhibitions in Moscow and studied the pictures acquired by Sergei Shchukin in Moscow and Vincenc Kramar in Prague. For the Formalists, Cubism was above all an art of the sign, providing a model for their new theories of poetic language. Jean Laude and Yve-Alain Bois have stressed the extent to which the example of Cubism predisposed the Formalists to accept Saussure's theory of language – and not, as one might have thought, the other way round. Roman Jakobson recalled, "It was the insistence, in Saussure's *Course*, on the question of relations which especially impressed me. It corresponds in a striking manner with the particular accent given by cubist painters such as Braque and Picasso, not on the objects themselves, but on their relation."[251]

Viktor Shklovsky, another Formalist, drew a different conclusion from the example of Cubism. Discussing Laurence Sterne's *Tristram Shandy* as an example of "the general laws governing plot structure," he wrote,

> Upon first picking up [the book], we are overwhelmed by a sense of chaos . . . But when you examine the structure of the book more closely, you perceive first of all that this disorder is intentional. There is method to Sterne's madness. It is as regular as a painting by Picasso. Everything in the novel has been displaced and rearranged. The dedication . . . makes its appearance on page 25. . . . The preface . . . is found not in the beginning of the book but in volume 3, chapter 20 . . . the exposition, the preparation of a given character comes only after we have already puzzled long and hard over some strange word or exclamation already uttered by this same character . . . It is the consciousness of form through its violation that constitutes the content of the novel.[252]

Evidently, for Shklovsky the structure of Cubist painting does not correspond to the structure of language, with its fixed relationships. Rather, what impresses Shklovsky is the way that Cubism invokes the conventions of traditional painting only in order to violate them. The tangled development of *Tristram Shandy* seems to him comparable to the combination of regularity and chaos in a painting by Picasso.

The key term in Shklovsky's criticism is "defamiliarization," introduced in his 1917 essay "Art as Technique." Here too Shklovsky proceeds by adopting arguments for advanced painting and translating them into literary terms. His essay begins within the intellectual framework of Impressionism. As perception becomes habitual, Shklovsky argues, it also becomes automatic, with the result that "eventually all of our skills and experiences function unconsciously." Thought becomes a kind of "algebra," with abstract symbols taking the place of actual experiences: "Life fades into nothingness. Automatization eats away at things, at clothes, at furniture, at our wives . . . "[253] Shklovsky's argument here closely echoes Taine's discussion of the fading of original perception and its replacement by a kind of algebraic notation.

The cure, Shklovsky suggests, lies in art: "Art exists that one may recover the sensation of life; it exists to make one feel things, to make the stone *stony*. The purpose of art is to impart the sensation of things as they are perceived and not as they are known." This requires an act of "defamiliarization," forcing us to see things afresh.[254] Here, Shklovsky echoes critics such as Fiedler, Bergson, and Fry, who saw Impressionism as a demonstration of how art could strip away conventional labels and recover perceptual experience. "The technique of art," Shklovsky writes, "is to make objects 'unfamiliar,' to make forms difficult, to increase the difficulty and length of perception because the process of perception is an aesthetic end in itself and must be prolonged." By emphasizing the importance of "difficulty," Shklovsky begins to draw a new meaning from the old arguments. "Art," he concludes, "is a way of experiencing the artfulness of an object." [255]

The Impressionist idea that art should allow us to recapture "the sensation of life" now gives way to an emphasis

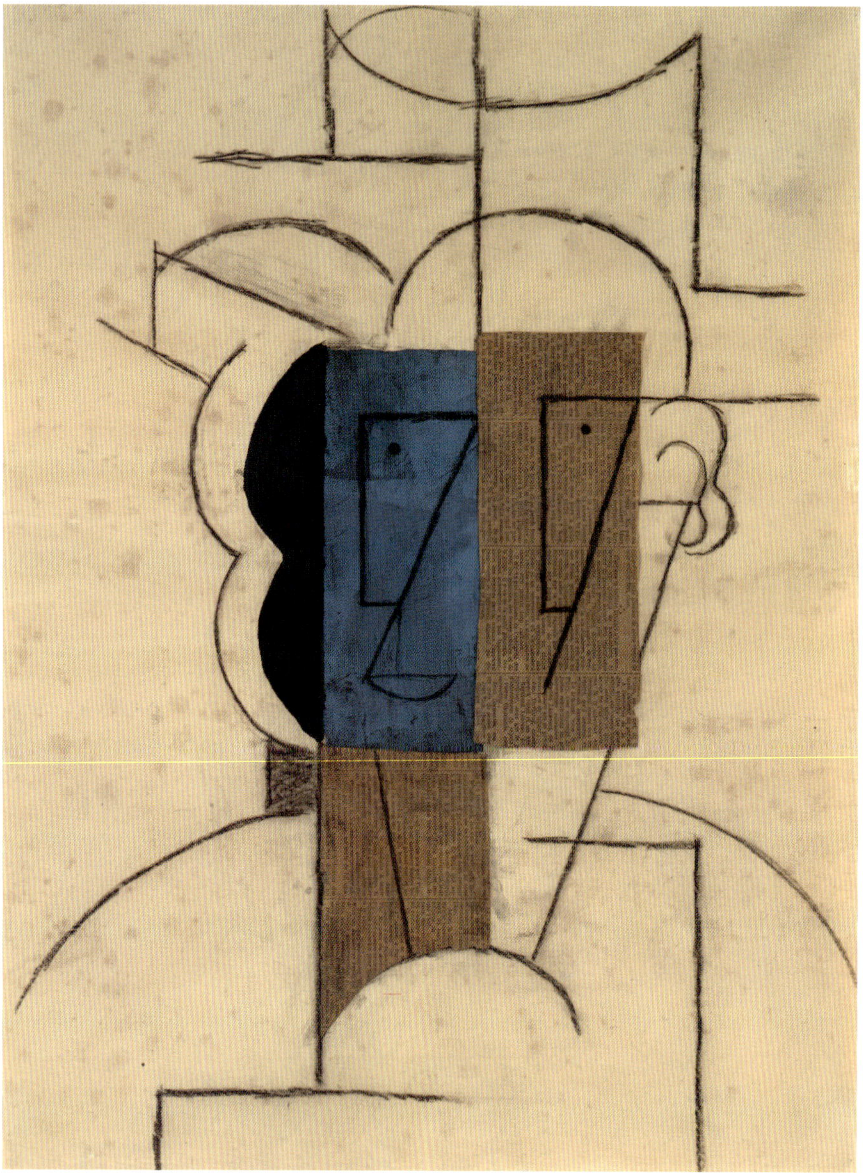

278 Picasso. *Man with a Hat.* Paris, after December 3, 1912. Pasted paper, charcoal and ink on paper, 62.2 × 47.3 cm. D.R. 534. The Museum of Modern Art, New York. Purchase

on the "process of perception" of "an object" – that is, the work of art itself. For this reason, Shklovksy argues, poetry requires a "difficult, 'laborious,' impeding language." Its rhythm is "the rhythm of prose *disrupted*."[256] Metaphor too focuses attention on language by making it harder to understand. Shklovsky's analysis reads like a catalogue of devices from Cubist painting:

In order to transform an object into a fact of art, it is necessary first to withdraw it from the domain of life . . . We must extricate a thing from the cluster of associations in which it is bound . . . Things are always in a state of revolt with poets, casting off their old names and adopting new names and faces. A poet . . . wrests the concept from the semantic cluster in which it is

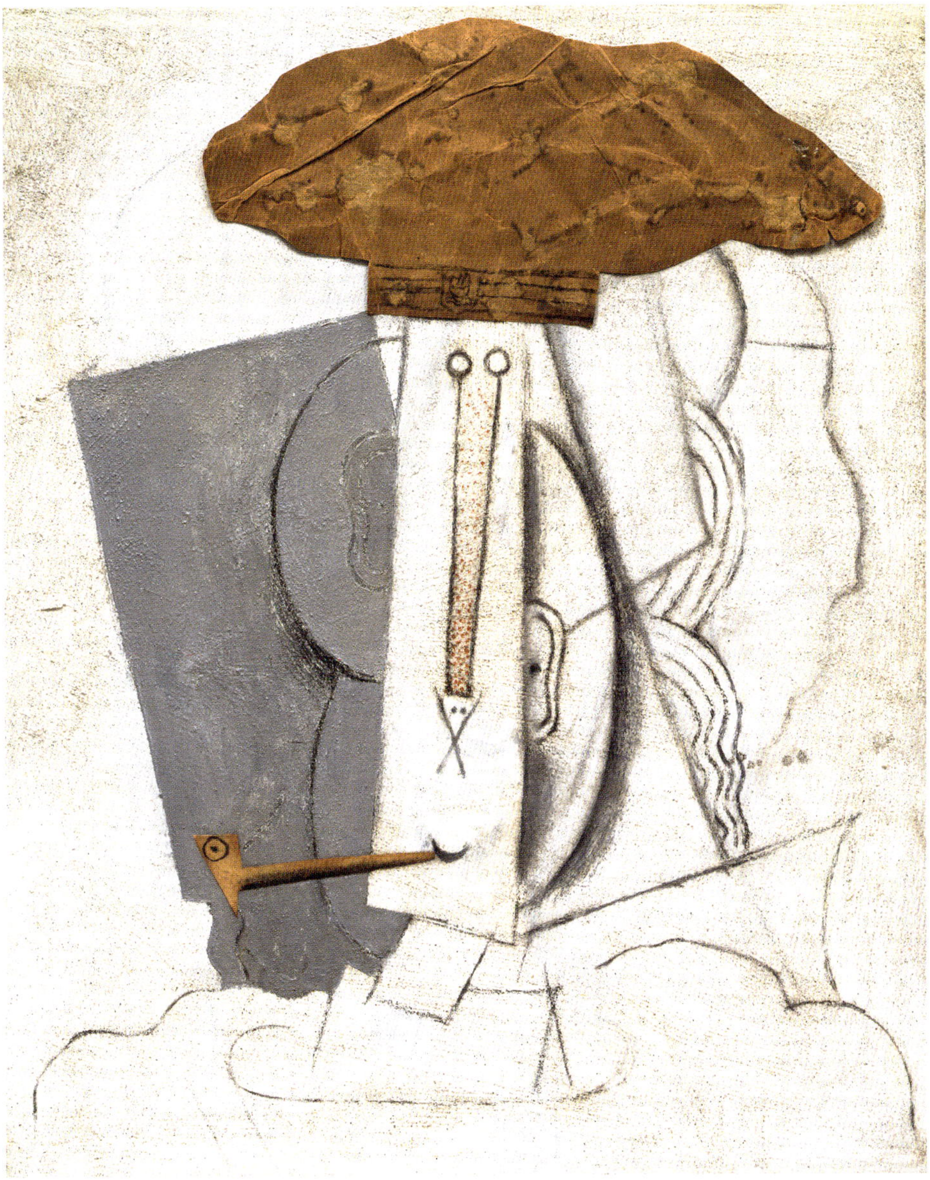

279 Picasso. *Student with Pipe*. Paris, March 1914. Gesso, sand, pasted paper, oil, and charcoal on canvas, 73 × 58.7 cm. D.R. 620. The Museum of Modern Art, New York. Nelson A. Rockefeller Bequest

> imbedded and reassigns it with the help of the word (figure of speech) to another semantic cluster . . . This is one of the ways in which an object can be transformed into something sensuous, into something capable of becoming an artifact.[257]

The break-up and transformation of language here parallels Picasso's break-up of the object into a series of different aspects and their recombination within the new structure of the Cubist painting. The reader's or viewer's pleasure now lies in the "sensuous" perception of the "artifact," not the sensuous perception of the original object.

In fact, this idea of finding pleasure in the reading of a difficult object had also been anticipated in the critical response to Impressionism. By presenting visual sensation in its raw, unmediated form, critics had observed,

Impressionist painting offered viewers the opportunity to participate actively in the completion of the image. In 1895, the Austrian scholar Franz Wickhoff argued that, since the "patches and spots" of Impressionist painting do not produce "self-contained forms" corresponding to recognizable objects, the viewer is compelled to "evolve the forms from them by the aid of unconscious (subconscious) reminiscences derived from our previous knowledge of the bodies themselves." The painter no longer integrates his visual sensations into a comprehensible image, but "forces the spectator to perform the final act which combines impressions into shape." The advantage of this style, Wickhoff commented, is that by making the viewer "help in the production of form," the painter "arouses in his mind the compelling conviction that what he sees is real." Viewers are encouraged to share in the creative activity of the artist, and take pleasure in the resulting mental image because it is in part their own creation.[258] Kahnweiler's description of how to read a Cubist picture offers a condensed account of the same process.[259]

Both Impressionism and Cubism thus demand the viewer's active participation in the construction of the image. This link between seemingly antithetical styles was noted by E. H. Gombrich in his analysis of the "beholder's share" in painting. As seen earlier, Gombrich analyzed the way that the beholder of an Impressionist canvas "must mobilize his memory of the visible world and project it into the mosaic of strokes and dabs on the canvas before him."[260] The process of transforming the canvas into an image of the world is actively pleasurable for the viewer, Gombrich argued, adding,

> It was in this enjoyment that a new function of art emerged gradually and all but unnoticed during the period we have discussed. The artist gives the beholder increasingly "more to do," he draws him into the magic circle of creation and allows him to experience something of the thrill of "making" which had once been the privilege of the artist. It is the turning point which leads to those visual conundrums of twentieth-century art that challenge our ingenuity and make us search our own minds for the unexpressed and inarticulate.[261]

Violin and Anchor is just the kind of "visual conundrum" that Gombrich alludes to. It challenges the viewer not merely to recognize the objects in it but also to find a coherent meaning in their juxtaposition. The very difficulty of the picture forces us to wrestle with its forms and symbols, trying to force them to release their hidden meaning. The struggle yields a kind of pleasure even if the picture throws us back, ultimately, into the realm of the "unexpressed and inarticulate."

This was a decidedly austere and refined kind of pleasure, however, and Picasso himself began to tire of it by fall 1913. He wanted his art to make more direct contact with lived experience. This meant not a return to naturalism but a modification of Cubism. From summer 1910 Picasso had situated his work in a geometric universe deliberately demarcated as different from the "real" world of organic form. He and Braque had created this alternate universe in part to escape the sense of distortion attached to their earlier experiments with geometric form. In 1913, breaking down the barrier between the Cubist universe and the real world, Picasso began to cultivate the sense of strangeness he had suppressed in 1910. The curved planes of *Woman with Chemise in an Armchair* (see fig. 123), painted in fall 1913, evoke the sensual contours of a woman's body without literally representing them. His spring 1914 painting *Student with Pipe* is virtually a parody of the austere geometric heads he had created in winter 1912–13 (figs. 278, 279). The face is still a rectangle, supplemented with the synecdochic sign of the reverse-*B*. But the rectilinear framework of the earlier work has dissolved, leaving the overlapping planes and curves of the student's face to tilt tipsily this way and that, deprived of external support. Without the screen of the Cubist grid, the oddness of Picasso's sign language becomes apparent. The absurdly long and narrow nose is formed by a pair of converging lines descending from the eyes, with a blush of pointillist dots suggesting the flush of excessive drinking. The flattened ears stick out like handles at either side of the face. *Student with Pipe* announces the end of the pure and austere Cubism of 1910–13, but it announces also the beginning of something new – a ribald, sensual Cubism, in constant dialogue with the real world. A dozen years later, this enlarged version of Cubism emerged from its chrysalis with a new name: Surrealism.

Notes

Preface

1 This explosion seems to have been provoked by the New York Museum of Modern Art's 1980 retrospective, organized by William Rubin. Among the earliest and most important responses were Linda Nochlin, "Picasso's Color: Schemes and Gambits," *Art in America*, vol. 68, no. 10, December 1980, pp. 105–23 and 177–83, and Rosalind Krauss, "Re-Presenting Picasso," in the same issue of *Art in America*, pp. 90–96. Patricia Leighten, *Re-ordering the Universe: Picasso and Anarchism, 1897–1914* (Princeton University Press, 1989) addressed the political implications of Cubism; it has been supplemented, and contested, by David Cottington, *Cubism in the Shadow of War: The Avant-Garde and Politics in Paris, 1905–1914* (New Haven and London: Yale University Press, 1998). The effects of World War I have been explored by Christopher Green, *Cubism and its Enemies: Modern Movements and Reaction in French Art, 1916–1928* (New Haven and London: Yale University Press, 1987) and Kenneth Silver, *Esprit de Corps: The Art of the Parisian Avant-Garde and the First World War, 1914–1925* (Princeton University Press, 1989). Jeffrey Weiss, *The Popular Culture of Modern Art: Picasso, Duchamp, and Avant-Gardism* (New Haven and London: Yale University Press, 1994) examines the links between high and low culture, while Elizabeth Cowling, "The Fine Art of Cutting: Picasso's *papiers collés* and constructions in 1912–14," *Apollo*, vol. 142, no. 405 (New Series), November 1995, pp. 10–18, reveals an unexpected link between Cubism and the practical aspects of fashion. Linda Dalrymple Henderson, *The Fourth Dimension and Non-Euclidean Geometry in Modern Art* (Princteon University Press, 1983) has now been complemented by Mark Antliff, *Inventing Bergson: Cutural Politics and the Parisian Avant-Garde* (Princeton University Press, 1993). The links among Cubism, linguistic theory, psychology, and modern educational philosophies are explored in Natasha Staller, *A Sum of Destructions: Picasso's Cultures and the Creation of Cubism* (New Haven and London: Yale University Press, 2001) and Norman Brosterman, *Inventing Kindergarten* (New York: Abrams, 1997).

2 John Richardson, with Marilyn McCully, *A Life of Picasso, Volume I: 1881–1906* (New York: Random House, 1991) and *A Life of Picasso, Volume II: 1907–1917* (New York: Random House, 1996).

3 For the semiological interpretation of Cubism, see esp. Rosalind Krauss, "Re-Presenting Picasso," and "The Motivation of the Sign," in William Rubin *et al*, eds., *Picasso and Braque: A Symposium* (New York: Museum of Modern Art, 1992), pp. 261–86; Yve-Alain Bois, "The Semiology of Cubism," in *Picasso and Braque: A Symposium*, pp. 169–208; and Christine Poggi, *In Defiance of Painting: Cubism, Futurism, and the Invention of Collage* (New Haven and London: Yale University Press, 1992).

4 This interpretation of Cubism as a stage on the road to abstraction seems implicit in the writings of such "canonical" critics as Douglas Cooper, Edward Fry, John Golding, Robert Rosenblum, and William Rubin. See Douglas Cooper, *The Cubist Epoch* (London: Phaidon, 1971); Edward Fry, *Cubism* (New York: McGraw-Hill, 1966); John Golding, *Cubism: A History and an Analysis, 1907–1914* (1959, repr. Cambridge, Mass.: Harvard University Press, 1988); and Robert Rosenblum, *Cubism and Twentieth Century Art* (New York: Abrams, 1959). As discussed in Chapter 4 below, Rosenblum's writings also provided the starting point for the "semiological" analysis of Cubism. William Rubin's influential analysis of Cubism was first proposed in "Jackson Pollock and the Modern Tradition," published in several 1967 issues of *Artforum* and reprinted in Pepe Karmel, ed., *Jackson Pollock: Interviews, Articles, and Reviews* (New York: Museum of Modern Art, 1999), pp. 118–75; on Cubism, see pp. 150–59. This was followed by "Cézannism and the Beginnings of Cubism," in William Rubin, ed., *Cézanne: The Late Work*, exh. cat. (New York: Museum of Modern Art, 1977), pp. 151–202; and by the "Introduction," in William Rubin, *Picasso and Braque: Pioneering Cubism*, exh. cat. (New York: Museum of Modern Art, 1989), pp. 15–62.

5 See e.g. Patricia Leighten, "Cubist Anachronisms: Ahistoricity, Cryptoformalism, and Business-as-Usual in New York," *Oxford Art Journal*, vol. 17, no. 2, 1994, pp. 91–102.

6 On the notion of the arbitrariness of the sign, and its application to Cubism, see Chapter 4 below.

7 See D. R., *passim*; and also the brilliant review by Edward Fry in *Art Journal*, vol. 41, no. 1, spring 1981, pp. 91–99.

8 See Clement Greenberg, "Towards a Newer Laocoon," originally published in *Partisan Review* in 1940 and repr. in John O'Brian, ed., *Clement Greenberg: The Collected Essays and Criticism. Volume 1: Perceptions and Judgments, 1939–1944*

(University of Chicago Press, 1986), pp. 32–35; and "Modernist Painting," a 1960 lecture, reprinted in *The Collected Essays and Criticism. Volume 4: Modernism with a Vengeance, 1957–1969*, 1993, pp. 86–87.

9 See Benjamin H. D. Buchloh, "The Primary Colors for the Second Time: A Paradigm Repetition of the Neo-Avant-Garde," *October* 37, Summer 1986, pp. 41–52.

10 See Yve-Alain Bois, "Kahnweiler's Lesson," in Bois, *Painting as Model* (Cambridge, Mass.: MIT Press, 1990), pp. 85–86.

11 In "What the Papers Say: Politics and Ideology in Picasso's Collages of 1912," *Art Journal*, vol. 47, no. 4, winter 1988, p. 354, David Cottington argues that Picasso, after 1909, began to make small pictures focused on "fundamentally conservative" formal concerns in order to please his collectors, who shared a "commitment to traditional aesthetic values." The nature of his market thus "entailed" Picasso's pursuit of "pictorial concerns of a technical and formal kind." In the corresponding passage of Cottington's more recent book, *Cubism in the Shadow of War*, pp. 132, this extreme claim is toned down to the less deterministic statement that the "radical formal inventiveness and esoteric intertextuality" of Cubism were "anchored to traditional pictorial genres and aesthetic values."

12 Douglas Cooper and Gary Tinterow, *The Essential Cubism: Braque, Picasso & their friends, 1907–1920*, exh. cat. (London: Tate Gallery, 1983, and New York: George Braziller, 1984).

13 Pepe Karmel, "Portraits of the Artist as Picasso," *Art in America*, vol. 68, no. 10, December 1980, pp. 26–29.

14 Pepe Karmel, "Picasso in Process," *Art in America*, vol. 74, no. 9, September 1986, pp. 108–15.

15 See n. 7 above.

16 See nn. 4 and 7 above.

17 A selection of this correspondence was originally published in *Daniel-Henry Kahnweiler: marchand, éditeur, écrirain*, the catalogue for the exhibition organized by Dominique Bozo and Isabelle Monod-Fontaine for the Musée National d'Art Moderne, Centre Georges Pompidou, in 1984. Further correspondence was transcribed and published in Judith Cousins, with Pierre Daix, "Documentary Chronology," in Rubin, *Picasso and Braque: Pioneering Cubism*, pp. 355–445. My visits to the Galerie Leiris allowed me to clarify and add to the information available from these sources.

18 Pepe Karmel, "Notes on the Dating of Works," in *Picasso and Braque: A Symposium*, pp. 322–49.

19 This topic is explored in the discussion following Rosalind Krauss's paper for the symposium, *Picasso and Braque: A Symposium*, pp. 300–04.

20 Pepe Karmel (Joseph Low Karmel), "Picasso's Laboratory: The Role of his Drawings in the Development of Cubism, 1910–1914," Ph.D. thesis, Institute of Fine Arts, New York University, 1993.

21 Daniel-Henry Kahnweiler, *The Rise of Cubism* (1920, trans. New York: Wittenborn, Schultz, 1949), pp. 10–13.

22 See Richard Shiff, *Cézanne and the End of Impressionism: A Study of the Theory, Technique, and Critical Evaluation of Modern Art* (University of Chicago Press, 1984), and Jonathan Crary, *Techniques of the Observer: On Vision and Modernity in the Nineteenth Century* (Cambridge, Mass.: MIT Press, 1990).

23 See Molly Nesbit, *Their Common Sense* (London: Black Dog, 2000); Natasha Staller, "Babel: Hermetic Languages, Universal Languges, and Anti-Languages in Fin de Siècle Parisian Culture," *Art Bulletin*, vol. 76, no. 2, June 1994, pp. 331–54, and *A Sum of Destructions.*

24 See below, Chapter 4, p. 115.

25 Pepe Karmel, "Beyond the 'Guitar': Painting, Drawing and Construction, 1912–14," in John Golding and Elizabeth Cowling, eds., *Picasso: Sculptor/Painter*, exh. cat. (London: Tate Gallery, 1994), pp. 189–97.

26 Pepe Karmel, "Mémoire et désir: Picasso . . . Céret, 1911–1913," in Joséphine Matamoros, ed., *Picasso: Dessins et papiers collés – Céret 1911–1913*, exh. cat. (Céret: Musée d'Art Moderne de Céret, 1997), pp. 10–21.

27 Pepe Karmel, "Pablo Picasso and Georges Braque, 1914–1915: Skeletons of Thought," in Sarah Greenough, ed., *Modern Art and America: Alfred Stieglitz and His New York Galleries* exh. cat. (Washington, D.C.: National Gallery of Art, 2001), pp. 185–201.

28 Alex Karmel, *A Corner in the Marais: Memoir of a Paris Neighborhood* (Boston: David R. Godine, 1998).

29 See Kirk Varnedoe and Pepe Karmel, *Picasso: Masterworks from The Museum of Modern Art* exh. cat. (New York: Museum of Modern Art, 1997); this exhibition appeared in Atlanta, Ottawa, and Los Angeles, but was not seen in New York. See also Kirk Varnedoe, with Pepe Karmel, *Jackson Pollock* exh. cat. (New York: Museum of Modern Art, 1998). My essay, "A Sum of Destructions," in Kirk Varnedoe and Pepe Karmel, eds., *Jackson Pollock: New Approaches* (New York: Museum of Modern Art, 1999), pp. 71–99, is devoted in part to Picasso's "curvilinear Cubism" of the 1920s and its influence on Pollock.

1 Ideas

1 Jacques de Gachons, "La peinture d'après-demain," *Je sais tout*, 15 avril 1912, pp. 349–51, photographically reproduced in Isabelle Monod-Fontaine, *Daniel-Henry Kahnweiler: marchand, éditeur, écrivain*, exh. cat. (Paris: Centre Georges Pompidou, 1984), pp. 27–29. All translations mine unless otherwise specified.

2 Salmon, a close friend of Picasso's, told the anecdote about a pair of painters visiting Kahnweiler's gallery and mistaking two Cubist figures – one by Picasso, the other by Braque – for landscapes. Salmon's text, originally published in the July 14, 1911 issue of *Paris-Journal*, is translated in the Documentary Chronology compiled by Judith Cousins with the collaboration of Pierre Daix, in William Rubin, *Picasso and Braque: Pioneering Cubism*, exh. cat. (New York: Museum of Modern Art, 1989), p. 375. For the *Accordionist* story see Alfred H. Barr, Jr., *Picasso: Fifty Years of His Art* (New York: Museum of Modern Art, 1946), p. 74. In fact, the inscription merely noted

the place where the canvas had been painted in the summer of 1911.

3 Jonathan Crary, *Techniques of the Observer: On Vision and Modernity in the Nineteenth Century* (Cambridge, Mass.: MIT Press, 1990).

4 Filiz Eda Burhan, "Vision and Visionaries: Nineteenth Century Psychological Theory, the Occult Sciences, and the Formation of the Symbolist Esthetic in France," Ph.D. dissertation, Princeton University, 1979; Natasha Staller, "Babel: Hermetic Languages, Universal Languages, and Anti-Languages in Fin de Siècle Parisian Culture," *Art Bulletin*, vol. 76, no. 2, June 1994, pp. 331–54.

5 Joseph Masheck, "The Carpet Paradigm: Critical Prolegomena to a Theory of Flatness," *Arts*, vol. 51, no. 9, September 1976, pp. 82–109.

6 See William Inness Homer, *Seurat and the Science of Painting* (Cambridge, Mass.: MIT Press, 1964); Meyer Schapiro, *Impressionism: Reflections and Perceptions* (written 1961–94, published New York: George Braziller, 1997), ch. 1: "The Concept of Impressionism;" José A. Argüelles, *Charles Henry and the Formation of a Psychophysical Aesthetic* (University of Chicago Press, 1972); Crary, *Techniques of the Observer*; and Margaret Olin, "Validation by Touch in Kandinsky's Early Abstract Art," *Critical Inquiry*, vol. 16, no. 1, autumn 1989, pp. 144–72.

7 David C. Lindberg, *Theories of Vision from Al-Kindi to Kepler* (Chicago and London: University of Chicago Press, 1976), esp. ch. 6, "The Optical Synthesis of the Thirteenth Century," and ch. 7, "Visual Theory in the Later Middle Ages." See also Erwin Panofsky, *Idea: A Concept in Art Theory*, trans. Joseph J. S. Peake (New York: Harper & Row, 1968), pp. 19–43.

8 See Lindberg, *Theories of Vision*, pp. 175–200, and Vasco Ronchi, *Optics: The Science of Vision*, trans. and rev. Edward Rosen (New York University Press, 1957), ch. 2, "The Basis of Seventeenth-Century Optics," esp. pp. 32–43.

9 John Locke, *An Essay Concerning Human Understanding*, 1690 (London: Dent, 1974), vol. 1, p. 112.

10 Ibid., pp. 113–14.

11 Ibid.

12 Ibid., pp. 104–11. On p. 107, Locke explicitly describes light as a secondary quality. In contrast, solidity, experienced via touch, is a primary quality; see p. 93.

13 Ibid., p. 113.

14 Ibid., p. 114. The question about the experience of a blind man who has regained his sight, attributed by Locke to a Dr. Molyneux, has spawned a critical literature of its own.

15 "Our ideas [are] nothing but actual perceptions in the mind . . . the mind has a power in many cases to revive perceptions which it had once had . . . in this sense it is that our ideas are said to be in our memories." Ibid., p. 118.

16 George Berkeley, "An Essay Towards a New Theory of Vision" (1709), para. 77, in George Berkeley, *Works on Vision*, ed. Colin Murray Turbayne (Indianapolis: Bobbs-Merrill, 1963), pp. 57–58.

17 Berkeley, "The Theory of Vision, or Visual Language" (1733), para. 40, in *Works on Vision*, p. 138; and "Essay Towards a New Theory of Vision," para. 143, in *Works on Vision*, pp. 89–90. Berkeley proceeds to anticipate what Saussure later called the principle of relative motivation: "It is indeed arbitrary that, in general, letters of any language represent sounds at all; but, when that is once agreed, it is not arbitrary what combination of letters shall represent this or that particular sound." Compare Ferdinand de Saussure, *Course in General Linguistics* (1915), trans. Wade Baskin (New York: Philosophical Library, 1959; repr. New York: McGraw-Hill, 1966), p. 131.

18 Berkeley, "Essay Towards a New Theory of Vision," para. 117, *Works on Vision*, p. 76; para. 127, p. 81; para. 144, p. 90. See also "Theory of Vision," para. 39, *Works on Vision*, p. 138.

19 Heinrich Helmholtz's major work, the *Treatise on Physiological Optics*, appeared (in German) in 1866, and he popularized his ideas in lectures such as "The Recent Progress of the Theory of Vision," published in 1873; see Richard M. Warren and Roslyn P. Warren, *Helmholtz on Perception: Its Physiology and Development* (New York: Wiley, 1968). Helmholtz's influence is visible in French texts from the later nineteenth century; see e.g. Auguste Laugel, *L'Optique et les arts* (Paris: Germe et Baillière, 1869), p. 48, who discusses the similarities between the eye and a camera and the way that the inherent defects of natural vision are responsible for the appearance of seemingly photographic characteristics in paintings made before the invention of photography. It should be noted, however, that the Helmholtzian theory of vision has very little to do with its putative experimental underpinnings; it is, in fact, little more than a restatement of the theory of vision found in Locke and Berkeley. The reappearance in France of this empiricist perspective reflects a general revival of empiricist thinking, as opposed to the Romantic, Hegelian tendencies that had dominated French thought in the first half of the nineteenth century; on this point, see Hans Aarsleff, *From Locke to Saussure: Essays on the Study of Language and Intellectual History* (Minneapolis: University of Minnesota Press, 1982), "Introduction," pp. 32–33.

20 Hippolyte Taine, *On Intelligence* (Paris, 1870; trans. New York: Henry Holt, 1875; repr. New York: University Publications of America, 1977), vol. 2, p. 63.

21 Ibid., pp. 64–65, 70.

22 Emile Zola, "Une nouvelle manière en peinture: Édouard Manet," first published in the *Revue du XIXe siècle*, January 1, 1867; repr. in Gaëtan Picon and Jean-Paul Bouillon, eds., *Emile Zola: Le bon combat, de Courbet aux impressionistes: anthologie d'écrits sur l'art* (Paris: Hermann, 1974), p. 81.

23 Taine, *On Intelligence*, vol. 2, p. 63. Taine's argument here derives from Locke, who had argued that children slowly learned to see, by forming associations between their optical experience of light and color and their tactile experience of the actual three-dimensional forms of things. In childhood, Locke said, "habitual custom" formed unconscious associations between the three-dimensional forms of objects, which we know from touch, and the two-dimensional shapes that they present to the eye. As a result, we are so "accustomed to perceive what kind of appearance convex bodies are wont to make in us"

that we no longer see the two-dimensional shapes that are actually imprinted on our eyes. Locke, *Essay*, vol. 1, pp. 113–14.

24 Laugel, *L'Optique et les arts*, p. 58.

25 "The whole technical power of painting depends on our recovery of what may be called the *innocence of the eye*; that is to say, of a sort of childish perception of these flat stains of color, merely as such, without consciousness of what they signify, – as a blind man would see them if suddenly gifted with sight." John Ruskin, *The Works of John Ruskin*, vol. 15, p. 27; cited in Crary, *Techniques of the Observer*, p. 95.

26 Lilla Cabot Perry, "Reminiscences of Claude Monet from 1889 to 1909," *The American Magazine of Art*, March 1927, repr. in Charles F. Stuckey, ed., *Monet: A Retrospective* (New York: Park Lane, 1985), p. 183. The same point is made in a story that seems to have passed into studio lore. "Remember Courbet and the story about the bundle of firewood," Cézanne told his friend Joachim Gasquet. "He put down a tone, without knowing that it *was* firewood. He wondered what it was he was painting. So he went to take a look. And it was a bundle of firewood." Joachim Gasquet, "Ce qu'il ma dit," in *Cézanne*, written 1912–13, published 1921; repr. in P. M. Doran, ed., *Conversations avec Cézanne* (Paris: Macula, 1978), p. 119. Georges Braque retold this story in Jacques Lassaigne, "Entretien avec Braque" (1961), in Gilberte Martin-Mery, Jacques Lassaigne, and Bernadette Contensou, *Les Cubistes*, exh. cat. (Bordeaux: Galerie des Beaux-Arts and Paris: Musée d'Art Moderne de la Ville de Paris, 1973), p. xvii. The story seems to originate in the memoirs of Francis Wey, published in Pierre Courthion, ed., *Courbet raconté par lui-même et ses amis* (Geneva, 1948), vol. 2, pp. 190–91; cited in Schapiro, *Impressionism*, ch. 2, n. 2.

27 Jules Laforgue, "Impressionism," 1883; repr. in Linda Nochlin, ed., *Impressionism and Post-Impressionism, 1874–1904: Sources and Documents* (Englewood Cliffs: Prentice-Hall, 1966), pp. 14–16. Laforgue offers a much condensed version of earlier accounts of vision, such as those found in Laugel, *L'Optique et les arts*, pp. 57–59, and Taine, *On Intelligence*, vol. 2, pp. 70–72.

28 Leo Larguier, "Cézanne parle," in *Le Dimanche avec Paul Cézanne: souvenirs* (Paris: L'Edition, 1925), extracts repr. in Doran, *Conversations avec Cézanne*, p. 16.

29 Helmholtz, "Concerning the Perceptions in General," 1866, repr. in Warren and Warren, *Helmholtz on Perception*, p. 178. This passage is cited also in Paul Vitz, "Visual Science and Modernist Art," in Calvin F. Nodine and Dennis F. Fisher, eds., *Perception and Pictorial Representation* (New York: Praeger, 1979), pp. 137–38.

30 O. N. Rood, "On the Relation between our Perception of Distance and Color," *American Journal of Science* (2nd series), vol. 32, 1861, p. 184; cited in Vitz, "Visual Science and Modernist Art," p. 137. Vitz draws the connection between Rood and Helmholtz, and notes the similarity between their remarks and Monet's remarks to Lilla Cabot Perry, discussed above.

31 Taine, *On Intelligence*, vol. 1, p. 1.

32 Louis Leroy, p. 12. "L'Exposition des impressionnistes," *Charivari*, April 25, p. 12. 1874, trans. in John Rewald, *The History of Impressionism*, rev. ed. (New York: Museum of Modern Art, 1961), p. 320; repr. in Nochlin, *Impressionism and Post-Impressionism, 1874–1904: Sources and Documents*, p. 12.

33 E. H. Gombrich, *Art and Illusion: A Study in the Psychology of Pictorial Representation*, 2nd ed., rev. (Princeton University Press, 1961), Part Three: "The Beholder's Share," p. 202. As Gombrich points out, the suppression of contour introduces an unprecedented difficulty to the reading of Impressionist paintings, because "the direction of the brushstroke is no longer an aid to the reading of forms." Gombrich's larger argument here, that the recognition of pictorial form always takes place via a process of "guided projection," derives directly from the scientific-empiricist tradition, which exercised a strong influence on the Vienna school of art history.

34 Bernard Berenson, *The Italian Painters of the Renaissance*, 4 vols., 1894–1907 (combined ed. London: Phaidon, 1952), pp. 40–41. Berenson's praise for Giotto's tactile style is immediately followed by a rehearsal of the Lockean theory of perception: "Psychology has ascertained that sight alone gives us no accurate sense of the third dimension. In our infancy long before we are conscious of the process, the sense of touch, helped on by muscular sensations of movement, teaches us to appreciate depth, the third dimension, both in objects and in space . . . The child is still dimly aware of the intimate connexion between touch and the third dimension . . . Later, we entirely forget the connexion, although it remains true that every time our eyes recognize reality, we are . . . giving tactile values to retinal impressions." The painter's task, Berenson argues, is also giving tactile values to retinal sensations. A painting should give the viewer "the illusion of being able to touch a figure . . . the illusion of varying muscular sensations in my palm and fingers corresponding to the various projections of this figure."

35 See Meyer Schapiro's 1977 lecture, "Cézanne and the Philosophers," in Schapiro, *Worldview in Painting – Art and Society: Selected Papers* (New York: George Braziller, 1999), pp. 75–105. See also chapter 2, p. 27, below.

36 In an 1891 article, Emile Bernard described a portrait of Mme Cézanne as: "Essentially hieratic and of a purity of line known only to the pure, primitive masters." Emile Bernard, "Paul Cézanne," *Les Hommes d'aujourd'hui*, vol. 7, no. 387, 1891, n.p., trans. in Nochlin, *Impressionism and Post-Impressionism*, p. 101. Bernard returned to this topic in 1904, writing that Cézanne's style is characterized by "a Giottesque candor and grace [that] shows things in the essential of their beauty." Emile Bernard, "Paul Cézanne," *L'Occident*, July 1904, repr. in Doran, *Conversations avec Cézanne*, pp. 38–39. Cézanne himself compared his work to that of the early cave painters, and described himself as "the primitive of my own style." He also referred to Gothic art as "essentially invigorating." Joachim Gasquet, "Ce qu'il ma dit," in Doran, *Conversations avec Cézanne*, p. 114.

37 Berenson's earliest published reference to Cézanne appears in

The Central Italian Painters, where he stresses Cézanne's "exquisite modelling" of the natural landscape: "[he] gives the sky its tactile values as perfectly as Michelangelo has given them to the human figure." Cited in Mary Ann Calo, *Bernard Berenson and the Twentieth Century* (Philadelphia: Temple University Press, 1994), p. 76.

38 Leo Stein, *Appreciation: Painting, Poetry & Prose* (New York: Crown Publishers, 1947; repr. Lincoln: University of Nebraska Press, 1996), pp. 154–55. This intersection between the avant-garde and the Italian "primitives" is also evident in Braque's interview with André Verdet, where he discusses the "tactile sense" abandoned by Impressionism and goes on to comment that this tactile sense "went quite far back in the history of painting." André Verdet, *Entretiens, notes et écrits sur la peinture: Braque, Léger, Matisse, Picasso* (Paris: Editions Galilée, 1978), pp. 19, 28. Picasso and Braque may also have been influenced, in this regard, by the 1904 exhibition "Les Primitifs Français."

39 Kandinsky, *Reminiscences*, 1913, trans. Hilla Rebay and adapted by Robert L. Herbert, in Herbert, ed., *Modern Artists on Art: Ten Unabridged Essays* (Englewood Cliffs: Prentice-Hall, 1964), p. 26.

40 Ibid., p. 32.

41 Lucien Arréat, preface to Georges Hirth, *Physiologie de l'Art* (Paris: Alcan, 1892), p. v.

42 Taine, *On Intelligence*, vol. 1, pp. 224–25; cited also in Burhan, "Vision and Visionaries," pp. 79–80 (see n. 4 above).

43 Helmholtz, "Concerning the Perceptions in General," 1866, in Warren and Warren, *Helmholtz on Perception*, pp. 191–92.

44 Laugel, *L'Optique et les arts*, p. 14.

45 See Gombrich's discussion of "The Beholder's Share," *Art and Illusion*, p. 202.

46 Taine, *On Intelligence*, vol. 2, p. 69.

47 Laugel, *L'Optique et les arts*, p. 32.

48 G.-Albert Aurier, "Symbolism in Painting: Paul Gauguin," *Mercure de France*, 2 (1891), trans. in Herschel B. Chipp, ed., *Theories of Modern Art: A Source Book* (Berkeley: University of California Press, 1968), pp. 90–92.

49 Natasha Staller traces the way that a fascination with esoteric languages, requiring special skill to decipher, permeated the visual culture of *fin-de-siècle* Paris in "Babel," pp. 331–54.

50 See Burhan, "Vision and Visionaries."

51 Jules Antoine Castagnary, "L'Exposition du boulevard des Capucines: Les Impressionnistes," *Le Siècle*, April 29, 1874; cited in Richard Shiff, *Cézanne and the End of Impressionism* (University of Chicago Press, 1984), p. 2.

52 Mallarmé's statement, in a letter of 1864, is cited in Daniel-Henry Kahnweiler, *Juan Gris* (Paris: Gallimard, 1946; trans. Douglas Cooper, New York: Curt Valentin, 1947; rev. ed. New York: Abrams, 1969) p. 98.

53 Maurice Denis, "The Influence of Paul Gauguin," *L'Occident*, October 1903, trans. in Chipp, *Theories of Modern Art*, p. 101; and Denis, "De Gauguin et de Van Gogh au Classicisme," *L'Occident*, May 1909, trans. in Chipp, *Theories of Modern Art*, p. 105. Gauguin's and Denis's theory of the "equivalent" should be compared with Taines' theory of the expressive sign, discussed in chapter 4, p. 112.

54 Clara T. MacChesney, "A Talk with Matisse," *New York Times Magazine*, March 9, 1913; repr. in Jack D. Flam, *Matisse on Art* (New York: Dutton, 1978), p. 51. Matisse's example was not hypothetical: he was in fact working on two versions of a composition, *Nasturtiums with Dance*, depicting a jar of flowers atop a sculpture-stand (identified by MacChesney as a table), standing in front of his earlier painting.

55 Masheck, "Carpet Paradigm," pp. 82–109.

56 Ibid., pp. 82–85.

57 In 1874, reviewing the first Impressionist exhibition, Louis Leroy, discussing Monet's *Impression, Sunrise*, had an imaginary visitor proclaim: "Wallpaper in its embryonic state is more finished than that seascape." "L'Exposition des impressionnistes," trans. in Nochlin, *Impressionism and Post-Impressionism*, p. 13; cited in Masheck, "Carpet Paradigm," p. 86.

58 Maurice Denis, "A Definition of Neo-Traditionism," *Art et critique*, August 1890, trans. in Nochlin, *Impressionism and Post-Impressionism*, p. 187; also in Chipp, *Theories of Modern Art*, p. 94.

59 Hippolyte Taine, "On the Ideal in Art," in *Philosophie de l'art*, 1864, trans. as *Lectures on Art* (New York: Henry Holt, 1875), vol. 1, pp. 338–39. (I have modified the translation to conform better to the original French.)

60 Masheck, "Carpet Paradigm," p. 93, notes Denis's dependence on Taine and earlier writers, and points out that this dependence has also been noted by Chipp and Gombrich.

61 Taine, "On the Ideal in Art," pp. 336–37.

62 Roger Fry, "An Essay on Aesthetics," in *Vision and Design* (London: Chatto & Windus, 1920; repr. Mineola: Dover, 1998), pp. 23–24.

63 Maurice Denis, "Cézanne," *L'Occident*, September 1907; repr. in Doran, *Conversations avec Cézanne*, p. 170. It was in this sense – of a severe reduction of coloristic means – that Denis understood Cézanne's statement, "J'ai voulu faire de l'impressionnisme quelque chose de solide et de durable comme l'art des Musées," which appears in the same passage of Denis's essay.

64 See Emile Bernard, "Paul Cézanne," *L'Occident*, July 1904; repr. in Doran, *Conversations avec Cézanne*, p. 34, and "Souvenirs sur Paul Cézanne," written 1904–06, published in *Mercure de France*, October 1907; repr. in Doran, *Conversations avec Cézanne*, pp. 59 and 61. The comparison to tapestry also appears in the writings of other critics.

65 Denis, "Cézanne," p. 170.

66 Zola, "Une nouvelle manière en peinture," pp. 87–88.

67 Gottfried Semper, chapter on "Dyeing and Printing," from *Der Stil in den technischen und tektonischen Künsten, oder praktische Ästhetik: ein Handbuch für Techniker, Künstler und Kunstfreunde*, 1860, excerpted in Semper, *The Four Elements of Architecture and Other Writings*, trans. Harry Francis Mallgrave and Wolfgang Herrmann (Cambridge University Press, 1989), pp. 234–40.

68 Bernard Bosanquet, *Three Lectures on Aesthetics* (London 1915;

repr. New York, 1968), p. 19; cited in Masheck, "Carpet Paradigm," pp. 92–93. Cf. Semper's remark that "Every material conditions its own particular manner of formation by the properties that distinguish it from other materials and that demand a technical treatment appropriate to it." See Semper, "Materials Used Formatively for Monumental Purposes," chapter 61 in *Der Stil*, excerpted in *Four Elements of Architecture*, p. 258.

69 Semper, *Der Stil*, chapters 54 and 60 ("Weaving" and "The Most Primitive Formal Principle in Architecture") in *Four Elements of Architecture*, pp. 229–30 and 254. See the discussion in Masheck, "Carpet Paradigm," p. 89.

70 See the "Purkersdorf" armchair designed by Moser in 1902, reproduced in Kirk Varnedoe, *Vienna 1900: Art, Architecture, Design*, exh. cat. (New York: Museum of Modern Art, 1986) p. 83, and the similar plant stand reproduced on p. 116.

71 Masheck, "Carpet Paradigm," p. 89, and Masheck, "Mondrian the New Yorker," *Artforum*, vol. 13, no. 2, October 1974, p. 65. As Masheck points out in "Mondrian the New Yorker," Reyner Banham, in *Theory and Design in the First Machine Age*, 2nd ed. (Cambridge, Mass.: MIT Press, 1981), pp. 142–43, suggests that Semper's influence was transmitted to the De Stijl group via the architect H. P. Berlage.

72 Greenberg, "Modernist Painting," 1960, in John O'Brian, ed., *Clement Greenberg: The Collected Essays and Criticism: Modernism with a Vengence, 1957–1969* (University of Chicago Press, 1993). Volume 4, p. 86.

73 Semper, *Der Stil*, chapter 58, "The Contrast of Greek Free Drapery to Barbarian Dress," in Semper, *Four Elements of Architecture*, p. 244.

74 Charles Blanc, *Grammaire des arts décoratifs* (Paris: Renouard, 1882), pp. i–xl. According to the title page, this is a second edition, augumented by "une introduction sur les lois générales de l'ornement." However, I have been unable to locate the earlier edition lacking this preface. The *Grammaire des arts décoratifs* was a sequel to Blanc's *Grammaire des arts du dessin* (Paris: Renouard, 1870).

75 Blanc, *Grammaire des arts décoratifs*, pp. xxx–xxxi.

76 Daniel-Henry Kahnweiler, *Mes Galeries et mes peintres* (1961; repr. Paris: Gallimard, 1982), p. 63, and "Huit entretiens," in *Le Point*, special issue on Picasso, vol. 7, no. 42, October 1952, p. 22.

77 Fernande Olivier, *Picasso and His Friends* (1933; trans. Jane Miller, New York: Appleton-Century, 1965), p. 139.

78 *Paris-Journal*, January 1, 1912; cited in Rubin, *Picasso and Braque: Pioneering Cubism*, p. 41; also reproduced in Cousins, "Documentary Chronology," ibid., p. 388.

79 Leo Stein, *Appreciation*, p. 176.

80 Gelett Burgess, "The Wild Men of Paris," *The Architectural Record*, vol. 27, no. 5, May 1910, p. 408.

81 Marius de Zayas, "Pablo Picasso," 1911; repr. in Marius de Zayas, *How, When, and Why Modern Art Came to New York*, ed. Francis M. Naumann (Cambridge, Mass.: MIT Press, 1996), pp. 212–21.

82 Françoise Gilot and Carleton Lake, *Life with Picasso* (New York: McGraw-Hill, 1964), p. 76, and an August 11, 1912 letter from Picasso to Kahnweiler, cited in Rubin, ibid., pp. 47–48. Apollinaire's remarks are cited in ibid., p. 42; his 1912 statement that "Picasso's discoveries were corroborated by the good sense of Braque" is also translated by Susan Suleiman in Leroy C. Breunig, ed., *Apollinaire on Art: Essays and Reviews, 1902–1918* (New York: Viking, 1972), pp. 257–58.

83 Dora Vallier, "Braque, la peinture et nous," *Cahiers d'art*, vol. 29, no. 1, October 1954, p. 14; cited in Rubin, *Picasso and Braque: Pioneering Cubism*, p. 41.

84 Daniel Henry [Kahnweiler], "Der Kubismus," in *Die Weissen Blatter* (Zurich-Leipzig), vol. 3, no. 9, September 1916, pp. 209–22; expanded version published as *Der Weg zum Kubismus* (Munich: Delphin, 1920); trans. as *The Rise of Cubism* (New York: Wittenborn, Schulz, 1949), p. 7.

85 The sequence and timing of the studies for the *Three Women*, and of the actual canvas, are discussed at length in Chapter 2 below.

86 Gilot and Lake, *Life with Picasso*, pp. 75–76.

87 Burgess, "The Wild Men of Paris," p. 405; cited in Edward F. Fry, *Cubism* (New York: McGraw-Hill, 1966), p. 53; and in Masheck, "Carpet Paradigm," p. 100.

88 Kahnweiler, *Rise of Cubism*, p. 7. On the preceding page, Kahnweiler wrote: "In the year 1906, Braque, Derain, Matisse and many others were still striving for expression through color, using only pleasant arabesques, and completely dissolving the form of the object. Cézanne's great example was still not understood. Painting threatened to debase itself to the level of ornamentation; it sought to be 'decorative,' to 'adorn' the wall." It should be noted that the corresponding passages of Kahnweiler's 1916 article, "Der Kubismus," pp. 211–14, describe the development of Picasso's work at this time in similar terms, but without explictly attacking the ideas of decoration or ornamentation.

89 The currency of this Neo-Platonic theory, in the years before World War I, is evident from the comments in Leo Stein, *Appreciation*, pp. 176–77 and 204–05; from Huntly Carter's article, "The Plato-Picasso Idea," *The New Age* (London), November 23, 1911, p. 88; and from John Middleton Murry's response, "The Art of Pablo Picasso," *The New Age*, November 30, 1911, p. 115. The articles by Carter and Murry are reprinted in Marilyn McCully, ed., *A Picasso Anthology: Documents, Criticism, Reminiscences* (London: Arts Council of Great Britain, 1981; repr. Princeton University Press, 1982), pp. 81–84.

90 Note Kahnweiler's comments, in *Rise of Cubism*, p. 8: "Thus Picasso [in 1908] painted figures resembling Congo sculptures, and still lifes of the simplest form. His perspective in these works is similar to that of Cézanne. Light is never more than a means to create form – through chiaroscuro . . . Of these paintings one can no longer say, 'The light comes from this side or that side,' because light has become completely a means. The pictures are almost monochromatic; brick red and red brown, often with a gray or a gray green ground, since the color is

meant to be only chiaroscuro" (i.e. the colors are meant to express form, not to capture the actual play of light on the model).

91 Kahnweiler, *Rise of Cubism*, p. 12; and see Locke, *Essay*, pp. 104–114.

92 In *Rise of Cubism*, pp. 10–11, Kahnweiler writes, rather cryptically: "Closed form accepts objects as contained by their own surfaces, viz., the skin; it then endeavors to paint this 'skin' as the contact point between the body and light where both merge into color . . . The painters of the Renaissance, using the closed form method, endeavored to give the illusion of form by painting light as color on the surface of objects. It was never more than 'illusion.'" The reader is left to infer that Picasso and Braque objected to this mode of "illusion." Kahnweiler made this point more clearly and explicitly in his later writings. In "L'Art nègre et le cubisme," for instance, he wrote: "Les peintres cubistes . . . répugnaient aux moyens illusionnistes. Parmi ceux-ci, le clair-obscur les choquait tout particulièrement par son caractère d'imitation, d'une part, et par l'alteration du ton local qu'il imposait, d'autre part." Kahnweiler, *Confessions esthétiques* (Paris: Gallimard, 1963), p. 229. Similarly, in his discussions with Francis Crémieux, he said that Picasso and Braque considered the evocation of three-dimensional form by chiaroscuro shading as a "dishonest method." Kahnweiler, *Mes galeries et mes peintres: entretiens avec Francis Crémieux*, 1961, trans. as *My Galleries and Painters* (New York: Viking, 1971), p. 62. This aversion to chiaroscuro might seem to contradict Kahnweiler's statement in *Rise of Cubism*, p. 8, that the light in Picasso's 1908 pictures is "a means to create form . . . through chiaroscuro." However, as discussed in n. 90 above, Kahnweiler distinguishes Picasso's Cubist chiaroscuro, which has no fixed light source, from conventional chiaroscuro, which does.

93 In *Rise of Cubism*, p. 10, Kahnweiler notes rather cryptically that "in the actual three dimensional world the object is there to be touched even after light is eliminated." That is, its three-dimensional form remains perceptible in the dark, albeit perceptible by touch rather than by sight. In this sense, 1908–09 Cubism can be understood as an attempt to represent bodies and objects as they appear in the dark. Indeed, this is the argument presented by Jean Paulhan in "Petite aventure en pleine nuit," in *La Peinture cubiste* (Paris: Denoël, 1970; repr. Paris: Denoël/Folio, 1990), pp. 61–81.

94 Kahnweiler, *Rise of Cubism*, p. 10. This key observation had already appeared in "Der Kubismus," the original 1916 version of Kahnweiler's text, p. 217: "Der wichtigere Vorgang aber, der entscheidende Schritt überhaupt, der den Kubismus loslöst von der bisherigen 'Sprache' der Malerei, vollzieht sich in Cadaquès . . . Picasso hat die *geschlossene Form durchbrochen*."

95 Vallier, "Braque, la peinture et nous," pp. 14–16. See also n. 38 above.

96 As Theodore Reff notes in "The Reaction Against Fauvism: The Case of Braque," in William Rubin *et al*, eds., *Picasso and Braque: A Symposium* (New York: Museum of Modern Art, 1992), p. 17: "what we now perceive as a reaction against Fauvism was perceived then as a reaction against the more widely known Impressionism." Indeed, Picasso told Françoise Gilot: "Cubism . . . was really the manifestation of a vague desire on the part of those of us who participated in it to get back to some kind of order, yes. We were trying to move in a direction opposite to Impressionism. That was the reason we abandoned color, emotion, sensation, and everything that had been introduced into painting by the Impressionists, to search again for an architectonic basis in the composition, trying to make an order of it . . ." Gilot and Lake, *Life with Picasso*, p. 75.

97 Vallier, "Braque, la peinture et nous," pp. 14–16.

98 Lassaigne, "Entretien avec Braque," pp. xvi–xvii.

99 Verdet, *Entretiens*, pp. 19, 28.

100 Albert Gleizes wrote that "the valuable but affected indications of Picasso and Braque did not, in spite of all, leave behind an impressionism of form which, however, they opposed to that of color," in "L'Art et ses répresentants, Jean Metzinger," 1911; cited in Daniel Robbins, "Jean Metzinger: At the Center of Cubism," in Joann Moser, ed., *Jean Metzinger in Retrospect* (Iowa City: University of Iowa Museum of Art, 1985), p. 19. Similarly, Claude Lévi-Strauss, serving as ghost-writer for the Socialist deputy George Monnet, wrote in 1930 that: "Cubism extends impressionism. Both displace the picture from canvas to viewer. But whereas the latter depends upon the retina's reestablishment of the image as it should be seen, as true, and as it has by no means been represented by the blending of colors, the former requires restoration of the work's meaning by the mind of the viewer. For the organic recomposition of impression, cubism substitutes a process of intellectual reconstruction." See Georges Monnet [in fact, Claude Lévi-Strauss], "Picasso and Cubism," in *Documents*, vol. 2, no. 3, 1930, trans. Dominic Faccini and annotated in *October*, no. 60, spring 1992, p. 51.

101 Willard Bohn, "In Pursuit of the Fourth Dimension: Guillaume Apollinaire and Max Weber," *Arts Magazine*, vol. 54, no. 10, June 1980, pp. 166–69, was the first scholar to note that Apollinaire's discussion of the "fourth dimension," in his 1913 volume *Cubist Painters*, was based on a text by the American painter Max Weber, published in *Camera Work* in 1910. Weber had been part of the Stein circle in Paris in 1905–08, beginning as a student of Matisse but ultimately arriving at a personal style based on Picasso's *Three Women*. Weber describes the "fourth dimension" as a "dimension of infinity," explaining this as a "boundless sense of space or grandeur." He argues that this is what makes it possible for a "Tanagra, Egyptian, or Congo statuette" to give "the impression of a colossal statue." Apollinaire, similarly, writes that "the dimension of infinity . . . is what gives objects their plasticity," and explicitly applies this argument to Cubism. Bohn's article is recapitulated in Linda Dalrymple Henderson, *The Fourth Dimension and Non-Euclidean Geometry in Modern Art* (Princeton University Press, 1983), pp. 60–64 and 167–73. As Henderson demonstrates, contemporary critics used the "fourth dimension" in at least three different senses: to evoke the enlarged perception of spaces and

objects; to allude to non-Euclidean geometry with its facet-like angles; and to describe the Cubist synthesis of multiple views perceived at a series of different moments (hence bringing the "fourth dimension" of time into painting).

To the accounts given by Bohn and Henderson, it should be added that Weber's description of space as a source of grandeur probably derives from Berenson's comments about "space-composition . . . this art comes into existence only when we get a sense of space not as a void . . . but . . . as something very positive and definite." (*The Italian Painters of the Renaissance*, 4 vols., 1894–1907 [combined edition London: Phaidon, 1952], p. 120; cited in Frank Stella, *Working Space* [Cambridge, Mass.: Harvard University Press, 1986], p. 19).

102 Cousins, "Documentary Chronology," in Rubin, *Picasso and Braque: Pioneering Cubism*, pp. 354–55.

103 Lassaigne, "Entretien avec Braque," pp. xvi–xvii.

104 Kahnweiler, *Gris*, p. 111.

105 Gilot and Lake, *Life with Picasso*, pp. 72–73.

106 Waldemar Georges, interview with Braque, *L'Esprit nouveau*, no. 6, 1921, p. 644; cited in John Golding, *Cubism*, 3rd ed. (Cambridge, Mass.: Harvard University Press, 1988), p. 124. Another Cubist, Juan Gris, made the same argument at greater length in the preceding issue of *L'Esprit nouveau*: "I compose with abstractions (colors) and make my adjustments when these colors have assumed the forms of objects. For example, I make a composition with a white and a black and [then] . . . adjust the white so that it becomes a paper and the black so that it becomes a shadow." Evidently, the idea of a white patch becoming a sheet of paper was a familiar *topos* in Parisian studios. The same text includes Gris's often quoted remark, "Cézanne turns a bottle into a cylinder, but I begin with a cylinder and . . . make a bottle." This makes the same point in different words. Gris, biographical notes, in *L'Esprit nouveau*, no. 5, 1921, pp. 533–34; reprinted in Kahnweiler, *Gris*, p. 193.

107 Kahnweiler, *Rise of Cubism*, pp. 11–13.

108 For "guided projection," see Gombrich, *Art and Illusion*, p. 202. Obviously, Kahnweiler had not read Gombrich. Other than Locke himself, the only identifiable source for Kahnweiler's knowledge of the empiricist tradition is the British literary critic George Henry Lewes, whose name appears in *Rise of Cubism*, p. 13, mis-spelled as H. G. Lewes. Best-known today as the partner of novelist George Eliot, Lewes published five volumes of essays on *Problems of Life and Mind*. "Preperception," the term cited by Kahnweiler, does not occur in any of the major essays reprinted in the first two volumes of this series, but in a fragment from a later volume. Here, in *Problems of Life and Mind*, 3rd series, vol. 2 (Boston: Houghton, Osgood, 1880), p. 106, Lewes uses "preperception" to express the idea that "each perception is itself the revival of many past experiences." This is a commonplace of late nineteenth-century psychology, found in Taine and countless other writers.

109 Writing in 1920, Le Corbusier and Ozenfant argued: "Our concept of the object comes from total knowledge of it, a knowledge acquired by experience of our senses, tactile knowledge, knowledge of its materials, its volume, its profile, of all its properties. And the usual perspective view only acts as the shutter-release for the memory of these experiences." See Le Corbusier and Ozenfant, "Purism," from *L'Esprit nouveau*, no. 3, trans. in Herbert, *Modern Artists on Art*, p. 65.

110 Apollinaire, "Art and Curiosity: The Beginnings of Cubism," *Le Temps*, October 14, 1912; trans. in Breunig, *Apollinaire on Art*, p. 260. What Apollinaire meant by "conceptual reality" seems to have been something akin to the world of Platonic forms. A few months later, in his essay "Modern Painting," published in *Der Sturm* in February 1913, he explained Cubism by noting that "a chair, from whatever angle one looks at it, will always have four legs, a seat, and a back," and that, to give a true representation of the chair, the artist would be therefore required to "disclose all the facets of the [chair's] geometric surface." *Apollinaire on Art*, pp. 268–69. This description of Cubism as a "conceptual" art did not go unchallenged. Kahnweiler in *Gris*, p. 121, acknowledged that "there was talk of 'conceptual' painting" at this time, but insisted that Picasso and Braque "were still empiricists." Their paintings, he said, "did not express 'concepts,' objects conceived by the mind, but gave a great variety of information, derived from previous visual impressions."

111 Apollinaire, "Modern Painting," in *Apollinaire on Art*, pp. 268–69.

112 See n. 2 above; the journalist Jacques de Gachons, "La peinture d'après-demain," pp. 27–29.

113 Marius de Zayas, "Pablo Picasso," *Camera Work*, no. 34, 1911; repr. in de Zayas, *How, When, and Why Modern Art Came to New York*, p. 216.

114 See pp. 6–7 above.

115 Burgess, "Wild Men of Paris," p. 405.

116 Gilot and Lake, *Life with Picasso*, pp. 119–20.

117 Yve-Alain Bois, "The Semiology of Cubism," in Rubin *et al.*, *Picasso and Braque: A Symposium*, p. 188.

118 Maurice Raynal, *Anthologie de la peinture en France de 1906 à nos jours*, 1927, trans. as *Modern French Painters* (New York: Brentano's, 1928), pp. 95–96. Christopher Green notes, in *Juan Gris* (London: Whitechapel Art Gallery, and New Haven: Yale University Press, 1992), p. 63 and n. 61, that the chapter on Gris in *Anthologie de la peinture* is adapted from an article that Raynal had originally published in *Feuilles libres* in April 1923.

119 On the influence of Mallarmé and Vendryes, see Green, *Gris*, pp. 83–85, and nn. 47–59.

120 Kahnweiler, *Gris*, pp. 63–86.

121 André Warnod, "En peinture tout n'est que signe, nous dit Picasso," *Arts*, no. 22, June 29, 1945, p. 1; trans. in Dore Ashton, ed., *Picasso on Art: A Selection of Views* (New York: Viking, 1972), pp. 18–19.

122 Kahnweiler, *Les Sculptures de Picasso* (Paris, Éditions du Chêne, 1948), n.p.

123 See J. M. Nash, "The Nature of Cubism: a study of conflicting explanations," *Art History*, vol. 3, no. 4, December 1980, pp. 435–37, and Paul Crowther, "Cubism, Kant, and Ideology," *Word & Image*, vol. 3, no. 2, April–June 1987, pp. 195–201.

124 Kahnweiler, *Rise of Cubism*, p. 11.

125 Ibid., pp. 11–12. Although the English here translates a later ver-

sion of Kahnweiler's essay, the key sentence – "Instead of an analytical description, the painter can, if he prefers, also create in this way a synthesis of the object" – appears in the original German text of 1916, "Der Kubismus," p. 219: "So kann die neue Malerei . . . von dem Objekte eine analytische Beschreibung geben, oder, falls sie das vorzieht, von ihm eine Synthese schaffen." Kahnweiler goes on to explicate the idea of "a synthesis of the object" by saying that the painter can, "in the words of Kant, 'put together the various conceptions and comprehend their variety in one perception.'" This statement seems to be based on a misunderstanding or a faulty recollection of Kant, who discusses, rather, the way that multiple perceptions can be comprehended in a single concept.

126 John Golding, in his *Cubism*, pp. 118–19, reviews the way that "analytic" and "synthetic" were employed by various Cubist critics, concluding that "it was in the writings of Gris that the difference between an analytical and synthetic approach was elaborated." Gris's response to the questionnaire, the key document here, was published in *Bulletin de la Vie Artistique*, January 1, 1925; trans. in Kahnweiler, *Gris*, p. 202–03.

127 Kenneth E. Silver, *Esprit de Corps: The Art of the Parisian Avant-Garde and the First World War, 1914–1925* (Princeton University Press, 1989), pp. 344–50.

128 Kahnweiler, *Gris*, p. 117.

129 *Documents* (Paris), vol. 2 (1930), no. 3, pp. 180–81; cited in Rubin, *Picasso and Braque: Pioneering Cubism*, n. 23. Rubin here endorses Lynn Gamwell's suggestion, in her *Cubist Criticism* (Ann Arbor: UMI Press, 1980), p. 106, that this anonymous outline of Picasso's career was drafted by the critic Carl Einstein.

130 Golding, *Cubism*, p. 118, credits Ozenfant and Jeanneret, in their 1925 survey *La Peinture Moderne*, with being the first critics to note this important shift in the appearance of Cubism.

131 Alfred H. Barr, Jr., *Picasso: Forty Years of His Art* (New York: Museum of Modern Art, 1946), p. 80. This seemingly mistaken use of "analytic" and "synthetic" was rationalized by later scholars, who argued that the technique of beginning with an abstract composition and then conferring realistic details upon its elements originated with Braque's *papiers collés* of fall 1912. See Golding, pp. 123–24, and Chapter 4, pp. 152–56 below.

2 Spaces

1 Jacques Lassaigne, "Entretien avec Braque" (1961), in Gilberte Martin-Mery, Jacques Lassaigne, and Bernadette Contensou, *Les Cubistes*, exh. cat. (Bordeaux: Galerie des Beaux-Arts, and Paris: Musée d'Art Moderne de la Ville de Paris, 1973), pp. xvi-xvii.

2 Daniel Henry [Kahnweiler], "Der Kubismus," *Die Weissen Blatter* (Zurich-Leipzig), vol. 3, no. 9, September 1916, p. 218: "Einerseits konnte durch Picassos neue Methode eine deutliche Darstellung der Tiefendimension gegeben werden auf nicht illusionistischem Weg. Dies Darstellungsweise läßt sich in ihrer etwas später erreichten endgültigen Form etwa so beschreiben: anstatt von einem angenommenen Vordergrunde auszugehen und von diesem aus mittels perspektivischer Mittel eine scheinbare Tiefe vorzutäuschen, geht der Maler vor einem festgelegten und dargestellten Hintergrunde aus, einer Wand z.B., von der er dann in möglichst anschaulicher Weise eine Art Formenschema nach vorn arbeitet, mittels Flächen etc., die durch ihre Stellung gegeneinander und durch ihre Richtung ein deutliches plastisches Bild geben."

3 See Erwin Panofsky, *Renaissance and Renascences in Western Art* (Stockholm: Almqvist & Wiksells; repr. New York: Harper & Row, 1969), pp. 122–23. Panofsky's argument treats Descartes's idea of uniform space as a precursor to Alberti's geometrical perspective; in reality, of course, Alberti preceded Descartes by almost two hundred years.

4 See e.g. the "Diagram of Picture Space," fig. 27, in Marilyn Stokstad, *Art History*, rev. ed. (New York: Prentice-Hall and Abrams, 1999), a typical textbook.

5 George R. Kernodle, *From Art to Theater: Form and Convention in the Renaissance* (University of Chicago Press, 1943); Pierre Francastel, *Peinture et société* (Lyon: Audin, 1951; repr. Paris: Denoël, 1977), esp. part 1, "Naissance d'un espace."

6 For an illustration of the fixed stage of the Renaissance festival, see Kernodle, *From Art to Theater*, fig. 51; as Kernodle notes, the arcade backdrop can be traced back to the Greek and Roman stage.

7 For illustrations, see George Kernodle, *The Theater in History* (Fayetteville: University of Arkansas Press, 1989), pp. 224–25.

8 The curtain descending without visible support in the background of Bellini's *Madonna and Child* was presumably part of a simple wood and fabric canopy like that visible in Perugino's *Virgin and Child with Four Saints* (1493, Vienna Kunsthistorische Museum). Bellini's "close-up" point of view eliminates the wooden framework which would otherwise have appeared at the sides and top of the composition.

9 William Rubin originally presented the idea of Cubist space as a kind of bas-relief in "Jackson Pollock and the Modern Tradition," published in the February, March, April, and May 1967 issues of *Artforum*; repr. in Pepe Karmel, ed., *Jackson Pollock: Interviews, Articles, and Reviews* (New York: Museum of Modern Art, 1999); see pp. 157–58. He again touched on it in "Cézannism and the Beginnings of Cubism," in William Rubin, ed., *Cézanne: The Late Work*, exh. cat. (New York: Museum of Modern Art, 1977), p. 187; and developed it at further length in "Pablo and Georges and Leo and Bill," *Art in America*, vol. 67, no. 2, March–April 1979, pp. 131–32.

10 Roger Fry, "Renoir," 1920, in *Vision and Design* (London: Chatto & Windus, 1920; repr. Mineola: Dover, 1998), pp. 188–89.

11 See Lawrence Gowing, "The Logic of Organized Sensations," in Rubin, *Cézanne: The Late Work*, pp. 56–61.

12 Bernard Berenson, *The Central Italian Painters*, cited in Mary Ann Calo, *Bernard Berenson and the Twentieth Century* (Philadelphia: Temple University Press, 1994), p. 76.

13 See Cézanne's remarks to his son, cited in Leo Larguier, "Cézanne parle," in *Le Dimanche avec Paul Cézanne: souvenirs*

(Paris: L'Edition, 1925), extracts reprinted in P. M. Doran, ed., *Conversations avec Cézanne* (Paris: Macula, 1978), pp. 14–17.

14 Maurice Denis, "Cézanne," *L'Occident*, September 1907; repr. in Doran, *Conversations avec Cézanne*, p. 178. The procedure described by Denis is evident in a seemingly unfinished canvas like the late portrait of a *Peasant in a Blue Blouse* (Kimbell Art Museum, Fort Worth); John Rewald, with Walter Feilchenfeldt and Jayne Warman, *The Paintings of Paul Cézanne: A Catalogue Raisonné* (New York: Abrams, 1996), cat. no. 826, where the lines of the model's arms (and the contours of the woman in the background) have been drawn on top of an already existing field of colors.

15 On the similar opposition between optical and tactile signs in another influential modernist, see Margaret Olin, "Validation by Touch in Kandinsky's Early Abstract Art," *Critical Inquiry*, 16, Autumn 1989, pp. 144–72.

16 On Cézanne as a model for "conservative" art, see Theodore Reff, "The Reaction Against Fauvism: The Case of Braque," in William Rubin *et al*, eds., *Picasso and Braque: A Symposium* (New York: Museum of Modern Art, 1992), pp. 25–29. On p. 38 (and n. 93), Reff quotes Braque's 1957 statement that "Cubism was essentially a reaction against the Impressionists" (originally published in Georges Braque, "The Power of Mystery," interview with John Richardson, *The Observer*, December 1, 1957, p. 16), and also Picasso's statement to Françoise Gilot that he and Braque "were trying to move in a direction opposite to Impressionism" (originally published in Françoise Gilot and Carlton Lake, *Life with Picasso* [New York: McGraw-Hill, 1964], p. 69). As Kenneth Silver has demonstrated, this "return to order" became even more important after the outbreak of war in 1914, which imbued "classicism" with a new patriotic fervor; see Kenneth Silver, *Esprit de Corps: The Art of the Parisian Avant-Garde and the First World War, 1914–1925* (Princeton University Press, 1989), and also Christopher Green, *Cubism and Its Enemies* (New Haven and London: Yale University Press, 1987).

17 Leo Stein, *Appreciation: Painting, Poetry & Prose* (New York: Crown Publishers, 1947; repr. Lincoln: University of Nebraska Press, 1996), p. 174.

18 Leo Steinberg, "Resisting Cézanne: Picasso's 'Three Women,'" *Art in America*, vol. 66, no. 6, November–December 1978, p. 125 and n. 9. The crux of Steinberg's argument is that "Picasso may have loved the late visionary Cézannes" which reduced all experience to the flux of color sensations, but may nonetheless have "experienced these paintings as depredations, spoilers of native character and inherent diversity" (p. 122). I would amend Steinberg's argument by saying that if Cézanne provided a model for a style of painting that dissolved individual objects into the optical field, he also provided a series of models for reasserting the character of individual objects and places.

19 Bernard Berenson, *The Italian Painters of the Renaissance*, 4 vols., 1894–1907 (combined ed., London: Phaidon, 1952), p. 40.

20 *Picasso* (Basel: Editions Beyeler, 1967), p. 32; cited in Steinberg, "Resisting Cézanne," p. 123.

21 I have gathered these quotations from Hélène Seckel, "Anthology of Early Commentary on *Les Demoiselles d'Avignon*," in William Rubin *et al*, *Studies in Modern Art 3: Les Demoiselles d'Avignon* (New York: Museum of Modern Art, 1994), pp. 213–56. For the subsequent fate of the painting, see "Chronology" by Seckel and Judith Cousins, pp. 145–75.

22 Gertrude Stein, *The Autobiography of Alice B. Toklas* (1933; repr. New York: Vintage, 1960), pp. 18, 22, 64. The pictures that Braque and Derain showed at the spring 1908 Salon des Indépendants were figure paintings deriving from Picasso's not yet completed *Three Women*, which the Steins later purchased. See Judith Cousins with Pierre Daix, "Documentary Chronology," in William Rubin *et al*, eds., *Picasso and Braque: Pioneering Cubism*, exh. cat. (New York: Museum of Modern Art, 1989), pp. 348–51.

23 Anatoly Podoksik, *Picasso: The Artist's Work in Soviet Museums* (New York: Abrams, 1989), gives the provenance of the *Three Women* (cat. 28) as: "1909 L. and G. Stein collection, Paris; 1913 D.-H. Kahnweiler Gallery, Paris; 1914 S. Shchukin collection, Moscow; 1918 First Museum of Modern Western Painting, Moscow; 1923 State Museum of Modern Western Art, Moscow; since 1948 The Hermitage, Leningrad. Inv. No. 9658." The photograph of the *Three Women* in the Kahnweiler archives (photo #155) bears the inscription, "Coll. Stein 1909–Acheté à Gertrude Stein; Stschoukine; Hermitage." However, there does not appear to be an entry for the *Three Women* in Kahnweiler's stockbook (the "petit carnet noir" or "pcn"). It is possible that Kahnweiler was acting as Shchukin's agent, so that the painting never formally entered his gallery stock. In summer 1912, Kahnweiler had sold another Picasso, probably *Composition with Skull*, 1908, to Shchukin for 10,000 francs; see letter of June 12, 1912 from Kahnweiler to Picasso, reprinted in Cousins, "Documentary Chronology," in Rubin, *Picasso and Braque: Pioneering Cubism*, exh. cat. (New York, Museum of Modern Art, 1989), p. 400 and n. 151.

24 On the long eclipse of the *Three Women* from critical awareness, see Rubin, "Cézannism and the Beginnings of Cubism," p. 184, and Steinberg, "Resisting Cézanne," pp. 115–17.

25 Leo Steinberg, "The Philosophical Brothel," *Art News*, vol. 71, September and October 1972; repr. in *October*, no. 44, spring 1988, pp. 17–74; and "Resisting Cézanne," pp. 121–23.

26 See, e.g. Derain's *The Turning Road, L'Estaque* of 1906, Friesz's *The Terrace* of 1907 (painted from the same vantage point as Braque's *View from the Hôtel Mistral, L'Estaque*), and Dufy's *Green Trees* of 1908. These are reproduced on pp. 114, 122, 133, respectively, of John Elderfield, *The "Wild Beasts": Fauvism and Its Affinities* (New York: Museum of Modern Art, 1976).

27 Léal, vol. 1, cat. no. 8, pp. 4r and 4v.

28 See e.g. *Musée Picasso: Carnets*, sketchbook MP 1861, p. 29r.

29 See Zervos II**, 644 (Kunstsammlung Basel, Kupferstichkabinett. Gift of Douglas Cooper).

30 The most detailed and comprehensive overview of the development of the *Three Women* appears in Pierre Daix, "Les trois périodes de travail de Picasso sur *Les Trois Femmes* (automne

1907-automne 1908), les rapports avec Braque, et les débuts du Cubisme," *Gazette des Beaux-Arts*, series 6, vol. III, nos. 1428–29 (January–February 1988), pp. 148–51. However, the sequence proposed here differs in important details from that proposed by Daix.

31 Many of the numerous studies for the *Three Women* are watercolors or gouaches; few have been published in color. However, my examination of the examples in the Musée Picasso, Paris, reveals the coloristic evolution – from pinks, blues, and yellows recalling the *Demoiselles* to the brick reds and leafy greens found in the finished *Three Women* – discussed here. The studies in question are reproduced (mostly in black and white) in Richet, cat. nos 151, 156, 159, 162, 163, 165, 169, 171, 172, 182–89 (not necessarily created in that order).

32 In several related studies, discussed in Chapter 3, pp. 60 below, Picasso experimented with inserting a turning figure – making the composition more dramatic but less unified.

33 Pierre Daix and Yve-Alain Bois have noted the importance of this "unitary system of notation," in which the same signifier (here, a curve) serves to indicate a series of different signifieds (arm, leg, breast, head, curtain). The original French text, in Pierre Daix and Joan Rosselet, *Le Cubisme de Picasso: catalogue raisonné de l'oeuvre peint, 1907–1916* (Neuchâtel: Ides et Calendes, 1979), p. 68, refers to "l'écriture unitaire de formes objectives et du contenant spatial" and to "une écriture picturale unitaire." These are translated in D.R., p. 68, as "a unitary idiom applicable to both solid objects and the surrounding space" and "a unitary pictorial idiom." Yve-Alain Bois, in "The Semiology of Cubism," in Rubin, *Picasso and Braque: A Symposium*, p. 180, suggests that the phrase might best be translated as a "unitary system of notation," and I have adopted this usage. Bois goes on to note that "the same geometric sign . . . is used over and over with a different semantic function, each time determined by its context . . . this system will be generalized in 1909."

34 As Leo Steinberg suggests, in "Resisting Cézanne," p. 128, the overall field seems to have been formed by a process of division, and the figures seem then to have been born from these divisions. Describing the finished canvas, Steinberg observes: "Triangulation . . . becomes the first move, followed . . . by a process of continuing subdivision. In other words, it is the field that divides into segments and, in so doing, engenders a woman's thigh . . . the larger units of the depicted anatomies are treated as sectors generated in the partitioning of the field."

35 Gert Schiff, in *Picasso at Work at Home: Selections from the Marina Picasso Collection, with additions from the Los Angeles County Museum and The Museum of Modern Art, New York*, exh. cat. (Miami: Center for the Fine Arts, 1985) , cat. 13, argues: "As the squaring indicates, Picasso used this sketch to ensure correct proportions when transferring the composition to canvas."

36 Daniel-Henry Kahnweiler, *The Rise of Cubism* (New York: Wittenborn, Schulz, 1949), p. 7.

37 Picasso's lack of commitment to the total pictorial integration he had achieved in the *Three Women* is evident from the so-called "Rhythmic Version" of the composition (see fig. 61), and from several related studies of *Bathers in a Forest* (e.g. Zervos XXVI, 292). Here, he sacrifices the unifying interlace of the figures in order to give them a greater sense of spatial projection. In particular, the figure on the right is detached, brought forward, and given a new pose, turning forcefully in three dimensions (see e.g. figs. 77–79).

38 Note the brushwork in Braque's *Large Nude* (reproduced in Rubin, *Picasso and Braque: Pioneering Cubism*, p. 87); this image corresponds to the leftmost of the three figures in *Woman* (see fig. 4).

39 Reff, "Reaction Against Fauvism," p. 26.

40 See n. 11 above.

41 See the remarks by Vauxcelles and Matisse in Cousins, "Documentary Chronology," in Rubin, *Picasso and Braque: Pioneering Cubism*, pp. 354–56.

42 D.R., p. 66.

43 Dora Vallier, "Braque, la peinture et nous: Propos de l'artiste recueillis," *Cahiers d'art*, vol. 29, no. 1, October 1954, p. 16.

44 Ibid.

45 See Picasso, *Le Sacré-Coeur*, winter 1909–10 (D.R. 339).

46 See Chapter 1, pp. 14–15 above.

47 Daniel-Henry Kahnweiler, with Francis Crémieux, *My Galleries and Painters* (1961, trans. Helen Weaver, New York: Viking, 1971), p. 57.

3 Bodies

1 Daniel-Henry Kahnweiler, *The Rise of Cubism* (New York: Wittenborn, Schulz, 1949), p. 10.

2 Leo Steinberg criticizes the idea that Cubism can be seen as progressing in a single direction in "[Resisting Cubism:] The Polemical Part," *Art in America*, vol. 67, no. 2, March–April 1979, p. 125.

3 See Chapter 1, pp. 3–5 above.

4 Cézanne's *The Large Bather*, c. 1885 (Rewald 555; Museum of Modern Art, New York) provided the model for Picasso's large canvas *Boy Leading a Horse*, winter 1905–06 (D.B. XIV.7; Museum of Modern Art, New York); see Anthony Blunt and Phoebe Pool, *Picasso: The Formative Years – A Study of His Sources* (London: Studio Books, 1962), figs. 161–66 and commentary.

5 See James Johnson Sweeney, "Picasso and Iberian Sculpture," *Art Bulletin*, 23, September 1941, pp. 191–98; Susan Mayer, "Ancient Mediterranean Sources in the Works of Picasso, 1892–1937," Ph.D. dissertation, New York University, 1980, and "Greco-Roman and Egyptian Sources in Picasso's Blue Period," *Arts*, vol. 53, June 1979, pp. 130–37; William Rubin, "Picasso," in William Rubin, ed., *"Primitivism" in Twentieth Century Art* (New York: Museum of Modern Art, 1984), vol. 1, pp. 247–51.

6 For an example of the kind of vase painting that might have influenced Picasso, see the vase of c. 460 BC from the Louvre reproduced in Giovanni Becatti, *The Art of Ancient Greece and*

Rome: From the Rise of Greece to the Fall of Rome (Englewood Cliffs: Prentice-Hall, and New York: Abrams, n.d.), p. 147. The exaggerated musculature of Picasso's figures may also be seen as a tacit, humorous reference to his friend Guillaume Apollinaire, who in 1905 enjoyed a brief, improbable stint as editor of the magazine *La Culture physique*, illustrated with photographs of body-builders whose rippling muscles were intended to reproduce the canon of classical statuary. A sketch by Picasso depicts Apollinaire as a latter-day Zeus, holding a copy of his newspaper; see the reproductions in D.B. D.XII.24; Zervos XXII, 286; and in Gertrude Stein, *Picasso* (London: T. Batsford, 1938; repr. New York: Dover 1984), fig. 15 (there dated 1906). On *La Culture physique*, see Tamar Garb, *Bodies of Modernity: Figure and Flesh in Fin-de-Siècle France* (London: Thames and Hudson, 1999), ch. 2, "Modelling the Male Body: Physical Culture, Photography and the Classical Ideal," pp. 54–79. See also the related drawings evoking bacchanals in Zervos XXII, 246, 291–94.

7 As Leo Steinberg noted in "Resisting Cézanne: Picasso's 'Three Women,'" *Art in America*, vol. 66, no. 6, November–December 1978, pp. 119–20, many of Picasso's nudes of 1907–08 display a curiously androgynous character, as if meant to evoke a primeval epoch before sexual differentiation. David Lomas, in "A Canon of Deformity: *Les Demoiselles d'Avignon* and Physical Anthropology," *Art History*, vol. 16, no. 3, September 1993, p. 437, suggests that Picasso's heavy-set nudes of this period are meant to exemplify the sociological view that "female prostitutes display features of atavistic return to a more masculine type." However, the asexual character of the *Two Nudes* might equally well be traced back to other sketches of 1906 where Picasso depicts pairs of children (see for instance Zervos I, 358), whose long torsos and short legs seem to provide the prototype for the *Two Nudes*. The symbolism of Picasso's anatomies cannot, in any case, be understood in isolation, but must be considered in the context of contemporaries such as Maillol and Bourdelle.

8 The sketchbook containing this first geometric figure of the *Demoiselles* studies also contains two sketches of a statuette in the nearby Egyptian galleries of the Louvre. The relation between the statuette and the sketches is noted by William Rubin in "La Genèse des Demoiselles d'Avignon," in Seckel, vol. 2, pp. 374–75; trans. and rev. in William Rubin, Hélène Seckel, and Judith Cousins, *Studies in Modern Art 3: Les Demoiselles d'Avignon* (New York: Museum of Modern Art, 1994), pp. 120–21.

9 *Picasso* (Basel: Editions Beyeler, 1967), p. 32; cited in Steinberg, "Resisting Cézanne," p. 123. Picasso's association between the decorative qualities of rhythm and polarity and the "intrinsic value" of painting echoes earlier writers such as Taine and Denis; see Chapter 1, p. 7 above.

10 See Chapter 1, p. 9 above.

11 Charles Blanc, *Grammaire des arts décoratifs*, 2nd ed. (Paris: Renouard, 1882), p. viii.

12 Léger used the phrase "Contrast of Forms" as the collective title for his paintings of 1912–14. His discussion of the idea, in the 1913 essay "The Origins of Painting and Its Representational Value," seems to derive directly from Blanc's discussion of "contrasting forms." See Fernand Léger, *Functions of Painting*, trans. Alexandra Anderson (New York: Viking, 1973), p. 7.

13 It should be noted that the frontality of archaic art – indeed, the concept of "frontality" per se – was an idea of relatively recent vintage; it was not until the 1890s that a Danish archaeologist, Julius Lange, pointed out that the Egyptian, Oceanic, and Mexican statues tended to be constructed around a rigidly vertical axis, shunning the torque of Hellenistic and Renaissance figures: "They may represent the body in a great number of different positions: walking, stationary, upright or leaning forward or backward, seated on a piece of furniture or on the ground, on horseback, kneeling, sleeping on the back, etc.: but, whatever position the figure takes, it is subjected to this rule, that *the median plane which one can construct, going from the summit of the head, the nose, the dorsal ridge, the sternum, the navel and the sexual organs, and which divides the body into two symmetrical halves, remains invariable, neither curving nor turning to either side.* A figure may well curve forward or backward; the median plane will remain a plane, but *it produces neither flexion nor lateral torsion either in the neck nor in the abdomen.* The legs are not always placed symmetrically; a figure may, for example, advance one foot in front of the other, kneel with one knee on the ground and the other raised, etc.; but the position of the legs will nonetheless indicate the same direction as the trunk and head of the figure." Julius Lange, *Darstellung des Menschen in der älteren griechischen Kunst*, trans. into German from Danish by Mathilde Mann (with a partial translation into French), (Strassburg: Heitz & Mündel, 1899), pp. xi–xii. Some years earlier, Henri Lechat had given a *compte-rendu* of Lange's original Danish publication in a pamphlet published as "Une loi de la Statuaire primitive: la loi de la frontalité," *Revue des universités du Midi*, vol. 1, 1895, 1.

14 Kahnweiler, *Rise of Cubism*, p. 7.

15 Close examination of the canvas of the *Demoiselles* suggests that the striations at one point extended across the face and upper torso of the standing figure at the center of the composition, but were subsequently overpainted with the present flesh color.

16 Kahnweiler, *Rise of Cubism*, p. 6.

17 See Seckel, vol. 1, carnet II, p. 8v.

18 Pierre Daix, in "L'Historique des Demoiselles d'Avignon revisé à l'aide des carnets de Picasso," in Seckel, vol. II, pp. 538–42, proposes that the sketchbook containing fig. 54 should be dated to 1908 rather than 1907.

19 Steinberg, "Resisting Cézanne," p. 127, argues that the faceting of the figure found in studies by Albrecht Dürer and other Renaissance artists is fundamentally different in conception from the faceting in Picasso's 1908–09 work. Yve-Alain Bois, "Painting as Trauma," *Art in America*, vol. 76, no. 6, June 1988, p. 140, compares fig. 55 to Renaissance "studies of proportion" by Dürer and Luca Pacioli, but argues that Picasso's goal was a "purging of such almost-academic procedures."

20 Ernst Brücke, *The Human Figure: Its Beauties and Defects* (trans. London: H. Grevel, 1900), pp. 74–76.

21 See Stephen Jay Gould, "Petrus Camper's Angle," in *Bully for Brontosaurus: Reflections in Natural History* (New York: W. W. Norton, 1991), pp. 229–40.

22 This geometric diagram of the face seems to lie behind a pair of drawings and paintings of 1911, see figs. 168, 169.

23 Leo Steinberg, "Drawing as if to Possess," section III of "The Algerian Women and Picasso at Large," in Steinberg, *Other Criteria: Confrontations with Twentieth-Century Art* (New York: Oxford University Press, 1972), pp. 174–81; in n. 33, Steinberg explains that "the phrase, 'que je les possède' was used by Picasso explaining his figure drawings" in a conversation with William Rubin.

24 See the drawing from the Marina Picasso collection reproduced in William Rubin, *Picasso and Braque: Pioneering Cubism*, p. 110, upper left.

25 John Richardson, with Marilyn McCully, *A Life of Picasso*, vol. II: *1907–1917* (New York: Random House, 1996), pp. 108–09. Richardson proposes that the setting of Picasso's 1909 *Bather* was suggested by Matisse's early 1908 painting of *Bathers with a Turtle*. Matisse's picture may well have been an influence, but it should be recalled that Picasso had employed similar beach settings in Blue Period pictures such as *Maternity* (Goetz collection, Los Angeles, D.B. VI.28) and *The Tragedy* (National Gallery of Art, Washington, D.C., D.B. IX.6).

26 See Chapter I, p. 6 above.

27 See Chapter I, pp. 14–15 and Chapter 2, pp. 44–47 above. Although Picasso did not develop the idea of superimposition at this time, the image of a flat, "playing card" figure plays a role in drawings and paintings of spring 1909 such as *Seated Woman* (Zervos XXVI, 370) and *Two Nudes* (D.R. 244).

28 Since childhood, Picasso had played the pictorial game of drawing animals with a continuous, interlacing line. See Roland Penrose, *Picasso: His Life and Work* (London: Gollancz, 1958), pp. 36 and 215–16. It is not clear whether this was a game that Picasso invented, or (more likely) whether it was a parlor game widespread at the time. Picasso's childhood drawings are lost, but examples of such interlaced animals from 1906–07 can be found in Zervos VI, 924, 931, 932, 939, 940, 948, 949, 964, 965; and Zervos XXVI, 176, 181–83, 185. Susan Grace Galassi, in *Picasso's One-Liners* (New York: Artisan, 1997) reproduces similar works from the years 1917–78.

29 Steinberg, "Resisting Cézanne," p. 127, uses the term "arris" rather than "border" to describe the line where two planes meet; he argues, furthermore, that these lines become the primary element in Picasso's compositions as early as 1908, with the *Three Women*.

30 Leo Stein, *Appreciation: Painting, Poetry & Prose* (New York: Crown Publishers, 1947; repr. Lincoln: University of Nebraska Press, 1996), pp. 176–77; see also his remarks on pp. 204–05. Kahnweiler, *Rise of Cubism*, pp. 7–8. Picasso's Platonic ambitions seem to have made their way from Paris to London via the Stein circle; see Huntly Carter, "The Plato-Picasso Idea," *The New Age* (London), November 23, 1911, p. 88, and John Middleton Murry, "The Art of Pablo Picasso," *The New Age*, November 30, 1911, p. 115; both repr. in Marilyn McCully, ed., *A Picasso Anthology: Documents, Criticism, Reminiscences* (London: The Arts Council, 1981, and Princeton University Press, 1982), pp. 81–84.

31 Roland Penrose, *The Sculpture of Picasso* (New York: Museum of Modern Art, 1967), p. 19.

32 On this movement, see Carmen Gimenez, ed., *Picasso and the Age of Iron* (New York: Solomon R. Guggenheim Museum, 1993). The term "drawings in space" (*dessins dans l'espace*), seems to have appeared for the first time in Daniel-Henry Kahnweiler, *Les Sculpture de Picasso* (Paris: Editions du Chêne, 1948), n.p.

33 Roland Penrose, *Sculpture of Picasso*, p. 19.

34 On the casting history of this work, see Elizabeth Cowling's entry for catalogue no. 5 in John Golding and Elizabeth Cowling, eds., *Picasso: Sculptor/Painter*, exh. cat. (London: Tate Gallery, 1994), p. 256.

35 On Nadelman's relations with Picasso, see Lincoln Kirstein, *Elie Nadelman* (New York: Eakins Press, 1973), pp. 183–85. On pp. 168–69, Kirstein describes how Seurat's simplification and harmonization of linear form, displayed in retrospectives of 1905 and 1908–09, provided a crucial example for Nadelman and, by implication, other Parisian artists such as Picasso. This is a topic that deserves further investigation. (I am grateful to Eric Larsen at the Salander-O'Reilly Gallery for informing me of the debate about the degree of Nadelman's influence on Picasso; this is a topic that looms large in the minds of Nadelman scholars and is not even on the radar screen for Picasso scholars.)

36 Brancusi began to use incised drawing as an expressive device in his now lost *Head of a Girl* of 1907; this was his first experiment with "direct carving"; see Sidney Geist, *Brancusi: A Study of the Sculpture* (New York: Grossman, 1968), p. 28. He returned to the device in *The Kiss* of 1907–08 and *Wisdom of the Earth* of 1908, reproduced in Geist, pp. 28–29, and, more legibly, the works reproduced in Friedrich Teja Bach *et al*, *Constantin Brancusi: 1876–1957* (Philadelphia Museum of Art, 1995), cat. nos. 9 and 10.

37 See the 1906 *Head of a Man* (Spies 11), the 1907 *Mask* (Spies 13), the 1906 *Woman Dressing her Hair* (Spies 17), and the 1908 *Mask of a Woman* (Spies 22).

38 Françoise Gilot and Carleton Lake, *Life with Picasso* (New York: McGraw-Hill, 1964), pp. 59–60.

39 Kahnweiler, *Sculptures de Picasso*, n.p.

40 Kahnweiler, *Rise of Cubism*, p. 10. Specifically, Kahnweiler writes that Picasso had "pierced the closed form . . . [which] accepts objects as contained by their own surfaces, viz., the skin." This terminology is misleading, insofar as it implies that Picasso began with a conventional image of a figure or object, and then cut away part of its surface. This description might apply to the fall 1909 *Head of a Woman*, with its gouged out areas exposing the inner volume of the head, or to the *Guitar* of 1912 (see fig. 229), where the front of the guitar is "cut away"

to reveal its interior. But it does not really apply to the figures of summer 1910, which give no sign of having ever possessed a continuous, self-enclosing "skin."

41 See fig. 146, a photograph showing Braque seated in Picasso's studio. Braque performed his required military service (as a member of the reserves) from March 27 through April 12, 1911, so the fact that he appears in uniform in this picture probably places the photograph at one end or the other of this period. Picasso had previously reproduced the floral-patterned curtain visible in this photograph in his Cézannian still life, *Bread and Fruit Dish on a Table* (D.R. 220), of winter 1908/09.

42 The door in figs. 83–85 seems to be modeled on an unframed door cut directly into the wall and molding of Picasso's studio; this is visible in another photograph from the Laurens Archive, reproduced in Anne Baldassari, *Picasso Photographe, 1901–1916*, exh. cat. (Paris: Musée Picasso, 1994), no. 152.

43 Fernande Olivier, *Picasso and His Friends* (1933; trans. Jane Miller, New York: Appleton-Century, 1965), pp. 132–37.

44 See Manet's *Fifer* or his *Woman with Parrot*, posed against blank fields of green or gray. This was a compositional device borrowed from Velasquez.

45 Edward Fry pointed out to me during the installation of "Picasso and Braque: Pioneering Cubism" (1989), that the spring 1910 canvas *Standing Nude with Raised Arm* (fig. 88) repeated the pose of the spring 1909 *Bather*. The drawing discussed here (fig. 86) is a study for the canvas.

46 Gilot and Lake, *Life with Picasso*, p. 118.

47 There is a small canvas of a *Standing Nude* (D.R. 350; Picasso estate) based on this drawing (see fig. 90).

48 Fig. 90 seems to derive from a slightly smaller drawing in the National Gallery, Prague (Zervos II**, 723). There is also a three-quarter view of this figure (D.R. 351; ex-Dutilleul). These works are probably contemporary with Picasso's oval canvas *Woman with Mandolin* (D.R. 341; Rubin, *Picasso and Braque: Pioneering Cubism*, p. 154); it seems likely that this canvas provoked Braque to paint his own *Woman with Mandolin* (Romilly 71; Rubin, *Picasso and Braque: Pioneering Cubism*, p. 155), which integrates Picasso's new mode of figuration with the rectangular grid newly developed by Braque.

49 William Rubin, *Picasso in the Collection of The Museum of Modern Art* (New York: Museum of Modern Art, 1972), p. 206.

50 Ibid., pp. 205–06: "This type of brushwork originated in Signac's basket-weave variation on Seurat's *points*. But, unlike Picasso, the Neo-Impressionists had used it in the form of a consistent, molecular screen. Matisse, too, frequently used such neo-impressionist brushwork with varying degrees of consistency until about 1905."

51 Picasso, July 25, 1911 letter to Braque, translated in Cousins, "Documentary Chronology," in Rubin, *Picasso and Braque: Pioneering Cubism*, p. 376. The canvas in question seems to be *The Accordionist*, which never in fact received its "treatment" of Signac-style bricks.

52 In "L'art nègre et le cubisme," *Confessions esthétiques* (Paris: Gallimard, 1963), p. 229, Kahnweiler mentions a 1909 work in which "Picasso tried to introduce *real* relief – a very slight relief . . . in order to avoid *fake* shadows."

53 Kahnweiler, *Rise of Cubism*, p. 11.

54 This estimate of the Steins' acquisitions is based on the collection notations in Kahnweiler's photographic files. The estimate of Kahnweiler's purchases is based on a review of his gallery stockbook for the years 1907–09. The 90 Picassos found in these pages constitute a significant fraction of the 443 works by all artists (including Picasso, Braque, Derain, and Vlaminck) that Kahnweiler acquired during this time.

55 See the account of Picasso's move from the Bateau-Lavoir to a larger, more elegant apartment and studio on the Boulevard Clichy, in Olivier, *Picasso and His Friends*, pp. 132–37. On Picasso's prosperity, see also John Berger, *The Success and Failure of Picasso* (Harmondsworth: Penguin, 1965; repr. New York: Pantheon, 1980), p. 5.

56 This was not the first economic squeeze Picasso had experienced since 1905. His expenses had occasionally outstripped his rising income; and these crises were usually resolved by an emergency sale of his work at bargain-basement prices. One such crisis, in 1908, allowed André Level to buy Picasso's 1905 *Saltimbanques* for a mere 1,000 francs. Level's account, in *Souvenirs d'un collectionneur* (Paris: Mazo, 1959), p. 23, makes it clear that Picasso expected to sell the picture for two or three times this sum to a German or Russian collector, but let Level have it for less because he urgently needed the cash. Later that year Picasso sold the *Three Women* to the Steins, presumably for a significantly higher sum. Spring 1910 seems to have been the first time since 1905 that Picasso experienced a financial crisis specifically because he could not sell his new work.

57 Stein, *Appreciation*, p. 187.

58 Gertrude Stein, *The Autobiography of Alice B. Toklas* (1933; repr. New York: Vintage, 1960), p. 111, describes visiting Picasso's studio in spring 1912: "One day we went to see him there. He was not in and Gertrude Stein as a joke left her visiting card. In a few days we went again and Picasso was at work on a picture on which was written ma jolie and at the lower corner painted in was Gertrude Stein's visiting card." By painting in Stein's visiting card and marking the painting as "her" canvas, Picasso was in effect asking her to buy it, ending her boycott of his work. (The sale turned out to be quite complex, because the canvas was already owned by Kahnweiler, who demanded a higher price than the Steins were accustomed to paying when they bought from Picasso directly.) The two-year gap between 1910 and 1912 supports Leo Stein's claim that he, not Gertrude, had always taken the leading role in their joint activity as collectors. In a 1934 letter to Albert Barnes, Leo Stein commented that "Until Gertrude bought a cubist Picasso, she was never responsible for a single picture that was bought, and always said so." Leo Stein, *Journey into the Self: being the letters, papers & journals of Leo Stein* (New York: Crown, 1950), p. 148.

59 Kahnweiler's spring 1910 purchases include 11 paintings: stockbook nos. 444–51 (D.R. 332, 324, 277, 320, 310, 309, 334, and an unidentified work, possibly a drawing rather than a

painting), stockbook nos. 470 and 472 (two more unidentified works, probably from the Blue Period, to judge by their titles), and stockbook no. 480 (D.R. 293). Of these only D.R. 324 and 334 were 1910 works, and only the latter was truly in Picasso's new style. (D.R. 277 is dated on Kahnweiler's photograph to spring 1910 but is placed more plausibly by Daix in spring–summer 1909.) These paintings are followed in the stockbook by a group of 18 drawings, whose titles and dates are not recorded. Some of these may have been 1910 works.

60 Although it is difficult to establish which pictures these collectors bought before 1910 and which after, the pattern of their holdings is significant. Dutilleul's collection ultimately included 11 Picassos done in the years 1908–09, but only one work from 1910; this was a drawing, D.R. 351 (a variant on fig. 90), acquired in 1912 by Kahnweiler, who subsequently sold it to Dutilleul (information from the entry for D.R. 351). Shchukin bought no 1910 or 1911 works by Picasso, a fact of which the artist was very much aware. In 1912, when Shchukin bought the 1908 canvas *Composition with Skull*, Picasso mentioned the sale in a letter to Gertrude Stein, commenting that, "He doesn't understand the more recent things." (Letter translated in Cousins, "Documentary Chronology," in Rubin, *Picasso and Braque: Pioneering Cubism*, p. 403; the vague description of *Composition with Skull* in the letter is confirmed by a contemporary entry for the picture in Kahnweiler's stockbook.) Shchukin later acquired two canvases from spring 1912 (D.R. 460 and 483) and continued buying Picasso's new work at a modest pace in 1913 and 1914. The halt in Shchukin's buying is noted in Rubin, ibid., p. 68.

61 Haviland bought a large *Seated Female Nude* directly from Picasso, while Uhde relieved Kahnweiler of one of the two 1910 canvases he had purchased, a small bust of *Girl with Raised Left Arm*. Haviland's purchase was the *Seated Female Nude* (see fig. 85 now in the Tate Gallery; Uhde's was *Girl with Raised Left Arm*, D.R. 334.

62 Cousins, "Documentary Chronology," in Rubin, *Picasso and Braque: Pioneering Cubism*, p. 365. Uhde's support was rewarded by a large portrait (D.R. 338) in which Picasso softened his new style just enough to produce a legible image.

63 Fernande Olivier, in *Picasso and His Friends*, pp. 143–44, writes: "One day, when he [Picasso] needed a pretty large sum of money, he sold his sculptures to Vollard . . . It was about this time that he began to paint cubist portraits." Indeed, as in Uhde's case, Picasso expressed his gratitude for Vollard's purchases by painting the dealer's portrait. Despite his notorious narcissicism, Vollard does not seem to have cared much for the picture, which he sold in 1913. Anatoli Podoksik, *Picasso: The Artist's Work in Soviet Museums* (New York, Abrams, 1989), entry 55, states that Picasso's 1910 *Portrait of Ambroise Vollard* was acquired by Shchukin in 1913, but the entry in D.R. 337 says that it was acquired by another Russian merchant, Ivan Morosov, in 1913, for 3,000 francs. By way of comparison, Isabelle Monod-Fontaine, in *Daniel-Henry Kahnweiler: Marchand, éditeur, écrivain*, exh. cat. (Paris: Musée National d'Art Moderne, Centre Georges Pompidou, 1984), p. 110, records that Picasso's *Violin and Anchor*, a somewhat smaller picture, was sold to Vincenc Kramar in June 1912; Kahnweiler's stockbook, entry 791, assigns a price of 4,000 francs, although it is not certain that Kramar actually paid that much.

64 None of the Cadaqués pictures appears in Kahnweiler's stockbook, except for a small, relatively legible view of boats in the Cadaqués harbor, purchased in early 1911. The four Cadaqués paintings acquired by Vollard were *Woman with Mandolin* (see fig. 91), *The Rower* (D.R. 360), *The Guitar Player* (D.R. 362), and *The Dressing Table* (D.R. 356). On the December exhibition, see ibid., p. 259, and *Apollinaire on Art*, pp. 122–23. (I am grateful to Judith Cousins for bringing Apollinaire's review to my attention.)

65 Vollard's comment is recorded in Level, *Souvenirs*, p. 28.

66 Kahnweiler, *Rise of Cubism*, p. 12.

67 Gilot and Lake, *Life with Picasso*, pp. 72–73.

68 I would date the Washington National Gallery's *Nude* (see fig. 43) to August 1910, because of the similarity between its facture (dark thin washes over a linear lay-in) and the facture of fall 1910 canvases such as *Daniel-Henry Kahnweiler* (see fig. 8).

69 Isabelle Monod-Fontaine, *Donation Louise et Michel Leiris: Collection Kahnweiler-Leiris* (Paris: Musée National d'Art Moderne, Centre Georges Pompidou, 1984), p. 103; Cousins, "Documentary Chronology," in Rubin, *Picasso and Braque*, p. 367; Richardson, *A Life of Picasso*, vol. II, p. 159.

70 See *Mlle Léonie* (D.R. 347).

71 *Girl with Mandolin* appears in the Kahnweiler photographic files, no. 32, as "'Femme à la Mandoline,' Paris, hiver 1910"; the same dating appears in Zervos II*, 235, although Zervos gives the title as "Jeune Fille à la Mandoline (Fanny Tellier)."

72 In the original edition of Barr's catalogue, *Picasso: Forty Years of His Art* (New York: Museum of Modern Art, 1939), pl. 91, the picture is identified as *Woman with a Mandolin* and placed in 1910, the date inscribed on the canvas. In the rev. ed., *Picasso: Fifty Years of His Art* (New York: Museum of Modern Art, 1946), p. 70, Barr changed the title to *Girl with a Mandolin (Fanny Tellier)*, adding, "1910 (dated); Paris, late (Z) but seeems early 1910 in style."

73 Penrose, *Picasso: His Life and Work* (see n. 28 above), pp. 155–56.

74 Rubin, *Picasso in the Collection*, p. 66; D.R. 346.

75 The link between *Girl with Mandolin* and the "Mlle Léonie" studies is implicitly acknowledged by Daix, who places the canvas *Mademoiselle Léonie* (D.R. 340) and the associated watercolor of the full-length figure (D.R. 347) in early 1910.

76 In the Kahnweiler photo files, Uhde is identified as the picture's owner in the years 1910–14. (Uhde's collection, like Kahnweiler's, was seized by the French government at the outbreak of World War I.)

77 See e.g. Fernand Léger's *Woman Sewing* of late 1909, reproduced in Douglas Cooper and Gary Tinterow, *The Essential Cubism: Braque, Picasso & their friends, 1907–1920*, exh. cat. (London: Tate Gallery, 1983; repr. New York: George Braziller, 1984), no. 94.

78 Barr, *Picasso: Fifty Years*, p. 73. Barr also compares the drawing to "a geometrized anatomical chart in which transparent cross sections of the body are superimposed on the silhouette," and to "a construction or perhaps, more accurately, plan, elevations, and sections of one structure combined in the same drawing." The immediate stimulus for this architectural comparison is Barr's recollection that the members of Stieglitz's circle had nicknamed Picasso's drawing "the fire-escape." However, the true source of the comparison is almost certainly Burgess's article "The Wild Men of Paris," *The Architectural Record*, vol. 27, no. 5, May 1910, p. 405, in which Braque is cited as saying that "to portray every physical aspect of [a woman] . . . require[s] three figures, much as the representation of a house requires a plan, an elevation, and a section." The "skeleton" and "X-ray" comparison is explored in greater depth in Linda Dalrymple Henderson, "X-Rays and the Quest for Invisible Reality in the Art of Kupka, Duchamp, and the Cubists," *Art Journal*, vol. 47, no. 4, Winter 1988, pp. 323–40.

79 William Rubin remarked in a fall 1986 seminar at the Institute of Fine Arts in New York that the "T"s of works like the *Daniel-Henry Kahnweiler* (see fig. 8) and the *Standing Nude* (see fig. 100) represented the origin of the Cubist grid. This is not literally true (since the grid appears in numerous earlier pictures of 1910) but, as argued here, it is effectively the case. Rubin also noted that the "T" marks in Picasso's 1910 work appear to have been the source for Mondrian's "plus and minus" style of 1914–16.

80 *Woman with Mandolin* (D.R. 390), *Seated Woman with a Mandolin* (see fig. 103), *Man with Mandolin* (see fig. 105), *Monk with Mandolin* (see fig. 186), *Mandolin and Three Glasses* (D.R. 386), *Mandolin with a Glass of Pernod* (D.R. 387), and a horizontal, oval still life entitled *The Architect-Musician* depicting a mandolin on a table (visible in a photograph of Picasso's studio [see fig. 182]); this was subsequently repainted and rotated to a vertical, becoming *The Architect's Table* (D.R. 456).

81 Picasso seems to have continued work on the enlarged canvas until sometime in early 1912, and it is dated by Zervos to "winter, 1911–12." (However, the lower section of the enlarged canvas was never brought to a state of finish comparable to that of the upper section.) The original upper section can be dated to early 1911, not only because of its compositional links to *Seated Woman with a Mandolin* (see fig. 103), but also because it appears in the March–April 1911 photograph of Braque seated in Picasso's studio (see fig. 146). The framed canvas is resting on the floor, upside down, behind the circular table with a mandolin and a fringed tablecloth. Only the bottom edge is visible (at top), but within this area the claw-like hand of the extended forearm is recognizable.

82 Braque's *Le Portugais* (see fig. 147) expands on the compositional structure of Picasso's *Mandolin Player* (see fig. 104), reproducing the triangular silhouette, the horizontal forearm, and the distinctive motif of cord-and-tassel (which migrated from left to right, multiplying in the process). As in the Beyeler Picasso, a dark trapezoidal form rises on the left side of the figure, creating a shadowy vacancy exactly where one might expect to find corporeal substance. The differences lie mainly in the narrative details: the musician grasps a guitar rather than a mandolin, and the café setting has been ornamented with stenciled letters announcing a "[GRAN]D BAL" and other events. The chronology of Braque's production is less certain than that of Picasso's. However, *Le Portugais* has been dated to spring 1911 by Henry Hope, Douglas Cooper, Jean Leymarie, and Edwin Mullins. This is supported by its place (no. 712) in the sequence of Kahnweiler's stockbook, after a group of spring 1911 works by Picasso but before Picasso's works of summer 1912.

Braque's so-called *Man with Guitar* (Romilly 99) seems to have been painted as a pendant to *Le Portugais*. It has almost exactly the same dimensions (116 × 81 cm); and the two works appear together in a photograph from Braque's studio (reproduced in Rubin, *Picasso and Braque: Pioneering Cubism*, p. 18). Kahnweiler photograph no. 1019 shows *Man with Guitar* but is labeled as "le joueur de mandoline." It seems to correspond to the work described in the stockbook (no. 757) as "le Mandoliniste," which, like *Le Portugais*, is bracketed by Picasso's production of spring and summer 1911. It should be said that the dimensions given for "le Mandoliniste" (46 × 38) do not correspond to those of "le joueur de mandoline" (116 × 81). However, the value assigned to the work in the stockbook (1,200 frs.) is identical to the value assigned *Le Portugais*, suggesting that the two works were in fact the same size. A smaller work would have been assigned a lower value.

Formally, *Man with Guitar* is quite different from *Le Portugais*. The body is dominated by a grid that resolves into a series of vertical strips, shaded and topped by curves so that they seem almost like a row of cylinders, standing side by side. On the right, the musician's fingers grasp the neck of the mandolin just below its inclined peg-board. On the left, the forearm descends at an angle, and terminates in a hand described by a single, elegantly curling plane. The figure is seated in a chair with a spiral armrest, visible at lower left. The organization of the body into vertical strips, the treatment of the arm and hand on the left, and the spiral of the armrest echo the distinctive features of Picasso's *Man with Mandolin* (see fig. 105) from the Musée Picasso (although the spiral armrest has been moved from right to left). To put it another way, the formal differences between Braque's *Man with Guitar* and *Le Portugais* reproduce the antinomy between Picasso's *Man with Mandolin* and his *Mandolin Player* (see fig. 104). Together, the two artists were exploring the range of styles possible within the general Cubist idiom of the grid.

83 Mila Gagarine, in the captions to Zervos XXVIII, 63 and 99, dates fig. 108 to 1912 and fig. 109 specifically to Sorgues, summer 1912. However, she dates Zervos XXVIII, 27 (see fig. 155), which shares the same structure of planes with fig. 108, and which is on the same size sheet, to Céret, summer 1911. Given the resemblance between fig. 108 and the summer 1911 painting *The Poet* (Peggy Guggenheim Collection, D.R. 423), it seems likely to me that all three drawings were done in summer 1911.

84 The sketch (fig. 111) appears in the summer 1912 notebook (Léal, vol. 1, cat. 16) that serves as the source for much of Picasso's work of summer and fall 1912. It is further discussed in Chapter 4, pp. 130–33 below.

85 Stein, *Appreciation*, p. 177.

86 Jacques Lassaigne, "Entretien avec Braque," in Gilberte Martin-Mery, Jacques Lassaigne, and Bernadette Contensou, *Les Cubistes*, exh. cat. (Bordeaux: Galerie des Beaux-Arts, and Paris: Musée d'Art Moderne de la Ville de Paris, 1973), pp. xvi–xvii.

87 Hofmann's stress on the importance of composing with superimposed planes is not well documented in the standard collection of his writings, *Search for the Real* (Andover: Addison Gallery of American Art, 1948; repr. Cambridge, Mass: MIT Press, 1967). It is discussed, however, in Cynthia Jennifer Goodman's 1982 dissertation, "The Hans Hofmann School and Hofmann's Transmission of European Modernist Aesthetics to America," pp. 72–79, and pl. 27. Furthermore, Hofmann's teaching diagrams, illustrating the use of superimposed planes, were published and discussed by his student, Sheldon Cheney, in *Expressionism in Art* (New York: Tudor, 1934; rev. ed. 1948), pp. 175–81.

88 Leo Stein, *Appreciation*, p. 186. Stein begins this passage by saying that, "In 1911 or 1912 Gertrude bought a cubist Picasso [*The Architect's Table* (D.R. 456)] . . . I have of course seen a lot of them." This seems to indicate that the following comments apply to work of the years 1911 and after.

89 Braque's fall 1913 work, e.g. *Woman with a Guitar* (Romilly 198), remains much closer to his work of 1910–11 than does Picasso's fall 1912 *Female Nude: "J'aime Éva"* (fig. 116).

90 Pierre Daix, *Picasso Créateur*, p. 143. In the Kahnweiler photo files (no. 361), the picture is described as "Femme en chemise dans un fauteuil," and it has traditionally been known as *Woman in a Chemise in an Armchair*. Since the woman is obviously not wearing the chemise, I have modified this to *Woman with Chemise in an Armchair*.

91 Paul Eluard, *A Pablo Picasso* (Geneva and Paris: Trois Collines, 1944), p. 36.

92 Kahnweiler, *Rise of Cubism*, pp. 11–12.

93 Benjamin H. D. Buchloh, "Figures of Authority, Ciphers of Regression: Notes on the Return of Representation in European Painting," in Benjamin H. D. Buchloh *et al*, eds., *Modernism and Modernity: The Vancouver Conference Papers* (Halifax: Press of the Nova Scotia College of Art and Design, 1983), pp. 86 and 84.

94 Rosalind Krauss, *The Picasso Papers* (New York: Farrar, Straus and Giroux, 1998), pp. 18, 96ff.

95 Daniel-Henry Kahnweiler, with Francis Crémieux, *My Galleries and Painters* (Paris: Gallimard, 1961; trans. Helen Weaver, New York: Viking, 1971), p. 54.

96 Stein, *Appreciation*, p. 188. Stein reported this conversation as taking place shortly after he had sold some of his Picassos to buy a Renoir, an event which seems to have occurred in 1913. Stein also said that he soon afterwards left Paris to live in Settignano; this move may have occurred in early 1914. See Stein, *Journey into the Self*, pp. 51 and 58.

97 Similarly, Pierre Daix, in D.R., p. 147, discusses "the confrontation of Cubist space and natural space" in Picasso's still lifes of spring 1914.

4 Signs

1 Raymond Cogniat, "Problème du jour: le cubisme et Picasso," *Arts*, no. 22, June 29, 1945, p. 1.

2 André Warnod, "En peinture tout n'est que signe, nous dit Picasso," ibid.; repr. in Marie-Laure Bernadac and Androula Michael, eds., *Picasso: propos sur l'art* (Paris: Gallimard, 1998), p. 53. Earlier, in a 1933 conversation with Kahnweiler, Picasso had remarked that the Surrealists "n'ont pas compris ce que j'entendais par 'surréalisme' quand j'ai inventé ce mot, qu'Apollinaire a ensuite imprimé: quelque chose de plus réel que la réalité." Kahnweiler, "Conversations avec Picasso," 1959; repr. in *Picasso: propos sur l'art*, p. 91. A similar remark appears in Brassaï, *Picasso & Company* (Garden City: Doubleday, 1966), p. 163.

3 Warnod, "En peinture," p. 1; repr. in *Picasso: propos sur l'art*, pp. 53–54.

4 Warnod, p. 4; repr. in *Picasso: propos sur l'art*, p. 56.

5 Kahnweiler, *Juan Gris* (Paris: Gallimard, 1946; trans. Douglas Cooper, New York: Curt Valentin, 1947; rev. ed. New York: Abrams, 1969), pp. 78–79. Realism, Kahnweiler argued on pp. 64–65, has never been a yardstick by which art could be judged. Indeed, the demand for "the identity of the graphic, plastic or vocal sign with the thing signified" is a kind of atavism, a hold-over from a primitive belief in the "magical" power of the sign.

6 Kahnweiler, *Gris*, pp. 79–80. Sooner or later, Kahnweiler suggested, the waning influence of the Academy would cause the blinders to drop from the public's eyes; at that point, modern art would seem as natural and realistic as any style that preceded it. The passage of time has not confirmed this prediction.

7 Kahnweiler, *Les Sculptures de Picasso* (Paris: Editions du Chêne, 1948), n.p. See p. 19 above.

8 Françoise Gilot and Carleton Lake, *Life with Picasso* (New York: McGraw-Hill, 1964), p. 221.

9 John Golding, *Cubism: A History and an Analysis, 1907–1914* (1959), rev. 3rd ed. (Cambridge, Mass.: Harvard University Press, 1988), pp. 128–31.

10 Robert Rosenblum, *Cubism and Twentieth-Century Art* (New York: Abrams, 1960), p. 66. Two later articles by Rosenblum, "Picaso and the Coronation of Alexander III: A note on the dating of some papiers collés," *Burlington Magazine*, vol. 113, no. 823, October 1971, pp. 604–07, and "Picasso and the Typography of Cubism," in Roland Penrose and John Golding, eds., *Picasso in Retrospect* (New York: Praeger, 1973), pp. 49–75, also provided an impetus to the semiological reading of Cubism.

11 William Rubin, *Picasso in the Collection of The Museum of Modern Art* (New York: Museum of Modern Art, 1972), p. 84.

12 Ironically, Lévi-Strauss himself wrote a brief article discussing Cubism, not as a linguistic system, but as an art of memory and association. See Chapter 1, n. 100 above.

13 Ferdinand de Saussure, "Phonological Species," chapter 1, *Course in General Linguistics* (1915), trans. Wade Baskin (New York: Philosophical Library, 1959; repr. New York: McGraw-Hill, 1966), pp. 38–49.

14 Saussure, "Linguistic Value," parts i and ii, ibid., pp. 111–17. On the other hand, the English word "lamb" is used, like the French "*mouton*," to signify both the animal and the meat derived from it.

15 On the arbitrariness of the sign, see Saussure, "Nature of the Linguistic Sign," ibid., p. 67. Later, however, discussing "Absolute and Relative Arbitrariness," p. 133, Saussure wrote: "Everything that relates to language as a system must, I am convinced, be approached from this viewpoint, which has scarcely received the attention of linguists: the limiting of arbitrariness."

16 Saussure, "Linguistic Value from a Conceptual Viewpoint," ibid., p. 118: "Since one vocal image is no better suited than the next for what it is commissioned to express, it is evident, even *a priori*, that a segment of language can never in the final analysis be based on anything except its noncoincidence with the rest. *Arbitrary* and *differential* are two correlative qualities."

17 Saussure, "The Sign Considered in Its Totality," ibid., p. 120.

18 Saussure, "Linguistic Value from a Material Viewpoint," ibid., p. 119.

19 Saussure, "The Vocal Apparatus and Its Functioning," ibid., pp. 42–44. Saussure points to another instance of this kind of distinctively unmarked feature on p. 86, where he notes that certain Czech words such as woman (*ena*) take a genitive plural (*-en*) distinguished by the *absence* of the usual suffixes *a, u, y*, etc. However, this "purely negative" marking can be perceived only by contrast to its "positive" alternatives.

20 Saussure, "Syntagmatic and Associative Relations," ibid., pp. 122–27, esp. p. 123.

21 Saussure, "Linguistic Value from a Conceptual Viewpoint," ibid., pp. 114–15.

22 Roland Barthes, "The Death of the Author," originally published in English in *Aspen* no. 5/6, fall–winter 1967; repr. in French in *Mantéia*, 5, 1968; retrans. in Roland Barthes, *Image/Music/Text* (New York: Hill and Wang, 1977), pp. 143 and 146.

23 Barthes, "Death of the Author," pp. 146–47.

24 Harold Bloom, *The Anxiety of Influence: A Theory of Poetry* (London: Oxford University Press, 1973).

25 Pierre Dufour, "Actualité du cubisme," *Critique* (Paris), nos. 267–68, August–September 1969, pp. 814, 815, 818.

26 Ibid., p. 815. It was clear to Dufour that the originality and materiality of the Cubist sign made it different from the conventional, immaterial sign of Saussurean semiology. This distinction was largely forgotten in the writings of later critics. Dufour's skepticism about structuralism is evident in his introduction to *Picasso, 1950–1968* (Geneva: Skira, 1969), p. 17, where he complains about "the pressure brought to bear at present by the fashion for linguistics in favor of the assimilation of art to a 'language.'" Citing Picasso's statement to François Gilot that, "A painting is a sign – just like the sign that indicates a one-way street," Dufour observes: "When we compare Cubist signs with those of the highway code or even with those of the ancient code of heraldry, we are struck by the obvious indigence of utilitarian signs. Cubist signs too are poor compared with the images of traditional painting, but they are amazingly rich in comparison with non-aesthetic signs . . . the fashion for linguistics . . . can do nothing to diminish this discrepancy."

27 Jean Laude, "Picasso et Braque, 1910–1914: la transformation des signes," in *Le Cubisme* (Centre Interdisciplinaire d'Études et de Recherche sur L'Expression Contemporaine, Université de Saint-Etienne, 1973), p. 24.

28 Ibid., p. 18.

29 Ibid., p. 21.

30 Ibid., pp. 13–14.

31 Françoise Will-Levaillant, "La Lettre dans la peinture cubiste," in *Le Cubisme* (Saint-Etienne), pp. 47 and 51.

32 Regarding Mallarmé and absence, see n. 125 below.

33 See the quotations from Rosenblum in D.R., pp. 93 and 123. Daix's awareness of what might be called the "Anglo-Saxon" approach to the sign is also apparent in his citation, on p. 132, of Rubin's comments on the role of the pre-existing sign in Synthetic Cubism; see Rubin, *Picasso in the Collection*, p. 84.

34 D.R., p. 123. The phrase "Manet's pictorial silence" is an allusion to George Bataille's discussion of Manet's *Olympia*: "The meaning of the picture is not in the text behind it but in the obliteration of that text. . . . [Olympia's] real nudity (not merely that of her body) is the silence that emanates from her, like that from a sunken ship. All we have is the 'sacred horror' of her presence – presence whose sheer simplicity is tantamount to absence." Georges Bataille, *Manet* (1955), (trans. Austryn Wainhouse and James Emmons, New York: Rizzoli, 1983), p. 62.

35 D.R., p. 113.

36 Ibid., pp. 116–18. The translation in the U.S. ed. of D.R. reads: "the shape of the guitar," but I have changed "shape" to "space" in order to reflect the original French, which says "La définition de l'espace de la guitare."

37 See Edward Fry, "Pierre Daix and Joan Rosselet, *Picasso: The Cubist Years 1907–1916*," *Art Journal*, vol. 41, no. 1, spring 1981, pp. 91–99; for a survey of new approaches, see the special Picasso issue of *Art in America*, vol. 68, no. 10, December 1980.

38 In "Re-Presenting Picasso," *Art in America*, vol. 68, no. 10, December 1980, p. 94, Krauss praises Daix for initiating a semiological reading of Cubism (she seems to be unaware of the earlier semiological readings by Laude and Will-Levaillant). However, in "In the Name of Picasso," *October* no. 16, spring 1981; repr. in Rosalind E. Krauss, *The Originality of the Avant-Garde and Other Modernist Myths* (Cambridge, Mass.: MIT

Press, 1985), p. 32, she criticizes him for not giving "a rigorous presentation of the concept of the sign."

39 Krauss, "Re-Presenting Picasso," pp. 93–94.

40 Saussure, *Course*, pp. 45–49.

41 Krauss, "In the Name of Picasso," pp. 34–35.

42 Ibid., pp. 35–37.

43 Saussure, "Absolute and Relative Arbitrariness," *Course*, p. 133.

44 Krauss, "In the Name of Picasso," p. 33.

45 Ibid.

46 Gilot and Lake, *Life with Picasso*, pp. 59–60 and 118.

47 Krauss, "In the Name of Picasso," p. 39.

48 See Rubin's discussion of the deliberate "depersonalization of the act of painting" in *Picasso and Braque: Pioneering Cubism*, exh. cat. (New York: Museum of Modern Art, 1989), pp. 19–20.

49 D.R., p. 132; Rubin, *Picasso in the Collection*, p. 84.

50 Kahnweiter, *Gris*, p. 125.

51 D.R., p. 132.

52 Yve-Alain Bois, "Kahnweiler's Lesson" was first published in English in *Representations*, no. 18, spring 1987; an enlarged version appeared in French in *Cahiers du Musée national d'art moderne*, no. 23, spring 1988; this version, trans. into English, was published in Yve-Alain Bois, *Painting as Model* (Cambridge, Mass.: MIT Press, 1990), pp. 65–97. Bois's essay, "The Semiology of Cubism," was first delivered as a paper in fall 1989, at the symposium organized in connection with the exhibition "Picasso and Braque: Pioneering Cubism"; the essay was published in William Rubin *et al*, eds., *Picasso and Braque: A Symposium* (New York: Museum of Modern Art, 1992), pp. 169–208.

53 Bois, "Kahnweiler's Lesson," pp. 86–90, and 94–95.

54 Bois, "Semiology of Cubism," p. 174.

55 See ibid., pp. 174–75 and 188, for "metaphorical displacement" and "polysemy," respectively.

56 Ibid., pp. 175–76.

57 Charles Sanders Peirce, "Icon, Index, and Symbol," Part 3 of "Logic as Semiotic: The Theory of Signs," in *The Philosophy of Peirce: Selected Writings*, ed. Justus Buchler (London: Routledge and Kegan Paul, 1940), repr. as *Philosophical Writings of Peirce* (New York: Dover, n.d.), pp. 104–15.

58 Charles Sanders Peirce, "On the Nature of Signs," 1873, in *Peirce on Signs: Writings on Semiotic by Charles Sanders Peirce*, ed. James Hoopes (Chapel Hill: University of North Carolina Press, 1991), pp. 116–43. This was written as a review of a new edition of the works of George Berkeley. As Peirce's comments suggest, a serious history of the idea of the arbitrary sign would have to take into account its links with the scholastic debate between nominalism and realism, and with the later British empiricist tradition. Indeed, Hume's theory of the association of ideas provides the model for Peirce's categories of icon, index, and symbol. As Peirce writes in "Some Consequences of Four Incapacities," 1868, repr. in *Peirce on Signs*, p. 80: "The association of ideas is said to proceed according to three principles – those of resemblance, of contiguity, and of causality. But it would be equally true to say that signs denote what they do on the three principles of resemblance, contiguity, and casuality." Evidently, resemblance is the underlying principle of the "icon," causality of the "index," and contiguity of the "symbol."

59 Bois, "Semiology of Cubism," p. 175. Besides associating the iconic sign with 1908–12 Cubism, Bois deploys the Peircian concept of the index to characterize the lattice or grid as a kind of sign of the pictorial field as a whole (pp. 180–81, no. 34, and no. 46). This seems to me a misuse of the term. Insofar as the grid parallels or resembles the pictorial field, it is a special kind of icon (a "diagram," as Bois himself says in no. 34). Insofar as it constitutes a syntactic convention, it might be described as a conventional "symbol." However, since there is no causal relationship between the picture surface and the grid inscribed, it cannot be described as an index.

60 Ibid., p. 187. Similarly, on p. 175, Bois writes: "For five years, from 1907 to 1912, Picasso has been exploring the elasticity of iconicity . . . But the artist arrived at the conclusion, in the fall of 1912, that the signified (meaning) of a sign is not entirely subsumed by its referentiality, hence his departure from a strictly iconic system to a symbolic one (in Peircian terminology) or to a semiological one (in Saussurian terms)."

61 Ibid., p. 173.

62 Ibid., p. 187.

63 Ibid., p. 176.

64 Ibid., p. 190.

65 Ibid., p. 175. Similarly, on p. 187, Bois writes: "Picasso's new system is almost entirely realized in his first proper *papier collé, Guitar, Sheet Music, and Glass* . . . What is at stake is . . . the search for greater differentiation of formal marks."

66 Ibid., pp. 173–74.

67 "Discussion," *Picasso and Braque: A Symposium*, p. 215.

68 Bois, "Semiology of Cubism," p. 175. See also p. 177.

69 Ibid., p. 188.

70 As Bois writes, in ibid., p. 174: "Signs are eminently contextual. Their meaning and function are determined not only by a relationship *in absentia* with all the other possible signs of the system to which they belong, but by their relationship *in praesentia* with their direct surroundings." Evidently, Bois is paraphrasing Saussure's statement: "The syntagmatic relation is *in praesentia*. It is based on two or more terms that occur in an effective series. Against this, the associative relation unites terms *in absentia* in a potential mnemonic series." Saussure, "Syntagmatic and Associative Relations," *Course*, p. 123.

71 See *Bread and Fruit Dish on Table*, winter 1908–09 (D.R. 220).

72 Bois, "Elements of Semiology," p. 188. What Bois actually says here is that the "black section of a circle . . . will return later in other works as the sign for the drop leaf of a table." He seems to be thinking of the wall construction documented in a photograph taken in Picasso's Boulevard Raspail studio in early 1913 (reproduced in Rubin, *Picasso and Braque*, p. 279, but mistakenly captioned "rue Schoelcher"). I have substituted the 1908–09 *Bread and Fruit Dish on Table* because it provides an earlier and clearer example.

73 Note from one of Saussure's lectures, quoted by René Amacker,

"Sur la notion de 'valeur,'" *Studi saussuriani per Robert Godel* (Bologna: Il Mulino, 1972), p. 15; cited in Bois, "Semiology of Cubism," p. 174, and in "Kahnweiler's Lesson," p. 88.

74 Bois, "Semiology of Cubism," p. 174.

75 F. Max Müller, *Three Introductory Lectures on the Science of Thought*, 1887 (Chicago: Open Court, 1888); hereafter *Science of Thought*. These offer a popularized summary of his longer *Lectures on the Science of Language*, first delivered in 1861–63 and published in 1869.

76 Hippolyte Taine, *On Intelligence* (Paris, 1870; trans. New York: Henry Holt, 1875; repr. New York: University Publications of America, 1977). Discussing the influence of *De l'Intelligence*, Hans Aarsleff notes that it had gone into nine editions by 1900; at that time, 12,000 copies were in print. See Hans Aarsleff, "Taine and Saussure," in *From Locke to Saussure: Essays on the Study of Language and Intellectual History* (Minneapolis: University of Minnesota Press), 1982, p. 364; I am grateful to Molly Nesbit for bringing this essay to my attention.

77 Taine, *On Intelligence*, vol. 1, pp. 15–17.

78 Ibid., p. 18.

79 Ibid., pp. 10–12. Taine's emphasis on the role of literal mimicry in the process of *mimesis* seems to reflect the influence of Auguste Comte, who wrote in the section on "Human Language," in *System of Positive Polity, or Treatise on Sociology* (Paris, 1852; trans. London, 1875; repr. New York: Burt Franklin, n.d.), vol. 2, pp. 190–91, 194, 197: "The cerebral organ of language can only employ two systems of external signs; the one addressed to the sense of sight, the other to that of hearing . . . it gives rise to the two fundamental arts: the mimic [which Comte identifies as sculpture and painting], and the musical. . . . The language addressed to the Eye, which at first was in use, ends by being a mere auxiliary of the language of the Ear . . . [However,] the language of the Ear . . . is naturally even more evanescent [than the language of the eye] . . . It is therefore forced . . . to borrow this indispensable instrument [picture-making] for fixing its signs."

80 Taine, *On Intelligence*, vol. 1, pp. 10–12.

81 Ibid., pp. 4–5.

82 Hippolyte Taine, *The Philosophy of Art*, 1864 (trans. as *Lectures on Art*, 1865; rev. 1875; repr. New York: AMS, 1971), vol. 2, pp. 61–63.

83 William Dwight Whitney, *The Life and Growth of Language: An Outline of Linguistic Science* (New York: D. Appleton, 1875; repr. New York: Dover, 1979), pp. 12, 27.

84 Arsène Darmesteter, *La Vie des mots etudiés dans leur significations*, 3rd ed. (Paris: Delagrave, 1889), pp. 5–6.

85 Michel Bréal, *Semantics: Studies in the Science of Meaning*, 1897 (trans. 1900, repr. New York: Dover, 1964), p. 243.

86 Müller, *Science of Thought*, pp. 32–33.

87 "If there is no such thing as a mere name, neither is there such a thing as a mere thought or a mere concept. The two are one and inseparable. We may distinguish them as we distinguish the obverse from the reverse of a coin; but to try to separate them would be like trying to separate the convex from the concave surface of a lens." Ibid., p. 50.

88 Ibid., p. iv.

89 William Dwight Whitney, *Max Müller and the Science of Language: A Criticism* (New York: D. Appleton, 1892), pp. 36–37.

90 Bréal, *Semantics*, p. 176.

91 In his *Semantics*, pp. 172–73, Bréal pointed out that the debate over the nature of language and the sign began in the *Cratylus* of Plato: "Socrates alternately supports either of two opinions: first, that there exists for each thing a name by nature belonging to it; next that the propriety of a name is wholly dependent on the consent of men. This discussion lasted as long as there were schools of grammar in Greece and Rome."

92 Whitney, *Life and Growth of Language*, pp. 38 and 74–75. See the similar explanation in Darmesteter, *La Vie des mots*, pp. 9–10.

93 Darmesteter, *La Vie des mots*, pp. 40–41. Darmesteter's discussion expands on the point made by Whitney, *Life and Growth of Language*, pp. 82–83.

94 Darmesteter, *La Vie des mots*, pp. 42–43.

95 Bréal, *Semantics*, pp. 171–72.

96 Ibid., pp. 146–47.

97 Darmester, *La Vie des mots*, p. 31.

98 Ibid., p. 46. Whitney, *Life and Growth of Language*, p. 111, noted in general terms that "the particular mode of transfer by which new expression is most abundantly won is the figurative," and gave numerous examples; however, he did not distinguish among different mechanisms of figuration.

99 Darmesteter, *La Vie des mots*, pp. 46 and 57.

100 Ibid., p. 49.

101 Ibid., p. 63.

102 Ibid., pp. 76–77.

103 Ibid., pp. 63–64. Darmesteter gave as an example the French idiom, "une feuille [leaf] de papier"; I have adapted this to its English counterpart, "a sheet of paper." Whitney made a similar point in the *Life and Growth of Language*, p. 87: "It is an important item in this process of transfer [of meaning] that we gradually lose our sense of the figure implied, and come to employ each sign as if it had always been the simple and downright representative of its idea."

104 Darmesteter, *La Vie des mots*, pp. 163–64.

105 Whitney, *Life and Growth of Language*, p. 87.

106 Ibid., p. 110.

107 Bréal, "The History of Words" (review of Darmesteter, *La Vie des mots*), 1887, repr. in *Semantics*, p. 282.

108 Bréal, *Semantics*, p. 30.

109 Saussure, *Course*, pp. 1–5, and 76. In *Life and Growth of Language*, p. 19, Whitney stated: "every word handed down in every human language is an arbitrary and conventional sign."

110 Compare Whitney, *Life and Growth of Language*, p. 67, with Saussure, *Course*, pp. 41–64. Of course, both writers are drawing on a long tradition of phonological analysis.

111 Aarsleff, "Taine and Saussure," p. 359.

112 Saussure, "Static and Evolutionary Linguistics," *Course*, pp. 79–85. Compare Saussure's emphasis on the importance of synchronic relations to Bréal's argument that "The actual and

present value of a word exercises such a power over the mind that it deprives us of all feeling for the etymological signification." Bréal, *Semantics*, p. 176.

113 Hippolyte Taine, 1866 preface to his *Essais de critique et d'histoire*, 12th ed. (Paris: Hachette, 1913), p. xviii; cited in Aarsleff, "Taine and Saussure," p. 362.

114 Saussure, "Linguistic Value," *Course*, pp. 114–15.

115 Whitney, *Life and Growth of Language*, p. 143.

116 Saussure, "Linguistic Value," *Course*, p. 114.

117 Bréal, "Chapter II: The Law of Differentiation," in *Semantics*, pp. 27–38.

118 Saussure, "Linguistic Value," *Course*, p. 118: see n. 16 above.

119 Bréal, *Semantics*, pp. 140–45.

120 Roman Jakobson, "Two Types of Language and Two Types of Aphasic Disturbances," in Roman Jakobson and Morris Halle, *Fundamentals of Language* (The Hague: Mouton, 1956), pp. 55–82. Jakobson's use of "metaphor" and "metonymy" corresponds closely to the mental mechanisms that Freud called "condensation" and "displacement."

121 Taine, *On Intelligence*, vol. 2, pp. 69 and 74.

122 See Chapter 1, pp. 4–5.

123 G.-Albert Aurier, "Symbolism in Painting: Paul Gauguin," *Mercure de France*, 2 (1891), trans. in Herschel B. Chipp, ed., *Theories of Modern Art: A Source Book* (Berkeley: University of California Press, 1968), pp. 90–92.

124 Laugel, *L'Optique et les arts* (Paris: Germe et Baillière, 1869), p. 32.

125 Mallarmé, "Vide, variations sur un sujet," in *Oeuvres complètes de Mallarmé* (Paris: N.R.F. Pléiade, 1945), p. 185: "Je dis: une fleur! Et, hors de l'oubli où ma voix relègue aucun contour, en tant que quelque chose d'autre que les calices sus, musicalement se lève, idée même et suave, l'absente de tous bouquets . . ." Cited in Kahnweiler, *Gris*, p. 128.

126 Maurice Denis, "A Definition of Neo-Traditionism," *Art et critique*, August 1890; trans. in Linda Nochlin, ed., *Impressionism and Post-Impressionism, 1874–1904: Sources and Documents* (Englewood Cliffs: Prentice-Hall, 1966), p. 187–88. Denis's argument here echoes the famous passages in Pascal's *Pensées* where the seventeenth-century philosopher argues that "Custom is our nature . . . Custom is a second nature, which destroys our first. But what is this nature? Why should not custom be natural? I fear that nature itself is nothing but an initial custom." Pascal, *Pensées*, nos. 89, 93.

127 Aurier, "Symbolism in Painting," pp. 90–92.

128 Paul Gauguin, *Avant et Après*, 1903; trans. 1952; repr. in Nochlin, *Impressionism and Post-Impressionism*, p. 167.

129 Emile Bernard, *Souvenirs inédits sur l'artiste peintre Paul Gauguin et ses compagnons*, 1939; cited in Hendrik Roelof Rookmaaker, *Synthetist Art Theories: Notes in Letters*; cited in Nochin, *Impressionism and Post-Impressionism*, p. 151, no. 34. Even Signac (more a disciple of Seurat than of Gauguin) noted that "the scenery I created from memory proves to be much closer to the subject than that in the watercolor which I bring back from a sitting on the spot." See John Rewald, ed., "Excerpts from the Unpublished Diary of Paul Signac: III (1898–1899)," *Gazette des Beaux-Arts*, 42, July–August, 1953, pp. 72–80; trans. in Nochlin, *Impressionism and Post-Impressionism*, p. 132.

130 Lucien Arréat, preface to Georges Hirth, *Physiologie de l'art* (trans. Arréat, Paris: Alcan, 1892), pp. ii and v. Taine, in *On Intelligence*, vol. 1, pp. 224–25, places an even heavier emphasis on the role of memory, arguing that by far the largest share of perceptual experience consists of remembered images. As he puts it, "external perception is an internal dream which proves to be in harmony with external things" – or, even more dramatically, "external perception is a true hallucination."

131 E.g. Emanuel Löwy in his influential *The Rendering of Nature in Early Greek Art* argued that the profile view was typical of archaic Greek art because it most clearly captured the essential character of a motif, and this is what memory retained. An insistence on strict profile offered a way to show the parts of the body in their natural dimensions, as the mind remembers them, instead of subjecting them to the perspectival distortions of vision. The "memory-picture" of an object is equivalent, Löwy writes, to its Platonic idea; and "the graphic expression of this would be a scheme of lines and planes approaching as nearly as possible simple geometric forms." Emanuel Löwy, *Die Naturwiedergabe in der älteren griechischen Kunst* (Rome, 1900); trans. as *The Rendering of Nature in Early Greek Art* (London: Duckworth, 1907), p. 10.

This argument appeared in the scientific literature as early as 1867, when the philosopher Ernst Mach wrote that perspective was not a natural mode of representation but an intellectual system of denotation; to children and members of non-Western cultures, who had not been schooled in the system, perspectival pictures seemed violently distorted. See Ernst Mach, "Why Has Man Two Eyes?," 1867, trans. in Ernst Mach, *Popular Scientific Lectures* (Chicago: Open Court, 1898), pp. 76–79 (the original publication date of the lecture is given in the translator's note to the 3rd ed., p. vii). A similar discussion of this point appears in Mach's later but better-known *The Analysis of Sensations, and the Relation of the Physical to the Psychical* (trans. Chicago and London: Open Court, 1914), p. 232.

132 See Chapter 1, p. 8 above.

133 Saussure, "The Object of Linguistics," *Course*, pp. 14–15, 17–18.

134 Albert Gleizes and Jean Metzinger, "On Cubism," 1912; trans. in Robert Herbert, ed., *Modern Artists on Art: Ten Unabridged Essays* (Englewood Cliffs: Prentice-Hall, 1964), p. 15.

135 On the Symbolist concept of the pictorial sign, see Chapter 1, pp. 6–7 above.

136 Waldemar George, "Juan Gris," *L'Amour de l'art*, November 1921, p. 351; cited in Christopher Green, *Juan Gris* (London and New Haven: Whitechapel Art Gallery, in association with Yale University Press, 1992), p. 84.

137 Léon Werth, *Quelques Peintres* (Paris: G. Crès, 1923), p. 205.

138 Green, *Gris*, pp. 83–87.

139 According to the author's preface (p. 4), the manuscript of Joseph Vendryes's *Le Langage, introduction historique à l'histoire*, was completed in 1914, but because of the eruption of war the

book was published only in 1921, as vol. 3 in a comprehensive series on *L'Evolution de la humanité.* It was rapidly translated into English, appearing as *Language: A Linguistic Introduction to History* (London: Routledge & Kegan Paul, 1925); all references here are to the English edition. Vendryes's discussion of phonetics, pp. 17–70, is particularly close to the corresponding section of Saussure's *Course*, pp. 32–64; in a note on p. 54, Vendryes praises Saussure's discussion of phonetics, but notes that his own text had been completed before the 1916 publication of the *Course*.

140 On pp. 194–95 of *Language* Vendryes writes that: "The etymology of isolated words is of no interest in itself . . . The defect of Darmesteter's book is that it inculcates a belief in a sort of internal logic which governs the semantic transformation of words." This is mistaken, Vendryes says, because, "words are not arranged in the mind as isolated entities." In other words, language must be understood as a system. Earlier, on pp. 176–77, he restates Whitney's formalist position: "Words are not used according to their historical value . . . words always have a *current* value." Vendryes here cites Charles Bally's *Précis de stylistique* (Geneva, 1905), pp. 21 and 47; it seems likely that Bally also provided a source for Saussure's concept of "synchronic" analysis.

141 See Vendryes, *Language*, pp. 315–43. See the related passages in Kahnweiler, *Gris*, pp. 68–74; Kahnweiler's discussion here is also indebted to Granet's *La Pensée chinoise* (Paris, 1934), vol. 25 in *L'Evolution de l'humanité.*

142 See the chapter "La Figuration de la pensée," in Jacques de Morgan, *L'Humanité préhistorique: esquisse de préhistoire générale* (Paris, 1921), vol. 2 in *L'Evolution de l'humanité*, pp. 271–83. Although the intellectual framework of Morgan's discussion is less comprehensive than Vendryes's, he provides numerous illustrations of hieroglyphic symbols on the border between figuration and convention; these may have influenced Joan Miró and the Surrealists. On this topic, see Sidra Stich, *Joan Miró: The Development of a Sign Language*, exh. cat. (Saint Louis: Washington University Gallery of Art, 1980), and Christopher Green, "The Infant in the Adult: Joan Miró and the Infantile Image," in Jonathan Fineberg, ed., *Discovering Child Art: Essays on Childhood, Primitivism, and Modernism* (Princeton University Press, 1998), pp. 210–34.

143 Maurice Raynal, "Juan Gris," *Feuilles libres*, no. 31, April 1923, cited in Green, *Gris*, p. 63, n. 61. As Green notes, this review was reprinted in modified form in Raynal's survey *Anthologie de la peinture en France de 1906 à nos jours* (Paris: Montaigne, 1927); trans. as *Modern French Painters* (New York: Brentanos, 1928), pp. 93–100. The discussion of "plastic metaphor" appears on pp. 96–97. As Green notes, p. 63, Raynal's idea of "confrontation" derives in part from Pierre Reverdy's influential essay on "The Image," in *Nord-Sud*, no. 13, March 1918, which emphasized the poetic importance of "analogy," arguing that a powerful image can result only from the "comparison of two distant realities, whose relationship is grasped only by the spirit." Read in isolation, Reverdy's essay seems to refer solely to poetry, but it was published in conjunction with two drawings by Braque, suggesting that it applied to modern art as well. (The Braque drawings were the first illustrations to appear in *Nord-Sud*, which switched to a larger format, beginning with the March 1918 issue, in order to accommodate the visual arts. See Etienne-Alain Hubert's notes to the reprint edition of *Nord-Sud*, published in 1980 by Jean-Michel Place.)

144 Raynal, "Gris," in *Modern French Painters*, p. 97.

145 Compare Darmesteter, *La Vie des mots*, pp. 66–67. In the original French, both Darmesteter and Raynal (*Anthologie de la peinture*, p. 176) refer to a "feuille" rather than a "sheet" of paper. The same point about the forgetting of underlying metaphors appears in Vendryes, *Language*, pp. 178–79, but without the example of the "sheet" of paper and without the invocation of the rhetorical trope of catachresis (although this term appears in another context on p. 200).

146 See Henri Focillon, *La Vie des formes* (Paris: Presses Universitaires de France, 1934); trans. as *The Life of Forms in Art* (New York: Zone Books, 1989), p. 40, where Focillon takes Darmesteter's linguistic argument as a model for his discussion of the evolution of forms in art. Focillon in turn provided the conceptual model for George Kubler's *The Shape of Time: Remarks on the History of Things* (New Haven: Yale University Press, 1962), so that it might be said that Darmesteter's influence crossed the ocean and persisted into the 1960s.

147 Bois, "Semiology of Cubism," pp. 180–81, citing D.R. p. 68.

148 Kahnweiler, *The Rise of Cubism* (New York: Wittenborn, Schulz, 1949), p. 12.

149 Gilot, *Life with Picasso*, pp. 59–60, discussed in Chapter 3, p. 68 above.

150 Ibid., p. 118.

151 Gleizes and Metzinger, "On Cubism," p. 9. The widespread currency of Gleizes and Metzinger's remark about curves and straight lines may be judged by its reappearance, twenty-five years later, in a list of modern esthetic discoveries compiled by the German Expressionist Gottfried Benn: "Deciphering of the Assyrian clay cylinders; new excavations at Babylon, Ur, Samara; the first coherent presentation of Egyptian sculpture – an analysis of composition methods in the reliefs leads to the surprising perception that they correspond exactly to the theories of Cubism: 'the art of drawing consists in establishing relationships between curves and straight lines.'" Gottfried Benn, "Art and the Third Reich," in E. B. Ashton, ed., *Primal Vision: Selected Writings of Gottfried Benn* (New York: New Directions, 1971), p. 90.

152 Mondrian spent the years 1912–13 in Paris, where he showed with Gleizes and Metzinger in the Salon des Indépendants of spring 1912.

153 Malevich's three-part series of etchings, "Construction of Axes of a Model," published in Malevich's 1919 book, *On New Systems of Art*, seems to be based on Picasso's "Mlle Léonie" etchings of 1910; and many of the etchings illustrating his 1927 book, *The Non-Objective World*, are literal redrawings of Cubist pictures by Picasso and Braque.

154 Kahnweiler, *Rise of Cubism*, p. 14.

155 Fernande Olivier, *Picasso and His Friends* (1933; trans. Jane Miller, New York: Appleton-Century, 1965), p 175.

156 This interpretation seems first to have been elucidated in Rosenblum, *Cubism and Twentieth-Century Art*, pp. 57–58.

157 The imitation of printed lettering was not in itself an innovation. Cézanne had reproduced printed lettering in his 1866 portrait of his father reading the newspaper *L'Evénement*.

158 Rosenblum, *Cubism and Twentieth Century Art*, p. 57.

159 Kahnweiler, *Rise of Cubism*, pp. 11–12.

160 Adam Gopnik and Kirk Varnedoe, "Caricature," in *High and Low: Modern Art and Popular Culture*, exh. cat. (New York: Museum of Modern Art, 1990), p. 123. A note on p. 4 identifies Gopnik as the principal author of "Caricature." Gopnik supports his point with a 1905 sheet containing multiple caricatures. I have taken the liberty of substituting fig. 156, a version of which appears on the sheet reproduced by Gopnik, because it relates more directly to my subsequent argument.

161 Adam Gopnik, "High and Low: Caricature, Primitivism, and the Cubist Portrait," *Art Journal*, vol. 43, no. 4, winter 1983, p. 126; cited in William Rubin, "Picasso," in William Rubin, ed., *"Primitivism" in 20th Century Art: Affinity of the Tribal and the Modern*, exh. cat. (New York: Museum of Modern Art, 1984), vol. 1, p. 285.

162 Félix Fénéon quoted in Roland Penrose, *Picasso: His Life and Work* (London: Victor Gollancz, 1958), p. 126.

163 Gopnik, "Caricature," in *High and Low*, p. 133.

164 Amedeo Modigliani, *Study for the Portrait of Frank Burty-Haviland*, 1914, reproduced in Emily Braun, ed., *Italian Art in the 20th Century: Painting and Sculpture, 1900–1988*, exh. cat. (Munich: Prestel and London: Royal Academy of Arts, 1989), no. 59. Manolo Hugué, *Portrait of the Painter Frank Burty Haviland*, 1908–09, reproduced in *Manolo Hugué*, exh. cat. (Barcelona: Museu d'art modern, 1990), no. 4. Haviland's distinctive features and hairstyle (parted in the middle) suggest that an otherwise untitled *Head* by Jacques Lipchitz, sculpted in 1914, is also a portrait of him; see *Jacques Lipchitz: The Paris Years*, exh. cat. (New York: Marlborough Gallery, 1996), no. 4.

165 The drawings labeled "Study for a Portrait of Frank Haviland" are reproduced in Zervos XXVIII, 28 (fig. 162), 176, and 178. Presumably Mila Gagarine, the editor of this volume, gave them that title because the drawings (or the photographs of them) were inscribed in this fashion. Of the five related drawings, two are reproduced in Zervos VI, 1147 and 1161 (fig. 163), and two more in Zervos XXVIII, 154 (fig. 164) and 168 (fig. 161); the fifth is recorded in the files of the Picasso estate (neg. no. 1148–322).

166 Picasso, *Shells on a Piano*, completed spring 1912, now in the Yale Art Gallery. (It is listed as "present collection unknown" in the entry in D.R. 461.)

167 See Jean Loize, "Frank Burty," *Reflets du Roussillon*, vol. 13, no. 53, spring 1966, pp. 4–5.

168 Olivier, *Picasso and His Friends*, p. 135. A photograph of Max Jacob seated at this piano permits its identification as a Gaveau, with its distinctive scrolled candelabra. A print of this photograph is reproduced in *Max Jacob et Picasso*, exh. cat. (Quimper: Musée des Beaux-Arts, and Paris: Musée Picasso, 1994), cat. 101, p. 75, where the caption states that Jacob is seated at his family's piano in Quimper. However, the archives of the Musée Picasso include what appears to be the original of this photograph (catalogued as neg. no. 90 DN 12.100), suggesting that it was taken by Picasso, probably in the Boulevard Clichy apartment where he moved in 1909. Olivier, in *Picasso and His Friends*, p. 135, describes their "little drawing room, with a sofa, a piano, and a pretty Italian cabinet . . ."

169 Patrick O'Brian, *Picasso* (New York: Putnam's, 1976), p. 184, seems to have been the first to observe that the so-called clarinet of Picasso's Céret paintings was really a *tenora*. Lewis Kachur, "Themes in Picasso's Cubism," Ph.D. diss., Columbia University, 1988, pp. 244–49, linked the imagery of the *tenora* to Picasso's friendship with Déodat de Séverac, mentioned in Olivier, *Picasso and His Friends*, p. 134. See also Blanche Selva, *Déodat de Séverac* (Paris: Delagrave, 1930) and *Déodat de Séverac*, exh. cat. (Céret: Musée d'Art Moderne, 1972); I am grateful to Claudine Caritg of the Musée d'Art Moderne de Céret for providing me with a copy of the 1972 catalogue. On the symbolism of Picasso's Céret pictures more generally, see Pepe Karmel, "Mémoire et désir: Picasso à Céret, 1911–1913," in Joséphine Matamoros, ed., *Picasso: dessins et papiers collés – Céret 1911–1913* (Céret: Musée d'Art Moderne de Céret, 1997), pp. 10–21.

170 See David Douglas Duncan, *Picasso Paints a Portrait* (New York: Abrams, 1996), which records the creation of the *Portrait of Jacqueline*, painted on July 1, 1957. As the photograph on pp. 22–23 makes clear, Picasso began not by looking at his model but by copying a previously created painted sculpture. He arrived at a new image by repeating and then modifying this earlier composition.

171 The spring 1911 date of this photograph can be established by the unfinished oval canvas at upper right, *Fish with African Instrument* (D.R. 385). The vertical oval canvas on the floor at lower right is an early state of *Man with Pipe* (D.R. 422), completed in fall 1911. (The framed rectangular canvas has not been identified.) The horizontal oval canvas of a mandolin on a table, at lower left, was originally sold to Kahnweiler under the title *The Architect-Musician*; reclaimed by Picasso, it was heavily repainted, becoming the vertical still life now known as *The Architect's Table* (D.R. 456). In its original state it resembled the spring 1911 canvas *Mandolin and Glass of Pernod* (D.R. 387).

172 The title *Monk with Mandolin* appears in the caption to Kahnweiler photograph no. 83. This is crossreferenced to stockbook no. 700, where the title is given as *Buffalo Bill*. In the stockbook it immediately follows *L'homme au chapeau melon à la mandoline*, no. 699, the Beyeler *Mandolin Player* (fig. 104) and is followed in turn by a small canvas entitled *Tête de Buffalo Bill*, no. 701 (D.R. 396).

173 Juan Gris, *Man in a Café*, 1912; reproduced in Green, *Gris*, no. 21.

174 On the suite of paintings including *Man with Mandolin*

and *Man with Guitar*, see William Rubin, "The Library of Hamilton Easter Field," in *Picasso and Braque: Pioneering Cubism*, pp. 63–69.

175 Fragson's song is identified in Maurice Jardot, *Picasso: peintures, 1900–1955* (Paris: Musée des Art Décoratifs, 1955), no. 28, cited in Varnedoe and Gopnik, *High and Low*, ch. 1, n. 21. Its lyrics are reproduced in part in the memoirs of Alice Halicka, *Hier: souvenirs* (Paris: Pavois, 1946), p. 35: "O Manon ma jolie/Mon coeur te dit bonjour/Pour nous les Tziganes jouent m'amie/La chanson d'amour, la chanson d'amour." *Ma Jolie* has sometimes been identified as *Woman with Guitar* rather than *Woman with Zither*, but the original title in both Kahnweiler's stockbook (no. 962) and photo files (no. 180) is unambiguous: "Femme à la Cithare."

176 See Braque's November 1912 contract with Kahnweiler, reproduced in Isabelle Monod-Fontaine, "Braque: The Slowness of Painting," in M.F./C., p. 57.

177 Leo Stein, *Appreciation: Painting, Poetry & Prose* (New York: Crown, 1947; repr. Lincoln: University of Nebraska Press, 1996), p. 186.

178 Gilot and Lake, *Life with Picasso*, p. 75; cited in Rubin, "Introduction," *Picasso and Braque: Pioneering Cubism*, p. 19. Rubin here discusses the extensive evidence that Picasso and Braque were both drawn to the idea of an "anonymous art" at this time.

179 On the link between Picasso's 1912 work and the "machine style" drawings of Picabia and Duchamp, see Pepe Karmel, "Francis Picabia, 1915: The Sex of a New Machine," in Sarah Greenough, ed., *Modern Art and America*, exh. cat. (Washington, D.C: National Gallery of Art, 2001), pp. 203–19.

180 Kahnweiler, *Gris*, p. 125.

181 Jean Paulhan, *Braque le patron* (1946; rev. ed. Paris: N.R.F., 1952), p. 76.

182 Douglas Cooper, "Braque as Innovator: The First *Papier Collé*," in M.F./C. *Fruit Dish and Glass* belonged to Cooper himself, who says in the essay that he had acquired it in the winter of 1946–47, but did not at first understand its significance. Braque and his wife came to dinner at Cooper's villa on the evening of September 7, 1957, and it was on that evening, Cooper writes, that he learned from the artist that "this was the first *papier collé* he had made" (pp. 17–18). This is very odd. Cooper was surely familiar with Paulhan's *Braque le patron*, published in 1946, and with Henry Hope's catalogue for the Museum of Modern Art's Braque retrospective of 1949, both of which had identified *Fruit Dish and Glass* as the first *papier collé*. Furthermore, Cooper himself had identified the work as "the first *papier collé*" in his catalogue for a Braque exhibition at the Tate Gallery (entry no. 33), held in 1956. Braque's 1957 comment cannot have been news to Cooper.

183 Braque's priority was acknowledged in an October 9, 1912 letter from Picasso, who had returned to Paris. "I have been using your latest papery and powdery procedures," Picasso wrote. Judith Cousins, "Documentary Chronology," in Rubin, *Picasso and Braque: Pioneering Cubism*, p. 407.

184 Dora Vallier, "Braque, la peinture, et nous: propos de l'artiste recueillis," *Cahiers d'art*, vol. 29, no. 1, October 1954, p. 17.

185 See the reproductions in Douglas Cooper, *Picasso: Theater* (New York: Abrams, 1967, repr. 1987), nos. 332–35.

186 John Golding, *Cubism*, p. 109.

187 Ibid., pp. 123–24. Golding argues that Braque was already employing, in 1913–14, the technique described by Waldemar George in 1921; see Chapter 1, p. 17 above.

188 The problem here is that Braque's rhetoric is at odds with his actual working procedure. He proclaimed in 1917 that "the painter thinks in forms and colors," that "the point is not to *reconstitute* an anecdotal fact but to *constitute* a pictorial fact," and that "the *papiers collés* [glued-on papers], the *faux-bois* – and other similar materials – that I have used in certain drawings make an impression . . . by their factual simplicity." Georges Braque, "Pensées et réflexions sur la peinture," *Nord-Sud*, no. 10, December 1917, pp. 3–5. These statements give the impression that he used the collage elements of his pictures to make abstract compositions, and only later transformed them into representational images.

It is evident from the *papiers collés* themselves, however, that the representational elements of Braque's pictures came before the collaged elements. The borders of the printed papers are frequently cropped to conform with the surrounding elements of the drawn composition. This is noted by Christopher Green in his *Gris*, p. 86, and Golding in *Cubism*, p. 109 notes that: "the small pencil marks around the fragments of paper [in *Fruitdish and Glass*] . . . indicate that the composition was worked out with care before the paper was finally pasted on." If the papers had really served as "facts" establishing the basic elements of the composition, Braque would probably not have been so ready to modify them.

It is possible that Braque first positioned the printed papers, then marked their positions, then developed the composition around their outlines, then replaced the papers, and then drew additional elements atop them. However, it seems simpler to assume that the drawings were done first, without any preliminary positioning of the papers; the printed papers were then trimmed to fit into the appropriate area of the composition; and elements of the drawings concealed by the printed papers were redrawn atop them.

189 The same repeated outlines also appear in a fourth still life *papier collé*, *Composition* (M.F./C. 11).

190 See Chapter 2, pp. 45–46 above.

191 Leo Stein, *Appreciation* (as in n. 177), pp. 176–77.

192 On serialism, see Michael Fried, *Three American Painters: Kenneth Noland, Jules Olitski, Frank Stella*, exh. cat. (Cambridge, Mass.: Fogg Art Museum, 1965), and John Coplans, *Serial Imagery*, exh. cat. (Pasadena Art Museum, 1968); the introductory essay from the latter is reprinted in *Artforum*, vol. 7, no. 2, October 1968, pp. 34–43.

193 In "The Motivation of the Sign," in Rubin *et al.*, *Picasso and Braque: A Symposium*, p. 261, Rosalind Krauss points out that the two strips of newsprint were originally two halves of a sin-

gle piece of the same sheet. After cutting them, Krauss observes, Picasso flipped one, thereby implying the existence of three-dimensional space in a composition otherwise composed of two-dimensional shapes. Krauss does not, however, note that the resulting negative space, between the neck of the violin and the adjacent piece of newsprint thereby assumes a profile that is the mirror image of the other piece of newsprint, representing the side of the violin. It is this negative space (rather than the adjacent newsprint, as Krauss suggests) that represents the back of the violin. In effect, the instrument is sandwiched between mirroring front and back planes, much like the "sandwich-man" version of the spring 1909 *Bather* (see fig. 67).

194 Kahnweiler, *Gris*, p. 119. Similar comments appear in several other texts by Kahnweiler. See *Les Sculptures de Picasso* (Paris, 1948), n.p. [p. 4]; "L'Art nègre et le cubisme," in *Confessions Esthetiques* (Paris, 1963), p. 234; and "Cubism: The Creative Years," *Art News Annual*, no. 24, 1955, p. 115. Kahnweiler specifies that Braque's reliefs were made from paper, and Picasso's from cardboard, wood, and iron.

195 In *Cubism and Twentieth-Century Art*, pp. 294–95, Rosenblum describes the "Guitar" as a metal "cutout" which "paralleled the technique of pasting papers." Similar comments about the relationship between collage and construction appear in Roland Penrose, *The Sculpture of Picasso*, exh. cat. (New York: Museum of Modern Art, 1967), p. 20, and Alan Bowness, "Picasso's Sculpture," in Penrose and Golding, *Picasso in Retrospect*, pp. 130–32.

196 Paulhan, *Braque le patron*, p. 47; Picasso's declaration (made to William Rubin) is cited in Rubin, *Picasso in the Collection*, p. 108. Douglas Cooper, who had the opportunity to discuss this question with both artists, stated unequivocally that Picasso's and Braque's constructed sculptures of 1912 were "forerunners of *papier collé*." Cooper, *The Cubist Epoch*, exh. cat. (London: Phaidon, and Los Angeles County Museum, 1971), p. 234.

197 In *Picasso in the Collection*, p. 74, Rubin dated the *Guitar* to early 1912, and this dating was adopted by Daix and Rosselet in their 1979 *catalogue raisonné*. In his 1981 review of this catalogue, Fry argued for a dating of summer or fall 1912, and in subsequent publications he and Rubin converged on a dating of October 1912 for the original cardboard maquette of the "Guitar," and some months later for the more permanent, sheet-metal version. See Fry, "Pierre Daix and Joan Rosselet, *Picasso: The Cubist Years 1907–1916*" (see n. 37 above), pp. 92–93, and n. 21, and "Picasso, Cubism, and Reflexivity," *Art Journal*, vol. 47, no. 4, winter 1988, pp. 296–310; see also Rubin, *Picasso and Braque*, pp. 31–32.

198 Clement Greenberg, "The Pasted Paper Revolution," originally published in *Art News*, September 1958; rev. version in *Art and Culture*, 1961; original repr. in *Clement Greenberg: The Collected Essays and Criticism*, vol. IV: *Modernism with a Vengeance, 1957–1969*, ed. John O'Brian (University of Chicago Press, 1993), pp. 61–66. On Semper's theories of the origins of decorative patterning, and their influence, see Chapter 1, pp. 8–9 above.

199 Kahnweiler, *Les Sculptures de Picasso*, n.p. [p. 4]. See Kahnweiler, *Rise of Cubism*, pp. 15–16, and William Rubin, "Modernist Primitivism," in Rubin, *"Primitivism" in 20th-Century Art*, pp. 18–20. Rubin's first, more anecdotal account of his discussions with Picasso was published as "Visits with Picasso at Mougins," *Art News*, vol. 72, no. 6, summer 1973, pp. 42–46.

200 Bois, "Kahnweiler's Lesson," p. 91.

201 Picasso's August 11, 1912 letter to Kahnweiler is transcribed in Isabelle Monod-Fontaine, *Daniel-Henry Kahnweiler: marchand, éditeur, écrivain*, exh. cat. (Paris: Centre Georges Pompidou, 1984), p. 112.

202 On the two Grebo masks owned by Picasso, see William Rubin, "Modernist Primitivism: An Introduction" and "Picasso," in Rubin, *"Primitivism" in 20th-Century Art*, pp. 20 and 305–07. Rubin in fact suggests that the mask purchased in August 1912 was the second Grebo mask acquired by Picasso.

203 Kahnweiler, *Rise of Cubism*, p. 10: "The decisive advance . . . occurred in Cadaqués . . . he had pierced the closed form." What is new in 1913–14 [i.e. 1912–14], Kahnweiler writes, p. 15, is the amalgamation of painting and sculpture, and in particular the technique of planar relief: "instead of having to demonstrate through shadows how one plane stands above, or in front of a second plane, they could now superimpose the planes one on the other and illustrate the relationship directly."

204 The literary evidence regarding Braque's constructions of 1911 and 1912 is fragmentary and complex. It is brilliantly summarized by Rubin in *Picasso and Braque: Pioneering Cubism*, pp. 30–41.

205 Cited in Ron Johnson, *The Early Sculpture of Picasso 1901–1914* (New York: Garland, 1976), p. 115. Johnson suggests that Salmon's remark applies to the series of *Guitar* sculptures, an interpretation based on the early 1912 dating of the metal *Guitar* in Rubin, *Picasso in the Collection*, p. 207. However, as the *Guitar* sculptures were actually done in fall-winter 1912–13, Salmon's remark must apply to something else.

206 The crossbar at the base of this head marks it as part of the spring 1912 sculpture series; compare Zervos XXVIII, 144.

207 Rubin, "Modernist Primitivism," in *"Primitivism" in 20th-Century Art*, p. 18.

208 In a 1923 interview, Picasso told Florent Fels, "the African sculptures that hang around almost everywhere in my studio are more witnesses than models." Cited in Rubin, "Picasso," in ibid., p. 260.

209 Picasso seems to have considered inscribing such graphic signs on the spring 1912 guitarist. See the sculpture sketch belonging to the Museum of Modern Art (inventory no. 80.81), where the face is represented as a flat circle, inscribed with a vertical line and two dots indicating the nose and eyes. This drawing is reproduced along with a group of other sketches in Zervos II*, 296 (middle row, second from right).

210 Picasso's winter 1908–09 transformation of the *Carnival at the*

Bistro (D.R. 218 and 219) into a still life of *Bread and Fruit Dish on a Table* (D.R. 220) still followed this "Arcimboldo" model: arms became loaves of bread, a hand became an apple, a breast became a melon.

211 Edward Fry was the first to note that the drawings and paintings of summer 1912 were closely related to *Guitar*; he also noted the appearance of the other drawings for constructed figures; see the works reproduced in the articles by Fry listed in n. 197 above.

212 In *The Cubist Epoch*, p. 58, Douglas Cooper wrote: "In the summer of 1912, [Braque] cut pieces of paper and cardboard and made some models of objects (guitars, violins) which he then painted . . . Picasso followed his example." Cooper's account seems to be confirmed by a late August letter to Kahnweiler, in which Braque writes: "I am working well and taking advantage of my stay in the country to do things that cannot be done in Paris, such as paper sculpture." Cousins, "Documentary Chronology," in Rubin, *Picasso and Braque*, p. 403.

213 Cousins, "Documentary Chronology," ibid., p. 407; retrans. from French ed., p. 385. The importance of this letter for the dating of the *Guitar* (fig. 299) is emphasized in Rubin, ibid., p. 32. As noted above, Picasso's reference to "techniques for working with paper" cannot apply to his first *papiers collés*, since these were not done until November, several weeks after he wrote this letter.

214 André Salmon, *Souvenirs sans fin* (Paris: N.R.F., 1955), p. 82, quotes Picasso as saying: "Tu vas voir. Je garde *el guitarron*, mais je vendrais *el* plan; tout le monde pourra faire la même." The passage is cited in Rubin, "Introduction," *Picasso and Braque*, p. 20.

215 For the other series of paintings deriving from fig. 227, see the series of still lifes reproduced in D.R. 565–69.

216 The paper reliefs visible in an early 1913 photograph of Braque's Hotel Roma studio (reproduced in Kahnweiler, "Cubism: The Creative Years," *Art News Annual*, no. 24, 1955, p. 108) may, similarly, have provided the models for several of Braque's 1913 canvases.

217 For Picasso's spring 1913 notebook, see Léal 17.

218 The disposition of the relevant sketches suggests that the two projects were not pursued simultaneously. The sketches related to the free-standing wooden construction appear in a more or less coherent sequence filling pp. 40–49 of the 1913 notebook. In each case, the sketch appears on the right-hand page. In contrast, the sketches related to the wall relief are scattered throughout the book, appearing on the verso of pp. 17, 67, 68, 76, and the recto of pp. 68 and 75. Picasso seems, when doing the second series, to have flipped through the more or less completed notebook, looking for blank pages on which to draw.

219 The newspaper fragment in the relief seems to be three columns wide. As the standard column width in papers such as *Le Journal* and *Excelsior* was around 7 cm, it is possible to estimate the overall dimensions of Picasso's construction.

220 Compare the drawings Zervos XXVIII, 321, 322, 331, and Zervos XXIX, 56, with the relief reproduced in Spies 56 (=D.R. 631).

221 The reliefs published in *Soirées de Paris* are reproduced in D.R. 629–31, 633, dated to fall 1913, when they were published, rather than the spring, when they were executed. They are also catalogued in Spies 34, 33a, 48, and 56.

222 Clipping from a February 1912 issue of *L'Assiette au beurre*, in the Galerie Kahnweiler archives; reproduced in Monod-Fontaine, *Daniel-Henry Kahnweiler*, p. 109.

223 Kahnweiler, *Gris*, p. 80.

224 Kahnweiler, *Rise of Cubism*, pp. 11–13.

225 George Berkeley, "An Essay Towards a New Theory of Vision," para. 77 (1709), in George Berkeley, *Works on Vision*, ed. Colin Murray Turbayne (repr. Indianapolis: Bobbs-Merrill, 1963), p. 57–58.

226 Conrad Fiedler, *On Judging Works of Visual Art* (1876; trans. Henry Schaefer-Simmern and Fulmer Mood, Berkeley: University of California Press, 1949), pp. 33, 39, 43, 51, and passim.

227 Henri Bergson, "Laughter" (1900) in Wylie Sypher, ed., *Comedy* (trans. Garden City: Doubleday, 1956), pp. 159–60. See the discussion of this passage in Mark Antliff, *Inventing Bergson: Cultural Politics and the Parisian Avant-Garde* (Princeton University Press, 1993), pp. 58–59.

228 Bergson, *Laughter*, p. 161.

229 Roger Fry, "An Essay in Aesthetics," 1909; repr. in *Vision and Design* (London: Chatto & Windus, 1920; New York: Dover, 1998), p. 18.

230 Scholars continue to debate just how much meaning should be attributed to the particular articles that Picasso used in his *papiers collés*. For a sample of this argument, see the "Discussion" in Rubin, *et al., Picasso and Braque: A Symposium*, pp. 74–79.

231 Olivier, *Picasso and His Friends*, p. 172. Earlier in her memoirs (p. 125), Olivier comments, "As for orchestral music, he [Picasso] never went to a concert."

232 "Le Violon d'Ingres" is no. 791 in Kahnweiler's stockbook. In his photo files, it appears as "Nature morte avec 'Soirées de Paris' ou le Violin et l'ancre." The July 5, 1912 letter to Kahnweiler is reproduced in Karmel, "Notes on the Datings," in Rubin, *et al., Picasso and Braque: A Symposium*, p. 341.

233 Ingres's violin appears as no. 263 in the catalogue of the Petit exhibition, under "Meubles et Objets Divers."

234 "On April 28 . . . a gala will take place in the George Petit galleries at four o'clock sharp. Before the assembled works of the famous painter, on Ingres's violin Kubelik will play those pieces of which the painter was particularly fond." André Salmon, "Courrier des ateliers," *Paris-Journal*, April 23; reproduced in Cousins, "Documentary Chronology," in Rubin, *Picasso and Braque: Pioneering Cubism*, pp. 373–74.

235 The paintings in question here are Braque's *Violin* (Romilly 93) and Picasso's *Glass, Violin, and Fan* (D.R. 411), both of spring–summer 1911; Braque's *"Mozart/Kubelik"* (Romilly 121) of early 1912; and Picasso's *Man with Violin* (see fig. 107), and Braque's *Man with a Violin* (Romilly 125), both of spring 1912.

236 *Les Soirées de Paris* was launched as a literary journal in February 1912. After a financial crisis, it folded in June

1913; Apollinaire found new backers and relaunched it in November 1913 with a broader focus including the visual arts. The first issue of this new series included the four photographs of Picasso's constructed reliefs, listed in n. 221 above.

237 Guillaume Apollinaire, "On the Subject in Modern Painting," *Les Soirées de Paris*, February 1, 1912; trans. in Leroy C. Breunig, ed., *Apollinaire on Art: Essays and Reviews, 1902–1918* (New York: Viking, 1972), pp. 197–98.

238 Apollinaire, "The Art World: The Italian Futurist Painters," *L'Intransigeant*, February 7, 1912; translated in *Apollinaire on Art*, pp. 199–200. See also Rosalind Krauss's discussion of Picasso, Apollinaire, and the Futurists, in "The Motivation of the Sign," in Rubin, *et al.*, *Picasso and Braque: A Symposium*, pp. 275–82.

239 Picasso, *Souvenir du Havre*, May 1912 (D.R. 458).

240 Gino Severini later recalled: "When I painted *Ricordi di Viaggio* in 1911 I showed it to Picasso, and shortly afterwards he painted *Souvenirs du Havre*, of course in quite a different style." *Cinquanti disegni di Pablo Picasso*, 1943, p. 22; cited in Marilyn McCully, ed., *A Picasso Anthology: Documents, Criticism, Reminiscences* (London: Arts Council of Great Britain, 1981; repr. Princeton University Press, 1982), p. 74.

241 For the documents establishing the date of this trip, see Cousins, "Documentary Chronology," in Rubin, *Picasso and Braque*, p. 389.

242 Pierre Daix, "Les trois séjours 'cubistes' de Picasso à Céret," in *Picasso et la paix*, exh. cat. (Céret: Musée d'Art Moderne, 1973), p. 120, suggests that Picasso accompanied Braque on a February 1912 visit to Le Havre, when Braque brought his fiancée Marcelle Lapré to meet his family. There does not seem to be any documentation of this visit, however. A January 6, 1912 letter from Braque to Marcelle demonstrates that he alone was in Le Havre on that date (see Cousins, "Documentary Chronology," in Rubin, *Picasso and Braque*, p. 388); and a June 6, 1912 letter from Picasso to Kahnweiler mentions that "Braque is at Le Havre, as you know. I've received a few postcards from him. He has to dance with sailors at the Scandinavia Bar and at St. Joseph. I believe he went for the First Communion of his little nephew." Cousins, ibid., p. 394.

243 *Violin and Anchor* appears as no. 791 in Kahnweiler's stockbook, along with a group of paintings from winter 1911–12. Picasso seems to have given this group to Kahnweiler before leaving for Céret in late May. It seems unlikely that a canvas as large as *Violin and Anchor* could have been begun and finished in the relatively brief period between Picasso's return from Le Havre and his departure for Céret. Furthermore, the May 9, 1912 issue of the German periodical *Pan* includes a letter from the critic Max Raphael mentioning that "Picasso has shown me recent pictures in which he has used pure blue and red as the pure matter of painting." McCully, *Picasso Anthology*, p. 93; summarized in Cousins, "Documentary Chronology," in Rubin, *Picasso and Braque*, p. 390. Given the exigencies of publication, Raphael must have visited Picasso's studio no later than mid-April, i.e. before Picasso's visit to Le Havre. Of course, this description applies to other works as well as *Violin and Anchor*, but it seems likely that the pictures containing brightly colored Ripolin paint were begun, as a group, before April. The aviation imagery in several of these pictures, such as *The Scallop Shell: "Notre Avenir est dans l'air"* (D.R. 464) may link them to the Carnival of February 1912, which included a float with a full-sized airplane, sponsored by the newspaper *Le Matin*; see Alain Faure, *Paris Carême-Prenant* (Paris: Hachette, 1978), pl. 15. The aviation motif too leads back to Braque. See the discussion in Rubin, *Picasso and Braque: Pioneering Cubism*, pp. 33–34 .

244 Despite its close iconographic links with *Violin and Anchor*, the *Souvenir du Havre* is dated in Kahnweiler's photo archives to "Paris, automne 1912." It is listed as no. 1160 in his stockbook, where it appears among a group of works transferred to Kahnweiler in late 1912.

245 H. P. Roché, "Souvenir sur Braque," *La Parisienne*, vol. 26, March 1955, p. 355. Braque also boasted of being able to play Beethoven symphonies on his accordion. Kahnweiler, *My Galleries and Painters* (Paris: Gallimard, 1961; trans. Helen Weaver, New York: Viking, 1971), p. 44. As Patricia Leighten has argued, *Re-Ordering the Universe: Picasso and Anarchism* (Princeton University Press, 1989), p. 116, Braque's identification with the accordion suggests that we read Picasso's summer 1911 *Accordionist* as, in part, a symbolic portrait of Braque.

246 October (?) 14, 1911 letter from Braque in Céret to Kahnweiler: "I read the cameo about me in *Paris-Journal*; it is not lacking in vividness. All that is missing is the accordion." Cousins, "Documentary Chronology," in Rubin, *Picasso and Braque*, p. 383.

247 Alexandra Parigoris, in "Les constructions cubistes dans *Les Soirées de Paris*: Apollinaire, Picasso et les clichés Kahnweiler," *Revue de l'art*, no. 82, 1988, p. 64, interprets the "BO" in fig. 265 as a fragment from the label of a bottle of the liqueur Bols. This is plausible, but it does not take into account the "BOX" in fig. 271; nor does it account for the "W" that appears with "BO" in both fig. 271 and fig. 265, nor the "S" that appears nearby in the painting.

248 The photograph in fig. 274 comes from the archives of the Bibliothèque Nationale (collection Rol 17510), where it is described as a picture of a fight between Carpentier and Willie Lewis that took place on December 13, 1911. In his autobiography, *Ma Vie de Boxeur* (Amiens: Roger Léveillard, 1921), p. 26, Carpentier wrote that, beginning in 1908, "Paris experienced a veritable invasion of American boxers, suddenly making the 'noble art' [i.e. Anglo-Saxon-style boxing] more popular than it had ever been in France. Among these foreigners, the incontestable king of our rings at that time was Willie Lewis." Carpentier went on to describe Lewis as "the man of whom one could say that he had inculcated the meaning of the pugilistic art into our athletes . . . the teacher of us all." After winning the European championship in October 1911, Carpentier eagerly looked forward to a match with Lewis. There is some uncertainty about its precise date, however. In his autobiography (pp. 67 and 79–80), Carpentier states that he fought another American boxer, Harry Lewis, on December 13, 1911, and that his match with Willie Lewis took place on May 23, 1912 – too

late for it to be the subject of the inscriptions in Picasso's spring 1912 work. It is possible that Carpentier confused these two matches, and that he fought Willie Lewis in December 1911, as the records of the Bibliothèque Nationale suggest. Alternatively, the inscriptions may have been inspired by a poster for a match between Willie Lewis and some other European fighter. Or Picasso may have misread the poster advertising the fight between Carpentier and Harry Lewis.

249 Olivier, *Picasso and His Friends*, pp. 104, 127–28. The small canvas sometimes known as *Boxer* (D.R. 469) also testifies to Picasso's interest in the sport, although it probably represents a boxing aficionado rather than an actual boxer.

250 Salmon, *Paris-Journal*, October 13, 1911; cited in Cousins, "Documentary Chronology," in Rubin, *Picasso and Braque*, p. 382. Roché, "Adieu, brave petite collection," *L'Oeil*, vol. 51, March 1959, p. 38. Picasso and his circle apparently thought that Braque resembled a well-known African-American boxer, Sam McVea, who frequented the Café de l'Hermitage on the Boulevard Clichy, and Oliver reinforces this association by referring to Braque as a "white negro." Olivier, *Picasso and His Friends*, pp. 103 and 172–73. This image also appears in Salmon's profile, where Braque is desribed as "a black king . . . come to bleach himself at the École des Beaux-Arts" and a "good-hearted colossus, who hides a Bushman head of hair under . . . a Tyrolian hat." Cousins, "Documentary Chronology," ibid., p. 382.

251 Roman Jakobson, "Structuralisme et téléologie," 1975, in *Selected Writings*, vol. 7 (Berlin, New York, Amsterdam: Mouton, 1985), p. 125; cited in Bois, "Kahnweiler's Lesson," p. 86. See also Laude, "Picasso et Braque," pp. 13–14.

252 Viktor Shklovksy, "The Novel as Parody," in Viktor Shklovsky, *Theory of Prose* (1929; trans. Benjamin Sher, Elmwood Park: Dalkey Archive Press, 1990), pp. 147–49.

253 Viktor Shklovsky, "Art as Technique," 1917. First translated into English by Lee T. Lemon and Marion J. Reis in *Russian Formalist Criticism: Four Essays* (Lincoln: University of Nebraska Press, 1965); new translation as "Art as Device" by Benjamin Sher in Shklovsky, *Theory of Prose*, pp. 4–5. Each of these translations of Shklovsky's essay has its own virtues and defects; I have quoted now from one, now from the other.

254 Shklovsky, "Art as Technique," in *Russian Formalist Criticism*, pp. 12–13.

255 Ibid., p. 12.

256 Shklovsky, "Art as Device," in *Theory of Prose*, pp. 3–4 and 13–14.

257 Shklovsky, "The Structure of Fiction," in ibid., pp. 61–62.

258 Franz Wickhoff, *Die Wiener Genesis*, 1895, trans. as *Roman Art: Some of its Principles and their Application to Early Christian Painting* (London, 1895), pp. 120–21.

259 Kahnweiler, *Rise of Cubism*, p. 12.

260 E. H. Gombrich, *Art and Illusion: A Study in the Psychology of Pictorial Representation* (Princeton University Press, 1956), p. 202. See the discussion of this passage in Chapter 1, p. 5 above. See also chapter 1, n. 100.

261 Ibid.

Index

Q

R

Photograph Credits

All works by Picasso © 2003 Estate of Pablo Picasso / Artists Rights Society (ARS), New York

Albright-Knox Art Gallery, Buffalo, New York: fig. 87.
Courtesy Thomas Ammann Fine Art, Zurich: fig. 207.
Art Institute of Chicago: figs. 8, 76.
The Barnes Foundation, Merion Station, Pennsylvania: fig. 19.
Basel, Oeffentliche Kunstsammlung: figs. 23, 36, 114, 143, 147, 150, 204.
Photographs by Michele Bellot © Réunion des Musées Nationaux / Art Resource, NY: frontispiece, figs. 34, 50, 165, 231, 236, 275.
Photograph by J. G. Berizzi © Réunion des Musées Nationaux / Art Resource, NY: fig. 232.
Bern, Kunstmuseum: fig. 33.
Fondation Beyeler, Riehen/Basel: figs. 30, 104, 145, 152.
Bibliothèque Nationale, Paris: fig. 274.
Chrysler Museum of Art, Norfolk, VA: fig. 59.
Cincinnati Art Museum: figs. 6, 12.
Columbus Museum of Art, Ohio: fig. 116.
© CNAC/MNAM/ distributed by Réunion des Musées Nationaux / Art Resource, NY: figs. 120, 211.
Fogg Art Museum, Harvard University Art Museums: fig. 9.
Museum Folkwang, Essen: fig. 151.
Photographs by Beatrice Hatala © Réunion des Musées Nationaux / Art Resource, NY: figs. 81, 127, 131, 179, 230, 233, 237, 264, 268, 273.
Hood Museum of Art, Dartmouth College, Hanover, NH: fig. 240.
Photographs courtesy of The Sidney Janis Gallery, New York: figs. 103, 148, 189.
Rijksmuseum Kröller-Müller, Otterlo: fig. 141.
Courtesy Galerie Jan Krugier, Ditesheim & Cie, Geneva: figs. 26, 98.
© Erich Lessing / Art Resource, NY: fig. 15.
Photographs by Hervé Lewandowski © Réunion des Musées Nationaux / Art Resource, NY: figs. 153, 174.
Musée d'art moderne de Lille Métropole, Villeneuve d'Ascq: figs. 29, 38, 214, 215.
Museum Ludwig, Cologne: fig. 91.
McNay Art Museum, San Antonio: figs 133, 209.
The Menil Collection, Houston: fig. 89.
Photograph © 1996 The Metropolitan Museum of Art: fig. 83.
The Metropolitan Museum of Art, New York: figs. 100, 140, 142, 202.
Moderna Museet, Stockholm: fig. 132.
Digital Images © The Museum of Modern Art / Licensed by SCALA / Art Resource, NY. Museum of Modern Art, New York: figs. 10, 16, 17, 21, 25, 51, 65, 78, 80, 99, 130, 149, 217, 227, 229, 235, 242, 278, 279.
The Patsy R. and Raymond D. Nasher Collection, Dallas, Texas: fig. 79.
National Gallery of Art, Washington, D.C.: fig. 43.
Nordenfjeldske Kunstgewerbemuseum, Trondheim: fig. 2.
Photographs by R.G. Ojeda © Réunion des Musées Nationaux / Art Resource, NY. Musée Picasso, Paris: figs. 105, 188, 208.
Philadelphia Museum of Art: figs. 18, 107, 135.
Picasso Archives, Musée Picasso, Paris: page vi, figs. 146, 160, 182, 228, 245, 246, 252.
Prague, National Gallery: figs. 40, 265.
Private collection: figs. 134, 206.
© Réunion des Musées Nationaux / Art Resource, NY: figs. 3, 20, 22, 24, 44, 45, 46, 48, 49, 54, 63, 94, 106, 111, 144, 157, 175, 196, 197, 198, 199, 200, 201, 219, 223, 224, 247, 249, 251, 254, 255, 256, 257, 258, 267, 271, 272.
The David and Peggy Rockefeller Collection: fig. 35.
Photograph by Adam Rzepka © CNAC/MNAM, distributed by the Réunion des Musées Nationaux / Art Resource, NY: fig. 84.
San Francisco Museum of Modern Art: figs. 7, 39.
SCALA / Art Resource: figs. 14, 27, 28, 52, 136.
Scottish National Gallery of Modern Art, Edinburgh: figs. 117, 222.
The Solomon R. Guggenheim Foundation, New York. Peggy Guggenheim Collection, Venice, 1976: fig. 1.
The Solomon R. Guggenheim Museum, New York: figs. 119, 221.
Sprengel Museum, Hannover: figs. 61, 221.
Stuttgart, Staatsgalerie: figs. 42, 95.
The Tate Gallery, London: figs. 37, 85.
Tel Aviv Museum of Art: fig. 31.
© Museo Thyssen-Bornemisza, Madrid: fig. 181.
Photograph by Malcolm Varon © 1984 The Metropolitan Museum of Art: fig. 82.
Kunstmuseum Winterthur: figs. 112, 158, 203.
Yale University Art Gallery, New Haven, Conn.: figs. 41, 213.
The Richard S. Zeisler Collection, New York: fig. 173.